• NATIONAL ARCHIVES OF INDIA •
Archives in India Historical Reprints

INDIAN TRAVELS OF THEVENOT AND CARERI

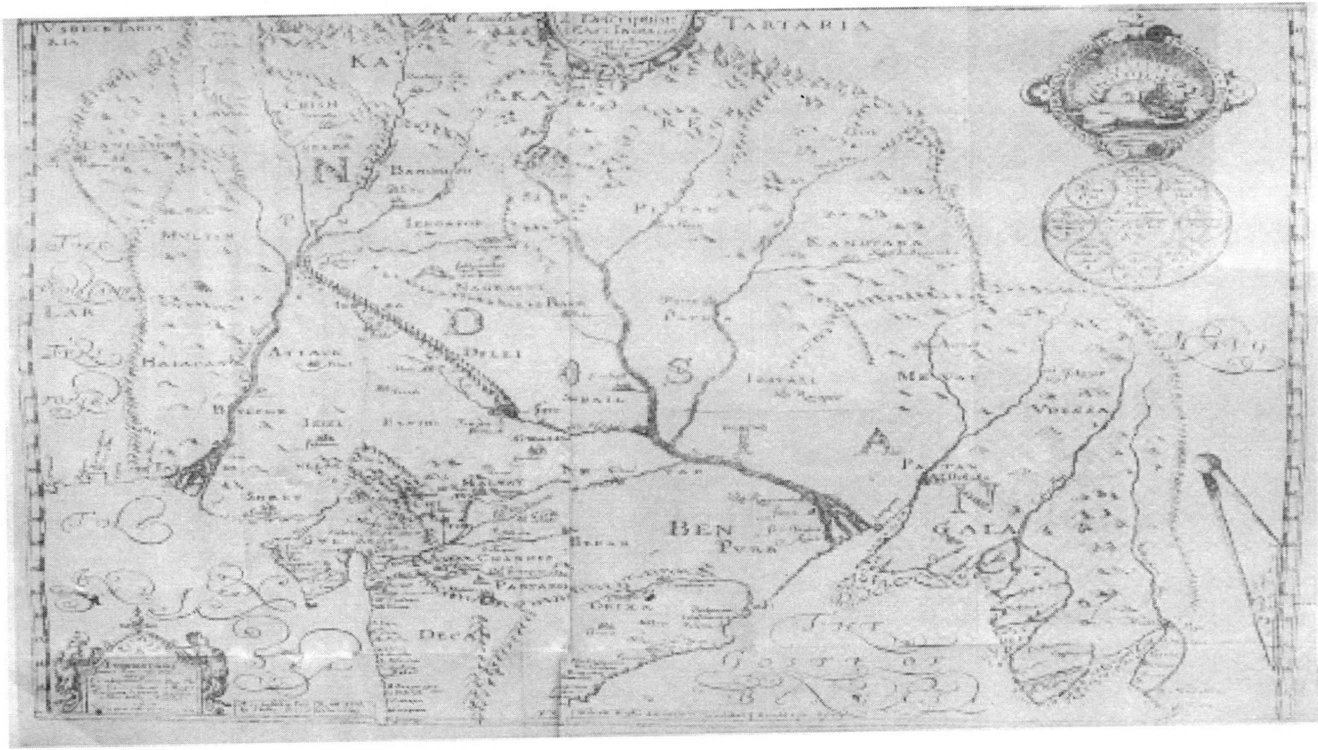
TARTARIA
DELLI
BEN
DECAN
LAR

• NATIONAL ARCHIVES OF INDIA •
Archives in India Historical Reprints

INDIAN TRAVELS OF THEVENOT AND CARERI

being the third part of the travels of
jean de thebenot
into the levant

and the third part of a voyage
round the world by
john francis gemelli careri

EDITED BY
SURENDRANATH SEN

GYAN

Published by

GYAN

Gyan Publishing House
5, Ansari Road
Daryaganj, New Delhi-110002
Phone: 011-47034999, 9811692060
E-mail: books@gyanbooks.com

Distribution Network
gyanbooks.com
India, USA, Canada, UK, Australia, France

ISBN : 978-81-212-3621-8 (PB)
First Published, New Delhi 1949

2nd Impression 2020

Printed at: Gyan Press, Delhi.

Indian Travels of Thevenot and Careri
Editor: Surendranath Sen

INDIAN RECORDS SERIES

INDIAN TRAVELS OF THEVENOT AND CARERI

BEING THE THIRD PART OF THE TRAVELS OF M. DE THEVENOT INTO THE LEVANT AND THE THIRD PART OF A VOYAGE ROUND THE WORLD BY DR. JOHN FRANCIS GEMELLI CARERI

EDITED BY
SURENDRANATH SEN,
Director of Archives, Government of India

PUBLISHED BY THE NATIONAL ARCHIVES OF INDIA
QUEENSWAY, NEW DELHI
1949

PREFACE

In June 1900 the Royal Asiatic Society of England drew the attention of the Government of India to the desirability of publishing a series of volumes bearing upon Indian history. The object of the Society was "to foster the growth of historical researches in India by publishing monographs summarizing the historical data scattered through the numerous oriental texts and these documents," which, according to the sponsors of the scheme, would "form the material out of which the social, industrial and political history of India could be reconstructed." The idea found favour with the Government of India and it was decided to publish through the Society two different series, *viz.*, "The Indian Text Series" and "The Indian Records Series." An annual grant of Rs. 15,000 for five years was sanctioned, but the Government retained the right to decide as to what books should be published in either series and in what order. In 1905 it was noticed that the Society was indifferent to the Records Series and the Secretary of the State entrusted this part of the publication to Messrs John Murray and the work proceeded under the direct supervision of the India Office. In the course of the next eight (1905-1913) years S. C. Hill's *Bengal in 1756-1757* (3 vols), C. R. Wilson's *Old Fort William* (2 vols), H. D. Love's *Vestiges of Old Madras* (4 vols), and the *Diaries of Streynsham Master* (3 vols) were duly published and then the series came to an abrupt end. In January 1942 the recently reconstituted Indian Historical Records Commission urged upon the Government of India the necessity of resuming their long interrupted publication activities and presented a comprehensive scheme envisaging the printing *in extenso* of the General Letters to and from the Court of Directors in 21 volumes, the revival of the Indian Records Series, and the publication through private agencies of documents in oriental languages in the custody of the National Archives of India (then Imperial Record Department). The new Records Series was to consist in the first instance of (*a*) Minutes of the Governor-Generals, (*b*) Browne Correspondence and (*c*) The Indian Travels of Thevenot and Careri. Travellers' accounts cannot be classed as records in the technical sense of the term, but as they are of undoubted value as raw materials of social and economic history of seventeenth century India the Commission was of opinion that they should have a place in the new series. The Government of India lent their support to the scheme but it could not be immediately implemented on account of the abnormal conditions caused by the war. But the preliminary work was at once taken in hand and steps were taken in September 1942 to terminate the existing contract with Messrs John Murray.

Under the scheme prepared by the Commission and adopted by the Government of India the entire responsibility of editing and publishing the Indian Records Series devolved upon their Director of Archives (formerly Keeper of Records). For obvious reasons the editing of the

B

Governor-Generals' Minutes and Browne Correspondence had to wait for the conclusion of the war and the Indian Travels of Thevenot and Careri was given precedence over the rest. Both the works were available in early English versions and it was considered undesirable to interfere with them, but a cursory comparison with the original French and Italian texts revealed omissions and inaccuracies which could not be left unnoticed. Principal J. D. Ward of Aitchison College, Lahore, then on military duty at New Delhi, very kindly placed his scanty leisure and linguistic gifts unreservedly at my disposal and readily volunteered to compare the extant English translation with the originals. But for his kind assistance the publication of this volume might have been indefinitely delayed and for all textual improvement the credit is entirely his.

In editing and annotating the present volume I have received cordial co-operation from so many quarters that an adequate acknowledgment of all my obligations is well nigh impossible. Sir William Foster despite the weight of four score years promptly replied to all my enquiries and often took the trouble of hunting up the information I sought in different libraries of London. I should also like to record here my indebtedness to the following for information relating to their particular branches of study and loan of books and supply of bibliographical data from their respective libraries:—Dr B. N. Chopra, D.Sc., F.N.I., Director, Zoological Survey of India; Cavaliero Panduranga Pissurlencar, Curator, Historical Records of Portuguese India; Dewan Bahadur Professor C. S. Srinivasachari, M.A., Principal, Shivaganga College, Shivaganga (South India); Mr A. J. Macdonald, B.Sc., B.Sc. (Agri), N.D.A., Imperial Veterinary Research Institute, Izatnagar; Mr Q. M. Munir, B.A., F.L.A., Archaeological Survey of India; Dr H. G. Randle, Librarian, India Office; Prof. C. V. Joshi, M.A., Rajdaftardar, Baroda; Mr P. M. Joshi, Bombay University Library; Mr M. W. H. DeSilva, Ceylon Government Representative in India; Senhor A. B. De Braganca Pereira, Presidente da Comissao Permanente de Arqueologia, Nova Goa; Dr T. A. Cockburn, Assistant Superintendent, Zoological Society of London; Mm. Professor D. V. Potdar, Bharata Itihasa Samsodhaka Mandala, Poona; Dr Ghulam Yazadani, M.A., D.Litt., O.B.E., Hyderabad (Deccan); Professor Jagdish Narain Sarkar, M.A., Patna College, Patna; Mr V. N. Damodaran Nambier, B.A., B.L., Superintendent, Central Records, Ernakulam; Prof. Girija Prasanna Majumdar, M.Sc., B.L., Ph.D., Presidency College, Calcutta; Mr K. S. Srinivasan, Indian Museum, Calcutta; Dr B. S. Guha, Director, Anthropological Survey of India; Dr B. Ch. Chhabra, Government Epigraphist for India; Mr Willy Heimann, Stockholm; Mr E. J. Dingwall, Honorary Assistant Keeper, Printed Books and Mr A. I. Ellis, Deputy Keeper of Printed Books, British Museum; Mr M. Rieunier, Bibliothèque Nationale, Paris; Miss Althea Warren, City Librarian, Los Angeles Public Library; Mr Lyle H. Wright, Bibliographer, Henry E. Huntington Library and Art Gallery, San Marino, Calif; Mr Horace I. Poleman, Chief, Indic Section, Library of Congress, Washington, D.C.; Mr Paul North Rice, Chief of the Reference Department, The New York Public Library, New York; Mr R. Gopalan, M.A., L.T., of the Central

Secretariat Library, New Delhi and Mr Des Raj Sharma, M.A., of the Central Archaeological Library, New Delhi.

It will be redundant to mention here my colleagues of the National Archives of India whose ungrudging assistance has considerably lightened my labour and facilitated my work.

A word may be added here about the notes. All omissions and errors in the translation have been corrected in the notes without any specific indication in all cases. Synonyms of archaic words, where considered necessary, have also been supplied. It is hoped there will be no difficulty in distinguishing them from the corrections.

National Archives of India,
New Delhi,
the 23rd December, 1948.

SURENDRANATH SEN

CONTENTS

	PAGE
PREFACE	v
INTRODUCTION	xvii

Indian Travels of Thevenot (being THE THIRD PART OF THE TRAVELS OF M. DE THEVENOT containing the Relation of *Indostan*, the *New Moguls*, and of other People and Countries of the *Indies*) 1—152

BOOK I

Chapter I	—Arrival at Surrat	1
Chapter II	—Of the Indies	4
Chapter III	—Of the Great Mogul	5
Chapter IV	—The Province of Guzerat	8
Chapter V	—Of Amedabad	11
Chapter VI	—Departure from Amedabad to go to Cambaye	17
Chapter VII	—Of Surrat	21
Chapter VIII	—Of Tary	24
Chapter IX	—Of the Weights and Money of Surrat ...	25
Chapter X	—Of the Officers of Surrat	26
Chapter XI	—Bad Offices done to the French Company at Surrat	29
Chapter XII	—Of the Marriage of the Governour of the Town's Daughter	31
Chapter XIII	—Of Burying-places, and the Burning of Dead Bodies	33
Chapter XIV	—Of Diverse Curiosities at Surrat	34
Chapter XV	—The Port of Surrat	37
Chapter XVI	—Of the Irruption of Sivagy	38
Chapter XVII	—Of Father Ambrose A Capucin	43
Chapter XVIII	—Of the Other Towns of Guzerat, and the Siege of Diu by the Turks, which was Defended by the Portuguese	44
Chapter XIX	—Of the Province and Town of Agra ...	46
Chapter XX	—Of the Habits at Agra	50
Chapter XXI	—Of Other Curiosities at Agra	53
Chapter XXII	—Of the Province or Town of Dehly, or Gehan-Abad	57
Chapter XXIII	—Of the Arms of the Mogul's	61
Chapter XXIV	—Of the Beasts at Dehly	62
Chapter XXV	—Of Other Curiosities at Dehly	65
Chapter XXVI	—Of the Festival of the Kings Birth-day ...	66
Chapter XXVII	—Of the Province and Town of Azmer ...	68
Chapter XXVIII	—Of the Feast of the New Year	70
Chapter XXIX	—Of the Beasts of the Country of Azmer, and of the Saltpetre	72
Chapter XXX	—Of the Province of Sinde or Sindy ...	74
Chapter XXXI	—Of Palanquins	76

BOOK I PAGE

Chapter XXXII —Of the Province of Multan 77
Chapter XXXIII —Of the Province of Candahar 78
Chapter XXXIV —Of the Province of Caboul, or Caboulistan 80
Chapter XXXV —Of the Province of Cachmir or Kichmir ... 82
Chapter XXXVI —Of the Province of Lahors and of the Vartias 84
Chapter XXXVII —Of the Provinces of Ayoud, or Haoud; Varad or Varal 87
Chapter XXXVIII —Of the Province of Becar, and of the Castes or Tribes of the Indies 88
Chapter XXXIX —Of the Province of Halabas, and of the Faquirs of the Indies 92
Chapter XL —Of the Province of Oulesser or Bengala, and of the Ganges 94
Chapter XLI —Of the Province of Malva 97
Chapter XLII —Of the Province of Candich 99
Chapter XLIII —Of the Province of Balagate 101
Chapter XLIV —Of the Pagods of Elora 104
Chapter XLV —Of the Province of Doltabad and of the Feats of Agility of Body 107
Chapter XLVI —Of Chitanagar 111
Chapter XLVII —Of the Province of Telenga 113
Chapter XLVIII —Of the Province of Baglana, and of the Marriages of the Gentiles 116
Chapter XLIX —Of the Usage of the Dead 119

BOOK II

Chapter I —Of Decan and Malabar 121
Chapter II —Of the Revolutions of Decan 126
Chapter III —Of Goa 129
Chapter IV —Of the Kingdom of Golconda Of Bagnagar 130
Chapter V —Of the Inhabitants of Bagnagar 135
Chapter VI —Of the Castle of Golconda 137
Chapter VII —Of the King of Golconda that Reigns ... 140
Chapter VIII —Of the Omras or Omros of Golconda ... 143
Chapter IX —The Authors Departure from Bagnagar for Masulipatan 146
Chapter X —Of the Authors Departure from Bagnagar for Surrat, and of Mordechin 150

Indian Travels of Careri (being PART III OF A VOYAGE ROUND THE WORLD BY DR JOHN FRANCIS GEMELLI CARERI, containing the most Remarkable Things he saw in *Indostan*) ... ... 153—276

BOOK I

Chapter I —The Description of Damam, A City belonging to the Portugueses in Indostan 157
Chapter II —The Authors Short Voyage to Suratte, and Return to Damam 163

BOOK I PAGE

Chapter III —The Authors Short Voyage to Bazaim, and Description of that City 166
Chapter IV —The Description of the Pagod in the Island of Salsete by the Portugueses Call'd the Canarin 171
Chapter V —The Author's Voyage to Goa 183
Chapter VI —The Description of the City Goa, and its Delightful Channel 186
Chapter VII —Of the Antient and Modern Dominion of the Portuguese in India 194
Chapter VIII —Of the Fruit and Flowers of Indostan ... 199

BOOK II

Chapter I —The Author's Journey to Galgala ... 207
Chapter II —The Author's Arrival at Galgala, Where the Great Mogul was Incamp'd 217
Chapter III —The Artifices, and Cruel Practices of the Mogul now Reigning, to Possess Himself of the Empire 222
Chapter IV —The Genealogy of the Great Moguls, and Other Things the Author Observ'd at That Court 234
Chapter V —Of the Government of the Great Mogul ... 240
Chapter VI —Of the Revenues and Wealth of the Great Mogul 241
Chapter VII —Of the Weapons, and Forces of the Great Mogul 242
Chapter VIII —The Manners, Habit, Marriages and Funerals of the Moguls 245
Chapter IX —Of the Climate, Fruit, Flowers, Minerals, Beasts and Coin, of Indostan ... 250

BOOK III

Chapter I —Of the Several Religions in Indostan ... 254
Chapter II —Of the Opinions and Superstitions of the Idolaters 259
Chapter III —Of Several Pagods of the Gentils ... 262
Chapter IV —The Author Continues the Account of What He Saw in the Camp of Galgala ... 264
Chapter V —The Author's Return to Goa, the Same Way He Came 267
Chapter VI —The Author's Voyage to Malaca ... 273

NOTES
Indian Travels of Thevenot 279
Indian Travels of Careri 337
ADDITIONAL NOTES 392
ITINERARY OF M. DE THEVENOT 393
ITINERARY OF DR GEMELLI CARERI 395
BIBLIOGRAPHY 397
INDEX 405
CORRIGENDA 433

LIST OF ILLUSTRATIONS

PAGE

1. M. de Thevenot ... ... *Facing page* 1
2. Title page of "Les Voyages de Mr. de Thevenot Aux Indes Orientales, Troisième Partie" *Facing Plate* 1
3. The sepulchre of Shah Alam at Sarkhej ... *Facing page* 11
4. Tapping toddy 24
5. The marriage of the daughter of the Governor of Surat 31
6. The Moor's headgear 50
7. A woman robber 57
8. The weighing of the Emperor 66
9. Indian conveyances 76
10. A Holi ritual—A boy representing Krishna shooting at the effigy of a giant 80
11. A strange way of covering distance as penance 94
12. Juggler's feat 107
13. Sati 119
14. The sepulchre of the King of Golcunda 137
15. The Malabar Cyphers 130
16. The Malabar Alphabet 130
17. The Consonants 130
18. Dr. John Francis Gemelli Careri 157
19. Title page of "Giro Del Mondo del dottor D. Gio: Francesco Gemelli Careri—Parte terza, Nell I'ndostan" ... ... *Facing Plate* 18
20. Kanheri—Cave No. 3 (2nd. century A.D.) Sculptured capitals of 7th. & 8th. pillars, from west in north row, view from south *Facing page* 171

NOTE:—Plates Nos. 1-14 have been reproduced from the French edition of Travels of M. de Thevenot, published in Paris, 1689; Nos. 15-17 from the English edition of his Travels, London, 1687 and Nos. 18-19 from the Italian edition of Dr. Gemelli Careri's Travels, (Naples, 1699 and 1700) and Plate No. 20 by the courtesy of the Department of Archaeology, India.

MAPS

William Baffin's map: 'A description of East India conteyninge th' Empire of the Great Mogoll' [Original at the British Museum—No. K 115(22)] ... ... *Frontispiece*

Map illustrating the itinerary of M. de Thevenot Facing Page 152

Map illustrating the itinerary of Dr. Gemelli Careri Facing page 276

INTRODUCTION

INTRODUCTION

I

The seventeenth century found many European travellers in India. They were a motley crowd of merchants and medicos, envoys and ecclesiastics, soldiers and sailors, fortune hunters and adventurers of all descriptions. They came from diverse countries by diverse routes on diverse missions ; some in quest of trade, others in search of a career, and yet others, a small minority, to seek diversion in new countries among new peoples with strange manners and novel customs. Tom Coryat, the eccentric but "unwearied walker", hiked all the way from Aleppo to Ajmer and "hath not left a pillar or tombe nor ould character unobserved almost in all Asia." "His notes," already "too great for portage" were left "some at Aleppo, some at Hispan" for he travelled light, his daily expense being limited to two copper pence. The German Mandelslo was better provided. A man of noble birth and liberal education, he accompanied, of his own accord, the Holstein embassy to Ispahan and subsequently sailed to Surat. The Italian Pietro della Valle traversed the wide plains of Egypt, Palestine, Assyria and Persia and thence crossed over to India not to shake the proverbial pagoda tree but to forget frustrated love under a new sun and a new sky in more congenial environments. Probably their wander-lust was inflamed by the legends of the gorgeous east and reinforced by the lure of the unknown, but they were all seekers of knowledge loyal and true. To this rare company belonged Jean de Thevenot and Giovanni Francesco Gemelli Careri. Neither greed nor cupidity not even their country's interest but natural curiosity brought them to the east and with uncommon fidelity they recorded what they saw and heard.

II

Jean de Thevenot was born at Paris on the 6th June 1633. He died near the small town of Miana in Persia while returning to his native land after an arduous journey of about four years on the 28th November 1667. During this brief span of thirty-four years he had visited more countries of Europe, Asia and Africa than many of his contemporaries ever heard of. An ardent student of geography and natural sciences, he assiduously studied the accounts of early travellers in which his uncle Melechisedech was keenly interested. The elder Thevenot long survived his nephew but he never crossed the limits of his own continent. If not so well known as an explorer, Melechisedech de Thevenot may claim to have vitally influenced his famous nephew's career by his literary enterprise. In emulation of Richard Hakluyt and Samuel Purchas he undertook to compile exhaustive accounts of famous travels under the title of

"Relations of diverse curious voyages hitherto unpublished which have been translated or extracted from the original works of French, Spanish, German, Portuguese, Dutch, Persian, Arab and other Travellers." Jean de Thevenot probably inherited his taste for strange lands and strange languages from his scholarly uncle. A man of independent means he could travel wherever he liked without any financial worry. In 1652 he set out on his European tour and visited in succession England, Holland, Germany and Italy. In 1655 he met at Rome Herbelot, "the most learned Man of his own, or perhaps of any Age, in every Branch of Oriental Literature",[1] according to the editor of Harris's *Navigation,* and they planned a trip to the east. For reasons unknown to us Herbelot could not go but Thevenot left Rome on 31st May to embark at Civita Vecchia on a galley commanded by Count Gaddi. After five months in Sicily and Malta he sailed for Constantinople. On the 30th August of the next year (1656) he set out for Anatolia whence he proceeded by sea to Egypt. The voyage proved unusually long but Thevenot ultimately reached Alexandria. In Egypt he saw the Nilometres and visited the Pyramids. He then joined a caravan bound for Suez as he wanted to have a look at the Red Sea. While returning his boat was set upon and plundered by Arab pirates but he eventually reached Cairo and sailed to Tunis in an English ship. A visit to the ruins of Carthage concluded his first voyage to the east but the journey home was not without the usual adventures. The boat in which he left Tunis encountered three Spanish corsairs and in the sanguine conflict that followed the young traveller almost lost his life. The corsairs, however, were worsted and Thevenot safely reached Livourne and returned to France through Italy in 1662. His friends and relatives fondly hoped that seven years of unmitigated hardship had sufficiently cooled his passion for foreign countries but the east called him back before long and he readily responded. As soon as his private affairs were settled Jean de Thevenot was out of Paris (16th October 1663) but he did not finally leave France till 24th January 1664 when he embarked at Marseilles. The 24th of the next month found him at Alexandria. He did not tarry there long and went east to visit Damascus, Aleppo and Mosul and then sailed down the Tigris to Bagdad. From Bagdad Thevenot went to Persia and after five months at Ispahan left for Bandar Abbas to catch a boat for India. Thwarted in his object Thevenot retraced his steps and visited the ancient monuments at and around Shiraz. The voyage to India was only postponed but not abandoned. On the 6th November 1665 he boarded at Basra an English built ship the *Hopewell* owned by an Armenian and commanded by an Italian, Captain Bernardo. The fare from Basra to Surat was 40 Abbasis or 60 shillings per head which was

1. Barthelemy d'Herbelot, born at Paris 1625, died 1695, studied Hebrew, Chaldean, Syriac, Arabic, Persian and Turkish. Ferdinand II, Grand Duke of Tuscany, invited him to his court and presented him a rich collection of oriental manuscripts. He later became Professor of Syriac at College de France. He had a large number of publications on oriental subjects to his credit. He went to Rome in 1655 with a view to contacting oriental people visiting the ports of Italy.

three times as high as a Muslim ship would charge. On the New Year's Day 1666 the ship arrived near Diu, a Portuguese port off the coast of Gujarat, and four days later another Portuguese station Bassein was sighted and then the *Hopewell* sailed north past Daman and reached the Surat Bar on Sunday the 10th January. Soon afterwards the ship was boarded by a customs officer and the French traveller had his first experience of the Great Moghul's agents. From Surat he travelled overland to Ahmadabad and Cambay farther north when he retracted his steps to the starting port. But he was not to stay there long. Across the Deccan peninsula he journeyed to Masulipatam on the eastern coast passing through Burhanpur, Aurangabad and Golkonda, cities noted for their commerce and industry, and visited on his way the far famed rock-cut temples of Ellora. He was the first European to describe these wonderful caves[2] and if his account of the sculptures and images are somewhat vague and inadequate we must not forget that few westerners were at that date sufficiently conversant with Indian iconography to identify Hindu and Buddhist idols and Thevenot spent only two hours at Ellora. By the end of the year he was back at Surat whence he sailed for Bandar Abbas in February 1667 en route to France but the rigours of his unceasing travels had seriously impaired his health and he passed away in Persia at the early age of thirty four. Thevenot's premature decease was a serious loss to science and oriental learning. But if death cut short his career so early the immortal fame that was his by right was not denied a moment too long. His *Voyage to the Levant,* published at Paris in 1664, proved a great success and definitely established his reputation as a keen observer and an able writer and his posthumous publications not only ensured but considerably added to that renown. Conversant with the principal languages of the Middle East, Turkish, Arabic and Persian, Thevenot freely moved among the people of those countries and he could not have experienced much inconvenience in India on the score of language as most of the Muslim officers and some Hindu dignitaries as well spoke at least one of these tongues. If his physique succumbed to the rigours of twelve years of toil and discomfort in foreign lands his indomitable will refused to own defeat until the last moment. In spite of failing health and approaching death Thevenot continued to write his journal and "described his Journey as far as the Bourg of *Farsank,* where he lodged the 16th of November." After his death the remaining parts of Thevenot's manuscripts were arranged and published by two of his friends, Sieur de Luisandre and the French Orientalist Petis. They passed through many editions and were translated into English, Dutch and German. To the students of Indian history Thevenot's *Voyages* is a work of abiding interest for nothing illustrates so well the merits and demerits of a foreign traveller's account of a country so vast with a history so chequered and a culture so ill-comprehended. But Thevenot did not

2. Seely remarks "M. Thevenot was but two hours inspecting them (the rock cut temples of Ellora); and speaks of his fear in passing under the excavated mountains. Without wishing to detract from the merit of former travellers, I must observe, that from personal observation I have discovered much inaccuracy, and occasionally wilful exaggeration." *Wonders of Elora,* p. 327.

confine himself to a general account of India and its people, he tried to describe in a general way its fauna and flora as well. The Indian flora however aroused his interest most and he essayed a separate scientific work in which each of the plants was to have a full and graphic description.

The Voyages of Jean de Thevenot were issued in successive parts from 1664 to 1684. *Relation d'un Voyage fait au Levant dans laquelle il est . . . . traité des états sujets au Grand-Seigneur, de l'Archipel, Terre Sante, Egypte, Arabie*—Paris 1664—4°.

Do., Rouen and Paris 1665.

Suite du même voyage où il est traité de la Perse—Paris, 1674.

Relation de l'Indoustan, des nouveaux Mogols et des autres peuples et pays des Indes—Paris, 1684.

These three parts were later collected under one title and issued in 5 vols. in 1689.

Voyages de M. de Thevenot tant en Europe qu'en Asie et en Afrique—Paris, 1689, 5 vols. 12°.

Five successive editions in five volumes each appeared at Amsterdam in 1705, 1723, 1725, 1727 and 1729.

A Dutch translation published at Amsterdam in 1681 is mentioned in *Biographie Universelle.*[3]

At least one German version is known. It consisted of three parts separately numbered and was published at Frankfort in 1693. The third part relates to Thevenot's Indian travels and has 228 pages. The title page is as follows:

Dess/Hn THEVENOTS/Reysen/In/Ost-Indian/Dritter Theil/In sich haltend/Eine genaue Beschreibung des Konigreichs Indostan/, der/neuen Mongols und anderer Völcker und Länder in Ost Indien/Nebenst/Ihren Sitten, Gesetzen, Religionen, Festen, Tempeln, Pagoden, Kirchhöfen/Commercien, und andern merckwurdigen Sachen/

Mit Röm. Kayserl Majest und Chur-Sachsis. gnädiger Freyhit/Franckfurt am Mayn/Gedruckt und Verlegt durch Phillipp Fievet Buchhandlern/Anna M.D. CXCIII.

It appears that Thevenot's *Voyages* was first rendered into English by A. Lovell and printed in 1687 at London by H. Clark for H. Faithorne, J. Adamson, C. Skegnes and T. Newborough, Booksellers in St. Paul's Churchyard. It was in three parts (*i*) Turkey (*ii*) Persia and (*iii*) The East-Indies.

Extracts appeared in Harris's *Navigation,* 1742, 1744-1748, 1750 and 1764, in John Knox's *A New collection of Voyages, Discoveries and Travels* 1767 and in John Newbery's "*World Displayed*" 1774 but the Indian part was not included in any of these compilations.

III

Giovanni Francesco Gemelli Careri was eighteen years younger than Jean de Thevenot. He was born of a noble family of Radicena (Calabria)

3. Volume 45, p. 384.

in 1651 and unlike the Frenchman lived to a ripe old age and died at Naples in 1725, long after he had concluded his tour round the world (1698). A student of jurisprudence and a lawyer by profession, Careri had attained the highest distinction his University had to confer, for his learned labours had earned him the degree of Doctor of Civil Law. For a few years he practised law and then some misfortunes at home which he does not specify drove him abroad to seek peace. But as the editor of Churchill's *Voyages and Travels* affirms he did not go "as a vagabond trusting to Fortune, but well provided with Mony to make him acceptable in all Parts, and gain Admittance where others under worse Circumstances could not." Like Thevenot again he started by visiting European countries first. Between 1685 and 1687 he travelled in Italy, France, England, Belgium, Holland and Germany. He is believed to have served as a volunteer in Hungary in 1687 and then went to Portugal and Spain and returned home in 1689 but his account of his European travels was published much later.[4] He had apparently resumed his practice but "the ill treatment and perpetual persecution to which he was subjected in his family" again sent him on a longer journey away from the uncongenial environments. When he left Radicena in June 1693 he told his brother that he intended to visit the Holy Lands alone but he had already made up his mind not to return until he had gone round the world. Careri was familiar with the published works of Thevenot. We do not know to what extent his tour programme was based on that of the French traveller but it is interesting to note that like Thevenot he also began his eastward voyage by visiting Sicily and Malta and then proceeding to Alexandria. He travelled up the Nile to see the ancient monuments of the country. From Egypt Careri went to Palestine. After visiting the sacred sites he returned by sea to Alexandria where he embarked for Smyrna on the 12th October. He left that town two months later and went to Gallipoli. From there he travelled as far as Adrianople and early in January of the next year (1694) reached Constantinople. Careri next came back to Smyrna where his luggage had been left and then set out for Trebizond. After crossing the mountains of Armenia and Georgia he entered Persia and arrived at Ispahan on the 17th July. While there Careri exploited his friendship with the Polish ambassador and in his train twice visited the court of the Shiah. Like Thevenot again he visited Shiraz and the ruins of Persepolis and then went *via* Lar to Bandar Congo where he took a boat for Daman on the 26th November 1694. But it was not until the 10th January 1695 that Careri arrived at his destination. The journey was not without its excitements. Careri had been advised to take his passage in an English boat bound for Surat but he preferred a Moorish ship going to Daman instead. The English were then at war with the French and he apprehended that French men-of-war might be lying in wait near Surat for their enemies but the Moors were at peace with all nations and it was safer to travel in one of their vessels. He had been also told that the customs house men at Surat were exceptionally strict as pearls were often smuggled from Persia through

4. *Viaggi per Europa*, 2 Vols, first published at Naples in 1701.

that port. Moreover the English boat had yet to take its cargo while the ship of his choice was ready to sail immediately. The fare from Congo to Daman says Careri was "according to the usual rate a Toman for me and thirty *Abassis*" for the servant but through the good offices of the Portuguese Commissioner he got his passage free. The sea was infested by corsairs. The Baloche pirates operated in their home waters while the notorious Sanganians cruised along the coast from Sind to Gujarat and sometimes extended their lawless activities as far as the Bay of Surat. The pilot a former trader in tobacco knew nothing about things nautical. No wonder the ship lost its bearing and an overdose of opium did not help to restore the confused pilot's sang-froid. Every sail on the distant horizon caused an alarm and Careri had no doubt that more than once they narrowly escaped the Sanganians. He had only one thing to say in their favour, while the Baloche pirates made slaves of their prisoners and treated them with barbarous cruelty the Sanganians being Hindus were content with the prize and left the passengers alone. At last when the coast line was in view and the captain and crew were under the erroneous impression that they were somewhere between Bassein and Daman Careri volunteered to go ashore and ascertain their position. He found to his dismay that they were off Mangrol, a small port of Gujarat, far to the north of Daman and the point they had sighted a few days earlier was not Diu as they had persuaded themselves but probably a stronghold of the dreaded Sanganians. It is no small credit to him that in the midst of all this confusion Careri did not fail to note when he first saw a flying fish. Once at Daman Careri was among friends for throughout his journey in the east he experienced nothing but kindness from the Portuguese. From Daman he went to Bassein where the Superior of the Jesuits invited him to settle and resume his legal practice. He was assured not only of a number of wealthy clients but also of an advantageous marriage but the prospects of a happy home and a busy practice could not tempt the restless wanderer. He moved on and visited the famous Buddhist caves at Kanheri which his fellow countryman Pietro della Valle had left unnoticed. Careri wrongly imagined that he was the first European to describe this wonder of industry and stone carvers' art for long before him Garcia da Orta had given a brief account of the cave temples of Mandapeshwar and Kanheri. The Dutchman John Huyghen van Linschoten almost literally reproduced Da Orta's account but Careri can rightly claim that no writer, Indian or European, had previously described the caves in such minute details with such unerring accuracy.[5] Thevenot's accounts of Ellora compares but

5. Sir Thomas Herbert probably refers to the Mandapeshwar caves when he writes of a temple "by incredible toil cut out of the hard Rock", which "was divided into three Isles and Galleries", and "the idols so exceeding ugly as would affright an *European* Spectator; nevertheless, this was a celebrated place, and so abundantly frequented by idolaters, as induced the *Portuguese* in zeal with a considerable force to master the Town and to demolish the Temples, breaking in pieces all the monstrous brood of misshapen Pagods."—p. 40. The demolition however was not thorough and complete as Herbert suggests for some of the figures were simply plastered over. Recently the removal of the plaster revealed a remarkable Naṭaraja group.

unfavourably with Careri's graphic discourse on Kanheri which may still serve as an excellent guide for the visitors of to-day so far as the general aspects are concerned. It is true he mistook Buddhas and Bodhisattvas for Greek giants and ascribed the rock-hewn temples to Alexander. But Indology was a science yet to be born when Careri rode to Kanheri and the average educated European knew the story of Alexander's Indian campaign and things of a gigantic dimension were naturally associated with the Greek hero just as Indians were wont to credit to Bhima all performances involving superhuman exertion. But Careri was not alone in his error. William[6] Finch thought that the Asoka pillar in the Allahabad fort "seemeth to have been placed by Alexander or some other great conqueror, who could not passe further for Ganges". Coryat laboured under a triple delusion when he asserted that he had been to a city called "Detee (Delhi) where Alexander the Great Joyned battell with Porus, King of India, and conquered him ; and in token of his victorie erected a brasse pillar, which remaineth to this day."[7] Alexander did not fight Porus at Delhi, he did not set up a pillar there and the one to which Coryat alludes was of polished sandstone and not of brass. Once a legend gains sufficient currency it is apt to be accepted without criticism, and we are not surprised when Sir Thomas Herbert[8] says that the Allahabad pillar was "probably fixt there for ostentation by *Alexander* or *Bacchus*" and quotes in support Ovid's verses :

> Whose conquest through the Orient are renowned
> Where tawny India is by Ganges bound.

Careri did not fail to notice the inscriptions of Kanheri though he did not care to give an exhaustive list. In his days neither the script nor the subject matter of these strange writings were known but they have since been all deciphered. He followed the same road from Mandapeshwar as a modern visitor does to-day, the road is still bad, but the jungle has been thinned and the wild animals have all disappeared with the exception of perhaps a few jackals. When Lord Valentia went to Kanheri in the early years of the nineteenth century the jungle was still haunted by tigers.[9] A few hamlets or to be more accurate, miserable huts are still to be found in the forest between Borivili and Kanheri but it is not possible to identify the villages Careri passed through. The caves were deserted long before he came to India and they still remain completely untenanted though most of them are in an excellent state of preservation and may serve as good dormitories for people seeking solitude. Careri then proceeded to Goa. Like other travellers he refers to the decline of Portuguese power in India but there is hardly any hint about that moral depravity of which Francois Pyrard de Laval and Pietro della Valle made

6. Foster—*Early Travels in India*, p. 177.
7. Foster, *op. cit.*, p. 248.
8. Herbert—*Some Yeares Travels*, pp. 66-67.
9. Valentia—*Voyages and Travels*, Vol. II, p. 198 (London 1809).

so much.[10] At Ispahan, Congo, Daman, Bassein and Goa, Careri had enjoyed the unbounded hospitality of Portuguese priests and laymen alike and although he writes of the stinginess of two Augustinian fathers the Portuguese had every claim on his gratitude. Careri left Goa before long for his cherished object was yet unattained. He wanted to have an audience of the Great Moghul himself. Aurangzeb was then encamped at Galgala waging a war against the Hindu and Muslim powers of the south that was ultimately to prove the ruin of his empire. To Galgala then Careri turned his unwearied steps accompanied by a Kanarese porter from Goa and a Hindu interpreter from Golkonda. Through the good offices of the Christian soldiers in the Moghul army Careri at last obtained admission to the court of the Emperor of whom he has left a fairly good pen-picture. His ambition fulfilled, Careri returned to Goa by a partly different route and embarked for China. He visited Macao, Canton, Nanking and Peking. While in China he was suspected to be an emissary of the Pope specially deputed to enquire into the differences then prevailing among the missionaries of different orders. Unfounded as it was, the suspicion cost him the good feelings of the Jesuits. None the less he managed to get an introduction to the Emperor and thus had audience of three of the mightiest rulers in Asia, a good luck that fell to the lot of few travellers. It is needless to add that a man of Careri's enterprise and inquisitiveness could not leave China without visiting the great wall. He left Peking on the 25th November, 1695 and set out from Macao on the 9th April 1696 to arrive at Manilla on the 8th May. A Spanish galleon took him across the Pacific and after a long voyage of five months he reached Acapulco in Mexico on the 12th January 1697. Then he went to Mexico city where he was warmly received by the Viceroy, Count of Montezuma, a nobleman of mixed descent as his name indicates. But the charms of the metropolis could not hold him long and he was on his way again intent on seeing the mines of Pachuca and the pyramids of Tezcuco. After witnessing many of the wonders of the two worlds he at last turned homewards and reached Cadiz on the 4th June 1698. He then travelled across Spain to France and took a boat at Marseilles for Genoa. From Genoa he proceeded to Milan and from Milan to his home town of Naples where Careri reached on the third of December. According to his own calculation, Careri completed his tour round the world in five years five months and twenty days. A man of untiring energy Gemelli Careri had kept his journal with strict punctuality and even in the midst of a stormy voyage he did not fail to note anything worth recording. After his return home he did not take long to revise his journal put it in the proper form and get it ready for the press. *Giro del Mondo* was published in six volumes at Naples in 1699-1700. Each volume dealt specially with one particular country and was dedicated to a separate personage. The first volume was dedicated to Don Luigi, Duke of Medina and the volume on Indostan (Hindusthan) to Don Carlos Sanseverino, Prince of Biriguano

10. Pyrard, Vol. II, Part I, pp. 114-115.
Pietro della Valle—Vol. I, p. 161.

and Duke of Sao Marco. The publication attained an unprecedented popularity and a second edition quickly followed. The Italian text went through eight editions within thirty years, six in the author's lifetime and two after his death.

Giro del Mondo	6 vols.	Naples,	1699-1700
	6 vols.	Venice,	1700
	9 vols.	,,	1710
	9 vols.	,,	1719
	6 vols.	Paris,	1719
	6 vols.	Naples,	1721
	6 vols.	Paris,	1727
	9 vols.	Venice,	1728

The last edition, that of 1728, is usually considered to be the best.

Careri's fame as a writer and traveller soon spread across the limits of his own country and his work was translated into English, French, German, Spanish and Portuguese. Within four years of the publication of the Italian text an English version appeared in Awnsham and John Churchill's *A Collection of Voyages and Travels* (1704) and reappeared in the subsequent editions of that collection in 1732, 1744, 1745 and 1752. Extracts from Careri's account of China were printed in Thomas Astley's *New General Collections of Voyages and Travels* in 1745-47 and the *Travels round the World* found a place in *A Compendium of Authentic and Entertaining Voyages* edited by Tobias Smollett, published in 1756 and re-published ten years later (in 1766). Obviously Careri had lost none of his original popularity. John Harris mentions him and may have utilised his work but did not reprint any part of it, James Burney commented on Careri's account of his voyage from Manila to Mexico in Vol. IV of his *Chronological History of Discoveries in the South Sea* (1803-1817) and Plates of Mexican antiquities reappeared in Vol. IV of Aglio's *Antiquities of Mexico* (1830-48). The first French version was published at Paris in six volumes in 1719 under the title of *Voyage autour du Monde.* It went through two more editions in 1727 and 1776-1777 and again found a place in Vol. 16 of Antoine Francois Prevost's *Histoire Génèrale des Voyages* (1747-80) and Vol. 15 of J. F. Laharpe's *Abrège de l'histoire génèrale des Voyages* (1816). A German rendering *Reise um die Welt* is available in Vol. IV of *Allgemeine Historie der Reisen zu Wasser und Lande* (Leipzig 1747-77) and a Portuguese version *Naufrage d'une Patache Portugues* in Vol. 3 of *Voyages Imaginaires* (Amsterdam 1787-1789). The Spanish translation of the part relating to Mexico *Viaji a la Neuva Espana* was published at Mexico as recently as 1927.

If Careri found a wide circle of readers in Western Europe both before and after his death some of the later critics had not been very kind to him. He has been roundly accused of literary piracy and unscrupulous mendacity. It has been suggested that he had never been to the court of Peking and his account was based entirely on the works of previous writers. One critic went so far as to insinuate that Gemelli Careri had never been out of Naples and the whole of his voyage was an outrageous invention. Careri makes no secret of his indebtedness to his predecessors. In fact he refers by name to Maffaeus (pp. 27, 69, 73, 75, 94, 209 and 304). Thevenot (pp. 13, 196, 214 and 230), Tavernier (pp. 85, 187, 188 and 223), Bernier (pp. 136, 196 and 212) and Teixeira (p. 196) in Part III of his *Giro del Mondo* and also mentions *Vida de Affonso de Albuquerque* (p. 96) and *Asia Portugueza* (p. 95), though the author's (Fariya e Souza) name is not given. But it is preposterous to suggest that Careri produced a work so informative and accurate without ever leaving his native city. His detailed description of Kanheri alone would give a lie to the charge.[11] Whether he was actually introduced to Aurangzeb at Galgala or to the Chinese Emperor at Peking it is difficult to prove or disprove at this distance of time but how could he learn that Aurangzeb was at Galgala, a place by no means widely known, in March 1695 without ever leaving Naples is a question that is not easy to answer. Careri had certainly been to India and no less an authority than Humboldt asserts that he must have been to Mexico as well. "I shall not discuss the question whether Gemelli had been to China and Persia", says he "but having travelled in the interiors of Mexico, mainly by the road the Italian traveller describes so minutely I can affirm that Gemelli had as undoubtedly been to Mexico, to Acapulco, and in the small villages of Matzlan and San Augustin de les

11. A brief winter day was all that Careri could spare for Kanheri and the journey back had to be completed before darkness added to the dangers of a tiger infested jungle path. That probably explains the omission of a few interesting details which we notice in his account of the Chaitya hall. Evidently he had not the time to examine more carefully the figures ranged on either side of the main door of the spacious cave nor did he realise that they were the conventional effigies of the donors and their wives and that is why he failed to recognise that on the right as well as on the left there are two male figures with the complement of a couple of the other sex. Though the upper part of one of the female figures on the right side of the door is missing a cursory glance at the anklets on the legs and the clothes leave no doubt about its real character. Careri correctly says that seventeen of the pillars in the Chaitya hall "have capitals" but his account remains incomplete when he adds that they had "figures of elephants on them." Elephants there are and plenty of them but they form parts of sculptured groups depicting different scenes. Sometimes the elephants are seen pouring water on stupas while two naga figures hold *Purna Kalasas* or pitchers filled with water. In other cases they pay their homage to the sacred Bodhi tree. In one group royal personages are seen riding elephants obviously to a place of worship; in another a worried *mahout* anxiously attempts to control an infuriated tusker. The figures on another capital depict riders gliding down the flanks of the beast and elsewhere a frightened lady is being coaxed to mount it. Two other animals sacred to the Buddhists, a lion and a horse, both couchant, are seen on the first pillar to the proper left while on another a bull is seen on the back side. Thus the Kanheri capitals bear all the four animals which are found on Asoka pillars. Since Careri visited Kanheri one pillar in Cave No. 10 has disappeared and of the four figures he saw in Cave No. 31 the outline of the seated ones alone remain while the standing figures are entirely gone. Otherwise the caves remain as the Italian traveller found them more than two hundred and fifty years ago.

Ceuves as Pallas to Crimea and M. Salt to Abyssinia." Abbe Clavigero, who traversed Mexico fifty years before Humboldt, pertinently asked how the author of *Giro del Mondo* could so accurately describe persons living at the time, the convents of Mexico, and churches of many villages unknown even by name in Europe without ever leaving Italy.[12] Whatever may be the shortcomings of his account Careri was no charlatan but that does not mean that each and every one of his statements must be accepted without a careful scrutiny.

IV

Both Thevenot and Careri had eyes to see and ears to hear, they were blessed with an unusually retentive memory, they wielded a facile pen and commanded a charming style. Careri had not, it is true, the linguistic abilities of Thevenot but he made up for this deficiency by his social virtues which earned him the friendship of Europeans of all nationalities resident in the east. His narrative was all the more readable, interpersed as it was with the gossips of the market place and scandals whispered at the dinner table. But both of them suffered from one common handicap. They were expected to deal with subjects beyond their personal experience and they wrote not only of what they saw but also of what came to their knowledge through less dependable sources. In assessing the historical value of their evidence it is therefore essential to remember that things heard are not things seen and to see things is not to comprehend them properly.

Our travellers were not more gullible than their learned contemporaries. Sometimes they rightly refused to accept doubtful statements at their face value. Careri for instance did not believe that the cupolas at Kanheri were tombs of deceased persons, for hewn out of solid rock they could not possibly have any hollow chamber inside. But they lived and worked in an age by no means oversceptical and could not always rise above the easy credulity that characterised it. Careri unhesitatingly repeated the story of Nuno da Cunha "encountering the city *Diu,* in the year 1635, found an old Man of 335 years of Age, who had a Son of 90. He had chang'd his Teeth three times, and his Beard as often grew Grey, after having been Black."[13] No less astounding is the "apish miracle" though Sir Thomas Roe had not the least suspicion about its authenticity.[14] "A juggler of Bengala (of which craft there are many and rare) brought to the King a great ape, that could, as hee professd, divine and prophesy (and to this beast by some sects is much divinitie ascribed). The King tooke from his finger a ring, and caused it to bee hid under the girdle of one among a dozen other boys, and bad the ape divine ; who went to the right child, and tooke it out. But His Majestie (somewhat more curious) caused in twelve several papers in Persian letters to bee written the names

12. Humboldt quoted in *Biographie Universelle,* Vol. 17, p. 53.
13. Careri, Book III, Chap. V, p. 192.
14. Foster, *The Embassy of Sir Thomas Roe,* p. 280.

of twelve lawgivers, as Moses, Christ, Mahomett, Aly, and others, and, shuffling them in a bagg, bad the beast divine which was the true law; who, putting in his foote, tooke out that inscribed the Christ. This amazed the King, who, suspecting that the apes master could reade Persian, and might assist him, wrote them anew in court characters, and presented them the second tyme. The ape was constant, found the right, and kissed it. Wherat a principal officer grew angry, telling the King it was some imposture, desiering hee might have leave to make the lotts anew, and offered him selfe to punishment if the ape could beguile him. Hee wrote the names, putting only eleven into the bagg, and kept the other in his hand. The beast searchd, but refusd all. The King commanded to bring one; the beast tore them in fury, and made signes of the true lawgivers name was not among them. The King demanded wher it was; and hee rann to the nobleman and caught him by the hand in which was the paper inscribed with the name of Christ Jesus. The King was troubled, and keepes the ape." Roe affirms that the miracle of the Christian ape was witnessed by thousands of spectators. Nor was this attitude limited to spheres spiritual. Necromancy being a recognised art(?), Thomas Coryat had no difficulty in believing a story about Akbar's sorcery, "who beeing once in a strange humour, to shew a spectacle to his nobles, brought forth his chiefest queene, with a sword cut off her head, and after the same, perceiving the heavinesse and sorrow of them for the death of her (as they thought), caused the head by vertue of his exorcisms, to be set on againe, no signe appearing of any stroke with his sword."[15] This is not indeed a contemporary account of Akbar's proficiency in the black magic but between the emperor's death and Coryat's arrival in India there was hardly a decade's interval. Mandelslo did not believe in the existence of two-headed snakes except as a freak[16] but William Finch writes of "bucklers and divers sorts of drinking cups" made of "Indian asse-horne."[17]

V

It is no wonder that the seventeenth century travellers should be inadequately informed about the geography of India. They did not know the country as a whole and in most cases their stay was all too brief. The knowledge of the Greek authors, which many of them could not claim, was of little use. Herbert quotes Strabo, Pliny, Curtius and Herodotus but he puts the southern limit of Alexander's advance at Daman[18] and identifies Surat with Muziris.[19] Thevenot's reference to *murdakhors* or the anthropophagi is also to be attributed to his classical studies. He probably relied on Herodotus who mentions an Indian tribe that lived

15. Foster, *Early Travels in India*, pp. 276-277.
16. Mandelslo, p. 27.
17. Foster, *Early Travels in India*, p. 176. Foster suggests that the Indian Rhinoceros is meant.
18. *Some Yeares Travels*, p. 41.
19. *Ibid*, p. 43.

on raw flesh and practised cannibalism.[20] Yet some of them, like Herbert, interrupted their narrative and paused to give an account of the country, its people and their history. When they set to write of the entire sub-continent they had naturally to rely on the available literature on the subject. But unfortunately the earlier writers were not better informed and they had in their time blindly drawn upon their predecessors. Thus wrong information passed from traveller to traveller and gained wider currency and greater credence as uncritical acceptance was apt to be misconstrued as independent corroboration. A few travellers more enterprising than the rest like Tavernier, Bernier and Manucci spent long years in India and had first hand knowledge of many of the provinces. The employees of the English, French and the Dutch East India Companies like Hedges, Methwold, Paelsert and Martin had wide experience of persons and places in their own particular spheres. But none of them had the industry, scholarship or critical acumen that marked the eleventh century Muslim mathematician Abu Rihan Alberuni and their credulity and carelessness often landed them in serious blunders. These were accepted as authentic facts by unwary writers and were repeated by them sometimes without any reference to the original sources. Nor were all the late comers content with a faithful recital of their predecessors' tales and they often essayed to embellish them with additional details. Hawkins despite his intimate association with Jahangir did not know that the Mughal empire had more than five sub-divisions[21] but fortunately his account went unnoticed by many of the more popular later travellers. Herbert writing of the same reign extends the north-western boundary of the empire "to the *Caucasus* and the *Maurenahar, Tartar* and *Persian*" and asserts that India had "thirty eight large Provinces (petty kingdoms of old)."[22] Peter Mundy had Baffin's map before him and excluded the Deccan from India.[23] But there was a remarkable agreement among Roe, Terry, De Laet and Mandelslo[24] as to the number of provinces into which the empire was divided in their days. They all affirm that the provinces numbered thirty-seven but on important details vital divergence of opinion is noticed. The chaplain very likely made better use of his leisure than His Excellency

20. Rawlinson, *The History of Herodotus*, Vol. II (1858), pp. 489-490. Elphinstone heard from some travelling merchants that 'one Afghan tribe (the Vizeerees) were savages and ate human flesh'. *Kingdom of Caubul*, Vol. I, p. 45.
21. Foster, *Early Travels*, p. 100. They are, the Punjab, Bengal, Malwa, the Deccan and Gujarat.
22. p. 58.
23. *Travels of Peter Mundy*, Vol. II, p. 305.
24. Foster, *The Embassy of Sir Thomas Roe*, pp. 490-496; Foster, *Early Travels*, pp. 291-295; Hoyland and Banerjee, *De Laet's Empire of the Great Mogol*, pp. 5-14; Mandelslo, pp. 14-16. Terry mentions the following thirty-seven provinces: (1) Candahar, (2) Cabul, (3) Multan, (4) Hajacan, (5) Buckor. (6) Tatta, (7) Soret, (8) Jesolmeere, (9) Attack, (10) Penjab, (11) Chishmere, (12) Banchish, (13) Jengapor, (14) Jenba, (15) Delli, (16) Bando, (17) Malway, (18) Chitor, (19) Guzarat, (20) Chandis, (21) Berar, (22) Narvar, (23) Gwaliar, (24) Agra, (25) Sanbal, (26) Baker, (27) Nagracutt, (28) Syba, (29) Kakares, (30) Gor, (31) Pitan, (32) Kanduana, (33) Patna, (34) Jesual, (35) Menat, (36) Udessa, (37) Bengala.

the Ambassador in testing the information that possibly came from a common source. Between Roe's and Terry's lists there is but one discrepancy and that a very minor one. "Jeselmeere" No. 8 in Terry's list found no place in Roe's, while Roch, Roe's No. 27 is omitted by Terry. De Laet did not come to India at all. His account of *The Empire of the Great Mogol* is professedly a compilation and his list agrees with Terry except for greater details. As De Laet's work on the Moghul empire was published in 1631 Mandelslo made free use of it only with one variation in the list of provinces, Narwar, No. 28 of De Laet being Mandelslo's 26. Otherwise the two lists agree not only in sequence but in all the main details. But Mandelslo was less careful in checking his facts and rashly committed himself to statements the more cautious Dutch geographer warily avoided. Two instances will suffice to illustrate the point. De Laet writes of Kashmir "The capital of this province is called Siranakar. The province lies upon both sides of the river Behat or Phat which winds in a meandering course with many islands, and finally falls into the Indus, or as others declare into the Ganges though this latter appears to me less probable. The province is mountainous (it marches with Kabul) and rather cold, though less so than the kingdom of Thebet which adjoins it on the east. At a distance of 8 leucae from the capital lies a large lake 5 leucae in circumference, in the middle of which is an island upon which a royal palace has been built for the convenience of those hunting wild geese; these birds abound in the lake in vast numbers. Near to the river which flows through the middle of this lake towards the west, enormous trees are to be seen, whose leaves are somewhat similar to those of the chestnut, though their wood is different. When it is cut into planks, this wood presents the appearance of waves, and is very well suited for the making of boxes."[25] Terry's note being the earlier is more precise and brief—"the chiefe citie is called Siranakar. The river Phat passeth through it, and so, creeping about many ilands, slides to Indus."[26] Roe agrees that "The Cheefe city is called Sirinakar" but he makes the Jhelum a tributary of the Ganges. "The river of Bhat passeth thorough it and findeth the sea by Ganges or, some say, of itself in the north part of the Bay of Bengala."[27] Mandelslo closely copies De Laet but without his circumspection commits the same error as Roe. His note on Kashmir is as follows: "The Province of *Chismer*, or *Quexmer*, the chief City whereof is called *Syranakar*, is seated upon the River of *Bezat* or *Badt* which makes a great number of Isles in their Province, and after a great compass falls into the *Ganges*. It touches some part of the Province of *Kabul*, and is cold enough by reason of its Mountains, though it may be affirm'd, that in comparison of the kingdom of Tiebet, which is as it were its Frontiers on the East side, it is very temperate. About eight *Cos* (which make four Leagues) from the chief City, in the midst of a Lake which is three miles about, there is a little Isle, where the *Mogul* hath built a very fair House, for the convenience of hunting the wild Goose. All along the *River* which

25. Hoyland and Banerjee, *De Laet's Empire of the Great Mogol*, pp. 7-8.
26. Foster, *Early Travels*, p. 292.
27. Foster, *The Embassy of Sir Thomas Roe*, p. 491.

runs through the middle of this Lake, there is a kind of a tree, whose leaves are like that of Chestnut, but the wood which is somewhat of a brownish colour, is chequer'd with small streaks of several colours, which makes it much sought after by persons of Quality."[28] De Laet had the scholarly integrity and decency of frankly owning his indebtedness to Terry. He does not deny his knowledge of Roe's Journal, on the contrary he compares the two lists and makes a pointed reference to their general agreement. Mandelslo relied solely on De Laet but he had not the fairness of acknowledging his obligations to the Dutch scholar. He made such omissions and alterations in the plagiarized note as would give it a semblance of originality but in doing so he committed an egregious factual mistake which the more cautious scholar had avoided. This is not the sole instance of Mandelslo's incompetent pilfering. In a note that he appended to his list of the thirty seven provinces De Laet observed: "Peter Texeira, in his account of the kingdom of Persia, enumerates several provinces of India, but not nearly so many as I have just mentioned. He speaks of the province of Utrad on the Jaxartes with a capital of the same name, but does not say where it is situated. He also writes that the kingdom of Cache produces most excellent horses. These are called Cachy after that kingdom which seem to be situated to the north of Cambay."[29] With the circumspection characteristic of a true scholar De Laet refrains from making any comment on Teixeira's statement and leaves it to his readers to take it for what it is worth. Not so the traveller. He had been to Cambay and felt himself competent to hazard a guess about the neighbouring regions, and here is the result: "*Texeira,* in his description of *Persia,* speaking of certain Provinces of the *Indies,* names that of *Utrat,* with its chief City, but he only names it, without giving any account of its situation. He speaks also of the kingdom of *Caeche,* and sayes it is considerable for the Race-horses it breeds, near *Cambaya,* towards the North: but certainly, it is no other than the Province of *Candisch,* before spoken of."[30] Teixeira was right in saying that Cutch was noted for its horses and lay to the north of Cambay though the peninsula of Kathiawad intervened between the island of Cutch and the Gulf of Cambay but Khandesh was nowhere near it and certainly could not boast of a special breed of race-horses. To confuse Cutch with Khandesh is to betray the grossest possible ignorance about Indian provinces. It is unnecessary to labour this point further. All that is needed is to remember that even a contemporary account cannot be more reliable than its sources and neither Thevenot nor Careri was more conscientious or less confident than Mandelslo. The average European traveller had no scruple about plagiarism and it was practised without any compunction throughout the century. Of course journals kept by resident merchants fall under a different category and are not to be confused with travellers' accounts.

It will be unfair to suggest that no seventeenth century traveller ever questioned the accuracy of current heresies, historical and geographical.

28. Mandelslo, p. 14.
29. Hoyland and Banerjee, *De Laet's Empire of the Great Mogol*, p. 15.
30. Mandelslo, p. 16.

In his letter to Lord Carew dated January 17, 1615(16) Sir Thomas Roe drew his lordship's attention to certain errors in the maps of India.[31] "I have one observation more to make of the falseness of our maps, both of Mercator and all others, and their ignorance in this countrey. First, the famous River Indus doeth not emptie himselfe into the sea at Cambaya as his chiefe mouth but at Sinde. My reason is: Lahor stands upon Indus, from whence to Sinde it is navigable, to Cambaya not so. Lahor in the maps is also falsely set downe, it lying north from Surat about a thousand miles." Roe was both right and wrong, for the Indus flows into the sea through the province of Sind but Lahore is on the banks of one of its principal tributaries and not on the Indus itself. William Finch was better informed and correctly stated that "The Castle (of Lahore) is seated on Ravee, a goodly river which falleth into Indus, downe which go many boats of sixty tunne or upwards, for Tatta in Sind after the fall of the raine, being a journey of some fortie days alongst by Multan, Seetpore, Buchur, Rauree[32] etc." Finch had been to Lahore himself but Roe wrote from Ajmer. Finch also knew that "Indus passeth in great beautie" by "Attock, a citie with a strong castle."[33] Coryat crossed the Indus on his way to Lahore and knew that the river had its source somewhere outside India.[34] Pietro della Valle added further to the extant knowledge and pointed out that "the River which disembogues in the inmost part of this Gulph (Cambay) is not *Indus,* but this *Mehi,* which I speak of, a River of handsome but ordinary greatness, and which hath not the least correspondence with Indus."[35] Thevenot also crossed the Mahi but was not apparently worried by these topographical errors. In his account of Kashmir he confuses the Chenab with the Jhelum and makes it flow into the Indus at Attock and confidently warns others not to mistake it for the Moselle which flows through Kabulistan and should be identified with Behat, which again is the Muslim name for the Jhelum. The source of Thevenot's error is not difficult to trace. His own personal knowledge was limited to the tract between Surat and Cambay and the road from Surat to Masulipatam. For information about other regions he usually turned to two of his countrymen Tavernier and Bernier, while he specifically mentions Bernier as one of his authorities more than once, Thevenot does not extend the same courtesy to Tavernier. Bernier does not mention the name of the river that flows by Srinagar but correctly indicates its course. "It winds gently around the kingdom, and passing through the capital, bends its peaceful course towards *Baramoule,* where it finds an outlet between two steep rocks, being then joined by several smaller rivers from the mountains, and dashing over precipices it flows in the direction of Atek, and joins the *Indus.*"[36] Earlier while describing the journey to Kashmir Bernier had written, "Some will pitch their tents on the banks of the *Tchenau,* others

31. Foster, *The Embassy of Sir Thomas Roe,* p. 91 and also p. 104.
32. Foster, *Early Travels,* p. 161.
33. *Ibid,* p. 168.
34. *Ibid,* p. 243.
35. Pietro della Valle, *Travels in India,* Vol. I, p. 64.
36. Bernier, *Travels in the Mogul Empire,* pp. 396-97.

will repair to the adjacent towns and villages, and the rest will be under the necessity of encamping in this burning *Bember*." Thevenot, in his anxiety to improve upon Bernier supplied the name of the river that flowed by Srinagar and Baramula and tried to indicate more definitely where it met the Indus, not pausing to think that if Berneir was not so precise in his statement he might have good reasons for remaining vague.

Bernier names twenty provinces into which Aurangzeb's empire was divided.[38] These were Delhi, Agra, Lahore, Hasmer (Ajmer), Gusaratte, Candahar, Maloua, Patna or Beara, Elabas (Allahabad), Haoud (Oudh), Moultan, Jagannat in which is included Bengale, Kachemire, Caboul, Tata, Aurengabad formerly Dauletabad, Varada (Berar), Candeys, Talengand (Telengana) and Baganala (Baglan). It would have been wise of Thevenot faithfully to follow a guide generally so reliable, but evidently he was familiar with the works of the earlier writers who mentioned no less than thirty-seven provinces. Thevenot made confusion worse confounded in his attempt to reconcile the earlier lists with the later. Roe was included in his uncle's *Relations of diverse curious voyages* and Roe claimed to have derived his information from a state paper preserved in the library of the Imperial Moghul. He was supported by Terry and Mandelslo and the discrepancy between the old list and the new might have caused no little bewilderment to the new enquirer. He arranged his chapters according to Bernier's list and then tried to locate the missing provinces in some of the new subahs, possibly with the help of Baffin's map, an easy solution, no doubt, but liable to serious inaccuracies in the absence of precise knowledge. He naturally started with the province of Gujarat as Surat, where he landed, and Ahmadabad and Cambay, cities he visited immediately after his arrival in India, were all within that province. He next described the province and town of Agra no doubt because it was the metropolis of the empire. Dehly or Gehanabad, Azmer, Sinde (Tatta of Bernier's list), Multan, Candahar, Caboul, Cashmir, Lahors, Ayoud with which he added Varad, Halabas, Becar, Oulesser (Orissa) or Bengala, Malava, Candich, Balagate (Bernier's Aurangabad), Dolatabad, of which Thevenot makes a separate province, Telenga and Baglana completed the list. Thus the tally of a score remained unaffected though Varad was joined with Oudh to make room for Daulatabad and a new province, Becar, was substituted for Bihar. In the joint province of Oudh and Varad which however were not geographically contiguous Thevenot placed some of the northern provinces of the Moghul empire mentioned by De Laet on the authority of Terry and Roe, and by Mandelslo on the authority of De Laet—Caucares, Bankich, Nagarcut, Siba, Gor, Pitan, Canduana and some others. In the mysterious province of Becar were included Douab, Jesuat and Udesse. Three more provinces, Gualear, Chitor and Mando were located in Malava. Thus thirteen out of the seventeen remaining provinces were accounted for but this created an insuperable difficulty for the modern student. He is called upon to solve the jigsaw puzzle of the composite provinces of Ayoudh, Varad and Becar.

37. Bernier, *Travels in the Mogul Empire*, p. 391.
38. *Ibid*, pp. 456-458.

It should be noted that even with this ingenious makeshift, Thevenot failed to provide for all the additional provinces of Roe and Terry as a cursory comparison will show. To add to our difficulty Thevenot's Becar cannot be safely identified with Bakar of the earlier writers on the ground of similarity or with Bernier's Beara or Bihar which a process of elimination would indicate. According to Thevenot, "The province of *Becar,* which comprehends the Countries of *Douab, Jesuat* and *Udesse,* is also watered by the Rivers that discharge themselves into the *Ganges.* It lies not only to the East of *Dehly,* but is also the most Eastern Province of *Mogolistan,* by the countrey of *Udesse,* which shuts it in with its Mountains. And that great Province being rich, by reason of the fertility thereof, yields to the *Great Mogul* Yearly above fourteen Millions. It contins several good Towns; but the best are *Sumbal, Menapour, Rageapour, Jehanac* and above all *Becaner,* which at present is the Capital, standing to the West of the Ganges." Terry says of Bakar "the chiefe citie called Bikaneer. It lyeth on the west side of Ganges."[39] Roe affirms that "The cheefe citty is called Bikanir. It bordereth north-west on Ganges."[40] There is therefore no difference between Terry and Roe, if Bikaner is not in the near neighbourhood of the Ganges it is certainly to the west of that river. But Thevenot placed the province to the east of Delhi and still maintained that Bikaner was its capital at the time he wrote. Of the other cities in this mysterious province Sambal is the chief town of a province of the same name, according to Roe (his No. 19) and Terry (No. 25). Rageapour (Roe's Ragepur) is the capital of Jesual (Thevenot's Jesuat and Nos. 16 and 34 of Roe and Terry respectively) and Terry places it east of Patna. Neither Roe nor Terry is a safe guide for they make two separate provinces of Gor (Gaur) and Bengala and commit other mistakes, but Thevenot's confusion was probably due to too much reliance on Baffin's map. Baffin places Udessa, with its capital Jekanat to the north east of Bengala. To its immediate west he places Mevat, and next to that province Jesuoll and Sanball. Baffin's Bakar is to the north of Sanball and north east of Delhi. No province of the Moghul days even approximately corresponded to this geographical fiction. But as Thevenot went mainly by Bernier's list he probably made an ineffective attempt to reconcile Baffin and Bernier, for Baffin's Udessa is the easternmost province of India, by including Sambal, Bikaner (located east of Delhi by Baffin) Rajápur and Udessa in Bernier's province of Patna or Beara (modern Bihar).

Nor is it possible to identify Thevenot's Varad or Varal with Bernier's Varada (Berar). It is like Becar another fictitious province that comprised the north-eastern region of Baffin's map "to wit *Gor, Pitan, Canduana* and some others." But why Thevenot placed Nagarcut (Nagarkot) and Calamac (Jwalamukhi) in the province of Ayoudh and Nerval (Narwar) and Gehud (Gohad) in the province of Halabas (Allahabad) is more than what we can guess.[41]

39. Foster, *Early Travels,* p. 294.
40. Foster, *The Embassy of Sir Thomas Roe,* p. 493.
41 Curiously enough with all the guides and popular handbooks at their disposal even modern travellers are not always free from geographical confusion. Ibanez,

Bernier's scheme, limited, as it was, to an inventory of the provinces with their Sarkars and Parganas and the estimated revenue, was too modest for Thevenot. He tried to embody in his account of the provinces all information that he could gather about the curiosities of the region, the habit of the people, the agricultural and industrial products as well as plants and animals. But in spite of his best efforts this ambitious plan suffered from serious inaccuracies. Not knowing that the musk deer was not an animal of the plains he extends its habitat to the province of Azmer (Ajmer) and confidently states: "There is in these countries, a Beast like a Fox, in the Snout, which is no bigger than a Hare ; the Hair of it, is of the colour of a Stags, and the Teeth like to a Dogs. It yields most excellent Musk." The musk deer has it is true two protruding canine teeth but it is a denizen of the Himalayan regions and not to be found anywhere near Ajmer. Careri knew that the musk deer or, as he called it the musk goat, occurred in Bhutan and in regions bordering on China, but not knowing all the facts he could not dismiss Thevenot's statement as utterly unfounded and unhesitatingly copied it almost word for word. Roe mentions musk among other costly articles to be found at Ajmer[42] and Thevenot might have been under the impression that the musk yielding animal also lived in the neighbourhood. Thevenot and Careri at least knew that the musk came from a "Bladder full of corrupt Blood, and that Blood maketh the Musk or is rather the Musk itself," but Francois Pyrard gives the most queer account of the animal and the process of extracting the scent. "Musk," he asserts, comes from China alone. It proceeds from a little animal of the size of a cat. To get musk they kill this animal and beat it all over in its skin and so let it rot ; when rotten they make little purses of the skin, and fill them with the flesh, minced small, and thus sell it."[43] This information probably originated with a Jesuit writer Michael Boyen who makes a similar statement in his *La Flore Chinoise*.[44]

One of Thevenot's very curious mistakes can be traced to Tavernier. Writing of the province and town of Agra, Thevenot asserts that the emperor Jehangir "was Interred in a Garden" of Agra "where his Tomb is only painted upon the portal." How Tavernier came to commit so astounding an error we cannot explain, but had not Thevenot inadvertently appropriated some of his worst mistakes the younger traveller's indebtedness to the older would not only have remained unacknowledged but also unestablished.

Careri came to India nearly thirty years after Thevenot but unlike his French predecessor he did not undertake an ambitious survey of the Moghul empire. He furnishes graphic descriptions of cities and camps he visited himself and his minute account of the churches and convents of Goa is accurate in every detail. Two earlier travellers Francois Pyrard of Laval and Pietro della Valle might have served as excellent guides but

---

the Spanish Nobel Laureate, places Colombo on the east coast of Ceylon and the late Lord Lytton after five years in India located Puri in Bihar.

42. Foster, *The Embassy of Sir Thomas Roe*, p. 116.
43. *The Voyage of Francois Pyrard of Laval*, Vol. II, part II, p. 359.
44. Mandelslo's *Travels*, p. 24.

Careri knew his Goa well and not only described the city and its monuments but its flowering plants and fruit trees as well. Not that he does not refer to towns and regions he did not visit but such references are neither numerous nor important. Like Thevenot he also depended on hearsay particularly for the history of the ruling dynasties and the civil administration of the country and naturally his account is not free from occasional errors. But on one important subject that may not be entirely without any interest to the Indian students Thevenot and Careri squarely contradicted each other. Neither of them had any personal knowledge of the notorious Sanganian pirates. Thevenot had not even had a distant glimpse of their sails. Careri suspected that he had. But while Thevenot gave them the worst possible character Careri credited them with a more humane behaviour. Writes Thevenot: "they Board and leap into the Bark, putting every living soul to the Sword (for they have no other Arms but Swords and Arrows:) and if any have a mind to save their lives, there is no other way to it, but to jump into the Sea, and so avoid their fury until they be wholely Masters of the Vessel, for till then, they give no Quarter: but when they find themselves sure of their Prize, they shed no more blood, and make Prisoners of all that remain alive; to hinder whose escaping, they cut the great Tendon that is above the Heel in each Leg, which renders them for ever unable to run away, and indeed it is not possible for a Man who has these Nerves cut, to go. Then they carry them to their Habitations, and set them to keep their flocks, without any hopes whilst they live of being delivered from that Bondage which is worse than death itself."[45] Careri on the contrary contends that these pirates did not make slave of the people they robbed. "The Pirates call'd *Sanganos* and *Ranas*, who are Gentils of Religion, and make no Slaves, but take what they find Aboard without hurting any Body. They live in some Islands, and on the Continent in marshy and inaccessible Places as also in Woods near *Syndi* and the kingdom of *Guzaratte*."[46] We do not know which of the two travellers was more correctly informed but in the absence of corroboration from more dependable sources it is not safe to accept one version in preference to the other.

VI

If our travellers were indifferent geographers they were no better naturalists. Duarte Barbosa mentions flying serpents of the kingdom of Narsyngua (Vijayanagar) in all seriousness. "There are as well serpents which fly in the air, whereof the mere breath and aspect are so deadly as to stay any man who comes near them, which serpents alight on trees or wheresoever they will."[47] Mandelslo believed that the crocodile of the Indian rivers had "no *Vertebre* or *joynts* either in his neck or back."[48] The flying foxes or fruit bats of India were noticed by most of the

45. *The Travels of Monsieur de Thevenot*, Part II, Book IV, Chap. II, p. 176.
46. Careri, *A Voyage round the World*, Book III, Chap. V, p. 190.
47. *The Book of Duarte Barbosa*, Vol. I, p. 199.
48. Mandelslo, p. 27.

travellers ; Linschoten and Fryer[49] referred to the enormous size they attain, Mandelslo and Pietro della Valle[50] found "batts as big as crows", Francois Pyrard de Laval used slightly different language and wrote that "bats there are as large as ravens."[51] But Finch had strange ideas about this common but curious mammal's method of reproduction. "This fowle" he writes, "the people say ingendreth in the eare."[52] Tom Coryat claimed to have seen two unicorns, mistaking rhinoceros for the mythical beast.[53] Roe was not less credulous. He offered to sell in all seriousness "a unicorn's horne" to an imperial prince.[54]

Not only were they prepared to believe whatever they were told about unfamiliar birds and beasts but many of them could not properly describe even domesticated animals they had seen at close quarters. It is not at all difficult to describe the peculiar features of an elephant but Nicholas Downton's account can certainly be improved upon. "(He) hath a body like a house, but a tayle like a ratte, erecting it like a cedar ; little eyes, but great sight ; very melancholly, but wise (they say) and full of understanding (or subtility rather) for a beast. Sometimes they become madd (of what I know not) and breaking loose endanger multitudes. (He) is fed somewhat costly, as with good bread, musk millions, sugarcanes, sweete stalkes, and sower grasse or sedge of the worst. (He) steeres like a hulke, stif-necked, almost all of one peice ; feeds himselfe with his trunck or snoute (that deadly instrument for his rage) being of a just length to the ground ; taking his meat with the end thereof and winding it up (or under, rather) to his mouth, so eates it ; but drinkes there with at length."[55] Though Downton takes the trouble of describing in details how the elephant eats and drinks and moves it is not easy to visualise the animal with "a body like a house and a tail like the rat's that moves like a hulk and eats and drinks with its snout." Terry's description of the second biggest Indian animal, the rhinoceros is not more helpful. The "Rhynocerts" "are large beasts as bigge as the fayrest oxen England affords ; their skins lye platted or as it were in wrinkles upon their backs"[56] is all that we are told. Peter Mundy's account though equally brief is more life-like. He writes of the "Ghendas, whose skinne is very thick and hard, lyeinge in plates over his bodye, with one horne standinge on his nose, as high as a tall horse, but made in proportion like a hogge."[57] Better still is Linschoten's[58] pen picture but neither of them had actually seen the animal and the credit of accurately describing the pachyderm belongs not to the travellers but to their informants. Thevenot's descrip-

49. *Voyage of Linschoten to the East Indies*, Vol. I, p. 302.
Fryer's East India and Persia, Vol. II, p. 99.
50. *Mandelslo*, p. 27; *Travels of Pietro della Valle in India*, Vol. I, p. 103.
51. *Voyage of Francois Pyrard of Laval*, Vol. I, p. 115.
52. Foster, *Early Travels in India*, p. 135.
53. *Ibid*, p. 246.
54. Foster, *The Embassy of Sir Thomas Roe*, p. 254.
55. *The Voyage of Nicholas Downton*, p. 145.
56. Foster, *Early Travels in India*, p. 304.
57. *The Travels of Peter Mundy*, Vol. II. p. 171.
58. *Voyage of Linschoten to the East Indies*, Vol. II, Chap. 47, pp. 8-11.

tion of a tame bat however leaves no doubt that he could give an accurate account of a strange animal in minute details when carefully observed.

Both Thevenot and Careri were also careless about the nomenclature of the animals they saw. They write indiscriminately of apes, baboons and monkeys. In India there is only one ape or man-like monkey, the gibbon or hoolock, and that does not occur in the parts they visited. Of baboons, dogheaded monkeys, there is none in this country. Among the wild beasts that infested the forest near Kanheri Careri mentions tigers and lions. There is no doubt that tigers haunted the neighbourhood of the caves when the Neapolitan traveller visited India and even much later but whether lions survived in the woodlands south of the Narbada in the closing years of the seventeenth century must remain a subject of enquiry. Careri took careful notes of the ancient monuments he saw. His account of the rock-hewn caves and the colleges, convents and cathedrals of Goa leaves little to be desired but his description of the birds he saw as he rode through the lonely forest on his way to Kanheri is extremely vague. Having no guide with him he naturally left them unnamed and only says "some were Green and as big as a Thrush, and sang very well, others bigger, black as velvet, and with vast long Tails ; others Red and Green ; some Black and Green, as big as a Turtle-dove, and many more never seen in Europe." One may guess the identity of the bird with a long tail and velvety black feathers. Careri in all probability saw the ubiquitious king crow but the forest to-day is not very rich in bird life and it is not safe to hazard a guess about the green songster and his red and green and black and green confrères. Probably the latter two were paraqueets and Careri having only a fleeting glimpse of them could not describe them better.

Thevenot devotes one chapter each to the beasts at Delhi and the beasts of the country of Ajmer but he describes only four animals in any detail, the horse, the elephant, the ox and the musk deer. Of these the musk deer alone is wild and uncommon and as we have already noted it has been given a habitat other than its own. The elephant naturally attracted the curiosity of foreign visitors and most of them had something to say about it. Much was not known about the period of gestation or the longevity of this huge beast and it is no wonder that Thevenot and others imagined that its method of mating was different from that of other quadrupeds. Nor was Thevenot alone in attributing rare physiological and psychological peculiarities to the elephant. Peter Mundy believed that "the females (different from other animals) in their place of generation which lyes right under their bellies where the Cowe's adders are placed, and the duggs of these are close to the fore legs."[59] Francois Pyrard ascribes to it almost a human abhorrence of indecency when he asserts that "the animal never covers the female in whatever heat he be, while any one is by."[60] Terry goes one better and says that "The males testicles lye about his forehead ; the females teates are betwixt her forelegges,"[61] though he

59. *Travels of Peter Mundy*, Vol. II, p. 234.
60. *Voyage of Francois Pyrard of Laval*, Vol. II, Pt. II, p. 346,
61. Foster, *Early Travels in India*, p. 307,

claims to have seen several of them.[62] Mundy and Terry were right as to the position of the teats, as for the rest their statement should be taken with more than the proverbial pinch of salt. The story of an elephant run amuck that had the good sense to gently put aside a helpless baby out of gratitude to its mother, which Terry heard from "an English merchant of good credit" was recounted in every detail by Linschoten.[63] No less fanciful is Tavernier's assertion that "at certain seasons the female elephant collects all kinds of leaves and grass, with which she makes for herself a bed with a kind of bolster, elevated 4 or 5 feet from the ground, where contrary to the nature of all other beasts, she lies to await the male."[64] Careri closely follows Thevenot in his account of the elephant but there is good reason to believe that he did not know all the animals he mentions. He seems to think that the Roz and the Meru are the same animal. "Rozes" he writes, "with the Body like a *Cow,* so call'd from a Rose they have on the Breast; the Male of this Species is call'd *Meru,* and has Horns half a span long, and the Body and Tail like a Horse." The Sambhar is called Meru in the Bombay presidency and the Roz is the same animal as the Nilgau. While the former is a deer the latter is an antelope. There is no difference in the general build of the male and female nilgau though they differ in colour and the English rose has nothing to do with one of its names. Its tail no more resembles that of the horse than the elephant's is like the rat's. Curiously enough Peter Mundy mentions at one place the Roż and Nilgau as two different animals[65] although earlier he had noted that they were but different names of the same antelope. Such instances of carelessness are however not rare among seventeenth century travellers.

Careri gave one whole chapter to the "fruit and flowers of Indostan". His account of the common plants of India suffers from the same defects as his description of the animals. The most noticed plants were the cocoa palm, the toddy palm, the areca palm, the betel vine and the pepper vine and here Careri had excellent guides in earlier writers. It is not clear whether he knew Linschoten's *Voyage to the East Indies* where the Indian plants are described in great details with rare scientific accuracy nor does it appear that he had access to the first scientific treatise on medicinal plants and herbs published at Goa by Garcia da Orta more than a century earlier[66] though Pietro della Valle refers to Orta and other botanists of repute.[67] It is however difficult to identify some of the plants of Careri's list without extraneous information. The omlam tree for instance bears according to him "a long Flower beautiful and fragrant enough." The flower is beautiful and fragrant no doubt but by no stretch of imagination can it be described as long. Similarly the tindolim flower is white and not red. Nor does one get a clear idea of papayas growing round the trunk of the tree near the top when Careri says that "they hang like clusters of Grapes about the

62. Foster, *Early Travels in India,* p. 304.
63. *Voyage of Linschoten to the East Indies,* Vol. II, pp. 6-7.
64. Tavernier's *Travels in India,* Vol. I, p. 222.
65. *Travels of Peter Mundy,* Vol. II, pp. 182 and 307.
66. *Coloquios dos Simples e drogas e cousas medicinais da India,* Goa, 1563.
67. *Travels of Pietro della Valle,* Vol. I, p. 37.

top of the Trunk." Careri's identification of the saffron plant with the Arbore Triste of Goa is as fantastic as Thevenot's association of the musk deer with Ajmer. His grounds for appending his chapter on Indian plants to his account of Goa deserves more than a passing notice. "Because all those sorts, which are found in the several Parts of that Tract, being to be had about Goa, and even some that are not elsewhere; it is proper we should give an account of them before we leave that city." This is corroborated by Peter Mundy when he said that "I saw here Sundry sorts off Fruites which I had not seene in North India, butt For any thatt grew there, they Might here bee Found."[68] Careri could not possibly have any knowledge of Peter Mundy's manuscript which was not published until recently.

VII

Travellers do not always bring an unprejudiced mind to a foreign land. People apt to ignore the inconsistencies of their own faith may be keenly alive to the absurdities of others. Familiarity does not always breed contempt; it often engenders tolerance as well. Unfamiliarity on the other hand may sometimes lead to misunderstanding. Unfortunately there is no infallible standard of social conduct and a foreigner may without fully comprehending its inner significance ridicule a long established custom which the native finds perfectly innocuous. It is no wonder that most of the foreign travellers were superficial if not perfunctory in their observation on the social customs and religious practices of India. Only the most striking features could have attracted their notice during their brief sojourn and they had neither the time nor the learning to examine them carefully. But it will be unfair to suggest that all of them approached the subject with superciliousness and contempt. François Pyard in fact paid the Indians he knew a very high compliment when he said "I have never seen men of wit so fine and polished as are these Indians: they have nothing barbarous or savage about them, as we are apt to suppose. They are unwilling indeed to adopt the manners and customs of the Portuguese; yet do they readily learn their manufactures and workmanship, being all very curious and desirous of learning. In fact the Portuguese take and learn more from them than they from the Portuguese; and they that come fresh to Goa are very simpletons till they have acquired the airs and grace of the Indies."[69] How far these encomiums were inspired by genuine admiration for South Indians and to what extent they reflected the bitterness caused by Pyrard's sufferings at the hands of the Portuguese it is difficult to determine at this distance of time. But when he spoke highly of the manners and customs of Bengal where the people, both men and women were according to him, "more cultivated than elsewhere" we should not attach much importance to his testimony as he had not been to that province and had no personal knowledge of its people.

68. *The Travels of Peter Mundy,* Vol. III, Pt. I, p. 59
69. *Voyage of Francois Pyrard of Laval,* Vol. II, Pt. I, pp. 248-249.

The better educated travellers, among whom Thevenot and Careri should be counted, usually took the trouble of reading the earlier writers. This had its advantage and corresponding disadvantage as well, for if they were not absolutely uninformed about India and Indians their views were likely to be influenced by the author of their choice and they could not under the circumstances take an objective view of things. Students of classical literature on the other hand were often prepared to find parallels between Hindu and Greek ideas and strove to discover evidence of Greek influence on Hindu thought and rites without pausing to find out which was earlier. Good Christians were naturally unwilling to recognise anything commendable in other religions but it will be unfair to accuse the ecclesiastics of blind fanaticism. Terry for instance had nothing but praise for those Muslim divines who "spend their dayes in meditation or else in giving good morall precepts unto others."[70] He further commended to his brothers in faith the example of those who, "what impediment soever they have either by pleasure or profit, pray five times everyday."[71] He had also great admiration for those "Mahometans and Gentiles" who "will rather die (like the mother and her seven sonnes : 2 *Mac.* 7) then eate or drinke anything their law forbids. Such meate and drinke as their law allowes they use onely to satisfie nature, not appetite ; hating gluttonie, and esteeming drunkennesse (as indeed it is) a second madnesse, and therefore have but one word in their language (*mest*) for a dunkard and a mad man."[72] But every one had not Terry's broad-mindedness to appreciate the good points in misguided heathens. Downton had no doubt that the filthy fakirs were "really possesst with devils."[73] Herbert thought that the "*Shaster* of the *Bannyans* is a depraved story of the Bible" and in their customs and religious rites he perceived the "delusion Satan charms them with."[74] Roe found "no civil arts" at Ajmer "but such as straggling Christians have lately taught."[75] The customs and manners of the country were, according to him, "either ordinary, or mingled with much barbarisme." "The Gentile, not knoweing any religion" "worshipped after their severall idolatryes all sorts of creatures." "No herecye in the world show so strange examples, nor bragg of such voluntarie poverteyes, punishments, sufferings and chastisements" as Islam. The race of Muhammad, Roe unhesitatingly asserted, was "imposturous."[76] But in comparison with one of his protégés Roe appears exceedingly mild and moderate. Coryat's Christian zeal could not brook even the Muslim call to prayer in the Muslim metropolis and he boldly climbed up a turret and loudly sent forth a defiant cry—"No God but one God and Christ the son of God" thus contradicting the Muezzin's proclamation that Muhammad was the prophet of God.[77] Nothing could conceivably outdo his denun-

70. Foster, *Early Travels in India*, p. 316.
71. *Ibid*, p. 317.
72. *Ibid*, p. 317.
73. *The Voyage of Nicholas Downton*, p. 137.
74. Herbert, *Some Years Travels*, p. 49.
75. Foster, *The Embassy of Sir Thomas Roe*, p. 116.
76. Foster, *The Embassy of Sir Thomas Roe*, pp. 104, 274 and 612.
77. Foster, *Early Travels in India*, p. 315.

ciation of Islam in reckless bravado, blind extravagance and fanatic intolerance. Referring to the life of the prophet he told a Muslim: "The truth whereof if thou didst know as well, I am perswaded thou wouldest spit in the face of thy Alcaron (*al Kuran*) and trample it under thy feete, and bury it under a Jaxe (i.e. *privy*), a booke of that strange and weake matter that I my selfe (as meanely as thou dost see me attired now) have already written two better bookes (God be thanked), and will hereafter this (by Gods *gratious* permission) write another better and truer."[78] A man with a mind so perverse could hardly be expected to take an impartial view of strange customs and novel faiths. But fortunately Coryat formed a class by himself and his record of complacent vanity and foolish fanaticism remains unbeaten.

By the middle of the seventeenth century the travellers' accounts had been more or less stereotyped and every one of them sought to describe the social customs and the religious rites of the countries they visited, as well as the dress, the dwellings, the staple food and the common diversions of the people. Every traveller therefore referred to the early marriage, that prevailed among the Hindus and Muslims alike, the caste system that characterised the Hindus alone, the theory of transmigration in which the "Banias" or, as Roe preferred to call them, the Pythagorians, implicitly believed, the consequent Jain practice of strict vegetarianism or abstention from animal food, the absurd length to which respect for animal life was carried and its abuse and exploitation by less scrupulous persons of other communities and above all the Sati or the practice of self-immolation on the funeral pyre of the deceased husband. Nor was the Hindu doctrine of trinity always overlooked and as it is easier to appreciate physical feats and acrobatic skill than to comprehend the philosophy of the Hindus, no traveller failed to notice the exploits of the jugglers and tumblers and their roadside open air performances as well as the strange habits of and severe self-mortification to which both the Muslim and the Hindu mendicants were wont to subject themselves.

The Indian habits, both Hindu and Muslim, have been described by Thevenot and Careri as well as many of their predecessors. Some of the travellers, Manucci, Thevenot and Tavernier, to mention only three of them, found the Indian or rather the Muslim garb quite suitable and, if Mandelslo is to be credited, many *European* merchants resident in the country dressed in the Indian fashion.[79] Downton's brief but picturesque lines will bear quotation: "This river wee past, and landed right before the Alfondica or custom house; and so along through many streets (humming like bees in swarmes with multitudes of people in white coates, men and women, close bodied and full of gathering to the mid-leg, with breeches and stockings in one, ruffling like gootes and all of one single callico; this being their generall or most neate or angelicall habite, which sparkles, of their kinde of starching, like silver spangles)."[80] Obviously

78. Foster, *Early Travels in India*, p. 272.
79. Mandelslo's *Travels*, pp. 20-21.
80. *The Voyage of Nicholas Downton*, p. 134.

the newcomers landing at Swally did not find the country habits either disagreeable or unbecoming.

The food varied from community to community, caste to caste and province to province. Mandelslo twice dined with the Governor of Ahmadabad, a native of Persia. When he wanted to take his leave of the Governor after the first visit Mandelslo was asked to stay for the dinner. "He caused some Fruit to be brought, while his people were laying the cloath, which was of cotton, laid upon a large Carpet of red *Turkie*-leather. The dinner was very noble, and serv'd up and drest according to the *Persian* way, the Meat being laid in dishes, all Porcelane, upon Rice of several colours, in the same manner as we had seen at the Court of *Ispahan*."[81] On his second visit he found the governor smoking tobacco who later took some opium and *bhang* as well. When the dinner began, "The Carver sate in the middle of the great Vessels wherein the meat was brought up, and with a great spoon put of it into little dishes, to be serv'd up to us. The *Chan* himself would needs also put in some, to assure us of his being pleasd' with our company."[82]

It is interesting to note that both coffee and tea had gained favour with the Indians in the earlier part of the seventeenth century though the exact date of their advent cannot be ascertained. Coffee was importd from Yemen, for India had trade relations with Persia and Arabia from the earliest times. The Indian ships used to bring *Kahwa* or Coffee berries on their return journey from Aden if Mandelslo is to be credited.[83] Terry informs us that "Many of the people who are strict in their religion drinke no wine at all. They use a liquor more healthful then pleasant, they call Cahha (Coffee: Arabic *Kahwa*): a blacke seed boyled in water, which doth little alter the taste of the water. Notwithstanding, it is very good to helpe digestion to quicken the spirits, and to clense the bloud."[84] The coffee habit does not seem to have been very popular. Tavernier says "as for India, it is but little used there."[85] Fryer found this drink very popular in Persia and noticed that if the Muslims of the Deccan "invite a Christian, they order Dishes apart, and between meals Entertain with *Coho,* Tobacco, *Pawn,* which makes a fragrant Breath, and gives a rare Vermilion to the Lips."[86] But the custom was not confined to the Muslims alone. Ovington says "The *Bannians* are not restain'd from the liberal Draughts of Tea and Coffee to revive their wasted Spirits any part of the Day." "Tea," he adds, "is a common Drink with all the Inhabitants of *India,* as well *Europeans* as Natives."[87] Ovington came to Surat in 1689. An earlier traveller, Mandelslo, also claimed to have found tea in common use in this country. "At our ordinary meetings every day," he wrote, "we took only *The,* which is commonly used all over the Indies, not only

81. Mandelslo's *Travels,* p. 28.
82. *Ibid,* p. 29.
83. *Ibid,* p. 69.
84. Foster, *Early Travels in India,* p. 300.
85. Tavernier's *Travels in India,* Vol. II, p. 20.
86. Fryer's *East India and Persia,* Vol. I, p. 234.
87. Ovington, *A Voyage to Surat,* p. 180.

among those of the Country, but also among the *Dutch* and *English*, who take it as a Drug that cleanses the Stomach, and digest the superfluous humours, by a temperate heat particular thereto."[88] Mandelslo arrived at Surat in April 1638. The popularity of tea among the indigenous people seems to have declined since then to be revived again in more recent times. As Tavernier informs us coffee was not grown in India. Indigenous wild tea plants were discovered in the hills of Assam in the thirties of the nineteenth century but it is doubtful whether they were cultivated in this country in the days of Thevenot and Careri.

The poor man's drink was toddy, but every poor man was not permitted this luxury, as the caste rules among the Hindus interdicted in many cases all alcoholic beverage. Thevenot devotes one chapter to this liquor which Terry found "as pleasing to the taste as any white wine, if drunke betimes in the morning."[89] But others refer to its pernicious effects. Nicholas Downton attributed the death of seven of his crew to "fluxe, which I conceave proceedeth of their inordynate drynkinge of a sorte of wine that distilleth out of the palmyto trees called Tadie."[90] Half a pint of tari (toddy) sufficed to cause Tavernier a terrible headache that lasted for two successive days.[91]

Neither black coffee nor brown tea, not even white toddy was so popular as *pan*. It was a universal favourite and was commended by many European travellers for its beneficient qualities. According to Roe, "it bytts in the mouth, avoydes rume, cooles the head, strengthens the teeth, and is all their phisicke ; it makes one unused to it giddy, and makes a man's spittle redd, and in tyme coullers the teeth which is esteemed a beawty."[92] Terry writes: "There is yet another helps to comfort the stomacke for such as forbeare wine, as herbe called Beetle or Pawne. It is in shape somewhat like an ivie leafe, but more tender. They chew it with a hard nut somewhat like a nut-megge, and a little pure white lime among the leaves ; and when they have sucked out the Juyce, put forth the rest. It hath many rare qualities ; for it preserves the teeth, comforts the braine, strengthens the stomacke, and cures and prevents a tainted breath."[93] Obviously Terry had not seen the leaf in its natural state or he would not have likened it to an ivy leaf. It is equally certain that Fryer, had not seen it either when he wrote that "The Natives chew it (betelnuts) with *chinam* (Lime of calcined Oyster-Shells) and *Arach*, a *Convolvulus*, with a Leaf like the largest Ivy, for to preserve their Teeth and Errect an unsavoury Breath: If swallowed, it inebriates as much as Tobacco."[94] Mandelslo thought that the "leaves are like those of the Orange-tree."[95] According to Pietro della Valle, "leaves of Betle" are "to the sight not

88. Mandelslo's *Travels*, p. 13.
89. Foster, *Early Travels in India*, p. 298.
90. *The Voyage of Nicholas Downton*, p. 196.
91. Tavernier's *Travels in India*, Vol. II, p. 242.
92. Foster, *The Embassy of Sir Thomas Roe*, p. 11.
93. Foster, *Early Travels in India*, p. 300.
94. Fryer's *East India and Persia*, Vol. I, p. 110.
95. Mandelslo's *Travels*, p. 33.

unlike the leaves of Cedars."[96] He also had not apparently seen the unprepared leaf but he referred to a ceremonial significance of presenting it to a visitor—"the custom being so in *India* for the person visited to give *Betle*-leaves to the visitant, wherewith the visit ends."[97] People of all castes, creeds and communities irrespective of their station in life, in all parts of India enjoyed the *pan* and it was freely distributed on festive occasions.

If Mandelslo left us a picture of a governor's dinner he did not forget to write of the poor man's daily fare. "Tradesmen (he really means artisans) are in the saddest condition, in as much as the Children cannot be put to any other Trades then what their fathers are of, and there is this inconvenience withall, that a piece of work must pass through three or four hands before it is finished ; so that all that they can do is to get five or six pence a day. They must accordingly fare very poorly, their ordinary Diet being only *Kitsery,* which they make of Beans, pounded and Rice, which they boyl together in water till the water be consumed. Then they put these to a little Butter melted, and this is their Supper, for all day they eat only Rice and Wheat in the grain."[98] Mandelslo could not claim an intimate knowledge of the poor artisans of Gujarat but his account is based, though without acknowledgement on that of a Dutch Factor who spent seven years at Agra. Francisco Palsaert said the same thing almost in identical words—"For their monotonous daily food, they have nothing but a little *Khichri,* made of 'green pulse' mixed with rice, which is cooked with water over a little fire until the moisture has evaporated, and eaten hot with butter in the evening ; in the day time they munch a little parched pulse or other grain, which they say suffices for their lean stomachs."[99] Pelsaert left India before Mandelslo came, nor could the Dutch merchant's *Remonstiantie* have been accessible to the German nobleman and the latter's debt to the former was not therefore direct. But De Laet was permitted to use Pelsaert's work for his chapter on the character, customs, institutions and superstitions of the Indian people and Mandelslo extracted from De Laet's *De Imperio Magni Mogolis* the passage quoted above with such verbal changes as he considered necessary.[100]

If the daily fare of the ill-paid artisans was extremely poor that of some Hindu castes and sects, by no means indigent, appeared very strange to newcomers from Europe. The "Baniyans" as they are collectively and indiscriminately called by the travellers, scrupulously refrained from all animal food and subsisted on vegetables and fruits. For people of the west meat and food were synonymous but these Hindus would not on any account hurt the meanest of the living creatures and would if possible redeem them at great expense from persons with scant respect for animal life. They built hospitals for ailing and old beasts and birds and as Fryer scoffingly remarked, "They have Hospitals here for Cows ; and are Charit-

96. *Travels of Pietro della Valle,* Vol. II, p. 226.
97. *Ibid,* p. 226.
98. Mandelslo's *Travels,* p. 64.
99. Moreland and Geyl, *Jahangir's India,* pp. 60-61.
100. De Laet's *Empire of the Great Mogol,* pp. 88-89.

able to Dogs, ... being more merciful to Beasts than Men."[101] This strange conduct was noticed by many writers and naturally caused comments not always complimentary. Herbert writes of the Bania's strict abstinence from meat and fish. "Full of phlegmatick fear they be and superstition: They are indeed merciful, grieving to see other people so hard-hearted as to feed upon Fish, Flesh, Raddish, Onions, Garlick, and such things as either have life or resemblance of blood. They for their parts will not kill so much as a Louse, a Flea, a Kakaroch or the like; *Non usus erat carnium ante diluvium,* saith *Comestor;* but contrariwise buy their liberty of such Sailors, and others, as of necessity must crush them: Yea, they have Hospitals for old, lame, sick or starved Creatures, Birds, Beasts, Cats, Rats, or the like; and have no worse men to oversee them than the *Pushelans,* the best respected sorts of *Bramins.*"[102] Similarly Mandelslo observes, "the Benjans abstain from the killing of living creatures, even to the Insects, how dangerous or troublesome soever they may be. They also forbear keeping any Fire and lighting Candles in the night time out of a fear that Flies or Moths should burn themselves therein; nay they make some difficulty to make pits on the Ground, for fear of drowning the Fleas and other Insects, which might lie in the way. What is yet more superstitious, they do not only redeem the Birds, which *Mahumetans* had taken, but they also built Hospitals for Beasts that are hurt and wounded."[103] Linschoten who came earlier and knew the country better also testified that "They eate not any thing that hath life or blood in it, neither would they kil it for all the goods in ye worlde, how small or unnecessarie soever it were, for that they stedfastly beléeve that every living thing hath a soule, and are next [after men to be accounted of] accordingly to Pythagoras law, and know it must die; and sometimes they do buy certain fowles or other beastes of the Christians or Portingals, which they meant to have killed, and [when they have bought them], they let them flée and run away."[104] This weakness on the part of the Banians was sometimes exploited by unscrupulous knaves to their own advantage and Careri claims to have actually seen a "rogue" at Surat who whenever he wanted to make some easy money went knife in hand with a hen to the Bania quarters so that some one might pay to save its life. Mundy heard of a bird hospital at Cambay[105] and Tavernier saw several such institutions for sick and disabled animals at Ahmadabad.[106]

This unusual solicitude for mute animals demanded an explanation and the travellers found an easy one in the Hindu belief in the immortality and transmigration of soul. Very few of them ever realised that this creed, or to be more accurate, theory was not confined to any particular caste or sect and reverence for animal life prevailed in its most extreme form among the Jainas, Mandelslo would include even the Rajputs among

101. Fryer's *East India and Persia,* Vol. I, p. 138.
102. Herbert, *Some Yeares Travels,* p. 52.
103. Mandelslo's *Travels,* pp. 53-54.
104. *Voyage of Linschoten,* Vol. I, p. 253.
105. *The Travels of Peter Mundy,* Vol. II, p. 310.
106. Tavernier's *Travels in India,* Vol. I, pp. 63-64.

the Banias[107] but all the seventeenth century travellers agreed that these tender hearted superstition was derived from the teachings of Pythagoras. "These are of *Pythagoras* his doctrinating, believing the Metempsychosis or transanimation or passage of Souls into Beasts," said Herbert and others concurred.[108] Roe repeats "The severest sect of these are Pythagorians for the opinion of the soules transmigration, and will not kyll any living creature, no, not the virmine that bites them, for feare of disseising the speiritt of some frend departed."[109] None of them even suspected that the theory might have originated in India in an age much earlier than that of the Greek philosopher and Pietro della Valle informs us that one of his acquaintances actually went so far as to suggest that Hindu superstition had made a god of Pythagoras and he and Brahma were identical.[110] But no one would credit the shrewd businessmen that the Banias were with any philanthropic or humanitarian motive. They were merely inspired by considerations of self interest in their unreasoning care for beasts, birds and insects. It was insinuated that they would not kill anything in fear of causing inconvenience to one of their own departed relatives whose soul might have found accommodation in the body of that particular creature. Mandelslo says that the Rajputs "believe in particular that the Souls of Men go into Birds, who afterwards give their Friends notice of the good and evil which is to befall them: upon which account it is, that they so superstitiously observe the flight and singing of those Creatures." "They have no compassion but what they have towards irrational creatures, especially Birds, which they take the pains to keep and feed, out of a perswation, that one day when their Souls shall be lodg'd in Creatures of that kind, some or other will have the same charity towards them. And this is their employment particularly on Holy-dayes, as also for ten or twelve dayes after the decease of their nearest kindred, and upon the anniversary dayes of their death."[111] Yet Mandelslo had their grounds for extraordinary abhorrence for blood shed and slaughter from the Banias themselves. While travelling from Agra to Lahore—"one day with a Pistol shot I kill'd a great Serpent, which I met with in the way and afterwards a Leopard and a Roebuck: but the *Benjans,* of whom there were many in our Company, took it very ill at my hands, and reproach'd me with my cruelty, in that I deprived those Creatures of a life which it was not in my power to give them, and which God had not bestow'd on them, but that he might be thereby glorified."[112] Here was a rational sentiment easily intelligible which Mandelslo and his fellow travellers found difficult to reconcile with the notorious superstition of the Hindus and ascribed their solicitude for helpless animals to their anxiety for their departed kindreds' welfare, not knowing that one of the precepts of Hinduism was to look upon all living beings as one's ownself.

---

107. Mandelslo's *Travels,* p. 57.
108. Herbert, *Some Years Travels,* p. 52.
109. Foster, *The Embassy of Sir Thomas Roe,* p. 271.
110. *Travels of Pietro della Valle,* Vol. I, p. 76.
111. Mandelslo's *Travels,* pp. 57-58.
112. *Ibid,* p. 45.

Early marriage was a notorious social evil which did not escape the notice of foreign travellers, but here also their account often suffered from absurd exaggeration. Herbert observed, "Marriage is here so honoured that most times they contract at seven, and at ten years old are often Parents ; which puts me in mind of that which *Pliny* in his 6 and 8 *lib, ch.* 17 and 14 writes concerning the *Calinge* whom he places hereabouts, and would have us believe that the women are pregnant at five and seldome live above eight ; but this is certain, that if an infant dye ere he be married his Parents procure a Virgin (to whom they give some Dynaes of Gold) to be his Bed-fellow or Wife for one Night, to avoid the reproachful Proverb, *He dyed unmarried.*"[113] In fairy tales we hear of such weddings and the selfless devotion of the saintly bride which miraculously restores the princely groom deceased before his time once again to life and health but in sober history we do not come across any such instance. Yet a more rational explanation was not wanting. Fitch was told—"they marry their children so young, because it is an order that when the man dieth, the woman must be burned with him, so that if the father die, yet they may have a father in lawe to helpe to bring up the children which bee married."[114] Withington says: "The reason whye they marrye them so younge, they say, is in regard they would not leave their children wiveless ; if yt should please God to take the parents away of either of the children, yet (say they) they have other parents to ayde them till they come to yeares of discretion."[115] However Herbert was not the only person to give credence to stories of early conception. Mandelslo also writes, "they marry their Children very young, which is the less to be wondered at, in as much as it is very certain that the *Indians* of both Sexes are capable of engendring much sooner than any other Nation: so that there are not any but are fit for the work of generation at ten or twelve years of age." In confirmation of his statement he cites the story of a child of three giving birth to a boy and "*Sheich Choram* sent for both Mother and Child, and ordered them to be brought up at the Court."[116] He also thought "the climate which derives to the *Bodies* living in it no great disposition to Chastity."[117]

If Indian girls conceived long before they attained puberty, some of the travellers were of opinion that nature compensated them with very easy labour. Terry writes "The women in those parts have a great happiness above all I know, in their easie bringing forth of children ; for it is a thing common there, for women great with childe one day to ride, carrying their infants in their bodies, the next day to ride againe, carrying them in their armes."[118] This blessing was not denied to the fair ladies of the Deccan if Methwold is to be believed. "They (the children) come into the

---

113. Herbert, *Some Yeares Travels,* p. 45.
114. Foster, *Early Travels in India,* pp. 16-17.
115. *Ibid,* p. 221.
116. Mandelslo's *Travels,* p. 58.
117. *Ibid,* p. 51.
118. Foster, *Early Travels in India,* p. 309.

world without much trouble to their mothers, for they are up againe about their business in three or four dayes, some the same day."[119]

Every one of the travellers claims to have witnessed at least one case of voluntary Sati. Roe writes of "*Gentills* of sundry idolatryes, theyr wives adorning the pyle, and entring the funerall fyres with great joy and honor"[120] but his evidence rests on common report. The testimony of Hawkins is more authoritative though he does not seem to have attended any such funeral. He says "I have seene many proper women brought before the King, whom (by his commandment) none may burn without his leave and sight of them; I meane those of Agra. When any of these commeth, hee doth perswade them with many promises of gifts and living if they will live, but in my time no perswasion could prevaile, but burn they would. The King, seeing that all would not serve, giveth his leave for her to be carried to the fire, where she burneth herselfe alive with her dead husband."[121] The most lamentable case is the one cited by Nicholas Withington for the girl widow was "not above ten yeares of age."[122] Her husband, a soldier, died in action and she burnt herself with his clothes and turban and the Governor's orders prohibiting the Sati could not influence her decision. Pietro della Valle in his romantic chivalry resolved, when he saw at Ikkeri a woman who had decided to burn herself with her husband's dead body, to honour by his presence her funeral "with that compassionate affection which so great Conjugal Fidelity and Love seem to me to deserve."[123] The Italian traveller carried with him the coffin of his dead wife until he returned home and the resolution was quite in keeping with his own temperament. Mandelslo relates a case which occurred at Cambay during his visit to that city. "The next day, the *English* Merchants came to my Lodging, whence we went together to the River side, without the City, where this voluntary execution was to be done. The Womans Husband was a *Rasboute,* and had been kill'd near *Lahor,* 200 Leagues from *Cambaya.* As soon as she had heard of his death, she would needs do his Obsequies, by causing her self to be burnt alive; but whereas the *Mogul* and his Officers are *Mahumetans,* who endeavour by degrees to abolish this heathenish and barbarous Custom, the Governour had a long time oppos'd her desires, under pretence that the news of her Husbands death being uncertain, he could not consent to the doing of an inhumane action, whereof there would afterwards haply be cause to repent. The Governours design was to see, whether time would abate anything of her passion, and the earnestness she was in to follow her husband into the other World: but seeing she was daily more and more instant to do it, he permitted her to comply with the Laws of her own Religion. She was not above twenty years of age, yet we saw her come up to the place of her execution with so much confidence, and a chearfulness so extraordinary to those who go to present and inevitable death, that I was much inclin'd to believe, that

119. Moreland, *Relations of Golconda,* p. 26.
120. Foster, *The Embassy of Sir Thomas Roe,* p. 105.
121. Foster, *Early Travels in India,* p. 119.
122. *Ibid,* p. 219.
123. *Travels of Pietro della Valle,* Vol. II, p. 267.

she had dull'd her senses with a dose of *Opium*, which is as commonly used in the *Indies* as in *Persia*."[124] It is needless to add further instances of this well-known practice. Fryer also suspected that the widow's own people drugged her with Datura, "when half mad she throws herself into the Fire, and they ready with great Logs keep her in his Funeral Pile."[125] Although Fryer does not speak from his personal experience there must have been many cases of such inhumanity and one wishes that Withington had been as observant as Mandelslo for it is very unlikely for a child of ten to persist in her mad resolution to burn herself to death though women of maturer years might have willingly gone to the pyre. Manucci claims to have rescued with the aid of an Armenian friend a widow about to be burnt, the mute appeal of whose pathetic eyes beseeching help had not gone unnoticed. The Armenian afterwards married the lady and had a son by her.[126] It is to be noted that the Moghul emperor and his officers viewed this practice with unconcealed disfavour and tried their best to prevent it by persuasion if possible. If they did not forbid it altogether they must have been influenced by the same considerations as actuated the early Governors-General of the East India Company, who hesitated to interfere with a social evil sanctified by old tradition and longstanding custom. The Muslim rulers of the Deccan were not less averse to this practice than their brethren of the north. Methwold mentions a Masulipatam case where the Kotwal definitely refused to give his consent and the woman afterwards circumvented the law by hanging herself.[127] An anonymous writer asserts that the Sati "is not permitted in places where Moslems are numerous, being against their rule ; and I have myself seen on two occasions that it was prevented when the women were practically ready to jump into the fire."[128]

It will not be irrelevant to refer here to the religious tolerance that ordinarily prevailed in the country. Commenting on Coryat's foolhardy attack on Islam and its prophet, Terry observes "which bold attempt in many other places of Asia, where Mahomet is more zealously professed, had forfeitted his life with as much torture as tyrannie could invent. But here every man hath libertie to professe his owne religion freely and, for any restriction I ever observed, to dispute against theirs with impunitie."[129] For such blasphemy as Coryat uttered against the religion of the state he might have been pilloried and burnt in his own country and in other parts of Europe. In the seventeenth century India, however, if we leave out of account some of the deplorable lapses of Aurangzeb, everybody was at liberty to profess his own faith without any let or hindrance from the state for the sovereign was expected, irrespective of his own religion, to give an unbiassed verdict on any disputed point relating to social customs or religious practices.

124. Mandelslo's *Travels*, p. 31.
125. Fryer's *East India and Persia*, Vol. I, p. 96.
126. Manucci, *Storia do Mogor*, Vol. II, p. 97.
127. Moreland, *Relations of Golconda*, p. 29.
128. *Ibid*, p. 75.
129. Foster, *Early Travels in India*, p. 315.

The travellers need not be blamed if in the interminable mazes of the polytheistic practices and primitive cults of popular Hinduism they failed to discover its higher teachings. Terry was told that the Brahmans "acknowledge one God, whom they describe with a thousand hands, with a thousand feete, and as many eyes, thereby expressing his power."[130] The real significance of the imagery was entirely lost upon him for neither could he comprehend nor could the ignorant Brahman whom he consulted explain the philosophy of the Gita and its conception of the Supreme Being pervading the entire universe and guiding the course of countless lives that emanated from and ultimately terminated in Him. Both Herbert and Mandelslo learnt, not from their Hindu acquaintances but from the treatises written by previous European scholars that the Hindus believed in the unity of godhead[131] but the myths and legends in which Hindu theology is intricately enveloped reached them in a garbled version. Here is the fable of the elephant-headed Ganesha, the god of success as Pietro della Valle heard it. "He is the son of Mahadeu, who finding him one day with *Parveti* his wife, but his own Mother, and not knowing who he was, kill'd him out of jealousie, cutting off his Head; but afterwards understanding that he was his own Son, he repented him of his error, and resolv'd to bring him to life again. Wherefore meeting with an Elephant, (as he had purpos'd to do with what he first happen'd upon) he cut off his Head, and placed it on his dead Son's shoulders."[132] Such stories were not calculated to bring the denizens of the Hindu Olympus into repute though Pietro della Valle was prepared to concede that some truth may lie behind these apparent absurdities. He writes: "Some of these Idolets sat upon Sundry Animals, as Tygers and the like, and even upon Rats; of which things the foolish and ignorant Indians relate ridiculous stories. But I doubt not that, under the veil of these Fables, their ancient Sages (most parsimonious of the Sciences, as all Barbarians ever were) had hid from the vulgar many secrets, either of Natural or Moral Philosophy, and perhaps also of History: and I hold for certain that all these so monstrous figures have secretly some more rational significations, though express'd in this uncouth manner."[133] But everyone was not prepared to take such tolerant views of "pagan" gods and "heathenish" mummeries. Roe writes of "sundry idolatryes and worshipping the creaturs of heaven and earth promiscuously" and scoffingly refers to the pilgrimage to the Ganges to which "all ascribe a kinde of divinity."[134] It was easier to admire the cunning of the jugglers and the "tumbling tricks of Men that use dauncinge, tumblinge etts. Feats." In the world of sports all races and creeds meet on a common ground and willingly pay homage to exceptional skill and uncommon courage.

The concept of caste is so alien to Christian society that this novel feature of Hinduism could not possibly escape the notice of any of our

130. Foster, *Early Travels in India*, p. 321.
131. Herbert, *Some Yeares Travels*, p. 47; Mandelslo's *Travels*, p. 52.
132. *Travels of Pietro della Valle*, Vol. I, p. 73.
133. *Ibid*, Vol. I, pp. 73-74.
134. Foster, *The Embassy of Sir Thomas Roe*, pp. 270-271.

travellers. They were aware of its rigidity and restrictions and both Thevenot and Careri attempted to give exhaustive inventories of existing castes and their subdivisions. Herbert knew that originally there were only four principal castes and he associated the later subdivisions with crafts thus indicating their professional character. He says "these never marry out of their own Casts ; Bramins marry the Daughters of *Bramins* ; Cuttery's the Daughters of Cuttery's ; Shuddery's *Shuddery's* ; and *Wyses* not only so, but also compere in their own Trades, as Taylors, the Daughters of Taylors ; *Barbers,* Barbers Daughters, etc. And contrary to the custome of *Mahometans,* their Wives live not under such subjection."[135] The last observation applied to West and South India alone where the Hindu women were not expected to put on the veil. According to Herbert the Brahmans were divided into eightytwo and the Vaishyas into thirtysix sub-castes[136] and he was under the impression that none but the "*Rajaes*" (Kshatriyas, *i.e.,* Rajputs) and the "*Wyses*" cared to contract more than one marriage.[137] "Polygamy here is odious," says he, "in which respect they cease not to vilifie the *Mahometans* as people of an impure soul."[138] Terry says "These Gentiles take but one wife ; of which they are not so fearefull as the Mahometans of their multitude, for they suffer their to goe abroad."[139] Mandelslo was better informed and definitely asserts that the Hindu was not debarred from polygamy. "The *Benjan* Law permits men, not only to marry a second or third time, in case of death, but also to wed a second or third Wife, if the first and second proves barren ; the first retaining nevertheless a certain pre-eminence, as being Mother of the Family."[140] This indicates the general practice rather than the legal restriction to matrimony, for while the Muslim is by law limited to four wives at a time, the Hindu may, if he likes, marry as many wives as he can comfortably maintain. Hamilton who came much later knew that "there are no Laws against Polygamy" among "the Gentiles."[141] Aware as he was of the exclusiveness and rigidity of the caste system Mandelslo still suggests that the Banias could sometimes convert Muslims,[142] but on what authority we do not know.

A small community that inhabited the sea coast of Gujarat was specially mentioned by many foreign writers because they "neither burne nor interre their dead" but "incircle pieces of ground with high stone walls, remote from houses or roadewayes, and therein lay their carkasses wrapped in sheetes ; thus having no other tombes but the gorges of ravenous fowles."[143] The Parsees form but an infinitesimal fraction of the teeming population

135. Herbert, *Some Yeares Travels,* p. 51.
136. Terry's total of four score and four is probably based on the number of species through which the soul according to popular belief migrate before attaining salvation.
137. Herbert, *Some Yeares Travels,* p. 46.
138. *Ibid,* p. 46.
139. Foster, *Early Travels in India,* p. 322.
140. Mandelslo's *Travels,* p. 52.
141. Hamilton, *A New Account of the East Indies,* Vol. I, p. 94.
142. Mandelslo's *Travels,* p. 57.
143. Foster, *Early Travels in India,* p. 323.

of India but they can rightly claim to be the most progressive and wealthy community in the country. To-day they are well-known for their industrial enterprise and commercial ventures but early in the seventeenth century they still eked out an honest livelihood as agriculturists, skilled artisans and small tradesmen. Mandelslo writes: "Their habitations are for the most part along the Sea-Coast, and they live very peaceably, sustaining themselves by the advantage they make out of the *Tobacco* they plant, and the *Terry* they get out of the Palms of those parts, and whereof they make *Arak,* in regard they are permitted to drink Wine. They intermeddle also with Merchandise, and the exchange of Money and keep Shops, and are of all Trades, except those of Farriers, Blacksmiths and Locksmiths; in regard it is an unpardonable sin among them to put out the fire."[144] When Fryer came to India towards the close of the century they still continued to rely mainly on agricultural pursuits. "They are rather Husbandmen than Merchants" testifies the sailor physician, "not caring to stir abroad."[145] Early the next century came another sailor, Captain Alexander Hamilton and he found more craftsmen among the Parsees than peasants. "They are very industrious and diligent in their Vocation, and are bred to Trades and manuring Ground. They are good Carpenters or Shipbuilders, exquisite in Weaver's Trade and Embroidery, which may be seen in the rich Atlasses, *Bottadaars* and *Jemewars* made by them, as well as fine *Baroach* and *Nunsaree Bastas* that come from their Manufactories. They work well in Ivory and Agate, and are excellent Cabinet-makers. They distil strong Waters, but that they do clandestinely, because that Trade is prohibited by the Government they live under; yet some of them get a good Livelyhood by it."[146] Still later Grose found that "The manufactures peculiar to that province of Guzarat are chiefly carried on by the industry of the Parsees."[147] When Bishop Heber came to Bombay in the first quarter of the nineteenth century the Parsees had already become the foremost Indian mercantile class in Western India.[148] The gradual emergence of this enterprising people from agriculture to industry makes an extremely interesting story. Compelled to abandon their ancestral home by religious persecution the Parsees found a happy asylum in the hospitable shores of India and contributed in no small degree to the wealth and welfare of the land of their adoption. While standing steadfastly by their ancient faith they did not falter for a moment in their fidelity to the new country.

VIII

Travellers' accounts often suffer from historical inaccuracy for obvious reasons. They had no access to authentic chronicles of the country and for current events they had to depend mainly, if not solely, on *bazar*

144. Mandelslo's *Travels,* p. 59.
145. Fryer's *East Indies and Persia,* Vol. I, p. 295.
146. Hamilton, *A New Account of the East Indies,* Vol. I, p. 95.
147. Grose, *A Voyage to the East Indies,* Vol. I, p. 123.
148. Heber's *Journal,* Vol. II, pp. 175, 194.

gossip. Moreover they were apt to get confused with unfamiliar foreign names and the seventeenth century corruption of Indian nomenclature probably made confusion worse confounded. Herbert makes Taj Mahal Jahangir's "best beloved wife" and Malik Ambar "a son of Nezam Shah."[149] According to Mandelslo *"Schach Achobar"* (Shah Akbar) was great-grandfather of "Schach Choram" (Khuram=Shah Jahan) and *"Schach Choram,* who was living at my being in those parts was a younger Son of *Scach Jahan's."*[150] But all such errors were not due to ignorance, sometimes they must be attributed to lack of elementary care. While relating the story of the Moghul conquest of Gujarat Mandelslo confidently asserts that the last reigning monarch of that kingdom was Mahmud Begara (Sulthan Mahomed Begeran)[151] but later correctly says that Madosfher (Muzaffar)[152] was the name of the last sultan who was carried prisoner by Akbar but he later managed to effect his escape and caused the emperor no little trouble. But even the *bazar* gossip preserved by contemporary travellers is not always without its value. The obscene story of the incestuous father[153] which Mandelslo relates in all its revolting details seems to have been the origin of the scandal to which Bernier gave wide currency in the reign of Aurangzeb. Only the builder of the Taj was substituted for a nameless sinner entombed at Ahmadabad and an accomplished princess was made to personate for a young lady unknown to history. Travellers had neither the time nor the training for testing historical evidence or checking doubtful chronology and accepted for sober truth many of the entertaining tales that went round the sarais and market places. That contemporary history also suffered badly at their hands will be evident from a cursory scrutiny of Thevenot's account of Shivaji and Carré's *History of Shivaji* and *Sequel to the History of Shivaji.*[154] Yet we cannot ignore the information they have unconsciously left about the economic condition of the country. Many of them noted the prices current at the time of their visit of food grains and other necessities of life. All of them are not silent about the prevailing wage rates at industrial centres. And it is not altogether impossible to prepare a schedule of prices and wages for different parts of India at different dates from the materials left by foreign travellers and resident merchants in the employment of the European trading companies. But this is hardly the place for an enquiry into the economic conditions of India during the seventeenth century.

IX

The most valuable part of Thevenot and Careri's travels, as indeed of all other travellers, is where they record their personal experiences and write of the roads they traversed, the towns they visited, the men they

149. Herbert, *Some Yeares Travels,* pp. 65 and 68.
150. Mandelslo's *Travels,* pp. 37 and 42.
151. *Ibid,* p. 25.
152. *Ibid,* p. 48.
153. *Ibid,* p. 25.
154. Sen, *Foreign Biographies,* pp. 187-258; also *The Travels of Abbé Carré,* Vol. I, pp. 229-30 and Vol. II, pp. 319-23.

met, the things they saw, the amenities they enjoyed, the discomforts they suffered and the difficulties they encountered. In those days there was no swift transport, the road was not always good and the country did not afford all the comforts and conveniences that the foreigner could expect in his own home land. The sea had its corsairs, the land its highwaymen and few travellers could afford to carry with them the much-needed cash; the utility of letters of credit depended on contingencies no one could foresee. But despite all these difficulties the lure of the unknown proved too strong for many adventurous spirits and in the far-off lands of the east they were warmly welcomed not only by their own countrymen but by all Europeans in general and even by their dusky brethren in faith. Careri was befriended by Portuguese officials and clergymen, Mandelslo was received with open arms by the English and the Dutch merchants, Pietro della Valle found never-failing friends in the Dutch and even Carré, employed on a political mission, was not infrequently helped by the enemies of his country. A white man travelling in the Moghul's country could normally count on the friendship and assistance of other white men.

The first annoyance that awaited the traveller at the port of disembarkation was the customs officer, not a popular figure in any country at any time. The duties were not high but the search was in some places exceptionally strict. Surat had a bad name among strangers on this account. Roe heard of "the custome of the Kings officers to search everie thing that came ashoare, even to the pocketts of mens cloathes on their backs, for custome."[155] His ambassadorial rank spared him all indignity and discourtesy but the average stranger could not expect any special consideration. Pietro della Valle, however, testifies that an exception was made in the case of his lady companion, doubtless on account of her sex. "Near the place where the boats land," he informs us, "stands the *Dogana,* or Custom-house, and it took us up some time to dispatch there, because they observe very narrowly, all goods that are brought in, (although they be but Clothes for change) to see whether there be anything coming to the Customes; nor will they suffer strangers to enter till they be first known, and have license as 'tis also practis'd in *Venice.* In all things they proceed with so great wariness, and good order, that it being known that I conducted with me Sigra Mariuccia although a girl very young, the *Capo* or President of the *Dogana,* requir'd likewise to be informed of her quality and gave order that she should not be conducted with any violence, or other disorder: otherwise in lawful things, there is no difficulty, either through diversity of Religion, or upon any other account."[156] Pietro della Valle had no merchandise with him, but Nicholas Downton who had, had less pleasant experience at the customs house of Surat. Mandelslo says that a duty of 2% was levied on bullion and 3½% on everything else[157] but he had no compliments to pay to the men of the customs. "We came ashore near the *Sulthan's* (governor's) Palace," says he, "and went immediately to the Custom-house to have our things search'd by the Officers

155. Foster, *The Embassy of Sir Thomas Roe,* pp. 28-29.
156. *Travels of Pietro della Valle,* Vol. I, pp. 23-24.
157. Mandelslo's *Travels,* p. 18.

there; which is done with such exactness in this place that they think it not enough to open Chests and Portmantles, but examine peoples clothes and pockets. The *Sulthan* or Governour, nay the Customers themselves, oblige Merchants and Passengers to part with, at the price they shall think fit to put upon them, those Goods and Commodities which they had brought for their own private use." Thus Mandelslo had to part with a pair of yellow amber bracelets for the time being at least.[158] Obviously the merchants were more rigorously searched than ordinary passengers. But the customs house people had to be very much on the alert as pearls were often smuggled through the port of Surat. It is needless to say that despite all vigilant scrutiny the professional smugglers and the more respectable merchants did not always find it difficult to pass unnoticed articles of high value and small dimensions like pearls. Roe admits that Richard Steele and Mr Jackson brought with them "the pearle and some other small matters stollen ashoare, according to my order, which I received and gave quittance for."[159] Tavernier mentions the case of an English captain who smuggled gold on several occasions and observes that "the merchants who import it (gold) use so much cunning in order to conceal it, that but little of it comes to the knowledge of the customs officers. The former do all they can to evade paying the customs, especially as they do not run so much risk as in the custom-houses of Europe."[160]

Different countries have different ways of catering to the travellers' needs. The lack of inns in India was a subject of common complaint among newcomers from the west. Nicholas Downton says that "they have not the use of innes, as in Christendome" and travellers had to lodge in Serais instead.[161] Terry elaborates the inconveniences in more explicit terms. "In this kingdome there are no innes to entertaine strangers. Onely in great townes and cities are faire houses built for their receit (which they call Sarray) not inhabited; where any passengers may have roome freely, but must bringe with him his bedding, his cooke, and other necessaries wherein to dresse his meate; which are usually carried on camels, or else in carts drawne with oxen, wherein they have tents to pitch when they meate with no Serras."[162] Mandelslo also found that "There are no common Inns in all the Kingdom of *Guzuratta,* nor indeed in all the Mogul's countrey, but instead thereof in Cities, as also in some Villages, there are certain publick Buildings, called *Sarai,* built by some persons out of Charity, for the convenience of Strangers and Travellers, who were it not for those, would be forc'd to lie in the open Air. These are the *Caravanseras,* which have only the four walls, and a covering overhead; so that to be accommodated therein, a Man must bring along with him what is not to be had there."[163] But all serais were not of this type as we learn from Nicholas Withington.

158. Mandelslo's *Travels,* p. 12.
159. Foster, *The Embassy of Sir Thomas Roe,* p. 405.
160. Tavernier's *Travels in India,* Vol. I, p. 9.
161. *The Voyage of Nicholas Downton,* p. 138.
162. Foster, *Early Travels in India,* p. 311.
163. Mandelslo's *Travels,* p. 65.

"Between Adgemere and Agra", he says, "at everye ten courses (which is an ordinarye days journeye) there is a serralia or place of lodging boothe for man and horse, and hostesses to dresse our victuals if we please, paying a matter of 3*d.* both for horse and meate dressinge."[164] Peter Mundy also confirms that "Metrannes or Betearees are certen Women in all Saraes, that looke to the little roomes there and dresse the Servants meate, accomodateinge them with Cottes etts. needful to bee had ; of these some have 2, some 3 or 4 roomes a peece, for which in the morninge wee pay 1 pice or 2 pice each."[165] Tavernier describes another type of Serais. "The word sera", says he, "signifies a great enclosure of walls or hedges, within which 50 or 60 thatched huts are arranged all round. Here there are some men and women who sell flour, rice, butter, and vegetables who make it their business to prepare bread and cook rice. If by chance any Musalman arrives, he goes into the village to seek for a piece of mutton or a fowl, when those who supply the food to the traveller clean out for him the room which he wishes to occupy, and they place in it a small bed of girths, upon which he spreads the mattress which he carries with him on his journey."[166] But even the best equipped serai compared but ill with the village inns of Europe where a traveller could expect a comfortable bed, a cheery fire, a jug of ale and a roast joint of meat. Bernier complains, "The Eastern *Karavans-Serrah* resemble large barns, raised and paved all round, in the same manner as our Pont-neuf. Hundreds of human beings are seen in them, mingled with their horses, mules, and camels. In summer these buildings are hot and suffocating, and in winter nothing but the breath of so many animals prevents the inmates from dying of cold."[167] The picture is doubtless overdrawn, for the good Frenchman was pining for the excellent inns between Paris and Lyons. The inn and the serai were the inevitable products of the social customs prevailing in their respective regions and the oriental more accustomed to the open-air life did not find it inconvenient to sleep in the uncovered courtyard and the Hindu had necessarily to cook his own food, for in most cases the caste rules would not permit him to sit at a common table and be served by a common cook. But even such comforts as the serais afforded were not to be had everywhere. Peter Mundy says there was no serai between Agra and Ahmadabad[168] and at Mandu Sir Thomas Roe had to lodge in a ruined tomb where his peace and rest were nightly disturbed by a lion and a wolf.[169] In the Deccan, mosques and temples often offered shelter to the passing strangers.[170]

In these days of high speed and quick transport an ox-drawn coach may be contemptuously dismissed as an antediluvian contrivance, slow, inconvenient and uncomfortable. In the seventeenth century the Indian ox was a noble animal fleet of foot, strong of limbs and inured to long

164. Foster, *Early Travels in India,* p. 225.
165. *The Travels of Peter Mundy,* Vol. II, p. 121.
166. Tavernier's *Travels in India,* Vol. I, p. 45.
167. Bernier, *Travels in the Mogul Empire,* p. 233.
168. *The Travels of Peter Mundy,* Vol. II, p. 264.
169. Foster, *The Embassy of Sir Thomas Roe,* p. 365.
170. Tavernier's *Travels in India,* Vol. I, p. 123.

journeys[171] and the ox chariot was not deemed unworthy of royalty. The merry monarch Jahangir once had a joyride with his beloved Nurmahal "in open waggon," "drawne by bullocks, himselfe carter and no man neare",[172] as Roe tells us. It may be argued that the cart was selected on this occasion more for fun than for comfort but Mundy once saw twenty "Coaches for the kinge's owne use, whereof 2 only were drawne by 2 horses" and "the rest by Oxen some of Extraordinarie greatnes, and some againe as little, chosen of purpose."[173] The English President at Surat sent an "*Indian* Coach, drawn by two white Oxen" to bring Mandelslo to his house[174] and when the German aristocrat visited Ahmadabad, Benjamin Roberts, the chief of the English factory there, came to receive him with his coach. "His Coach made after the *Indian* fashion, was gilt all over, covered with several pieces of *Persian* Tapistry, and drawn by two white Oxen, which express'd as much metal as we could have expected from the best Horses in Germany."[175] At another place Mandelslo writes, "In travelling through the Countrey, they make use of Camels, Mules, Horses and Oxen. They have also a kind of Coaches, for two or three persons, which are drawn by Oxen, whereto they are so accustomed, that they easily get ten or twelve leagues a day. The upper part of covering of these Coaches is of Cloath or Velvet ; but those which carry Women are close of all sides."[176] Herbert mentions chariots drawn by buffaloes[177] and poorer people not infrequently rode buffaloes and oxen which Mandelslo found exceedingly uncomfortable.[178] But Tavernier thought otherwise. "Oxen," he says, "take the place of horses, and there are some of them whose paces are as easy as those of our hacks."[179] Wealthy people had of course more stately conveyances. They could travel in Palanquins and Chaudalas with greater ease and ride the elephant if they liked, but for the common folk and the ordinary traveller the homely cart was the coach *par excellence*. Pietro della Valle and his Mariucca travelled from Surat to Cambay in two of these country chariots and crossed a shallow part of the Gulf of Cambay at low tide without even wetting the floor,[180] for the water did not come above the belly of the big oxen. Pietro and the lady squatted inside their chariots in good Indian fashion but Downton's lack of care "in letting one legge hang out of the coach, and (in talke) moving it to and fro" almost cost him that limb.[181] Coach oxen were not at all in-

171. According to the *Ain-i-Akbari* the Gujarat breed was the best "Though every part of the empire produces cattle of various kinds, those of Gujarat are the best. Sometimes a pair of them are sold at 100 muhurs. They will travel 80 kos in 24 hours and surpass even swift horses." Blochman, *Ain-i-Akbari*, Vol. I, p. 149.
172. Foster, *The Embassy of Sir Thomas Roe*, p. 426.
173. *The Travels of Peter Mundy*, Vol. II, p. 193.
174. Mandelslo's *Travels*, p. 12.
175. *Ibid*, p. 22.
176. *Ibid*, p. 65.
177. Herbert, *Some Yeare's Travels*, p. 42.
178. Mandelslo's *Travels*, p. 45.
179. Tavernier's *Travels in India*, Vol. I, pp. 35-36.
180. *Travels of Pietro della Valle*, Vol. I, p. 65.
181. *The Voyage of Nicholas Downton*, p. 141.

expensive, a pair cost Tavernier nearly 600 rupees but he warns the reader not to be surprised for some of them "make journeys lasting sixty days, at 12 or 15 leagues a day, and always at the trot."[182] Bullock *jhatkas* or covered carts are still in common use in South India. One of the mural paintings in a building adjoining the great Shiva temple of Tanjore depicts a queen of the place seated on a chariot drawn by a pair of oxen.

The coaches naturally lead us to the roads some of which at least received high appreciation from foreign travellers. The highway from Agra to Lahore was by common consent the best in the country. Coryat was not a blind admirer of things Indian and he could claim to be a competent judge of roads as he had hiked through many countries of Europe and Asia. His admiration of this long avenue extending over hundreds of miles was as unbounded as genuine. "From the famous citie of Lahore I have twentie daies journey to another goodly citie, called Agra, through such a delicate and even tract of ground as I never saw before, and doubt whether the like bee to be found within the whole circumference of the habitable world. Another thing also in this way being no lesse memorable than the plainenesse of the ground ; a row of trees on each side of this way where people doe travell, extending it selfe from the townes end of Lahore to the townes end of Agra ; the most incomparable shew of that kinde that even my eies survaied."[183] Herbert, while recording the distance from Agra to Lahore, does not forget to add "most of the way being through a shade of Trees."[184] Mandelslo found travelling from Agra to Lahore "so much the more pleasant, in that our way was but one continued Alley, drawn in a streight line, and planted on both sides with Date-trees, Palm-trees, *Cocos*-trees, and other kind of Fruit-trees, which gave us a continued refreshing shade against the heat of the Sun."[185] But other roads were not probably so good or so pleasant. In every likelihood the road from Agra to Lahore was better looked after for it was the king's highway *par excellence* being frequently used by the Emperor himself and his principal nobles. At the other extreme were rough tracks hardly deserving the name of public thoroughfares. Roe writes to Sir Thomas Smythe while in the entourage of the Emperor, "I am yet followeing this wandering King over mountaynes and through woods, so strange and unused wayes that his owne people, who almost know no other god, blaspheame his name and hers that (it is said) conducts all his actions."[186] Sometimes they had to "cutt the way through the woods, but with soe much trouble and inconvenience to the baggage that it was left behind."[187] But Jahangir was obviously travelling by unfrequented byeways or his nobles would not be cursing and grumbling.

In those days people had to travel in company and with guards, for the roads were not safe. Sometimes, the qafilla or caravan would grow in

182. Tavernier's *Travels in India*, Vol. I, p. 37.
183. Foster, *Early Travels in India*, p. 244.
184. Herbert, *Some Yeares Travels*, p. 62.
185. Mandelslo's *Travels*, p. 45.
186. Foster, *The Embassy of Sir Thomas Roe*, p. 337.
187. *Ibid*, p. 338.

size as it progressed, for fresh people would join it at different points for the security it offered. Peter Mundy says that a qafilla of moderate size that left Surat with fifteen to twenty coaches gradually swelled into a crowd of 250 to 300 carts by the time it reached Nandurbar and became all the more vulnerable as the rear had hardly any effective contact with the van.[188] The region from Surat to Cambay which Thevenot and Pietro della Valle covered at different dates was far from safe in the earlier decades of the seventeenth century. Downton heard of robbery and murder in the near neighbourhood of Broach.[189] He describes the road from Broach to Chormondo as "the most theveshest waie in those partes" and his party was provided with a guard of twenty five horsemen.[190] Downton was detained at Ahmadabad after obtaining the Governor's leave to depart, "but that night, divers beinge robbed and murdred close by the cittie gates, order againe was given we should not departe untill such time as a sufficient guarde was provided."[191] Mandelslo says: "The Rasboutes make the way between *Amadabath* and *Cambaya* very dangerous, which made me take for my Convoy eight foot-souldiers arm'd with pikes and Bucklers. This kind of Souldiers do also the office of Lacqueys, running just before the Horses; and may be hired for a small matter ; for I gave them but eight Crowns for the whole journey, though I had them three dayes in which time I travell'd thirteen of the Country Leagues."[192] Once the highway-men extorted one hundred rupees from a qafilla that Mandelslo[193] met and on another occasion he encountered a party of Rajput robbers near Anklesar.[194] Peter Mundy describes the country between Agra and Ahmadabad as "Theivish" and heard of a number of robberies near Abu.[195] Three witnesses therefore agree that the country near about Ahmadabad was rather insecure.

Downton and Mandelslo had armed men to protect them and their goods against the predatory Rajputs and Kolis. Thevenot mentions another class of guards, the *Charans,* whose novel method of defence was quite as effective and could be purchased at two rupees a day. But the armed guards were not expensive either, as Mandelslo points out. As for their fidelity, Terry's testimony is quite conclusive. "I must needes commend the Mahumetans and Gentils for their good and faithfull service ; amongst whom a stranger may travell alone, with a great charge of money or goods, quite through the countrey and take them for his guard, yet never be neglected or injured by them. They follow their masters on foote carrying swords and bucklers or bowes and arrows for their defence ; and by reason of great plentie of provision in that kingdome, a man may hire them upon easie conditions, for they will not desire above five shillings

188. *The Travels of Peter Mundy,* Vol. II, p. 45.
189. *The Voyage of Nicholas Downton,* pp. 25-26.
190. *Ibid,* p. 103.
191. *Ibid,* p. 113.
192. Mandelslo's *Travels,* p. 30.
193. *Ibid,* p. 35.
194. *Ibid,* p. 46.
195. *The Travels of Peter Mundy,* Vol. II, pp. 264 and 246.

the moone, paide the next day after the change, to provide themselves all necessaries, and for it doe most diligent service."[196]

But the Rajputs who extorted money from travellers in Gujarat and in the neighbouring regions were not necessarily common robbers. Many petty chieftains had their traditional right of levying tolls or transit duties on goods and men passing through their territories. Thevenot mentions the Grassia Raja who in lieu of the duties he received extended free hospitality to the caravan. The Rajputs of Champanir who infested the Broach-Baroda road owed no allegiance to the Emperor, as Mandelslo was told,[197] and were more like the bold barons of medieval Europe than the armed ruffians who stopped coaches on the King's highway. The garrison of an old castle near Baroda used to levy an impost of a Rupee and half per wagon and those who resisted the claim would no doubt be despoiled of their belongings.[198] Mandelslo also relates how a second band of the so called robbers lightly let off a Bania caravan when they were told that earlier a sum of one hundred rupees had been paid to another party of armed men.[199] In certain cases rebel leaders regularly collected *Zakat* or taxes from all passersby and Mundy tells us how near Sirohi his party had to halt one day "to pay our custome to Chanda."[200] Similarly when customs were demanded of Mundy and his friends by Raja Shiv Das's men near Allahabad they vainly invoked the authority of the Emperor and his Viceroy on whom the most filthy abuses were showered.[201] Tavernier definitely states that "there are Rajas, or petty tributary Princes, who interfere with trade, each claiming that the goods ought to traverse his territory and pay him custom."[202] The powerful Zemindars, far away from the seat of imperial authority were at liberty to exercise their customary right of exacting tolls and transit duties and those who had the temerity of refusing their claims would naturally be relieved of all their earthly goods. But if the highways of India were not quite safe for lonely travellers in the seventeenth century conditions in other countries were not much better. About the same time Mundy found the country between Phillipopolis and Sophia particularly robber ridden[203] and Des Hayes observes that in most parts of Serbia and Bulgaria villages had strong enclosures where people took shelter when robbers were about.[204] About six miles from Chambéry Coryat passed a castle where all strangers had to pay a small sum. The city of Venice according to him was infested by armed ruffians at night. Similarly Coryat heard on his way to Abbeville in France that the forest of Veronne through which he had to travel had lurking in it "false knaves" who "suddenly set upon travellers."[205] The town of Mirandula in Italy

196. Foster, *Early Travels in India*, p. 313.
197. Mandelslo's *Travels*, p. 19.
198. Mandelslo's *Travels*, p. 21.
199. *Ibid*, p. 35.
200. *The Travels of Peter Mundy*, Vol. II, pp. 258-259.
201. *Ibid*, p. 118.
202. Tavernier's *Travels in India*, Vol. I, p. 31.
203. *The Travels of Peter Mundy*, Vol. I, p. 61.
204. *Ibid*, pp. 205-206.
205. *Coryat's Crudities*, Vol. I, p. 160.

was "very desolate and unpeopled: the reason is, because the Bandits which are the murdering robbers upon the Alps, and many places of Italy, make their aboad in it as it were their safe sanctuary and refuge, where they live in the castle of the Towne, who because they doe often times violently break out upon the townsmen and other passengers, depriving them both of life and goods, they minister such occasion of feare to the inhabitants, that there dwell but few people in the towne."[206] Coryat further states that it was not wise to take more than a specified sum of money to some parts of Italy. "At the townes end certain searchers examined us for money, according to a custome that is used in many other townes and cities in Italy. For if a man carry more money about him then is warranted or allowed in the country, it is ipso facto confiscated to the Prince or Magistrate, in whose territory a man is taken."[207]

The seventeenth was a century of war and turmoil both in Europe and in India, law and order could not be as strictly enforced then as in later times, and that sense of citizenship which alone ensures social security was yet to be developed. The arm of the state was nowhere long enough to reach every corner of the country. The Rajputs and Kolis who have been indiscriminately classed as robbers or highwaymen really took advantage of the weakness of the administration. They fall under three categories, chieftains exercising hereditary rights of levying tolls, rebels blackmailing the defenceless travellers, and petty princes in the role of the guardians of peace, like the Grassias and the Koli rajas, forcing merchants and travellers to purchase their protection and forbearance. Besides them there was the ordinary highwayman who terrorised the countryside. But on the whole conditions in many parts of India permitted organised bands of merchants and travellers to move about in comparative safety. We must not forget that Thevenot traversed the Deccan when the Maratha menace was still unabated and Careri passed through the southern Maratha country when the Moghul and the Marathas were engaged in a life and death struggle. It also appears that the highroads of Gujarat had become safer since the days of Downton and Mandelslo for Pietro della Valle and Thevenot hardly encountered any danger on their journey from Surat to Cambay. Oaten's remarks are not unworthy of consideration when he says: "From one point of view there is nothing that gives us such an insight into the comparatively high state of civilisation in India during the medieval period as the immunity with which strangers from a foreign country were able to take their women-folk with them on their travels in India. In the fifteenth century we saw Conti doing so with perfect safety; at the beginning of the seventeenth Pietro della Valle supplies us with a second example. Had the positions been reversed and an Indian traveller attempted to travel with his family through any of the more civilised countries of Europe between the beginning of the fifteenth and the close of the sixteenth century, it is doubtful whether the treatment he would have received would have been in any way comparable to that which the

206. *Coryat's Crudities*, Vol. I, p. 261.
207. *Ibid*, p. 227.

natives of India, Hindu and Mohammedan alike, meted out to their 'Feringhi' visitors."[208]

Terry also testifies to the civility of the common people and the general security of the road. "The truth is," he says, "that the people there in general are very civil, and we never had any affronts or ill usage from them, if we did not first provoke them." Unfortunately such provocations were not always wanting though ruffled tempers did not ordinarily lead to any untoward result if amends were made in time. Terry cites three such cases. Sir Thomas Roe had brought with him an English cook to Surat. The day he arrived at the port the cook found his way to an Armenian's house and got drunk. While "staggering homeward" he met the governor's brother and reviled him as a "heathen dog." That gentleman not understanding the language enquired what he said. "The cook answered him with his sword and scabbard, with which he struck at him." He was immediately seized, disarmed and lodged in the local gaol but was sent home unpunished when the ambassador "sent word unto the governor's brother that he was not come hither to patronise any disorderly person, and therefore desired him to do with him what he pleased." On another occasion an Englishman who claimed to know the country and its people better had brought troubles on Terry's party by his unwarranted rudeness. "In our journey towards the Court (after we had been in our way about seven days from Surat) we rested at a place called Ditat, where many of the inhabitants offered to guard us and our goods, though we (observing there was no danger) desired it not, but they would do it, and in the morning expected and asked something of us by way of recompense. One of our company (who had been in East-India a year or two before) told them, that what they had done they did without our desire, and therefore they should have nothing from us, but some ill language, which he then gave them. We set forward in the morning, according to our wonted custom ; they followed after us, to the number at the least of three hundred men, (for the place was great and populous) and when we were gone about a mile from that town, stopped our carriages ; he of our company who told them they should have no recompence, was presently ready to shoot at them with his musket, which made them all to bend their bows at us." The impending disaster was however averted by Terry's intervention, and a few kind words with a paltry present (worth three shillings of English money) sufficed to put the angry mob in a better mood and they left with mutual good wishes. The third trouble was caused by a young man of aristocratic birth who had proved a disgrace to his family and had been sent to the east to die of drink or hardwork. He whipped a servant of Prince Khurram for refusing to hold his horse and again "with a little money, and great many good words, we so quieted this man, that we never after heard any more complaining from him. So that, as I before observed, we were not at any time in any dangers of suffering by that people, but some of our own nation was the procuring cause of it." It is presumed that too many

208. Oaten, *Travels in India*, pp. 137-138.

scapegraces were not sent abroad to save troubles at home and such instances as Terry recorded were by no means common.[209]

X

Everything taken into consideration the foreign travellers had one great advantage over the chroniclers of the court. Having nothing to fear or to expect from the powers that were they could fearlessly tell the unvarnished truth regardless of official frowns and favours. Having come from other lands they recorded with meticulous care matters seemingly unimportant which a native of India would have ordinarily dismissed as commonplace. But they had their limitations as well. Their knowledge of the country and its people was in most cases superficial and the value of their accounts necessarily depended upon the sources of their information. They suffered from the common credulity of their age and they were not always in a position to verify or test the accuracy of what they were told. Their veracity is not to be questioned but we need not accept anything on trust. No authority can be more reliable than his sources and in assessing the historical merit of Thevenot and Careri's travels we should always bear this salutary principle in mind. Their learning, their integrity, their sincerity are not suspected. Yet we may not be able to accept all their statements as equally authentic without a sifting enquiry as to their sources that may not always be equally irreproachable. This is however not to minimise the value of foreign travellers' accounts of India. As a contemporary source of Indian history they will always remain indispensable, but what cannot be dispensed with is not necessarily infallible.

---

209. Terry, *Voyage to East India* (London 1655), pp. 160-69.

INDIAN TRAVELS OF THEVENOT

THE THIRD PART OF THE TRAVELS OF Mr. de Thevenot,

CONTAINING

The Relation of *Indostan*, the *New Moguls*, and of other People and Countries of the *Indies*.

M. de Thevenot

VOYAGES

DE M^{R}

DE THEVENOT.

CONTENANT LA RELATION de l'Indoſtan, des nouveaux Mogols ; & des autres Peuples & Pays des Indes.

A PARIS,

Chez LA VEUVE BIESTKINS, ruë de la Harpe, à l'Imprimerie des Roziers.

M. DC. LXXXIV.

Avec Privilege du Roy.

THE

THIRD PART

OF THE

TRAVELS

OF

Mr. de THEVENOT,

containing

The Relation of *Indostan,* the *New Moguls,* and of other People and Countries of the *Indies.*

BOOK I

CHAPTER I

ARRIVAL AT SURRAT

I set out from *Balsora*[1] in the Ship *Hopewel,*[2] the sixth of *November,* 1665, six Days before[3] the beginning of the *Monson,*[4] and the tenth of *January* 1666, arrived at the Bar of *Surrat ;*[5] so that I had above two Months Voyage of it. That place which is about six French Leagues from *Surrat,* is called, the Bar, because of the many Sand-banks that hinder great Ships from entring the River, before they be unloaded ; and the proper season for Sailing on the Indian-Sea, is called *Mousson* or *Monson,* by corruption of *Moussem.* I have mention'd in the Second Part of my Travels, that that season wherein there is a constant Trade-Wind upon that Sea, begins commonly at the end of October ; that it lasts to the end of *April,* and that that is the time to go from *Persia* to the *Indies,* if one would avoid the Tempests.

Bar of *Surrat.*

Monson.

Next Day, being the Eleventh, about half an hour after two a Clock[6] in the Morning, I went with the rest of the Passengers into a Boat, and at Eight at Night we arrived before *Surrat,* near to the Custom-house, where coming to an Anchor, I past the Night in the Boat ; and next Day, the twelfth of *January,* about ten of the Clock in the Morning the Custom-house being open, our Boat upon the signal given, put in to

Land as near as it could: From thence we were carried ashore upon Mens backs, who came up to the middle[7] in the Water to take us up, and immediately[8] we were led into a large Court; having crossed it, we entred into a Hall, where the Customer waited for us, to have us searched.

A strict search.

Visited[9] we were; but in so severe and vexatious a manner, that tho' I did expect it, and had prepared my self for it before hand, yet I had hardly patience enough to suffer the Searchers to do whatsoever they had a mind to, tho' I had nothing about me but my Cloaths; and indeed, it is incredible what caution and circumspection those People use to prevent being cheated. And in this manner they proceed.[10]

The Bar is six Leagues from the Town.

So soon as a Ship comes to an Anchor at the *Bar*, the Master is oblig'd to to go ashore in his Boat, and acquaint the Custom-house with his arrival, and presently[11] he is search'd from Head to Foot, at the same time a Waiter[12] is sent on board the Vessel, to hinder them from breaking bulk, running any thing ashore, or on board another Ship that hath been already searched; and in the mean time, if they have still time enough, they send off several Barks to bring the Men and Goods ashore to the Custom-house. The Waiter[13] has for his dues from every Passenger an *Abassy*[14] which is worth about eighteen Pence; and the Bark has half a *Roupie* a Head, that is, about fifteen Pence for the passage. If when the Passengers come to the Town, the Custom-house be not as yet shut, they presently[15] come ashore; but if it be, they must tarry in the Bark: In the mean while it is never open but from ten in the Morning till Noon,[16] and it requires a whole Tide to come from the Bar to the Town, unless by good luck one have the Wind and Tide with him.

Abassy 18 pennce. Half a *Roupie* 15 pence.

Seeing the rest of the Day and all the following Night are to be spent in the Bark, Waiters are set over it, Who keep constant Watch to see that none enter in or go out. When the Custom-house is opened, and the Passengers suffered to come ashore, then double diligence is used, and the number of Waiters encreased. One[17] Bark advances at a time, and the[18] lands just against the Custom-house Gate which is upon the Key.[19]

There is a *Kiochk*,[20] or covered Pavillion, where Sentinels are placed to observe and view all that goes in or comes out of the Bark; and the Custom-house Porters go into the Water, and bring the Men and Goods ashore upon their Backs.

Pions.

In the mean time, there are upon the River-side, a great number of *Pions*,[21] who are Men ready to be employ'd in any kind of Service, and to be hired by the Day, if one pleases, as the *Staffieri*[22] in *Italy* are. These *Pions* of the Custom-house have great Canes in their Hands to keep off the People with, that those who come ashore may not have the least communication with any body; and for the greater security, they draw up in both sides, and make a Lane for the Passengers. This is no inconsiderable service to new comers, for if any body came near them, they would certainly be accused of smuggling Goods; and then besides the Caning they would be expos'd to, they must also expect to be roundly fined, and some have been fined in above Ten thousand Livres,[23] though, in reality they had not saved a bit of Goods. And, indeed, they who have a mind to conceal any thing, and defraud the Custom-house, order their Affairs more truly:[24] They stay not[25] till they come to *Surrat*, there to beg the assistance of their Friends. I have known some bring in a great many precious Stones, and other rich Jewels, which the Officers of the Custom-house never saw, nor got one Farthing by, because the Dutch Commander was their Friend, and had assisted them.

From that Court of the Custom-house, one is led into the Hall, where the chief Customer sits on his *Divan*,[26] after the manner of the Orientals, and his Clerks underneath him. I shall say nothing of the *Indian Divans* in this place, because they are like to those of *Turky* and *Persia*. The Passengers enter into that place one after another, and but one at a time. Presently[27] they write down in a Register the name of him that enters, and then he is searched. He must take off his Cap or Turban, his Girdle, Shoes, Stockins, and all the rest of his Cloaths, if the Searchers think fit. They feel his Body all over; and handle every the least inch of stuff about him with all exactness if they perceive any thing hard in it, they immediately rip it up, and all that can be done, is to suffer patiently. That search is long, and takes up above a quarter of an Hour for every Person severally, though at that time they only examine what they have about them. If they find Gold or Silver, they take two and a half *per cent*. and give back the rest;[28] then the partie is let go, but must leave his Goods and Baggage. He that hath been searched marches out by the Wicket of a Gate that opens into the Street, where there is a Guard that suffers him not to pass without Orders from the Customer.

Next Day, all who have left their Goods or Baggage, fail not to come to the same Gate. The Customer comes also about ten of the Clock in the Morning, and having considered whether the Seal which the Day before he put upon two great Padlocks that hold the great Gate and Wicket shut, be whole or not, he causes both to be opened. He and his Men go in; the Gate is shut again, and the Wicket only left open. So all wait without till they be called in; and it was my good fortune to be introduc'd with the first.

They presently[29] bid me own what belong'd to me, and my Cloakbags being brought into the middle of the Hall, they were opened and emptied; every thing was examined one after another: Though I had no Merchant-goods, yet all was searched; my Quilt was ript up, they undid the Pommel of one of my Pistols, with Pegs of Iron felt in the Holsters; and the Clerks at length, being satisfied with the view of my things, I was let go, and pay'd only Custom for my Money. It was no small fortune for me to be so soon dispatched; for Men may wait sometimes a Month before they can get out their Baggage, and especially they who have Merchants-goods, for which at that Custom-house they pay Four in the Hundred, if they be Christians, and Five in the Hundred if they be *Banians*.[30]

What is pay'd at the Custom-house.

CHAPTER II

OF *THE* INDIES

The limits of *India*.

Before I enter into a particular Description of what I have seen in the *Indies*, it is necessary for the understanding of the Countrey, that I describe the Limits thereof, and say somewhat of their Extent. If one would comprehend in the *Indies* all the Countries which to the *West* border on the Provinces of *Macran*,[1] or *Sinde*,[2] *Candahar* and *Kaboul*;[3] to the *North*, or[4] *Tartary*; to the East, on *China* and the Sea; and to the *South*, on the *Ocean*, there is no doubt but that so great a number of Kingdoms and Provinces must make a very vast Countrey: But it may be truly said, that to the *East* the extent of it, (which is very large) is not as yet well known, seeing the Traders of *Indostan*, who traffick in *China*, spend above a Year in Travelling from their own Countrey into that; and that long Journey is a good Argument that there are several Kingdoms betwixt the *Great Mogul's* Countrey, and that of the Emperour of *China*.

The Division of the Limits of *Indostan*.

In the usual Division of the *Indies*, that Eastern part is called *India* beyond the *Ganges*[5], as the *Western* is named *India* on this side of *Ganges*. This latter part is best known, and is called *Indostan*[6], having for its natural Limits to the *West* and *East*, the *Ganges* and *Indus*, which have their Sources[7] in the Mountains of *Zagatay*[8] and *Turquestan*. These two last Countries border *Indostan* on the North-side, as the Indian-Sea limits it on the *South*, round the Cape of *Comory*[9], from the Mouths of Ganges to those of *Indus*.

The Source of *Ganges*.

The Empire of the *Great Mogul* which in particular is called *Mogulistan* is the largest and most powerful Kingdom of the *Indies ;* and the Forces of the other Kings of *Indostan* ought the less to be compared to his, that most of them are in some dependance on that Prince. I shall write what I know of their Kingdoms, when I have treated of his and of himself.

CHAPTER III

OF THE GREAT MOGUL

The *Great Mogul*[1] descends in direct line from *Tamerlan,*[2] whose Successours that setled in the Indies, took to themselves the Name of *Moguls,* that they might be distinguished from those to whom that Prince left *Zagatay, Corassan,*[3] *Persia,* and other Countries to be Governed after him. They thought that that Name might contribute much to the Glory of their Family, because by taking it they would more easily perswade Men, that they are of the Race of *Ginguis Can,*[4] the First Emperour of the Ancient Moguls, who had carried it above Twelve Ages[5] before them, and who under that Title began the Greatest and most Powerful Empire in the World. *Ginguis Can.*

Mogul was heretofore the Name of a mighty People, who inhabited a vast Country at the extremity of East *Tartary,* towards the North, which some have called *Mogul,* others *Mongul* and *Mongal,* and others *Mogulistan,* where *Ginguis Can* was Born. That Emperour or Great *Chan,* reduced it wholly under his Obedience, before he undertook the Conquest of the rest of *Asia ;* and his Subjects, as well as he, were called *Moguls.* This gave occasion to those of *India,* to take the same Name, thereby to signifie that they are descended from him. *Mogul.*

As for the Genealogy of *Tamerlan,* it must be examined some where else than in the relation of Travels, if one would know the truth of it, because of the diversity of opinions that are to be found amongst the Oriental writers upon that subject. *Tamerlan.*

Tamerlan had already given great jealousie to the Indians, by Conquering the Province of *Gazna,*[6] which had been sometimes in their dependance, though lying a great deal on this side of the *Indies,* and which in his own lifetime was Possessed by *Pir Muhemmed,*[7] Son of his Eldest Son *Gayeteddin ;*[8] but when *Mirza Baber,* who descended from the Third Son of that Emperour,[9] retreated thither after the loss of *Maurenahor*[10] or *Zagatay,* he bestirred himself so well in setling his Dominion there, as he did in some other Countries of the *Indies* that lay next to him, and were,[11] according to the *Lebeltaric,*[12] (he Reigned Fourty three Years,) that his Son *Humayon* had no *Gazna. Pir-Muhemmed. Gayeteddin. Mirza Baber. Humayon.*

great difficulty to get Footing in *Indostan* after the death of his Father, which happened in the Year 1530. and who had already made some unsuccessful attempts in that Country.

This young Prince made himself Master of *Candahar, Caboul,* and many other Towns, the greatest part whereof he lost sometime after by the Valour of *Chaalem*[13] King of *Bengale* and *Deran* ;[14] but he recovered them in process of time by the means of *Tahmas*[15] Kings of *Persia,* whose Sister he Married, and having carried his Conquest farther on, he made *Delhy*[16] the Capital of his Kingdom.

Ecbar.

His Son *Ecbar*[17] Succeeded him ; and having joyned a great many Provinces of *Indostan* to those which his Father left him, died in the Year 1604.[18]

Gehanguir.

Selim his Eldest Son, was immediately Crowned by the Name of *Gehanguir* ;[19] and having Reigned Three and twenty Years, and enlarged the Conquest, he died in the Year 1627.

Bulloquoy.

After his death, his Grandson *Boulloquoy*[20] Reigned about Three Months, but he was strangled by Order of *Sultan Corom,*[21] a Rebel Son of *Gehanguir,* who having made sure of the Empire, took to himself the Name of *Chagehan*[22] in the Year 1628.

Corom.
Chagehan.

Seeing Blood and Rebellion raised him to the Throne, he had experience of the same disorders amongst his Children,[23] which he had caused to his Father ; for through their jealousie his Empire was almost always in confusion, and at length fell into the hands of *Auranzeb*[24] the Third of his Four Sons, who Reigns at present.

Auranzeb.

In mounting to the Throne, this Prince imitated the crimes of his Father ; for he put to death *Dara* his Eldest Brother, imprisoned *Mourad*[25] his other Brother who confided in him, and clapt up his own Father in Prison, who died Five or Six Years after, about the end of the Year 1666.

The death of *Chagehan.*

The Power of the *Mogul.*

The *Great Mogul* is certainly a most Powerful Prince, as we may Judge by his Riches, Armies, and the number of People that are within the extent of his Empire. His yearly Revenues, they say, mount to above Three hundred and thirty French Millions.[26] The *Canon Name,*[27] which is a Register containing a List of his Forces, makes it appear, that that Prince entertains Three hundred thousand Horse,[28] of which betwixt Thirty and Thirty five thousand, with ten thousand Foot are for a Guard to his Person both in time of Peace and War, and are commonly quartered in those places where he keeps his Court. This Empire extends from East to West above Four hundred Leagues, and from North to South above Five hundred, and that vast space, (excepting some Mountains and Deserts,) is so full of Towns, Castles, Burroughs and Villages, and by consequence of Inhabitants who till the Land,

The Registered Forces of the *Mogul.*

or emprove it by manufactures, and the commerce which that Country affords, that it is easie to judge of the Power of the King who is Master thereof.

The true bounds of his Empire are to the West, *Macran* or *Sinde* and *Candahar ;* to the East, it reaches beyond the Ganges ; to the South it is limited by *Decan,* the great Sea and the Gulf of *Bengale ;* and to the North by the *Tartars.* The exageration of many Travellers, concerning the extent of the Countries of this great King of the *Indies,* was the cause that I made it my business to consult the most knowing Men, that I might learn what they thought of the greatness of it, and what now I write is their Opinion.

The bounds of *Mogulistan.*

They affirm not as some do, that when the *Mogul* makes War, he sends Three hundred thousand Horse into the field. They say, indeed, that he pays so many ; but seeing the chief Revenues, or to say better, the rewards of the Great Men, consist particularly in the pay which they have for more or fewer Troopers, it is certain that they hardly keep on Foot one half of the Men they are appointed to have ; so that when the Great *Mogul* marches upon any expedition of War, his Army exceeds not an Hundred and fifty thousand Horse, with very few Foot, though he have betwixt Three and four hundred thousand Mouths in the Army.

The true Forces of the *Mogul.*

Besides, I was informed by any Indian who pretends to know the Map of his Country, that they reckon no more but twenty Provinces[29] within the extent of *Mogulistan* in the Indies, and that they who have reckoned more, have not been well informed of their number, since of one Province they have made two or three.

This Indian had a list of the Princes Revenues calculated for the twenty Provinces, and I made no doubt of the truth of his System ; but I had rather call them Governments, and say that every Government contains several Provinces. I shall observe the Revenues of the Governments, in the Discription I give of them, and shall call each Government a Province, that I may not vary from the memoires which I have ; and as I entered the Indies by the Province of *Guzerat,* so I shall describe it before the others.

Twenty Provinces or Governments in *Mogulistan.*

CHAPTER IV

THE PROVINCE OF GUZERAT

Guzerat.

The Province of *Guzerat*,[1] which was heretofore a Kingdom, fell into the Possession of the *Great Mogul Ecbar*, about the year 1565.[2] He was called into it by a great Lord,[3] to whom the King of *Guzerat, Sultan Mamoet*[4] gave the general Government thereof, when being near his death, he trusted him with the tuition and regency of his only Son, in the Year 1545, or 1546 during the Reign of *Humayon* the Father of *Ecbar*.

Government.

The ambition of that Governour who was envied by all the great Men[5] of the Kingdom of *Guzerat*, that were his declared Enemies, and against whom he resolved to maintain himself at the cost of his own lawful Prince, made him betake himself to the King *Mogul*, under pretext of soliciting his protection for his Pupil named *Mudafer*,[6] who was already of Age,[7] but not yet of sufficient Authority to maintain his Guardian against the faction of the great Men whom he had provoked.

Mudafer King of *Guzerat.*

Ecbar seizes *Guzerat.*

Ecbar entered Guzerat with an Army, and subdued all those who offered to make head against him, and whom the Governour accused of being Enemies to his King: But instead of being satisfied with one Town[8] which with its Territories had been promised him, he seized the whole Kingdom, and made the King and Governour Prisoners. That unfortunate Prince being never after able to recover it again; not but that having made his escape, he attempted once again to have reestablished himself,[9] but his efforts were in vain, for he was overcome, and made Prisoner a second time, so that despair at length made him destroy himself.

Mudafer kills himself.

Guzerat a pleasant Province.

This is the pleasantest Province of *Indostan*, though it be not the largest. The *Nardaba, Tapty*,[10] and many other Rivers that water it, render it very fertile, and the Fields of *Guzerat* look green in all the seasons of the Year, because of the Corn and Rice that cover them, and the various kinds of Trees, which continually bear Fruit.

The Ports *Surrat* and *Cambaye.*

The most considerable part of *Guzerat* is towards the Sea, on which the Towns of *Surrat* and *Cambaye*[11] stand, whose Ports are the best of all *Mogulistan*. But seeing *Amedabad* is the Capital Town of the Province, it is but reasonable we should treat of it before we speak of the rest.

Departure from *Surrat* to *Amedabad.*

February the First I parted from *Surrat* to go to that Town, and going out at *Baroche Gate*,[12] I marched streight North. Two hours after I crossed the River *Tapty*, in a Boat big enough, but very incommodious for taking in of Chariots, because the sides of it were two foot high. Eight Men were

The Boats on the

forced to carry mine, after they had taken out the Oxen, and I was about half an hour in crossing that River. I continued my journey by the Town of *Beriao,*[13] the River of *Kim,*[14] which I crossed with the same trouble that I had done the *Tapty,* by the Town *Ouclisser,*[15] the River of *Nerdaba,* and at length I arrived at the Town of *Baroche,* which is distant from *Surrat* and the Sea, Twenty *Cosses* which makes about Ten French Leagues, because a *Cosse*[16] which is a Measure amongst the Indians for the distance of places, is about half a League. *Tapty* incommodious. *Beriao* a Town. *Kim* a River. *Ouclisser* a Town. *Nerdaba* a River. *Cosse.*

Baroche[17] lies in 21 degrees 55 minutes North Latitude. The fortress of *Baroche* is large and square, standing on a Hill, which makes it to be seen at a great distance. It is one of the chief strengths of the Kingdom, and had heretofore a very large Jurisdiction. The Town lies upon the side,[18] and at the foot of the Hill, looking towards the River of *Nerdaba.* It is environed with Stone-Walls about three Fathom high, which are flanked by large round Towers at Thirty or Thirty five Paces distance one from another. The *Bazards*[19] or Market-places are in a great Street at the foot of the Hill ; and there it is that those Cotten-Stuffs are made, which are called *Baftas,*[20] and which are sold in so great plenty in the *Indies.* *Baroche.* *Baftas.*

The Hill being high and hard to be mounted, it might be a very easie matter to put the fortress in a condition not to fear any Attack, but at present it is so much slighted, that there are several great breaches in the Walls[21] to the Land side, which no body thinks of repairing. In that Town there are *Mosques* and *Pagodes,*[22] that's to say, Temples of the Heathen, as well above as below. The River-water is excellent for whitening of Cloaths, and they are brought from all parts to be whitened there. There is little or no other Trade there, but of Agates ; but most of those are Sold at *Cambaye.* There is great abundance of Peacocks in the Country about *Baroche.*[23] The Dutch have a Factor[24] there for the quick dispatch and clearing at the Custom-house, the other sorts of Cloaths that come from *Amedabad* and elsewhere, because since all Goods must pay duties[25] as they enter and come out of *Baroche,* there would always happen confusion, if the care of that were referred to the carriers who transport them. Peacocks at *Baroche.*

Leaving *Baroche,* I continued my Journey Northwards, to the little Town of *Sourban,*[26] which is seven Leagues distant from *Baroche,* and then having crossed the Brook *Dader,*[27] and several Villages, I arrived at *Debca*[28] which lies on the side of a Wood seven Leagues from *Sourban.* The inhabitants of this Town were formerly such as are called *Merdi-Coura* or *Anthropophagi,*[29] Man-eaters, and it is not very many Years since Mans flesh was there publickly sold in the Markets. That place seems to be a nest of Robbers ; the Inhabitants who are *Sourban.* *Debca.* *Anthropophagi.*

for the most part Armed with Swords, are a most impudent sort of People: In what posture soever you be, they continually stare you in the Face, and with so much boldness, that let one say what he pleases to them, there is no making of them to withdraw: Passengers that know them, are always upon their Guard, nay, and are obliged to carry a Lance with them, when they go to do their needs.

Petnad.

Next day we parted from thence and went to *Petnad,*[30] a little Town seven Leagues and a half from *Debca,* and arrived there, having first past the Gulf or River of *Mai,*[31] where there is a Watch to secure the Rode.[32] We found in our way two great *Tanquiez*[33] and a great number of Monkies of an extraordinary bigness. These *Tanquiez* are standing Ponds or reservations[34] of Rain-water; there are many of them in the *Indies,* and commonly there is great care taken in looking after them, because Wells being rare in that Country, there is an extream need of these publick reservatories, by reason of the continual thirst which the heat causes in all Animals there, and some of them are as big as Lakes or large Ponds.

Tanquiez.

An account of the Road from *Surrat* to *Amedabad.*

One must go out by *Baroche* gate and cross the River of *Tapty* a league and a half from *Surrat.*

Next we came to the Town of *Sousentra,*[35] where we say a very lovely Well, which I shall not describe in this place, because it is almost like to that of *Amedabad,* whereof I shall speak in its proper place. From thence we went to *Mader*[36] which is six Leagues and a half from *Petnad.* Upon the Road we saw an infinite number of Apes of all sorts, not only upon the Trees in the Fields, but even those also by the way side, which were not in the least afraid of any body. I severall times endeavoured to make them flie with my Arms, but they stirr'd not, and cried their *pou pou* like mad, which is, as I think, the *houp houp* of which *Monsieur de la Boulaye*[37] speaks.

There is a great Wartree[38] four leagues from *Surrat* where one may repose. *Kim* a River. *Ouclisser* a Town. *Nerdaba* a River are to be past, and then one comes to *Baroche,* 10 leagues from *Surrat.* *Sourban* a Town 7 leagues from *Baroche.* *Dader* a River or Brook. *Debca* 7 leagues from *Sourban.* *Mai* a River. *Petnad* 7 leagues and a half from *Debca.* *Sousentra* a Town. *Mader* 6 leagues and a half from *Petnad.* *Matrous* a River.

Gitbag 5 leagues from *Mader.*

We went next to *Gitbag,*[39] five Leagues from *Mader,* we met a great many *Colies,*[40] which are a People of a *Caste* or tribe of Gentiles, who have no fixed Habitation, but wander from Village to Village, and carry all they have about with them. Their chief business is to pick and clean the Cotten, and when they have no more to do in one Village they go to another. In this Village of *Gitbag,* there is a pretty handsome Garden of the Kings: I walked in it; it lies along the side of a reservatory, and I saw a great many Monkies and Peacocks therein. The dwelling which remains appears to have been

The sepulchre of Shah Alam at Sarkhej

handsome, but it is let run to ruin ; and a Royal-house, not far off, is in very bad repair also. It is but two Leagues and a half from *Gilbag* to *Amedabad*.

Amedabad two Leagues from Gilbag.

CHAPTER V

OF AMEDABAD

Amedabad is distant from *Surrat* fourscore and six Cossess, which make about fourty three French Leagues. It is not improbable but that this Capital of *Guzerat* is the *Amadavistis* of *Arian*,[1] though modern Writers say, That it hath its name from a King called *Ahmed* or *Amed*,[2] who caused it to be rebuilt, and that it was called *Guzerat*[2a] as well as the Province, before that King reigned. King *Chagehan* named it *Guerdabad*,[3] the Habitation of Dust, because there is always a great deal there. This Governour of the Province has his residence in it, and he is commonly a Son of the *Great Mogul ;* but at present a great *Omra* called *Muhabbat-Can*[4] is the Governour ; and the Kings of *Guzerat* resided there also, before King *Ecbar* seized it.

Amedabad the Capital of Guzerat.

Guerdabad.

This Town lies in twenty three Degrees and some Minutes North-Latitude.[5] It is built in a lovely Plain, and Watered by a little River called *Sabremetty*,[6] not very deep, but which in the time of the Rains prodigiously overflows the Plains.[7] There you may see many large Gardens, enclosed with Brick-walls, and which have all a kind of Pavillion at the entry. After that I saw a very spacious Reservatory,[8] that hath in the middle a lovely Garden fourscore Paces square, into which one enters by a Bridge four hundred Paces long, and at the end of the Garden there are pretty convenient Lodgings.

The Scituation of Amedabad. Sabremetty a River.

A Reservatory of Water, with a Garden in the middle.

Then you see several Houses here and there, which makes, as it were, a great Village, and a great many Tombs[9] indifferently well built. This might be called an Out Suburbs, because, from thence one enters by a Postern into a Street with Houses on each side, which leads streight into the Town, and is on that side the true Suburbs of *Amedabad*.

The Town is enclosed with Stone and Brick-walls, which at certain distances are flanked with great round Towers and Battlements all over. It hath twelve Gates, and about a League and a half in its greatest length, if you take in the Suburbs. It is one of the places of *Guzerat* that is most carefully kept in order, both as to its Walls and Garrison, because it lies most conveniently for resisting the incursions of some neighbouring Rajas. They are afraid particularly of the Inrodes of the *Raja*

The Walls and Towers of Amedabad.

Raja of *Badur.*

of *Badur,*[10] who is powerful by reason of the Towns and Castles which he hath in the Mountains, and which are not accessible but by narrow passes that can be most easily defended. King *Ecbar* used all endeavours during the space of seven Years to ruin that *Raja;* but he could not accomplish it, and was forced to make Peace with him. However his People are always making Incursions, and he comes off by disowning them. His usual Residence is in the Province of *Candich.*[11]

Dutch in *Amedabad.*

So soon as I arrived at *Amedabad,* I went to lodge in *Quervanseray,*[12] where I found the Monument of the Wife of a King of *Guzerat:*[13] After I had taken a little repose there, I went to see the Dutch Factors, for whom I had Letters from the Commander of *Surrat.* They detain'd me, and no excuse would serve, but that I must needs lodge with them ; nay, they were so kind, as to accompany me by turns to all the places of *Amedabad,* wither my Curiosity led me: They are lodged in the fairest and longest Street of the Town. All the Streets of *Amedabad* are wide, but this is at least thirty Paces over, and at the *West* end of it there are three large Arches that take up its whole breadth.

The *Meidan* of *Amedabad.*

Going from their Lodgings, one enters by these high Arches into the *Meidan-Chah,*[14] which signifies the Kings Square. It is a long Square having four hundred Paces in breadth, and seven hundred in length, with Trees planted on all sides. The Gate of the Castle is on the *West* side, opposite to the three Arches,[15] and the Gate of the *Quervanseray* on the *South.* On the same side there are six or seven pieces of Canon mounted, and on the other, some more great Gates which are at the Head of pretty fair Streets. In this *Meidan* there are several little square Buildings about three Fathom high, which are Tribunals for the *Cotoual,*[16] who is the Criminal Judge. In the middle of the place there is a very high Tree, purposely planted for the exercise of those who learn to shoot with the Bow, and who with their Arrows strive to hit a Ball which for that end is placed on the top of the Tree.

The Castle of *Amedabad.*

Having viewed the *Meidan,* we entered the Castle by a very high Gate, which is betwixt two large round Towers about eight fathom high. All the Appartments of it signifie but little,[17] though the Castle be walled about with good Walls of Freestone, and is as spacious as a little Town.

The fair *Quervanseray* of the *Meidan* of *Amedabad.*

The *Quervanseray* in the *Meidan,* contributes much to the beautifying of that place. Its Front is adorned with several Lodges and Balcony's supported by Pillars, and all these Balcony's which are of Stone, are delicately cut to let in the Light. The entry is a large eight-square[18] Porch arched over like a Dome, where you may find four Gates, and see a great many Balcony's: These Gates open into the body of the

Building, which is a Square of Freestone two Stories high, and varnished over like Marble, with Chambers on all sides, where Strangers may lodge.

The Kings Palace in *Amedabad.*

Near the *Meidan,* is a Palace belonging to the King, which hath over the Gate a large Balcony for the Musicians, who with their Pipes, Trumpets, and Hoboys, come and play there, in the Morning, at Noon, in the Evening, and at Midnight. In the Appartments thereof there are several Ornaments of Folliages, where Gold is not spared. The English Factory is in the middle of the Town. They are very well lodged, and have fair Courts. Their Ware-houses commonly are full of the Cloaths of *Lahors* and *Dehly,* with which they drive a great trade.

Juma-mesgid Fridays Mosque.

There are many Mosques great and small in *Amedabad,* but that which is called *Juma-mesgid,*[19] *Fridays* Mosque,[20] because the devout People of all the Town flock thither on that Day, is the chief and fairest of all. It hath its entry from the same Street where the Dutch-house is built, and they go up to it by several large Steps. The first thing that appears is a square Cloyster of about an hundred and forty Paces in length, and an hundred and twenty in breadth, the Roof whereof is supported by four and thirty Pillasters. The Circuit of it is adorn'd with twelve Domes, and the Square in the middle paved with great square Bricks. In the middle of the Front of the Temple, there are three great Arches, and at the sides two large square Gates that open into it, and each Gate is beautified with Pilasters, but without any order of Architecture. On the outside of each Gate there is a very high Steeple, which hath four lovely Balcony's, from whence the *Muezins*[21] or Beadles of the Mosque, call the People to Prayers. Its chief Dome is pretty enough, and being accompanied with several little ones, and two *Minarets,* the whole together looks very pleasant ; all that pile is supported by forty four Pillars placed two and two, and the Pavement is of Marble. The Chair of the *Imam*[22] is there as in other Mosques, but besides that, in a corner to the Right hand there is large *Jube*[23] resting upon two and fourty Pillars eight Foot high apiece, which must only have been built to hide the Women that go to the Mosque, for that *Jube* is closed up as high as the Sealing with a kind of Pannels of Plaster with holes through ; and there I saw above two hundred *Faquirs,*[24] who held their Arms cross ways behind their Head, without the least stirring.

Santidas, Pagod. The Ceremonie of King *Auranzeb,* for converting a Pagod

Amedabad being inhabited also by a great number of Heathens, there are *Pagods,* or Idol-Temples it it. That which was called the *Pagod* of *Santidas*[25] was the chief, before *Auranzeb* converted it into a Mosque. When he performed that Ceremonie, he caused a Cow to be killed in the place, knowing very well, that after such an Action, the Gentiles according to

into a Mosque.

their Law, could worship no more therein. All round the Temple there is a Cloyster furnished with lovely Cells, beautified with Figures of Marble in relief, representing naked Women sitting after the Oriental fashion. The inside Roof of the Mosque is pretty enough, and the Walls are full of the Figures of Men and Beasts ; but *Auranzeb*, who hath always made a shew of an affected Devotion, which at length raised him to the Throne, caused the Noses of all these Figures which added a great deal of Magnificence to that *Mosque*, to be beat off.[26]

Chaalem a Burying place.

The *Chaalem*[27] is still to be seen in *Amedabad ;* it is the Sepulchre of a vastly rich Man whom the Indians report to have been a Magician, and the Mahometans believe to be a great Saint ; so that it is daily visited by a great many out of Devotion : It is a square pile of Building, having on each side seven little Domes which set off a great one in the middle, and the entry into that place is by seven Ports which take up the whole front. Within this Building there is another in form of a Chappel, which is also square, when one is within the first which is paved with Marble, one may walk round the Chappel that hath two Doors of Marble, adorned with Mother of Pearl, and little pieces of Chrystal : The Windows are shut with Copper Lattices cut into various Figures. The Tomb of the Mock-Saint which is in the middle of the Chappel, is a kind of a Bed covered with Cloath of Gold, the Posts whereof are of the same materials as the Doors of the Chappel are, and have the same Ornament of Mother of Pearls ; and over all there are six or seven Silken Canopy's, one over another, and all of different colours. The place is very much frequented, and is continually full of white Flowers brought thither by the Devout Mahometans, when they come to say their Prayers : A great many Estrige-Eggs[28] and hanging Lamps are always to be seen there also.

On the other side of the Court there is a like Building,[29] where some other Saints of theirs are Interred, and not many steps farther, a Mosque[30] with a large Porch supported by Pillars, with many Chambers and other Lodgings for the Poor ; and to compleat all, there is a spacious Garden at the backside of the Mosque.

There are many Gardens in *Amedabad ;* and are so full of Trees, that when one looks upon that Town from a high place, it seems to be a Forrest of green Trees, most of the Houses being hid by them ; and the Kings Garden[31] which is without the Town and by the River-side, contains all the kinds that grow in the *Indies*. There are long Walks of Trees planted in a streight line, which resemble the *Cours de la Reine* at *Paris*.

A spacious Garden.

It is very spacious, or rather, it is made up of a great many Gardens raised Amphitheatre-wise ; and in the uppermost there is a Terrass-Walk, from whence one may see Villages at several

Leagues distance. This Garden being of a very great extent, its long Walks yielded a very agreeable Prospect. They have in the middle Beds of Flowers, which are not above a Fathom and a half in breadth, but which reaches from one end of the Garden to the other. In the Centre of four Walks which makes a Cross, there is a Pavillion[32] covered with green Tiles. Thither go all the young People of the Town to take the fresh Air upon the Banks of a Bason[33] full of water underneath.

Going thither, we saw a pile of Building, where a King of *Guzerat* lies Interred.[34] It is a square Fabrick, and in the Opinion of the Indians, the Magicians and Sorcerers entertain the Devil there. It is covered with a great Dome, having five smaller ones on each side; and on each front of the Building, there are Pillars which support these Domes. Some Streets from thence there is to be seen a Sepulchre, where a Cow is interred under a Dome standing upon six Pillars.

The Sepulchre of a King of *Guzerat* at *Amedabad*.

The Sepulchre of a Cow.

They would have me go next to *Serquech*,[35] which is a small Town about a League and a half from the City. The Indians say, that in ancient times that place was the Capital of *Guzerat*,[36] because of the vast number of Tombs of Kings and Princes[37] that are there; but it is far more probable, that that place was only destin'd for their Burying, and that *Amedabad* hath always been the Capital. I observ'd there a Building much of the same structure as that of *Chaalem*. It hath the same Ornaments, and is dedicated also to one of their Saints;[38] and all the difference is, that this has thirteen Domes[39] on each side, and the Dome which covers the Chappel, is painted and guilt in the inside. Opposite to this Fabrick, there is another like to it, and dedicated also to a Saint.

Serquech.

Near to these Sepulchres, I saw a Mosque[40] like to that which I viewed at *Amedabad*, and the only difference is, that it is less. It hath adjoyning to it[41] a great *Tanquies*[41a] or Reservatory; in the Chappels on the sides whereof, are the Tombs of the Kings, Queens, Princes and Princesses of *Guzerat*, to which they descend by several Steps of very lovely Stones.[42] They are all of good solid work, whereby it sufficiently appears, that they have been made for Kings and Princes; but they are framed[43] according to the same Model. They consist commonly of a large square Building that hath three great Arches on each Front, and over them a great many little ones. There is a large Dome in the middle, and a great many little ones in the sides, and in every corner, a Tower with a little pair of Stairs in the thickness of the Wall, to go up to Terras-Walks which are at certain distances upon the Building; the Tomb being exactly under the great Dome. Most of these places are full of the marks of the Peoples Devotion, both Mahometans and Indians, who on certain days flock thither, of whom the

Sepulchre of the Kings and Princes of *Guzerat*.

Indigo at *Serquech.*

latter bewail the loss of their Princes. There are a great many *Pagods* in those quarters, and from *Serquech* comes all the Indigo[44] which is sold at *Amedabad.*

An extraordinary Well.

Without the City of *Amedabad* there is a lovely Well,[45] the Figure of it is an oblong square; it is covered with seven Arches of Freestone, that much adorn it: There are six spaces betwixt the Arches to let light in, and they are called, the Mouths of the Well. It is four Fathom broad, and about four and twenty long. At each end there is a Stair-case two Foot broad to go down to it, with six Stories[46] or Landings supported by Pilasters eight Foot high: Each Storie hath a Gallerie, or place[47] of four Fathom extent, and these Galleries and Pilasters are of Freestone: Sixteen Pilasters support each Gallerie, and the Mouths of the Well are about the same length and breadth that the Galleries are: The Figure of the third Mouth differs from the rest, because it is an Octogone, and has near it a little turning[48] Stair-case that leads down to the Well; the Water of it rises from a Spring, and it was up to the middle of the fourth Story when I went down, several little Boys at that time swiming in it from one end to the other amongst the Pillars. The Indians say, that this Well was made at the charges of a Nurse of a King of *Guzerat,* and that it cost thirty Millions;[49] but I could discover no work about it that required so great expences.

An Hospital for Birds.

In this Town there is an Hospital for Birds.[50] The *Gentils* lodge therein all the sick Birds they find, and feed them as long as they live if they be indisposed. Four-footed Beasts have theirs also: I saw in it several Oxen, Camels, Horses, and other wounded Beasts, who were look'd after, and well fed, and which these Idolaters buy from Christians and Moors, that they may deliver them, (as they say,) from the cruelty of Infidels; and there they continue if they be incurable, but if they recover, they sell them to *Gentils* and to none else.

Panthers for Hunting.

There are a great many Forrests about *Amedabad,* where they take Panthers[51] for Hunting, and the Governour of the Town causes them to be taught, that he may send them to the King. The Governour suffers none to buy them but himself, and they whose care it is to tame them, keep them by them in the *Meidan,* where from time to time they stroak and make much of them, that they may accustom them to the sight of Men.

A rare Beast.

The Dutch shewed me a Beast they had, which is much esteem'd in that Countrey. It hath the Head of a Conie, and the Ears, Eyes and Teeth of a Hare; its Muzle is round and of a Flesh-colour, and hath a Tail like a Squirrel; but it is a Foot and a half long: In the Fore-feet it hath four Fingers, and a Claw in place of the fifth; its hind Feet have five Toes compleat, which are very long as well as the Claws: The

Sole of its Feet is flat like an Apes, and of a Flesh-colour: Its Hair is long and course, and of a dark Red; but that on its Belly and Fore-feet is greyish like the Wooll of a Hare; it will eat any thing but Flesh, and easily cracks the hardest Nuts: It is neither wild nor hurtful; will play with a Cat, and shew tricks like a Squirrel: It rubs its Snout with the Feet and Tail as they do, and has the same cry, but much stronger. The Dutch bought it of an *Abyssin,* who had it at *Moca,* though no body could tell the name of it, nor what kind of Beast it was. For my part, I make no doubt but that it is a particular kind of Squirril, though it be three times as big as those we have in *Europe.*

The Commodities of *Amedabad.*

The Commodities that are most traded in at *Amedabad,* are Satins, Velvets, Taffeta's, and Tapistries with Gold, Silk and Woollen Grounds: Cotten-Cloaths are sold there also; but they come from *Lahors* and *Dehly*: They export from thence great quantities of Indigo, dried and preserved Ginger, Sugar, Cumin, Lac, Mirabolans, Tamarins, Opium, Saltpetre and Honey. The chief trade of the Dutch at *Amedabad* consists in *Schites,*[52] which are painted Cloaths; but they are nothing near so fine as those of *Masulipatan*[53] and St. *Thomas.*[54]

CHAPTER VI

DEPARTURE FROM AMEDABAD *TO GO TO* CAMBAYE

Departure from *Amedabad* to *Cambaye.*

Having seen what was curious and worth the seeing in *Amedabad,* and having thanked my Landlords for their Civilities, who at parting procured me an Officer of the *Catoual* to see me safe out at the Gates. I departed the sixteenth of *February* for *Cambaye* which is but two days easie Journey, that is, about fifteen or sixteen French Leagues from *Amedabad.* I followed the same way I came after I had visited the little Town of *Baredgia,*[1] which I left on the Left hand in coming. It is four Leagues from *Amedabad;* but I saw nothing in it remarkable. When I was got as far as *Souzentra* I took to the Right hand,[2] the way of *Cambaye,* and came to lodge all Night in the Village of *Canara,*[3] a League and a half from *Cambaye.*

Baredgia a Town.

The Way of *Cambaye.*

Cambaye.

Cambaye which some call *Cambage* is a Town of *Guzerat,*[4] lying at the bottom of a Gulf of the same name which is to the *South* of it. It is as big again as *Surrat;*[4a] but not near so populous; it hath very fair Brick-walls about four Fathom high, with Towers at certain distances. The Streets of it are large and have all Gates at the ends,[5] which are shut in the Night-time: The Houses are very high, and built of Bricks dried in the Sun, and the Shops are full of Aromatick Perfumes, Spices, Silken and other Stuffs. There are vast numbers of Ivory Bracelets, Agat-Cups, Chaplets and Rings made in this Town; and these Agats are got out of Quarries of a Village called *Nimodra,*[6] which are about four Leagues from *Cambaye,* upon the Road to *Baroche;* but the pieces that are got there are no bigger than ones fist.

Agats.

The Castle of *Cambaye.*

Most part of the Inhabitants are *Banions* and *Raspoutes,*[7] whom we shall describe in the sequel. The Castle where the Governour Lodges is large, but not at all beautiful. There are so many Monkies in this Town, that sometimes the Houses are covered over with them, so that they never fail to hurt some body in the Streets when they can find any thing on the Roofs to throw at them. The out skirts of the Town are beautified with a great many fair publick Gardens. There is a Sepulchre built of Marble,[8] which a King of *Guzerat* raised in Honour of his Governour, whom he loved exceedingly, but it is kept in bad repair. It contains three Courts, in one of which are several Pillars of Porphyrie, that still remain of a greater number. There are many Sepulchres of Princes there also. Heretofore there was in *Combaye* an Hospital for Sick Beasts, but it hath been neglected, and is now fallen to ruin.[9] The Suburbs are almost as big as the Town, and they make Indigo there.[10] The Sea is half a League distant from it, though heretofore it came up to the Town;[11] and that has lessened the trade of the place, because great Ships can come no nearer than three or four Leagues. The Tides[12] are so swift to the North of the Gulph, that a Man on Horse-back at full speed, cannot keep pace with the first Waves; and this violence of the Sea is one reason also why great Ships go but seldom thither. The Dutch come not there but about the end of *September,*[13] because along the Coast of *India* that looks to[14] *Arabia,* and especially in this Gulf of *Cambaye,* it is so bad for Ships in the beginning of this Month, by reason of a violent West-wind[15] that blows then, and which is always accompanied with thick Clouds which they call Elephants, because of their shape, that it is almost impossible to avoid being cast away.[16]

The Sepulchre of the Governour of the King of *Guzerat.*

An Hospital for sick Beasts.

Indigo at *Cambaye.*

Ways to return to *Surrat.*

Having satisfied my curiosity as to what is remarkable in *Cambaye,* I took leave of my Friends; and there being several ways to go from thence to *Surrat,* I advised[17] which I had best to take. One may go by Sea in four and twenty hours, in an *Almadie*[18] which is a kind of Brigantine used by the Portuguese for Trading along that Coast: But these Vessels go not commonly but in the[19] night-time, that they might not be discovered by the *Malabars.*[20] In the day-time they keep in Harbours, and in the evening the Master goes up to some height to discover if there be any *Malabar* Barks at Sea. The *Almadies* Sail so fast that the *Malabars* cannot come up with them, but

Almedie.

The Gulf of *Cambaye* dangerous.

they endeavour to surprise them, and when they discover any one in a Harbour, they skulk behind some Rock, and fall upon it in its passage. Many of these *Almadies* are lost in the Gulf of *Cambaye,* where the Tides are troublesome, and the Banks[21] numerous; and that's one reason why Men venture not to go to *Surrat* this way by Sea, unless extraordinary business press them. *Malabar* Corsars.

There is another way still by Sea, which is to pass through the bottom of the Gulf in a Chariot, over against *Cambaye,* at low Water; and one must go three Leagues and a half in Water, which then is betwixt two and three foot deep: But I was told that the Waves beat so rudely sometimes against the Chariot, that it required a great many hands to keep it from falling, and that some mischance always happened; which hindred me from undertaking that course, though I knew very well that when I was past it, I had no more but eight and twenty Leagues to *Surrat.* And therefore I chose rather to go by Land, what danger soever there might be of Robbers, as I was assured there was.

When my Friends found I was resolved to go that way, they advised me for my security to take a *Tcheron*[22] with a Woman of his *Caste* or tribe, to wait upon me till I were out of danger; but I refused to do it, and found by the success that I had reason to do as I did. These *Tcherons* are a Caste of Gentiles, who are highly esteemed amongst the Idolaters: They live, for most part at *Baroche, Cambaye,* and *Amedabad*: If one have any of these with him he thinks himself safe, because the Man acquaints the Robbers they meet, that the Traveller is under his guard, and that if they come near him, he will cut his own Throat, and the Woman threatens them that she'l cut off one of her Breasts with a Razor which she shews them; and all the Heathen of those places look upon it to be a great misfortune, to be the cause of the death of a *Tcheran,* because ever after the guilty person is an eye-sore[23] to the whole tribe; he is turned out of it, and for his whole life-time after upbraided with the death of that Gentil. Heretofore some *Tcherons* both Men and Women have killed themselves upon such occasions; but that has not been seen of a long time, and at present, they say, they compound with the Robbers for a certain Sum which the Traveller gives them, and that many times they divide it with them. The *Banians* make use of these People; and I was told that if I would employ them, I might be served for two *Roupies* a day: Nevertheless I would not do it, as looking upon it to be too low a kind of Protection. *Tcheron.*

So then I ordered my Coach-man to drive me the same way I came, and to return to *Souzentra* that I might go to *Surrat* by the ordinary way, though the compass he fetched[24] made my Journey longer by seven Leagues and a half. For all the caution I could use, my men lost their way beyond *Petnad,*[25] and we found ourselves at the Village of *Bilpar,*[25a] the inhabitants whereof who are called *Gratiates,*[26] are for the most part all Robbers. I met with one of them towards a little Town named *Selly* ;[27] he was a fellow in very bad cloaths,[28] carrying a Sword upon his Shoulder ; he called to the Coach-man to stop, and a Boy about Nine or Ten years old that was with him, ran before the Oxen: My men presently offered them a *Pecha*[29] which is worth about ten French Deniers, and prayed the little Boy to be gone ; but he would not, till the Coach-man growing more obstinate, obliged the Man to accept of the *Pecha.* These Blades go sometimes[30] in whole troops, and one of them being satisfied, others come after upon the same Road, who must also be contented, though they seldom use violence for fear of offending their *Raja.* I wondered how that *Gratiate* being alone, durst venture to set upon so many ; but he Coachman told me, that if the least injury had been offered to him, he would have given the alarm by knocking with his Fingers upon his Mouth, and that presently[31] he would have been assisted by his Neighbours: In the mean time this small rancounter convinced me that there was not so great danger upon the Roads, as some would have made me believe.

Gratiates.

We found our way again shortly after: We then crossed the River of *Mahy,* and coming out of it I gave half a Roupie to the same *Gratiates* whom I payed as I went to *Amedabad.* The tole[32] belongs to the *Raja* of the Country, who is to answer for the Robberies committed within his Territories. And the truth is, he is as exact as possibly he can be to hinder them, and to cause restitution to be made of what is taken, especially if it be Merchants Goods, or other things of consequence: And my Coach-man told me, that one day having lost an Ox, he went to the *Raja* to demand his Ox ; The *Raja* sent for those who he thought had stoln it, and causing them to be cudgelled, till one of them confessing he had it, he obliged him to bring it out, and restore it to the Coach-man, who was to give him only a *Roupie* for the blows he had received. But the *Raja* of the *Gratiates* do's much more ; for if he that comes to complain, have not time to stay till what he hath lost be found, it is enough if he tell the place of his abode, and he fails not to send it him back by one of his People, though it be eight days Journey off. He is so much a Gentleman, that most commonly he sends Presents to People of fashion who pass by *Bilpar,* and do's them all the good Offices they desire of him.

Mahy a River.

The *Raja* of the *Gratiates* makes good Robberies.

Seeing the Caravans that pass by that place on their way to *Agra,* pay him ten *Roupies* a Man, he treats the whole Caravan *gratis,* and sends Provisions and Victuals into the Camp ; which he orders his Cooks to dress. These do what they can to please the Caravan, and earn some *Pechas* from them, and they are

The *Raja* treats the Caravan *gratis.*

reckoned the best Cooks in the Countrey ; but in truth, their Ragoes[33] are not at all good: Nor do's their Master forget to send Dancing Girls to divert the Company ; and when they are ready to go, he furnishes the Caravan with several Horsemen for their security, until they be out of his Jurisdiction. His Territories comprehend all the Villages from *Cambaye* to *Baroche,* and all his Subjects are called *Gratiates.*

Next Day I came to the Town of *Baroche,* and stay'd only a few Hours to refresh my Men and Oxen. The Officers of the Custom-house asked me at parting, If I had any Merchants-goods, and having answered them that I had none ; they took my word, and used me civily: So I crossed the River at *Ouclisser,* from whence next day I went to *Surrat.*

CHAPTER VII

OF SURRAT.

The Town of *Surrat* lies in one and twenty Degrees and some Minutes of North Latitude,[1] and is watered by the River *Tapty.* When I came there, the Walls of it were only of Earth, and almost all ruinous ; but they were beginning to build them of Brick, a Fathom and a half thick ; they gave them but the same height ; and nevertheless they design'd to fortifie the place as strong as it could be made ; because of the Irruption that a Raja,[2] (of whom I shall speak hereafter) had made into it some time before. However the Ingeneer hath committed a considerable fault in the setting out of his Walls: He hath built them so near the Fort, that the Town will be safe from the Canon of the Castle, and those who defend it may easily be galled by Musquet-shot from the Town.

Surrat.

The Fortification of *Surrat.*

These new Walls[3] render the Town much less than it was before ; for a great many Houses made of Canes that formerly were within its Precinct are now left out, for which, those who are concerned pretend Reparation.[4] *Surrat* is but of an indifferent bigness,[5] and it is hard to tell exactly the number of its Inhabitants,[6] because the seasons render it unequal: There are a great many all the Year round ; but in the time of the *Monsson,* that is to say, in the time when Ships can go and come to the *Indies* without danger, in the Months of *January, February,*[7] *March,* and even in *April,* the Town is so full of People, that Lodgings[8] can hardly be had, and the three Suburbs are all full.

The bigness of *Surrat.*

It is inhabited by Indians, Persians, Arabians, Turks, Franks,[9] Armenians, and other Christians: In the mean time its usual Inhabitants are reduc'd to three Orders, amongst whom,

The Inhabitants of *Surrat.*

indeed, neither the Franks nor other Christians are comprehended, because they are but in a small number in comparison of those who profess another Religion. These three sorts of Inhabitants are either Moors,[10] Heathens,[11] or Parsis; by the word *Moors* are understood all the Mahometans, Moguls, Persians, Arabians or Turks that are in the *Indies*, though they be not uniform in their Religion, the one being *Sunnis* and the other *Chiais*:[12] I have observed the difference betwixt them in my Second Part.[13] The Inhabitants of the Second Order are called Gentils or Heathens, and these adore Idols, of whom also there are several sorts. Those of the third rank are the *Parsis*, who are likewise called *Gaures*[14] or *Atechperest*,[15] Adorers of the Fire: These profess the Religion of the Ancient Persians, and they retreated into the *Indies*,[16] when *Calyfe Omar*[17] reduced the Kingdom of *Persia* under the power of the Mahometans. There are People vastly rich in *Surrat*, and a *Banian* a Friend of mine, called *Vargivora*,[18] is reckoned to be worth at least eight Millions. The English and Dutch have their Houses there, which are called Lodges and Factories:[19] They have very pretty Appartments, and the English have settled the general Staple of their trade there. There may be very well an hundred Catholick Families in *Surrat*.

Moors at *Surrat*.

Gentils at *Surrat*.

Parsis at *Surrat*.

Rich Merchants in *Surrat*.

English and Dutch Factories at *Surrat*

The Castle of *Surrat*.

The Castle is built upon the side of the River at the South end of the Town, to defend the entry against those that would attack it, by the *Tapty*. It is a Fort of a reasonable bigness, square and flanked at each corner by a large Tower. The Ditches on three sides are filled with Sea-water, and the fourth side which is to the West is washed by the River. Several pieces of Canon appear on it mounted; and the Revenues of the King that are collected in the Province are kept there, which are never sent to Court but by express Orders. The entry to it is on the West side by a lovely Gate which is in the *Bazar* or *Meidan*: The Custom-house is hard by, and that Castle has a particular Governour, as the Town has another.[20]

The Houses of *Surrat*.

The Houses of this Town on which the Inhabitants have been willing to lay out Money, are flat[21] as in *Persia*, and pretty well built; but they cost dear,[22] because there is no Stone in the Countrey; seeing they are forc'd to make use of Brick and Lime, a great deal of Timber is employ'd, which must be brought from *Daman*[23] by Sea, the Wood of the Countrey which is brought[24] a great way off, being much dearer because of the Land-Carriage. Brick and Lime are very dear also; and one cannot build an ordinary House at less charge than five or six hundred Livres for Brick, and twice as much for Lime. The Houses are covered with Tiles made half round, and half an Inch thick, but ill burnt; so that they look still white when they are used, and do not last; and it is for that reason that the Bricklayers lay them double, and make them to keep whole.

Canes which they call *Bambous*[25] serve for Laths to fasten the Tiles to ; and the Carpenters work which supports all this, is only made of pieces of round Timber : Such Houses as these are for the Rich ; but those the meaner sort of People live in, are made of Canes, and covered with the branches of Palm-trees. *Bambous.*

Now, it is better building in the *Indies* in the time of Rain,[26] than in fair weather, because the heat is so great, and the force of the Sun so violent, when the Heavens are clear, that every thing dries before it be consolidate,[27] and cracks and chinks in a trice ; whereas Rain tempers that heat, and hindering the Operation of the Sun, the Mason-work has time to dry. When it rains the Work-men have no more to do, but to cover their Work with Wax-cloath, but in dry weather there is no remedy ; all that can be done is to lay wet Tiles[28] upon the Work as fast as they have made an end of it ; but they dry so soon, that they give but little help. The Streets of *Surrat* are large and even, but they are not paved, and there is no considerable publick Buildings within the Precinct of the Town. The time to Build in. The Streets of *Surrat.*

The Christians and Mahometans there eat commonly Cow-beef, not only because it is better than the Flesh of Oxen, but also because the Oxen are employed in Plowing the Land, and carrying all Loads. The Mutton that is eaten there, is pretty good ; but besides that, they have Pullets, Chickens, Pidgeons, Pigs, and all sorts of wild Fowl.[29] They make use of the Oyl of *Cnicus silvestris,*[30] or wild Saffron with their Food ; it is the best in the *Indies*, and that of *Sesamum*[31] which is common also, is not so good. The Meat at *Surrat.* Oyles at *Surrat.*

They eat Graps in *Surrat* from the beginning of *February*, to the end of *April*, but they have no very good taste. Some think that the reason of that is, because they suffer them not to ripen enough : Nevertheless the Dutch who let them hang on the Vine as long as they can, make a Wine of them which is so eager,[32] that it cannot be drunk without Sugar. The white Grapes are big and fair to the Eye, and they are brought to *Surrat*, from a little Town called *Naapoura,*[33] in the Province of *Balagate*, and four days Journey from *Surrat*. Grapes at *Surrat.* *Naapoura* a Town.

The Strong-water[34] of this Country is no better than the Wine, that which is commonly drunk, is made of *Jagre*[35] or black Sugar put into Water with the bark of the tree *Baboul,*[36] to give it some force ; and then all are Distilled together. They make a Strong-water also of *Tary*[37] which they Distil ; But these Strong-waters are nothing so good as our Brandy, no more than those they draw from Rice, Sugar and Dates. The Vinegar they use is also made of *Jagre* infused in Water. There are some that put Spoilt-raisins in it when they have any ; but to make it better, they mingle *Tary* with it, and set it for several days in the Sun. Vinegar at *Surrat*

CHAPTER VIII

OF TARY.

Tary. *Tary* is a liquor that they drink with pleasure in the *Indies*. It is drawn from two sorts of Palm-trees, to wit, from that which *Cadgiour.* they call *Cadgiour,*[1] and from that which bears the *Coco ;* the best is got from the *Cadgiour.* They who draw it gird their Loyns with a thick Leather-girdle, wherewith they embrace the trunk of the Tree, that they may climb up without a Ladder ; and when they are come to that part of the Tree from which they would draw the *Tary,* they make an incision one Inch deep and three Inches wide, with a pretty heavy Iron-Chizel, so that the hole enters in to the pith of the *Cadgiour,* which is white : At the same time they fasten an earthen Pitcher half a Foot below the hole, and this Pot having the back part a little raised, receives the Liquor which continually drops into it ; whil'st they cover it with Briars or Palm branches, least the birds should come and drink it. Then they come down, and climb not up the Tree again till they perceive that the Pitcher is full, and then they empty the *Tary* into another Pot fastened to their girdle. That kind of Palm-tree bears no Dates, when they draw *Tary* from it ; but when they draw none, it yields wild Dates.

Coco-tree. They take another course in drawing that Liquor from the *Coco*-tree.[2] They make no hole, but only cut the lower branches to a Foot length. They fasten Pots to the end of them, and the *Tary* Distils into the Vessels. Seeing the Operation I have been speaking of is but once a year performed on these Palm-tress, they whose Trade it is to sell *Tary,* have a prodigious number of these Trees, and there are a great many Merchants that Farm them. The best *Tary* is drawn in the Night-time ; and they who would use[3] it with pleasure, ought to drink of that, because not being heated by the Sun, it is of an acide sweetness, which leaves in the Mouth the flavour of a Chestnut, which is very agreable. That which is drawn in the day-time is eager,[4] and most commonly made Vinegar of, because *Coco.* it easily corrupts and decays. That kind of Palm, or *Coco*-tree, is fit for many other uses, for of its trunk they make Masts and Anchors, nay, and the hulks of Ships also ; and of its bark Sails and Cables. The Fruit that springs from its feathered branches, is as big as an ordinary Melon, and contains a very wholesome Juice, which hath the colour and taste of Whitewine. The Dutch have a great many of these *Coco*-trees in Batavia, which turn to great profit to them. The Revenue alone of those which belong to the Company near the Town, with the imposition on every Stand of those who sell any thing in the Market-place, is sufficient to pay their Garison ; But

Tapping toddy

they are so rigorous in exacting it, that if any one leave his Stand, to take a minutes refreshment in the Rain, or for any other necessary occasion, though he immediately come back, yet must he pay a second time if he will challenge[5] the same Stand.

At *Surrat*, are sold all sorts of Stuffs and Cotton-cloaths that are made in the *Indies*, all the Commodities of *Europe*, nay and of *China* also, as Purceline, Cabinets and Coffers adorned with Torqueises, Agats, Cornelians, Ivory, and other sorts of embellishments. There are[6] Diamonds, Rubies, Pearls, and all the other pretious Stones which are found in the East to be sold there also: Musk, Amber, Myrrh,[7a] Incense, Manna,[8] Sal-Armoniac,[9] Quick-Silver, Lac, Indigo, the Root Roenas[10] for dying Red, and all sorts of Spices and Fruits which are got in the *Indies* and other Countries of the *Levant*, go off here in great plenty; and in general all the Drogues that Foreign Merchants buy up to transport into all parts of the World. Commodities of *Surrat*.

CHAPTER IX

OF THE WEIGHTS AND MONEY OF SURRAT.

At *Surrat* as elsewhere, there are diverse kinds of Weights and Measures. That which is called *Candy*,[1] is of twenty *Mans*, but the most common Weight used in Trade is the *Man*,[2] which contains fourty *Serres*[3] or Pounds, and the Pound of *Surrat* contains fourteen Ounces, or five and thirty *Toles*. All Gold and Silver is weighed by the *Tole*,[4] and the *Tole* contains fourty *Mangelis*,[5] which makes fifty six of our *Caracts*,[6] or thirty two *Vales*,[7] or otherwise fourscore and sixteen *Gongys*.[8] The *Vale* contains three *Gongys*, and two *Toles* a third and a half, answers to an Ounce of *Paris* weight, and a *Tole* weighs as much as a *Roupie*.[9] The *man* weighs fourty Pound weight all the *Indies* over, but these Pounds or Serres vary according to different Countries: For instance, the Pounds of *Surrat* are greater than those of *Golconda*, and by consequence the *Man* is bigger also: The *Serre* or Pound of *Surrat* weighs no more but fourteen Ounces; and that of *Agra* weighs twenty eight. The weights of *Surrat*. *Candy* a measure. The *Man* a weight at *Surrat*. The Pound of *Surrat*. *Tole*. *Mangelis*. *Caracts*. *Vales*. *Gongy*. The Ounce of *Paris*.

Great sums of Money are reckoned by *Leks*,[10] *Crouls* or *Courous*,[11] *Padans*,[12] and *Nils*. An hundred thousand *Roupies* make a *Lek*, an hundred thousand Leks a *Courou*, an hundred thousand *Courous* a *Padan*, and an hundred thousand *Padans* a *Nil*. The great Lords have *Roupies* of Gold,[13] which are worth about one and twenty French *Livres*; but since they pass not commonly in Trade, and that they are only Coined for the The Money of *Surrat*. *Roupies* of Gold.

most part, to be made presents of, I shall only speak of those of Silver. The Silver *Roupie* is as big as an *Abassy* of *Persia,* but much thicker, it weighs a *Tole ;* It passes commonly for thirty French Sols,[14] but it is not[15] worth above nine and twenty. They yearly Coin *Roupies ;* and the new ones during the year they are Coined in, are valued a *Pecha* more than those of the foregoing year, because the Coiners pretend that the Silver daily wears : The truth is, when I came to *Surrat,* the *Roupies* were worth thirty three *Pechas* and a half,[16] and when I left it, the same were worth but thirty two and a half. They have *Roupies* and quarter pieces also.

Abassis. The *Abassis* that are brought from *Persia,* pass only for ninteen *Pechas,* which are about sixteen French *Sols* and a half. There is also a *Mogole* Silver-Coin, called *Mahmoudy,*[17] which is worth about eleven *Sols* and a half.

Pecha. The *Pecha* is a piece of Copper-Money as big and thick as a *Roupie,* it is worth somewhat more than ten French *Deniers,*[18] and weighs six of our *Drachms.*

Baden. They give threescore and eight *Baden*[19] or bitter Almonds for a *Pecha.* These Almonds that pass for Money at *Surrat,* come from *Persia,* and are the Fruit of a shrub that grows on the Rocks. There are also half *Pechas.*

The *Moguls* Money Very fine. It is to be observed that the Silver Money of the *Great Mogul* is finer than any other, for whenever a Stranger enters the Empire, he is made to change the Silver he hath, whether *Piastres*[20] or *Abassis,* into the Money of the Country, and at the same time they are melted down, and the Silver refined for the Coyning of *Roupies.*

CHAPTER X

OF THE OFFICERS OF SURRAT.

Officers of *Surrat.* There is a Mufty[1] at *Surrat,* who has the inspection[2] over all that concerns the Mahometan Religion, and a *Cady*[3] established for the Laws, to whom recourse is had in case of contest.[4] *Mufty. Cady.* The *Great Mogul* entertains[5] another great Officer there, whom the Franks call Secretary of State, and whose duty much resembles that of the Intendant[6] of a Province in France. He *Vaca-Nevis.* is called *Vaca-Nevis,*[7] that is who writes and keeps a Register of all that happens within the extent of the Country where he is placed. The King keeps one in every Government, to give him notice of all that occurs, and he depends on no Minister of State, but only on his Majesty.

There are two Governours or *Nabad*[8] at *Surrat*, who have no dependence one on another, and give an account of their actions only to the King. The one Commands the Castle, and the other the Town; and they encroach not upon one anothers rights and duties. The Governour of the Town Judges in Civil matters, and commonly renders speedy Justice: If a Man sue another for a Debt, he must either shew an obligation, produce two witnesses, or take an Oath: If he be a Christian, he swears upon the Gospel; if a Moor, upon the Alcoran,[9] and a Heathen swears upon the Cow: The Gentils Oath consists only in laying his hand upon the Cow, and saying, that he wishes he may eat of the Flesh of that Beast, if what he says be not true; but most of them chuse rather to lose their cause than to swear, because they who swear are reckoned infamous among the Idolaters.

Two Governours at *Surrat*. *Nabad.*

The way of suing for a Debt in the *Indies.*

The first time one goes to wait upon the Governour, as soon as they come they lay before him,[10] five, six, or ten *Roupies*, every one according to his Quality; and in the *Indies* the same thing is done to all for whom they would shew great respect. This Governour meddles not at all in Criminal Affaires; an Officer named *Cotoual* takes cognisance of them. In *Turkey* he is called *Sousbassa*,[11] and in *Persia Deroga*.[12] He orders the Criminals to be punished in his presence, either by Whipping or Cudgelling, and that correction is inflicted many times in his House, and sometimes in the Street at the same place where they have commited the fault. When he goes abroad through the Town, he is on Horse-back, attended by several Officers on Foot, some carrying Batons and great Whips, others Lances, Swords, Targets,[13] and Maces of Iron like the great Pestles of a Morter ; but all have a dagger at their sides. Nevertheless neither the Civil nor Criminal Judge can put any one to death. The King reserves that Power to himself; and therefore when any Man deserves death, a Courier is dispatched to know his pleasure, and they fail not to put his Orders in execution, so soon as the Courier is come back.[14]

The Criminal Judge *Cotoual*

The *Cotoual* is obliged to go about the Street in the Night-time, to prevent disorders; and sets guards in several places. If he find any Man abroad in the Streets, he commits him to Prison, and very rarely does he let him go out again, without being Bastonadoed or Whipt. Two of the Officers that wait on him, about nine of the Clock beat two little Drums, whilst a third sounds two or three times a long Copper-Trumpet, which I have described in my Voyage into *Persia*.[15] Then the Officers or Serjeants cry as loud as they can, *Caberdar*,[16] that's to say, *take heed*; and they who are in the Neighbouring Streets, answer with another[17] cry, to shew that they are not asleep. After that they continue their round, and begin to cry again afresh until they have finished it. This round is

The cry of *Caberdar.*

performed thrice a Night, to wit, at nine of the Clock, Midnight, and three in the Morning.[17a]

The *Cotoual* answers for Robberies.

The *Cotoual* is to Answer for all the Robberies committed in the Town;[18] but as generally all that are put into that Office, are very cunning, so they find always evasions[19] to come off without paying. Whil'st I was at *Surrat,* an *Armenian* Merchant was Robbed of two thousand four hundred *Chequins,*[20] his name was *Cogea Minas*:[21] Two of his Slaves absconding about the time of the Robbery, he failed not to accuse them of it; all imaginary[22] enquiry was made after them, but seeing there was no news to be had neither of them nor of the Money, the report run that these Slaves had committed the Theft; and that they were concealed by[23] some Moor that was in intelligence with them, who perhaps, to get all the Money had killed and buryed them, as it had already happened at *Surrat.*

In the mean time the Governour told the *Cotoual,* that he must forthwith pay the Money, because if the Emperour came to know of the matter, all the fault would be laid at their door, that perhaps they might be served worse than to be made pay the Money that had been stollen from *Cogea Minas,* and that therefore they had best send for the *Armenian,* and learn from him how much he had really lost. The *Cotoual* said nothing to the contrary, but at the same time asked leave to commit him to Prison, and to put him and his servants to the Rack, that so by torture he might discover whether or not he had really lost the Money, and if so, whether or not one of his own Men had Robbed him. The Governour granted what he demanded; but no sooner was the news brought to the *Armenian,* but he desisted from pursuing the *Cotoual,* and chose rather to lose all than to suffer the torments that were designed for him. In this manner commonly the *Cotoual* comes off.

The punishment of those who are suspected of Robbery.

When any one is Robbed, this Officer apprehends all the People of the House both Young and Old where the Robbery hath been committed, and causes them to be beaten severely. They are stretched out upon the Belly, and four Men hold him that is to be punished by the Legs and Arms, and two others have each a long Whip of twisted thongs of Leather made thick and round, wherewith they lash the Patient one after another, like Smiths striking on an Anvil, till he have received two or three hundred lashes, and be in a gore of Blood. If at first he confess not the Theft, they whip him again next day, and so for several days more, until he hath confessed all, or the thing stolen be recovered again; and what is strange, the *Cotoual* neither searches his House or Goods, but after five or six days, if he do not confess he is dismissed.

Prevost Foursdar.

At *Surrat* there is a *Prevost* who is called *Foursdar,*[24] and he is obliged to secure the Country about,[25] and to Answer for all the Robberies that are committed there ; but I cannot tell if he be so crafty as the *Cotoual*. When they would stop any Person, they only cry *Doa-padecha*,[26] which hath greater force than a *Hue-and-cry ;* and if they forbid a Man to stir out of the place where he is, by saying *doa-padecha*, he cannot go, without rendering himself Criminal, and is obliged to appear before the Justice.[27] This cry is used all over the *Indies* : After all, there are but Fines[28] imposed at *Surrat*, the People live there with freedome enough.

Doa-Padecha.

CHAPTER XI

BAD OFFICES DONE TO THE FRENCH COMPANY AT SURRAT.

Bad Offices done to the French Company at *Surrat*.

The Governour of *Surrat* was making strict enquiry into the French Company, when I came to the *Indies*. Seeing at first he applyed[1] himself to the other Franks, and particularly to those whose interest it was not to have it[2] established at *Surrat*, they told him a great deal of evil of the French ; so that by the Artifice of their Enemies he had conceiv'd a bad Opinion of them. He was thinking to sollicite their exclusion at Court, when Father *Ambrose*,[3] Superior of the *Capucins*,[4] being enform'd of it, went to undeceive him, telling him that he ought not to give credit to the Enemies of that Company, for that they were combin'd to ruin it if they could. He loved that Father because of his Probity, and therefore did not reject him ; only adjur'd him to tell him the truth without dissimulation concerning the matter, and whether the French, who were to come, were not pirates, as it was reported all over the Countrey, and as many Franks had assured him they were.

Lambert Hugo a Corsar.

This thought was suggested in *Surrat*, so soon as it was known that there was a Design in *France* of sending Ships to trade in the *East-Indies ;*[5] and the Calumny was easily believ'd, because one *Lambert Hugo*,[6] a Dutch-man, who had had French on Board of him,[7] and whom they brought fresh into the Peoples Minds, had been two Years before at *Moca*[8] with French Colours, and a Commission from the Duke of *Vendosme*[9] then Admiral of *France*, and had taken some Vessels : But that which offended most, was the story of the Ship that carried the Goods of the Queen of *Visiapour*,[10] and was stranded about *Socotra*,[11] an Isle lying in eleven Degrees forty Minutes Latitude, at the entry of the Red-Sea. That Queen who was going to *Mecha*,[12] was out of the reach of the *Corsar*, for luckily she had gone on Board of Dutch

The Queen of *Visiapour. Socotra.*

Ship;[13] but being satisfied with a Ship belonging to her self for transporting her Equipage; *Hugo* met that Ship, and persued her so briskly, that the Master was forced to run aground. It being difficult for the Corsar to approach the Ship in the place where she lay, he lost no courage,[14] but patiently expected[15] what might be the issue of her stranding: His expectation was not in vain; for the Indians wanting Water for a long time, and finding none where they were, suffered great extremity; and therefore having hid in the Sea what Gold, Silver, and pretious Stones they could,[16] they resolved to have recourse to the Corsar himself to save their lives, hopeing that he would be satisfied with what remained in the Ship.

The Cunning of *Hugo.*

Hugo being come up with them, cunningly found out that they had sunk somewhat in the Sea; and a false Brother told him, that none but the Carpenter and his Son knew where the Queens Treasure was, (for she had carried with her a great deal of Money, Jewels and rich Stuffs to make Presents at *Mecha, Medina, Grand Cheik,*[17] and other places,[18] resolving to be very magnificent.) In fine, *Hugo* having sufficiently tortured the Master, Carpenter, and the Carpenters Son, whom he threatened to kill in his Fathers presence, made them bring out what was in the Sea, and seized it, as he did the rest of the Cargoe. This Action had made so much noise in the Indies, that *Hugo,* who was there taken for a French-man, was abominated, and by consequence all French-men for his sake.

The Governour talked high of[19] that Corsar to Father *Ambrose,* who had much adoe to perswade him, that he was not a French-man, because he came with French Colours, and for certain had a great many French-men on Board. However, after much Discourse he believed him; but[20] for all that excused not the French from the Action wherein they had assisted him, and still maintained, that nothing but a design of Robbing had brought them into that Countrey: The Father denied that it was their design, but that they only came with *Lambert Hugo* to revenge an affront done to some French, in *Aden*[21] a Town of *Arabia the Happy,* lying in the eleventh Degree of Latitude; and thereupon he told him what was done in that Town to the French, some years before; How that a Pinnace of *Monsieur de la Meilleraye,*[22] being obliged in a storm to separate from her Man of War, and to put into *Aden.* The *Sunnis* by force and unparalell'd impietie, had caused all those that came ashore to be Circumcised, though at first they received them well, and promised to treat them as Friends. That notwithstanding that, the King of *France* as well as the *Indians* had disapproved the Action of the Corsar and French who were on Board of him, because they had put his Subjects into bad Reputation, by the Artifice of the Enemies of *France*; but that he was resolved to dispell that bad Reputation, by settling a Company to trade

Aden.

The marriage of the daughter of the Governor of Surat

to the *Indies*, with express Orders to exercise no Acts of Hostility there.

The Governour being satisfied with the Answer of Father *Ambrose*, prayed him to write down in the Persian Language all that he had told him ; and so soon as he had done so, he sent it to Court. The *Great Mogul* having had it read to him in the Divan, was fully satisfied therewith, as well as his Ministers of State, and then all desired the coming of the French Ships. The truth is, that Governour shewed extraordinary kindness to the *Sieurs de la Boullaye* and *Beber*,[23] the Companies Envoys, and told them, that on the Testimony of Father *Ambrose*, he would do them all the service he could. The English President,[24] an old Friend of that Fathers, shewed them also all the Honour he could, having sent his Coach and Servants to receive them, and he assured the Father, that they might command any thing he had. Thus the Capucin by the Credit that he had acquired in the Indies, dispersed the bad reports which the Enemies of France, had raised against the French.

The French justified by Father *Ambrose*.

Envoys from the French Company.

CHAPTER XII

OF THE MARRIAGE OF THE GOVERNOUR OF THE TOWN'S DAUGHTER.

Whil'st I was at *Surrat*, the Governour of the Town[1] married his Daughter to the Son of an *Omra*,[2] who came thither for that end. That young Lord made his Trumpets, Tymbals[3] and Drums play publickly during the space of twelve or fourteen days,[4] to entertain the People, and publish his marriage upon a *Wednesday* which was appointed for the Ceremony of the Wedding ; he made the usual Cavalcade about eight of the Clock at Night, first marched his Standards which were followed by several hundreds of Men carrying Torches, and these Torches were made of Bambous or Canes, at the end whereof there was an Iron Candlestick, containing Rolls of oyled Cloath made like Sausages. Amongst these Torch-lights there were two hundred Men and Women, little Boys, and little Girls, who had each of them upon their Head a little Hurdle of Ozier-Twigs, on which were five little Earthen Cruces that served for Candlesticks to so many Wax-Candles, and all these People were accompanied with a great many others, some carrying in Baskets, Rolls of Cloath and Oyl to supply the Flamboys, and others Candles.

The marriage of a great Lord at *Surrat*.

The Ceremonies of the Wedding.

The Cavalcade of the Wedding.

The Trumpets came after the Flamboy-carriers, and these were followed by publick Dancing-women, sitting in two

Machins made like Bedstids without Posts, in the manner of *Palanquins,* which several Men carried on their Shoulders. They sung and play'd on their Cymbals, intermingled with Plates and flat thin pieces of Copper, which they struck one against another, and[5] made a very clear sound, but unpleasant, if compared with the sound of our Instruments. Next came six pretty handsome led Horses, with Cloath-Saddles wrought[6] with Gold-thread.

The Bridegroom having his Face covered with a Gold-Fringe, which hung down from a kind of Mitre that he wore on his Head followed on Horse-back, and after came twelve Horse-men, who had behind them two great Elephants, and two Camels which carried each two Men playing on Tymbals ; and besides these Men each Elephant had his Guide sitting upon his Neck. This Cavalcade having for the space of two hours marched through the Town, passed at length before the Governours House, where they continued, as they had done all along the Streets where the Cavalcade went, to throw Fire-Works for some time, and then the Bridegroom retired.

Bonefires.

Sometime after, Bonefires prepared on the River-side before the Governours House were kindled ; and on the Water, before the Castle there were six Barks full of Lamps burning in tires ; about half an hour after ten these Barks drew near the House, the better to light the River : And at the same time, on the side of *Renelle,*[7] there were Men that put Candles upon the Water, which floating gently without going out, were by an Ebbing-Tide carried towards the Sea. *Renelle* is an old Town about a quarter of a League distant from *Surrat* : It stands on the other side of the *Tapty,* and though it daily fall into ruin, yet the Dutch have a very good Magazin there.

Renelle a Town.

There were five little artificial Towers upon the Water-side full of Fire-lances and Squibs, which were set on fire one after another ; but seeing the Indian Squibs make no noise no more than their Fire-lances, all they did, was to turn violently about, and dart a great many streaks of Fire into the Air, some streight up like Water-works,[8] and others obliquely, representing the branches of a Tree of Fire : They put fire next to a Machine which seemed to be a blew[9] Tree when it was on fire, because there was a great deal of Brimstone in the Fire-work : After that, upon a long Bar of Iron fixed in the ground they placed a great many artificial Wheels, which play'd one after another and spread abundance of Fire : They also burnt divers Pots full of Powder, from which large flakes of Artificial Lightning glanced[10] up in the Air ; and all this while, Squibs and Serpents flew about in vast numbers ; and with them many Fire-lances, in which was a great deal of Camphire, that yielded a whitish dazling flame.

These Fire-works play'd almost an hour ; and when they were over, the main business was performed. The Maid was married in her Fathers House by a *Moula,*[11] and about two of the Clock in the Morning was conducted upon an Elephant to her Husbands Lodgings. The Wedding.

There were a great many Dancers, Tumblers, and players at sleight of Hand in the open places ; but they acted nothing, as I could see, but what was dull, and yet I was advantageously placed in Windows to examin their play, being desirous to see, if what was told of their dexterity was true ; but I found nothing extraordinary[12] in it, and I should have had a bad Opinion of the Indian Dances, if I had not met with nimbler[13] afterwards in my Travels there. Dancers, Juglers.

The first time I saw Hermaphrodites was there. It was easie to distinguish them, for seeing there is a great number in that Town, and all over the *Indies,* I was enform'd before hand, that for a mark to know them by, they were oblig'd under pain of Correction,[14] to wear upon their Heads a Turban like Men, though they go in the habit of Women. Hermaphrodites.

CHAPTER XIII

OF BURYING-PLACES, AND THE BURNING OF DEAD BODIES.

The Burying-places of *Surrat* are without the Town, about three or four hundred Paces from *Baroche-Gate*. The Catholicks have their own apart ; and so have the English and Dutch, as well as some Religious Indians. The English and Dutch adorn[1] their Graves with Pyramids of Brick whitened over with Lime ; and whilst I was there, there was one a building for a Dutch Commander, which was to cost eight thousand Livres.[2] Amongst the rest, there is one of a great drinker,[3] who had been banished to the *Indies* by the *States General,* and who is said to have been a Kinsman of the Prince of *Orange*: They have raised a Monument for him, as for other Persons of note ; but to let the World see that he could drink stoutly, on the top of his Pyramid there is a large Stone-cup, and one below at each corner of his Tomb ; and hard by each Cup there is the Figure of a Sugar-loaf. When the Dutch have a mind to divert themselves at that Monument, they make, God knows, how many Ragoes in these Cups, and with other less Cups drink or eat what they have prepared in the great ones. Burying places. The Sepulchres of the English and Dutch. The Sepulchre of a Dutch drinker.

The Religious Gentils have their Tombs about two thousand Paces beyond the Dutch Burying-place. They are square, and The Tombs of the

Religious Gentils.

made of Plaister ; they are about two or three Foot high, and two Foot broad, covered some with a Dome, and others with a Pyramid of Plaister somewhat more than three Foot high ; on the one side there is a little Window, through which one may see the top of the Grave ; and because there are two Soles of Feet cut upon them, some have believ'd that the *Vartias*[4] were interred with the Head down and the Feet upwards, but having enform'd my self as to that, I learnt, that there was no such thing, and that the Bodies are laid in their Graves after the ordinary manner.

The place where Bodies are burnt.

The place where the *Banians* burn their dead Bodies, is by the River-side, beyond the Burying-places ; and when they are consumed, the Ashes are left there, on design,[5] that they may be carried away by the Tapty, because they look upon it as a Sacred River.[6] They believe that it contributes much to the Salvation of the Soul of the deceased, to burn his Body immediately after his Death, because, (as they say,) his Soul suffers after the separation from the Body till it be burnt: It is true, that if they are in a place where there is no Wood, they tye a Stone to the dead Body, and throw it into the Water, and their Religion allows them to bury it if there be neither Water nor Wood ; but they are still perswaded that the Soul is much happier when the Body hath been burnt.

They burn not the Bodies of Children that die before they are two Years old, because they are as yet innocent ; nor do they burn the Bodies of the *Vartias* nor *Jogues,*[7] who are a kind of Dervishes,[8] because they follow the rite of *Madeo,*[9] who is one of their great Saints, and who ordered the Bodies to be interred.

Madeo.

CHAPTER XIV

OF DIVERSE CURIOSITIES AT SURRAT.

A fair Well.

Towards the English Burying-place there is a great Well ; a *Banian* made it[1] for the convenience of Travellers, and it is of an oblong square Figure, like the Well of *Amedabad,* which I have described. There are over it diverse thin Brick-Arches, at some Feet distance one from another: Several Stairs go down to it, and the Light enters by the spaces that are between the Arches ; so that one may see very clearly from the top to the bottom. On the outside there is the Figure of a Red-face, but the Features are not to be distinguished. The Indians say, that it is the Pagod of *Madeo,* and the Gentils pay a great Devotion to it.

Daman-gate. *A lovely Tanquie.*

Towards *Daman-gate,* where the loveliest Walk in all the Countrey begins, there is a Reservatory[2] much esteemed. That Gate is covered and encompassed with the branches of a lovely War, which the Portuguese call the Tree of Roots, that furnishes the pleasantest Resting-place imaginable to all that go to the *Tanquie.* This great Reservatory of Water hath six[2a] Angles ; the side of every Angle is an hundred paces long, and the whole at least a Musket-shot in diametre. The bottom is paved with large Free-stone, and there are Steps almost all round in form of an Amphitheatre, reaching from the brim to the bottom of the Bason ; they are each of them half a Foot high, and are of lovely Free-stone that hath been brought from about *Cambaye ;* where there are no Steps there is a sloaping descent to the *Bason ;* and there are three places made for Beasts to water at.

A Building in the middle of the *Tanquie.*

In the middle of this Reservatory there is a Stone-Building about three Fathom every way,[3] to which they go up by two little Stair-cases. In this place they go to divert themselves, and take the fresh Air ; but they must go to it in Boat. The great *Bason* is filled with Rain-water in the season when the Rains fall, for after it hath run through the fields, where it makes a kind of a great Chanal, over which they have been obliged to make Bridges, it stops in a place enclosed within Walls, from whence it passes into the *Tanquie* through three round holes, which are above four Foot Diametre, and hard by there is a kind of Mahometan Chappel.[4]

Gopy.

This Tanquie was made at the charges of a rich *Banian* named *Gopy,*[5] who built it for the publick ; and heretofore all the Water that was drank in *Surrat* came from this Reservatory, for the five Wells which at present supply the whole Town, were not found out till long after it was built. It was begun at the same time the Castle was, and they say, that the one cost as much as the other. It is certainly a Work worthy of a King, and it may be compared to the fairest that the Romans ever made for publick benefit. But seeing the Levantines let all things go to ruine for want of repair, it was above six Foot filled with Earth when I saw it, and in danger sometime or other to be wholly choaked up, if some Charitable Banian be not at the charge of having it cleansed[6]

The Princesses Garden.

Having viewed that lovely Reservatory, we went a quarter of a League farther to see the Princesses Garden, so called, because it belongs to the *Great Moguls* Sister.[7] It is a great Plot of Trees of several kinds ; as *Manguiers,*[8] *Palms,*[9] *Mirabolans,*[10] *Wars, Maisa-trees,*[11] and many other planted in a streight line. Amongst the Shrubs I saw the *Querzehere*[12] or *Aacla,* of which I have treated at large in my Second Part, and also the *Accaria* of *Egypt.* There are in it a great many very fair streight Walks, and especially the four which make a Cross over the Garden, and have in the middle a small Canal of Water that is drawn by Oxen out of a Well. In the middle of the Garden there is a Building with four Fronts, each whereof hath its Divan, with a Closet at each corner ; and before every one of these Divans there is a square Bason full of Water, from whence flow the little Brooks which run through the chief Walks. After all, though that Garden be well contriv'd, it is nothing to the gallantry[13] of ours. There is nothing to be seen of our Arbours, Borders of Flowers, nor of the exactness of their Compartments, and far less of their[14] Water-works.

The War-tree.

About an hundred, or an hundred and fifty Paces from that Garden, we saw the War-tree[15] in its full extent. It is likewise called *Ber,* and the Tree of *Banians,* as also the Tree of Roots, because of the facility wherewith the branches that bear large Filaments, take Rooting, and by consequence produce other branches ; insomuch that one single Tree is sufficient to fill a great spot[16] of Ground ; and this I speak of, is very large and high, affording a most spacious shade. Its circuit is round, and is fourscore Paces in Diametre, which make above[17] thirthy Fathom. The Branches that had irregularly taken Root, have been so skilfully cut, that at present one may without any trouble walk about every where under it.

A Sacred Tree.

The Gentils of India look upon that Tree as Sacred ; and we might easily perceive that at a distance, by the Banners which the *Banians* had planted on the top and highest Branches of it. It hath by it a Pagod dedicated to an Idol which they call *Mameva ;*[18] and they who are not of their Religion, believe it to be a representation of *Eve.* We found a *Bramen* sitting there, who put some Red Colour upon the Foreheads of those who come to pay their Devotions, and received the Presents of Rice or Cocos that they offered him. That Pagod is built under the Tree in form of a Grot ; the outside is painted with diverse Figures representing the Fables of their false Gods, and in the Grot there is a Head all over Red.[19]

Charity towards Ants.

In that place I saw a Man very charitable towards the Ants : He carried Flower in a Sack to be distributed amongst them, and left a handful every where where he met with any number.

Whilst we were abroad in the Fields, we considered the Soyl of *Surrat,* it is of a very brown Earth ; and they assured us, that it was so very rich, that they never dunged it. After the Rains they sow their Corn, that is, after the Month of *September,* and they cut it down after *February.* They plant Sugar-Canes there also ; and the way of planting them, is to make great Furrows, wherein, before they lay the Canes, they put a great many of the little Fish called Gudgeons :[20] Whether

Sugar-Canes.

these Fish serve to fatten the Earth, or that they add some qualitie to the Cane, the Indians pretend, that without that Manure the Canes would produce nothing that's good. They lay their pieces of Canes over these Fish, end to end, and from every joint of Cane so interred, their[21] Springs a Sugar-cane, which they reap in their season.

The Soyl about *Surrat* is good for Rice also, and there is a great deal sown. *Manguiers* and Palm-trees of all kinds, and other sorts of Trees thrive well there, and yield great profit. The Dutch water their Ground with Well-Water, which is drawn by Oxen after the manner described in my Second Part; but the Corn-land is never watered, because the Dew that falls plentifully in the Mornings, is sufficient for it.

The River of *Tapty* is always brackish at *Surrat*, and therefore the Inhabitants make no use of it, neither for Drink nor Watering of their Grounds, but only for washing their Bodies, which they do every Morning as all the other Indians do. They make use of Well-water to drink, and it is brought in Borrachoes[22] upon Oxen. This River of it self is but little, for at High-water it is no broader than half of the River of *Seine* at *Paris*: Nevertheless it swells so in the Winter-time[23] by the Rain-water, that it furiously overflows, and makes great havock: It has its source in a place called *Gehar-Conde*,[24] in the Mountains of *Decan*, ten Leagues from *Brampour*.[25] It passes by that Town, and before it discharge it self into the Sea, it Waters several Countries, and washes many Towns, as last of all it does *Surrat*. At low Water, it runs to the Bar; but when it flows[26] the Sea commonly advances two Leagues over that Bar, and so receives the Water of the *Tapty*. The River of *Tapty*.

CHAPTER XV

THE PORT OF SURRAT.

The Bar of *Surrat*, where Ships come at present, is not its true Port; at best it can be called but a Road; and I had reason to say in the beginning of this Book, that it is called the Bar because of the Banks of Sand which hinder Ships from coming farther in. The truth is, there is so little Water there, that though the Vessels be unloaded, the ordinary Tides are not sufficient to bring them up, and they are obliged to wait for a Spring tide; but then they come up[1] to *Surrat*, especially when they want to be careen'd. Small Barks come easily up to the Town with the least Tides. The Port of *Surrat*.

The true Port of *Surrat* is *Soualy*,[2] two Leagues from the Bar. It is distant from the Town four Leagues and a half; *Soualy*.

and to go to it by Land, they cross the River at the Town. All Vessels heretofore came to an Anchor in this Port, where the Ground is good ; but because the Customs were often stolen there, it is prohibited, and no Ship hath gone thither since the Year One thousand six hundred and sixty, but the English and Dutch who are suffered to Anchor there still, and have their several Magazins in that place. That Port affords them a fair opportunity of getting ashore what they please Custom-free ; and the Coaches of the Governours, Commanders, or Presidents of these two Nations, who often take the Air thereabouts, might easily carry off any thing of small bulk from on board their Ships. They have even Gardens at *Soualy* by the Sea-side, and each a small Harbour, where they put their Boats or Barks ; so that it is their own fault if they save not a great many things without paying Custom.

Since the Prohibition made to other Nations of coming to Anchor at *Soualy,* there are always a great many vessels at the Bar, though it be an incommodious Road for them ; for ships come from *Persia, Arabia Faelix,* and generally from all Countries of the *Indies* as formerly ; so that the Prohibition of putting into *Soualy* hath nothing lessened the Customs which yield the King yearly twelve *Lecks* of *Roupies,* each *Leck* being worth about an hundred thousand French Livres.[3] The Master of the Custom-House is a *Moor,* and has his Commission from the Governour of *Surrat.* The Clerks are *Banians,* and the rest of the Officers of the Custom-House, as Waiters,[4] Porters. and others, are also Moors, and they are called the *Pions* of the Custom-House.

CHAPTER XVI

OF THE IRRUPTION OF SIVAGY.

Sivagy.

In *January* 1664. *Raja Sivagy* put the Customers and their Governour to a strange plunge[1]; and seeing he is become famous by his actions, it will not be amiss, I think, to give a short History of him. This *Sivagy* is the Son of a Captain of the King of *Visiapours,*[2] and born at *Bassaim*[3] being of a restless and turbulent Spirit, he rebelled in his Fathers life-time, and putting himself at the Head of several *Banditi,* and a great many debauched Young-Men, he made his part good in the Mountains of *Visiapour* against those that came to attack him,[4] and could not be reduced. The King thinking that his Father kept intelligence[5] with him, caused him to be arrested ;[6] and he dying in Prison,[7] *Sivagy* conceived so great a hatred against the King, that he used all endeavours to be revenged on him.

The History of *Raja Sivagy.*

In a very short time he plundered part of *Visiapour,* and with the Booty he took made himself so strong in Men, Arms and Horses, that he found himself able[8] enough to seize some Towns, and to form a little State in spight of the King, who died at that time. The Queen,[9] who was Regent having other Affairs in hand, did all she could to reduce *Sivagy* to duty ; but her endeavours being unsuccessful, she accepted of the Peace he proposed to her, after which she lived in quiet.

The Queen Regent of *Visiapour.*

In the mean while, the Raja, who could not rest, plundered some places belonging to the *Great Mogul ;* which obliged that Emperour to send Forces against him, under the conduct of *Chasta-Can*[10] his Uncle, Governour of *Aurangeabad. Chasta-Can* having far more Forces than *Sivagy* had, vigorously pursued him, but the *Raja* having his retreat always in the Mountains, and being extreamly cunning the *Mogul* could make nothing of him.

Chasta-Can Uncle to the *Mogul.*

However that old Captain, at length, thinking that the turbulent Spirit of *Sivagy* might make him make some false step, judged it best to temporize, and lay a long while upon the Lands of the *Raja.* This Patience of *Chasta-Can* being very troublesome to *Sivagy,* he had his recourse to a Stratagem. He ordered one of his Captains to write to that *Mogul,* and to perswade him that he would come over to the service of the *Great Mogul,* and bring with him five hundred Men whom he had under his Command. *Chasta-Can* having receiv'd the Letters, durst not trust them at first ; but receiving continually more and more, and the Captain giving him such reasons for his discontent as looked very probable, he sent him word that he might come and bring his Men with him. No sooner was he come into the Camp of the *Moguls,* but he desired a Passport to go to the King that he might put himself into his Service : But *Chasta-Can* thought it enough to put him in hopes of it, and kept him with him.

A Stratagem of War.

Sivagy had ordered him to do what he could to insinuate himself into the favour of *Chasta-Can,* and to spare no means that could bring that about, to shew upon all occasions the greatest rancour and animosity imaginable ; and in a particular manner to be the first in Action against him or his Subjects. He fail'd not to obey him : He put all to Fire and Sword in the *Raja's* Lands, and did much more mischief than all the rest besides ; which gained him full credit in the Mind of *Chasta-Can,* who at length made him Captain of his Guards. But he guarded him very ill, for having one Day sent word to *Sivagy,* that on a certain Night[11] he should be upon Guard at the General's Tent ;[12] the *Raja* came there with his Men, and being introduced by his Captain, came to *Chasta-Can,* who awaking flew to his Arms, and was wounded in the Hand ; however he made a shift to escape, but a Son of his was killed,[13] and

Sivagy surprizes *Chasta-Can.*

Sivagy thinking that he had killed the General himself, gave the signal to retreat: He marched off with his Captain and all his Horse in good order. He carried off the Generals Treasure, and took his Daughter,[14] to whom he rendered all the Honour he could. He commanded his Men under rigorous pains, not to do her the least hurt, but on the contrary, to serve her with all respect; and being informed that her Father was alive, he sent him word, That if he would send the Summ which he demanded for her Ransom, he would send him back his Daughter safe and sound; which was punctually performed.

Chasta-Can retires for fear of *Sivagy*.

He wrote afterwards to *Chasta-Can* praying him to withdraw, and owned that the stratagem that had been practised was of his own contrivance; that he hatched[15] a great many others for his ruine, and that if he drew not off[16] out of his Lands, he should certainly lose his life. *Chasta-Can* slighted not the Advice: He informed the King, that it was impossible to force *Sivagy* in the Mountains; that he could not undertake it, unless he resolved to ruine his Troops; and he received Orders from Court to draw off under pretext of a new Enterprize.[17] *Sivagy*, in the mean time, was resolved to be revenged on the *Mogul* by any means whatsoever, provided it might be to his advantage, and knowing very well that the Town of *Surrat* was full of Riches, he took measures how he might plunder it: But that no body might suspect his Design, he divided the Forces he had into two Camps; and seeing his Territories lie chiefly in the Mountains, upon the Road betwixt *Bassaim*[18] and *Chaoul*,[19] he pitched one Camp towards *Chaoul*, where he planted one of his Pavillions, and posted another at the same time towards *Bassaim*; and having ordered his Commanders not to plunder, but on the contrary, to pay for all they had, he secretly disguised himself in the habit of a *Faquir*.[20] Thus he went to discover the most commodious ways that might lead him speedily to *Surrat*: He entred the Town to examine the places of it, and by that means had as much time as he pleased to view it all over.

Sivagy's first Camp towards *Chaoul*. The other towards *Bassaim*.

Sivagy at Surrat in the habit of a *Faquir*.

Sivagy returns to his Camp.

And comes back to *Surrat* with four thousand men.

Being come back to his Chief Camp, he ordered four thousand of his Men to follow him without noise, and the rest to remain encamped, and to make during his absence as much noise as if all were there, to the end none might suspect the enterprise he was about, but think he was still in one of his Camps. Every thing was put in execution according to his orders. His march was secret enough, though he hastened it to surprise *Surrat*; and he came and Encamped near *Brampour-gate*. To amuse[21] the Governour who sent to him, he demanded guides under pretence of marching to another place; but the Governour without sending him any Answer, retired into the Fort with what he had of the greatest value, and sent for assistance on all hands. Most of the Inhabitants in consternation forsook their Houses and fled into the Country. *Sivagy's* Men entered the Town and plundered it[22] for the space of four days burning several Houses. None but the *English* and *Dutch* saved their quarters from the pillage, by the vigorous defence they made, and by means of the Cannon they planted, which *Sivagy* would not venture upon, having none of his own.

The Plundering of *Surrat*.

Nor durst he venture to attack the Castle neither, though he knew very well that the richest things they had were conveighed thither, and especially a great deal of ready Money. He was affraid that attack might cost him too much time, and that assistance coming in might make him leave the plunder he had got in the Town ; besides, the Castle being in a condition to make defence, he would not have come off so easily as he had done elsewhere. So that he marched off[23] with the Wealth he got:[24] And it is believed at *Surrat* that this *Raja* Carried away in Jewels, Gold and Silver, to the value of above thirty French Millions ;[24a] for in the House of one *Banian* he found twenty two Pound weight of strung Pearls,[25] besides a great quantity of others that were not as yet pierced.

22 lbs. of Pearls in the house of one *Banian*.

One may[26] indeed wonder that so populous a Town should so patiently suffer it self to be Plundered by a handful of Men ; but[27] the *Indians* for the most part are cowards.[28] No sooner did *Sivagy* appear with his small body of Men, but all fled, some to the Country to save themselves at *Baroche*, and others to the Castle, whither the Governour[29] retreated with the first. And none but the Christians of *Europe* made good[30] their Post and preserved themselves. All the rest of the Town was Plundered, except the Monastery of the *Capucins*. When the Plunderers came to their Convent, they past it by ; and had Orders from their General to do so, because the first day in the Evening, Father *Ambrose*, who was Superiour of it, being moved with compassion for the poor Christians living in *Surrat*, went to the *Raja* and spake in their favour, praying him at least not to suffer any violence to be done to their Persons. *Sivagy* had a respect for him, took him into his protection, and granted what he had desired in favour of the Christians.[31]

The Christians of *Europe* defended themselves against *Sivagy*. The *Capucins* escaped.

The *Great Mogul* was sensibly affected with the Pillage of that Town, and the boldness of *Sivagy ;* but his Affairs not suffering[32] him to pursue his revenge at that time, he dissembled his resentment and delayed it till another opportunity.

In the Year One thousand six hundred sixty six, *Auran-Zeb* resolved to dispatch him, and that he might accompish his design, made as if[33] he approved what he had done, and praised it as the action of a brave Man, rejecting[34] the blame upon the Governour of *Surrat*, who had not the courage to oppose him. He expressed himself thus to the other Rajas of Court, amongst whom he knew *Sivagy* had a great many Friends ; and told

Auran-Zeb praises *Sivagy* that he may allure him to his Court.

them that he esteemed that Raja for his Valour, and wished he might come to Court; saying openly that he would take it as a pleasure if any would let him know so much. Nay he bid one of them write to him, and gave his Royal word that he should receive no hurt; that he might come with all security, that he forgot what was past, and that his Troops should be so well treated, that he should have no cause to complain. Several *Rajas* wrote what the King had said, and made themselves in a manner sureties for the performance of his word; so that he made no difficulty to come to Court, and to bring his Son with him, having first ordered his Forces to be always upon their Guard, under the Command of an able Officer whom he left to head them.[35]

Sivagy's coming to Court.

At first he met with all imaginable caresses, but some Months after, perceiving a dryness[36] in the King, he openly complained of it, and boldly told him, that he believed he had a mind to put him to death, though he was come on his Royal word to wait upon him, without any constraint or necessity that obliged him to it; but that his Majesty might know what Man he was, from *Chasta-Can* and the Governour of *Surrat*: That after all if he Perished, there were those who would revenge his death; and that hopeing they would do so,[37] he was resolved to die with his own hands, and drawing his Dagger, made an attempt to kill himself, but was hindered and had Guards set upon him.[38]

The boldness of *Sivagy* in speaking to the King.

The King would have willingly put him to death, but he feared an insurrection of the *Rajas*. They already murmured at this usage notwithstanding the promise made to him; and all of them were so much the more concerned for him, that most part came only to Court upon the Kings word.[39] That consideration obliged *Auran-Zeb* to treat him well, and to make much of his Son. He told him that it was never in his thoughts to have him put to death, and flattered him with the hopes of a good Government[39a] which he promised him, if he would go with him to *Candahar*,[40] which then he designed to Besiege. *Sivagy* pretended to consent, provided he might Command his own Forces. The King having granted him that, he desired a Pass-port for their coming, and having got it, resolved to make use of it for withdrawing from Court. He therefore gave Orders to those whom he entrusted with that Pass-port, and whom he sent before under pretence of calling his Forces, to provide him Horses in certain places which he named to them, and they failed not to do it. When he thought it time to go meet them, he got himself and his Son both to be carried privately in Panniers[41] to the River-side. So soon as they were over, they mounted Horses that were ready for them, and then he told the Water-man,[42] that he might go and acquaint the King, that he had carried over *Raja Sivagy*. They Posted it[43] day

Sivagy's pretence.

His escape.

and night, finding always fresh Horses in the places he had appointed them to be brought to ; and they passed every where by vertue of the Kings Pass-port : But the Son unable to bear the fatigue of so hard Riding, died upon the Road.[44] The Raja left Money to have his body honourably Burnt, and arrived afterwards in good health in his own territories.

Auran-Zeb was extremly vext at that escape. Many believed that it was but a false report, and that he was put to death ; but the truth soon was known. This *Raja* is short and tawny, with quick eyes that shew a great deal of wit. He eats but once a day commonly, and is in good health ; and when he Plundered *Surrat* in the Year One thousand six hundred and sixty four, he was but thirty five years of Age. *Sivagy's shape and way of living.*

CHAPTER XVII

OF FATHER AMBROSE *A* CAPUCIN.

Father Ambrose[1] of whom I have spoken hath by his vertue and good services acquired a great Reputation in the Countries of the *Mogul*, and is equally esteemed of Christians and Gentils : And indeed, he hath a great deal of Charity for all. He commonly takes up[2] the difference that happen amongst Christians, and especially the Catholicks ; and he is so much Authorized by the *Mogul* Officers, that if one of the parties be so headstrong as not to be willing to come to an accommodation, by his own Authority he can make him consent to what is just. He makes no difficulty to cause a scandalous Christian to be put in Prison, and if complaint be made of it to the Governour or *Cotoual*, desiring that the Prisoner may be set at liberty, they both send the Petitioner to the Father, telling him that it is a matter they are not to meddle with. If the Supplicant find favour with them, they only offer their Intercession with the *Capucin ;* and one day I saw a Man whom he had let out of Prison at the entreaty of the *Cotoual* severely chid by that Officer, because he had incurred the indignation of Father *Ambrose*. Those whose lives are too irregular he banishes the Town, and the *Cotoual* himself gives him *Pions* to force them out, with Orders to conduct them to the place the *Capucin* shall appoint. *Father Ambrose a Capucin.* *The Authority of Father Ambrose.*

He employs his interest pretty often for the Heathen ; and I saw a Pagan whom they carried to Prison for a slight fault, delivered at his request. He disputes boldly concerning the Faith in the Governours presence ; and one day he reclaimed a Christian Woman debauched by one of the Queens Secretaries, who that she might live licentiously, had renounced her Religion and embraced the *Mahometan ;* and one Morning he himself went and rescued her out of the hands of that Gentil. Indeed, his life hath been always without reproach, which is no small praise for a Man who lives in a Country where there are so many different Nations that live in so great disorders, and with whom his charge obliges him to keep company.

A MAHOMETAN FESTIVAL.

I thought I had observed in my Book of *Persia* all the Festivals which the *Moors* or *Mahometans* celebrate, but they had one in this Town which I had never seen before. They call it the Feast of *Choubret*,[3] and believe that on that day the good Angels examine the Souls of the departed, and write down all the good that they have done in their life-times, and that the bad Angels sum up all their evil actions the same day. So that every one employs that day wherein they believe that God takes an account of the Actions of Men, in Praying to him, doing Alms-deeds,[4] and sending one another Presents. They end the Festival with Lights and Bon-fires kindled in the Streets and publick places, and a great many Fire-works which flie about on all hands, whil'st the Rich mutually treat one another with Collations and Feasts which they make in the very Streets or Shops.

The Feast of *Choubret*.

CHAPTER XVIII

OF THE OTHER TOWNS OF GUZERAT, *AND THE SIEGE OF* DIU *BY THE* TURKS, *WHICH WAS DEFENDED BY THE* PORTUGUESE

Besides the Towns of the Province of *Guzerat* whereof I have spoken, there are above thirty others, on which depend a great many Bourgs and Villages ; but those which lie near the Sea, are the most considerable. *Broudra*[1] is one of the best, lying betwixt *Baroche* and *Cambaye*, but more towards the East, in a most fertile though sandy Country : it is a large modern Town, and retains the Name of another ruined Town, which is but three quarters of a League from it, and has been called *Broudra* and *Rageapour* :[2] It hath pretty good Walls and Towers, is inhabited by a great many *Banians ;* and seeing the finest Stuffs in *Guzerat* are made in this Town, it is full of Artizans who are continually employed in making of them. It hath above two hundred Bourgs and Villages within its Jurisdiction, and there is store[3] of *Lacca*[4] to be found therein, because it is gathered in abundance in the territory of one of its Bourgs called *Sindiguera*.[5]

Broudra a Town.

Ragea-pour a Town.

The little Town of *Goga*[6] is on the other side of the Gulf, about eight and twenty or thirty Leagues from *Cambaye*. It abounds with *Banians* and Sea-men. *Goga a Town.*

Patan[7] lies more to the South, towards the great Sea ; it is a great Town, heretofore of much Trade, and affords still abundance of Silk-stuffs that are made there. It hath a Fort and very beautiful Temple wherein are many Marble-pillars. Idoles were Worshipped there, but at present it serves for a *Mosque*. *Patan a Town.*

The Town of *Diu*[8] belongs to the *Portuguese*, and lies also in the Province of *Guzerat*, fortified with three Castles. It stands at the entry of the Gulf of *Cambaye* to the right hand, in twenty two degrees eighteen minutes Latitude,[9] and two hundred Leagues from Cape *Comorin*. Before *Surrat* and *Cambaye* came into reputation, it had the advantage of most of the Commerce that at present is made in those two Towns. Its first Castle was built in the Year fifteen hundred and fifteen,[10] by *Albaquerque*[10a] a *Portuguese*. *Campson*[11] the last but one of the *Mammelukes* of *Egypt*,[12] set on[13] by the King of *Guzerat* sent an Army against the *Portuguese*, which perished there. They were not then Masters of the Town, and had no more but the Castle. *Campson Sultan of Egypt.* *Mammelukes.*

Sultan *Soliman*[14] Emperour of the *Turks*, sent and besieged it in the year One thousand five hundred and thirty eight,[15] at the desire of the same King of *Guzerat*, named Badur[16] (for that Country belonged not then to the *Moguls*) and his success was no better than that of the Sultan of *Egypt*. *Solimans* Fleet consisted of threescore and two Gallies, six Gallions, and a great many other smaller Vessels fitted out at *Suez* in the Red Sea, which had on board four thousand *Janisaries*,[17] and sixteen thousand other Soldiers, not to reckon Gunners, Sea-men, and Pilotes. It parted from *Suez* in *June*, and a Basha[18] called *Soliman*[19] who commanded it, in his passage Seized the Town of *Aden*, by horrible treachery, and hanged the King of it.[20] *Sultan Soliman.* *King of Guzerat.* *Solimans Fleet and Army.* *Aden.*

When this Fleet came before *Diu*, it was joyned by fourscore Sail of Ships of the Country, and so soon as the Forces were put a-shore, they landed fifty pieces of Cannon,[21] wherewith they battered the Citadel, which on the other side was besieged by a Land-army of the King of *Guzerat*. Many brave Actions happened during that Siege. The Governour of the Citadel called *Silveira*[22] a *Portuguese*, shew'd so much Valour and Prudence, in resisting the several assaults and attacks of the *Turks* and *Indians*, that he forced them to raise the Siege shamefully, and to forsake their Pavillions,[23] Ammunition and Artillery, to leave above a thousand wounded Men in their Camp, above a thousand more that were out a forraging, and fifty pieces of Cannon besides, which were Seized by the *Portuguese*. *Silveira a Portuguese.*

Stones of *Cobra*.

In this Town of *Diu* the so much famed Stones of *Cobra*[24] are made, they are composed of the Ashes of burnt roots, mingled with a kind of Earth they have, and once again burnt with that Earth, which afterwards is made up into a Paste, of which these Stones are formed. They are used against the stingings of Serpents and other venemous Creatures, or when one is wounded with a Poysonous Weapon. A little Blood is to be let out of the Wound with the prick of a Needle, and the Stone applied thereto which must be left till it drop off of it self. Then it must be put into Womans milk ; or if none can be had, into that of a Cow, and there it leaves all the Venom it hath imbibed ; for if it be not so used, it will burst.

Stingings of Serpents. The Remedy.

Nariad and *Mamadebad* Towns.

Betwixt *Broudra* and *Amedabad,* there are two Towns more, of indifferent bigness, the one called *Nariad,*[25] and the other *Mamadebad,*[26] where many Stuffs are made, and the latter furnishes the greatest part of Guzerat, and other Neighbouring Countries with Cotton-thread. I shall treat no more here of the other Towns of this Kingdom, because there being but little worth remarking in them, the discription would be tedious. It pays commonly to the Great *Mogul* Twenty Millions five hundred thousand French Livres a Year.

The Revenue of the Province of *Guzerat*.

CHAPTER XIX

OF THE PROVINCE AND TOWN OF AGRA.

Agra.

Agra is one of the largest Provinces of *Mogulistan,*[1] and its Capital Town which bears the same Name, is the greatest Town of the *Indies*. It is distant from *Surrat* about two hundred and ten Leagues, which they make commonly in five and thirty or six and thirty days Journey of Caravan, and it lies in the Latitude of twenty eight degrees and half[2] on the River *Gemna,*[3] which some call *Geminy,* and Pliny *Jomanes*. This River hath its source in the Mountains to the North of *Dehly,* from whence descending towards this Town, and receiving several rivulets in its course, it makes a very considerable River. It runs by *Agra,* and having traversed several Countries, falls into the *Ganges* at the great Town of *Halbas*.[4]

Gemna a River. *Jomanes* River. The course of *Gemna*.

Bacchus.

There is no need of taking the pains that some have done, to have recourse to *Bacchus* for illustrating *Agra* by an ancient Name.[5] Before King *Ecbar,* it was no more but a Bourg which had a little Castle of Earth, and pretended to no privilege over its Neighbours upon account of Antiquity ; and indeed, there were never any marks of that to be found.

That Prince being pleased with the seat of it, joyned several Villages thereunto : He gave them the form of a Town by other buildings which he raised, and called it after his own Name *Ecbar-Abad,*[6] the habitation of *Ecbar,* where he established the seat of his Empire, in the year One thousand five hundred threescore and six. His declaration of that was enough to People it; for when the Merchants came to understand that the Court was there, they came from all parts, and not only the *Banian* Traders flocked thither, but Christians also of all Perswasions, as well as Mahometans, who strove in emulation who should furnish it with greatest variety of Goods; and seeing that Prince called the *Jesuits* thither, and gave them a Pension to subsist on, Catholick Merchants made no scruple to come and live there, and to this day these Fathers take the care of Spirituals, and teach their Children.

Agra called *Ecbar-Abad.*

Merchants Flock to *Agra.*

Jesuits at *Agra.*

Though this Prince pretended[7] to make *Agra* a place of consequence, yet he Fortified it not neither with ramparts, Walls, nor Bastions, but only with a Ditch, hopeing to make it so strong in Soldiers and Inhabitants, that it should not need to fear the attempts of any Enemy. The Castle was the first thing that was built, which he resolved to make the biggest at that time in the *Indies;* and the situation of the old one appearing good and commodious, he caused it to be demolished, and the foundations of the present to be laid. It was begirt with a Wall of Stone and Brick terrassed in several places, which is twenty[8] Cubits high, and betwixt the Castle and River a large place[9] was left for the exercises the King should think fit to divert himself with.

Castle of *Agra.*

The Kings Palace is in the Castle. It contains three Courts adorned all round with Porches and Galleries that are Painted and Gilt; nay there are some peeces[10] covered with plates of Gold. Under the Galleries of the first Court, there are Lodgings made for the Kings Guards: The Officers Lodgings are in the second; and in the third, the stately appartments of the King and his Ladies; from whence he goes commonly to a lovely Divan which looks to the River, there to please himself with seeing Elephants fight, his Troops exercise, and Plays[11] which he orders to be made upon the Water, or in the open place.

The Kings Palace at *Agra.*

This Palace is accompanied with five and twenty or thirty other very large ones, all in a line, which belong to the Princes and other great Lords of Court; and all together afford a most delightful prospect to those who are on the other side of the River, which would be a great deal more agreeable, were it not for the long Garden-walls, which contribute much to the rendering the Town so long as it is.[12] There are upon the same line several less Palaces and other Buildings. All being desirous to enjoy the lovely prospect and convenience of the Water of the *Gemna,* endeavoured to purchase ground on that side, which is the cause that the Town is very long but narrow,

Palaces of the great men at *Agra.*

and excepting some fair Streets that are in it, all the rest are very narrow, and without Symmetry.

Square places at *Agra.*

Before the Kings Palace, there is a very large Square, and twelve other besides of less extent within the Town. But that which makes the Beauty of *Agra* besides the Palaces I have mentioned, are the *Quervanseras* which are above threescore in number ; and some of them have six large Courts with their Portico's, that give entry to very commodious Appartments, where stranger Merchants have their Lodgings: There are above eight hundred Baths in the Town, and a great number of Mosques, of which some serve for Sanctuary. There are many magnificent Sepulchres in it also, several great Men having had the ambition to build their own in their own life-time, or to erect Monuments to the memory of their Fore-fathers.

Quervanseras of *Agra.*

Baths of *Agra.*

Sepulchres of *Agra.*

The Sepulchre of King *Ecbar.*

King *Gehanguir* caused one to be built for King *Ecbar* his Father, upon an eminence of the Town.[13] It surpasses in magnificence all those of the *Grand Signiors,* but the fairest of all, is that which *Cha-Gehan* Erected in honour of one of his Wives called *Tadge-Mehal,*[14] whom he tenderly loved, and whose death had almost cost him his life. I know that the Learned and curious Mr. Bernier[15] hath taken memoires of it, and therefore I did not take the pains to be exactly informed of that work. Only so much I'll say that this King having sent for all the able Architects of the *Indies* to *Agra,* he appointed a Council of them for contriving and perfecting the Tomb which he intended to Erect, and having setled Salaries upon them, he ordered them to spare no cost in making the finest *Mausoleum* in the World, if they could. They compleated it after their manner, and succeeded to his satisfaction.

The beautiful *Mausoleum* of *Tadge-Mehal.*

The stately Garden[16] into which all the parts of that *Mausoleum* are distributed, the great Pavillions with their Fronts, the beautiful Porches, the lofty dome that covers the Tomb, the lovely disposition of its Pillars, the raising of Arches which support a great many Galleries, Quiochques and Terrasses, make it apparent enough that the Indians are not ignorant in Architecture. It is true, the manner of it seems odd to Europeans ; yet it hath its excellency, and though it be not like that of the Greeks and other Ancients, yet the Fabrick may be said to be very lovely. The Indians say that it was twenty years[17] in building, that as many Men as could labour in the great work[18] were employed, and that it was never interrupted during that long space of time.

The Tomb of King *Gehanguir.*

The King hath not had the same tenderness for the memory of his Father *Gehanguir,* as for that of his Wife *Tadge-Mahal ;* for he hath raised no magnificent Monument for him : And that *Great Mogul* is Interred in a Garden, where his Tomb is only Painted upon the portal.[19]

Now after all the Air of Agra is very incommodious[20] in the Summer-time, and it is very likely that the excessive heat which scorches the Sands that environ this Town, was one of the chief causes which made King *Cha-Gehan* change the Climate, and chuse to live at *Dehly*. Little thought this Prince that one day he would be forced to live at *Agra*, what aversion soever he had to it,[21] and far less still, that he should be Prisoner[22] there in his own Palace, and so end his days in affliction and trouble. That misfortune though befel him, and *Auran-Zeb* his third Son, was the cause of it,[23] who having got the better of his Brothers, both by cunning and force, made sure of the Kings Person and Treasures, by means of Soldiers whom he craftily slipt[24] into the Palace, and under whose Custody the King was kept till he died.

The Air of *Agra*.

King *Cha-Gehan* prisoner in his Palace.

Auran-Zeb imprisoned the King his Father.

So soon as *Auran-Zeb* knew that his Father was in his Power, he made himself be proclaimed King: He held his Court at *Dehly*, and no party was made[25] for the unfortunate King, though many had been raised by his bounty and liberalities. From that time forward *Auran-Zeb* Reigned without trouble; and the King his Father dying in Prison about the end of the year One thousand six hundred sixty six,[26] he enjoyed at ease the Empire, and that so famous Throne of the *Moguls*,[27] which he had left in the Prisoners appartment to divert him with. He added to the precious Stones that were set about it, those of the Princes his Brothers, and particularly the Jewels of *Begum-Saheb*[28] his Sister, who died after her Father; and whose death (as it was said,) was hastened by Poison. And in fine,[29] he became absolute Master of all, after he had overcome and put to death *Dara-Cha* his Eldest Brother, whom *Cha-Gehan* had designed for the Crown. That King is Interred on the other side of the River, in a Monument which he began, but is not finished.[30]

Auran-Zeb proclaimed King.

The death of King *Cha-Gehan*.

Begum-Saheb Sister to *Auran-Zeb*.

The Sepulchre of *Cha-Gehan*.

The Town of *Agra* is Populous as a great Town ought to be, but not so as to be able to send out Two hundred thousand fighting men into the Field, as some have written. The Palaces and Gardens take up the greatest part of it, so that its extent is no infallible Argument of the number of its Inhabitants. The ordinary Houses are low, and those of the commoner sort of People are but Straw, containing but few People a piece; and the truth is, one may walk the Streets without being crouded, and meet with no throng but when the Court is there: But at that time, I have been told there is great confusion, and infinite numbers of People to be seen; and no wonder indeed,[31] seeing the Streets are narrow, and that the King besides his Household, (who are many,) is always attended by an Army for his Guard; and the *Rajas, Omras, Mansepdars*[32] and other great Men, have great Retinues, and most part of the Merchants also follow the Court, not to reckon a vast number of Tradesmen, and thousands of followers who have all their subsistence from it.

Christians at *Agra.*

Some affirm that there are twenty five thousand Christian Families in *Agra,*[32a] but all do not agree in that. This indeed is certain, that there are few Heathen and *Parsis* in respect of[33] *Mahometans* there, and these[34] surpass all the other Sects in power, as they do in number. The Dutch have a Factory in the Town;[35] but the English have none now, because it did not turn to account.

Dutch Factory at *Agra.*

The Officers are the same as at *Surrat,* and do the same Duties, and it is just so in all the great Towns of the Empire. We told you[36] that the *Foursdar* or Prevost, is to answer for all the Robberies committed in the Country; And that was the reason why Mr. *Beber,* one of the Envoys to the great *Mogul,* for the concerns of the *East-India* Company in *France,* having been Robbed, demanded from that Officer of *Agra,* the Sum of thirty one thousand two hundred *Roupies,* which he affirmed were taken from him. That Sum astonished the *Foursdar* who told him that he did not believe he had lost so much; and because the Envoy made Answer that the sum would certainly encrease, if he delayed to pay down the Money, and if he gave him time to call to mind a great many things which he had forgot; He wrote to the *Great Mogul,* and informed him that it was impossible that that Envoy could have lost so great a Sum. *Monsieur Beber* had also made his addresses at Court; but it being pretty difficult to give an equitable sentence in the Case, the King, that he might make an end of it, commanded the *Foursdar* to pay the Envoy fifteen thousand *Roupies,* and because he was wounded when he was Robbed, he ordered him out of his Exchequer, ten thousand *Roupies* for his Blood.

Mr. *Beber* Robbed.

Liberality of the *Great Mogul.*

CHAPTER XX

OF THE HABITS AT AGRA.

Habits at *Agra.*

For so many different Nations as are at *Agra,* as well as in the rest of the Indies, there is pretty great uniformity in the manner of apparel; and none but the Mahometans called *Moors* by the *Portuguese,* distinguish themselves outwardly by a particular kind of Coif, or head-attire, but in all things else, they are cloathed as the rest. The Breeches of the Indians are commonly of Cotten-cloath, they come down to the mid leg, and some wear them a little longer, so that they reach to the Anckle. They who affect Rich Clothing, wear Silk breeches striped with different colours, which are so long that

Moors.

Breeches.

The Moor's headgear

they must be plated upon the Leg, much in the same manner as formerly Silk-stockings were worn in *France*.

The Shirt hangs over the Breeches, as the fashion is all over the *Levant*. These Shirts are fastened as the Persians are,[1] and heretofore had no greater opening than theirs; but because the Moors Shirts are open from top to bottom, as their upper Garments, which they call *Cabas*[2] are; many People at present wear them in that fashion, because they find them, more commodious,[3] being more easily put on and off: Besides that when one is alone, he may open them and take the fresh Air. Shirts.

When it is cold Weather, the Indians wear over their Shirt an *Arcaluck*[4] or *Just au corps* quilted with Cotten and Pinked, the outside whereof is commonly of a schite[5] or Painted stuff. The colours upon them are so good and lively, that though they be soiled by wearing, yet they look as fresh again as at first when they are washed. They make the Flowers and other motely colours that are upon the Stuffs with Moulds. *Arcaluck.*

Over the *Arcaluck* they put the *Caba,* which is an upper Garment, but then it must be supposed the weather is not hot; for if there be but the least heat, they wear no *Arcaluck,* and the *Caba* is put next the Shirt. The *Caba* of the *Indians* is wider than that of the *Persians,* and I cannot tell how to express the manner of it more intelligibly, then by saying it is a kind of gown with a long Jerkin[6] fastened to it, open before, and pleated from top to bottom, to hinder it from being too clutterly.[7] It hath a collar two fingers breadth high, of the same Stuff with the rest, they button not that Vest as we do our Coats, but they fold it cross ways over the Stomack; first from the right to the left, and then from the left to the right. They tie it with Ribbons of the same Stuff, which are two Fingers broad and a Foot long; and there are seven or eight of them from the upper part down to the Haunches, of which they only tie the first and last, and let the rest hang negligently as being more graceful. *Caba.*

These *Cabas* are commonly made of white Stuff, that's to say of Cotten-cloath, to the end they may be the lighter, and the neater by being often washed; and that agrees with the fashion of the Ancient *Indians*. I say of Cotton-cloath, because they use no other in the *Indies,* and have no Flax there: Nevertheless some wear them of Painted cloath, but that is not the Gentilest manner of Apparel, and when the Rich do not wear White they use Silk, and chuse the broadest Stuff they can find, which commonly is streaked with several colours. There is no Flax in the *Indies.*

They use only one Girdle, whereas the *Persians* have two, nay and it is not very dear neither, being only of White- Girdle.

cloath, and it is rare to see the Indians make use of the lovely Girdles of Persia, unless they be wealthy persons of Quality.

Cadeby, Lovely Vests at *Agra.*

When it is very cold, the Indians wear over all the Cloaths I have been speaking of, a Garment or Vest called *Cadeby,*[8] and then the Rich have very costly ones. They are of Cloath of Gold, or other Rich Stuff, and are lined with Sables which cost very dear.

Chal or Toilet.

At all times when they go abroad, they wear a *Chal*[9] which is a kind of toilet[10] of very fine Wool made at *Cachmir.*[11] These *Chals* are about two Ells[12] long and an Ell broad; they are sold at five and twenty or thirty Crowns a piece if they be fine, nay there are some that cost fifty Crowns but these are extraordinary fine.[13] They put that *Chal* about their Shoulders, and tie the two ends of it upon their Stomack, the rest hanging down behind to the small of their Back. Some wear them like a Scarf, and sometimes they bring one end to the Head, which they dress in manner of a Coif. They have of them of several colours, but those the *Banians* wear are most commonly *Fild-de-mort,*[14] and the Poor, or such as will not be at the[15] charges, wear them of plain Cloath.

The *Turban* of the *Indies.*

Cloath whereof 25 or 30 Ells do not weigh four Ounces.

The *Turban* worn in the *Indies* is commonly little. That of the Mahometans is always White, and the Rich have them of so fine a Cloath, that five and twenty or thirty Ells of it which are put into a *Turban,* will not weigh[16] four Ounces. These lovely Cloaths are made about *Bengale*: They are dear, and one single *Turban* will cost five and Twenty Crowns. They who affect a Richer attire, have them mixed with Gold; but a *Turban* of that Stuff costs several *Tomans,* and I have said elsewhere that a *Toman*[17] is worth about forty five French *Livres.*

The form of the *Turbans* at *Agra.*

These *Turbans* wreathed as they ought to be, much resemble the shape of the Head, for they are higher behind by four or five Fingers breadth than before,[18] so that the upper part of the Head is only well covered; and I have seen Paisant women in *France,* whose Coiffing lookt pretty like that kind of *Turban.*[19]

The *Indians* wear their Hair.

The Indians wear their Hair for Ornament, contrary to[20] the Mahometans who shave their Heads; and in that, as in many other things, the Indians imitate their Ancestours.

Hose and Shoes.

As for Stockings the Indians are at no charge, for they use neither Stockings nor Socks, but put their Shoes on their naked Feet. The stuff they are made of is *Maroquin,* or *Turkey*-leather, and they are much of the same shape as the *Papouches*[21] of the Turks; but the Persons of Quality have them bordered with Gold, and they have behind a kind of a heel of the same stuff as the instip, which most commonly they fold down, as they do who go with their Shoes slipshod. However the *Banians* wear the heel of theirs up because being men of business they would[22] walk with freedom, which is very hard to be done,[23] when the Foot is not on all sides begirt with the Shoe.

The Rich *Banians* cover the upper Leather of theirs with Velvet,[24] Embrodered with great Flowers of Silk ; and the rest are satisfied with red Leather and small Flowers, or some other Galantry[25] of little value.

The Shoes or Papouches of the *Banians*.

The *Mogul* Women who would distinguish themselves from others, are Cloathed almost like the Men ; however the sleeves of their Smocks, as those of the other *Indian* Women, reach not below the Elbow, that they may have liberty to adorn the rest of their Arm with Carkanets[26] and Bracelets of Gold, Silver and Ivory, or set with Precious Stones, as likewise they do the small of their Legs. The ordinary Smocks of the *Indian* Idolatrous Women reach down only to the middle, as does the Waste-coat of Sattin or Cloath, which they wear over it, because from the Waste down-wards they wrap themselves up in a piece of Cloath or Stuff, that covers them to the Feet like a Petticoat ; and that Cloath is cut in such a manner, that they make one end of it reach up to their Head behind their Back.

The Womens Apparel.

The *Indians* Smocks. Their Waste-coats.

They wear no other Apparel neither within Doors, nor abroad in the Streets, and for Shoes they have high Pattins.

They wear a little flat Ring of Gold or Silver in their Ears, with engraving upon it ; and they adorn their Noses with Rings which they put through their Nostril.

The *Indian* Women adorn their Nose and Ears with Rings.

Rings also are the Ornaments of their Fingers, as they are in other places : They wear a great many, and as they love to see themselves, they have always one with a Looking-Glass set in it,[27] instead of a Stone, which is an Inch in diametre. If these *Indian* Women be Idolators, they go barefaced ; and if *Mahometans,* they are Vailed. There are some Countries in the *Indies,* where the Women as well as Men go naked[28] to the middle, and the rest of their Body is only covered to the Knee.

A Finger Looking-Glass.

Indian Women naked to the middle.

CHAPTER XXI

OF OTHER CURIOSITIES AT AGRA.

There are a great many at *Agra,* who are curious in breeding up of Beasts, to have the pleasure to make them Fight together : But seeing they cannot reach to[1] Elephants and Lions, because it costs dear[2] to feed them, most part[3] content themselves with[4] He-goats, Weathers, Rams, Cocks, Quailes, Stags, and Antilopes, to entertain their Friends with the Fightings of these Beasts.

Fighting of Beasts.

Indian Antilopes.

The *Indian* Antilopes,[5] are not altogether like those of other Countries ; they have even a great deal more courage, and are to be distinguished by the Horns. The Horns of the ordinary Antilopes are greyish, and but half as long as the Horns of those in the *Indies,* which are blackish, and a large Foot and a half long. These Horns grow winding to the point like a screw ; and the *Faquirs* and *Santons*[6] carry commonly two of them pieced together ; they are armed with Iron at both ends, and they make use of them, as of a little Staff.[7]

Leopard.

When they use not[8] a tame Leopard for catching of Antilopes, they take with them a Male of the kind, that is tame, and fasten a Rope about his Horns with several nooses and doubles, the two ends whereof are tied under his Belly ; so soon as they discover a Heard of Antilopes, they slip this Male, and he runs to joyn them: The Male of the Heard advances to hinder him, and making no other opposition, but by playing with his Horns, he fails not to be pestered[9] and entangled with his Rival, so that it being uneasie[10] for him to retreat, the Huntsman cunningly catches hold on him, and carries him off ; but it is easier so to catch the Male than the Females.

Pidgeons.

A Screen for Fowling.

There are Pidgeons in that Country all over green,[11] which differ from ours only in colour: The Fowlers take them with Bird-lime, in this manner ; they carry before them a kind of light Shed or Screen, that covers the whole Body, and has holes in it to see through ; the Pidgeons seeing no Man, are not at all scared when the Fowler draws near, so that he cunningly catches them, one after another, with a Wand and Bird lime on it, none offering to flie away. In some places Parrocquets are taken after the same manner.

The catching of Water-fowl.

The *Indians* are very dexterous at Game ;[12] they take Waterfowl[12a] with great facility, as thus: The Fowlers swim almost upright, yet so, that they have their Head above Water, which they hide with a Pot full of holes, to let in the Air, and give them sight. Besides, this Pot is covered with Feathers, to cheat the Ducks, and other Fowl ; so that when the Fowler draws near them, they are not in the least scared, taking that floating head for a Fowl ; and then the Fowler makes sure of them by the Feet, which he catches hold of under Water, and draws them down: The other Ducks seeing no body, think that their comrades have only dived, and are not at all scared ; so that growing acquainted with the Feathered head, that still follows them, they are at length all taken, whil'st in vain they stay[13] for the return of those who have dived, before they flie away to another place.

Nerouer.

The Huntsmen of *Agrà* go five Days Journey from the Town, as far as a Mountain called *Nerouer,*[14] where there is a mine of excellent Iron ; but their business in going so far is only to catch a kind of Wild Cows which they call *Merous,*[15] that are to be found in a Wood round this Hill, which is upon the Road from *Surrat* to *Golconda;* and these Cows being commonly very lovely, they make great advantage of them.[16] *Merous,* Wild Cows.

One may see a great many Pictures in the Indies upon Paper and Past-board, but generally they are dull pieces, and none are esteemed but those of *Agra* and *Dehly*: However, since those of *Agra* are for the most part indecent, and represent Lacivious Postures, worse than those of *Aretin,*[17] there are but few civil Europeans that will buy them. Indian Pictures.

They have a way in this Town of working in Gold upon Agat, Chrystal, and other brittle matters,[18] which our Goldsmiths and Lapidaries have not. When the Indians would beautifie Vessels, Cups, or Coffers; besides the Circles of Gold they put about them, they engrave Flowers and other Figures, and also enchase Stones upon them. They cut leaves of Gold to fill up the void spaces of the Figures, lay several pieces one upon another, and enchase them so artificially[19] in the hollow places, with an Iron Instrument like a Graver, that when the void spaces are filled up, it looks like Massie[20] Gold. They do the same with Stones, they encompass them also with such pieces of Leaf-Gold, and press them in so close that the Stones hold very well. Working upon Agat and Chrystal.

They make Rings about Vessels, either about the middle or brims, of a kind of Gold made into little round Rods, which they beat upon an Anvil, till they be reduced into flat thin Plates; then they take the measure of the part of the Vessel which they would incircle,[21] and having most exactly bent the Ring, they Soulder the two ends of it together, and put it upon the part of the Vessel they intend it for; so that it holds very well, provided one have the skill to adjust it true to the place marked: If Handles be necessary to the Vessels, or Locks for the Coffers of Agat or Crystal, they soulder them to the Ring with the same Art that they souldered the two ends of it; but they do it after another way than our Goldsmiths do. For that end they make use of little red Beans which are black at the end, and are the fruit of a *Convolvulus,* called in Indian *Gomtchi,* and in the *Telenghi* Language, *Gourghindel.*[22] They peel off the Skin which is dry and hard, and taking the inside of the Bean that is yellowish, they grind it upon an Iron-Plate with a little Water till it be dissolved into a Liquid Solution; then they pound a little bit of Borax, mix it with that Solution, and with this mixture dawb the ends which they intend to soulder, and having heated them with a Coal, joyn them together; so that the two sides close fast and hold extraordinarily well.

This work is performed by poor People, and sometimes by little Boys, who do it very skilfully and quickly, for a matter of two Crowns for each tole of Gold; and something is also given to him that beats and flattens the Rods of Gold: However none of these People know how to Enammel Gold.

The Province of *Agra* hath above fourty Towns in its dependance, and, as they say, above three thousand four hundred Villages. *Fetipour. Sicari.* *Fetipour*[22a] is one of the Towns; it was heretofore called *Sicari,* and the Name *Fetipour,* which signifies, *The enjoyment of what one desires,* was given it by *Ecbar,* because of the happy news he received there of the birth of a Son,[23] when he was upon his return from a Warlike expedition. This Town is about six Leagues from *Agra;* it hath been very lovely, and that *Great Mogul* in the beginning of his Reign, having rebuilt the Walls of it, made it the Capital of his Empire. But the Ambition Kings have to make small things great, prompting *Ecbar* to build a Town where there was nothing but a *Agra* a Bourg. Village, or at most, but a Bourg named *Agra,*[23a] the Town of *Fetipour* was not only neglected, but hath been since wholly abandoned; for so soon as *Agra* was become a Town, and that *Ecbarabad.* the King had given it his Name, calling it *Ecbarabad,* a place built by *Ecbar,* he went to reside there and forsook *Fetipour.*

A lovely Meidan at *Fetipour.* Though this Town of *Fetipour* be much decay'd, yet there is still a large Square to be seen in it, adorned with fair Buildings; and the stately entry of *Ecbar's* Palace[24] is still entire, and has adjoyning to it one of the loveliest Mosques[25] in the A fair Mosque at *Fetipour, Calenders.* East, built by a Mahometan a *Calender*[26] by profession, who lies buried there as a Saint.[27] The *Calenders* are Dervishes who go bare-footed. This Mosque is still adorn'd with all its Pillars, and lovely Seelings, and indeed, with all that can beautifie a fair Temple. Near to it there is a great Reservatory[28] which The cause of forsaking *Fetipour.* supplied the whole Town with Water, and was the more necessary that all the Springs thereabouts are Salt; and the unwholsome Waters were one of the chief causes that obliged the *Great Mogul* to settle elsewhere.

Beruzabad, Chitpour. *Beruzabad*[29] is one of the Towns of *Agra. Chitpour*[30] is another, and has a great trade in Schites or painted Cloaths. *Bargant, Chalaour, Vetapour, Mirda, Ladona, Hindon, Canova, Byana,* and *Scanderbade,* all Towns of *Agra.* *Bargant*[31] is likewise one, which belongs to a *Raja* who exacts some dues. *Chalaour*[32] stands upon a Hill. At *Vetapour*[33] lovely Tapistry is made. *Mirda,*[34] *Ladona,*[35] *Hindon,*[36] *Canova,*[37] *Byana,*[38] and *Scanderbade,*[39] are also Towns of *Agra.* These last furnish the best Indigo of the Indies. Two Leagues from *Byana* there are to be seen the Ruins of Ancient Palaces, and other Buildings; as also some very considerable ones upon a little Hill some Leagues from *Scanderbade.* At the Foot of the Hill on the side of that Town, there is a lovely Valley walled in, divided into several Gardens, and the Ruins of several Buildings, which is not to be wondered at, seeing heretofore *Scanderbade* was several Leagues long, having been the Capital City of a powerful King of the Patans;[40] and the Hill it self made part of the Town, which was afterwards sack'd and ruin'd

A woman robber

by *Ecbar,* when he took it from *Raja Selim,*[41] who made it his chief Garrison and Magazin. *Raja Selim.*

Upon the Road from *Agra* to *Byana* there is a Royal-House, built by the Queen Mother of *Ecbar,*[42] with Gardens kept in very good order: There are also in *Byana* some *Serraglio*'s and a long *Meidan,* but that Town is thin of Inhabitants. *Seronge*[43] hath also been named to me amongst the Towns of the Province of *Agra,* and Schites are made there, which in beauty come near those of St. *Thomas.* There are a great many other Towns, whose Names I know not. The chief Rivers that water *Agra,* are the *Gemna* or *Geminy, Lanque,*[44] *Cham-Elnady,*[45] *Geogonady,*[46] *Singour;*[47] and a great many smaller. The Royal House of King *Ecbar*'s Mother. *Gemna* or *Geminy, Lanque, Cham-Elnady, Geogonady, Singour,* all Rivers of *Agra.*

The Kings Revenue in this Province of *Agra,* is reckoned to amount to above thirty seven Millions of French-Livres a Year. The Revenue of *Agra.*

CHAPTER XXII

OF THE PROVINCE OR TOWN OF DEHLY, *OR* GEHAN-ABAD.

The Province of Dehly bounds that of Agra to the North, and at present the *Great Mogul Auran-zeb* keeps his Court in the chief City of it, which is about fourty five Leagues distant from Agra. In *Indostan* it is called *Gehan-abad,*[1] and elsewhere *Dehly.* The Province of *Dehly.* *Gehan-Abad.*

The Road betwixt these two Towns is very pleasant; it is that famous Alley or Walk[2] one hundred and fifty Leagues in length, which King *Gehanguir* planted with Trees, and which reaches not only from *Agra* to *Dehly,* but even as far as *Lahors.* Each half League is marked with a kind of Turret: There are threescore and nine or threescore and ten of them betwixt the two Capital Cities, and besides there are little Serraglio's or Carvanseras, from Stage to Stage for lodging Travellers. However there is nothing worth the observing about these Serraglios, unless in that which is called *Chekiserai,*[3] which is six Leagues from *Agra.* In that place there is the Ancient Temple of an Idol, and it may be reckoned amongst the largest and fairest Pagods of the Indies. It was more frequented than now it is, when the *Gemna* washed the Walls thereof,[4] because of the convenience of Ablutions: But though that River hath fallen off[5] almost half a League from it, yet many Indians still resort thither, who forget not to bring with them Food for the Apes that are kept in an Hospital built for them. A Walk of 150 Leagues. The Pagod of *Chekiserai.* An Hospital for Apes.

Though the Road I have been speaking of be tolerable, yet it hath many inconveniencies. One may meet with Tygres,

The Robbers Snare.

Panthers and Lions upon it; and one had best also have a care of Robbers, and above all things not to suffer any body to come near one upon the Road. The cunningest Robbers[6] in the World are in that Countrey. They use a certain Slip with a running-noose, which they can cast with so much slight[7] about a Mans Neck, when they are within reach of him, that they never fail; so that they strangle him in a trice. They have another cunning trick also to catch Travellers with: They send out a handsome Woman upon the Road, who with her Hair deshevelled, seems to be all in Tears, sighing[8] and complaining of some misfortune which she pretends has befallen her: Now as she takes the same way that the Traveller goes, he easily falls into Conversation with her, and finding her beautiful, offers her his assistance, which she accepts; he had no sooner taken her up behind him on Horse-back, but she throws the snare about his Neck and strangles him, or at least stuns him, until the Robbers (who lie hid) come running in to her assistance and compleat what she hath begun. But besides that, there are Men in those quarters so skilful in casting the Snare, that they succeed as well at a distance as near at hand; and if an Ox or any other Beast belonging to a Caravan run away, as sometimes it happens, they fail not to catch it by the Neck.

Dangerous Women upon the Road from *Agra* to *Dehly*.

Three Towns of *Dehly*.

The first Town of *Dehly*.

There are three Towns of *Dehly*[9] near to one another:[10] The first (which is entirely destroy'd, and whereof some Ruins only remain,) was very ancient, and the learned Indians will have it to have been the Capital Town of the States of King *Porus*, so famous for the War which he maintained against *Alexander the Great*.[11] It was nearer the Source of the *Gemna* than the two others that have been built since. The Indians say it had two and fifty Gates, and there is still at some distance from its Ruins, a Stone-bridge, from whence a Way hath been made with lovely Trees on each side, which leads to the second *Dehly*, by the place where the Sepulchre of *Cha-Humayon*[12] is.

The Sepulchre of *Cha-Humayon*.

The Second Town of *Dehly*.

This Second Town of *Dehly* is that which was taken by the King, whom they call the first Conquerour of the *Indies* amongst the Modern Moguls, though his Father *Mirzababer* had invaded it before. It was then beautified with a great many stately Sepulchres of the *Patan* Kings, and other Monuments which rendered it a very lovely Town; but *Cha-Gehan* the Father of King *Auran-Zeb*, demolished it for the Building of *Gehan-Abad*. Towards the Sepulchre of *Humayon*, there is a Pyramide[13] or Obelisk of Stone, which by its unknown characters shews a great Antiquity, and which is thought in the Indies to have been erected by *Alexander*'s order, after the defeat of *Porus*. This I cannot believe, because I make no doubt, but that the Inscription would then have been in Greek, which is not so.

A Pyramide of great Antiquity towards *Dehly*.

The Third Town of *Dehly* is joyned to the remains of the Second: *Cha-Gehan* resolving to imitate King *Ecbar,* and to give his Name to a new Town, caused this to be built of the Ruines of the Second *Dehly,* and called it *Gehan-Abad*: So the Indians call it at present, though amongst other Nations it still retains the Name of *Dehly.* It lies in an open Champian Countrey upon the brink of the *Gemna,* which hath its source in this Province, and runs into the *Ganges.* The fortress of it is half a League in circuit, and hath good Walls with round Towers every ten Battlements, and Ditches full of Water, wharffed with Stone, as likewise lovely Gardens round it: And in this Fort[14] is the Palace of the King, and all the Ensignes[15] of the Royalty.

The Third Town of *Dehly.*

The Fort of *Dehly.*

The Kings Palace at *Dehly.*

This Town of *Dehly* or *Gehan-abad,* contrary to[16] that of *Agra* or *Ecbar-abad,* hath no Ditches but Walls filled up with Earth behind, and Towers. There is a place towards the Water-side for the fighting of Elephants, and other Exercises; and towards the Town there is another very large place where the *Raja's,* who are in the Kings Pay encamp and keep Guard, and where many exercises are performed. The Market is also kept in that Square, and there Puppet-players, Juglers and Astrologers shew their tricks.

Here I should give a description of the inside of the Fort and Palace, and having begun with the two Elephants at the entry which carry two Warriours,[17] speak of the Canal that enters into it; of the Streets that lead to the several Appartments; of the Officers and others who are upon the Parapets of these Streets on Duty; of the Portico's and stately Courts of Guard, where the *Mansepdars* and *Emirs* or *Omras* keep Guard; of the Halls where all sorts of Artisans, who have the Kings Pay work; of that great Court of the *Amcas*[18] with its Arches, and the Consort that's made there; of the *Amcas* it self, that stately Hall adorn'd with thirty two Marble-Pillars, where the King (having all his Officers great and small standing before him, with their Hands a-cross their Breasts)[19] gives every Day at noon Audience to all who have recourse to his Justice.

A Description of the Palace.

The Canal of the Palace of *Dehly.*

The posture of the Officers of the *Great Mogul.*

I should also describe that other Court, and Inner-hall[20] where the Prince gives Audience to his Ministers, concerning the Affairs of his State, and Household, and where the *Omras* and other great Men repair every Evening to entertain the King in the Persian Language though they be of different Nations. In fine, all the particulars of the Palace ought to be described, without forgetting that stately Throne of Massive Gold with its Peacock, so much talked of in the *Indies,* which the Moguls say was begun by *Tamerlan,*[21] though that be very unlikely: For to whom could King *Humayon* and his Father have entrusted it in the time of their disasters? Seeing the Spoils

The Throne of the *Great Mogul.*

of the *Patan* Kings and other Sovereigns of the *Indies,* who were overcome by the Mogul Kings, are converted into Jewels and Precious Stones to adorn it, it is said to be worth above twenty Millions of Gold ;[22] but who can know the value thereof? since it depends on the Stones that make the Riches as well as the Beauty thereof, whose weight and excellency must be particularly examin'd, if one would judge of their worth, and by consequence, of the value of the Throne.

Though I have had Memoirs given me of the Palace and that Throne, yet I'll say no more of them, because I make no doubt but that *Monsieur Bernier,* who hath lived many Years at the Court of the *Great Mogul,* in an honourable Employment, and commodious[23] for having a perfect knowledge of the Fort, Palace, and all that is in them, will give a compleat description of the same. I am confident also that he will not omit the Town, the chief places whereof are the great Mosque[24] with its Domes of white Marble, and the *Carvansery* of *Begum-Saheb,*[25] that Princess whom we mentioned before. The two chief Streets of *Dehly*[26] may be reckoned amongst the rarities of it,[27] for they are wide, streight, and very long: They have Arches all along on both sides, which serve for Shops for those who have their Ware-house backwards. Over these Arches there is a Terras-walk to take the Air on when they come out of their Lodgings ; and these Streets ending at the great Square and Castle, make the loveliest Prospect that can be seen in a Town. There is nothing else considerable in *Dehly.* The ordinary Houses are but of Earth and Canes ; and the other Streets are so narrow, that they are altogether incommodious.[28]

The great Mosque of *Dehly,* with its Domes of White Marble.

Streets of *Dehly.*

But that inconvenience seems to contribute somewhat to the Reputation of that Capital City of the Empire of the Mogul, for seeing there is an extraordinary croud in the Streets while the Court is there, the Indians are perswaded that it is the most populous City in the World ; and nevertheless I have been told, that it appears to be a Desart when the King is absent. This will not seem strange if we consider, that the Court of the *Great Mogul* is very numerous, because the great Men of the Empire are almost all there, who have vast retinues, because their Servants cost them but little in Diet and Cloaths ; that that Court is attended by above thirty five thousand Horse, and ten or twelve thousand Foot, which may be called an Army ; and that every Souldier hath his Wife, Children and Servants, who for the most part are married also, and have a great many Children as well as[29] their Masters. If to these we add all the drudges and rascally People which Courts and Armies commonly draw after them, and then the great number of Merchants and other Trading People, who are obliged to stick to them, because in that Countrey there is no Trade nor Money to be got but at Court. When I say, we consider *Dehly* void of all those

The *Great Mogul's* Court is very numerous.

Servants Diet costs little in the *Indies.*

An Army that follows the Court.

I have mentioned, and of many more still, it will easily be believed, that that Town is no great matter when the King is not there ; and if there have been four hundred thousand Men in it when he was there, there hardly remains the sixth part in his absence. Let us now see what Arms the *Moguls* use.

CHAPTER XXIII

OF THE ARMS OF THE MOGUL'S.

Their Swords are four Fingers broad, very thick, and by consequence heavy ; they are crooked a little, and cut only on the convexside. The Guard is very plain ; commonly no more but a handle of Iron, with a cross Bar of the same underneath the Pummel which is also of Iron,[1] is neither Round[2] nor Oval, but is flat above and below like a Whirligigg, that the Sword may not slip out of their Hands when they fight. The Swords made by the Indians are very brittle ; but the English furnish them with good ones brought from *England*. The *Mogul's* use Waste-belts for their Swords ; they are two Fingers broad and have two Hangers into which the Sword is put, so that the Point is always upwards ; and all the ordinary sort of People in the *Indies* carry them commonly in their Hand, or upon their Shoulder like a Musket.

Mogul's Arms.

The form of the *Mogul's* Swords.

It is their custom also to carry a Dagger by their sides, the Blade being near a Foot long, and above four Fingers broad at the Handle. They have an odd kind of Guard, and I don't remember that I have ever seen any thing in *France* relating to Arms that looks liker it than the handle of some Moulds for casting of Bullets, or small-shot,· it is made of two square Bars of Iron one Finger broad, and about a Foot long, which are paralell, and four Inches distant one from another ; growing round they joyn together at the upper part of the Blade, and have cross Bars of two little Iron-Rods two Inches distant from one another.[3]

The *Moguls* Dagger.

The Indians never want[4] one of these Daggers by their side, betwixt the Girdle and *Caba ;* they carry it always bending a little sideways, so that the end of the Guard comes pretty high, and the Point pretty low upon their Stomach. The Officers of War have also Daggers with an Iron-Guard, but it is damasked and guilt ; and Persons of great quality have of them after the Persian fashion, which are less[5] and richer.

Their other offensive Arms are the Bow and Arrow, the Javelin or *Zagaye,*[6] and sometimes the Pistol :[7] The Foot carry a Musket, or a Pike twelve Foot long.

The *Moguls* Cannon good for nothing.

They have Cannon also in their Towns, but since they melt the Metal in diverse Furnaces, so that some of it must needs be better melted than others[8] when they mingle all together, their Cannon commonly is good for nothing.

Defensive Arms.

The *Moguls* Buckler.

The defensive Arms of the *Indians,* are a round Buckler about two foot in diametre: It is made of Buff, varnished over with Black, and hath a great many Nails, the heads whereof are above an inch over; with it they defend themselves against Arrows and Swords.

Coat of Mail. The *Moguls* Vambrace.

They have likewise the Coat of Mail, the Cuirats, the Head-piece, and a Vambrace fastened to the Sword; this Vambrace is a piece of Iron covering the Handle almost round, and growing broader as it reaches from the Guard of the Sword, to the upper part of the Pummel, and sometimes higher. It is four or five inches in diametre at that place, and is lined with Velvet, or some such like thing in the inside, that it may not hurt the Hand: So that by means of that Engine,[9] both hand and handle are wholly covered from the Enemies blows.

CHAPTER XXIV

OF THE BEASTS AT DEHLY.

Beasts at *Dehly*.

At *Dehly* are all sorts of Beasts that are known. The King hath many, and private Men who are Rich, have some also. They have Hawks[1] there of all kinds; all kinds of Camels, Dromedaries, Mules, Asses, and Elephants. They have also Elks,[2] and Rhinoceroses which are as big as the largest Oxen. The ordinary Oxen there, are less than ours. Buffles they have also, and those of *Bengala* are the dearest, because they are very stout,[3] and are not at all afraid of Lions. Nor do they want Dogs of all sorts, but those which are brought from *Maurenahar,* or *Transoxiane,* are most esteemed for Hunting, though they be small: However the *Indian* Dogs are better for the Hare. They have also Stags, Lions and Leopards.

Elks. Rhinoceros. Buffles.

Dogs of *Maurenahar*.

Horses.

There is abundance of all sorts of Horses there. Besides the Country breed, which the *Moguls* make use of, and which are very good Horses; they have others also from the Country of the *Ulbecks,*[4] *Arabia,* and *Persia,* those of *Arabia* being most esteemed, and the loveliest of all are constantly reserved for the King. They have neither Oats nor Barley given them in the *Indies;* so that Foreign Horses when they are brought thither, can hardly feed. The way they treat them is thus: Every Horse has a Groom, he curries and dresses him an hour before day,[4a] and so soon as it is day[5] makes him drink;

The way of dressing and feeding the Horses.

at seven of the Clock in the Morning, he gives him five or six balls of a composition called *Donna,*[6] made of three Pounds of Flower, the weight of five *Pechas* of Butter, and of four *Pechas* of *Jagre;* these Balls are at first forced down his Throat, and so by degrees he is accustomed to that way of feeding, which in some Months after, he grows very fond of.

An hour after, the Groom gives the Horse Grass, and continues to do so at certain times, every hour of the day after: and about four of the Clock, after noon, he gives him three Pound of dried Pease bruised; he mingles Water with them, and sometimes a little Sugar, according to the disposition the Horse is in; and when Night is drawing on, he carefully prepares his Horses litter, which is of dry Dung, laid very thick, which he is very careful to provide. For that end, he gathers all that his Horse hath made, and when that is not sufficient, he buys from others, who are not so much concerned for the convenience of their Horses.

Litter of dry Horse-dung.

At *Dehly,* as elsewhere, they take care to adorn their Horses. The great Lords have Saddles and Housses[7] Embroadered, and set sometimes with Pretious Stones, proportionably to the charge they intend to be at: But the finest Ornament, though of less cost, is made of six large flying tassels of long white Hair, taken out of the Tails of wild Oxen,[8] that are to be found in some places of the *Indies.* Four of these large tassels fastened before and behind to the Saddle,[9] hang down to the ground, and the other two are upon the Horses head; so that when the Rider spurs on his Horse to a full speed, or if there be any wind, these tassels flying in the Air, seem to be so many wings to the Horse, and yield a most pleasant prospect.[10]

Flying tassels of white Hair, taken out of the tails of some Oxen.

There are several sorts of Elephants at *Dehly,* as well as in the rest of the *Indies;* but those of *Ceilan*[11] are preferred before all others, because they are the stoutest, though they be the least, and the *Indians* say that all other Elephants stand in awe of them. They go commonly in Troops and then they offer violence to no body, but when they straggle from the rest, they are dangerous. There are always some of them that have the cunning and inclination to do mischief; and in the Country these are called, Robbers on the Highways, because if they meet a Man alone, they'll kill and eat him.[12]

Elephants.

Elephants Robbers on the High ways.

Strong Elephants can carry forty *Mans;* at fourscore Pound weight the *Man.* Those of the Country of *Golconda, Siam, Cochin,* and *Sumatra,* are indeed, less esteemed than the Elephants of *Ceilan,* but they are much stronger, and surer footed in the Mountains; and that is the reason, why the great Men, (when they are to Travel,) provide themselves of those, rather than of the Elephants of *Ceilan.* However it may be said in general, that Elephants, of what Country or kind soever

An Elephants Load.

The choice of Elephants.

they be, are the surest footed of all Beasts of Carriage, because it is very rare to see them make a trip[13]: But seeing it is chargeable[14] to feed them, and that besides the Flesh they give them to eat, and the Strong-waters they drink, it costs at least half a *Pistol*[15] a day for the Paste of Flower, Sugar and Butter, that must be given to a single one; there are but few that keep them: Nay, the great Lords themselves entertain[16] no great number of them; and the *Great Mogul* has not above five hundred for the use of his houshold, in carrying the Women in their *Mickdembers*[17] with grates (which are a sort of Cages) and the Baggage; and I have been assured, that he hath not above two hundred for the Wars, of which some are employed in carrying small Field-pieces upon their Carriages.

The food that is given to an Elephant.

Mickdembers.

Elephants docile.

When an Elephant is in his ordinary disposition, his Governour can make him do what he pleases with his Trunck. That instrument, which many call a hand, hangs between their great Teeth, and is made of Cartilages or Gristles: He[18]'ll make them play several[19] tricks with that Trunck; salute his friends, threaten those that displease him, beat whom he thinks fit, and could make them tear a Man into pieces in a trice, if he had a mind to it. The governour sits on the Elephants Neck, when he makes him do any thing, and with a prick of Iron in the end of a Stick, he commonly makes him Obey him. In a word, an Elephant is a very tractable Creature, provided he be not angry, nor in lust; but when he is so, the Governour himself is in much danger, and stands in need of a great deal of art, to avoid ruin; for then the Elephant turns all things topsy-turvy, and would make strange havock, if they did not stop him, as they commonly do, with fire-works that they throw at him.

Elephants furious.

Elephant-hunting.

Elephant-hunting is variously performed. In some places they make Pit-falls for them, by means whereof they fall into some hole or pit, from whence they are easily got out, when they have once entangled them well.[20] In other places they make use of a tame Female, that is in season for the Male, whom they lead into a narrow place, and tie her there; by her cries she calls the Male to her, and when he is there, they shut him in, by means of some Rails made on purpose, which they raise, to hinder him from getting out; he having the Female in the mean time on his back, with whom he Copulates in that manner, contrary to the custom of all other Beasts. When he hath done, he attempts to be gone, but as he comes, and goes[21] to find a passage out, the Huntsmen, who are either upon a Wall, or in some other high place, throw a great many small and great Ropes, with some Chains, by means whereof, they so pester and entangle his Trunck, and the rest of his Body, that afterwards they draw near him without danger; and so having taken some necessary cautions, they lead him

Elephant-hunters.

to the company of two other tame Elephants, whom they have purposely brought with them, to shew him an example, or to threaten him if he be unruly.[22]

There are other Snares besides for catching of Elephants and every Country hath its way. The Females go a Year with their young, and commonly they live about an hundred Years. Though these Beasts be of so great bulk and weight, yet they swim perfectly well, and delight to be in the Water: So that they commonly force them into it by Fire-works, when they are in rage, or when they would take them off from Fighting, wherein they have been engaged. This course is taken with the Elephants of the *Great Mogul,* who loves to see those vast moving bulks rush upon one another, with their Trunck, Head, and Teeth. All over the *Indies,* they who have the management of Elephants, never fail to lead them in the Morning to the River, or some other Water. The Beasts go in as deep as they can, and then stoop till the Water be over their Backs, that so their guides may wash them, and make them clean all over, whilst by little and little they raise their bodies up again.

She-Elephants go a year with their young.

Elephants live 100 years.

CHAPTER XXV

OF OTHER CURIOSITIES AT DEHLY.

The Painters of *Dehly* are modester[1] than those of *Agra,* and spend not their pains about lascivious Pictures, as they do. They apply themselves to the representing of Histories, and in many places, one may meet with the Battels and Victories of their Princes, indifferently well[2] Painted. Order is observed in them, the Personages have the suitableness that is necessary to them,[3] and the colours are very lovely, but they make Faces ill.[4] They do things in miniature pretty well, and there are some at *Dehly* who Engrave indifferently well[5] also; but seeing they are not much encouraged,[6] they do not apply themselves to their work, with all the exactness they might; and all their care is to do as much work as they can, for present Money to subsist on.[7]

Painters of *Dehly*.

There are People in *Dehly,* vastly rich in Jewels, especially the *Rajas* who preserve their Pretious Stones from Father to Son. When they are to make Presents, they chuse rather to buy, than to give away those which they had from their Ancestors: They daily encrease[8] them, and must be reduced to an extream pinch, before they part with them.

People Rich in Jewels.

There is in this Town, a certain Metal called *Tutunac,*[9] that looks like Tin, but is much more lovely and fine, and is often taken for Silver; that Metal is brought from *China,*

Theban Stone or *Garnet.*

They much esteem a greyish Stone there, wherewith many Sepulchres are adorned; and they value it the more, that[10] it is like *Theban* Stone, or *Garnet.* I have seen in the Countries of some *Rajas,* and elsewhere, *Mosques* and *Pagods* wholly built of them.

Screws at *Dehli.*

The Indians of Dehly cannot make a Screw as our Locksmiths do; all they do, is to fasten to each of the two pieces that are to enter into one another, some Iron, Copper, or Silver wire, turned Screw-wise, without any other art than of souldering the Wire to the pieces; and in opening them, they turn the Screws from the left hand to the right, contrariwise to ours, which are turned from the right to the left.

Citrul Flowers drive away the Flies.

They have a very easie remedy in that Country, to keep the Flies from molesting their Horses, when the Grooms are so diligent as to make use of it: For all they have to do, is to make provision of Citrul Flowers,[11] and rub them therewith. But many slight that remedy, because it must be often renewed, seeing the Curry-comb[12] and Water takes it off. I cannot tell if these Flowers have the same vertue in our Country.

The Women of *Dehly.*

The Women of *Dehly* are handsome, and the Gentiles very chast; insomuch, that if the *Mahometan* Women did not by their wantonness dishonour the rest, the Chastity of the *Indians* might be proposed[13] as an example to all the Women of the *East.* These *Indian* Women are easily delivered of their Children; and sometimes they'll walk[14] about the Streets next day after they have been brought to Bed.

CHAPTER XXVI

OF THE FESTIVAL OF THE KINGS BIRTH-DAY.

The Festival of the Kings Birth-day.

The pomp of the Festival.

There is a great Festival kept yearly at *Dehly,* on the Birth-day of the King regnant. It is Celebrated amongst the People, much after the same manner as the *Zinez*[1] of *Turkey* which I described in my first Book, and lasts five days; It is Solemnized at Court with great Pomp. The Courts of the Palace are covered all over with Pavillions of Rich Stuffs; all that is magnificent in Pretious Stones, Gold and Silver is exposed to view in the Halls; particularly the great and glittering Throne, with those others that are carried about in progresses, which are likewise adorned with Jewels. The fairest Elephants decked with the richest Trappings, are from time to time brought out before the King, and the loveliest Horses in their turns also; and since the first *Mogul* Kings intro-

Decked Elephants.

The weighing of the Emperor

duced a custom of being weighed in a Balance,[2] to augment the pleasure of the solemnity, the King in being, never fails to do so. The King is weighed.

The Balance wherein this is performed, seems to be very Rich. They say that the Chains are of Gold, and the two Scales which are set with Stones,[3] appear likewise to be of Gold, as the Beam of the Balance does also, though some affirm that all is but Guilt. The King Richly attired, and shining with Jewels, goes into one of the Scales of the Balance, and sits on his Heels, and into the other are put little bales, so closely packt, that one cannot see what is within them: The People are made believe, that these little bales (which are often changed,) are full of Gold, Silver and Jewels, or of Rich Stuffs; and the *Indians* tell Strangers so, when they would brag of their Country, then[4] they weigh the King with a great many things that are good to eat; and I believe that what is within the Bales, is not a whit more Pretious. The Balance wherein the King is weighed

However when one is at the Solemnity,[5] he must make as if he believed all that is told him, and be very attentive to the Publication of what the King weighs; for it is published, and then exactly set down in writing. When it appears in the Register, that the King weighs more than he did the year before, all testifie their Joy by Acclamations; but much more by rich Presents, which the Grandees, and the Ladies of the *Haram* make to him, when he is returned to his Throne; and these Presents amount commonly to several Millions. The King distributes, first a great quantity of Artificial Fruit and other knacks of Gold and Silver, which are brought to him in Golden Basons; but these knacks are so slight, that the profusion (which he makes in casting them promiscuously amongst the Princes, and other Great men of his Court, who croud one another to have their share,) lessens not[6] the Treasure of his Exchequer; for I was assured that all these trifles would not cost one hundred thousand Crowns. And indeed, *Auran-Zeb* is reckoned a far greater Husband,[7] than a great King ought to be: during five days, there is great rejoycing all over the Town, as well as in the Kings Palace, which is exprest by Presents, Feastings, Bonefires and Dances; and the King has a special care to give Orders, that the best Dancing women and Baladines,[8] be always at Court. The presents of the Festival. Trifles given by the King. *Auran-Zeb* a great Husband. Publick rejoycing.

The Gentiles being great lovers of Play at Dice; there is much Gaming, during the five Festival days. They are so eager at it in *Dehly* and *Benara,*[9] that there is a vast deal of Money lost there, and many People ruined. And I was told a Story of a *Banian* of *Dehly,* who played so deep at the last Festival, that he lost all his Money, Goods, House, Wife and Children. At length, he that won them, taking pity of him, Play at Dice.

gave him back his Wife and Children ; but no more of all his Estate, than to the value of an hundred Crowns.

To conclude, The Province of *Dehly,* hath no great extent to the South-East, which is the side towards *Agra ;* but is larger on the other sides, especially Eastwards, where it hath a great many Towns : The Ground about it is excellent, where it is not neglected, but in many parts it is.

The Ground of *Dehly.*

The ground about the Capital City is very fertile ; Wheat and Rice grow plentifully there. They have excellent Sugar also, and good Indigo, especially towards *Chalimar,*[10] which is one of the Kings Countrey-houses, about two Leagues from *Dehly,* upon the way to *Lahors.* All sorts of Trees, and Fruit grow there also ; but amongst others, the *Ananas* are exceeding good. I shall speak of them in the Description of the Kingdom of *Bengala.*

Chalimar, one of the Kings Country Houses.

It is specified in my Memoire, that this Province pays the *Great Mogul* yearly, between thirty seven and thirty eight Millions.

The Yearly Revenue of *Dehly.*

CHAPTER XXVII

OF THE PROVINCE AND TOWN OF AZMER.

The Province of *Azmer,* lies to the North-East of *Dehly ;*[1] the Countrey of *Sinde* bounds it to the West : It hath *Agra* to the East, *Multan* and *Pengeab*[2] to the North, and *Guzerat* to the South. This Province of *Azmer,* hath been divided into three Provinces of *Bando,*[3] *Gesselmere*[4] and *Soret ;*[5] and the Capital City at present, is *Azmer,*[6] which is distant from *Agra,* about sixty two Leagues.

The Road from *Agra* to *Azmer.*[7]

It is Six Leagues from *Agra* to *Fetipour,* 6 Leag. to *Bramabad.* 7 Leag. to *Hendouen.* 7 Leag. to *Mogul-serai.* 6 Leag. to *Lascot.* 7 Leag. to *Chasol.* 4 Leag. to *Pipola.* 7 Leag. to *Mosa-baa.* 5 Leag. to *Bender-Sandren.* 6 Leag. to *Mandil.* 1 Leag. to *Azmer.*

This Town lies in twenty five Degrees and a half, North Latitude,[8] at the foot of a very high, and almost inaccessible Mountain :[9] There is on the top of it, an extraordinary strong Castle ;[10] to mount to which, one must go turning and winding for above a League ; and this Fort gives a great deal of reputation to the Province. The Town hath Stone-Walls, and a good Ditch ; without the Walls of it, there are several Ruins of Fair Buildings, which shew great antiquity. King *Ecbar* was Master of this Province,[11] before he built *Agra* : and before it fell into his hands, it belonged to a famous *Raja,* or *Raspoute,* called *Ramgend ;*[12] who came to *Fetipour,* and resigned it to him ; and at the same time, did him Hommage for it.

The Situation of *Azmer.*

Raja Ramgend

This *Raja* was *Mahometan,* as his Predecessors had been; and besides a great many ancient marks of Mahometanism, that were in that Country in his Time; the famous *Cogea Mondy,*[13] who was in reputation of Sanctity amongst the Mahometans, was reverenced at *Azmer;* and from all Parts, they came in Pilgrimage to his Tombe:[14] It is a pretty fair Building, having three Courts paved with Marble; whereof the first is extreamly large, and hath on one side, several Sepulchres of false Saints; and on the other, a Reservatory of Water, with a neat Wall about it. The second Court is more beautified, and hath many Lamps in it. The third is the loveliest of the three; and there the Tomb of *Cogea Mondy* is to be seen in a Chappel whose door is adorned with several Stones of colour, mingled with Mother of Pearl. There are besides, three other smaller Courts, which have their Waters and Buildings for the convenience and lodging of *Imans,* who are entertained[15] to read the *Alcoran.*

Cogea Mondy.

The Sepulchre of *Cogea Mondy.*

King *Ecbar* had a mind to try as well as the rest, the Vertue of this same *Cogea-Mondy;* and because he had no Male-Children, he had recourse to his Intercession to obtain them. He made a Vow to go and visit his Tomb, and resolved upon the Journey in the bourg of *Agra.*

Ecbars Vow for obtaining of Male-Children.

Though it be a walk of threescore and two Leagues from *Agra* to *Azmer,* yet he performed the Pilgrimage on foot,[16] having ordered Stone-seats to be made at certain distances, for him to rest on: Nevertheless, he was quite tired out; for being of a hot and stirring[17] Nature, he could hardly lay a constraint upon himself to walk softly,[18] so that he fell sick upon it. He entered bare-footed (as the rest did) into the Chappel of the *Mock-Saint:* There he made his Prayers, gave great Charity; and having performed his Devotion, and read the *Epitaph* of *Cogea Mondy,* which is written there in the *Persian* Language; he returned back to the place from whence he came.

King *Ecbar* made a Pilgrimage of 60 Leag. on foot.

As he passed by *Fetipour,* he consulted a certain *Dervish,* named *Selim,* who was esteemed very devout; and the *Mahometans* say, that this Man told him, that God had heard his Prayers, and that he should have three Sons,[19] at that, Ecbar was so well pleased with this Prophecy, especially when it began to be fulfilled, that he gave his Eldest Son the name of the *Dervish Selim;* that Town which was called *Sycary,* the name of *Fetipour,* which signifies a place of Joy and Pleasure; and that he built a very stately Palace there, with a Design to make it the Capital of his Empire.

Selim a *Dervish.*

The Prophecy of *Selim* the *Dervish.*

Sicary.

Azmer is a Town of an indifferent bigness, but when the *Great Mogol* comes there, there is no room to stir in it, especially when there is any Festival; because, besides the Court and Army, all the People of the Country about, flock thither, and some disorder always happens.

Neurous.

Let us speak a little of the Feast of *Neurous,*[20] which King *Gehanguir* Celebrated at *Azmer,*[21] where he happened to be one New Years day; for *Neurous,* signifies *New Day;* and by that, is meant, the First day of the Year, which begins in *March,* when the Sun enters into *Aries.*

CHAPTER XXVIII

OF THE FEAST OF THE NEW YEAR.

The Feast of the New Year.

The Memoires that were given me observe, that some days before the Festival, all the Palace was adorned; and especially, the Places and Halls, into which People were suffered[1] to enter: There was nothing all over but Sattin, Velvet, Cloath and Plates of Gold: The Halls were hung with rich Stuffs, Flower'd with Gold and Silver: And that where the *Great Mogul* appear'd in his Throne, was the most magnificent of all: The Cloath of State that covered it, was all set with Pretious Stones; and the Floor was covered with a Persian Carpet of Gold and Silver Tissue. The other Halls had in like manner, their Cloaths of State; Their Foot-Carpets, and other Ornaments, and the Courts were also decked (the most considerable of them) with lovely Tents pitched there; though they were not so Pompous as those which are pitched in the Capital Cities of the Empire, upon a like Solemnity. The first day of the Feast, the Throne was placed in the Royal Hall, and was covered all over with the Jewels of the Crown; the number of them was the greater, that there was but one of the Kings Thrones brought; and that (as it is usual) the Jewels of the other little Thrones had been taken off, for the adorning of this.

The Ornaments of *Neurous.*

A Fair of the Ladies of the *Serraglio.*

The Festival began in the *Serraglio,* by a Fair[2] that was kept there. The Ladies and Daughters of the great Lords, were permitted to come to it; and the Court-Ladies of less Quality, (who thought themselves witty enough to make their Court, by putting off the curious Things that they had brought thither) were the Shop-keepers: But these had not all the Trade to themselves; for the Wives of the *Omras* and *Rajas* (who were allowed to come in) opened Shop also, and brought with them the richest Goods they could find; and which they thought suited best with the King, and the Princesses of his *Serraglio.* Many had occasion by selling,[3] and disputing pleasantly and wittily, about the Price of the things, which the King and his Wives came to cheapen,[4] to make their Husbands Court; and to slip in Presents to those that could

The Great Ladies, Shop-keepers.

serve them in bettering their Fortune, or keeping them as they were.

The King and his *Begum,* pay'd often double value for a thing, when the Shop-keeper pleas'd them ; but that was, when they rallied wittily and gentilely (as People of Quality commonly do)[5] in buying and selling: And so it happened, that the wittiest and fairest were always most favoured. All these stranger Ladies, were entertained in the *Serraglio* with Feasting, and Dancings of *Quenchenies,*[6] who are Women and Maids of a Caste of that name, having no other Profession but that of Dancing: And this Fair lasted five days.

Begum.

Quenchenies.

It is true, The Commodities sold there, were not so fine, nor rich, as they would have been, had the Festival been kept[7] in *Dehly* or *Agra ;* but the best, and most pretious Things that were to be found in *Azmer,* and in the nearest Towns, were exposed to Sale there ; wherewith the King was very well satisfied.

During these rejoycings of the *Serraglio,* The great Men, who kept Guard, entertained themselves at their Posts, or elsewhere ; And there were a great many Tables served at the Kings charges, which gave them occasion[8] to Celebrate the *Neurous,* or New Years Feast merrily.

The King appeared daily in the *Amcas,* at his usual hour, but not in extraordinary Magnificence before the seventh day ; and then the Lords (who had every day changed Cloaths) appeared in their richest Apparel. They all went to salute the King, and His Majesty made them Presents, which were only some Galantries[9] of small value, that did not cost him Four hundred thousand French Livres. The eighth and ninth days, The King also sat on his Throne, (when he was not Feasting with his Princess (sic) and Omras, in one of the Out-Halls) where he made himself several times familiar with them ; but that familiarity excused them not from making him Presents[10]. There was neither *Omra,* nor *Mansepdar,* but made him very rich Presents ; and that of the Governour, or Tributary of *Azmer,* was the most considerable of all. These Presents were reckoned in all, to amount to fourteen or fifteen Millions. The Festival concluded at Court, by a review of the Kings Elephants and Horses, pompously[11] equipped ; and in the Town by a great many Fire-works, that came after their Feasting. *Gehanguir,* indeed, gave not the Princes, and great Lords, the equivalent of the Presents they made him at this Solemnity: But he rewarded them afterwards by Offices, and Employments. And this is the course the King commonly takes with them, and few complain of it.

The Kings Presents at *Neurous.*

The Presents of the Great Lords to the King.

CHAPTER XXIX

OF THE BEASTS OF THE COUNTRY OF AZMER, AND OF THE SALTPETRE.

There is in these Countries, a Beast like a Fox in the Snout, which is no bigger than a Hare: the Hair of it, is of the colour of a Stags, and the Teeth like to a Dogs. It yields most excellent Musk;[1] for at the Belly it hath a Bladder full of corrupt Blood, and that Blood maketh the Musk, or is rather the Musk it self: They take it from it, and immediately cover the place where the Bladder is cut, with Leather, to hinder the scent from evaporating: But after this Operation is made, the Beast is not long liv'd.[2]

The Musk Animal.

Pullets.

There are also towards *Azmer,* Pullets[3] whose Skin is all over black, as well as their Bones, though the Flesh of them be very white, and their Feathers of another colour.

Maids Marriageable at 8 or 9 years of age.

In the extremity of this Province, the Maids are very early Marriageable, and so they are in many other places of the *Indies,* where most part can enjoy Man,[4] at the age of eight or nine years,[5] and have Children at ten. That's a very ordinary thing in the Country, where the young ones go naked, and wear nothing on their Bodies, but a bit of Cloath to cover their Privities.

The Childrens playes.

Most of the Children in these Countries have the same playes to divert them with, as amongst us: they commonly make use of Tops, Giggs, and Bull-flies in the season; of Childrens Trumpets, and many other Toys of that nature. The People are rude and uncivil: The Men are great clowns, and very impudent; they make a horrid noise when they have any quarrel, but what Passion soever they seem to be in, and what bitter words soever they utter, they never come to blows. The Servants are very unfaithful, and many times rob their Masters.

Venemous Scorpions.

The remedy of Fire.

There are very venemous Scorpions in that Country, but the *Indians* have several remedies to cure their Stinging, and the best of all is Fire. They take a burning Coal, and put it near the wound; they hold it there as long and as near as they can: The venom keeps one from being incommoded by the heat of the Fire; on the contrary, the Poison is perceived to work out of the Wound by little and little, and in a short time after, one is perfectly cured.

The Oxen are shod.

The ways of this Country being very Stony, they shoe the Oxen when they are to Travel far on these ways. They cast them[6] with a Rope fastened to two of their Legs, and so soon as they are down, they tye their four Feet together, which they put upon an Engine[7] made of two Sticks in form of an X;

and then they take two little thin and light pieces of Iron, which they apply to each Foot, one piece covering but one half Foot, and that they fasten with three Nails above an Inch long, which are clenched upon the side of the Hooffs, as Horses with us are shod.

Indian Oxen.

Seeing the Oxen in the *Indies* are very tame, many People make use of them in Travelling, and ride them like Horses; though commonly they goe but at a very slow pace. Instead of a Bit, they put one or two small strings through the Gristle of the Oxes Nostrils, and throw over his Head a good large Rope fastened to these strings, as a Bridle, which is held up by the bunch he hath on the fore part of his back, that our Oxen have not. They Saddle him as they do a Horse, and if he be but a little spurred, he'll go very fast; and there are some that will go as fast as a good Horse. These Beasts are made use of generally all over the *Indies;* and with them only are drawn Waggons, Coaches and Chariots, allowing more or fewer, according as the load is heavier or lighter.

The Oxen are Saddled.

The Oxen serve to draw Coaches, as well as Carts and Waggons.

The Oxen are Yoaked by a long Yoak at the end of the Pole, laid upon their Necks; and the Coach-man holdeth in his hand the Rope to which the strings that are put through the Nostrils are fastened. These Oxen are of different sizes, there are great, small, and of a middle size, but generally all very hardy, so that some of them will Travel fifteen Leagues a day. There is one kind of them, almost six Foot high, but they are rare; and on the contrary another, which they call Dwarfs, because they are not three Foot high; these have a bunch on their Back as the rest have, go very fast, and serve to draw small Waggons.

White Oxen are very dear.

They have white Oxen there, which are extraordinary dear, and I saw two of them which the Dutch had, that cost them two hundred Crowns a piece; they were really, lovely, strong and good, and their Chariot that was drawn by them, made a great shew. When People of quality have lovely Oxen, they keep them with a great deal of care; they deck the ends of their Horns with sheaths of Copper; they use them to Cloaths as Horses are, and they are daily curried and well fed. Their ordinary Provender is Straw and Millet, but in the Evening they make each Ox swallow down five or six large Balls of a Paste made of Flower, Jagre and Butter kned together. They give them sometimes in the Country, *Kichery,*[8] which is the ordinary Food of the Poor; and it is called *Kichery,* because it is made of a Grain of the same name boiled with Rice, Water and Salt: Some give them dryed Pease, bruised and steeped in Water.

They have great care of the Oxen.

The food of the Oxen.

Kichery.

After all;[9] no part of this Province is fertile, but the Countries about *Azmer,* and *Soret,* for the Countries of *Gessel-*

The Saltpetre of *Azmer.*

mere, and *Bando,* are Barren. The chief Trade of *Azmer* is in Saltpetre,[9a] and there are great quantities of it made there, by reason of the black fat Earth that is about it, which is the properest of all other Soils to afford Saltpetre. The *Indians* fill a great hole with that Earth, and pound it in Water with great pounders of very hard Timber, when they have reduced it into a Liquid mash, they let it rest, to the end the Water may imbibe all the Saltpetre out of the Earth: This mixture having continued so for some time, they draw off what is clear, and put it into great Pots, wherein they let it boil, and continually scum it; when it is well boiled, they again drain what is clear out of these Pots, and that being congealed and dryed in the Sun, where they let it stand for a certain time, it is in its perfection; and then they carry it to the Sea-port Towns, and especially to *Surrat,* where the Europeans and others buy it to Ballast their Ships with, and sell elsewhere.

The way of making Saltpetre.

This Province of *Azmer,* pays commonly to the *Great Mogul,* thirty two or thirty three Millions,[10] notwithstanding the barren places that are in it.

CHAPTER XXX

OF THE PROVINCE OF SINDE *OR* SINDY.

The Province of *Sinde* or *Sindy.*

Sinde or *Sindy,* which some call *Tatta,*[1] is bounded with the Province of *Azmer* to the East; and the Mountains which border it on that side, belong to the one or other Country. It hath *Multan* to the North, to the South, a Desart and the *Indian* Sea;[2] and to the West, *Macran* and *Segestan.*[3] It reaches from South to North, on both sides the River *Indus,* and that River is by the Orientals called also *Sindy* or *Sinde.* On the banks of it was fought that famous Battel betwixt *Ginguis-Can,* first Emperour of the *Tartars* or Ancient *Moguls,* and the Sultan *Gelaleddin,*[4] which decided the destiny of the Empire in favour of the former, against the *Carezmian*[5] Princes, who had for a long time been Masters of the Kingdom of *Persia,* of all *Zagatay,* and of the greatest part of the Country of *Turquestan.*

The River *Sinde.* *Ginguis-Can.* *Gelaleddin.* *Carezmian* Princes.

Tatta. *Diul.* *Dobil.*

The chief Town of this Province is *Tatta,* and the most Southern Town, *Diul.*[6] It is still called *Diul-Sind,* and was heretofore called *Dobil.* It lyes in the four and twentieth or five and twentieth degree of Latitude. There are some Orientals, that call the Country of *Sinde,* by the name of the Kingdom of *Diul.* It is a Country of great Traffick,[7] and especially in the Town of *Tatta,* where the *Indian* Merchants buy a great many curiosities made by the Inhabitants, who are wonderfully Ingenious in all kind of Arts. The *Indus* makes a great many little Islands towards *Tatta,* and these Islands being fruitful and pleasant, make it one of the most commodious[8] Towns of the *Indies,* though it be exceeding hot there.

There is also a great trade at *Lourebender,*[9] which is three days Journey from *Tatta,* upon the Sea, where there is a better Road for Ships, than in any other place of the *Indies*. The finest *Palanquins*[10] that are in all *Indostan,* are made at *Tatta,* and there is nothing neater, than the Chariots with two Wheels, which are made there for Travelling. It is true, they have but few Coaches, because few *Europeans* go thither, and hardly any of the *Indians* make use of Coaches but they; but these Chariots are convenient enough for Travelling, and are not harder than Coaches. They are flat and even, having a border four fingers broad, with Pillars all round, more or fewer, according to the fancy of him for whom it is made; but commonly there are but eight, of which there are four at the four corners of the Engine,[11] the other four at the sides, and thongs of Leather are interwoven from Pillar to Pillar, to keep one from falling out. Some, (I confess,) have the Chariot surrounded with Ballisters of Ivory, but few are willing to be at the charges of that, and the Custom of making use of that Net-work of Leather, makes that most part cares not for Ballistérs, but go so about the Town, sitting after the Levantine manner, upon a neat Carpet that covers the bottom of the Chariot. Some cover it above with a slight Imperial, but that commonly is only when they go into the Country, to defend them from the Sun-beams.

Lourebender.

Chariots convenient for Travelling.

This Machine hath no more but two Wheels put under the side of the Chariot, and not advancing outwards, they are of the height of the fore Wheels of our Coaches; have eight square spoaks, are four or five fingers thick, and many times are not shod. Hackny-coaches to Travel in, with two Oxen, are hired for five and twenty pence, or half a Crown a day; but whatever ease the *Indians* may find in them, our Coaches are much better, because they are hung.

The Wheeles of the *Indian* Chariots.

The Wheels of Waggons or Carts, for carrying of Goods, have no Spoaks; they are made of one whole piece of solid Timber, in form of a Mill-stone, and the bottom of the Cart, is always a thick frame of Wood. These Carts are drawn by eight or ten Oxen, according to the heaviness of the Loads. When a Merchant conveys any thing of consequence, he ought to have four Soldiers, or four Pions, by the sides of the Waggon; to hold the ends of the Rope that are tyed to it, to keep it from overturning, if it come to heeld in bad way;[12] and that way is used in all Caravans, though commonly they consist of above two hundred Waggons.

Cart-Wheeles.

CHAPTER XXXI

OF PALANQUINS.

Palanquin.

Indians that are Wealthy, Travel neither in Chariots nor Coaches: They make use of an Engine which they call *Palanquin,* and is made more neatly at *Tatta,* than any where else. It is a kind of Couch with four feet, having on each side ballisters four or five Inches high, and at the head a feet a back-stay like a Childs Cradle, which sometimes is open like Ballisters, and sometimes close and Solid. This Machine[1] hangs by a long Pole, which they call *Pambou,*[2] by means of two frames nailed to the feet of the Couch, which are almost like to those that are put to the top of moving Doors, to fasten Hangings by ; and these two frames which are the one at the head, and the other at the opposite end, have Rings through which great Ropes are put, that fasten and hang the Couch to the *Pambou.*

The *Pambous* of *Palanquins.*

The *Pambous* that serve for *Palanquins,* are thick round Canes five or six Inches in Diametre, and four Fathom long, crooked Arch-wise in the middle, so that on each side from the bending, there remains a very streight end, about five or six foot long. On the bending of the *Pambou,* there is a covering laid of two pieces of Cloath sewed together, betwixt which at certain distances, there are little Rods cross-ways, to hold the Cloaths so, that they may conveniently cover the *Palanquin.* If a Woman be in it, it is covered close over with red-Searge, or with Velvet if she be a great Lady: And if they be afraid of Rain, the whole machine is covered over with a waxed Cloath. In the bottom of these *Palanquins,* there are Mats and Cushions to lie or sit upon, and they move or ease themselves by means of some Straps of Silk that are fastened to the Pambou, in the inside of the Machine.

The Ornament of *Palanquins.*

Every one adorns his *Palanquin* according to his humour, some have them covered with plates of carved Silver, and others have them only Painted with Flowers and other curiosities, or beset round[3] with guilt Balls ; and the Cases or Cages, wherein hang the Vessels that hold the Water which they carry with them to drink, are beautified in the same manner, as the Body of the *Palanquin.* These Machines are commonly very dear, and the *Pambou* alone of some of them, costs above an hundred Crowns ; but to make a-mends[4] for that, they have Porters at a very easie rate, for they have but nine or ten Livres a piece by the Month, and are obliged to Diet themselves : It requires four Men to carry a *Palanquin,* because each end of the *Pambou* rests upon the Shoulders of two Men ; and when the Journey is long, some follow after to take their turn, and ease the others when they are weary.

The Porters of *Palanquins.*

Indian conveyances

Sinde, of which we have been speaking, yields not the *Great Mogul,* above three Million four hundred thousand French *Livres* a Year.

The yearly Revenue of the Province of *Sinde.*

CHAPTER XXXII

OF THE PROVINCE OF MULTAN.

Multan.

Multan, which comprehends *Bucor,*[1] has to the South the Province of *Sinde,* and to the North the Province of *Caboul;* as it hath *Persia* to the West, and the Province of *Lahors* to the East. It is watered with many Rivers[2] that make it Fertile. The Capital Town which is also called *Multan,*[3] was heretofore a place of very great Trade, because it is not far from the River *Indus;* but seeing at present, Vessels cannot go up so far, because the Chanel of that River is spoilt in some places, and the Mouth of it full of shelves, the Traffick[4] is much lessened, by reason that the charge of Land-carriage is too great: However the Province yields plenty of Cotton, of which vast numbers of Cloaths are made. It yields also Sugar, Opium, Brimstone, Galls,[5] and store of Camels, which are transported into *Persia,* by *Gazna,* and *Candahar,* or into the *Indies* themselves by *Lahors;* but whereas the Commodities went heretofore down the *Indus* at small Charges, to *Tatta,* where the Merchants of several Countries came and bought them up, they must now be carried by Land as far as *Surrat,* if they expect a considerable price for them.

What *Multan* produces.

The Town of *Multan* is by some Geographers attributed to *Sinde,* though it make a Province by it self. It lies in twenty nine Degrees forty Minutes North Latitude,[6] and hath many good Towns in its dependance, as *Cozdar* or *Cordar,*[7] *Candavil,*[8] *Sandur,*[9] and others. It furnishes *Indostan* with the finest Bows that are to be seen in it, and the nimblest Dancers.[10] The Commanders and Officers of these Towns are *Mahometans* and by consequence, it may be said, that most part of the Inhabitants are of the same Religion: But it contains a great many *Banians* also, for *Multan* is their chief Rendezvous for Trading into *Persia,* where they do what the Jews do in other places; but they are far more cunning, for nothing escapes them, and they let slip no occasion of getting the penny,[11] how small soever it be.

The Town of *Multan.*

Cozdar or *Cordar. Candavil, Sandur Towns.*

Banians.

The Tribe of these *Banians,* is the fourth in dignity amongst the Castes, Tribes, or Sects of the Gentiles; of whom we shall treat in the sequel of this Relation. They are all Merchants and Broakers, and are so expert in business, that hardly any

The *Banians* useful.

body can be without them. They give them commissions of all kinds; though it be known that they make their profit of every thing, yet Men chuse rather to make use of them, than to do their business themselves; and I found often by experience, that I had what they bought for me, much cheaper, than what I bought myself, or made my servants buy. They are of a pleasing humour, for they reject no service, whether honourable or base, and are always ready to satisfie those who employ them; and therefore every one hath his *Banian* in the *Indies*, and some persons of Quality intrust them with all they have, though they be not ignorant of their Hypocrisie and Avarice. The richest Merchants of the *Indies* are of them and such I have met with in all places where I have been in that Country. They are commonly very Jealous of their Wives, who at *Multan* are fairer than the Men, but still of a very brown complexion, and love to Paint.

Catry.

At *Multan* there is another sort of Gentiles, whom they call *Catry*.[12] That Town is properly their Country, and from thence they spread all over the *Indies*; but we shall treat of them when we come to speak of the other Sects: both the two have in *Multan* a Pagod of great consideration,[13] because of the affluence of People, that came there to perform their Devotion after their way; and from all places of *Multan*, *Lahors*, and other Countries, they come thither in Pilgrimage. I know not the name of the Idol that is Worshipped there; the Face of it is black, and it is cloathed in red Leather: It hath two Pearls in place of Eyes; and the *Emir* or Governour of the Countrey, takes the Offerings that are presented to it. To conclude, The Town of *Multan* is but of small extent for a Capital, but it is pretty well Fortifi'd; and is very considerable[14] to the *Mogul*, when the *Persians* are Masters of *Candahar*, as they are at present.

The Pagod of *Multan*.

The Idol of *Multan*.

The yearly Revenue of *Multan*.

What the *Great Mogul* receives yearly from this Province, amounts to Seventeen millions, Five hundred thousand Livres.

CHAPTER XXXIII

OF THE PROVINCE OF CANDAHAR.

The Province of *Candahar*.

Before I speak of the Eastern Provinces of the *Indies*, I shall proceed to treat of those which are to the West of the *Indus*, or towards the Rivers that make part of it. *Candahar*[1] is one of them; tho' the chief Town of it belong at present to the King of *Persia*,[2] who took it from *Cha-Gehan*, contrary to the will of his Grand-mother, which cost her her Life. It is said, That that Lady got Money from the *Great Mogul,* to hinder the Siege of this Town. Her Grand-son being ready to march, she made him a thousand Entreaties to divert him from the expedition ; and finding that she could gain nothing of him by fair means, she fell into a passion, and upbraided him that he was going to squander away the Estate of Orphans. This Discourse so offended the King, that having asked her if that Estate belonged to any but to him, He cut her over the head with an Axe that he held in his hand, of which she died.[3]

The King of *Persia* kills his Grand-mother.

This Province hath to the North the Country of *Balc,*[4] whereof an *Usbec* Prince is Sovereign. To the East it hath the Province of *Caboul,* to the South that of *Bucor,* which belongs to *Multan,* and part of *Sigestan,* which is of the Kingdom of *Persia ;* and to the West, other Countries of the King of *Persia.* The Province is very mountainous, and *Candahar* its chief Town, lies in the twenty third degree of Latitude, though some Travellers have placed it in the four and thirtieth.[5]

The bounds of *Candahar.*

That Countrey produces abundantly all sorts of Provisions that are necessary for the subsistence of its Inhabitants, unless it be on that side which lies towards *Persia,* where it is very barren. Every thing is dear in the chief Town, because of the multitude of Forreign Merchants that resort thither, and it wants[6] good Water. The Town of *Candahar* is considerable by its Situation ; and every one knows that the *Persian* and *Mogul* both pretend to[7] it. The former has in it at present a Garrison of nine or ten thousand Men, least it should be surprized by the *Mogul ;* and being besides a Town of great importance, it is fortified with good Walls, and hath two Citadels.

Two Citadels at *Candahar.*

The Trade that it hath with *Persia,* the Country of the *Uzbecs* and *Indies,* makes it very rich ; and for all the Province is so little, it heretofore yielded the *Mogul* betwixt fourteen and fifteen Millions a year. There is no Province in *Indusfan* where there are fewer Gentiles. The Inhabitants are great lovers of Wine, but they are prohibited to drink any ; and if a *Moor* who hath drank Wine, commit any Scandal, he is set upon an Ass, with his Face to the Tail, and led about the Town, attended by the Officers of the *Cotoual,* who beat a little drum, and they are followed by all the Children,[8] who hoop and hallow after them. Though there be no Province of *Indostan,* where there are fewer Gentiles: yet there are *Banians* there, because of Traffick ;[9] but they have no publick Pagod: and their Assemblies for Religion are kept in a Private House, under the direction of a *Bramen,* whom they entertain for performing their Ceremonies.

Candahar, a rich Town.

The yearly Revenue of the *Mogul* from *Candahar.*

Wine-drinkers punished.

The King of *Persia* suffers not the Gentiles Wives there to burn themselves when their Husbands are dead. There are

The Wives are not burnt at *Candahar.*

a great many *Parsis* or *Guebres* there, but they are poor, and the *Mahometans* employ them in the meanest and most servile drudgeries: They perform the Ceremonies of their Religion on a Mountain not far distant from the Town, where they have a place, wherein they preserve the Fire which they worship. I have spoken of these People in my Book of *Persia.*[10]

The same Officers are in *Candahar,* as in the Towns of the Kingdom of Persia,[11] and do the same Duties: but above all things, they have special Orders to treat the People gently, because of the proximity of the *Moguls;* and if they oppress them in the least, they are severely punished for it.

There are some small *Rajas* in the Mountains, who are suffered to live in liberty, paying some easie[12] Tributes; And these Gentlemen have always stuck to the strongest side, when the Country came to change its Master. There is also a little Countrey in the Mountains which is called *Peria,*[13] that's to say, *Fairy-Land,* where Father *Ambrose* a *Capucin* spent a *Lent* upon the mission in two Bourgs, whereof the one is named *Cheboular,*[14] and the other *Cosne;*[15] And he told me That that country is pleasant enough, and full of good honest People: but that the Christians who are there, have but slight tinctures of Religion.

Peria.

CHAPTER XXXIV

OF THE PROVINCE OF CABOUL, OR CABOULISTAN.

Province of *Caboul.*

Caboulistan. *Zabulistan.*

Caboulistan is limited to the North by *Tartary,* from which it is separated by Mount *Caucasus,*[1] which the Orientals call *Caf-Dagai. Cachmire* lies to the East of it: It hath to the West *Zabulistan,*[2] and part of *Candahar;* and to the South; the Countrey of *Multan.*[3] Two of the Rivers that run into the *Indus,*[4] have their source in the Mountains thereof, from whence they water the Province, and for all that, render it nothing the more fruitful; for the Countrey being very cold, is not fertile, unless in those places that are sheltered by Mountains: Nevertheless it is very rich, because it hath a very great Trade with *Tartary,* the Countrey of the *Usbecs, Persia,* and the *Indies.* The *Usbecs* alone sell yearly above threescore thousand Horses there; and that Province lies so conveniently for Traffick, that what is wanting in it, is brought from all Parts; and things are very cheap there.

Caboul, a Town.

The chief Town of the Province is called *Caboul;* a very large place with two good Castles; And seeing Kings have

A Holi ritual—A boy representing Krishna shooting at the effigy of a giant

held their Courts there,[5] and many Princes successively have had it for their Portion ; there are a great many Palaces in it. It lies in thirty three degrees and a half North Latitude: *Mirabolans* grow in the Mountains of it, and that's the reason why the Orientals call it *Cabuly*. There are many other sorts of Drugs gathered there ; and besides that, they are full of aromatick Trees, which turn to good account to the inhabitants as also do the Mines of a certain iron, which is fit for all uses. From this Province especially come the Canes, of which they make Halbards and Lances, and they have many Grounds planted with them. *Caboulistan* is full of small Towns, Burroughs and Villages ; most of the Inhabitants are heathen: and therefore there are a great many Pagods there. They reckon their months by Moons, and with great Devotion celebrate their Feast, called *Houly*,[6] which lasts two days. At that time their Temples are filled with People, who came to Pray and make their Oblations there ; the rest of the Celebration consists in Dancing by companies in the Streets, to the sound of Trumpets. At this Feast, they are cloathed in a dark Red, and many go to visit their Friends in Masquarade.

Mirabolans.

Houly a Feast.

Those of the same Tribe eat together, and at night they make Bonefires in the Streets. That Feast is Celebrated yearly at the Full Moon in *February*, and ends by the destruction of the Figure of a Giant ; against which a little child shoots Arrows, to represent what the People are made to believe ; to wit, That God coming into the World under the name of *Cruchman*,[7] he appeared in shape of a Child, that a great Giant that feared to be undone by him, endeavoured to ruin him: But that that Child hit him so dexterously with an Arrow, that he laid him dead upon the ground. These people seem heretofore to have been Christians ; but if they have had any Tincture[8] of it, it is much corrupted by the Fables and strange Tales that have been told them concerning the same, to which they conform their Lives and Religion. Their chief Charity consists in digging a great many Wells, and in raising several Houses, at certain distances, upon the High-ways ; for the convenience of Travellers: And by these little Houses, there is always a place fit for those who are weary and heavy Loaded, to rest in ; so that they can put off, or take up their Burden without any bodies help.

God under the name of *Cruchman.*

A Giant killed by *Cruchman.*

The Charity of the *Indians* of *Caboul.*

This Countrey supplies the rest of the *Indies* with many Physicians, who are all of the caste of *Banians* : Nay, and some of them are very skilful, and have many secrets in Medicine ; and amongst other Remedies, they often make use of burning. The *Great Mogul* has not out of this Province above four or five Millions a year.

Physicians of the *Indies.*

The yearly Revenue of *Caboul.*

CHAPTER XXXV

OF THE PROVINCE OF CACHMIR OR KICHMIR.

The Province of *Cachmire.*

The Kingdom or Province of *Cachmir,*[1] hath to the West *Caboulistan,* to the East, part of *Tibet ;* to the South, the Province of *Lahors ;* and to the North, *Tartarie* : But these are its most remote limits ; for it is bounded and encompassed on all hands by Mountains, and there is no entry into it, but by by-ways and narrow passes. This Countrey belonged sometimes to the Kings of *Turquestan,* and is one of those which were called *Turchind,* that is to say, the *India* of the *Turks,* or the *Turky* of the *Indies.*

Turchind.

Tchenas, a River.

The Waters of the Mountains that environ it, afford so many Springs and Rivulets, that they render it the most fertile Countrey of the *Indies ;* and having pleasantly watered it, make a River called *Tchenas,* which having communicated its Waters for the transportation of Merchants Goods through the greatest part of the Kingdom, breaks out through the breach of a Mountain, and near the Town of *Atoc,* discharges it self into the *Indus ;* but before it comes out, it is discharged by the name of a Lake,[2] which is above four Leagues in circuit, and adorned with a great many Isles that look fresh and green, and with the Capital Town of the Province that stands almost on the banks thereof.[3] Some would have this River to be the *Moselle,*[4] but without any reason ; for the *Moselle* runs through *Caboulistan,* and is the same that is now called *Behat* or *Behar,*[5] because of the aromatick Plants that grow on the sides of it.

Atoc.

Cachmir, a Town. *Syrenaquer.*

The Town of *Cachmir,* which bears the name of the Province, and which some call *Syrenaquer,* lies in the five and thirtieth degree of Latitude, and in the hundred and third of Longitude.[6] This Capital City is about three quarters of a League in length, and half a League in breadth. It is about two Leagues from the Mountains, and hath no Walls. The Houses of it are built of Wood, which is brought from these Mountains, and for the most part are three Stories high, with a Garden, and some of them have a little Canal which reaches to the Lake, whither they go by Boat to take the Air.[7] This little Kingdom is very populous, hath several Towns, and a great many Bourgs. It is full of lovely[8] Plains, which are here and there intercepted by pleasant little Hills, and delightful Waters ; Fruits it hath in abundance, with agreeable Verdures. The Mountains which are all Inhabited on the sides, afford so lovely a prospect by the great variety of Trees, amongst which stand Mosques, Palaces, and other Structures, that it is impossible perspective can furnish a more lovely Landskip. The *Great Mogul* hath a House of Pleasure there, with a stately Garden,[9] and the Magnificence of all is so much

The beauty of *Cachmire.*

the greater, that[10] the King who built it, adorned it with the spoils of the Gentiles Temples, amongst which there are a great many pretious Things.

King *Ecbar* subdued this Kingdom, which was before possest by a King named *Justaf-Can*:[11] He being Victorious in all places, wrote to this Prince that there was no appearance he could maintain a War against the Emperour of the *Indies*, to whom all other Princes submitted; that he advised him to do as they had done; and that he promised him, if he would submit willingly, without trying the fortune of War, he would use him better than he had done the rest; and that his Power instead of being lessened, should be encreased, seeing he was resolved to deny him nothing that he should ask Justaf-can (who was a peaceable Prince) thinking it enough to leave his Son in his Kingdom, came to wait upon the *Great Mogul* at the Town of Lahors, trusting to his word: He paid him Hommage; and the Emperour having confirmed the Promise which he made to him in his Letters, treated him with all civility.

King *Ecbar* subdued *Cachmir*. *Justaf-can* King of *Cachmir*.

In the mean time Prince *Jacob*,[12] *Justafs* Son, would not stop there: For being excited by the greatest part of the People of the Kingdom, who looked upon the Dominion of the Moguls as the most terrible thing imaginable; he caused himself to be proclaimed King, made all necessary preparations in the Countrey, and at the same time secured the Passes and Entries into it; which was not hard to be done, because there is no coming to it, but by streights[13] and narrow passes which a few Men may defend. His conduct highly displeased the *Great Mogul*, who thought at first that there was Intelligence betwixt the Father and Son; but he found at length, that there was none: And without offering any bad usage to the Father, he sent an Army against *Cachmir*, wherein he employed several great Lords and Officers of War, who had followed *Justaf-can*. He had so gained them by his Civilities and Promises, that they were more devoted to him, than to their own Prince; and they being perfectly well acquainted with the streights[14] and avenues of the Mountains, introduced the *Moguls* into the Kingdom, some through Places that belong to them, and others by By-ways that could not possibly have been found, without the conduct[15] of those who knew the Countrey exactly. They succeeded in their Design the more easily, that King *Jacob* thought of nothing but guarding the most dangerous places, and especially the Pass of *Bamber*,[16] which is the easiest way for entring into *Cachmir*.

Jacob, the Son of *Justaf-can*.

Cachmirians, Officers introduce the *Moguls*.

The Moguls having left part of their Army at *Bamber*, to amuse Prince *Jacob*, and his Forces[17] marched towards the highest Mountains, whither the *Omras* of *Cachmir* led them: There they found small passages amongst the Rocks, that were

Bamber.

not at all to be mistrusted: By these places they entered one after another, and at length, meeting in a place where the Rendezvous was appointed; they had Men enough to make a Body sufficiently able to surprize (as they did in the Night-time) the Capital City which wanted Walls, where *Jacob Can* was taken. Nevertheless *Ecbar* pardoned him, and allowed Him and his Father, each of them a Pension for their subsistence: But he made sure of the Kingdom which he reduced into a Province. He annexed it to the Empire of *Mogolistan*, and his Successours have enjoyed it to this present, as the pleasantest Country in all their Empire. It yields not the *Great Mogul* yearly, above five or six hundred thousand *French* Livres.

The yearly Revenue of *Cachmir*.

CHAPTER XXXVI

OF THE PROVINCE OF LAHORS *AND OF THE VARTIAS.*

The Province of *Lahors*.

It is about forty eight or fifty Leagues from *Lahors* to the borders of *Cachmir*, which is to the North of it, as *Dehly* is to the South; and *Lahors* is a hundred *Leagues*[1] from *Dehly*, for they reckon Two hundred *Cosses* from the one Town to the other, and the *Cosses* or half Leagues are long in that Countrey. *Multan* lyes to the West of *Lahors*, and is distant from it threescore and odd Leagues; and to the East of it there are high Mountains, in many places Inhabited by *Rajas*, of whom some are tributary to the *Great Mogul*, and others not, because having strong places to retreat into, they cannot be forced, though the Merchants suffer much by their Robberies; and when they travel in that Countrey, they are obliged to have a guard of Soldiers to defend the *Caravanes* from these Robbers.

The Situation of *Lahors*.

Lahors, Town. *Ravy*, River. *Pangeab*.

Lahors lies in thirty one degrees fifty minutes Latitude,[2] near the River *Ravy*,[3] which falls into the Indus as the others do. The *Moguls* have given that Province the name of *Pangeab*, which signifies the five Rivers, because five run in the Territory of it. These Rivers have received so many particular names from the Moderns that have spoken of them, that at present it is hard to distinguish them one from another; nay, and most part of these names are confounded, though *Pliny*[4] distinguished them by the names of *Acelines, Cophis, Hydarphes, Zaradras* and *Hispalis*.[5] Some Moderns call them *Behat, Canab, Sind, Ravy, Van*;[6] and others give them other Appellations, which are not the names of the Countrey, or at least which are not given them, but in some places of it they run through. However, all these Rivers have their Sources in

Acelines, Cophis, Hydarphes, Zaradras, Hispalis. Rivers. *Behat, Canab, Sind, Ravy, Van.* Rivers.

the Mountains of the North, and make up the Indus, that for a long way, goes by the name of *Sinde,* into which they fall; and that's the reason why this River is sometime called *Indy,* and sometimes *Sindy*. The chief Town is not now upon the *Ravy* as it was for a long time, because that River having a very flat Channel, has fallen off from it above a quarter of a League.[7]

This hath been a very pretty Town when the Kings kept their Courts in it,[8] and did not prefer *Dehly* and *Agra* before it. It is large, and hath been adorned as the others are with *Mosques,* publick Baths, Quervanserais, Squares, Tanquies, Palaces and Gardens. The Castle[9] remains still, for it is strongly built, heretofore it had three Gates on the side of the Town, and nine towards the Countrey,[10] and the Kings Palace within it, hath not as yet lost all its beauty.[11] There are a great many Pictures upon the Walls, which represent the Actions of the *Great Moguls,* their Fore-fathers that are pompously Painted there; and on one Gate there is a Crucifix and the Picture of the Virgin on another, but I believe these two pieces of Devotion were only put there by the Hypocrisie of King *Gehanguir,* who pretended a kindness for the Christian Religion to flatter the Portuguese.[11a] Many of the chief Houses of the Town run into decay daily, and it is pity to see in some Streets (which are above a League in length) Palaces all ruinous. Nevertheless the Town is not old, for before King Humayon, it was at best but a Bourg: That King made a City of it, built a Castle,[12] and kept his Court there, and it encreased so in a short time, that with the Suburbs it made three Leagues in length. As there are a great many Gentiles in this Town, so are there many Pagods also; some of them are well adorned, and all raised seven or eight steps from the ground.

Pictures at *Lahors.*

A Crucifix at *Lahors.* The Picture of the B. Virgin.

Pagods at *Lahors.*

Lahors is one of the largest and most abundant Provinces of the Indies; the Rivers that are in it render it extreamly fertile, it yields all that is necessary for life; Rice, as well as Corn and Fruits are plentiful there; there is pretty good Wine in it also, and the best Sugars of all *Indostan*. There are in the Towns Manufactures, not only of all sorts of painted Cloaths, but also of every thing else that is wrought in the *Indies*;[13] and indeed, according to the account of my *Indian,* it brings in to the *Great Mogul* above thirty seven Millions a year,[14] which is a great Argument [15] of its fruitfulness. I have already said, that the great walk of Trees (which begins at *Agra*) reaches as far as *Lahors,* though these two Towns be distant from one another an hundred and fifty Leagues, that lovely Alley is very pleasant, because the *Achy* Trees[16] (wherewith it is planted) have long and thick Branches which extend on all sides, and cover the whole way; there are also a great many Pagods upon the Road from *Lahors* to *Dehly,* and

The product of *Lahors.*

Manufactures in *Lahors.*

The yearly Revenue of *Lahors.*

Achy, Tree.

Tanassar, a Town.

especially towards the Town of *Tanassar,*[17] where Idolatry may be said to be freely professed.

A Convent of *Vartias.*

The Vows of the *Vartias.*

There is a Convent of Gentiles there, who are called *Vartias,* that have their General, Provincial and other Superiours, they say that it is above Two thousand years since they were founded. They vow Obedience, Chastity and Poverty ;[18] they strictly observe their Vows, and when any one trespasses against them, he is rigorously punished. They have Brothers appointed to beg for all the Convent ; they eat but once a day, and change their House every three Months, they have no fixt time for their Noviciat ; some perform it in two years, some in three, and there are others who spend four years therein, if the Superiour think fit. The main point of their institution is not to do to others what they would not have others do to them ; that precept they observe even towards Beasts, for they never kill any, and much more towards Men, seeing if any body beat them, they do not resist, and if they be reviled, they make no answer. They obey the least Signal of their Superiour without murmuring, and it is forbidden to them to look a Woman or Maid in the face ; they wear nothing on their Bodies but a Cloath to cover their Privy Parts, and they bring it up to their heads to make a kind of a Coif like that of a Woman ; they can possess no Money, are prohibited to reserve any thing for to morrow to eat, and how hungry soever they may be, they patiently wait till their Purveyors bring them the Alms, which are daily given them at the Houses of the Gentiles of their Tribe ; they take but little, that they may not be troublesome to any body, and therefore they receive no more at every place but a handful of Rice, or some other eatable matter, and if more be offered them, they'll refuse[19] it ; they take nothing but what is boyled and drest,[20] for they kindle no Fire in their House, for fear some Flie may burn it self therein ; when they have got Charity enough, they return to the Convent, and there mingle all the Rice, Lentils, Milk, Cheese, and other Provisions they have got together. Then an Officer distributes all equally among the *Vartias,* who eat their Portions severally cold or hot, as it is given them, and drink nothing but water.

The Noviciat of the *Vartias.*

The conduct of the *Vartias.*

The *Vartias* live on Alms.

The *Vartias* eat but once a day.

They make their meal about noon, which serves them for the whole day ; let hunger or thirst press them never so much, they must wait till the same hour next day, before they either eat or drink.

The *Vartias* Dormitory.

The rest of the day they employ in Prayers, and reading of Books ; and when the Sun sets, they go to sleep, and never light a Candle. They all lie in the same Chamber, and have no other Bed but the Ground. They cannot of themselves leave the orders after they have once taken the Vows ; yet if they commit any fault contrary to their Vows, and especially against that of Chastity, they are expelled, not only the order, but also their tribe. The General, Provincials, and all the Officers change their Convent every four Months their Office is for Life; and when any of them dies, he names to the Religous, him whom he thinks fittest to succeed, and they follow his choice. These *Vartias* have above ten thousand Monasteries in the *Indies*; and some of them are more Austere than others: Nay their [sic] are some who think it enough to worship God in Spirit, and these have no Idols, and will have no Pagod near them. There are also Religious Nuns in some places, who live very exemplarily.

The Officers of *Vartias.*

Gentile Nuns.

CHAPTER XXXVII

OF THE PROVINCES OF AYOUD, *OR* HAOUD; VARAD *OR* VARAL.

The two Provinces of *Ayoud*[1] and *Varal,*[2] are so little frequented by the *Moguls,* that they (from whom I asked an account of them,) could give me none, though they were pretty well acquainted with the rest of *Mogulistan;* and therefore I cannot say much of them in particular. The Province of *Ayoud,* (as far as I could learn,) contains the most Northern Countries that belong to the *Mogul,* as *Caucares,*[3] *Bankich,*[4] *Nagarcut,*[5] *Siba,*[6] and others: And that of *Varal* consists of those which are most North-East ward, to wit, *Gor,*[7] *Pitan,*[8] *Canduana,*[9] and some others.

The Province of *Ayoud.*

The Province of *Varal.*

These two Provinces being every where almost watered with the Rivers which run into the *Ganges,* are very fertile; notwithstanding the Mountains that are in them, which makes them exceeding Rich. The Province of *Ayoud* yields the *Great Mogul* above ten Millions, and that of *Varal,* more than seven and twenty a year. The great gains that these two Provinces, and that which is next them, make from the Strangers of the North and East, are the cause of such considerable Revenues as the *Mogul* draws out of them, and they are so much the greater, that (these Countries being remote from the Sea,) no *Europeans* share with them therein.

The yearly Revenue of *Ayoud* and *Varal.*

There are many *Rajas* in both, who (for the most) part, own not the Authority of the *Great Mogul.* There are two Pagods of great reputation in Ayoud, the one at *Nagarcut,*[10] and the other at *Calamac*[11], but that of *Nagarcut* is far more famous than the other, because of the Idol *Matta,*[12] to which it is Dedicated; and they say that there are some Gentiles, that come not out of that Pagod without Sacrificing part of their Body. The Devotion which the Gentiles make shew of at the Pagod of *Calamac,* proceeds from this, that they look upon it

Rajas not Subjected.

The Pagods of *Nagarcut.*

The Idol *Matta.*

The Pagod of *Calamac.*

as a great Miracle, that the Water of the Town which is very cold, springs out of a Rock, that continually belches out Flames. That Rock of *Calamac*, is of the Mountain of *Balaguate*,[13] and the Bramens (who Govern the Pagod,) make great profit of it.

CHAPTER XXXVIII

OF THE PROVINCE OF BECAR, *AND OF THE CASTES OR TRIBES OF THE* INDIES.

The Province of *Becar*.

Douab, *Jesuat*, *Udesse*. The Towns of *Becar*, *Sambal*, *Menapour*, *Rageapour*, *Jehanac*, *Becaner*. Towns.

The Province of *Becar*,[1] which comprehends the Countries of *Douab*,[2] *Jesuat*[3] and *Udesse*,[4] is also watered by the Rivers that discharge themselves into the Ganges. It lies not only to the East of *Dehly*, but is also the most Eastern Province of Mogolistan, by the Countrey of *Udesse*, which shuts it in with its Mountains: And that great Province being rich, by reason of the fertility thereof, yields to the *Great Mogul* yearly above fourteen Millions. It contains several good Towns; but the best are *Sambal*,[5] *Menapour*,[6] *Rageapour*,[7] *Jehanac*,[8] and above all *Becaner*,[9] which at present is the Capital, standing to the West of the Ganges.

Castes or Tribes of the Gentiles. 84.

In this Province of *Becar*, and in the two former, there are of[10] all the Castes and Tribes of the *Indians*, which are reckoned in all to be fourscore and four in number.[11] Though all of them profess the same Religion, yet the Ceremonies of every one of these Castes, nay, and of the private Persons of each Caste, are so different, that they make an infinite number of Sects. The People of every one of these Tribes follow a Trade; and none of their Off-spring can quit it, without being reckoned infamous in his Tribe. For Example, The *Bramens* (who make the first Tribe) profess Doctrine, and so do their Children, without ever forsaking that Profession. The second, is the Tribe of the *Catry* or *Raspoutes*[12] who make profession of Arms: Their Children profess the same, or ought to do it, because they all pretend to be descended of Princes of the Gentiles; Not but some of them are Merchants,[13] nay, and Weavers in the Provinces of *Multan*, *Lahors*, and *Sinde*; but they are despised in the Tribe, and pass for base Fellows, void of honour. The third, is the Tribe of the *Soudr*[14] or *Courmy*, and these are the Labourers of the Ground; some of them carry Arms, and since that is an honourable Trade, and of a superiour Caste, it do's not reflect upon them; but because they love not to serve on Horse-back, they serve commonly for the Garisions of Places; and this Caste or Tribe is the greatest of all. The fourth, is the Tribe of the *Quens* or *Banians*; and they are all Merchants,

Bramens

Catry or *Raspoutes*.

Soudr or *Courmy*.

Bankers, or Brokers, and the expertest People in the World for making Money of anything.

Anciently there were no more Tribes but these four ; but in succession of time, all those who applied themselves to the same Profession, composed a Tribe or Caste, and that's the reason they are so numerous. The *Colis* or Cotton-dressers have made a distinct Caste: The *Teherons* or Travellers Guards, have theirs: The *Palanquin*-bearers have also made one, and they are called *Covillis* :[15] Bow-makers and Fletchers have also made another ; as also the Hammer-men, such as Goldsmiths, Armorers, Smiths and Masons. They who work in Wood, as Carpenters, Joyners and Bill-men, are all of one Caste: Publick Wenches, Tumblers, Vaulters, Dancers and Baladins, are of another. And it is the same with Taylors, and other Sheers-men, with Coach-makers and Sadlers: The *Bengiara,*[16] who are Carriers, Painters and (in a word) all other Trades-men.[17]

Colis. *Teherons.* *Covillis.* *Bengiara.*

The least esteemed of all the eighty four Tribes, are the *Piriaves*[18] and the *Der,*[19] or *Halalcour,*[20] because of their nastiness ;[21] and they who touch them, think themselves unclean. The *Periaves* are employed in taking off, and carrying away the Skins of Beasts, and some of them are Curriers.[22] The *Halalcour* are the Gold-finders[23] of the Towns ; they make clean the publick and private Houses of Office,[24] and are payed for it Monthly ; they feed on all sort of Meats prohibited or not prohibited ; they eat others leavings without considering what Religion or Caste they are of: And that's the reason why those who only speak *Persian* in the *Indies,* call them *Halalcour,* (that's to say) He that takes the liberty to eat what he pleases ; or according to others, He that eats what he has honestly got. And they who approve this last Application,[25] say, that heretofore the *Halalcour* were called *Haramcour,* eaters of prohibited Meats: (But that a King one day hearing his Courtiers Jear them, because of their nasty[26] Trade, said to them, Since these People gain their Bread better than you, who are lazy lubbards, their name of *Haramcour* ought to be given to you, and to them that of *Halalcour.*) And that they have retained that name.

Der. *Periaves.* *Halalcour.* *Haramcour,* or *Halalcour.*

There is a Caste of Gentiles, called *Baraguy,*[27] who damn[28] the yellow Colour ; and who in the Morning put white on their Fore-head, contrary to the custom of the other Castes, who have red put there by the *Bramens.* When a Gentile is Painted with this Red, he bows his Head three times, and lifts his joyned hands thrice up to his Fore-head ; and then presents the *Bramen* with *Rice* and a *Cocos.*

Baraguy. White and Red colours on the Fore-head.

All the Castes or Tribes go to their Devotions at the same time ; but they adore what Idol they please, without addressing themselves solely to him, to whom the Temple is dedicated, unless their Devotion invite them to do so, in so much that some carry their Idols along with them, when they know that he whom they Worship is not there. None of these Gentiles marry out of their own Tribe. A *Bramen* marries the Daughter of another *Bramen*, a *Raspoute* the Daughter of a *Raspoute*, a *Halalcour* the Daughter of a *Halalcour*, a Painter of a Painter, and so of the rest.

The alliance of the Gentiles.

The subordination of Tribes.

The eighty four Tribes, observe among themselves an Order of Subordination. The *Banians* yield to the *Courmis*,[29] the *Courmis* to the *Rajpoutes* or *Catrys*, and these (as all the rest do) to the *Bramens*; and so the *Bramens* are the chief and most dignified of the Gentiles. And therefore it is, that a Bramen would think himself prophaned, if he had eaten with a Gentile of another Caste than his own, though those of all other Castes may eat in his House. And so it is with the other Tribes in relation to their inferiours.

Brahmanes. *Gymnosophists.*

The *Bramens*, who are properly the *Brahmanes* or *Sages* of the Ancient *Indians*, and the *Gymnosophists* of *Porphyrius*,[30] are the Priests and Doctors of the Heathen in India. Besides Theologie (which they profess) they understand Astrology, Arithmetick and Medicine; but they who are actually Physicians, pay yearly a certain Tribute to their Caste, because Physick ought not to be their Profession. All these Gentiles have a respect for the *Bramens*; and they believe them in all things, because they have been always told that God sent the four *Bets*[31] to them, which are the Books of their Religion, and that they are the keepers of them.

Bets, or Books of Religion.

Philosophers.

Ram, a God of the Gentiles.

Several of these Doctors apply themselves to Philosophy, and love not to appear so extravagant as the rest in their Belief. When a Christian speaks to them of their God *Ram*, whom the Gentiles Worship; they maintain not that he is God, and only say that he was a great King, whose Sanctity and good Offices that he did to Men, have procured him a more particular communion with God, than other Saints have; and that so they shew him much more reverence: And if one speak to them of the Adoration of Idols, they answer, that they Worship them not; that their intention is always fixed upon God; that they only honour them, because they put them in mind of the Saint whom they represent; that one must not heed the ignorance of the Common People, who form to themselves a thousand idle fancies, their Imaginations being always stuffed with Errors and Superstitions; and that when one would be informed of a Religion, he ought to consult those that are knowing in it. That it is true, the ignorant believe that many great Men (under whose shape God hath made himself known) are Gods, but that for their part, they believe no such thing;[32] and that if God hath been pleased to Act so, it was only to facilitate the Salvation of Men, and to condescend to the capacity and humour of every Nation.

The Adoration of Idols.

The Belief of the understanding *Indians*.

Upon this Principle they believe that every Man may be saved in his Religion and Sect, provided he exactly follow the way which God hath set before him, and that he will be damned if he take another Course: They make no doubt but that their Religion is the first of all Religions; that it was Established in the days of *Adam*, and preserved in *Noah*:[33] They believe Heaven and Hell, but they affirm that none shall enter there before the Universal Judgment: They say also, that no body ought to find fault with them for the honour they shew to the *Cow*; that they prefer her before other Animals, only because she furnishes them more Food, by means of her Milk, than all the rest put together; and that she brings forth the Ox which is so useful to the World, seeing he makes it subsist by his Labour, and feeds Men by his Pains.

The *Indians* believe that their Religion is the first of all. Respect to the *Cow*.

The *Bramens* believe the *Metempsychosis* or *Transmigration* of Souls[34] into New Bodies, more or less noble, according to the merit of their Actions which they have done in their Life-time. And many of the other Castes follow that Opinion of *Pythagoras*;[35] They believe that every Soul must thus make many Transmigrations, but they determine not the number; and therefore there are some who kill no Beast, and never kindle Fire nor light Candle, for fear some Butterflie should burn it self thereat: It being possible (say they) that the Soul of a Butterflie may have lodged in the Body of a Man; and they have the same Sentiment of other Animals. In prospect of saving living Creatures, they often sollicite the *Mogul* Governours, to forbid Fishing on certain Festival days; and sometimes that prohibition is procured by Presents. They would willingly also hinder the killing of Cows, but they can never obtain that. The *Mahometans* will needs eat Flesh, and that of the Cow is the best of all the gross Meats of the *Indies*.

Metempsychosis.

Pythagoras.

After all, the vulgar Opinion of the Gentiles, touching the God Ram, is that he was produced, and came out of the Light, in the same manner as the Fringe of a Belt comes out of that Belt; and if they Assign him a Father whom they call *Dester*,[36] and a Mother named *Gaoucella*;[37] that is only for form sake, seeing he was not born: And in that consideration, the *Indians* render him divine Honours in their Pagods, and else where; And when they salute their Friends, they repeat his Name, saying, *Ram, Ram*. Their Adoration consists in joyning their hands, as if they Prayed, letting them fall very low, and then lifting them up again gently to their mouth, and last of all; in raising them over their head. They call *Chita*[38] the Wife of *Ram*; and seeing they know what respect Christians bear to the Holy Virgin, they have the boldness to compare that Wife to her; and if they meet with her Image, they take it to be the representation of *Chita*.

The Opinion of the Gentiles concerning their God *Ram*.

Chita the Wife of *Ram*.

Bassaim. An Image of the Virgin. Our Lady of Remedies.

In this Opinion many Gentiles go to *Bassaim,* a Town belonging to the *Portuguese,* where there is the Image of a Virgin, who is called our Lady of Remedies,[39] and where (they say) Miracles are wrought. When they come to the Church-door, they salute it, bowing to the ground; and having taken off their Shoes, and come in, they make many Reverences; they put Oyl into the Lamp that hangs before the Image; burn Wax-Candles, and cast some Money into the Box, if they be able. At first they would have added to this Oblation, Fruits, and the Anointing of their Body, that so they might call it Sacrifice, but the *Portuguese* hindred them. It may easily be concluded, from the aversion they have to the killing of Beasts, that their Sacrifices are never bloody; they only consist in bringing into their Pagods many things fit to be eaten. When they are come there, and have taken Directions from the *Bramen,* they Anoint their Body with Oyl, and say their Prayers, before the Idol they intend to Invocate; and having presented their Oblation to it, they return out of the Pagod again. The chief *Bramen* takes of it what he pleases, and then all that have a mind to eat of it, may, of what Religion soever they be. They perform also Sacrifices to the Sea.

The *Indian* Sacrifices.

CHAPTER XXXIX

OF THE PROVINCE OF HALABAS, *AND OF THE* FAQUIRS *OF THE* INDIES.

The Province of *Halabas.* *Narvar.* *Mevat.*

The Province of *Halabas*[1] was heretofore called *Purop:*[2] In it are comprehended *Narvar*[3] and *Mevat,*[4] which have *Bengala* to the South. The chief Town lying upon the side of the *Ganges,* at the mouth of the River *Gemini,* bears the name of the Province; for a long time it was one of the Bulwarks of the Kingdom of the *Patans,* and is the same Town which *Pliny* calls *Chrysobacra.*[5] It fell under the power of the Great Mogul *Ecbar,* after he had subdued the Kingdom of Bengala: He caused the strong Citadel to be built there,[6] which stands upon a tongue of Land, begirt with three Walls, whereof the last (I mean the outmost Wall) was of very hard red Stone. That Castle is adorned with a very ancient Obelisk;[7] it is above sixty Foot high from the ground, and has many Inscriptions upon it; but the Letters of it are so worn out, that one cannot so much as distinguish the Character.

Chrysobacra.

The King's Palace is also a fair pile of Building;[8] and underneath it there are places Arched, where the Pagods[9] are carefully kept, which the People of the Countrey attribute to *Adam* and *Eve,*[10] whose Religion they pretend to follow:

Adam, Eve.

Thither comes at certain times an incredible concours of People, in Pilgrimage from all parts of the *Indies;* and they are drawn thither by the belief they have, that *Adam* and *Eve* were created there: But before they approach that place (which they look upon to be holy) they throw themselves stark naked into the *Ganges* to be purified, and they have[11] their Beards and Hair, that they may merit the Honour of being introduced. That Province hath a great many good Towns, of which number are *Narval* and *Gehud;*[12] but the People there are so extravagant in point of Religion, that hardly any thing is to be understood of it: They are taken with every thing they see, and approve all the Actions of those that make any shew of Devotion, never minding whether it be true or false. It many times happens that a *Banian* will give a *Faquir* considerable Sums of Money, because he has the boldness to place himself near his Shop, and to protest that he'll kill himself if he be not supplied with what he demands: The *Banian* promises fair, and brings it him; but because the fantastical *Faquir* understands that several have contributed to that Charity, he openly[13] refuses it, and goes about to execute what he hath threatned, if the *Banian* alone furnish not the Sum; and the *Banian* knowing that some *Faquirs* have been so desperate as to kill themselves upon the like occasion, is so much a fool as to give it out of his own Purse, and to give the others back again what they had contributed.

The *Indians* Purification in the *Ganges*.

Narval, *Gehud* Towns.

Faquir.

These *Faquirs* (who give themselves out to be of a Religious Order) have commonly no place to retreat unto, unless it be some Pagods; and they cannot be better compared (if you'll set aside the Penances they do) than to *Gypsies*, for their way of Living is like theirs; and I believe their Profession has the same Original, which is *Libertinisme*. However, they attribute it to a Prince named *Revan*,[14] who had a Quarrel with *Ram;* and who being overcome and stript of all, by an Ape called *Herman*,[15] spent the rest of his Life in rambling over the World, having no other subsistence for himself and his followers but what was given him in Charity.

Gypsies, *Faquirs*.

Prince *Revan*.

Herman the Ape.

They are many times to be seen in Troops at *Halabas*, where they Assemble for Celebrating of some Feasts[16] (for which they are obliged to wash themselves in the *Ganges*) and to perform certain Ceremonies. Such of them as do no hurt, and shew signs of Piety are extreamly honoured by the Gentiles; and the Rich think they draw down blessings upon themselves, when they assist those whom they call Penitents. Their Penance consists in forbearing to eat for many days, to keep constantly standing upon a Stone[17] for several weeks, or several months; to hold their Arms a cross behind their head, as long as they live, or to bury themselves in Pits for a certain space of time. But if some of these *Faquirs* be good Men, there

The good *Faquirs* honoured.

Faquirs Rogues.

are also very Rogues amongst them; and the *Mogul* Princes are not troubled, when such of them as commit violences are killed.

One may meet with some of them in the Countrey stark naked with Colours and Trumpets, who ask Charity with Bow and Arrow in hand;[18] and when they are the strongest, they leave it not to the discretion of Travellers to give or refuse. These wretches have no consideration even for those that feed them; I have seen some of them in the *Caravans,* who made it their whole business to play tricks, and to molest Travellers, though they had all their subsistence from them. Not long since I was in a *Caravane,* where some of these *Faquirs* were, who took a fancy to suffer no body to sleep: All night long they did nothing but Sing and Preach; and instead of banging them soundly to make them hold their peace (as they ought to have been served) the Company prayed them civilly, but they took it ill; so that they doubled their Cries and Singing, and they who could not Sing, laugh'd and made a mock of the rest of the *Caravane.*

These *Faquirs* were sent by their Superiours, into I know not what Countrey full of *Banians,* to demand of them Two thousand *Roupies,* with a certain quantity of Rice and *Mans* of Butter; and they had orders not to return without fulfilling their Commission. This is their way all over the *Indies,* where by their *Mummeries,* they have accustomed the Gentiles to give them what they demand, without daring to refuse. There are a great many *Faquirs* among the *Mahometans,* as well as amongst the Idolaters, who are also Vagabonds, and worse than they: and commonly both of them are treated alike.

The *Moguls* Revenue from *Halabas.*

The Province of *Halabas* pays the *Moguls* yearly about fourteen Millions.

CHAPTER XL

OF THE PROVINCE OF OULESSER *OR* BENGALA, *AND OF THE* GANGES.

The Province of *Ouleser,* or *Bengala. Jaganat.*

The Province of *Oulesser,*[1] which we call *Bengala,* and which the Idolaters name *Jaganat;*[2] because of the famous Idol of the Pagod of *Jaganat* which is there, is Inhabited by Gentiles no less fantastical in point of Religion, than those of *Halabas;* and this one instance may serve for a proof of it. A *Faquir* intending to invent some new spell of Devotion that was never seen before, and which might cost him a great deal of pains, resolved to measure with his Body the whole extent of the *Moguls* Empire, from *Bengala* as far as *Caboul,* which are

Strange Penance of a *Faquir.*

A strange way of covering distance as penance

the limits of it from South East to North West. The pretext he had for so doing, was, that once in his life he might be present at the Feast of *Houly,* which I have already described, and he had a kind of novices to wait upon him and serve him.

The first Action he did when he set out upon his Journey, was to lay himself at full length on the ground upon his belly, and to order that the length of his Body might be marked there; that being done, he rose up, and acquainted his followers with his Design, which was to take a Journey as far as *Caboul,* by lying down and rising up again continually, and to walk no more at a time but the length of his Body; ordering his Novices to make a mark on the ground at the Crown of his Head, every time he lay down, to the end he might exactly regulate the March he was to make; all was punctually performed on both sides: The *Faquir* made a Cosse and a half a day, that's to say, about three quarters of a League; and they who related the Story, met him a year after his setting out, no farther off than at the utmost bounds of the Province of *Halabas.* In the mean time, he had all imaginable respect shewed him in the places he passed through; and was loaded with Charity, in so much, that he was obliged to distribute the Alms he got amongst the Poor, who in hopes of getting by him, followed him in his Journey.

Many *Mahometans* live there also, but they are no better than the Gentils. The People (for the most part) are extraordinarily voluptuous; they have a captious and subtil wit, and are much given to pilfring and[3] stealing: The Women themselves are bold and lascivious, and use all Arts imaginable to corrupt and debauch[4] Young Men, and especially Strangers, whom they easily trapan, because they are handsom and wear good Cloaths.[5]

The Inhabitants of *Bengala* voluptuous.

The people in this Province live much at their ease, because of its fruitfulness; and above Twenty thousand Christians dwell there. The Countrey was kept in far better order under the *Patan* Kings, (I mean) before the *Mahometans* and *Moguls* were Masters of it,[6] because then they had Uniformity in Religion. It has been found by experience, that disorder came into it with *Mahometanism;* and that diversity of Religions hath there caused corruption in Manners.

Mahometanism hath introduced disorder.

Daca, or *Daac,*[7] is properly the capital City of Bengala; it lies upon the banck of the *Ganges,* and is very narrow, because it stretches out near a League and a half in length, along the side of that River. Most of the Houses are only built of Canes, covered with Earth: The *English* and *Dutch* Houses are more solid, because they have spared no cost for the security of their Goods: The *Augustines* have a Monastery[8] there also. The Tide comes up as far as *Daca,* so that the Galleys which are

Daca, or *Daac.*

The *Augustins* have a Monastery at *Daca.*

Galleys of the Gulf of *Bengala*.

built there, may easily Trade in the gulf of *Bengala ;* and the *Dutch* make good use of theirs for their Commerce.

Towns of *Bengala*. *Philipatan*, *Satigan*, *Patane*, *Casanbazar*, *Chatigan*. Towns. The *Dutch* Factory at *Patan*.

The Countrey is full of Castles and Towns ; *Philipatan,*[9] *Satigan,*[10] *Patane,*[11] *Casanbazar*[12] and *Chatigan,*[13] are very rich ; and *Patane* is a very large Town, lying on the West side of the *Ganges* in the Countrey of *Patan,* where the Dutch have a Factory. Corn, Rice, Sugar, Ginger, long Pepper, Cotton and Silk, with several other Commodities, are plentifully produced in that Country, as well as Fruits ; and especially the *Ananas,* which in the out side is much like a Pine-Apple ; they are as big as Melons, and some of them resemble them also ; their colour at first is betwixt a Green and a Yellow, but when they are ripe, the Green is gone ; they grow upon a Stalk not above a Foot and a half high ; they are pleasant to the taste, and leaves the flavour of an Apricock in the mouth.

Ananas.

The *Ganges*.

The *Ganges* is full of pleasant Islands, covered with lovely *Indian* Trees ; and for five days Sailing on that River, Passengers are delighted with the beauty of them. In these Isles, and some other places of *Bengala,* there is a kind of bird called *Meina,*[14] which is much esteemed ; it is of the colour of a Blackbird, and almost as big as a Raven, having just such another Beak, but that it is yellow and red ; on each side of the neck, it hath a yellow streak which covers the whole Cheek till below the eye, and its Feet are yellow ; they teach it to speak like a Starling, and it hath the tone and voice much like ;[15] but besides its ordinary Voice it hath a strong deep Tone which seems to come from a distance ; it imitates the neighing of a Horse exactly, and feeds on dryed Pease which it breaks. I have seen some of them upon the Road from *Masulipatan* to *Bagnagar.*[16]

Meina, a bird.

The Water of the *Ganges*.

The Heathen *Indians* esteem the water of the *Ganges* to be sacred ; they have Pagods near it, which are the fairest of all the *Indies ;* and it is in that Countrey especially where Idolatry is triumphant: The two chief Pagods are that of *Jaganat,* (which is at one of the mouths of the *Ganges*[17]) and the other of the Town of *Benarous,*[18] which is also upon the *Ganges*. Nothing can be more magnificent than these Pagods, by reason of the quantity of Gold and many Jewels, wherewith they are adorned. Festivals are kept there for many days together, and millions[19] of People repair thither from the other Countreys of the Indies ; they carry their Idols in triumph, and act all sorts of Superstitions ; they are entertained by the *Bramens,* who are numerous there, and who therein find their Profit.

Pagods of *Jaganat*. Pagod of *Banarous*.

The *Great Mogul* drinks of the Water of the *Ganges*.

The *Great Mogul* drinks commonly of the Water of the *Ganges,*[20] because it is much lighter than other Waters ; and yet I have met with those who affirm that it causes Fluxes ; and that the *Europeans* (who are forced to drink it) boil it first. This River having received an infinite number of Brooks and

Rivers from the North, East and West, discharges it self by several mouths into the Gulf of *Bengala,* at the height of three and twenty degrees, or thereabouts; and that Gulf reaches from the eighth degree of Latitude to the two and twentieth, it being eight hundred Leagues over. On the sides thereof to the East and West, there are many Towns belonging to several Sovereigns, who permit the Traffick of other Nations, because of the profit they get thereby.

The Gulf of *Bengala.*

The Coasts of the Gulf of *Bengala.*

My *Indian* reckons the yearly Revenue of the *Mogul* in this Province, to amount to Ten millions; but I learnt from other hands, that it hardly makes Nine,[21] though it be far richer than other Provinces that yield him more: The reason given for that, is, that it lies in the extremity of his Empire, and is Inhabited by a capricious sort of People, who must be gently used, because of the Neighbourhood of Kings that are enemies, who might debauch them if they were vexed. The *Mogul* sends the Traitors thither, whom he hath condemned to perpetual Imprisonment;[22] and the Castle where they are kept, is strictly guarded.

The *Moguls* Revenue from *Bengala.*

Traitors.

CHAPTER XLI

OF THE PROVINCE OF MALVA.

Malva[1] is to the West of *Bengala* and *Halabas;* therein are comprehended the Countries of *Raja-Ranas, Gualear*[2] and *Chitor.*[3] The Town of Mando[4] is one of the fairest Ornaments of the Province: The *Mahometans* took it from the *Indians,* above Four hundred years before the *Moguls* came there,[5] and when they attacked it, it was in the possession of *Cha-Selim,*[6] King of *Dehly.* The first of the *Moguls* that took it, was King *Humayon,* who lost it again; but he afterwards made himself Master of it.[7] This Town is of a moderate bigness, and hath several Gates, which are esteemed for their structure and height: Most of the Houses are of Stone; and it hath lovely Mosques, whereof the chief is much beautified;[8] a Palace that is not far from that Mosque, (and which depends upon it) serves as a Mausoleum to four Kings,[9] who are interred in it, and have each of them a Monument; and close by, there is a Building in form of a Tower,[10] with Portico's and several Pillars.

The Province of *Malva.* *Raja-Ranas.* *Gualear,* *Mando.* Towns. *Cha-Selim,* King of *Dehly.*

Though this Town lying at the foot of a Hill, be naturally strong by its Situation, it is nevertheless fortified with Walls and Towers, and has a Castle on the top of the Hill, which is steep, and encompassed with Walls six or seven Leagues in circuit. It is a very neat Town at present,[11] but nothing to

The Castle of *Mando.*

The Ruins of *Mando*, shew that it hath been magnificent.

what it hath been heretofore: It appears by the Ruins all about, that it hath been much greater than it is, that it hath had two fair Temples,[12] and many stately Palaces; and the sixteen large *Tanquies* or Reservatories, which are to be seen still for keeping of Water,[13] shew (that in former times) it hath been a place of great consequence.

Ratispor, the Capital of *Malva*.

Traitors condemned to die.

This Province is very fertile, and produces all that grows in the other places of the *Indies*. *Ratispor*[14] is the Capital of the Province, and at present the Town of greatest Traffick; it stands also upon a Mountain, and thither the *Grand Signior* sends the Traitors whom he hath condemned to die: For a certain time they are kept Prisoners, and always one or other in the room with them; and the day they are to die, they make them drink a great quantity of Milk, and throw them down from the top of the Castle upon the declining side of the Hill, which is full of sharp pointed craggy Stones, that tear the Bodies of the wretches, before they can reach the bottom of the Precipice.

Chitor.

Raja-Ranas of the Race of *Porus*.

An hundred Temples in *Chitor*.

Antique Statues.

The Revenue of the Province of *Malva*.

The Town of *Chitor* is very famous also, but it is almost ruined; it long belonged to *Raja-Ranas*, who deduced his Genealogie from King *Porus*;[15] though that *Raja* had considerable Territories, and strong, by reason of the Mountains that almost encompassed them; yet could he not avoid the misfortune of other Princes, but fell (as they did) under the power of the *Moguls*, in the Reign of King *Ecbar*. At present, there are but few Inhabitants in *Chitor*, the Walls of it are low, and of a great many stately publick Buildings, nothing remains but the ruins. The hundred Temples or Pagods are still to be distinguished, and many antick Statues to be seen; it hath a Fort, where Lords of chief Quality are Imprisoned for small faults: In short, The remains of many Ancient Fabricks (that are to be seen there) make it apparent, that it hath been a very great Town. The Seat of it is very pleasant, and the top of the Hill (on which it stands) extreamly fertile; it hath still four Reservatories or *Tanquies* for the private use of the Inhabitants. There are a great many other Trading Towns in that Province, and the *Great Mogul* receives yearly out of it above fourteen Millions.

An extraordinary Bat.

There are two kinds of Bats in that Countrey, the one is like to that we have in *Europe*; but seeing the other differs much, I pleased my self in examining it in a Friends House, who kept one out of curiosity;[16] it is eight Inches long, and covered with yellowish Hair; the Body of it is round, and as big as a Ducks; its Head and Eyes resemble a Cats, and it has a sharp Snout like to a great Rat; it hath pricked black Ears and no Hair upon them; it hath no Tail, but under its Wings, two Teats as big as the end of ones little finger; it hath four Legs, some call them Arms, and all the four seem to be glued fast within the Wings, which are joyned to the Body along the sides, from the Shoulder downwards; the Wings are almost two Foot long, and seven or eight Inches broad, and are of a black Skin like to wet Parchment; each Arm is as big as a Cats thigh; and towards the Joynt, it is almost as big as a Mans Arm; & the two foremost from the Shoulder to the Fingers, are nine or ten Inches long; each of the two Arms is fleshed into the Wing, Perpendicularly to the Body, being covered with Hair, and terminating in five Fingers, which make a kind of hand; these Fingers are black and without Hair; they have the same Joynts as a Mans Fingers have; and these Creatures make use of them to stretch out their Wings when they have a mind to flie: Each hind Leg or Arm, is but half a Foot long, and is also fastened to the Wing parallel to the Body; it reaches to the lower part of the Wing, out of which the little hand of that Arm peeping, seems pretty like the hand of a Man; but that instead of Nails, it hath five Claws; the hind Arms are black and hairy (as those before[17] are) and are a little smaller. These Bats stick to the Branches of Trees, with their Talons or Claws; they fly high, almost out of sight, and some (who eat them) say they are good meat.[18]

CHAPTER XLII

OF THE PROVINCE OF CANDICH.

The Province of *Candich*, *Berar*, *Orixa*.

The Province of *Candich*[1] is to the South of *Malva*, and they who have reduced the Provinces, have joyned to it *Berar*, and what the *Mogul* possesses of *Orixa*.[2] These Countries are of a vast extent, full of populous Towns and Villages, and in all *Mogulistan*, few Countries are so rich as this. The Memoire[3] I have of yearly Revenues, makes this Province yield the *Mogul* above seven and twenty Millions a year. The Capital City of this Province is *Brampour*;[4] it lies in the twenty eighth degree of Latitude, about fourscore Leagues distant from *Surrat*.[5] The Governour thereof is commonly a Prince of the Blood, and *Auren-Zeb* hath been Governour of it himself.

The *Moguls* yearly Revenue from *Candich*.

Brampour, the Capital of *Candich*.

A Quarrel the *Sieurs La Boullaye* and *Beber* had with a *Banian*.

Here it was that the *Sieurs de La Boullaye* and *Beber* Envoy's from the *French East-India* Company, quarrelled with the *Banians*, to whom they were recommended. When they arrived at *Brampour*, these Banians met them with Basons full of Sweetmeats, and *Roupies* in their hands. The Gentlemen not knowing the custom of the Countrey, which is to offer Presents to Strangers whom they esteem; and imagining that the five and twenty or thirty *Roupies* that were offered them, was a sign that they thought them poor, fell into a Passion, railed at the *Banians,* and were about to have beat them, which was like to have bred the trouble enough: if they had been well informed of the custom of the Countrey, they would have taken the Money, and then returned some small Present to the *Banians;* and if they had not thought it fit to make a Present, they might have given it back again after they had received it; or if they would not take it, touch it at least with their Fingers ends, and thanked them for their civility.

I came to *Brampour* in the worst weather imaginable; and it had rained so excessively, that the low Streets of that Town were full of water, and seemed to be so many Rivers. *Brampour* is a great Town standing upon very uneven ground; there are some Streets very high, and others again so low, that they look like Ditches when one is in the higher Streets; these inequalities of Streets occur so often, that they cause extraordinary Fatigue. The Houses are not at all handsom, because most of them are only built of Earth; however, they are covered with Varnished Tiles, and the various Colours of the Roofs, mingling with the Verdure of a great many Trees of different kinds, planted on all hands, makes the Prospect of it pleasant enough. There are two *Carvanseras* in it, one appointed for lodging Strangers, and the other for keeping the Kings Money, which the Treasurers receive from the Province; that for the Strangers is far more spacious than the other, it is square, and both of them front towards the *Meidan.* That is a very large place, for it is at least Five hundred paces long, and Three hundred and fifty broad; but it is not pleasant, because it is full of ugly huts, where the Fruiterers sell their Fruit and Herbs.

The Ground of *Brampour.*

The House of *Brampour.*

The entry into the Castle[6] is from the *Meidan,* and the chief Gate is betwixt two large Towers; the Walls of it are six or seven Fathom high; they have Battlements all round, and at certain intervals there are large round Towers which jet a great way out, and are about thirty paces Diametre. This Castle contains the Kings Palace, and there is no entring into it without permission; the *Tapty* running by the East side of that Town, there is one whole Front of the Castle upon the River-side, and in that part of it the Walls are full eight Fathom high, because there are pretty neat Galleries on the top, where the King (when he is at *Brampour*) comes to look about him,[7] and to see the fighting of Elephants, which is commonly in the middle of the River; in the same place, there is a Figure of an Elephant[8] done to the natural bigness, it is of a reddish shining Stone, the back parts of it are in the Water, and it leans to the left side; the Elephant (which that Statue represents) died in that place, fighting before *Cha-Gehan* (the Father of *Auran-Zeb*) who would needs erect a Monument to the Beast, because he

The Castle of *Brampour.*

The Kings Palace at *Brampour.*

The Monument of an Elephant.

loved it, and the Gentiles besmear it with Colours, as they do their Pagods.

They drink not commonly the *Tapty* Water at *Brampour,* because it is very brackish ; but they are supplied from a large square Bason[9] (that is in the *Meidan*) the Water whereof comes from a distant Spring, and before it fills that Bason, passes by the *Carvansera* for Strangers which it furnishes ; it then runs under ground to the great Bason in the place, which many times is empty at night, because of the great quantity of Water which they fetch thence all day long ; but it fills again in the night-time, and so they seldom have any want. There are a great many Houses also on the other side of the River, and they may be said to be a second Town.

The great Trade of the Province is in Cotton-cloath, and there is as much Traffick at *Brampour,* as in any place of the *Indies.* Painted Cloaths are sold there, as every where else ; but the white are particularly esteemed, because of the lovely mixture of Gold and Silver that is in them, whereof the rich make Veils, Scarfs, Handkerchiefs and Coverings, but the white Cloaths so Adorned, are dear. In short, I do not think that any Countrey of *Indostan* abounds so much in Cotton as this do's[10] which bears also plenty of Rice and Indigo. The same Trade is driven at *Orixa, Berar,* and other Towns of this Province.

White Cloaths mingled with Gold and Silver at *Brampour.*

Indigo at *Brampour.*

CHAPTER XLIII

OF THE PROVINCE OF BALAGATE.

Balagate[1] is one of the Great *Moguls* rich Provinces, for it yields him Five and twenty Millions a year ; it lies to the South of *Candich.* To go from *Surrat* to *Aurangeabad,*[2] which is the Capital Town of *Balagate,* one must from *Duman*-Gate hold streight East, and soon after, turning towards the South-East, cross some Countries of the Provinces of *Benganala*[3] and *Telenga.*[4] Part of *Balagate* I saw, as I went to *Golconda ;* for this Journey I hired two Chariots, one for my self, and another for my Man and Baggage ; I payed about Seventeen Crowns a month for each Chariot, and I entertained two *Pions* in my Service, to whom I gave two Crowns a piece by the month, and two pence half penny a day for Board-wages (as the custom is,) these Men are always by the sides of their Masters Chariot or Waggon, that they may hold it up in bad way if it heel'd ; when one comes to any place to bait at,[5] they'll do any thing out of the Kitchin ; but they will not venture to dress Meat, which those of their Sect would not eat. In short, They are

The Province of *Balagate.* The yearly Revenue of *Balagate.*

The Pay of *Pions.*

The *Pions* do all things except Kitchin-work.

in all things else very serviceable ; they'll buy what is necessary, look after their Masters things exactly, and stand sentinel all night long ; they are Armed with Sword and Dagger, and have besides the Bow, Musket or Lance, and are always ready to fight against all sorts of Enemies. There are of them both *Moors* and *Gentiles* of the Tribe of the *Raspoutes ;* I took *Raspoutes,* because I knew they served better than the *Moors,* who are proud, and will not be complained of, whatsoever foppery or cheat they may be guilty of.

The *Pions* Arms.

The Heathen *Pions* are better than the *Moors.*

I made this Journey in company of Monsieur *Bazou,*[6] a *French* Merchant, a very civil and witty Man, who had with him ten Waggons or Chariots, and fourteen *Pions* for himself, his Servants and Goods ; we were eight Franks in company, and in all Five and forty Men. We parted from *Surrat* in the Evening, and encamped near the Queens Garden, which is without *Daman*-Gate ; so soon as we were got thither, we sent to the Town for what Provisions we wanted, for else we must have fared hard during our Journey. The Gentiles (who sell Provisions) will neither furnish Travellers with Eggs nor Pullets ; and instead of ordinary Bread, there is nothing to be got but ill baked Buns or Cakes, so that one must not fail to make provision of Bisket at *Surrat.*

Journey from *Surrat* to *Aurangeabad.*

The Countrey from *Surrat* to *Aurangabad,* is extreamly diversified ; there are in it a great many *Wars, Manguiers, Mahova,*[7] *Quiesou,*[8] *Caboul,*[9] and other sorts of Trees ; and I saw the *Querzeheray* there also, which I have described in my Book of *Persia.*

Trees. *Wars, Manguiers, Mahova, Quiesou, Caboul. Querzeheray* second Vol.

There are vast numbers of Antelopes, Hairs and Partridges, here and there in that Countrey ; and towards the Mountains *Merous,*[9a] or wild Cows, most part of the Land is arable Ground ; and the Rice (wherewith the Fields are covered) is the best in all the *Indies,* especially towards *Naopoura,*[10] where it has an odoriferous Taste, which that of other Countries has not. Cotton abounds there also, and in many places they have Sugar-Canes, with Mills to bruise the Canes, and Furnaces to boyl the Sugar.

Merous, wild Cows.

Places of Camping on the Road from *Surrat* to *Aurangeabad.*

Barnoly, a Bourg five Leagues from *Surrat. Balor,* a Village, 4 Leag. from *Barnoly. Biaraa,* Village, 3 Leag. and a half from *Balor. Charca* a Village, 2 Leag. and a half from *Biara. Naopoura* a Town, 6 Leag. from *Charca. Quanapour* a Village, 6 Leag. from *Naopoura. Pipelnar* a Town, 6 Leag. from *Quanapour. Tarabat* a Village, 4 Leag. from *Pipelnar. Setana* a Bourg, 4 Leag. and a half from *Tarabat. Omrana* a Village, 5 Leag. and a half from *Setana. Enquitenqui,* 6 Leag. from *Omrana. Deotcham* a Town, 6 Leag. from *Enquitenqui.* The *Sour,* a Town, 6 Leag. from *Deotcham: Aurangeabad,* 8 Leag. from the *Sour.*[11]

Now and then one meets with Hills that are hard to be crossed over, but there are lovely Plains also watered with many Rivers and Brooks. In this Road there are four Towns, and four or five and thirty Bourgs and Villages, pretty well Peopled. *Tchoguis,*[12] or Guards of the High-ways, are often to be met with here, who ask Money of Travellers, though it be not their due ; we gave to some and refused others, but that signifies no great matter in the whole.

In most places Inhabited, there are Pagods, and every now and then, we met with Waggons full of Gentiles, who were coming to perform their Devotions in them. The first Pagod (I saw) was by the side of a great *War ;* and before the Door of it, there was an Ox[13] of Stone, which a Gentile (who spake *Persian*) told me was the Figure of the Ox, which served to carry their God *Ram.* We found besides, many other Pagods like to that, but we saw others, which consisted of one single Stone about six Foot high,[14] on which the Figure of a Man is cut in relief: There are also a great many Reservatories and *Caravanserai* upon the Road, but we chose rather to Encamp, than Lodg in them, because of their nastiness.[15]

An Ox that carried the God *Ram.*

As we were encamped near the Bourg *Setana*[16] under *Manguiers,* not far distant from a small River, which is also called *Setana,* almost mid way betwixt *Surrat* and *Aurangeabad;* we met the Bishop of *Heliopolis,*[17] so much esteemed in the *Indies* for his Piety and Zeal ; he had in company with him Monsieur *Champson,* and a *Spanish Cordelier,* who had left the Bishop of *Barut,*[18] with several other Church-men, who laboured in converting the Gentiles at *Siam.* That Bishop was going to *Surrat,* in order to return to *France,* from whence he hoped to bring back new Missionaries with him ; and the *Cordelier* came from *China,* where he had lived fourteen Years ; we continually met *Caravans* of Oxen and Camels upon our Road, and some I saw that came from *Agra,* consisting of more than a thousand Oxen loaded with Cotton-Cloath. At length, the eleventh of *March* we arrived at *Aurangeabad,* threescore and fifteen Leagues from *Surrat,* which we Travelled in a fortnight.

Setana, a Bourg.

Bishop of *Heliopolis.*

Bishop of *Barut.*

Caravans of above a 1000 Oxen.

Aurangeabad, the Capital of *Balagate.*

This great Town (the Capital of the Province) has no Walls ; the Governour (who is commonly a Prince) has his Residence there, and King *Auran-Zeb* commanded there, as long as he did at *Candich* in the Reign of his Father.[19] His first Wife (whom he loved dearly) died in this Town ;[20] as a Monument to her, he erected a lovely *Mosque,* covered with a Dome, and beautified with four Minarets or Steeples. It is built of a white polished Stone, and many take it for Marble, though it come short of that, both in hardness and lustre. There are several other pretty fair *Mosques*[21] in this Town, and it is not destitute of publick places, *Carvanseras,* and *Bagnios* :[22] The buildings are for the most part of Free-stone, and petty high ; before the

The Sepulchre of *Auran-Zeb's* first Wife.

Doors there are a great many Trees growing in the Streets, and the Gardens are pleasant, and well cultivated, affording the refreshment of Fruit, Grapes, and Grass-plats. They have Sheep there without Horns, that are so strong, as that being Bridled and Saddled, they'll carry Children of ten years of Age up and down, wheresoever they please. This is a Trading Town, and well Peopled, with excellent Ground about it: Though it was but in the beginning of *March*, we found all the Corn cut down. I saw some Apes[23] much esteemed there, which a Man had brought from *Ceilan*: They valued them because they were no bigger than ones Fist, and differed in kind from the common Monkeys; they have a flat Forehead, big round Eyes, which are yellow and clear like the Eyes of some Cats; their Snout is very sharp, and the inside of their Ears yellow; they have no Tail, and their Hair is like to that of other Apes. When I looked upon them, they stood upon their hind Feet, and embraced one another often, eying the People stedfastly without being scared; their Master called them wild Men.

Sheep that are Saddled and Bridled.

Extraordinary Apes.

CHAPTER XLIV

OF THE PAGODS OF ELORA.

The Pagods of *Elora*.

At *Surrat* I was told great matters of the Pagods of *Elora*;[1] and therefore I had a mind to see them, so that so soon as I came to *Aurangeabad*, I sought out for an Interpreter to go along with me; but it being impossible for me to find one, I resolved to take my Servants with me, and make that little Journey alone. And because my Oxen were weary, I hired a little Waggon to carry me thither, and took two *Pions* more besides those I had: I gave all the four, half a Crown Piece, and leaving my Men to look after my Baggage, I parted about nine of the Clock at Night. They told me that there was some danger of meeting Robbers, but being well Armed, (as my Men also were,) I was not much concerned; and I chose rather to run some little risk, than to miss an opportunity of seeing those Pagods, which are so renowned all over the *Indies*: We marched softly[2] because of the unevenness of the Country, and about two of the Clock in the Morning, came near to *Doltabad*,[3] where we rested till five.

We had a rugged Mountain to ascend, and very hard for the Oxen to climb up, though the way cut out of the Rock, be almost every where as smooth, as if it were Paved with Freestone: It had on the side a Wall three Foot thick, and four Foot high, to hinder the Waggons and Chariots from falling down into the Plain, if they chanced to be overthrown. My

A lovely way in a Mountain.

Pions thrust forward the Waggon with all their force, and contributed as much as the Oxen to get it up to the top of the Hill. When I arrived there, I discovered a spacious Plain of well cultivated Land, with a great many Villages, and Bourgs amidst Gardens, plenty of Fruit-trees and Woods: We Travelled at least for the space of an hour over Plow'd Land, where I saw very fair Tombs[4] several stories high, and covered with domes built of large grayish Stones, and about half an hour after seven, having passed by a great *Tanquie*,[5] I alighted near a large Court paved with the same Stones. I went in, but was obliged to put off my Shoes; at first I found a little *Mosque*, where I saw the *Bismillah* of the *Mahometans* writ over the Door; the signification of that Inscription is, *In the Name of God*. There was no light into the *Mosque*, but what entered by that Door; but there were many Lamps burning in it, and several old Men that were there, invited me to come in, which I did. I saw nothing rare in it, but two Tombs covered with Carpet: And I was extreamly troubled for want of an Interpreter, for else I had known a great many particulars, that I could not be informed of.

Fair Tombs at *Elora*.

A large Court in *Elora* where one must put off his Shoes.

A little farther Westward, my *Pions* and I were above half an hour clambering down a Rock, into another very low Plain. The first thing I saw were very high Chappels, and I entered into a Porch cut out of the Rock, which is of a dark grayish Stone, and on each side of that Porch, there is a Gigantick figure of a Man cut out of the natural Rock,[6] and the Walls are covered all over with other figures in relief, cut in the same manner. Having passed that Porch, I found a Square Court,[7] an hundred paces every way: The Walls are the natural Rock, which in that place is six Fathom high, Perpendicular to the Ground-plat, and cut as smooth and even, as if it were Plaster smoothed with a Trewel. Before all things, I resolved to view the outside of that Court, and I perceived that these Walls, or rather the Rock hangs, and that it is hollowed underneath; so that the void space makes a Gallery almost two Fathom high, and four or five broad: It hath the Rock for Ground, and is supported only by a row of Pillars cut in the Rock, and distant from the floor of the Gallery, about the length of a Fathom, so that it appears as if there were two Galleries. Everything there, is extreamly well cut, and it is really, a wonder to see so great a Mass in the Air, which seems so slenderly underpropped, that one can hardly forbear to shiver at first entering into it.

Gigantick Figures of Men cut in the Rock.

A Gallery in the Rock.

Pillars cut in the Rock.

A Mass of Rock in the Air.

In the middle of the Court there is a Chappel, whose Walls inside and outside are covered with figures in relief. They represent several sorts of Beasts, as Griffons, and others cut in the Rock: On each side of the Chappel there is a Pyramide or Obelisk,[8] larger at the Basis than those of *Rome*, but they are

Diverse Antick Figures in a Chappel.

Lovely Pyramides.

not sharp pointed, and are cut out of the very Rock, having some Characters upon them, which I know not. The Obelisk on the left hand, has by it an Elephant as big as the Life, cut out in the Rock, as all the rest is; but his Trunck has been broken. At the farther end of the Court, I found two Stair-cases cut in the Rock, and I went up with a little Bramen, who appeared to have a great deal of Wit: Being at the top, I perceived a kind of Platform, (if the space of a League and a half, or two Leagues, may be called a Platform) full of stately Tombs, Chappels and Temples, which they call Pagods, cut in the Rock. The little Bramen led me to all the Pagods, which the small time I had allowed me to see: With a Cane he shew'd me all the Figures of these Pagods, told me their Names, and by some Indian words which I understood, I perceived very well, that he gave me a short account of the Histories of them; but seeing he understood not the *Persian* Tongue, nor I the *Indian* I could make nothing at all[9] of it.

An Obelisk with an Elephant.

The Pagods of *Elora*.

I entered into a great Temple built in the Rock;[10] it has a flat Roof, and adorned with Figures in the inside, as the Walls of it are: In that Temple there are eight rows of Pillars in length, and six in breadth, which are about a Fathom distant from one another.

A great Temple built in the very Rock.

The Temple is divided into three parts: The Body of it, (which takes up two thirds and a half of the length,) is the first part, and is of an equal breadth all over; the Quire, which is narrower, makes the second part; And the third, which is the end of the Temple, is the least, and looks only like a Chappel; in the middle whereof, upon a very high Basis, there is a Gigantick Idol, with a Head as big as a Drum, and the rest proportionable. All the Walls of the Chappel are covered with Gigantick Figures in relief, and on the outside all round the Temple, there are a great many little Chappels adorned with Figures of an ordinary bigness[11] in relief, representing Men and Women, embracing one another.

A Gigantick Idol.

Figures of Men and Women.

Leaving this place, I went into several other Temples of different structure, built also in the Rock, and full of Figures, Pilasters, and Pillars: I saw three Temples, one over another, which have but one Front all three;[12] but it is divided into three Stories, supported with as many rows of Pillars, and in every Story, there is a great door for the Temple; the Stair-cases are cut out of the Rock. I saw but one Temple that was Arched, and therein I found a Room, whereof the chief Ornament is a square Well, cut in the Rock, and full of Spring-water, that rises within two or three foot of the brim of the Well. There are vast numbers of Pagods all along the Rock, and there is nothing else to be seen for above two Leagues: They are all Dedicated to some Heathen Saints, and the Statue

For above two Leagues there is nothing to be seen but Pagods.

Juggler's feat

of the false Saint, (to which every one of them is Dedicated,) stands upon a Basis at the farther end of the Pagod.

In these Pagods I saw several *Santo's* or *Sogues*[12a] without Cloaths, except on the parts of the Body which ought to be hid: They were all covered with Ashes, and I was told that they let their Hair grow as long as it could. If I could have stayed longer in those quarters, I should have seen the rest of the Pagods, and used so much diligence, as to have found out some body, that might have exactly informed me of every thing; but it behoved me to rest satisfied as to that, with the information I had from the Gentiles of *Aurangeabad,* who upon my return told me, that the constant Tradition was, that all these Pagods, great and small, with their Works and Ornaments, were made by Giants, but that in what time it was not known.[13] **The time when these Pagods were made.**

However it be, if one consider that number of spacious Temples, full of Pillars and Pilasters, and so many thousands of Figures, all cut out of a natural Rock, it may be truly said, that they are Works surpassing humane force; and that at least, (in the Age wherein they have been made,) the Men have not been altogether Barbarous, though the Architecture and Sculpture be not so delicate as with us. I spent only two hours in seeing what now I have described, and it may easily be judged, that I needed several days to have examined all the rarities of that place; but seeing I wanted time, and that it behoved me to make haste, if I intended to find my company still at *Aurangeabad,* I broke off my curiosity, and I must confess it was with regret: I therefore got up into my Waggon again, which I found at a Village called *Rougequi,*[14] from whence I went to *Sultanpoura,*[15] a little Town, the Mosques and Houses whereof are built of a blackish Free-stone, and the Streets paved with the same. Not far from thence I found that so difficult descent, which I mentioned; and at length, after three hours march from the time we left *Elora,* we rested an hour under Trees, near the Walls of *Doltabad,* which I considered as much as I could. **Multitudes of Figures.** ***Rougequi. Sultanpoura.***

CHAPTER XLV

OF THE PROVINCE OF DOLTABAD *AND OF THE FEATS OF AGILITY OF BODY.*

This Town was the Capital of *Balagate,* before it was conquered by the *Moguls*: It belonged then to *Decan,* and was a place of great Trade; but at present the Trade is at *Aurangeabad,* whither King *Auran-Zeb* used his utmost endeavours to transport it, when he was Governour thereof. The Town is **Doltabad.** **Trade transported from**

Doltabad to *Aurangeabad.*

indifferently big[1] it reaches from East to West, and is much longer than broad; it is Walled round with Free-stone, and has Battlements and Towers mounted with Cannon. But though the Walls and Towers be good, yet that is not the thing that makes it accounted the strongest place belonging to the *Mogul*: It is an Hill of an oval Figure, which the Town encompasses on all sides, strongly Fortified, and having a Wall of a natural smooth Rock, that environs it at the bottom, with a good Citadel on the top, whereon the Kings Palace stands. This is all I could see from the place, where I was without the Town: But I learnt afterwards from a Frenchman who had lived two years therein; that besides the Citadel, there are three other Forts in the Place, at the foot of the Hill, of which one is called *Barcot,* the other *Marcot,* and the third *Calacot.*[2] The word *Cot* in Indian, signifies a Fort; and by reason of all these Fortifications, the Indians think that place Impregnable. I spent two hours and a half in coming from *Doltabad* to *Aurangeabad,* which are but two Leagues and a half distant. This was the third time that I crossed this last Town, and about an hour after, I came to the place where my company Encamped: They waited only for a Billet from the Customer, to be gone, but it could not be had that day, because it was *Friday,* and the Customer (who was a *Mahometan*) observed that day with great exactness.

A Hill in *Doltabad* fortified.

Barcot. *Marcot.* *Calacot.*

Calvar.

It is threescore[3] Leagues and more from *Aurangeabad* to *Calvar,*[4] which is the last Bourg or Village belonging to the *Mogul,* on the Frontiers of the Kingdom of *Golconda.* We found eight Towns, great and small, before we came to *Calvar,* to wit, *Ambar, Achty, Lasana, Nander, Lisa, Dantapour, Indour, Condelvaly,* and *Indelvay*;[5] and that Countrey is so Populous, that we continually met with Bourgs and Villages on our way. An hour and an halfs march from *Aurangeabad,* we encamped under the biggest *War*-tree, that I have seen in the Indies: It is exceedingly high, hath some branches ten Fathom long, and the circumference of it, is above three hundred[6] of my paces. The branches of it are so loaded with Pigeons, that it were an easie matter to fill a great many Pigeon-houses with them, if one durst take them; but that is forbidden, because they are preserved for the Prince's pleasure. There is a Pagod under that Tree, and many Tombs, and hard by a Garden planted with Citron-trees.

A fair *War.*

Ambar.

We saw a stately *Tanquie* at the Town of *Ambar,* it is square, and on three sides faced with Free-stone, with fair steps to go down to it: In the middle of the fourth side there is a Divan, that runs out into the Water about two Fathom; it is covered with Stone, and supported by sixteen Pillars a Fathom high: It stands at the foot of a fair House, from whence they go down into that Divan, by two fine pair of Stairs at the sides of it, there to take the Air and Divert themselves. Near the Divan there is a little Pagod under Ground, which receives day-light by the door, and by a square airie, and many Devout People are there,[7] because of the convenience of the Water. On the Road we met with a great many Troopers who were going to *Aurangeabad,* where there was a Rendez-vous appointed for an Army, which was to march against *Viziapour.*[8]

Five Leagues from the Town of *Nander,* near a Village called *Patoda,*[9] we had the Diversion of seeing Feats[10] of Agility of Body:[11] There was a great concourse of People, and we had a place given us, on an Eminence, under the shade of a great Tree, from whence we might easily see all the Plays. The Tumblers did all that the Rope-dancers of *Europe* do, and much more: These People are a supple as an Eel, they'll turn their whole body into a Bowl, and then others rowl[12] them with the hand. The finest tricks were performed by a Girl of thirteen or fourteen years of Age, who Played for the space of two hours and more. This amongst other Feats of Agility which she did, appeared to me extreamly difficult: She sat down upon the Ground, holding cross-ways in her Mouth a long cutting Sword; with the right Hand she took hold of her left Foot, brought it up to her Breast, then to her left side, and without letting go that Foot, she put her Head underneath her right Arm, and at the same time, brought her Foot down along the small of her Back: Then she made it pass under her sitting, and over the right Leg four or five times without resting, being always in danger of cutting her Arm or Leg with the edge of the Sword: And she did the same thing with the left Hand and right Foot.

Nander. Extra-ordinary feats of Agility of Body.

Whilst she was shewing of that trick, they dug a hole in the Ground two foot deep, which they filled with Water. So soon as the Girl had rested a little, they threw into the hole a little Hook made like a Clasp, for her to fetch out with her Nose, without touching it with her Hands: She put her two Feet on the sides of the Pit, and turned her self backwards, upon her two Hands, which she placed on the sides of the hole where her Feet had stood. Then she dived headlong into the Water, to search after the Hook with her Nose: The first time she missed it, but the pit being filled full of Water again, she plunged backwards into it a second time, and upholding her self only with the left hand, she gave a sign with the right hand, that she had found what she sought for, and she raised her self again with the Clasp at her Nose.

Then a Man took this Girl, and setting her upon his Head, ran at full speed through the place, she in the mean time not tottering in the least: Setting her down, he took a large Earthen pot, like to those round Pitchers that the Indian Maids make use to draw Water in; and put it upon his Head with the mouth upwards. The Girl got on the top of it, and he carried her about the place with the same security, as he had done without the Pot; Which he did twice more, having put the Pot with the mouth downwards once, and then with the mouth side-ways. The same trick he shewed in a Bason wherein he turned the Pot three different ways: Then he took the Bason and turned its bottom up upon his Head, with the Pitcher over it. The Girl shewed the same tricks upon it. And at length, having put into the Bason upon his Head, a little wooden Truncheon a foot high, and as big as ones Arm, he caused the Girl to be set upright upon that Stake, and carried her about as before; sometimes she only stood upon one Foot, taking the other in her Hand; and sometimes she hurkled down upon her Heels, nay, and sat down, though the carrier in the mean time, went on as formerly. Then the Man took the Bason[13] from under the Stake, and put it on the top of it, where the Girl likewise appeared: Then changeing the Play, he put into the Boson four Pins, or little Stakes of Wood, four Inches high, set square-ways with a Board upon each of them, two Fingers breadth, and upon these Boards four other Pins or little Stakes, with as many Boards more, making in all, two Stories over the Bason, supported with the great Stake or Pillar: And that Girl getting upon the upper Story, he ran with her through the place with the same swiftness as at other times, she not appearing in the least, afraid of falling, though the Wind was high. These People shew'd a hundred other tricks of Agility, which I shall not describe, that I may not be tedious; only I must say, that the finest I saw Acted, were performed by Girls. We gave them at parting three *Roupies,* for which they gave us a thousand Blessings: We sent for them at Night to our Camp, where they diverted us again, and gained two *Roupies* more.

Ila a Town. *Indour* a Town.

From thence we went to the Towns of *Ila* and *Dentapour,* and some days after we arrived at *Indour,*[14] which belongs to a *Raja,* who owns the *Mogul* no more than he thinks fit: He is maintained by the King of *Golconda,*[15] and in time of War, he sides always with the strongest. He would have had us pay two *Roupies* a Waggon; but after much dispute, we payed but one, and passed on. We came before a Village called *Bisetpoury*;[16] and being informed, that near to that place, on the top of a Hill, there was a very fair Pagod, we alighted and went on Foot to see it.

CHAPTER XLVI

OF CHITANAGAR.

That Pagod is called *Chitanagar*[1]: It is an oblong square Temple, forty five Paces in length, twenty eight in breadth, and three Fathom high; it is built of a Stone of the same kind as the *Theban*. It hath a Basis five Foot high all round, charged[2] with Bends and Wreaths, and adorned with Roses and Notchings, as finely cut, as if they had been done in *Europe*. It hath a lovely frontispiece, with its Architrave, *Cornish* and *Fronton*; and is Beautified with Pillars, and lovely Arches,[3] with the Figures of Beasts in relief, and some with Figures of Men. Then we viewed the inside; the contrivance of that Temple is like that of *Elora*, it hath a Body, a Quire,[4] and a Chappel at the end. I could perceive nothing in the Body and Quire, but the four Walls; though the Lustre of the Stones they are built of, renders the prospect very agreeable: The Floor is of the same Stone, and in the middle of it there is a great Rose well cut. This place like the other Pagods, receives light only by the door: On each side of the Wall of the Quire, there is square hole a foot large, which slopes like a Port-hole for a Piece of Od'nance, and in the middle of the thickness of it, a long Iron skrew, as big as ones Leg, which enters Perpendicularly into the Wall like a Bar, and I was informed, that these Irons served to fasten Ropes to, for supporting of those who performed voluntary Abstinence for seven days or longer. In the middle of the Chappel at the end, there is an Altar of the same Stone as the Walls are of; it is cut into several Stories, and Adorned all over with Indentings, Roses, and other Embellishments of Architecture, and on each side below, there are three Elephants Heads. There hath been a Pedestal prepared of the same Stone the Altar is of, to set the Idol of the Pagod upon; but seeing the building was not finished, the Idol hath not been set up.

The Pagod of *Chitanagar*.

The fair Temple of *Chitanagar*.

The Architecture of the Temple of *Chitanagar*.

The contrivance of the Temple of *Chitanagar*.

A Place for Penance.

When I came down, I perceived at the foot of the Hill, on the East side, a building, which I was not told of; I went thither alone with my *Pions*, but found nothing but the beginnings of a Palace, the Walls whereof were of the same Stone as the Pagod. The Threshold of each Door is of one piece of Stone, a Fathom and a half long: It is all Built of very great Stones, and I measured one of them, that was above four Fathom long. Near to that Building, there is a Reservatory as broad as the *Seine* at *Paris*; but so long, that from the highest place I went to, I could not discover the length of it. In that Reservatory, there is another little Tanquie, seven or eight Fathom square, and Walled in: This Water bring below the House, there is a large pair of Stairs to go down to it; and

A fair Building near *Chitanagar*.

A very great Reservatory.

about an hundred and fifty paces forward, in the great Reservatory opposite to the House, there is a square Divan or *Quiochque,* about eight or ten Fathom wide, the Pavement whereof is raised about a foot above the Water. That Divan is built and covered with the same Stone, that the House is built of: It stands upon sixteen Pillars, a Fathom and a half high, that's to say, each Front on four.

The Architecture of *Chitanagar* of a very good contrivance. *Chita.* Encampings upon the Road from *Aurangeabad* to *Calvar.*

Seeing my Company kept on their March, I spent but half an hour in viewing that Building, which very well deserves many, as well for examining the design of it, the nature of the Stones, their Cut, Polishing and Bigness; as for considering the Architecture, which is of a very good contrivance,[5] and though it cannot absolutely be said to be of any of our Orders, yet it comes very near the Dorick. The Temple and Palace are called *Chitanagar,* that is to say, the Lady *Chita,* because the Pagod is Dedicated to *Chita* the Wife of *Ram*: I learnt that both had been begun by a Rich *Raspoute,* who dying, left the Temple and House imperfect. After all, I observed, as well in the Ancient, as Modern Buildings of the *Indies,* that the Architectors make the Basis, Body, and Capital of their Pillars, of one single piece.

Tchequel Cane.

Tchequel Cane Leag. and a half from *Aurangeabad.* *Ambar* a Town, *Rovilag-herd* 6 Leag. from *Tchequel-Cane.* *Dabolquera* 5 Leag. from *Rovilag-herd.* *Achti* a Town, 8 Leag. from *Dabolquera.* *Manod* 6 Leag. from *Achti.* *Parboni* a Town, 5 Leag. from *Manod.* *Pournanadi* a River. *Lazana* a Town, 6 Leag. from *Parboni.* *Nander* a Town, 5 Leag. from *Lazana.* *Guenga Ganges* a River, *Patoda* a Town, 5 Leag. from *Nander,* *Condelvai* 9 Leag. from *Patoda.* *Mandgera* a River. *Lila* a Town. *Dentapour* a Town. *Indore* a Town, 9 Leag. from *Condelvai.* Coulan a River. *Indelvai* a Town, 4 leag. from *Indour.* *Calvar* 4 Leag. from *Indelvai.*[6]

We past next by the Town of *Indelvai,* of which nothing is to be said in particular, but that a great many Swords, Daggers, and Lances are made there, which are vended all over the *Indies,* and that the Iron is taken out of a Mine near the Town,[7] in the Mountain of *Calagatch.*[8] The Town (at that time,) was almost void of Inhabitants, for they were gone farther up into the Country, because of the Brother of *Sivagy,*[9] who made inrodes to the very Town. We Encamped beyond *Indelvai,* and next day being the six and twentieth of March, (having after four hours March passed over the pleasantest Hills in the World, by reason of the different kinds of Trees that cover them,) we arrived at *Calvar* which is the last Village of the *Moguls* Countrey. It is distant from *Aurangeabad,* about fourscore and three Leagues, which we Travelled in a fortnights time.

The rest of the Road to *Golconda* I shall describe, when I treat of that Kingdom. The way from *Aurangeabad,* that I have been now speaking of, is diversified by Hills and

Plains: All the Plains are good Ground, some sow'd with Rice, and the rest planted with Cotton-trees. *Tamarins, Wars, Cadjours, Manguiers, Quesous,* and others; and all Watered with several Rivers, which turn and wind every way, and with *Tanquies* also, out of which they draw the Water by Oxen: And I saw one of these Reservatories at *Dentapour,* which is a Musquet-shot over, and seven or eight hundred Geometrical paces long. We were incommoded during our whole Journey almost with Lightenings, Whirle-winds, Rains, and Hail-stones, some as big as a Pullets Egg;[10] and when we were troubled with none of these, we heard dull Thunderings, that lasted whole Days and Nights. We met every where Troops of Horse designed against *Viziapour,* the King whereof, refused to send the *Great Mogul,* the Tribute which he used to pay to him.

Very large Hail-stones.

The *Moguls* Horse against *Viziapour.*

To conclude with this Province, it is to be observed, that all the Rocks and Mountains I have mentioned, are only dependances of that Mountain which is called *Balagate,* which according to the *Indian* Geographers, divides *India* into the two parts of North and South,[11] as that of *Guate,* according to the same Geographers, environs it almost on all hands.

The Mountain of *Balagate.*

CHAPTER XLVII

OF THE PROVINCE OF TELENGA.

Telenga[1] was heretofore the principal Province of *Decan,* and reached as far as the *Portuguese* Lands towards *Goa,*[2] *Viziapour* being the Capital City thereof: But since the *Mogul* became Master of the Northern places of this Countrey, and of the Towns of *Beder*[3] and *Calion,*[4] it hath been divided betwixt him and the King of *Decan,* who is only called King of *Viziapour,* and it is reckoned amongst the Provinces of *Indostan,* which obey the *Great Mogul.* It is bordered on the East by the Kingdom of *Golconda* on *Maslipatan* side, on the West by the Province of *Baglana* and *Viziapour,* on the North by *Balagate,* and on the South by *Bisnagar.*[5] The Capital City of this Province is at present *Beder,* which belonged to *Balagate* when it had Kings and it hath sometime belonged to *Decan.*

The Province of *Telenga.*

Calion.

The borders of *Telenga.*

Beder is a great Town;[6] it is encompassed with Brick-Walls which have Battlements, and at certain distances Towers; they are mounted with great Cannon, some whereof have the mouth three Foot wide. There is commonly in this place a Garison of Three thousand Men, half Horse and half Foot, with Seven hundred Gunners; the Garison is kept in good order, because of the importance of the place against *Decan,* and that they are always afraid of a surprize. The Governour lodges in a

Beder.

Great Guns. The Garison of *Beder.*

Castle without the Town,[7] it is a rich Government, and he who commanded it when I was there, was Brother-in-law to King *Chagean, Auran-Zebs* Father ;[7a] but having since desired the Government of *Brampour,* (which is worth more) he had it, because in the last War, that Governour had made an Army of the King of *Viziapours,* raise the Siege from before *Beder.*

The Train of the Governour of *Beder.*

Some time after, I met the new Governour upon the Road to *Beder,* who was a *Persian* of a good aspect, and pretty well stricken in years ; he was carried in a *Palanquin* amidst Five hundred Horse-men well mounted and cloathed, before whom marched several Men on foot, carrying blew Banners charged with flames of Gold, and after them came seven Elephants. The Governours *Palanquin* was followed with several others full of Women, and covered with red Searge, and there were two little Children in one that was open. The *Bambous* of all these *Palanquin,* were covered with Plates of Silver chamfered ; after them came many Chariots full of Women, two of which were drawn by white Oxen, almost six Foot high ; and last of all, came the Waggons with the Baggage, and several Camels guarded by Troopers. This Province of *Telenga* is worth above Ten millions a Year to the *Great Mogul.*

The *Great Moguls* Revenue in *Telenga.*

No where are the Gentiles more Superstitious than here ; they have a great many Pagods with Figures of Monsters, that can excite nothing but Horror instead of Devotion, unless in those who are deluded with the Religion. These Idolaters use frequent Washings ; Men, Women and Children go to the River as soon as they are out of Bed ; and the rich have Water brought them to wash in. When Women lose their Husbands, they are conducted thither by their Friends, who comfort them ; and they who are brought to Bed, use the same custom, almost as soon as they are delivered of their Children, and indeed, there is no Countrey where Women are so easily brought to Bed ; when they come out of the Water, a *Bramen* dawbs their Forehead with a Composition made of Saffron, and the Powder of white Sawnders[8] dissolved in Water, then they return home, where they eat a slight Breakfast ; and seeing they must never eat unless they be washed, some return to the *Tanquie* or River, about noon ; and others perform their Ablutions at home, before they go to Dinner.

The washings of the Gentiles.

The feeding of the Gentiles.

As they have a special care not to eat any thing but what is dressed by a Gentile of their Caste, so they seldom eat any where but at home, and commonly they dress their Victuals themselves, buying their Flower, Rice, and such other Provisions in the Shops of the *Banians,* for they'll not buy any where else.

The Diet of some Castes.

These *Banians* (as well as the *Bramens* and *Courmis*) feed on Butter, Pulse, Herbs, Sugar and Fruit ; they eat neither Fish nor Flesh, and drink nothing but Water, wherein they put Coffee and Tea; they use no dishes, for fear some body of another Religion or Tribe, may have made use of the Dish, out of which they might eat; and to supply that, they put their Victuals into large Leaves of Trees, which they throw away when they are empty, nay, there are some of them who eat alone, and will not suffer neither their Wives nor Children at Table with them.

Nevertheless, I was informed, that in that Countrey one certain day of the year, the *Bramens* eat Hogs Flesh;[9] but they do it privately for fear of Scandal, because the Rules of their Sect enjoyn[9a] them so to do, and I believe it is the same all over the *Indies*. The *Bramens* sometimes eat Hogs Flesh.

There is another day of rejoycing, whereon they make a Cow of Paste, which they fill full of Honey, and then make a fashion of killing it, and break it to pieces; the Honey which distills on all sides, represents the Blood of the Cow, and they eat the Paste instead of the Flesh. I could not learn the Original of that Ceremony; as for the *Catris* or *Raspoutes*, except that they eat no Pullets, they (as the rest of the inferiour Castes do) make use of all kinds of Fish and Flesh, unless it be the Cow, which they all have in veneration. A Cow of Paste.

The Gentiles generally are great Fasters,[10] and none of them let a fortnight pass over without mortifying themselves by Abstinence, and then they Fast four and twenty hours; but that is but the ordinary Fast, for there are a great many Gentiles (and especially Women) who will fast six or seven days;[11] and they say, there are some that will Fast a whole month, without eating any more than a handful of Rice a day, and others that will eat nothing at all, only drink Water, in which they boyl a Root, called *Criata*,[12] which grows towards *Cambaye*, and is good against many distempers; it makes the Water bitter, and strengthens the Stomach. When a Woman is at the end of one of these long Fasts, the *Bramen* her director, goes with his companions to the House of the penitent, beats a Drum there, and having permitted her to eat, returns home again. There are such Fasts many times among the *Vartias*, the *Sogues*, and other religious Gentiles of that Province, and they accompany them with several other mortifications. The Gentiles Fasting. *Criata*, a Root.

Now I have mentioned these Religious Gentiles, I would have it observed, that in all the *Indies* there is no religious Community amongst the Gentiles, belonging particularly to one Caste or Tribe: For Example, There is not any, whereinto none are admitted but *Bramens* or *Raspoutes*; if there be a convent of *Sogues* any where, the Community will consist of *Bramens*, *Raspoutes*, *Comris*, *Banians* and other Gentiles; and it is the same in a convent of *Vartias*, or a company of *Faquirs*. I have already treated of both these, as occasion offered. Religious Communities.

CHAPTER XLVIII

OF THE PROVINCE OF BAGLANA, *AND OF THE MARRIAGES OF THE GENTILES.*

The yearly Revenue of *Baglana*.

The Province of *Baglana*[1] is neither so large, nor do's it yield so great a Revenue as the other nineteen ; for it pays the *Great Mogul* a year but Seven hundred and fifty thousand *French* Livres ; it is bordered by the Countrey of *Telenga*, *Guzerat*, *Balagate*, and the Mountains of *Sivagi* ; the Capital Town of it is called *Mouler*.[2] Before the *Moguls*, this Province was also of *Decan*, and at present it belongs to *Mogolistan* ; by it the *Portuguese* border upon the *Moguls* Countrey, and their Territories begin in the Countrey of *Daman*.

Mouler. The *Portuguese* border on the *Moguls* Countrey.

Daman.

The Town of *Daman*[3] that belongs to them, is one and twenty Leagues from *Surrat*, which is commonly Travelled in three days. It is indifferently big,[4] fortified with good Walls, and an excellent Citadel ; the Streets of it are fair and large, and the Churches and Houses built of a white Stone, which makes it a pleasant Town. There are several Convents of Religious Christians in it ; it depends on *Goa*, as the other *Portuguese* Towns do, especially as to Spirituals, and the Bishop keeps a Vicar General there. It lies at the entry of the Gulf of *Cambaye* ; and the *Portuguese* have Slaves there of both Sexes,[5] which work and procreate only for their Masters, to whom the Children belong, to be disposed of at their pleasure ; from *Daman* to *Bassaim* it is eighteen Leagues : This last Town lies in the height of about nineteen Degrees and a half, (upon the Sea,) being Walled round, and almost as big as *Daman* ; it hath Churches, and a College of Jesuits as *Daman* hath.

Portuguese slaves.

Bassaim.

From *Bassaim* to *Bombaim*,[6] it is six Leagues ; this last Town hath a good Port, and was by the *Portuguese* made over to the *English*, upon the Marriage of the *Infanta* of *Portugal* with the King of *England*, in the year 1662 ; it is six Leagues more from *Bombaim* to *Chaoul*. The Port of *Chaoul* is difficult to enter, but very safe and secure from all foul weather ; it is a good Town, and defended by a strong Citadel upon the top of a Hill, called by the *Europeans*, *Il Morro di Ciaul* ;[7] it was taken by the *Portuguese*, in the year One thousand five hundred and seven.

Bombaim made over to the *English*.

Chaoul.

Il Morro di Ciaul

Dabul.

From *Chaoul* to *Dabul*,[8] it is eighteen good Leagues. *Dabul* is an ancient Town, in the Latitude of seventeen degrees and a half ; it has its Water from a Hill hard by, and the Houses of it are low, it being but weakly fortified ; I am told *Sivagi* hath seized it,[9] notwithstanding its Castle, as also *Rajapour*, *Vingourla*, *Rasigar*,[10] and some other places upon that coast of *Decan*. It is almost fifty Leagues from *Dabul* to *Goa*, which is in *Viziapour*.

Rajapour, *Vingourla*, *Rasigar* Towns.

As all the People of that coast are much given to Seafaring, so the Gentiles offer many times Sacrifices to the Sea, especially when any of their Kindred or Friends are abroad upon a Voyage. Once I saw that kind of Sacrifice, a Woman carried in her hands a Vessel made of Straw, about three Foot long, it was covered with a Vail ;[11] three Men playing upon the Pipe and Drum accompanied her, and two others had each on their head a Basket full of Meat and Fruits ; being come to the Sea-side, they threw into the Sea the Vessel of Straw, after they had made some Prayers, and left the Meat they brought with them upon the Shoar, that the poor and others might come and eat it. I have seen the same Sacrifice performed by *Mahometans*. Sacrifice to the Sea.

The Gentiles offer another at the end of September,[12] and that they call to open the Sea, because no body can Sail upon their Seas from May till that time ; but that Sacrifice is peformed with no great Ceremonies, they only throw *Coco's* into the Sea and every one throws one. The only thing in that Action that is pleasant, is to see all the young Boys leap into the Water to catch the *Coco's ;* and whilst they strive to have and keep them, shew a hundred tricks and feats of Agility. Opening of the Sea.

In this Province (as in the rest of *Decan*) the *Indians* Marry their Children very young, and make them Cohabit much sooner that they do in many places of the Indies ; they Celebrate Matrimony at the Age of four, five or six Years, and suffer them to bed together when the Husband is ten Years old, and the Wife eight ;[13] but the Women who have Children so young, soon leave off Child-bearing, and commonly do not conceive after thirty Years of Age, but become extreamly wrinkly ; and therefore there are places in the *Indies* where the young Married couple are not suffered to lye together before the Man be fourteen Years old : After all,[14] a Gentile marries at any Age, and cannot have several Wives at a time as the *Mahometans* have ;[14a] when his Wife dies, he may take another, and so successively, provided she he takes be a Maid, and of his own Caste. The Marriage of Children. An *Indian* cannot have several Wives at a time.

There are many Ceremonies to be seen at the Weddings in *Indostan,*[15] because the Gentiles are numerous there ; there are certain times (when in great Towns) Five or six hundred are Celebrated a day, and nothing is to be seen in the Streets but Inclosures ; these Wedding Inclosures are just as big as the Front of the Husbands House to the Street, they are made of Poles and Canes hung in the inside, and covered with Tapistry or Cloaths, to preserve the Guests from the heat of the Sun, and there they feast and make merry. Great numbers of Marriages in *Indostan*. Wedding inclosures.

But before the Wedding Feast, they must make the usual Cavalcade through the Town ; Persons of Quality perform it in the manner I described in the Chapter of *Surrat,* and the Citizens with far less Pomp. This is their custom, First appear The Cavalcade of the Wedding.

a great many People playing on Instruments, some on Flutes, others on Timbals, and some have a long kind of Drums like narrow Barrels, which hang about their Neck; and besides these, others hold Copper-cups, which they strike one against another, and thereby render a very bad Harmony; though these Instruments together make a great noise, several little Boys of five, six or seven years of Age, come after on Horse-back, and Children two or three years Old in little Chariots, about a Foot high, or somewhat more, drawn by Goats or Calves and after them, the Husband appears upon the fairest Horse he can have, with a *Coco* in his hand; he is Cloathed in his best Apparel, his head covered with a Garland of Flowers, or a Cap in form of a Mitre, adorned with Painters Gold, and a Fringe that reaches down to the lower part of his Face; he hath about him a great many *Banians* on Foot, who have their Coif and *Caba* dawbed over with Saffron, and are mingled with those that carry *Umbrella's* and *Banners*, who make a great shew with them; after the bridegroom hath in this equipage made many turns about the Town, he goes to the House of his Bride, and there the Ceremony is performed.

The Ceremonies of the Marriage.

A *Bramen* having said some Prayers over both, puts a Cloath betwixt the Husband and the Wife, and orders the Husband with his naked foot to touch the naked foot of his Wife, and that Ceremony compleats the Marriage, the Consummation whereof is delayed till a competent Age, if the Parties be too young, after that, the Bride is conducted with her Face uncovered to the Bride-grooms Lodgings; her Train (which consists of several pieces of Stuff of different Colours,) is carried by Men; and amongst other pieces of Houshold Furniture,[16] they carry a Cradle for the Child that is to be born of that Marriage, Drums and Trumpets going before all the Procession. The rich make their Cavalcades by Torch-light in the night time for greater State, and are better accompanied. When they come to the Bride-grooms House, the Feasting begins, and because the Husbands are obliged to treat most of their Caste, the Solemnity lasts seven or eight days.

Women of the *Indies* fruitful.

They are easily brought to bed.

The Women all over the *Indies* are fruitful, because they live very frugally as well as their Husbands, and they are so easily brought to Bed, that some of them go abroad the same day they have been Delivered, to wash themselves in the River. Their Children are brought up with the same facility; they go naked till they be seven Years old, and when they are two or three Months old, they suffer them to crawl upon the ground till they be able to go;[17] when they are dirty they wash them, and by degrees they come to walk as streight as ours do, without the torture of Swathing-bands or Clouts.

Sati

CHAPTER XLIX

OF THE USAGE OF THE DEAD.

The *Indian* Wives have a far different fate from that of their Husbands, for they cannot provide themselves of a second, when their first Husband is dead ; they dare not Marry again, they have their Hair cut off for ever after ;[1] and though they be but five or six years old (they are obliged) if they will not burn themselves, to live in perpetual Widowhood, which happens very often ; but then they live wretchedly, for they incur the contempt of their Family and Caste, as being afraid of death ; what Vertue soever they make appear, they, can never regain the esteem of their Relations, and it is rare (though they be young and beautiful,) that they ever find another Husband ; not but that some of them transgress the Law of Widowhood, but they are turned out of the Tribe when it comes to be known ; and such of them as are resolved to Marry again, have recourse to the Christians or Mahometans, and then they forsake Gentilisme. In fine, The Gentiles make the glory of Widowhood, to consist in being burnt with the Bodies of their Husbands ;[2] when one asks them the cause of it, they say it is the custom ; they pretend it was always so in the Indies, and so they hide their cruel Jealousie under the vail of Antiquity. When a Heathen Man or Woman has committed a sin that makes them be expelled the Caste, as if a Woman had lay'n with a *Mahometan,* she must (if she would be readmitted into the Tribe) live upon nothing for a certain time, but on the Grain that is found amongst Cow-dung.

The Widowhood of the Women.

The glory of Widowhood consists in being burnt with their Husbands.

Penance for a Heathen Woman who hath sinned.

The most usual way of ordering the Bodies of Men, after their death in the *Indies,* is to wash them in the water of a River or Reservatory, near to which there is a Pagod, then to burn them, and throw the Ashes into the same water ; in some Countries they leave them upon the brink of the River, but the Ceremony of burying differs according to places ; in some places the Body is carried, (with beat of Drum) sitting uncovered in a Chair, cloathed in goodly Apparel, and accompanied with his Relations and Friends ; and after the usual Ablution, it is surrounded with Wood and his Wife who hath followed in triumph, hath her Seat prepared there, where she places herself Singing, and seeming very desirous to die : A *Bramen* ties her to a Stake that is in the middle of the Funeral Pile, and sets Fire to it ; the Friends pour odoriferous Oyles into it, and in a short time both the Bodies are consumed.

The ordering of dead Bodies.

Funerals differ according to places.

The way of burning the dead Husband with the living Wife.

In other places the Bodies are carried to the River-side in a covered Liter, and being washed, they are put into a hutt full of odoriferous Wood, if they who are dead have left enough to defray the Charges. When the Wife (who is to be burnt) hath

A Woman that endeavours to shew a fearlessness before she is burnt.

taken leave of her kindred, and by such Galantries as may convince the Assembly, (which many times consists of the whole Caste,) that she is not at all afraid of dying ; she takes her place in the Hutt under the head of her Husband, which she holds upon her knees, and at the same time recommending her self to the Prayers of the *Bramen,* she presses him to set fire to the Pile, which he fails not to do.

Pits, wherein the Bodies of the Husband and Wife are burnt.

Elsewhere they make wide and deep Pits, which they fill with all sorts of combustible Matter ; they throw the Body of the deceased into it, and then the *Bramens* push in the Wife after she hath Sung and Danced, to shew the firmness of her resolution ; and sometimes it happens, that Maid-Slaves throw themselves into the same Pit after their Mistresses, to shew the love they bore to them, and the Ashes of the burnt Bodies are afterwards scattered in the River.

Interment of Bodies.

In the other Places, the Bodies of the dead are interred with their Legs a cross ; their Wives are put into the same Grave alive, and when the Earth is filled up to their neck, they are strangled by the *Bramens.*[3]

There are several other kinds of Funerals among the Gentiles of the *Indies,* but the madness of the Women in being burnt with their Husbands, is so horrid, that I desire to be excused that I write no more of it.

Mahometanisme in the *Indies* is a happiness for the Women.

To conclude, the Women are happy that the *Mahometans* are become the Masters in the *Indies,* to deliver them from the tyranny of the *Bramens,*[4] who always desire their death, because these Ladies being never burnt without all their Ornaments of Gold and Silver about them, and none but they having power to touch their Ashes ; they fail not to pick up all that is pretious from amongst them. However, the *Great Mogul* and other *Mahometan* Princes, having ordered their Governours to employ all their care in suppressing that abuse, as much as lies in their power, it requires at present great Solicitations and considerable Presents, for obtaining the permission of being Burnt ; so that the difficulty they meet with in this, secures a great many Women from the infamy they would incur in their Caste, if they were not forced to live by a Superior Power.

The *Mahometan* Governours endeavour to hinder the burning of the *Indian* Women.

The end of *Mogolistan.*

THE

THIRD PART

OF THE

TRAVELS

OF

Mr. De THEVENOT

BOOK II

OF THE INDIES.

CHAPTER I

OF DECAN *AND* MALABAR.

Decan[1] was heretofore a most powerful Kingdom, if one may believe the *Indians ;* it consisted of all the Countries that are in that great Tongue of Land, which is betwixt the Gulfs of *Cambaye* and *Bengala,* all obeyed the same King ; nay, and the Provinces of *Balagate, Telenga* and *Baglana,* which are towards the North, were comprehended within it, so that it may be said, that at that time there was no King in the *Indies* more powerful than the King of *Decan ;* but that Kingdom in process of time hath been often dismembred ; and in the beginning of the last Age, (when the *Portuguese* made Conquests therein) it was divided into many Provinces,[2] for they found there the Kings of *Calecut,*[3] *Cochin,*[4] *Cananor*[5] and *Coulam*[6] upon the Coast of *Malabar.*[7] Another King Reigned at *Narsingue,*[8] there were some Common-wealths in it also ; and the Dominions of him[9] (who was called King of *Decan*) reached no further than from the limits of the Kingdom of *Cambaye* or *Guzerat,* to the borders of the principality of *Goa,* which did not belong to him neither.

Decan hath been a great Kingdom.

The Arrival of the Portuguese in the Indies.

Calecut was the first place of the *Indies,* which the *Portuguese* discovered in the year One thousand four hundred and ninety eight, under the conduct of *Vasco de Gama.*[10] The King of *Calecut,* who at first received them friendly, would at length, have destroyed them, at the instigation of *Arabian* Merchants, and the greatest Wars they had in the *Indies,* was against that King. The King of *Cochin* made Alliance with

Calecut.

them, and the Kings of *Cananor* and *Coulam* invited them to come and Trade with them.

Malabar.

Malabar (which is the Countrey of all these Kings) begins at *Cananor,* and ends at Cape *Comory ;* the most powerful of all these Princes, was the King of *Calecut,* who took the Quality of *Samorin* or Emperour.[11] The Port of *Calecut,* lying in the Latitude of eleven degrees twenty two minutes,[12] is at some distance from the Town ; before the coming of the *Portuguese,* it was the most considerable Port of the *Indies* for Commerce, and Ships came thither from all parts. The Town has no Walls, because there is no ground for laying a Foundation upon, for water appears as soon as they begin to digg. There are no good Buildings in *Calecut,* but the Kings Palace and some Pagods ; the Houses joyn not,[13] they have lovely Gardens, and of all things necessary for life, there is plenty in that Town.

Samorin, or Emperour.

The Town of *Calecut.*

Cochin. King of *Cochin.*

The King of *Cochin* was a most faithful Friend to the Portuguese,[14] for, for their sake he was deprived of his Kingdom by the King of *Calecut ;* but they restored him, and gained so much upon him, that he gave them leave to build a Fort in that part of the Town, which is called *Lower-Cochin* upon the Sea side, to distinguish it from the *Higher-Cochin* where the King resides, and from which it is distant a quarter of a League. The *Portuguese* have held that Fort a long time, but three or four years since, it was taken from them by the *Dutch.*[15]

The Fort of *Cochin,* taken from the *Portuguese* by the *Dutch.*

The Port of *Cochin.*

The Port of *Cochin* is very good, there is six Fathom water close by the Shoar, and upon a Planc one may easily come from on Board the Vessels. The Town of *Cochin* is about thirty six Leagues from *Calecut ;* it is watered by a River,[16] and there is plenty of Pepper in the Countrey about it,[17] which is fruitful in nothing else. There are People in that Countrey who have Legs like an Elephant,[18] and I saw a Man at *Cochin* with such a Leg ; the Son Inherits not after his Father, because a Woman is allowed by the custom to lye with several Men, so that it cannot be known who is the Father of the Child she brings forth ; and for Successions, the Child of the Sister is preferred, because there is no doubt of the Line by the Female. The Sisters (even of the Kings themselves) have liberty to chuse such *Nairs*[19] or Gentlemen as they please to lye with ; and when a *Nair* is in a Ladies Chamber, he leaves his Stick or Sword at the Door, that others (who have a mind to come) should know that the place is taken up, no body offers to come in then: And this custom is Establish'd all over *Malabar.*[20]

Abundance of Pepper at *Cochin.*

A Man with a leg like an Elephant.

Succession in *Malabar.*

The Women have liberty to chuse their Galants.

The Coronation of the King of *Cochin.*

Heretofore the King of *Cochin* was Crowned upon the Coast, though it was possest by the *Portuguese ;* but he who ought now to be King, would not be Crowned there, because it is in the power of the *Dutch:*[21] And he made them answer, when they invited him to follow the Custom, that he would have nothing to do with them ; and that when the *Portuguese* were restored to the possession of that coast, he would be Crowned there. In the meane time the *Dutch* have Crowned another Prince,[22] who is the Kings Kinsman, and have given him the Title of *Samorin* or Emperour, which the King of *Calecut* pretends to.

The true King of *Cochin* is retired to *Tanor*,[23] which is the first Principality of his House, to the Prince of *Tanor* his Uncle, eight Leagues from *Cochin*. They Sail from one Town to the other in little Barks, upon a pretty pleasant River. *Tanor.*

These *Naires* or Gentlemen we have been speaking of, have a great conceit of their Nobility, because they fancy themselves descended from the Sun ;[24] they give place to none but the *Portuguese*, and that precedency cost Blood. The *Portuguese* General (to compose the Debates that happened often betwixt them) agreed with the King of Cochin, that the Matter should be decided by a duel of two Men, and that if the *Naire* had the better on't, the *Portuguese* should give place to the *Naires* ; or if the contrary happened, the *Naires* should allow the *Portuguese* the advantage for which they fought, and the *Naire* being overcome, the *Portuguese* take place of the *Naires* ; they go stark naked from the girdle upwards, and have no other Clothing from the girdle to the knee, but a piece of Cloath ; their head is covered with a Turban, and they carry always a naked Sword and a Buckler. The *Naire* Women are cloathed like the Men, and the Queen her self is in no other dress.[25] The *Naires* have several degrees of Nobility amongst them, and the inferior make no difficulty to give place to those that are above them. The *Naires.* A duel betwixt a *Portuguese* and a *Naire* for the place. The Apparel of the *Naires.*

They have a great aversion to a Caste of Gentiles, who are called *Poleas*.[26] If a *Naire* come so near a *Poleas* as to have felt his breath, he thinks himself polluted,[27] and is obliged to kill him ; because if he killed him not, and it came to the Kings knowledge, he would cause the *Naire* to be put to death, or if he pardoned him as to life, he would order him to be sold for a Slave ; but besides that, he must make publick Ablutions with great Ceremonies. *Poleas.*

For avoiding any mischance that may happen upon that account, The *Poleas* cry incessantly when they are abroad in the Fields *Popo*,[28] to give notice to the *Naires* who may be there, not to come near. If a *Naire* hear the word *Popo*, he answers (crying) *Coucouya*,[29] and then the *Poleas* knowing that there is a *Naire* not far from him, turns aside out of the way, that he may not meet him. Seeing these *Poleas* cannot enter into Town, if any of them need any thing, they are obliged to ask for it without the Town, crying as loud as they can, and leaving Money for it in a place appointed for that Traffick ; when they have left it and told so, they are to withdraw, and a Merchant fails not to bring what they demand ; he *Popo.* *Coucouya.* The *Poleas* cannot enter into Towns.

takes the true value of his Commodity, and so soon as he is gone, the *Poleas* comes and takes it, and so departs.

No *Cavalrie* in *Cochin.*

Cavalrie are not used in the Wars, neither in *Cochin,* nor the rest of *Malabar;* they that are to fight otherwise than on Foot, are mounted upon Elephants, of which there are many in the Mountains, and these Mountain-Elephants are the biggest of the *Indies.* The Idolaters tell a false story at *Cochin,* which they would have no body to doubt of, because of the extraordinary respect they have for a certain Reservatory, which is in the middle of one of their Pagods. This great Pagod stands upon the side of a River, called by the *Portuguese Rio Largo,*[30] which runs from *Cochin* to *Cranganor,* it goes by the name of the Pagod of Swearing; and they say, that the Reservatory or *Tanquie,* which is in that Temple, has Communication under ground with the River, and that when any one was to make Oath judicially about a matter of importance, he that was to Swear, was brought to the *Tanquie,* where a Crocodile was called upon,[31] which commonly kept there, that the Man put himself upon the back of the Creature when he swore, that if he said truth, the Crocodile carried him from one end of the Reservatory to the other, and brought him back again sound and safe to the place where it took him up; and if he told a lie, that the Beast having carried him to one side of the *Tanquie,* carried him again into the middle, where it dived under water with the Man; and though at present there be no Crocodile in that Reservatory, yet they confidently affirm that the Story is true.

Mountain Elephants.

Rio Largo.

The Pagod of Swearing.

Coulam.

Coulam (which is the Capital Town of the little Kingdom of that name) is four and twenty Leagues to the South of *Cochin,* but the King keeps not commonly his Court there. Before *Calicut* was in reputation, all the Traffick of that Countrey was at *Coulam,* and then it was a flourishing Town, but it is much diminished now both in Wealth and Inhabitants. The Haven of it is safe, and the Tide runs a great way up in the River. There are a great many Christians of St. *Thomas*[32] at *Coulam* as well as at *Cochin;* they pretend that they have preserved the Purity of the Faith, which that Apostle taught their Ancestors; and there are a great many also in the Mountains that run from *Cochin* to St. *Thomas* by *Madura.*[33] In the divine Office they make use of the *Sariack* Language, and most of them are Subjects of the King of *Cochin,* as well as many Families of the Jews, who live in that Countrey. I have been also told of a little Kingdom (called *Carghelan*)[34] that is in those parts, where there is also another little Prince; and so these little Kingdoms terminate *Malabar* to the South, as *Cananor* begins it to the North.

Christians of St. *Thomas.*

Syriack Language.

Carghelan.

Cananor.

There is a good Harbour at *Cananor,* which is a large Town; the little King (who is called King of *Cananor*)[35] lives not there; he holds his Court towards a streight farther from the Sea ; his Countrey affords all things necessary for life ; the *Portuguese* have been always his Friends, and many of them live in his Countrey.

The *Malabars* of *Bergare,*[36] *Cougnales*[37] and *Montongue*[38] near *Cananor,* are the chief Pirats of the *Indian* Sea, and there are many Robbers also in the Countrey, though the Magistrates, do all they can to root them out. The truth is, They'll put Man to death for a single Leaf of Betlie stolen ; they tye his hands, and having stretched him out upon his belly, run him through with a Javelin of *Areca,*[39] then they turn him upon his back, and the Javelin being quite through his Body, they fasten it in the ground, and bind the Criminal so fast to it that he cannot stir, but dies in that posture.

Indian Pirats. *Bergare, Cougnales, Montongue.*

The punishment of *Malabar* Robbers.

All the *Malabars* write as we do (from the left to the right) upon the leaves of *Palmeras-Bravas,*[40] and for making their Characters, they use a Stiletto a Foot long at least ; the Letters which they write to their Friends on these leaves, are made up round, like a roll of Ribbons ; they make their Books of several of these leaves, which they file upon a String, and enclose them betwixt two Boards of the same bigness ; they have many Ancient Books (and all almost in Verse) which they are great lovers of. I believe the Reader will be glad to see their Characters, and I have hereto subjoyned the Alphabet : The *Bramens* are held in greater honour here than elsewhere ; what War soever there may be amongst the Princes of *Malabar,* Enemies do them no hurt, and nevertheless, there are many Hypocrites among them who are very Rogues. There are certain Festival days in *Malabar,* on which the Young People fight like mad-men,[41] and many times kill one another ; and they are perswaded, that such as die in those Combats are certainly saved.

The Leaf of the Palm-Tree on which Men write.

The *Bramens* much esteemed in *Malabar.*

The Kings of *Banguel*[42] and *Olala*[43] are to the North of that Countrey, and *Mangalor*[44] (which lies within ten degrees and some minutes of the Line) belongs to the King of *Banguel.* This is a little ill built Town twelve Leagues from *Barcelor,*[45] as *Barcelor* is twelve Leagues from *Onor,*[46] and the Countrey where these Towns lie, is called *Canara,*[47] all the rest of the coast (as far as *Goa*) signifies but very little, except the Town of *Onor,* which is about eighteen Leagues from *Goa ;* it hath a large and safe Harbour made of two Rivers, that fall into the Sea by one and the same mouth below the Fort, which stands upon a pretty high Rock. The Town is far worse[48] than the Fort ; the most considerable People live there with the Governour, and many *Portuguese* have their Residence in it ; it lies in the Latitude of fourteen degrees. The rest of *Decan* Northwards, within a little of *Surrat,* belongs to the King of *Viziapour,* or to the *Portuguese ;* the *English* (as I have said) hold *Bombaym* there and *Raja Sivagy* some other places. The Kings of that

Banguel, Olala Mangalor.

Barcelor.

Onor.

coast have hardly so much yearly Revenue a piece, as a Governour of a Province in *France*, and yet they hold out still, notwithstanding the Changes that have happened in the other Countreys of *Decan*.

CHAPTER II

OF THE REVOLUTIONS OF DECAN.

Tcher-Can. *Chahalem.* *Humayon.* *Selim.* *Daquem.*

He who may be called last King of *Decan*, or at least the last but one, was a *Raja* of the Mountains of *Bengale*, called *Tcher-Can*,[1] who rendered himself so powerful, that having taken to himself the haughty Title of *Chahalem*, (which signifies King of the World) he made all the Kings of the *Indies* to tremble ; that Captain having raised a great Revolt in the Kingdom of *Bengala*, put the King of it to death,[2] and not only usurped the Kingdom and all *Patan*, but also all the Neighbouring Dominions ; he even forced the first *Mogul* King *Humayon*[3] to flie from *Dehly*, which he had seized from an *Indian* King called *Selim*,[4] and all that (which at present is called the Kingdoms of *Viziapour*, *Bisnagar* or *Cornates*,[5] and *Golconda*) fell under his power, with the Title of the Kingdom of *Decan* ; but what is most surprizing of all, at the very time (when he was most dreaded all over the *Indies*,) he grew weary of Royalty, and gave his Dominions to a Cousin German of his own, called (as I think) *Daquem*, whom he made King, and then retired to a private life in *Bengala*.[6]

A great Treason.

But seeing he had been served in his Conquests by some *Mahometan* Captains, whom he much esteemed for their Valour, he contracted with his Successour that he should leave them in the Governments of the Countries, where he had placed them : The truth is, The new King not only confirmed them therein, but (that he might please *Chahalem* the more) augmented their Governments, and honoured them with a particular confidence. These Captains maintained splendidly the power of their Master, as long as *Chahalem* lived ; but after his death, which happened in the Year One thousand five hundred and fifty,[7] his Successour having been defeated by the *Mogul Humayon*, who returned into the *Indies*, with the assistance that *Chah-Tahmas*, King of *Persia*, gave him at the Sollicitation of his Sister ; these Traitors (instead of owning their Benefactor as they ought to have done by their Loyalty,) combined against him, and killed all his faithful Friends ; they seized his own person, and having shut him up in the Castle of *Beder*, kept him there till he died, under the strickt Guard of one of the Conspirators ; they next invaded his Countreys, divided amongst themselves his Provinces, and formed them into Kingdoms. The three chief Conspirators were *Nizam-Cha*,[8] *Cotb-Cha*[9] and *Adil-Cha*;[10] these three Usurpers made themselves Kings, and established the Kingdoms of *Viziapour, Bisnagar* or *Carnates*, and *Golconda*. *Viziapour* fell to the share of *Nizam-Cha*, who is said to have been an *Indian*, and of the Royal Blood; *Bisnagar* to *Adil-Cha*, and *Golconda* to *Cotb-Cha*; and the Successours of these several Kings have since continued to take the name of their Founders.

The Usurpers of *Decan*.

The settlement of three Kingdoms.

As many other Captains[11] were concerned in the Conspiracy, so were other Principalities erected in *Decan*, but most of them fell under the power of the first three, or of their Successours. These three Princes possessed their Kingdoms without trouble, so long as they lived together in good Intelligence, and they defeated the Army of the *Mogul* in a famous *Battel*,[12] but they fell a clashing amongst themselves about the end of their Reigns, and their Children succeeded to their Misunderstandings as well as to their Dominions, to which the cunning of the *Moguls* did not a little contribute. These have by degrees taken from them the Provinces of *Balagate*, *Telenga* and *Baglana*,[13] or at least the greatest part of them, and *Auran-Zeb* seized of a great many good Towns in *Viziapour*,[14] when he was no more as yet but the Governour of a Province, which would not have happened, if the King of *Bisnagar* had assisted his Neighbour as he ought to have done. The want of assistance on that Kings part, so exasperated the King of *Viziapour*, that he no sooner made peace with the *Mogul* in the year One thousand six hundred and fifty, but he made a League with the King of *Golconda* against the King of *Bisnagar*, and entered into a War with him; they handled him so very roughly, that at length, they stript him of his Dominions. The King of *Golconda* seized those of the coast of *Coromandel*,[15] which lay conveniently for him; and the King of *Viziapour* having taken what lay next to him, pursued his Conquest as far as the Cape of *Negapatan*,[16] so that *Adil-Cha* was left without a Kingdom,[17] and constrained to flie into the Mountains where he still lives deprived of his Territories. His chief Town was *Velour*,[18] five days Journey from St. *Thomas*, but that Town at present belongs to the King of *Viziapour*, as well as *Gengi*,[19] and several others of *Carnates*.

Auran-Zeb.

Velour.

Gengi.

This Kingdom of *Carnates* or *Bisnagar*, which was formerly called *Narsingue*, began three days Journey from *Golconda* towards the South; it had many Towns, and the Provinces thereof crossed from the coast of *Coromandel* to the coast of *Malabar*, reaching a great way towards the Cape of *Comory*; it had *Viziapour* and the Sea of *Cambaye* to the West, and the Sea of *Bengala* to the East; what of it belongs to the King of *Viziapour* is at present governed by an Enuch of Threescore and ten years of Age, (called *Raja-Couli*,)[20] who conquered it with extraordinary expedition. That *Raja* (to whom the King

Carnates. *Bisnagar*.

Raja Couli.

gave the Surname of *Niecnam-Can,*) which is as much as to say, *Lord of good renown,* is the richest Subject of the *Indies.*

Whilst I was in *Carnate,* the Kings of *Viziapour* and *Golconda* attacked a certain Raja,[21] who had a Fort whither he retreated betwixt the two Kingdoms, there he committed an infinite number of Robberies ; and in the last War that the *Great Mogul* made in *Viziapour,* that *Raja* (set on by the *Mogul*) made considerable incursions into the Countreys of the two Kings, which made them force him to the utmost extremity ; so that they took his Fort, made him Prisoner, and seized all his Riches.

Viziapour.

The Kingdom of *Viziapour* is bounded to the East by *Carnates,* and the Mountain of *Balagate ;* to the West by the Lands of the Portuguese ; to the North by *Guzerat* and the Province of *Balagate ;* and to the South by the Countrey of the *Naique* of *Madura,*[22] whose Territories reach to the Cape *Comory.* This *Naique* is tributary to the King of *Viziapour,* as well as the *Naique* of *Tanjahor,*[23] to whom belonged the Towns of *Negapatan, Trangabar,*[24] and some others towards the coast of *Coromandel,* when the King of *Viziapour* took them. *Negapatan* fell since into the hands of the *Portuguese,* but the *Dutch* took it from them, and are at present Masters of it. The *Danes* have also seized a place (where they have built a Fort towards *Trangabar*) which is distant from St. *Thomas* five days Journey of a Foot-post, which they call *Patamar.*[25]

The Pagod of *Trapety.*

As to the famous Pagod of *Trapety,*[26] (which is not far from Cape *Comory*) it depends on the *Naique* of *Madura ;* it consists of a great Temple, and of many little Pagods about it ; and there are so many Lodgings for the *Bramens,* and the Servants of the Temple, that it looks like a Town. There is a great deal of Riches in that Pagod.

The King of *Viziapour.*

The King of *Viziapour* is the most potent Prince of all those of *Decan,* and therefore he is often called King of *Decan.* His chief City is *Viziapour,* which hath given the name to the Kingdom, and he hath many other considerable Towns in his Provinces with three or four Ports, to wit, *Carapatan,*[27] *Dabul, Raja-pour,* and *Vingourla ;* but I am informed that *Raja Sivagy* hath seized some of them not long since.

The Town of *Viziapour.*

The Town of *Viziapour* is above four or five Leagues in circumference ; it is fortified with a double Wall, with many great Guns mounted, and a flat bottomed Ditch. The Kings Palace is in the middle of the Town, and is likewise encompassed with a Ditch full of water, wherein there are some Crocodiles.[28] This Town hath several large Suburbs full of Goldsmiths and Jewellers Shops, yet after all, there is but little Trade, and not many things remarkable in it.

An Orphan adopted and

The King (who Reigns in *Viziapour* at present)[29] was an Orphan, whom the late King and the Queen adopted for their

Son ; and after the death of the King, the Queen had so much interest as to settle him upon the Throne ; but he being as yet very young, the Queen was declared Regent of the Kingdom; Nevertheless, there has been a great deal of weakness during her Government, and *Raja Sivagy* hath made the best on't for his own Elevation. made King of *Viziapour.*

CHAPTER III

OF GOA.

The Town of *Goa* (with its Isle of the same name,) which is likewise called *Tilsoar,*[1] borders upon *Viziapour,* directly Southward ; it lies in the Latitude of fifteen degrees and about forty minutes[2] upon the River of *Mandoua,*[3] which discharges it self into the Sea two leagues from *Goa,* and gives it one of the fairest Harbours in the World ; some would have this Countrey to be part of *Viziapour,* but it is not ; and when the *Portuguese* came there, it belonged to a Prince called *Zabaim,*[4] who gave them trouble enough ; nevertheless, *Albuquerque* made himself Master of it in *February* One thousand five hundred and ten, through the cowardize of the Inhabitants, who put him into possession of the Town and Fort, and took an Oath of Allegiance to the King of *Portugal.* *Goa.* *Zabaim,* Prince of *Goa.*

This Town[5] hath good Walls, with Towers and great Guns, and the Isle it self is Walled round, with Gates towards the Land, to hinder the Slaves from running away, which they do not fear (towards the Sea) because all the little Isles and Peninsules that are there, belong to the *Portuguese,* and are full of their Subjects. This Isle is plentiful in Corn, Beasts and Fruit, and hath a great deal of good water. The City of *Goa* is the Capital of all those which the *Portuguese* are Masters of in the *Indies.* The Arch-Bishop, Vice-Roy and Inquisitor General, have their Residence there ; and all the Governours and Ecclesiastick and secular Officers of the other Countries (subject to the *Portuguese* Nation in the *Indies*) depend on it. *Albuquerque* was buried there in the year One thousand five hundred and sixteen, and St. *Francis* of *Xavier*[6] in One thousand five hundred fifty two. The River of *Mendoua* is held in no less veneration by the *Bramens* and other Idolaters, than *Ganges* is elsewhere, and at certain times, and upon certain Festival days, they flock thither from a far, to perform their Purifications. It is a great Town, and full of fair Churches, lovely Convents, and Palaces well beautified ; there are several Orders of Religious, both Men and Women there, and the Jesuits alone have five publick Houses ; few Nations in the World were so rich in the *Indies* The death of *Albuquerque.* The death of St. *Francis* of *Xavier.*

as the *Portuguese* were, before their Commerce was ruined by the Dutch, but their vanity is the cause of their loss ; and if they had feared the Dutch more than they did, they might have been still in a condition to give them the Law there, from which they are far enough at present.

There are a great many Gentiles about *Goa,* some of them worship Apes,[7] and I observed elsewhere that in some places[8] they have built Pagods to these Beasts. Most part of the Gentiles, Heads of Families in *Viziapour,* dress their own Victuals themselves ; he that do's it having swept the place where he is to dress any thing, draws a Circle,[9] and confines himself within it, with all that he is to make use of ; if he stand in need of any thing else, it is given him at a distance, because no body is to enter within that Circle, and if any chanced to enter it, all would be prophaned, and the Cook would throw away what he had dressed, and be obliged to begin again. When the Victuals are ready, they are divided into three parts, The first part is for the Poor, the second for the Cow of the House, and the third portion for the Familie, and of this third they make as many Commons[10] as there are Persons ; and seeing they think it not civil to give their leavings to the poor, they give them likewise to the Cow.

The way of the *Banians* dressing their Victuals.

CHAPTER IV

OF THE KINGDOM OF GOLCONDA, *OF* BAGNAGAR.

Golconda.

The most powerful of the Kings of *Decan,* next to *Viziapour,* is the King of *Golconda.* His Kingdom borders on the East side, upon the Sea of *Bengala ;* to the North, upon the Mountains of the Countrey of *Orixa ;* to the South, upon many Countries of *Bisnagar,* or Ancient *Narsingue,* which belongs to the King of *Viziapour ;* and to the West, upon the Empire of the *Great Mogul,* by the province of *Balagate,* where the Village of *Calvar* is, which is the last place of *Mogolistan,* on that side. There are very insolent collectors of Tolls at *Calvar,* and when they have not what they demand, they cry with all their force, their *Li, li, li,* striking their Mouth with the palm of their Hand, and at that kind of alarm-bell, which is heard at a great distance, naked Men come running from all parts, carrying Staves, Lances, Swords, Bows, Arrows, and some, Musquets, who make Travellers pay by force what they have demanded, and when all is payed, it no easie matter still to get rid of them.

Calvar.

Li, li, li.

The boundaries of *Mogulistan* and *Golconda,* are planted about a League and a half from *Calvar* ; They are Trees which

The bounds of *Mogulistan.*

THE

Malabar Cyphers.

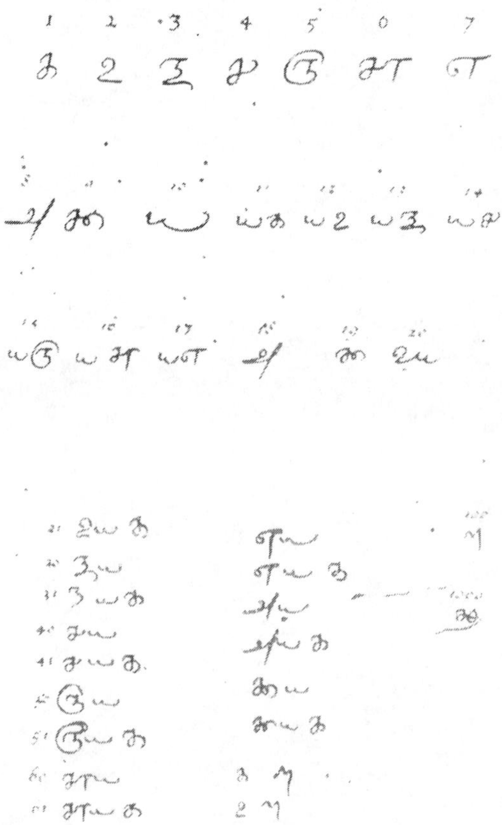

THE

Malabar Alphabet.

FIGURES.	NAMES.		POWERS.
	The VOWELS.		
	Aana	*a*	breve
	Auena	*a*	longum
	Iinà	*i*	breve
	Iena	*i*	longum
	Ououna	*ou*	Gallicum breve
	Ouuena	*ou*	Gallicum longum
	Eena	*e*	breve
	Eeaa	*e*	longum
	Ayena	*ay*	Gallicum
	Oona	*o*	breve
	Ouena	*o*	longum
	Auuena	*aou*	Gallicum
	Akena		*Non est vocalis, sed solummodo est figura quietis, sicut quando pronunciatur per, litera r est quiescens, quia pronunciatur cum vocali praecedente, & non habet vocalem sequentem; figura autem quietis est punctum superpositum literis.*

Insert this between Pag. 90, and 91. of the Third Part.

The CONSONANTS.

FIGURES.	NAMES.	POWERS.
ந	Naana	*nostrum* n.
ப	Paana	*nostrum* p.
ம	Maana	*nostrum* m.
ய	Jaana	J *consonans.*
ர	Raana	*nostrum* r *simplex, ut in verbo gallico* pere, mere.
ல	Laana	*nostrum* l.
வ	Vaana	V *consonans.*
ழ	Raana	*pronuntiatio blæsorum qui non possunt pronuntiare* r.
ள	Laana	l *in medio palati tangendo cum extremitate linguæ medium palati.*
ற	*i Græcorum aspiratum.* Raana	*nostrum* r *duplex, ut in verbo gallico* terre.
ன	Naana	*parva differentia pronuntiationis hujus literæ à pronuntiatione nostra* n, *& non potest benè adverti illa differentia nisi ab ipsis naturalibus.*
க	Caana	x *græcorum, & quando est simplex pronuntiatur ut* g *cum* a, ga, *vel* go, gue, gui, gou.
ங	Naana	*ista litera est propria Indorum, nec in ullâ aliâ linguâ nobis cognitâ reperitur talis pronuntiatio.*
ச	Chaana	*sicut* ch *Gallorum in verbo gallico* cherté.
ஞ	Gnaana	*sicut* gn *Gallorum in verbo gallico* compagnie.
ட	Daana	*quasi* dad *Arabum, pronuntiatur in medio palati, tangendo cum extremitate linguæ medium palati.*
ண	Naana	*etiam pronuntiatur in medio palati, tangendo cum extremitate linguæ medium palati.*
த	Taana	*nostrum* t, *& quando est simplex, multoties pronuntiatur ut nostrum* d.

Mahoua.

they call *Mahoua ;* these mark the outmost Land of the *Mogul,* and immediately after, on this side of a Rivulet, there are *Cadjours,* or wild Palm-trees, planted only in that place, to denote the beginning of the Kingdom of *Golconda,* wherein the insolence of collectors is far more insupportable than in the confines of *Mogolistan ;* for the duties not being exacted there, in the Name of the King, but in the Name of private Lords, to whom the Villages have been given, the Collectors make Travellers pay what they please. We found some Officers, where they made us give fifty *Roupies,* in stead of twenty, which was their due, and to shew that it was an Extortion of the Exactors, they refused to give us a note for what they had received, and in the space of three and twenty Leagues betwixt *Calvar* and *Bagnagar,* we were obliged with extream rigour, to pay to sixteen Officers ; *Bramens* are the Collectors of these Tolls, and are a much ruggeder sort of People to do with, than the *Banians.*

16 Officers in 23 Leagues.

The Road from *Calvar* to *Bagnagar.*[4]
Malaredpet 3 or 4 Leag. from *Calvar.*
Bouquenour a Town.
Mellinar 6 Leag. from *Malaredpet.*
Degelpeli 6 Leag. from *Mellinar.*
Marcel 3 Leag. *Degelpeli.*
Bagnagar 4 Leag. from *Marcel.*

In our way from *Calvar* to *Bagnagar* we found no other Town but *Buquenour,*[1] but there are others to the right and left ; we passed by eighteen Villages. The Nadab[2] or Governour of the Province, lives in the little Town of *Marcel,*[3] and we made that Journey in six days of Caravan : In short, there are few or no Countries, that delight Travellers with their verdure, more than the Fields of this Kingdom, because of the Rice and Corn that is to be seen every where, and the many lovely Reservatories that are to be found in it.

Bagnagar.
Aider-abad.

The Capital City of this Kingdom is called *Bagnagar,* the *Persians* call it *Aider-abad ;*[5] it is fourteen or fifteen Leagues from *Viziapour,* situated in the Latitude of seventeen Degrees ten Minutes,[6] in a very long plain, hemmed in with little Hills, some Cosses distant from the Town, which makes the Air of that place very wholesome, besides that, the Countrey of *Golconda* lies very high. The Houses of the Suburbs, where we arrived, are only built of Earth and thatched with Straw, they are so low and ill contrived, that they can be reckoned no more than Huts. We went from one end to the other of that Suburbs, which is very long, and stopt near the Bridge which is at the farther end of it. There we stayed[7] for a note from the *Cotoual* to enter the Town, because of the Merchants Goods of the Caravan, which were to be carried to the *Cotouals* House to be searched : But a *Persian* named *Ak-Nazar,*[8] a favorite of the Kings, who knew the chief of the Caravan, being informed of its arrival, sent immediately a Man with orders, to let us enter with all the Goods, and so we past the Bridge,[9] which is only three Arches over. It is about three Fathom broad, and is paved with large flat Stones : The River of *Nerva*[10] runs under that Bridge, which then seemed to be but a Brook, though in time of the Rains, it be as broad as the

Nerva.

Seine before the *Louvre* at *Paris*. At the end of the Bridge, we found the Gates of the City, which are no more but Barriers: Being entered, we marched a quarter of an hour through a long Street with Houses on both sides, but as low as those of the Suburbs, and built of the same materials, though they have very lovely Gardens.

We went to a *Carvanseray* called *Nimet-ulla*,[11] which has its entry from the same Street: Every one took his lodging there, and I hired two little Chambers, at two *Roupies* a Month. The Town makes a kind of Cross, much longer than broad, and extends in a streight line, from the Bridge to the four Towers;[12] but beyond these Towers the Street is no longer streight, and whilst in walking I measured the length of the Town, being come to the four Towers, I was obliged to turn to the left, and entered into a Meidan, where there is another Street that led me to the Town-Gate, which I looked for. Having adjusted my measures, I found that *Bagnagar* was five thousand six hundred and fifty Paces in length, to wit, two thousand four hundred and fifty from the Bridge to the Towers, and from thence, through the *Meidan* to the Gate which leads to *Masulipatan*, three thousand two hundred Paces. There is also beyond that Gate, a Suburb eleven hundred Paces long.

The *Meidan* of *Bagnagar*.

There are several *Meidans* or Publick places in this Town, but the fairest is that before the Kings Palace: It hath to the East and West two great Divans very deep in the Ground, the Roof whereof being of Carpenters work, is raised five Fathom high, upon four Wooden Pillars; this Roof is flat, and hath Balisters of Stone cast over Arch-ways, with Turrets at the corners. These two Divans serve for Tribunals to the *Cotoual*, whose Prisons are at the bottom of these Divans, each of them having a Bason of Water before them. The like Balisters go round the Terrass-walks of the place: The Royal Palace is to the North of it, and there is a Portico over against it, where the Musicians come several times a day to play upon their Instruments, when the King is in Town.

Fightings of Elephants.

In the middle of this place, and in sight of the Royal Palace, there is a Wall built, three Foot thick, and six Fathom in height and length, for the fighting of Elephants, and that Wall is betwixt them, when they excite them to fight; but so soon as they are wrought up to a rage, they quickly throw down the Wall. The ordinary Houses there, are not above two Fathom high; they raise them no higher, that they may have the fresh Air during the heats, and most part[13] of them are only of Earth; but the Houses of Persons of Quality are pretty enough.

The Palace of *Bagnagar*.

The Palace which is three hundred and fourscore Paces in length, takes up not only one of the sides of the Place, but is continued to the four Towers, where it terminates in a very loftly Pavillion. The Walls of it which are built of great Stones, have at certain distances half Towers, and there are many Windows towards the place, with an open Gallery to see the shews. They say it is very pleasant within, and that the Water rises to the highest Appartments: The Reservatory of that Water, which is brought a great way off, is in the top of the four Towers, from whence it is conveyed into the House by Pipes. No Man enters into this Palace, but by an express Order from the King, who grants it but seldom ; nay, commonly no body comes near it, and in the place there is a circuit staked out, that must not be passed over. There is another square *Meidan* in this Town, where many great Men have well built Houses. The *Carvanseras* are generally all handsome, and the most esteemed is that which is called *Nimet-ulla* in the great Street opposite to the Kings Garden: It is a spacious square, and the Court of it is adorned with several Trees of different kinds, and a large Bason where the *Mahometans* performe their Ablutions.

The four Towers.

That which is called the four Towers, is a square building, of which each face is ten Fathom broad, and about seven high : It is opened in the four sides, by four Arches, four or five Fathom high, and four Fathom wide, and every one of these Arches, fronts a Street, of the same breadth as the Arch. There are two Galleries in it, one over another, and over all a Terrass that serves for a Roof, bordered with a Stone-Balcony ; and at each corner of that Building, a Decagone Tower about ten Fathom high, and each Tower hath four Galleries with little Arches on the outside ; the whole Building being adorned with Roses and Festons pretty well cut: It is vaulted underneath, and appears like a Dome, which has in the inside all round Balisters of Stone, pierced and open as the Galleries in the outside, and there are several Doors in the Walls to enter at. Under this Dome there is a large Table placed upon a Divan, raised seven or eight Foot from the Ground, with steps to go up to it. All the Galleries of that Building, serve to make the Water mount up, that so being afterwards conveyed to the Kings Palace, it might reach the highest Appartments. Nothing in that Town seems so lovely as the outside of that Building, and nevertheless it is surrounded with ugly shops made of Wood,[14] and covered with Straw, where they sell Fruit, which spoiles the prospect of it.

Gardens near *Bagnagar*.

There are many fair Gardens in this Town, their beauty consists in having long walks kept very clean, and lovely Fruit-trees ; but they have neither Beds of Flowers nor Water-works,[15] and they are satisfied with several Cisterns or Basons with Water. The Gardens without the Town are the loveliest, and I shall only describe one of them, that is reckoned the pleasantest of the Kingdom. At first one enters into a great place which is called the first Garden ; it is planted with Palms and *Areca*-trees, so near to one another, that the Sun can hardly pierce through them. The Walks of it are streight and neat, with borders of white Flowers which they call *Ghoul Daoudi,*[16] the *Flowers of* David, like Camomile-Flowers ; there are also *Indian* Gilly-flowers, with some other sorts. The House is at the end of this Garden, and has two great Wings adjoyning the main Body of it: It is two Story high, the first consisting in three Halls, of which the greatest is in the middle, the main Body of the House, and in each Wing there is one, all three having Doors and Windows, but the great Hall has two Doors, higher than the others, which open into a large *Kioch* or Divan, supported by eight great Pillars in two rows. Crossing the Hall and Divan, one goes down a pair of Stairs into another Divan of the same form, but longer, which (as the former) hath a Room on each side, opened with Doors and Windows. The second Story of the Building is like the first, save that it hath but one Divan ; but it hath a Balcony that reaches the whole length of that front of it. The House is covered with a flat Roof of so great extent, that it reaches over the outmost Divan of the lower Story, and is supported by six eight-cornered Wooden Pillars, six or seven Fathom high, and proportionably big.

From the lower Divan, a Terrass-walk two hundred Paces long, and fifty broad, faced with Stones runs along all the Front of the House ; and two little groves of Trees, that are on the sides of it. This Terrass that is at the head of the second Garden, (which is much larger than the first,) is raised a Fathom and a halfe above it, and has very neat Stairs for going down into it. The first thing that is to be seen (looking forwards,) is a great square Reservatory or *Tanquie,* each side whereof is above two hundred Paces long ; in it there are a great many Pipes that rise half a Foot above Water, and a Bridge upon it, raised about a Foot over the surface of the Water, and above six Foot broad, with wooden Railes. This Bridge is fourscore Paces long, and leads into a Platform of an Octogone figure in the middle of the Reservatory, where there are Steps to descend into the Water, which is but about a Foot lower than the Platform: There are Pipes in the eight Angles of it, and in the Pillars of the Railes, from whence the Water plays on all sides, which makes a very lovely sight. In the middle of the Platform there is a little House built two Stories high, and of an Octogone figure also ; each Story hath a little Room with eight Doors, and round the second Story there is a Balcony to walk in: The Roof of this Building which is flat, is bordered with Balisters, and covers the whole Platform also: That Roof is supported by sixteen wooden Pillars, as big[17] as a Mans Body, and about three Fathom high, (if you comprehend[18] their Capitals,) and there are two of them at each Angle, of which one rests upon the Wall of the House, and the other is near the Railes that go round it.

The Garden wherein this Reservatory is, is planted with Flowers and Fruit-trees: All are in very good order, and in this, as well as in the first Garden, there are lovely Walks well Gravelled, and Bordered with divers Flowers: There runs a Canal in the middle of the great Walk, which is four Foot over, and carries away what it receives from several little Fountains of Water, that are also in the middle of that Walk, at certain distances: In short, this Garden is very large, and bounded by a Wall which hath a great Gate in the middle that opens into a Close of a large extent, Planted with Fruit-trees, and as neatly contrived as the Gardens.

CHAPTER V

OF THE INHABITANTS OF BAGNAGAR.

There are many Officers and Men of Law at *Bagnagar*, but the most considerable is the *Cotoual*: He is not only Governour of the Town, but also chief Customer of the Kingdom. He is besides, Master of the Mint-house, and Supream Judge of the City, as well in Civil as Criminal matters; he rents all these places of the King, for which he pays a good deal of Money. There are in this Town many Rich Merchants, Bankers and Jewellers, and vast numbers of very skilful Artisans. Amongst the Inhabitants of Bagnagar, we are to recken the forty thousand Horse, *Persians, Moguls*, or *Tartars*, whom the King entertains, that he may not be again surprised, as he hath been heretofore by his Enemies.

The Inhabitants of *Bagnagar*.

Besides the *Indian* Merchants that are at *Bagnagar*, there are many *Persians* and *Armenians*, but through the weakness of the Government, the *Omras* sometimes squeeze them; and whil'st I was there, an *Omra* detained in his House a Gentile Banker whom he had sent for, and made him give him five thousand *Chequins;* upon the report of this Extortion, the Bankers shut up their Offices, but the King Commanded all to be restored to the Gentile, and so the matter was taken up.

The Tradesmen of the Town, and those who cultivate the Land, are Natives of the Country. There are many Franks also in the Kingdome, but most of them are *Portuguese*, who have fled thither for Crimes they have committed: However the *English*[2] and *Dutch*[3] have lately setled there, and the last make great profits. They established a Factory there, (three years since) where they buy up for the Company, many *Chites* and other Cloaths, which they vent elsewhere in the *Indies*. They bring from *Masulipatan* upon Oxen, the Goods which they know to be of readiest sale in *Bagnagar ;* and other Towns of the Kingdom, as Cloves, Pepper, Cinnamon, Silver, Copper, Tin, and Lead, and thereby gain very much ; for they say, they get five and twenty for one, of profit ; and I was assured that this profit amounted yearly to eleven or twelve hundred thousand *French Livres*. They are made welcome in that Countrey, because they make many Presents, and a few days before I parted from *Bagnagar,* their Governour began to have Trumpets and Tymbals,[4] and a Standard carried before him, by Orders from his Superiours.

Publick Women.

Publick Women are allowed in the Kingdom,[5] so that no body minds it when they see a Man go to their Houses, and they are often at their Doors well drest, to draw in Passengers: But they say most of them are spoiled. The common People give their Wives great Liberty: When a Man is to be Married, the Father and Mother of his Bride, make him promise that he will not take it ill, that his Wife go and walk through the Town, or visit her Neighbours, nay and drink *Tary,* a drink that the *Indians* of *Golconda* are extreamly fond of.

The liberty of Wives in *Golconda.*

When a Theft is committed at *Bagnagar,* or elsewhere, they punish the Thief by cutting off both his Hands ; which is the Custome also in most Countries of the *Indies*.[6]

The Money of *Golconda.*

The most currant Money in this Kingdom, are the *Pagods,*[7] *Roupies* of *Mogul,* the halfe *Roupies,* quarter *Roupies* and *Pechas*. The *Pagods* are pieces of Gold, of which there are old and new ones ; when I was at *Bagnagar,* the old were worth five *Roupies* and a half, that's to say, about eight French *Livres,* because they were scarce then, and the new were only worth four *Roupies,* that's about six *Livres ;* but both rise and fall, according as People stand in need of them: And the *Roupies* which in *Mogulistan* are worth but about half a Crown, pass in *Golconda* for five and fifty *Pechas,* which are worth six and forty or seven and forty *Sols*. This Money of *Pechas* is Coyned at *Bagnagar ;* but the *Dutch* at present furnishing the Copper, these *Pechas* are for them, which afterward by the way of Trade they change into *Pagods* and *Roupies*.

Pechas.

The Price and Weight of Diamonds. *Mangelin* a weight. *Carat.*

Seeing the Kingdom of *Golconda* may be said to be the Countrey of Diamonds,[8] it will not be amiss to know the Price that is commonly given for them proportionably to their weight. The chief weight of Diamonds, is the *Mangelin ;*[9] it weighs five grains and three fifths, and the *Carat* weighs only four *Grains,*[10] and five *Mangelins* make seven *Carats*. Diamonds that weigh but one or two *Mangelins,* are commonly sold for fifteen or sixteen Crowns the *Mangelin ;* such as weigh three *Mangelins,* are sold for thirty Crowns[11] the *Mangelin ;* and for five Crowns one may have three Diamonds, if all the three weigh but a

The sepulchre of the King of Golcunda

Mangelin: However the price is not fixt, for one day I saw fifty[12] Crowns a *Mangelin* payed for a Diamond of ten *Mangelins*, and next day there was but four and forty a *Mangelin*, payed for another Diamond that weighed fifteen *Mangelins*: Not long after, I was at the Castle with a Hollander who bought a large Diamond weighing fifty *Mangelins*, or threescore and ten *Carats*, he was asked seventeen thousand Crowns for it; he bargained for it a long while, but at length drew the Merchant aside to strike up a bargain, and I could not prevail with him to tell me what he payed for it. That Stone has a grain in the middle, and must be cut in two. He bought another at Bagnagar, which weighed thirty five *Mangelins* or *eight*[13] and forty *Carats*, and he had the *Carat* for five hundred and fifty five *Guilders*.[14]

CHAPTER VI

OF THE CASTLE OF *GOLCONDA*.

The Castle where the King commonly keeps his Court, is two Leagues from *Bagnagar*; it is called *Golconda*,[1] and the Kingdom bears the same name. *Cotup-Cha* the first,[2] gave it that name, because after his Usurpation seeking out for a place where he might build a strong Castle, the place where the Castle stands was named to him by a Shepheard, who guided him through a Wood to the Hill where the Palace is at present; and the place appearing very proper for his designe, he built the Castle there, and called it *Golconda*, from the word *Golcar*,[3] which in the *Telenghi* Language signifies a Shepheard: all the Fields about *Golconda* were then but a Forest, which were cleared by little and little, and the Wood burnt. This place is to the West of *Bagnagar*; the plain that leads to it, as one goes out of the Suburbs, affords a most lovely sight, to which the prospect of the Hill that rises like a Sugar-loaf in the middle of the Castle, which has the Kings Palace all round upon the sides of it, contributes much by its natural situation. This Fort is of a large compass,[4] and may be called a Town; the Walls of it are built of Stones three Foot in length, and as much in breadth, and are surrounded with deep Ditches, divided into *Tanquies*, which are full of fair and good Water.

Golconda a Castle.

But after all, it hath no works of Fortification but five round Towers, which (as well as the Walls of the place) have a great many Cannon mounted upon them, for their defence. Though there be several Gates into this Castle, yet two only are kept open, and as we entered, we crossed over a Bridge built over a large *Tanquie*,[5] and then went through a very narrow place betwixt two Towers, which turning and winding, leads to a great Gate[6] guarded by *Indians* sitting on seats of Stone, with their Swords by them. They let no Stranger in, if he have not a permission from the Governour, or be not acquainted with some Officer of the Kings. Besides the Kings Palace[7] there is no good building in this Castle, unless it be some Officers lodgings; but the Palace is great, and well situated for good Air, and a lovely Prospect; and a *Flemish* Chirurgeon[8] who is in the Kings service, told me, that the Chamber where he waited on the King, hath a *Kiock,* from whence one may discover not only all the Castle and Countrey about, but also all *Bagnagar,* and that one must pass through twelve Gates before one comes to the appartment of the Prince. Most part of the Officers lodge in the Castle, which hath several good *Bazars,* where all things necessary, (especially for life) may be had, and all the *Omras,* and other great Lords have Houses there, besides those they have at *Bagnagar.*

The King will have the good Workmen to live there, and therefore appoints them lodgings, for which they pay nothing: He makes even Jewellers lodge in his Palace, and to these only he trusts Stones of consequence, strictly charging them not to tell any what work they are about, least if *Auran-Zeb* should come to know that his workmen are employed about Stones of great value, he might demand them of him: The Workmen of the Castle are taken up about[9] the Kings common Stones, of which he hath so many that these Men can hardly work for any body else.

The cutting of Saphirs.

They cut Saphirs with a Bow of Wire; whil'st one Workman handles the Bow, another poures continually upon the Stone very liquid solution of the Powder of white *Emrod*[10] made in Water; and so they easily compass their Work. That white *Emrod* is found in Stones, in a particular place of the Kingdom, and is called *Coriud* in the *Telenghy* Language: It is sold for a Crown or two *Roupies* the pound, and when they intend to use it, they beat it into a Powder.

White *Emrod.*

To take a spot out of a Diamond.

When they would cut a Diamond to take out some grain of Sand, or other imperfection they find in it, they saw it a little in the place where it is to be cut, and then laying it upon a hole that is in a piece of wood, they put a little wedge of Iron upon the place that is sawed, and striking it as gently as may be, it cuts the Diamond through.

Bezoars.

The King hath store of excellent *Bezoars*:[11] The Mountains where the Goats feed that produce them, are to the North-East of the Castle, seven or eight days Journey from *Bagnagar;* they are commonly sold for forty Crowns the pound weight. The long are the best: They find of them in some Cows, which are much bigger than those of Goats, but of far less value, and those which of all others are most esteemed, are got out of a kind of Apes that are somewhat rare, and these *Bezoars* are small and long.

The Sepulchres[12] of the King who built *Golconda*, and of the five Princes who have Reigned after him, are about two Musquet-shot from the Castle. They take up a great deal of Ground, because every one of them is in a large Garden ; the way to go thither is out at the West Gate, and by it not only the Bodies of Kings and Princes, but of all that die in the Castle are carried out ; and no interest can prevail to have them conveyed out by any other Gate. The Tombs of the six Kings are accompanied with those of their Relations, their Wives, and chief Eunuchs. Every one of them is in the middle of a Garden ; and to go see them, one must ascend by five or six steps to a walk built of those Stones, which resemble the *Theban*. The Chappel which contains the Tomb is surrounded by a Gallery with open Arches : It is square, and raised six or seven Fathom high ; it is beautified with many Ornaments of Architecture, and covered with a Dome, that at each of the four corners has a Turret ; few people are suffered to go in, because these places are accounted Sacred. There are *Santo's* who keep the entry, and I could not have got in, if I had not told them that I was a Stranger. The floor is covered with a Carpet, and on the Tomb there is a Satten Pall with white Flowers, that trails upon the Ground. There is a Cloath of State of the same Stuff a Fathom high, and all is lighted with many Lamps. The Tombs of the Sons and Daughters of the King are on the one side, and on the other all that Kings Books, on folding seats, which for the most part are *Alcorans* with their Commentaries, and some other Books of the *Mahometan* Religion. The Tombs of the other Kings are like to this, save only that the Chappels of some are square in the inside as on the outside, and of others built in form of a Cross ; some are lined with that lovely Stone I have mentioned, others with black Stone, and some others with white, so Varnished as that they appear to be Polished Marble, nay, some of them are lined with Purslane.[13] The Tomb of the King that died last is the finest of all,[14] and its Dome is Varnished over with Green. The Tombs of the Princes their Brothers, of their other Relations, and of their Wives also, are of the same form as their own are ; but they are easily to be distinguished, because their Domes have not the crescent which is upon the Domes of the Monuments of the Kings. The Sepulchres of the chief Eunuchs are low and flat Roofed without any Dome, but have each of them their Garden : All these Sepulchres are Sanctuaries, and how criminal soever a Man may be that can get into them, he is secure. The *Gary*[15] is rung there as well as in the Castle, and all things are most exactly regulated amongst the Officers. That *Gary* is pretty pleasant, though it be only rung with a stick, striking upon a

The Sepulchres of the Kings and Princes of *Golconda*.

large Plate of Copper that is held in the Air ; but the Ringer strikes artfully, and makes Harmony with it ; the *Gary* serves to distinguish time. In the *Indies* the natural day is divided into two parts. The one begins at break of day, and the other at the beginning of the night, and each of these parts is divided into four Quarters, and each Quarter into eight Parts, which they call *Gary*.

CHAPTER VII

OF THE KING OF GOLCONDA *THAT REIGNS.*

The King that Reigns is a *Chiai*[1] by Religion, that's to say, of the Sect of the *Persians ;* he is the seventh since the Usurpation[2] made upon the Successour of *Chaalem* King of *Decan,*[3] and he is called *Abdulla Cotup-Cha.* I have already observed, that the name of all the Kings of *Golconda* is *Cotup-Cha,* as *Edel-Cha* is the name of the Kings of *Viziapour.* This King is the Son of a *Bramen* Lady,[4] who hath had other Princes also by the late King her Husband, and was very witty. He was but fifteen years of Age[5] when his Father (who left the Crown to his Eldest Son) died ; but the Eldest being less beloved of the Queen than *Abdulla* his younger Brother,[6] he was clapt up in Prison, and *Abdulla* placed upon the Throne. He continued in Prison until the year One thousand six hundred fifty eight ;[6a] when *Auran-Zeb* coming into the Kingdom with an Army, the captive Prince had the boldness to send word to the King, that if he pleased to give him the command of his Forces, he would meet the *Mogul* and fight him. The King was startled at that bold proposal, and was so far from granting him what he demanded, that he caused him to be poysoned.

The number of Soldiers.

The King of *Golconda* pays above Five hundred thousand Soldiers ;[7] and that makes the Riches of the *Omras,* because he who has Pay for a thousand Men, entertains but Five hundred, and so do the rest proportionably. He allows a Trooper (who ought to be either a *Mogul* or *Persian*) ten *Chequins* a month, and for that Pay, he ought to keep two Horses and four or five Servants. A Foot-soldier (of these Nations) hath five *Chequins,* and ought to entertain two Servants, and carry a Musket. He gives not the *Indians* (his own Subjects) above two or three *Roupies* a month, and these carry only the Lance and Pike. Seeing the late King gave his Soldiers better Pay than this do's, he was far better served : He entertained always a strong Army, and the number of Men he payed was always compleat. By that means he easily hindred the *Great Mogul* from attempting any thing against him, and was not tributary to him as his Son is.[8]

Heretofore the King went ever now and then to his Palace of *Bagnagar*, but he hath not been there this eight years ; since *Auran-Zeb* (who was then but Governour of a Province) surprized him in it, having marched his Forces with so great diligence, that they were at the Gates of *Bagnagar*, before the King had any News that they were marched from *Aurangeabad*, so that he easily made himself Master of the Town :[9] Nevertheless, the King in disguise, escaped by a private door, and retreated to the Fort of *Golconda*. The *Mogul* plundered the Town and Palace, carrying away all the Riches, even to the Plates of Gold, wherewith the Floors of the Kings appartment were covered. The Queen Mother (at length) had the Art to appease the Conquerour ; she treated with him in name of the King, and granted him one of his Daughters in Marriage for his Son,[10] with promise that he should leave the Kingdom to him, if he had no Male issue, and he hath none. Had it not been for that Accommodation, he was upon the point of losing his Kingdom, and perhaps his life too. Since that time he is apprehensive of every thing ; and next to the Queen-mother, he trusts no body but *Sidy Mezafer*[11] (his favourite) and the *Bramens*, because that Queen is of the *Bramen* caste, and continually surrounded by them. The King knows of nothing but by them, and there are some appointed to hearken to what the *Vizier* himself, and other Officers have to say to the King ; but his fear is much encreased since the *Great Mogul* hath been in War with the King of *Viziapour*,[12] whom in the beginning he assisted with Two hundred thousand Men, commanded by an Eunuch, who was almost as soon recalled as sent, upon the complaints made by the *Moguls* Embassadour at *Golconda*. The King (to excuse himself) said, that that Army was sent without his knowledge ; and he is still in great apprehension of having the *Moguls* upon his back, if they succeed against the King of *Viziapour*, who hath hitherto defended himself very bravely. This shews the weakness of that King ; he dares not put to death his *Omras*, even when they deserve it ; and if he find them guilty of any Crime, he condemns them only to pay a Fine, and takes the Money. Nay, the Dutch begin to insult over him, and it is not long since they obliged him to abandon to them an *English* Ship,[13] which they had seized in the Road of *Masulipatan*, though he had undertaken to protect her.

There is a Prince also at his Court, who begins to create him a great deal of trouble, and it is he whom they call the Kings little Son-in-law,[14] who hath married the third of the Princesses his Daughters, because he is of the Blood Royal : He pretends to the Crown, what promise soever hath been made to the *Great Mogul ;* he makes himself to be served as the King himself is, who hitherto loved him very tenderly; but at present he is jealous of that Son-in-law as well as of the rest, and fancies that he intends to destroy him, that he himself may Reign, tho' he be reckoned a Man of great integrity. There was in *Bagnagar* a Moorish *Santo*[15] that lived near the Carvansery of *Nimet-Ulla,* who was held in great veneration by the *Mahometans ;* the House he lived in was built for him by a great *Omra,* but he kept his Windows shut all day, and never opened them till towards the Evening, to give his Benedictions to a great many people, who asked them with cries, prostating themselves,[16] and kissing the ground in his presence. Most part of the *Omras* visited that cheat every evening; and when he went abroad (which happened seldom) he went in a *Palanquin,* where he shewed himself stark naked after the *Indian* fashion, and the People reverenced him as a Saint. The great Lords made him Presents, and in the Court of his House he had an Elephant chained, which was given him by a great *Omra.* Whil'st I was in my Journey to *Carnates,* the Kings little Son-in-law gave to this *Santo* a great many Jewels belonging to the Princess his Wife, Daughter to the King; and since no Man knew the motive of so great a Present, which perhaps was only some Superstitious Devotion, it was presently given out that it was to raise Forces against the King, that with the concurrence of the *Santo* he might invade[17] the Crown. Whether that report was true or false, it is certain that the King sent to the *Santo's* House, to fetch from thence his Daughters Jewels and the Elephant, and ordered him to depart out of the Kingdom. The Kings eldest Daughter was married to the Kinsman of a *Cheik* of *Mecha ;*[18] the second married *Mahmoud,* eldest Son to *Auran-Zeb,*[19] for the Reasons I mentioned already; and the third is Wife to the little Son-in-law *Mirza Abdul-Cossin,* who has Male-Children by her;[20] and they say, the fourth is designed for the King of *Viziapour.*[21]

A Moorish *Santo.*

The King of *Golconda* has vast Revenues; he is proprietory of all the Lands in his Kingdom, which he Rents out to those who offer most, except such as he gratifies his particular Friends with, to whom he gives the use of them for a certain time. The Customs of Merchants Goods that pass through his Countrey, and of the Ports of *Masulipatan* and *Madrespatan*[22] yield him much, and there is hardly any sort of Provisions in his Kingdom, from which he hath not considerable dues.

Customs.

Diamond Mines.

The Diamond-Mines pay him likewise a great Revenue,[23] and all they whom he allows to digg in; those that are towards *Masulipatan* pay him a Pagod every hour they work there, whether they find any Diamonds or not. His chief Mines are in *Carnates*[24] in divers places towards *Viziapour,* and he hath Six thousand Men continually at work there, who daily find near three Pound weight, and no body diggs there but for the King.

This Prince wears on the Crown of his head, a Jewel almost a Foot long, which is said to be of an inestimable value; it is a Rose of great Diamonds, three or four Inches diameter; in the top of that Rose there is a little Crown, out of which issues a Branch fashioned like a Palm-Tree Branch, but is round; and that Palm-Branch (which is crooked at the top) is a good Inch in Diameter, and about half a Foot long; it is made up of several Sprigs, which are (as it were) the leaves of it, and each of which have at their end a lovely long Pearl shaped like a Pear; at the Foot of this Posie, there are two Bands of Gold in fashion of Table-bracelets, in which are enchased large Diamonds set round with Rubies, which with great Pearls that hang dangling on all sides, make an exceeding rare shew; and these Bands have Clasps of Diamonds to fasten the Jewels to the head: In short, that King hath many other considerable pieces of great value in his Treasury, and it is not to be doubted, but that he surpasses all the Kings of the *Indies* in pretious Stones; and that if there were Merchants (who would give him their worth,) he would have prodigious Sums of Money.

A rich Jewel of the King of *Golconda*.

CHAPTER VIII

OF THE OMRAS *OR* OMROS *OF* GOLCONDA.

The *Omras* are the great Lords of the Kingdom, who are (for the most part) *Persians*, or the Sons of *Persians*; they are all rich, for they not only have great Pay yearly of the King for their Offices, but they make extream advantage also by the Soldiers, scarcely paying one half of the number they are obliged to entertain; besides that, they have gratifications from the King, of Lands and Villages, whereof he allows them the Use, where they commit extraordinary extractions by the *Bramens*, who are their Farmers.

These *Omras* generally make a very handsome Figure; when they go through the Town, an Elephant or two goes before them, on which three Men carrying Banners are mounted; fifty or sixty Troopers well cloathed, and riding on *Persian* or *Tartarian* Horses, with Bows and Arrows, Swords by their sides, and Bucklers on their backs, follow them at some distance; and after these come other Men on Horse-back, sounding Trumpets, and playing on Fifes.

After them comes the *Omra* on Horse-back, with thirty or forty Footmen about him, some making way, others carrying Lances, and some with fine Napkins driving away the Flies,

One of them holds an Umbrello over his Masters head, another carries the Tobacco-Pipe, and others Pots full of water in hanging Cases of Canes. The *Palanquin* carried by four Men, comes next with two other Porters for change; and all this pomp is brought up[1] by a Camel or two, with Men beating of Timbals on their backs.

When the *Omra* pleases, he takes[2] his *Palanquin*, and then his Horse is led by him.[3] The *Palanquin* is sometimes covered with Silver, and its Canes or *Bambous* tipt with Silver at both ends; the Lord is to be seen lying in it, holding Flowers in his hand, smoaking Tobacco, or else chewing *Betle* and *Areca*, shewing by that soft and effeminate Posture a most supine dissoluteness. All (who have any considerable Pay, whether Moors or Gentiles) imitate the Gentiles, and are carried through the Town in *Palanquins* well attended; and the Dutch Interpreter at *Bagnagar* (who is a Gentile,) goes at present with such an equipage, save only that instead of Camels, he hath a Chariot; but (at least) there is not a Cavalier, but hath his Umbrello bearer, his two Flie-drivers, and his Cup-bearer.

The *Betle*[4] (which these Gentlemen chew in their *Palanquin*) is a Leaf not unlike to an Orange-Tree Leaf, though it be not so broad; the Stalk of it being weak, it is commonly planted near the *Areca*-Tree, to which it clings; and indeed, the *Indians* never take Betle without an *Areca*-Nut, and they are sold together. The *Areca* is very high, and much like to an ordinary Palm-Tree; it carries its Nuts in clusters, and they are as big as Dates, and insipid. This *Betle* and *Areca* keep all the *Indians* in countenance, and they use it in the Streets and every where. They pretend that it is an excellent thing for the Stomach, and for the sweetness of Breath.

All that are called *Omras* at *Golconda*, have not the ability[5] of those whose Train and Equipage I have now observed; there are those who being not so rich, proportion their Train to their Revenue; besides, the quality of *Omra* is become so common, and so much liberty allowed to take that Title, that the *Indians* who guard the Castle and the outside of the Kings Palace, to the number of a Thousand, must needs be called *Omras* also, though their Pay be no more than about a Crown a month: But in short,[6] some of the great *Omras* are exceeding rich.

Emir-Gemla, or Mir-Gemla.

There was the *Omra*, or rather the *Emir Gemla*,[7] the Son of an Oyl-man of *Ispahan*, who had the wealth of a Prince: He left the Service of the King of *Golconda*, went over to the *Mogul*, and died Governour of *Bengala*. It is well known, that he had a design to make himself King of *Bengala*, where he was very powerful, and that he only waited for a fabourable occasion to get his Son[8] from the Court of the *Great Mogul*, where he was detained as an hostage. He had twenty *Mans* weight of Diamonds, which make Four hundred and eight

Pounds of *Hollands* weight; and all this Wealth he got by the Plunder he formerly made in *Carnates,* when he was at the head of the Army of the King of *Golconda,* at the time when that King (in conjunction with the King of *Viziapour*) made War against the King of *Bisnagar*. This General took a great many places there in a short time, but the Fort of *Guendicot*[9] standing upon the top of an inaccessible Rock, put a full stop to his Conquests. The Town is upon the side of the Hill: one must (in a manner)[10] crawl up to come to it, and there is no way to enter it but by one narrow Path. *Mir-Gemla* being unable to force it, made use of his cunning and Money, and so managed those (whom the *Naique* sent to him to negotiate a Peace,) that he wheedled out the Governour, under pretext of entring into a League with him for great Designs; but no sooner was he come to the place of meeting, but the *Omras* made sure of his Person, contrary to the Promise he had given, and kept him constantly with him till he put him in possession of *Guendicot*. This place is within ten days Journey of St. *Thomas,* upon the main Land. *Guendicot.*

I had been two months in the Countrey when Winter came on; it began in *June* by Rain and Thunder, but the Thunder lasted not above four days, and the Rain poured down with great storms of Wind till the middle of *July,* though now and then we had some fair weather: The rest of that month was pretty fair; in *August, September* and *October,* there fell great Rains, but without any Thunder; the Rivers overflowed so prodigiously that there was no passing over the Bridges, no not with the help of Elephants. The River of *Bagnagar*[11] beat down almost two thousand Houses, in which many People perished. The Air was a little cold in the night-time and morning, there was some heat during the day, but it was as moderate as it is in *France* in the month of May, and the Air continued in this temper until February the year following, when the great heats began again. Winter in *Golconda.*

These Rains render the Land of this Kingdom exceeding fertile, which yields all things in abundance, and especially Fruits. Vines are plentiful there, and the Grapes are ripe in *January,* though there be some that are not gathered but in *February, March* or *April,* according as the Vines are exposed to the heat; they make White-wine of them. When the Grapes are gathered, they Prune the Vines, and about Midsummer thay yield Verjuice. In this Countrey also they have two Crops a year of Rice, and many other Grains.

CHAPTER IX

THE AUTHORS DEPARTURE FROM BAGNAGAR *FOR* MASULIPATAN.

Having stayed long enough at *Bagnagar,* I had a design to see some Countries of the coast of *Coromandel ;* and notwithstanding it was Winter, I resolved to set out for *Masulipatan.* Seeing there was no Travelling neither in Coach nor Chariot, because of the badness of the Ways, and the frequent overflowings of the Rivers and Brooks, I hired a Horse for my self, and two Oxen for my Servant and Baggage, and I parted with some Merchants. We came to a Bourg called *Elmas-Kepentch,*[1] eight Leagues from *Bagnagar*: They who have a mind to go to the Diamond-mines of *Gany,*[2] take their way by *Tenara,*[3] where the King has a stately Palace, consisting of four large Piles of Stone-building, two Stories high, and adorned with *Portico's,* Halls and Galleries, and before the Palace there is a large regular Square ; besides these Royal Appartments, there are Habitations for Travellers, and unalienable Rents for entertaining the poor, and all Passengers that please to stop there.

Diamond-mines. *Tenara,* a stately Palace.

Having no business at these Diamond-mines, which are six or seven days Journey from *Golconda,* we went the other way. In all our Journey, we found but three small Towns, which are *Panguel,*[4] *Sarchel*[5] and *Penguetchepoul ;*[6] but we met with several Rivers, the most considerable of which are *Kachkna*[7] and *Moucy ;*[8] we went through sixteen or seventeen Villages, about which the Fields are always green and pleasant to the eye, though the way be very bad. There I saw Trees of all kinds that are in the *Indies,* and even *Cassia-*Trees,[9] though they are scarce in other Countries of the *Indies ;* at length (in ten days time) we arrived at *Masulipatan,*[10] the whole Journey makes about fifty three *French* Leagues, and in fair weather they perform it in a weeks time.

Masulipatan lies on the coast of *Coromandel,* in sixteen degrees and a half North-Latitude. This Town is Situated upon the Gulf of *Bengala* East South-East from *Bagnagar,* though the Town be but small, yet it is well Peopled ; the Streets are narrow, and it is intollerably hot there from *March* till *July.* The Houses are all separated one from another, and the Water is brackish, because of the Tides that come up to it ; there is great Trading there in *Chites,* because, besides those that are made there, a great many are brought from St. *Thomas,* which are much finer, and of better Colours than those of the other parts of the *Indies.*

The Road from *Bagnagar* to

Elmas-Quipentche, eight Leagues from *Bagnagar. Tchellapeli* 6 Leag. from *Elmas. Panguel,* a Town. *Amanguel* 6 Leag. and a half from *Tchellapeli. Surchel-Quipentche,* a Town, Half a Leag. from

Amen. *Mousi,* a River. *Gougelou* 3 Leag. from *Sarchel.* *Anendeguir* 4 Leag. from *Gougelou.* *Penguetchpoul,* a Town, 5 Leag. from *Anendeguir.* *Pantela,* 5 Leag. and a half from *Penguetch.* *Matcher,* 4 Leag. from *Pantela.* *Quachgna,* a River. *Ovir* 4 Leag. from *Matcher.* *Milmol,* 4 Leag. from *Ovir.* *Goroupet,* 2 Leag. from *Milmol.* *Masulipatan,* half a Leag. from *Goroupet.* *Masulipatan.*[11]

The Coast is excellent,[12] and therefore Ships come thither from all Nations, and go from thence into all Countries. I saw there *Cochinchinese,* Men of *Siam, Pegu,* and of many other Kingdoms of the East.

The Countrey of *Masulipatan* (as all the rest of the Coast) is so full of Idolaters, and the Pagods so full of the lascivious Figures of Monsters, that one cannot enter them without horrour; it is exceeding fruitful, and Provisions are very cheap there. The people of our *Caravan* had a Sheep for Twelve pence, a Partridge for a Half penny, and a Fowl for less than Two pence; it is the same almost all over the coast of *Coromandel,* wherein there is no more commonly comprehended but what reaches from the Cape of *Negapatan* to the Cape of *Masulipatan*: But some Authors carry it further, and will have it to reach from Cape *Comory* to the Western mouth of the *Ganges,* though others make it to end at the Cape, which the *Portuguese* call *Das Palmas.*[13] Idolaters. Figures of Monsters. The extent of the Coast of *Coromandel.* The Cape *Das Palmas.*

There are several Towns on this Coast, some of which are good, and amongst others *Negapatan,* which lyes in the Latitude of twelve degrees:[14] *Trangabar,* which is almost in the same Latitude; *Meliapour* or St. *Thomas* which lyes in the heighth of thirteen degrees and a half, and which the *Moors* (with the assistance of the *Dutch*) took back from the *Portuguese* in the year One thousand six hundred sixty two. *Negapatan.* *Trangabar.* *Meliapour* or St. *Thomas.*

The Kingdom of *Golconda* reaches not above two Leagues beyond St. *Thomas.* They say that St. *Thomas* suffered Martyrdom in that Town which bears his name; at St. *Thomas* they make Lime of such Shells as are brought from St. *Michael* in *Normandy,* and for that end they burn them with Hogsdung.

The Small-pox is very frequent in that Countrey; but there is another more violent Distemper that commonly commits greater ravage there. It is called *Akeron,*[15] and only seizes Children; it is an inflammation of the Tongue and Mouth, proceeding from too great heat; their Parents are careful to cool them from time to time with Herbs that are good against that Disease, for otherwise it seizes the Guts, reaches to the Fundament, and kills the Child. There are many *Naiques* to the South of St. *Thomas,* who are Sovereigns: The *Naique* of *Madura* is one; he of *Tangiour* is at present a Vassal to the King of *Viziapour.* *Naique* properly signifies a Captain; heretofore they were Governours of Places, and Officers of the King; but having Revelled, they made themselves Sovereigns. *Akeron,* a distemper. *Naiques* that are Sovereigns.

Poliacate. *Poliacate*[16] is to the North of St. *Thomas,* and the Factory (which the *Dutch* have established there) is one of the best they have in the *Indies,* by reason of the Cotton-cloaths, of which they have great Ware-houses full there. At *Poliacate* they re- Salt-Petre. fine the Salt-Petre which they bring from *Bengala,* and made the Gun-powder, with which they furnish their other Factories · they refine the Salt-Petre that they send to *Europe* in *Batavia.* *Gueldria.* The Governour of *Gueldria,*[17] which is the Fort of *Poliacate,* has of the *Dutch* fifty Crowns a month Pay, with fifty Crowns more for his Table, Provisions of Wine and Oyl, and his Cloaths, which he can take when he pleases out of the Companies Ware-houses. The current Money at *Poliacate,* are *Roupies* and *Pagods,* which are there worth four Roupies, that *Fanons,* Money. is almost six *French* Livres ; they have *Fanons*[18] also which are small pieces, half Gold and half Silver ; they have the same Stamp as the Pagods have ; six and a half of them (with half a Quarter-piece) make a *Roupie,* and six and twenty and a half a *Gazer,* Money. *Pagod* : They have also *Gazers,*[19] which are small Copper-pieces, as big as a *Fanon,* forty of which go to a *Fanon ;* and the *Dutch* at present Coin all these pieces of Money.

Palicole. *Dacheron.* Their Company has a Factory also at *Palicole,*[20] two days Journey Northward from *Masulipatan,* and another at *Dacheron*[21] on the same Coast. *Bimilipatan*[22] is four days Journey Northwards of *Masulipatan.* The Traffick of those parts consists in Rice, fine Cloaths, Iron, Wax and Lacre, which is as good as at Pegu ; and from abroad they import Copper, Tin, Lead and *Bimilipatan.* *Cicacola.* Pepper : From *Bimilipatan* to *Cicacola*[23] it is fifteen hours travelling by Land, and that is the last Town of the Kingdom of *Golconda,* on the side of *Bengala.* The Governours of that Countrey are great Tyrants, and if any one threaten to inform the King of their exactions they'll laugh at it, and say that he is King of *Golconda,* and they of their Governments ; from *Cicacola* to *Bengala* it is a months Journey by Land.

In many places of the Kingdom of *Golconda* the people are much infested by Serpents ; but one may cure himself of their Sting, provided he neglect not the wound, and hold a burning Coal very near the part that is stung ; the Venom is perceived to work out by degrees, and the heat of the Fire is not at all troublesome : They make use also of the Stone of Cobra,[24] which hath been spoken of before.

When I thought my self sufficiently informed of the places on the Coast of *Coromandel,* I returned from *Masulipatan* to *Bagnagar,* and stayed there three weeks longer, because I would not go from thence but in company of *Monsieur Bazon,* who had some business still remaining to make an end of ; so that I had as much time as I needed to see the Celebration of The Festival of *Hussein* in *Golconda.* the Festival of *Hussein,* the Son of *Aly,*[25] which fell out at that time. The *Moors* of *Golconda* celebrated it with more

Fopperies than they do in *Persia ;* there is nothing but Masquarades for the space of ten days ; they erect Chappels in all the Streets with Tents, which they fill with Lamps, and adorn with Foot-Carpets ; the Streets are full of People, and all of them almost have their Faces covered with Sifted ashes ; they who are naked cover their whole Body with them, and they who are cloathed their Apparel ; but the Cloaths they wear on these days are generally extravagant, and their Head-tire much more ; they all carry Arms ; most part have their Swords naked, and the poor have Wooden ones ; several drag about the Streets long Chains as big as ones Arm, which are tied to their Girdle ; and it being painful to drag them, they thereby move the pity of Zelots who touch them, and having kissed their Fingers, lift them up to their Eyes, as if these Chains were holy Relicks. They make Processions, wherein many carry Banners, and others have Poles, on which there is a Silver-Plate that represents *Husseins* hand ; some with little Houses of a light wood upon their heads, skip, and turn at certain Cadences of a Song ; others dance in a round, holding the point of their naked Swords upwards, which they clash one against another, crying with all their force *Hussein* : The publick Wenches themselves come in for a share in this Festival, by their extravagant Dances, Habits and Head-tire.

The Heathen Idolaters celebrate this Feast also for their diversion, and they do it with such Fopperies as far surpass the *Moors ;* they drink, eat, laugh, and dance on all hands, and they have Songs which savour little of a doleful pomp, that the *Moors* pretend to represent : They observe only not to shave themselves during the ten days ; but though it be prohibited to sell any thing except Bread and Fruit, yet there is plenty of all things in private Houses.

This Festival is hardly ever celebrated without Blood-shed ; for there being several *Sunnis* who laugh at the others, and the *Chyais* not being able to endure it, they often quarrel and fight, which is a very proper representation of the Feast ; and at that time there is no enquiry made into Man-slaughter, because the *Moors* believe, that during these ten days the Gates of Paradise are open to receive those who die for the *Musselman* Faith. At *Bagnagar* I saw one of these quarrels raised by a Tartar, who spake some words against *Hussein* : Some *Chyais* being scandalized thereat, fell upon him to be revenged, but he killed three of them with his Sword, and many Musket-Shot were fired : A Gentleman (who would have parted them) received a wound in the Belly that was like to have cost him his life, and seven were killed out-right : Nay, some of the Servants of the *Grand Vizir* were engaged in it ; and this chief Minister passing by that place in his *Palanquin,* made haste down that he might get on Horse-back and ride away. Next day after the Feast they make other processions, sing doleful Ditties, and carry about Coffins covered with divers Stuffs, with a Turban on each Coffin, to represent the interment of *Hussein* and his Men, who were killed at the Battel of *Kerbela* by the Forces of *Calif Yezid.*[26]

CHAPTER X

OF THE AUTHORS DEPARTURE FROM BAGNAGAR *FOR* SURRAT, *AND OF* MORDECHIN.

No sooner was this Feast ended, but *Monsieur Bazon* advertised me to prepare for my return to *Surrat,* which I did, so that *November* the thirteenth we parted from *Bagnagar,* with a Pass-port he had obtained from the King, to pay no Duties throughout the whole Kingdom ; but we went another way than we came. When we came to *Danec*[1] they demanded Duties for three Villages, but with so much eagerness, that it seemed we were in the fault that we had not our Money ready in our hands to give it them ; however, when the Man (whom *Sidy Muzafer* had given *Monsieur Bazon* to make good the Passport) had shew'n it to the Collectors, they were satisfied and only asked some small gratuity to buy *Betle ;* and it was just so with us in all places where Toll is payed. We continued our Journey by most ugly ways ; and after seven days March arrived at the Town of *Beder,* mentioned before which is but two and twenty Leagues distant from *Bagnagar.* In this Road we found the Rivers of *Nerva, Penna* and *Mousi,* two little Towns, called *Moumin* and *Pendgioul,*[2] and a great many Villages. The Kingdom of *Golconda* ends on this side, betwixt the Bourgs *Couir* and *Senjavour'd.*[3]

Campings or Lodgings from *Bagnagar* to *Beder.*[4]

From *Bagnagar* to *Danec* five Cosses. *Nervna,* a Riv. To *Tchelcour* 7 Cosses. *Penu,* a River. To *Squequerdeh* 6 Cosses. To *Yacout-Kepentch* 3 Cosses. To *Yenquetala* 6 Cosses. *Moumin,* a Town. *Pendgioul* a Town. To *Couir* 8 Cosses. *Senjavour'd.* To *Dediqui* 6 Cos. To *Beder* 4 Cos. The Cosses reduced make 22 Leag. and a half. Lodgings from *Beder* to *Patry.* To *Etour* 12 Coss. *Manjera* a River. To *Morg* 8 Coss. To *Oudeguir* 6 Coss. to *Helly* 6 Coss. to *Rajoura* 6 Coss. to *Saourgaon* 6 Coss. *Careck* a River. *Ganga* a River. To *Caly* 8 Coss. to *Raampouri* 6 Coss. to *Patry* 8 Coss. the whole 33 Leagues.[5] The way from *Patry* to *Brampour.* To *Gahelgaon* 9 Coss. *Doudna* a River. *Patou* a Town, 6 Coss. *Ner* a Town, 6 Coss. *Seouny* 8 Coss. *Chendequer* a Town, 2 Coss. *Ourna* a River. *Zafravad* a Town, 10 Coss. *Piply* 10 Coss. *Deoulgan* 6 Coss. *Rouquera* a Town, 6 Coss. *Melcapour* a Town, 2 Coss. *Nervar* a River. *Pourna* River. *Japour* 12 Coss. *Tapty* Riv. *Brampour* a Town, 2 Coss. The whole 39 Leag. and a half.[6]

We parted from *Beder* the twentieth of *November,* and I travelled thirty three Leagues more with *Monsieur Bazon ;* but because he had business at *Aurangeabad,* and I at *Brampour,* we parted the thirtieth of *November* at the Town of *Patry,*[7] after we had passed the Rivers *Manjera, Careck* and *Ganga.*[8] We found upon our Road the Towns of *Oudeguir,*[9] *Rajoura*[10] and *Patry,* where the Governours took great care to guard themselves from the Parties of the King of *Viziapours* Army, with whom the Mogul was in War. For my part, (having taken another Servant) I took my way by the Towns of *Patou, Ner, Chendequer, Zafravad, Rouquera* and *Melcapour,* all which six are not so good as one of our ordinary Cities ; and on *Thursday* the ninth of *December* I arrived at *Brampour,* which I have described before. In my way from *Patry* to *Brampour,* I found the Rivers *Doudna, Nervar, Pourna* and *Tapty,*[11] and I spent nine and twenty days in that Journey, though in another season of the year it be performed in two and twenty.

I parted from *Brampour* (the Capital City of the Province of *Candiche*) to return to *Surrat* by the common Road, and falling sick of a Cholick by the way, I learned a cure for it. The *Portuguese* call the four sorts of Cholicks that people are troubled with in the *Indies* (where they are frequent) *Mordechin.*[12] The first is a bare Cholick, but that causes sharp Pains ; the second, besides the Pain causes a Loosness. They who are troubled with the third, have violent Vomitings with the Pains ; and the fourth produces all the three Symptomes, to wit, Vomiting, Loosness, and extream Pain ; and this last I take to be the *Cholera morbus.* These distempers proceed most commonly from Indigestion, and cause sometimes such cutting Pains, that they kill a Man in four and twenty hours. The Remedy which is used in the *Indies* against it, is to heat a Peg of Iron about half as big as ones Finger red hot, clap it to the sole of the Patients heel, and hold it there till he be no longer able to endure it, so that the Iron leave a mark behind it: The same must be done to the other heel with the same red hot iron, and that Remedy is commonly so effectual that the Pains instantly cease. If the Patient be let Blood with that burning, his life will be in evident danger ; and several People have told me that when they let Blood before they burn the heel, the Patient infallibly dies, just as many days after he hath been let Blood, as he was ill before ; but Blood-letting is not dangerous two days after the Operation: There are some who make use of Ligatures for this distemper, and bind the Patients head so fast with a Swathing-band, as if they had a mind to squeeze out his Brains ; they do the same with his Back, Reins, Thighs and Legs ; and when the Patient finds no good of this Ligature, they think him past cure.

Mordechin.

A Remedy for the Cholick.

A Flux alone is also a common and very dangerous distemper in the *Indies,* for many die of it, and the least overheating brings it upon one. The Remedy is to take two Drachms

A Flux or Loosness. A Remedy for a Flux.

of torrified *Rhubarb*,[13] and a Drachm of Cummin-seed ;[14] all must be beat into a Powder, and taken in Limon-water, or (if that be wanting) in Rose-water. The common people of the *Indies* have no other remedy against this distemper, but Rice boyled in water till it be dry, they eat it with Milk turned sower, and use no other Food as long as the distemper lasts ; the same they use for a Bloody Flux.[15]

I travelled from *Brampour* to *Surrat* with a *Banian* and a *Mula* that came from Court. This *Mula* having represented his poverty to the King, obtained a Pension from him of Five hundred *Roupies*, which amount to about seven hundred and fifty *French* Livres, which was assigned to him upon a Village. It is three-score and fifteen Leagues from *Brampour* to *Surrat*, and we spent a fortnight in the Journey ; we found many Towns and Castles on our Road, and were never an hour without seeing some Bourg or Village ; and seeing Lions many times happen to be in the way, there were Sheds or Cottages under Trees, whither the *Indians* betook themselves in the night-time ; we crossed also some Mountains and eight Rivers ; I saw nothing else but what was very common. We were put in fear of the Troopers of the *Raja* of *Badur*, who skulk in the Mountains of *Candiche*, and roam about every where, though at present their Master renders obedience to the *Great Mogul* ; but we met with none of them, and arrived safely at *Surrat*.

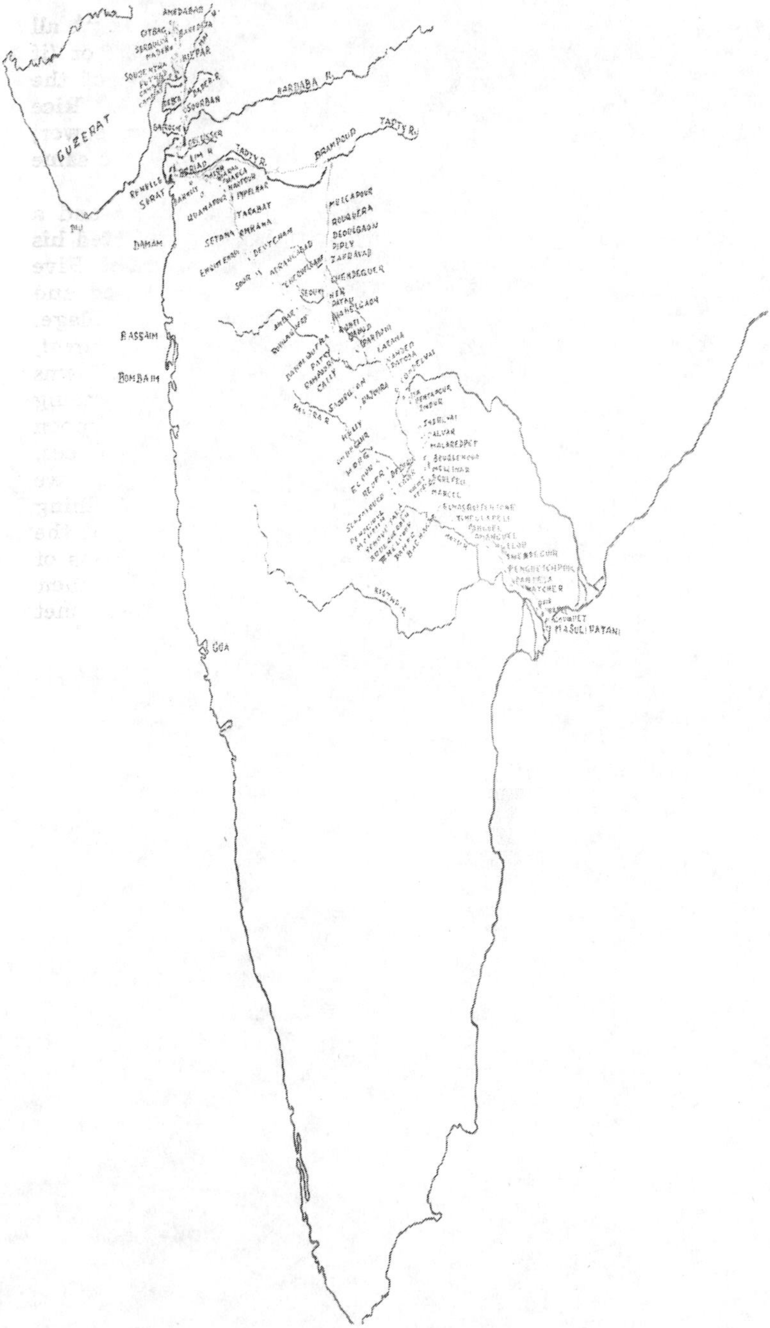
GUZERAT
AMEDABAD
BARDABA R.
SOURBAN
TAPTY R.
BRAMPOUR
TAPTY R.
SURAT
TARABAT
DAMAM
ORANGABAD
BASSAIM
BOMBAIM
CHENDEGUER
MALAREDPET
MARCEL
GOA
MASULIPATAN

INDIAN TRAVELS OF CARERI

A
VOYAGE
Round the WORLD
By Dr. *John Francis Gemelli Careri.*
PART III.
Containing the most Remarkable Things he saw in *INDOSTAN.*

Dr Gemelli Careri

A VOYAGE ROUND THE WORLD

By Dr. JOHN FRANCIS GEMELLI CARERI.

PART III

Containing the most Remarkable Things he saw in

INDOSTAN

BOOK I

CHAPTER I

THE DESCRIPTION OF DAMAM, *A CITY BELONGING TO THE* PORTUGUESES *IN* INDOSTAN.

Never was Traveller better pleas'd, after enduring many hardships, for a considerable time in far distant Countries, in being safely restor'd to his native Soil,[1] enjoying the company of dearest Friends, and relating what he had seen; than I was at my Landing in *Indostan,* which made me forget the Toils of my troublesome Voyage. If it be extraordinary delightful to feed the Ears with the Relation of what precious things Nature has bestow'd on that wealthy Country, for the ease of humane Life; you may judge how great a satisfaction it was to me, to be upon the spot where I might actually see and be acquainted with them. Being therefore lodg'd in the Monastery of the *Augustinians*[2] in *Damam,*[3] and having a little rested me after my Voyage, on *Munday*[4] the 11th of *January* 1695, I apply'd my self to landing of my Equipage. The *Portuguese* Factor was so civil that as at *Bander-Congo*[5] my Portmantues had not been search'd for the sake of the Commissioner; so neither were they open'd at *Damam* through his courtesy. He obligingly told me, he could wish I had brought the value of 100000 Crowns; for in regard I was a stranger he would not have taken any Custom of me; for had I been a *Portuguese,* I must have paid 10 *per cent.*[6] (which to say the Truth would have been considerable) to the Gentils,[7] who farm'd the Customs. When I acquainted *F. Francis*[7a] with this Generosity of the Factors, he told me, that notwithstanding his being a

Gemelli, 1695.

Religious Man, having brought two Bales of Carpets, for the service of their Church, the Custom-house Officers had stopp'd them for their Duties. I apply'd my self to the Factor, to have them restor'd to him, representing *F. Francis*'s great worth, and how much he was esteem'd at *Ispahan* by all the great ones; so that at length through my inter-cession he recover'd his Bales.

Damam City.

The City *Damam* is seated on the left side of the River of that Name,[8] in 20 degrees of Latitude. Tho' but ill peopled, it is Beautiful enough, and built after the *Italian* manner. Three broad Streets divide it in length, and four across them; all so regularly built, that the corners of the Houses (which are for the most part trench'd about)[9] do not jut out an Inch one beyond another; 'tis true most of them have only a Ground Floor, very few having any Rooms above, and they are generally Til'd. Instead of Glass their Windows are made of Oyster Shells curiously Wrought and Transparent. Every House has its Garden or Orchard with Fruit Trees.

Air.

The Air of *Damam* is very good, being North of *Goa;* and tho its Summer and Winter be at the same time as it is at *Goa*[10] (for whilst I stay'd it was Summer in those parts, and the Winter is from *May* till the end of *September,*[11] with continual Rain and Storms) yet during that time I call'd Summer, there is some sort of Coolness in the Morning, which is not at *Goa.*

Fortification.

It has four modern and well Built Bastions;[12] but 'tis somewhat irregular, and ill provided with Cannon. The Compass is about two Miles, without any Ditch on the East and South sides, but with a low Work, or Intrenchment Breast high. On the other sides the Ditch is fill'd by an Arm of the River, towards which there are two Gates, and before the first a Draw-Bridge. All the Walls are back'd with Ramparts.

Government.

The Government is in a Captain, or Commandant,[13] and it is kept by a good Garrison. The Factor before mention'd has the charge of the King's Revenue. It is inhabited by *Portugueses, Mestizos,*[14] who are born of white Fathers and black Mothers, *Pagans* and *Mahometans;* but these two last are not allow'd the free exercise of their Religion. There are several good Monasteries, as those of the *Jesuits,* the *Recolets,*[15] the *Augustinians,* and the Parish Church; but none of them has above three Altars opposite to the Door. The Monasteries are convenient enough for the religious Men. That of *S. Augustin,* where I resided, had an excellent square Cloister, with twelve good Stone Columns, besides the four great Pillars at the Angles. Above in the Dormitory there are twenty eight smaller Columns.

Monasteries.

Old *Damam.*

All that has been here mention'd belongs to new *Damam;* for the old is on the right of the aforesaid River, consisting of poor low Houses, or rather Cottages with Mud Walls, and cover'd with Palm Tree Leaves. Here most of the *Moors* and *Gentils* live, having their Shops of several Trades along the ill contriv'd Streets.

Between the old City and the new is the Harbour made by the River *Damam ;* but no Vessels either great or small can come in but at Flood, during six Hours of the Day, as was said in the foregoing Book, as it is at *Ostend* in *Flanders*[16] and *Çalis* in *Picardy.*[17] The Stream is so rapid at Ebb that no Oars can stem it, but they must needs come to an Anchor (unless the Wind sets in very hard,)[18] and stay till the next Flood. This is to be understood of Vessels of small Burden ; for great Ones can neither go in or out but twice a Month, that is, when the Moon is new and at the full, because of the Spring Tides,[19] which there they call great Tides. The Port.

The Entrance into this Harbour is defended by a small Castle seated on the side of old *Damam.* It is longish[20] and has three Bastions, well enough furnish'd with Cannon. On the North side of the City is a small Suburb, consisting of Cottages cover'd with Palm-Tree-Leaves, and inhabited by Christian Blacks ; and at a small distance from it, a Village of *Gentils,* with a *Bazar,*

In the Year 1535. *Martin Alfonso de Sousa*[21] took and destroy'd *Damam* in three Days. In 1559. *D. Constantin* Son to the Duke of *Braganza*[22] Viceroy of *India,* retook it from *Asid Bosita Abyssino,*[23] who had revolted from his Sovereign, and made it of considerable Strength. The great *Mogul* has attempted to reduce it several times ;[24] and particularly fifty Years[25] ago *Aurenge-Zeb-Alanguir* afterwards King, lay'd Siege to it with an Army of eighty thousand Men ;[26] but the *Portugueses* defended it so bravely, making a terrible Slaughter of the Enemy with their continual Sallies at Night, that he was forc'd after lying three[27] Months before it, to march off with the loss of half his Army. The occasion of it was, that the *Moguls* resolving to make the last Effort to take it, and having to this purpose plac'd two hundred Elephants in the Front with long sharp Swords in their Trunks ; the Beasts frighted with the Fire of the *Portugueses* Muskets,[28] ran disorderly upon the *Mahometan* Army, cutting in pieces abundance of Men, with the same Weapons they were Arm'd to destroy the Christians. The Barbarians being but in a bad condition by their own Contrivance ; the *Portugueses* retiring into the Town, began in scorn to throw Cockle-shells,[29] which the *Mahometans* abhor, into the Enemies Camp, with an Engine they call *Papagayo,*[30] made of Pastboard strengthened with Canes, and carry'd up into the Air by the Wind and guided by a Rope. *Maff. Hist. Ind.* page 252 *lit. F.*

The *Portugueses* Live very great[31] in *India,* both as to their Tables, Cloathing, and number of *Cafres,*[32] or Slaves to serve them ; having some of these to carry them in *Palanchines* *Portugueses* way of Living.

on their Shoulders, and others great Umbrelloes of Palm-Tree Leaves. The *Palanchine* is like a wooden Bier painted and gelt, seven Spans long, and four in breadth, with two well wrought Risings at both ends. On it they lay a *Persian* Carpet, and over that a piece of *Russian* Leather, that it may not heat their Backs, and two Silk Pillows, on which they lie along.[33] There are Ropes, or Iron Rings fastned to the ends, through which they run a *Bamboa*,[34] or thick *Indian* Cane, to lay on the Shoulders of the Blacks, two before, and two behind, all in a Row or File ; very few being carry'd by two. The Person in the *Palanchine* is cover'd with an Umbrelloe of eight Spans Diameter, carry'd by a Slave, or else fastned to the *Bamboa* that crosses the *Palankine*, and may be turn'd to that side the Sun is on. In rainy Weather they use another sort of Carriage call'd *Andora*,[35] with a Covering made of Palm-Tree Leaves, sloaping like the Ridge of a House, fix'd upon the *Bamboa* ; there are two small Windows or Doors on the sides, that may be open'd to see who goes along the Street. The *Andora* differs from the *Palankine* in nothing, but the *Bamboa* ; because the latter has a crooked one, that he who is carry'd may sit up ; and that of the *Andora* is strait, so that he must lye along as if he were in Bed. This would be a convenient way of Travelling on those soft Pillows for an effeminate European, who should find fault with the joulting of the *Neapolitan* Sedans, and would desire to travel in Safety and Sleep. They are generally us'd there by Women, Religious Men, and all other Persons ; a Religious Men [*sic.*] of any note, never being seen abroad in *India*, but in an *Andora* or *Palankine*, attended by many Slaves, there being but few Converts. Besides, the Charge is very inconsiderable, for they that have no Slaves, pay four *Indians* but twelve *Coslines* of *Naples*[36] a Month for carrying them.

Palankines and Andoras.

Coaches.

When they go out of Town, or travel some Days Journey, they use a sort of Coach drawn by Oxen, guided by a Cord run through their Nostrils. These Coaches are square like a Chair, and can hold but two ; the top of it is commonly cover'd with Silk,[37] three of the sides open, and the back clos'd with Canes interwoven one within another.

Provisions.

They have no good Flesh to Eat in *Damam* ; because the Beef and Pork is ill tasted : They seldom kill Sheep or Goats ; and every Body cannot go to the Price of Fowls. Fish is also scarce, and none of the best ; besides they have no Oil of Olives to dress it, but instead thereof make use of that of *Coco*-Nuts. The Bread[38] is Extraordinary good, even that they make of Rice. Thus a Stranger at *Damam*, who is not entertain'd by some Body, has but an ill time of it, if he expects for his Mony to furnish himself in the Market ; because the Gentry have all their Provisions in their Houses, and the meaner Sort makes a shift with Rice and *Sura*,[39] that is, Palm-Tree Wine, scarce ever tasting Bread all the Year about.

Fruits and Herbs.

There is not any one sort of our *European* Fruits, but all *Indian*, as *Coco*-Nuts,[40] *Mansanas, Giambos, Undis, Ananasas, Atas, Anonas,* and others we shall describe in their proper Place, and give the Cuts of them. As for Herbs there are many of the *European*, and of the Country; among which the Roots of that call'd *Cassaras*,[41] being like white Tartuffs, or Pignuts; of the bigness and taste of a Chestnut, are excellent.

Beasts.

Damam is also very famous for all sorts of Game; for besides all the *European* Creatures of[42] wild Boars, Wolves, Foxes, and Hares; in the Mountains there are those they call *Baccareos*,[43] in shape like Bucks, and in taste like Swine; *Zambares*,[44] whose Bodies are like Oxen, and their Horns, and Feet like those of a Stag; *Gazelles*,[45] which are like Goats; *Dives*[46] like Foxes; *Roses*, with the Body like a Cow, so call'd from a Rose they have on the Breast; the Male of the Species is call'd *Meru*, and has Horns half a Span long, and the Body and Tail like a Horse;[47] Wolves like Stags with hairy Horns;[48] *European* Stags; black wild Cats with Wings[49] like those of the Bats, with which they skip and fly from one Tree to another, tho' they be far distant; wild Horses and Cows. There are three sorts of Tigers, call'd *Bibo*,[50] *Cito*,[51] and the Royal,[52] each differing from the other in bigness of Body, and variety of Spots. It being their Property to be continually in search of wild Boars, these taught to defend themselves by Nature, tumble in the Mire, and dry themselves in the Sun so often, till the Mud is crusted hard on them. Being thus arm'd, instead of being made a Prey, they often gore the Tygers with their sharp Tusks; for they working with their Claws on the hard Mud, are a long time pulling it off, and by that means give the Boars time to kill them.

The *Portugueses* have two ways of killing Tygers, one is lying conceal'd in a Ditch, near the Water where they come to Drink; the other going in a Cart drawn gently[53] through the Wood by Oxen,[54] and thence shooting them. But they use all their Endeavours to hit them on the Forehead, for if the Tyger falls not the first Shot, it grows so enrag'd with the Hurt, that it certainly tears the Hunter in pieces.

Birds.

Besides four footed Beasts, there is great plenty in the Woods of Peacocks, Patridges of two sorts, Ducks, Pigeons, Turtle-Doves, Swallows, Rooks, and other sorts known in *Europe*. They for Pastime keep a sort in Cages about as big as a Thrush, call'd *Martinhos*[55] of the City, and of the Country. The first are black and white; the latter of an ash Colour, with a red Breast.

Diseases.

A Man[56] in *India* must be very regular in Eating, or he will fall into some incurable Distemper; or at least such as must be cure[d] after the Country fashion[57] with Fire ; Experience having shewn that *European* Medicines are of no use there. The Disease they call *Mordazin*[58] is a complication of Fever, Vomiting, Weakness in the Limbs, and Head-ach. It always proceeds from too much Eating, and is cur'd by burning both the Heels with a red hot Spit, till the Patient feels the heat of the Fire. That they call *Bombaraki,* and *Naricut,*[59] swells and causes a violent pain in the Belly, and to cure it, Fire is also apply'd to the Swelling, so that those who have the good Fortune to recover carry the signs of the Fire afterwards on their Belly. For this reason the Physitians that go out of *Portugal* into those parts, must at first keep company with the *Indian* Surgeons to be fit to Practice ; otherwise if they go about to cure those Distempers, so far different from ours after the *European* manner, they may chance to Kill more than they Cure. For fear of these Diseases on Flesh Days they only eat Flesh at Dinner, and generally Fish at Night.

Thevenot Voyage disc. Indies c. 10 p. 319.

Habit.

The Habit of the *Portugueses* that have setled their aboad in *India*[60] is very odd, for under their Coats or Vests they wear a sort of Breeches, call'd *Candales,*[61] the like whereof I never saw in any part of *Europe ;* for when they are ty'd they leave something like the tops of Boots on the Leg. Others under a short Doublet, wear wide Silk[62] Breeches ; and some have them hang down to their Ankles, so that they serve for Hose.

The *Gentils* wear a long Silk Garment, gather'd about the Wast like a Petticoat. It is ty'd with Ribbons before upon the Breast, and under the left Arm like the *Persian Cabayas ;*[63] and with a Girdle about the middle ; under it they have long Breeches down to their Heels. On their Shoulders hangs a piece of Silk or Woollen,[64] which they wrap about their Head when it is cold, the Turbant being but very small. Others go naked, only covering their Privities with a Clout.

The Women have no other Garment but a long piece of Stuff, wherewith they cover all their Body, except their Legs and part of their Belly. Some add a little sort of Smock with half Sleeves ; adorning their bare Arms with Bracelets, and Strings of Glass and Latton ;[65] their Ears with large Silver Pendents, and their Ankles with Rings of the same Metal.

Wednesday 12th, I went to visit the King's Factor, being much oblig'd to him for his Civility. The same Day I went with *F. Constantin* to old *Damam* for Pastime. *Thursday* 13th, we went to take the Air in a Garden of the *Augustinians,* as well the religious Men, as their Guests and others, in five of the Country Coaches, *F. Francis* treated us generously.[66] Coming home I saw them on the Shore building a Vessel they call Galavetta,[67] which was all Pinn'd with Wood, and Caulk'd with Cotton,

CHAPTER II

THE AUTHORS SHORT VOYAGE TO SURATTE, *AND RETURN TO* DAMAM.

Having a curiosity to see *Suratte,* and it being easie to go thither ; because the Convoy was ready to sail for *Cambaya* and other Parts,[1] I went on *Friday* 14th, to give a visit to the Commadore of the Galliots that were to Convoy the Trading Vessels, and desir'd him to give me my Passage aboard his, which was built Frigot[2] fashion and carry'd twenty Guns. He civilly granted it, so Courteous is the *Portuguese* Nation, and therefore having return'd thanks I went home to make ready. *Saturday* 15th, after Dinner, leaving my Luggage with *F. Francis* to avoid all Trouble of that severe Custom-House, I imbark'd with my Man aboard the Commadore's Galliot, and the great Stream carrying us out of the Harbour presently after Noon,[3] we Sail'd with a fair Wind which continu'd all Night.

Sunday 16th, about break of Day we came in sight of the Bay of *Suratte,* that City being but sixty Miles from *Damam,* and entring it with a fair Wind, came to an Anchor at *Suali,*[4] twelve Miles from the City. I immediately went a Shore with the Commadore's Nephew, where the Custom-House Officers search'd our Bags narrowly for Pearls, or *Zecchines.*[5] Then I went to see the Director of the *French* Company,[6] who kept me with him.[6a]

Suratte is seated in twenty Degrees of Latitude, and a hundred and five of Longitude,[7] at the Mouth of the Bay of *Cambaya* and Kingdom of *Guzaratte.* It is not large, enclose'd by a weak Wall, built after it was Plunder'd by *Savagi,* or *Kacagi.*[8] The Castle is no better, having four Towers but no Ramparts, but either coming from Sea or Land it must be pass'd by to come at the City. The Governor of it only commands the Garrison Souldiers ; the City being govern'd by a *Nabab,*[9] who receives the King's Taxes throughout the whole Province. The private Houses are built with Mud mixt with Cows Dung, and small Brush-wood broke ; there are not above a dozen good ones belonging to *French, English, Dutch* and *Mahometan* Merchants. Nevertheless *Suratte* is the prime Mart of *India,* all Nations in the World Trading thither, no Ship sailing the *Indian* Ocean, but what puts in there to Buy, Sell, or Load ; for in the Port of *Suratte,* there is a Trade not only for all sorts of Spice, and among them for Ginger, but of very rich Gold and Silk Stuffs, of very fine Cottons and other Commodities brought thither from remote Parts. There are such rich Merchants, that they can load any great Ship out of one of their Ware-Houses. I may say without enlarging, that all the rich Silks and Gold Stuffs curiously wrought with Birds and

Suratte City.

Flowers; all the Brocades, Velvets, Taffetas, and other sorts made in *Amadabat*,[10] are convey'd to *Suratte*, which is but four Days Journey from it. I say those of *Amadabat*, which is the greatest City in *India*, and nothing inferior to Venice for this Trade; tho' its Houses are low and made of Mud and *Bamboo;* and the Streets Narrow, Crooked, and full of Dirt. But I forgot the fine Muslins of *Cambaya*, and the Curiosities made in the most valuable Agate that is brought into[11] *Europe*.

Amadabat City.

Cambaya City.

Cambaya the Metropolis of that Kingdom was a large and rich City, whilst the *Portugueses* were possess'd of it, *Baroche* and *Suratte;*[12] for this brave Nation govern'd it well enough, the Gate being still standing that People made for its security; but after they abandon'd it and retir'd to the Sea[13] it lost much of its Splendor[14] and Magnificence; for the Vessels Anchor twelve Miles from it, and cannot come up to the City but with the Flood; which is so violent and swift that a Horse can scarce outrun it. For this reason the Ships often do not go up, because they must do it against Wind, to check the violence of the Tide that drives so impetuously.

Barosce City.

Barosce[15] above mention'd is famous for its excellent white and stain'd Calicoes, as also for Ginger, and the best Market for its Commodities is at *Suratte*[16] ten miles distant from it. Its Port is the River,[17] which falls into the Sea fifteen Miles lower, up which small Barks can go with the Tide.

I purposely omit to mention particularly so many Countries, which like Rivers to the Sea convey all their Wealth to *Suratte*, because of the good Vent they find for it there; this being a matter well known to *Europeans*. But there would be a much greater Resort, were its port better, and that the Vessels when they have run six Miles up the River, were not forc'd to lye at *Suali*, ten Miles from the City; whence and whither Commodities are convey'd in small Boats.

Monday 17th, I saw the Church of the *Capucins*[18] which is decently adorn'd, and their House convenient, those good Men having built it after the manner of *Europe*.

Banians Tree and Pagods.

Tuesday 18th, I went to see the Tree of the *Gentils*, we call *Banians*,[19] under which they have the Pagods of their Idols, and Meet to perform their Ceremonies. It is of the same bigness and sort as that describ'd at *Bander-Congo;* but the Pagods differ, for under this I found four, one call'd of *Mamaniva*,[20] which has a mighty Front; two others of *Rio-Ram*,[21] and the fourth a retiring Place for *Fachires* that do Pennance; whereas under the Tree at *Bander-Congo* there is but one.

Under this Tree and in the neighbouring Parts there are many Men, who have enjoyn'd themselves and do perform such dreadful Pennances, that they will seem fabulous to the Reader, and impossible to be gone through without the assistance of the

Fachires or Penitents.

Devil. You may see one hanging by a Rope ty'd under his Arms and to the Tree, only his Feet touching the Ground, and the rest of his Body being Bow'd, and this for many Years without changing Place or Posture Day or Night. Others have their Arms lifted up in the Air, so that in process of Time there grows such a Stiffness or Hardness in the Joynts that they cannot bring them down again. Some sit with their Hands lifted up without ever moving them. Others stand upon one Foot, and others lye along with their Arms under their Heads for a Pillow. In short, they are in such Postures, that sometimes a Man can scarce believe his Eyes, but fancies it is an Illusion. Thus they continue Naked all Seasons of the Year, with vast long Hair, and Nails grown out, expos'd to the Rain, and burning Rays of the Sun, and to be stung by Flies, whom they cannot drive away. Other *Fachirs* who take that Employment supply their Necessities of Eating and Drinking. These Penitents are not asham'd to go quite Naked,[22] as they came out of their Mothers Wombs. The Women go devoutly to kiss those Parts Modesty forbids us to name, and tho' they take them in their Hands they feel not the least Motion of Sensuality, but they roul their Eyes in a most dreadful manner without taking notice of them, as I saw one on *Wednesday* 19th, beset by some silly *Pagan* Women, who paid their Respects to him with great Humility.

Thursday 20th, a young *French* Man conducted me to see an *Hospital*[23] of the *Gentils*, where abundance of irrational Creatures were kept. This they do because they believe the Transmigration of Souls, and therefore imagining those of their Forefathers may be in the vilest, and filthiest living Creatures they provide them with Food. Thus the wild Monkeys come to eat what is provided for them. Besides the prodigious number of Birds and Beasts maintain'd there, particular care is taken of the Lame and Sick. But that which most amaz'd me, tho' I went thither to that purpose, was to see a poor Wretch naked bound Hands and Feet, to feed the Bugs or Punaises, fetch'd out of their stinking Holes to that purpose. The best of it is that any Man should voluntarily expose himself to be so devour'd, for a small reward given him, according to the Hours he will continue under it. An Hospital for Birds and Beasts.

Friday 21th, going home, after walking about a while, I saw abundance of People got together before a *Pagan* Merchant's Shop, and in the midst of them a jugling Fellow with a Hen in one Hand and a Knife in the other. Inquiring into the meaning of it, they told me, that Man was a Rogue, who when he had a Mind to get Mony, carry'd that Hen through the Streets where the *Gentils* liv'd, threatning to kill it, that they might give him Mony to save its life, each of them believing the Soul of some of his Kindred might be in that Hen. In A Foolish piece of Knavery.

short, I saw him receive some Mony, and go on still threatning the same.

Saturday 22d, all the Vessels from *Diu, Cambaya, Baroche* and other Places being come together to Sail for *Goa* and other Dominions of *Portugal,* and the Galiots being ready to Convoy them, I again went aboard the same that brought me. Sailing out of the Mouth of the River with a fair Wind we got into the open Sea, and after lying by two Hours for the small Vessels to go a head of us, we held on our Course gently all Night.

Sunday 23d. at break of Day we found our selves many Miles from *Damam* and too late to hear Mass. The Galiots came to an Anchor after Noon[24] without the Mouth of the River, some small Barks going up it. I found *F. Francis* expected me with Impatience, who receiv'd me with Expressions of great Affection.

Monday 24th, I took leave of Friends that had been kind to me, there being an opportunity to Imbark for *Bazaim.*

CHAPTER III

THE AUTHORS SHORT VOYAGE TO BAZAIM, *AND DESCRIPTION OF THAT CITY.*

Having long since resolv'd to see *Goa,* on *Thursday*[1] 25th, I caus'd my Baggage to be carry'd down to the Shore by *Boes,*[2] so they call Porters in *India,* and thence[3] into a Vessel at *Diu* that carry'd Oars, lying without the River, as the Fathers *Francis,* and *Constantin* had done. Having with them taken leave with Thanks of the Prior and Religious[3a] of the Monastery, we went down to the Shore, and thence in a Boat to the *Navillo,* which was a long Boat of the King's, with six Oars and a square Sail in the middle, having[4] one Falconet aboard, and seventeen *Portuguese* and *Canarine* Souldiers. At Ebb, which fell out[5] when the Moon was vertical, we set forwards with the help of a small Gale, and of the Tide that set towards *Bazaim ;*[6] for from the Time the Moon first appears above the Horizon till she comes to the mid-Heaven the Flood runs towards *Suratte ;* and when the Moon goes down, towards *Bazaim.*

Trapor Town.

Wednesday 26th, at break of Day we were off the Town and Fort of *Trapor,*[7] a Place well Inhabited, with Monasteries of *Dominicans* and *Recolets.* Ten Miles from this[8] the *Portugueses* have another impregnable Castle call'd *Asserim ;*[9] for besides its being seated on the Top of the Hill, where there is no other higher Ground to command it, a crooked Path cut out of the Mountain, along which two Men cannot go abreast, leads up to it, and is defended by several Guards, who may withstand an Army only rowling down the Stones plac'd there to that purpose.

The Wind continuing fair we Sail'd by the Fort and Village of *Maim*,[10] and several other Towers and Dwellings, and then by the little Island *De la Vaca*,[11] or of the Cow, three Miles in Compass, and not far distant from *Bazim*. Much Time being lost waiting for the Barks, and[12] *Parancos*[13] that came under Convoy and were mere Slugs, we could not reach *Bazaim* after seventy Miles Sail till Midnight. We came to an Anchor before the Channel form'd by the small Island[14] and the Continent, for fear of running a Ground in the dark, and[15] *Thursday* 27th, went in with the Flood. *Maim.*

There being no Houses of Entertainment in the City, we were receiv'd by *F. Felicianus* of the Nativity, born at *Macao* in the Kingdom of *China*, and Prior of the Monastery of the *Augustinians*, who treated us all very courteously and like a true *Portuguese*.

Bazaim a City in the Kingdom of *Cambaya* is seated in 19 deg. of Latitude, and 104 of Longitude.[16] *Nuno de Acuna*[17] in the Year 1535 took it for King *John* of *Portugal*,[18] from *Badar*[19] King of *Cambaya*, who terrify'd by the Valour of the *Portuguese* Nation, surrendered it to them with the neighbouring Islands, whilst *Martin Alfonso de Sousa*, undauntedly attack'd and took *Damam* and its Fortress, cutting in pieces all the *Turkish* Garrison, and afterwards levelling the Castle with the Ground in 3 Days. The Compass of *Bazaim* is 3 Miles, and has eight Bastions,[20] not all quite finish'd. On them I saw some Pieces of Cannon, with the Arms of *Philip* the 4th,[21] of happy Memory King of *Spain*. On the North-side the Walls are rampard, and the other Fortifications are not yet finish'd; on the South side towards the Chanel, there is only a single Wall, that Place being less expos'd to the Danger of Enemies, and sufficiently defended by the Ebb and Flood. One third of the City towards the North is Unpeopled, by reason of the Plague which some Years rages in it.[22] The Streets are wide and strait, and the great Square or Market has good Buildings about it. There are two principal Gates, one on the East and the other on the West, and a small one towards the Channel or Streight. The Harbour is on the East side, form'd as was said, by the Island and Continent. *Bazaim City.* *Maff. Hist. Ind. lib.* 11, page 252.

The Government is in a Captain,[23] as they call him, or Governor,[24] and the Administration of Justice in a *Veedor*,[25] and the *Desembargador*,[26] who is a Gown Man, and Judge of Appeals from all the *Veedors* of the Northern Coast; along which in every City there are Factors and Treasurers for the Revenue of the Crown of *Portugal*. The *Portuguese* General resides at *Bazaim,* with sovereign Authority over the Captain of that and all the other Northern Places, whence he is call'd General of the North.

A Monster.

Friday 28th, I Walk'd about the City with the Fathers,[27] but saw nothing so extraordinary, as I did on[28] *Saturday* 29th, which was a *Pagan* born in *India,* who had an Infant sticking fast to his Navel, with all his Limbs, perfect except the Head, which was in the Man's Belley, and made its Excrements apart like every other perfect Creature. Whether the Man or Infant was struck, they both felt the Pain.

Habit of the People.

Sunday 30th, Mass was sung at the *Augustinians* with Musick, which being in *India* was not disagreeable, and much Gentry was there. The Heat was greater than at *Damam ;* so that as well Women as Men went about the Streets naked ; the Men covering their Privities with a Clout, and the Women their Bodies and Thighs with a piece of Linnen. The People of Fashion at that Time wear Silk and[29] very thin Muslins, having long[30] Breeches down to their Heels so that they need no Stockings. Instead of Shooes they wear Sandals like the Fryars.

The *Gentils.*

All the *Gentils* bore their Noses to put Rings through, as they do to the Buffaloes in *Italy.* Every Beggar, much more those that are well to pass, rubs his Teeth every Morning betimes with a Stick,[31] and spends two Hours at that Work, according to the Custom of the Country. They use no Quilts because of the Heat, but lay Blankets[32] and Sheets on the Bed, made of[33] Cords without Boards, as is us'd by the *Persians* of *Lar*[34] and *Bander-Congo.*

Monday the last of the Month, I went with *F. Peter* of the *Martyrs*[35] to the Village of *Madrapur,*[36] to see some vagabond *Moors,* who vaulted and perform'd feats of Activity[37] like our Tumblers and Rope-Dancers. The most wonderful thing was to see a Man who turn'd round upon a Cane, held up by another on his Girdle ; and what most amaz'd me was that he who supported the Cane went on without putting his Hands to guide it, and he that was on the top of it did not help himself with his Hands neither, and yet the Cane or *Bamboo* was thirty Spans high. At last after giving two skips in the Air he lighted on a very high Beam, fix'd to that purpose ; I know not how he could do all this without some supernatural Assistance.

A Wonderful Tumbler.

Tuesday the first of *February,* a Messenger from the *Nabab,* or Governour of *Suratte* came in a *Palankine* with thirty *Souldiers,* to treat about some Business with the Governour, and deliver him two Letters.

The Country Houses of *Bazaim.*

Wednesday 2d,[38] I went in an *Andora* of the Monastery to see the *Cassabò,*[39] which is the only Diversion at *Bazaim:* nothing appearing for fifteen Miles but delightful Gardens, Planted with several sorts of the Country Fruit Trees, as Palm,

Fig, Mangas, and others, and abundance of Sugar Canes. The Soil is cultivated by Christian, *Mahometan,* and *Pagan* Peasants, inhabiting the Villages thereabouts. They keep the Gardens always Green and Fruitful, by Watering them with certain Engines ; so that the Gentry allur'd by the cool and delightful Walks, all have their Pleasure Houses at *Cassabò,* to go thither in the hottest Weather to take the Air, and get away from the contagious and pestilential Disease call'd *Carazzo,*[40] that uses to infect all the Cities of the Northern Coast. It is exactly like a *Bubo,* and so violent that it not only takes away all means of preparing for a good End, but in a few Hours depopulates whole Cities, as witness, *Suratte, Damama, Bazaim, Tana*[41] and other Places, which often suffer under this Calamity.

In this Territory of *Cassabò* I saw the Sugar Canes Press'd between two great wooden Roulers, turn'd about by Oxen, whence they came out thoroughly squeez'd. Then the Juice is boil'd in Cauldrons, and being set out to cool at Night in earthen Vessels it hardens into white Sugar.

Thursday, 3d, I went to visit the Image of our Lady *De los Remedios,* standing in a Parish Church belonging to the *Dominicans,*[42] on the Road to *Cassabò.* About five Years since this Church was Burnt by *Kacagi,*[43] a *Gentil* Subject to the *Great Mogul,* who with a great Multitude of Outlaws, and four thousand Souldiers, went about like a Rover, Plundering and Burning Villages. Thence I went to see another miraculous Image of our Lady *da Merce,*[44] in a small Church founded and serv'd by an *Augustinian* who did the Office of Curate.

Friday 4th, I saw the Church of the *Jesuits,*[45] in *India* call'd *Paulistas.*[46] It is richly Gilt, not only the three Chappels, but the Walls and Arch ; but the Workmen knew not how to make that rich Metal shew it self to the best advantage. The Dormitory and Cloister are the best in the City.[47] In the Garden, besides the *Indian,* there are some sort of *European* Fruit ; and among the rest Figs and Grapes, which the F. Rector told me came to Maturity twice a Year, that is, in December and March. ***Jesuits.***

Saturday 5th, I visited the Monastery of the *Dominicans,*[48] with the famous Dormitory. The Church was large and had but three Altars, as we said was us'd in *India,* opposite to the great Gate, and all well adorn'd. ***Dominicans.***

Sunday 6th, I heard Mass in the Church of the *Misericordia*[48a], which is the Parish of the City ; and continuing to visit Churches came on *Monday* 7th to that of the *Franciscans.*[49] Both Church and Monastery are built after the manner of *Europe,* the Church having many Chappels, contrary to the Custom of *India.* ***Franciscans.***

Hospitallers.

Tuesday 8th, I heard Mass in the Parish of our Lady *de la Vida*,[50] where there are three very good Altars well adorn'd. The Monastery of the Fathers, Hospitallers,[51] or *S. John de Dios*, where I was on *Monday*, 9th,[52] is so Poor that it can maintain but three Fryars.

Thursday 10th, understanding there was a Wedding of People of Quality at the Church of our Lady *de la Vida*, I[53] went to see the Ceremony. I observ'd the Bridegroom did not give his Bride the right Hand, and thinking it an extravagant custom, as being only us'd by Crown'd Heads, I ask'd the reason of it of some *Portugueses*; who told me the same was practis'd in *Portugal*, and this that the Gentlemen might have his right Hand at liberty, to put to his Sword in Defence of the Lady. The Bride was richly clad, after the *French* fashion; but some Trumpets went along, founding such a doleful Tone, as little differ'd from that they use in conducting Criminals to Execution. I return'd to the Monastery in the *Andora*; and here it is to be observ'd that the manner of saluting those they meet, when they are carry'd in this sort of conveniency, in *Italy* would be taken for an affront, and laugh'd at; for in token of respect they shut to the little Door of the *Andora* upon them. This in *Naples* would certainly produce a Duel, and in *India* is done out of respect even to the Vice-Roy himself.

Friday 11th, I heard Mass in the Parish Church of our Lady *da Se*,[54] where there are several Altars, and two Chappels.

There are no Doctors of the Civil Law throughout the *Portuguese* Dominions in *India*, and those few *Canarins*, who follow this Employment, through their Ignorance prove bad Advocates, or Councellors, and Sollicitors, and some times Plead both for Plaintiff and Defendant. Besides, for the most part Causes are decided by Ignorant Captains or Governors without the approbation of an Assessor. This happens for want of an University and Colleges to teach the Law; and because the *Portuguese* Doctors will not go so far from their Country, by reason of the little profit they should make in *India*. *F. Felicianus* the Prior understanding that I was a Doctor of the Civil Law, on *Saturday* 12th, propos'd a Match to me with a Portion of 20000 pieces of Eight,[55] and with a Promise that I should be Advocate to the Monasteries, and to some Families of Note, which would yield about 600 pieces of Eight a Year. Having no inclination to live in those hot Countries, I answer'd, that tho' he had offer'd me 100000 Pieces of Eight Portion, I should never be induc'd to quit *Europe* for ever.

Kanheri—Cave No. 3 (2nd century A.D.)
Sculptured capitals of 7th & 8th pillars, from west in north row, view from south

CHAPTER IV

THE DESCRIPTION OF THE PAGOD *IN THE ISLAND OF* SALSETE,[1] *BY THE* PORTUGUESES *CALL'D THE* CANARIN.

The *Pagod* or Temple of the *Canarin,*[2] whereof I intended to give an exact and true account, is one of the greatest wonders in *Asia ;* as well because it is look'd upon as the Work of *Alexander* the Great,[3] as for its extraordinary and incomparable Workmanship, which certainly could be undertaken by none but *Alexander.* What I most admire is that it is almost unknown to *Europeans ;* for tho' I have made much enquiry, I do not find that any *Italian,* or other *European* Traveller has writ of it ;[4] and it is very strange to me that so Ingenuous a Man as our *Peter de la Valle*[5] should omit to see both this *Pagod,* and the Palace of *Darius,*[6] with the Antiquities of *Celmenar,*[7] that were but a few Leagues out of his way, since he travell'd for his Pleasure, and made nothing of spending Thousands of Crowns to satisfy his Curiosity.[8] Tho' a poor Man I spar'd no Cost or Labour, that I might see all and inform the Publick. As for *Tavernier,*[9] it is no wonder he minded not to see these things, because his principal End was Trade, and buying of Jewels, and therefore he only went to those places where his business lay, and he could make most profit ; and tho' he made several Voyages to *India,* he minded not to see Antiquities tho' he pass'd close by them.

I had a mind to go to *Tana,* and pass over from thence to the *Pagod ;* but the Fathers Visitor and Prior dissuaded me, saying, it was better going by *Deins.*[10] Accordingly *Sunday* 13th, hiring a Boat I went over to the Village of *Gormandel,*[11] in the Island *Salzete.* The Houses are scatter'd on both sides of the Mountains, on the top whereof is the Palace of the Lord of the Village. I went thence upon the Streight to the Village of *Deins,* belonging to the Nuns of *S. Monica* at *Goa,* 6 Miles distant from *Bazaim* : *F. Edward* an *Augustinian* Procurator to those Nuns, receiv'd me into his House on account of a Letter of recommendation I had from the F. Visitor. *Gormandel* Village.

Being hot and dry,[12] *F. Edward* brought out two Citron Peels preserv'd ; and I without considering eat one and drank a great Glass of Water ; but he afterwards offering me the other, I call'd to mind, I had swallow'd down some Hundreds of Pismires, which cover'd the said Peels and perhaps dislodg'd the Souls of so many dead Idolaters residing in those little Bodies. I therefore refus'd the other with Thanks, desiring him to keep that Sweat-meat, which was as old as the Village, to treat some other Guest ; because I would not upon any account be guilty again of such a Slaughter of Ants. After

A Church in a Rock.

this Poor Refreshment I went to the Village of *Monoposser,*[13] a Mile distant, to see a Church under Ground,[14] formerly a *Pagod* cut in the Rock, on which stands the College and Monastery of the *Franciscans.*[15] It is a 100 Spans long, and in Breadth thirty. The side Walls, as has been said are of the natural Rock, and only the Front is made by Art. Close by is another *Pagod* cut in the Rock, formerly serving for their[16] Idolatrous Worship.

The Church and Monastery are like all the rest in *India.* Five Religious Men live there, to whom the King of *Portugal* allows 200 *Murais*[17] of Rice, all which they give to the Poor, except only as much as serves for their own sustenance. One of these Fathers[18] does the Office of a Curate, in the Village of *Cassi,*[19] two Miles distant, and has a good dwelling there. On the Mountain near the said College is another Hermitage, with a Chappel.

Returning to *Deins, F. Edward* told me, that tho' he had us'd all his endeavours he could not find Men to carry me in an *Andora,* for his People were fled, and there were no others at *Monoposser;* by which perceiving that the Father was an Exception of the general Civility of the *Portuguese,* I was forc'd to take up with an ill House.[20]

Monday 14th, the Owner who was a *Pagan,* brought me the Horse very late, because none of them goes out of his House, till he has perform'd his Idolatrous Ceremonies, and thinking to take some little Meat[21] before I set out, good sparing *F. Edward* told me the Bread was not come yet; and I answering I would send to buy some, he reply'd it was not yet bak'd; and I might dine in a Village half way. Desiring him further to appoint some Peasant to shew me the *Pagod,* because the *Gentil* knew not the way well,[22] he would neither send a Country Man, nor one of his Servants; whereupon I set out in Danger of losing my way for want of a Guide, travelling on a Mountain full of Monkeys, Tygers, Lions, and other wild Beasts and venomous Creatures. Coming to the Village, where I design'd to eat, I found nothing but a little Rice half boil'd in fair Water; the place consisting of only four Cottages in the thickest of the Wood; so that I went on fasting. By the way I met strange Birds. Some were Green and as big as a Thrush, and Sang very well; others bigger, black as Velvet, and with vast long Tails; others Red and Green; some Black and Green, as big as a Turtle-dove, and many more never seen in *Europe;* there were also an innumerable company of Parrots, and Monkeys, and Apes, with very long Tails leaping from Tree to Tree.

After riding eight Miles thro' the thick Wood, we knew not where the *Pagod* was, or what way to take to find it. It pleas'd Providence, we hapned to meet with some naked *Pagan* Women, carrying Loads of Wood, who put us into the Road.[23] Being come to the Foot of the Rock, I was worse puzzl'd for want of some Body to hold my Horse, the Idolater being to guide me through the Labyrinth of so many *Pagods*. At last I found a Peasant wandering about the Mountain, and giving him the Horse to hold, I climb'd the bare[24] Craggy Rock with the Idolater, at the top whereof on the East[25] side the great *Pagod* is hewn out, with other small ones by it.

The wonderful *Pagod*.

The first piece of Workmanship that appears, consists of two large Columns,[26] 2 Spans[27] high, the third part of them from the bottom upwards is square, the middle part Octangular, and the top round. Their Diameter is six Spans; they are fifteen Spans distant from one another, and each of them eight from the Rock, which is cut after the same manner. These Columns support a Stone Architrave forty four Spans long, four in thickness and eight in breadth; cut like the rest out of the same Rock. These 3 Porticos lead into a sort of Hall or Passage Room, four Spans[28] long, cut in the same Rock. At the end of it are three Doors, one fifteen Spans high, and eight in Breadth, which is the middlemost, and two others four Spans square on the sides, which are the way into a lower place. Over these Doors is a Cornish four Spans broad, of the same Stone; over which thirty Spans above the Ground, there are other such Doors, or Windows cut in the Rock. At the same height, there are little Grots,[29] or Dens, six Spans high,[30] of which the middlemost is the biggest. Thirty four Spans above the Ground, in the same place is such another Grot. It is no easy matter to conceive what the use of all this was.

Advancing ten Paces towards the Right, I saw a sort of Grot, open on two sides, twenty four Spans in length, and fifteen in breadth, over which was a round *Cupula* fifteen Spans high, and ten wide, with a square Cornish, like that about the Grot. Here there is an Idol cut in the Rock, in half Relieve, which seems to hold something in its Hand, but what it is does not appear.[31] The Cap it has on, is like that of the Doge of *Venice*. By it stand two Statues in a submissive Posture, as if they were Servants. They have Conical, or Sugar-Loaf Caps on. Over their Heads are two small Figures, like the Angels we Paint in the Air; below two little Statues, holding their Hands on a Staff, and two Children by their sides, with their Hands put together, as if they pray'd;[32] on their Backs is something like a piece of Wood. Close by is another round *Cupula* all of one Stone, and shap'd like the other, but the top of it is broke. Both this and the other are suppos'd to have been Sepulchres of the Antient *Gentils*; but there is no Ground to make this out, no opening appearing to put in the Bodies or Ashes; but on the contrary it is visible they are not hollow within, but only cut without, in the shape of *Cupulas*. About this second,[32a] there are 4 great Figures Carv'd in half Relief, holding in the left Hand something like a Garment, and the same sort of Caps on their Heads, with small Figures at their Feet, and 2 above. Opposite to them, there are three little ones sitting, and 6 other large ones, and 3 of a midling Size standing, all cut in the Rock after the same manner: But that in the middle, which seems to be the Idol, in its left holds a Tree with Fruit on it.[32b] On the other side there are 16 Figures,[32c] all sitting with both Hands on their Breasts, and the same Caps ; one of them seems to be superior to the rest, because there are two Figures standing by its side,[32d] and two Children above.

At a small distance Northward is a little Grot eight Spans square, and in it, as it were a Bed of the same, Stone, four Spans broad, and eight long. On the other Frontispiece is a Statue sitting on its Legs, after the manner of the East, with the Hands together on the Breast ; and another standing with the Branch of a Fruit-Tree in its Hand, and above a wing'd Infant.

Beyond the Grot, and on the same Front, which runs sixty Spans within the Rock, there are two Statues sitting after the same manner, their Hands plac'd the same way, with Conical Caps on their Heads, and two like Servants standing by them.[32d]

On the same side is the Famous *Pagod* of the *Canarin.*[33] The Entrance to it is through an opening forty Spans long, in a Wall of the same Stone, fifty Spans long, and eight Spans thick,[34] on which there are three Statues.[35] On the right Hand before you go into the *Pagod,* is a round Grot, above fifty Spans about,[36] in which round the Wall, there are many Statues sitting, and some standing, and one on the left, is bigger than the rest. In the middle rises a round *Cupula,* cut out of the same Rock, like a Pillar of the same Stone, with several Characters carv'd about it, which no Man can ever explain.[36a] Going into the first Porch of the *Pagod,* which is 50 Spans square, there are on the sides two Columns 60 Spans high, with their Capitals, and six Spans Diameter. On that upon the Right Hand coming in, there are two Lions, with a Shield by them ; on the other upon the left two Statues. Beyond these Columns at the entrance of a Grot, on the left there are two great Statues standing, and looking at one another. Still further in are 2 vast big Statues on the Left, and one on the Right of the Door, all standing, with several little Statues by them, only within the space of that Porch ; for going into the adjoyning Grot, which is 24 Spans square, there is nothing worth observing. On the right Hand, where the Lions are, there are no Statues, but two large Vessels upon convenient Pedestals.

Hence there are[37] three equal Doors thirty Spans high, and eight broad, but that in the middle even with the Floor, those on the sides five Spans above it, into another plain[38] Place. Here there are four Columns twelve Spans high, standing on the Rock it self, between the five Windows that give Light to the *Pagod*. On the right side of the Door there are some unknown Letters worn with Age,[38a] as is all the rest of the Work. In this Place on the sides, besides several small Figures, there are two vast Statues of Giants standing,[39] above twenty five Spans high ; shewing their right Hands open, and holding a Garment in the left, on their Heads the same Caps, and in their Ears Pendents after the *Indian* Fashion.

At the Entrance of the great Gate of the *Pagod,* which is fifteen Spans high, and ten in breadth, there are on the Right four Statues standing, one of which is a Woman holding a Flower in her Hand ; and twelve other less, some sitting and some standing, with their Hands on their Breasts, and something in them. On the left are four other Statues, two whereof are Women, with large Rings about their Ancles of the same Stone, and sixteen little Statues on their sides, some sitting, some standing, and some with their Hands on their Breasts, as was said before. Over the said Door there are other two great ones, and as many opposite to them, with three little ones standing. On the left Hand within is another Inscription in the same Character :[39a] Over the Arch of this Door is a Window forty Spans wide, which is the width of the *Pagod,* with a Stone like an Architrave in the middle, supported on the inside by two Octangular Pillars.

The *Pagod* is Arch'd, forty Spans in breadth, and one Hundred in length, and rounded at the end, besides the four Columns at the Entrance, there are thirty more within, which divide it into three Isles ; seventeen of them have Capitals, and Figures of Elephants on them, the rest are Octangular and Plain. The space between the Columns and the Rock, that is, the breadth of the side Isles[40] is six Spans. At the end of the *Pagod,* there is a sort of round *Cupola,* thirty Spans high, and sixteen of my Paces about, cut in the same Rock, but not hollow within. I believe it serv'd for some use, which we being Ignorant of the ancient Customs of those Times cannot guess at. I know not what Judgment *Portuguese* Authors make of it, because their Books are scarce at *Naples ;* but they it is certain are well acquainted with it, the Viceroys themselves sometimes coming from *Goa* to see it ; yet it is most likely they could never[41] discover the Truth.

All that has been hitherto Describ'd is Cut in the very Rock, without any Addition to the Statues, or any thing that may be parted. But on the Floor of the *Pagod* there are several hew'd Stones, which perhaps serv'd for Steps to some Structure.

Coming out of the *Pagod,* and ascending fifteen Steps, all cut in the Rock, I found two Cisterns of Rain-Water, good to Drink ; and as many Steps above that, a Grott sixteen Spans square, and a great one further on with much Water standing in it. Mounting twenty Spaces higher, I found another Grott twenty Spans square, which led to another of the same Dimensions, and that into one of twelve. In the first was a rising Window with Steps to it cut in the Rock, with two Columns near a small Cistern.

At a small distance from these Grotts is another *Pagod,*[42] with a handsome plain Place before it, and little Walls about to sit down, and a Cistern in the middle. Five Doors cut in the Rock lead into the first Arch ; and between them are four Octangular Pillars ; all but the middle Door are two Spans above the Ground. On the sides of this Arch, whose length is the breadth of the *Pagod,* that is, eight Spans,[43] there are on the left several Statues sitting, like those above mention'd, and others on the right standing. All about the Frontispiece there are many sitting and standing, no way different from the rest already Describ'd. Then there are three Doors to the *Pagod,* that in the middle twelve Spans high, and six in breadth, the two on the sides ten Spans high, and four broad. The *Pagod* is sixty Spans square, no way proportionable, being but twelve Spans high. On both the sides, and over the Entrance there are above 400 Figures great and small carv'd, some sitting, some standing, like those before spoke of ; but two on the right bigger than the rest are standing, as is that in the middle of the Frontispiece, which is of the biggest Idol ; and another on the left in the same Posture ; but all worn with Age, which destroys every thing. On both sides there are two Grotts fourteen Spans square, with a low Wall within two Spans above the Ground.

Going up ten Steps further Northward is a Grott, and within that another less. On the right is another like it, with another little on within it, in which is a low Wall like those before mention'd. The great one is about twenty Spans in length, and ten in breadth ; the other ten square, and all of them with small Cisterns. On the right side is another of the same bigness, with two small Pillars before it, two little Grotts, and three Cisterns, one on the right, and two on the left ; and another adjoining to it, with another within it, and a Cistern of the same Dimensions of the other. It is likely these were the Dwellings of the Priests of the *Pagod,* who there led a penitential Life, as it were in a *Pagan Thebaida.*

Descending from that great height, fifteen Steps cut in the Rock, there is a little *Pagod,* with a Porch before it thirty Foot square, which leads into it through three Doors, between which there are two square Pilasters. On the left Hand there are four

Statues ; two sitting, and two less in the middle standing. On the right Hand a little open Grott, and another *Pagod,* with a Cistern before it, the way into which is first, through a Door ten Spans in height, and six in breadth, into a Room twenty Spans square ; which has on the right another very dark Room twelve Spans square, which makes the *Pagod* somewhat Dark. In the midst whereof is a round *Cupola* of one solid Piece, fifteen Spans high, which is the height of the *Pagod.* Descending fifty upright Steps, there is a plain Space cut in the Rock, which is not very hard, and eight Octangular Columns twelve Spans high, which leave nine Intervals to ascend five Steps that lead into an Arch. In this Place on the left side, which is ten Spans, is a great Idol sitting Bareheaded ; two other great Statues standing, and some small ones ; on the right side two other Statues sitting, and two standing, besides many little ones about them. Then the way into the *Pagod* is through three Doors, twelve Spans in height, and six in breadth with two Windows over them. The *Pagod* is 100 Spans in length, fifty in breadth, and ten in height. About it runs an Arch eight Spans broad, with ten square Columns. Here are four Rooms, or Grotts, twelve Foot square ; besides seven in the Front, and left side of the *Pagod,* where the Cistern is ; all which I suppos'd to be Rooms for the Priests of the Temple. In the *Niche* of it, which is ten Foot square, is a great Idol sitting, with two Statues standing, and another sitting on the left, by which also there are two Statues standing, and several small Figures in half Relief about it. Ascending ten Spans over against it is a little Grott, supported by two small Columns, ten Spans high. There is a Door ten Spans high, and four in breadth out of it into a Room, or Grott sixteen Spans square, and thence into another of twelve, where there is a large Idol sitting, holding his Hands on his Breast.

Then descending twenty Steps there is a plain Space, whence four Steps on the left lead up into an Arch, where there are four Pilasters twelve Spans high, the Distances between which are the way into three little Rooms cut in the Rock. Twenty Steps lower there are other Grotts cut in the Rock, with small Cisterns, but for what use cannot be imagin'd unless we suppose all these Cavities were Dwellings of the Idolaters. It is only reported, That this wonderful Work was made with a vast Expence, by *Alexander* the Great, who was of the same Religion.

Descending from the high Rock, I mounted a Horse-back, with a good Stomach, having fasted that Day against my Will, and made haste away to satisfy Hunger. By the way I saw abundance of Monkeys, and Apes, and being about to kill one, the Pagan pray'd me not to Hurt them. Near the Road were two Palm-trees, rising out of the Trunk of one great Tree five[44] Spans, and spreading abroad their fruitful Branches.

Near the Village of *Canarin,* which gives its Name to the *Pagod* here describ'd, is a Rock 100 Paces about, with several Grotts and Cisterns under it, which might formerly be Dwellings ; the antient Gentils affecting to have their Habitations in Rocks, to save the Expence of Materials in Building. On the East side before the largest Grott is a great Idol sitting, with his Hands a-cross on his Legs.

Returning to *Deins,* I met *F. Edward* of St. *Antony* walking. He instead of getting me something to Eat, began to Discourse after an odd manner ; inquiring concerning Particulars of the *Pagod ;* but I left him to Prate by himself, telling him it was not time to Talk upon an empty Belly. Alighting, and going up to my Chamber, the first thing I said to the Servant of the House, was to ask him, Whether there was any thing to Eat. He told me there was none ; and bidding him go fetch me a little Bread at least, he set before me a small Loaf, with the same Citron Peels cover'd with Pismires, these Vermin leaving nothing untouch'd in *India ;* for which reason the *Indians,* to save some Preserves, set them under[45] a Table, whose Feet are in wooden Bowls full of Water,[46] to keep them off. I made but two Mouth-fulls of the Bread ; yet had not the Courage to do so by the sweet Meat, which I fancy was made when first Preserving was invented ; and therefore I bid the Servant keep that Rarity from the Pismires, against his Master had some other Stranger to Entertain. The worst of it was, the wretched Village afforded nothing for Mony to satisfy[47] Hunger, and therefore being spent with Weariness and Fasting, I lay down on the Bed, expecting Supper. *F. Edward* in the mean while, having walk'd about a long time, without thinking of me ; at length, two Hours and a half after it was Night,[48] came to the dark Room. I hearing a Noise between Sleeping and Waking, and not seeing who it was, ask'd, Who was there, and he very soberly answer'd Truly, Sir, I did not think you were here (tho' we talk'd[49] together when I came into the Village) and being told I had Eaten nothing but a little Bread, he order'd the Cloth to be laid. This Word made me recover my faint Spirits ;[50] when I saw two Plates of small fry'd Fishes appear, and that which had the least was set before me, the other with the larger before the Father. I was twice about[51] changing Plates with him, but Modesty prevail'd, and I arm'd my self with Patience. After Supper *F. Edward* kept me up till Midnight, with a Thousand idle Tales, not satisfy'd that he had spent three Hours in needless Chat, with the Peasants ; and I having given him the Hearing against my Will, at last fell a Sleep without making any Answer. When I awak'd, finding he was gone. I stripp'd a pace, and went to Bed, quite spent with Hunger and Weariness, wishing for the next Day, that I might fly from that wretched Place.

The Island *Salzete,* in which the aforesaid *Pagod* is seated, is about seventy Miles in compass, twenty in length, and fifteen in breadth. Being very low, it is cut by several Channels running in from the Sea ; but there are high Mountains in it cover'd with Trees. The Soil is very fruitful, and produces abundance of Sugar-Canes, Rice, and Fruit ; such as *Mangos, Cocos, Transolins,*[52] *Giacccharas,*[53] *Tamarinds, Ananas,*[54] *Papais,*[55] and other Sorts, which shall be describ'd elsewhere. There are in it several Villages of Poor wretched *Gentils, Moors,* and Christians, Living in Houses Built with Wattles crusted over with Mud, and cover'd with Straw, or Palm-tree Leaves. They go Naked, both Men and Women covering their Privities with a Clout, and their Breasts with another, or else with a short Jerkin that does not reach below the Navel, leaving the Arms, Thighs, and Legs bare. On their Arms they wear Bracelets of Silver and Glass, and thick Silver Rings about the Legs. The Peasants are worse than Vassals to the Lords of the Villages ; for they are bound to Till the Land, or to Farm as much as may put them in a Condition to Pay the Landlord ; thus like Slaves[56] they fly from one Village to another, and[56] their Landlords bring them back by force. They generally Pay for their Land, four, six, or twelve *Morais* of Rice, so call'd when the Husk is off, and *Vate*[57] when it is on, which is the way they usually deliver it. A *morais* is 25 *Paras,* and the *Para* 24 Pounds *Spanish ;* Measures the *Portuguese* use for Provisions, as they do the *Covedo,*[58] for long Measure.[59] If the Peasants take the Land to Till in the Place of their Abode, they Pay no other Duty to King or Landlord (tho' some Exact some Days of personal Service) ; but those that hold in Fee, Pay an Imposition according to what they are worth[60] every four Months to the Kings Factors or Treasures, residing in all the Northern Cities. These Villages are given in Fee to Soldiers who have Serv'd long ; or to other Persons that have well deserv'd of the Crown, for three Lives, after which they generally endeavour to Renew ; but to the Church they are given for ever.

Salzete Island.

Besides so many Villages, there are in this Island several Places of Consequence ; and among the rest the City and Fortress of *Bombaim,*[61] which is several Miles about. It is parted from *Salzete* by a Channel,[62] which at low Water is Fordable. This Island was given by the King of *Portugal,* in Dower to Queen *Catherine* of *England,* and accordingly that King has been Possess'd of it, ever since the Year 1662.[63] There are also in *Salzete* the Forts of *Bandora,*[64] and *Versava*[65] with their Villages ; as also *Tana,* about which there are five small Forts garrison'd and furnish'd with Cannon. The Country, tho' open, is excellent good for *India,* and has three Monasteries of *Dominicans, Augustinians* and *Recolets.* It is famous for Calicoes,[66] no Place in the *Portuguese* Dominions exceeding it

Bombaim.

in this Particular, even for Table Service.[67] Eight Years since one Brother kill'd another at *Tana,* about the Possession of a Village. The *Jesuits* are Possess'd of the best part of this Island of *Salzete,* having almost all the Point that looks towards the East, and the Channel of *Bazaim;* and it is reported for a certain Truth, that they have more Revenues in India, than the King of *Portugal.*

Tana.

From *Bazaim* to *Tana,* and from *Tana* to *Bombaim* runs a Channel of Salt Water, in some Places half a Mile over, in others more or less; and because near *Goadel,*[68] it runs through the midst of a Rock, the *Portugueses* generally say, That *Alexander* the Great, coming, as some will have it, several times to *Bazaim,* caused the Rock to be cut through to give a Passage to the Water;[68a] and that it was he who had the neighbouring *Pagod* of the Elephant[69] cut out of the solid Rock.

Jo. Bapt. Nicol. Hist. p. 3. Verb. Bazaim.

Tuesday 15th, as soon as ever Day began to appear I set out. Coming to *Gormandel,* I found no Boat to carry me over to *Bazaim,* and going further, I saw one setting out; therefore running down to the Shore, I made Signs to the *Moors* and *Gentils* in it to come back, and take me Aboard, which they refusing, rather than be left to endure more Hardship on the Shore, I made use of the *Portuguese* Authority, making as if I would Fire at them with my Gun, which they perceiving, came about to take me up. I went over to *Bazaim,* and[70] being ask'd by the Father's Visitor, and Prior how *F. Edward* had treated me, I answer'd their Recommendation had but an ill Effect; and they desiring to hear all Particulars, I took out my Pocket Book, and Read to them all that has been here said concerning *F. Edward's* ill Usage. The Fathers Laugh'd heartily, but were inwardly much Displeas'd that his extravagant Behaviour should blemish the Reputation of the *Portuguese* Civility.

Wednesday 16th, the Count *de Villa Verde,* Viceroy of India,[71] Sailing by with four great Ships, and ten small ones towards *Diu,* visiting the Northern Coast, the City saluted him with all its Cannon. He answer'd with seven Guns, and the City again fir'd round.[72] By the way he had gain'd a Victory over the *Arabs* of *Mascate,*[73] after this manner. These Barbarians discovering the *Portuguese* Ships; stranded three of their Vessels in the Bay and River of *Zanghisara,*[74] being in the Territory of *Savagi,* and carrying off in the Night what was most Valuable in two of them, fortify'd the third, planting Cannon on the Shore to defend it. The *Portugueses* could not Attack them on the same Day, because it was late; but the next Morning, being the 25th of *January,* fell on, and whilst the Fire set to them by the *Arabs* themselves Burn'd the other two Vessels, they run in with eight Long-Boats full of Men, because the great Ships could not come up, and after a long Fight, and much Blood spilt in the Attack of the third Vessel,

and *Arabs* on the Shore, they Boarded, and made themselves Masters of her, cutting in Pieces some Hundred of Barbarians. They took in her 14000 *Roupies,* and thirty Pieces of Cannon. Only four *Portugueses* were kill'd in the Action, and twenty wounded; and so great a Number of the Enemy, that the River and Shore were all dy'd with their Blood.

A barbarous Murder.

The return of some small Vessels that went to carry Refreshments to the Viceroy, brought us certain Intelligence of the Murder of *Antony Machado de Brito,*[75] Admiral of the *Portuguese* Fleet, which hapned on the 30th of *December,* 1694. after he had behav'd himself with unparallell'd Bravery against his Enemies. His sharp Tongue had gain'd him the ill Will of almost all the Gentry of *Goa,* and along the Coast, but more particularly of the Family of *Melo,*[76] which was powerful in Kindred, and great by Birth. His Affronts becoming insupportable, they conspir'd to the Number of fifty to Murder him, and having agreed on the Time, Place, and Manner of Executing their Design, they made several Loop-Holes in the Houses of the Quarter and Parish of St. *Peter,*[77] that they might Shoot him with more Safety. The General, or rather Admiral[78] perswading himself, that Gentlemen could not harbour Thoughts of taking an ungenerous Revenge, tho' warn'd to be upon his Guard, because there were treacherous Practices against him, would never admit any Soldiers to attend him, and Particularly two Captains that were willing to share in his Dangers. Thus being carry'd in a *Palankine* alone, only with one Black that carry'd his Umbrella, a Shot was made at him from a House,[79] which giving him a slight Wound, he leap'd out of the *Palankine,* and taking the Snuff he held betwixt his Fingers, said, *Who is it you aim at?* *Tristan de Melo* at these Words, coming out of his House, answer'd, *At you,* and fir'd a Blunderbus upon him. He with an undaunted Courage fended it with his Cloak, and bowing his Body; then drawing his Sword, and falling on his Enemy, he struck him five times, but to no Purpose, because he had on a Coat of Mail; whereupon he Cleft his Head, and with a back Stroak cut him over the Face, which made him fall. Then taking him by the Hair, he set his Feet on him, and was going to run his Sword into his Breast; but *Tristan* begging his Life, he generously Granted it; saying he would not imbrew his Hands in such base Blood. In the mean while, out came *Tristan's* Son, and a *Mulatto*[81] (so they call those that are got betwen Blacks and Whites) and Firing two Blunderbus's,[82] lodg'd several Bullets in the Admiral's[83] Breast, breaking in pieces the Cross he wore as a Badge of Knighthood, but still he stood, and defended himself; when a Slave came up, and run him into the Side with a Javelin.[84] Nor did he go unpunished, for the General with a back Stroak ripp'd open his Belly, whereof he Dy'd at Night. *Machado* being ready to

Expire, drew near to the *Palankine,* and setting his Peruke to rights the best he could, laid himself in it. The Murderers fearing he might yet Live, one of them who was a Priest, came with a Blunderbuss in his Hand to make an End of him ; but seeing him ready to breath out his Soul, ask'd whether he would make his Confession. The Admiral call'd him *Jew,* and bid him go about his Business. Afterwards a *Dominican*[85] coming to him, he gave Signs of Repentance, and grasping his Hands, Dy'd with these Words, *The Blood of Christ save me.* They found in his Breast about 30 Bullets ; whereupon People admiring his Valour, said, He must need have more vital Spirits than other Mortals, since there must go so much to the killing of him. The Soldiers of the Fleet, who were most of them Aboard,[86] hearing so many Shot, and afterwards that their Admiral was kill'd, ran to the Place, and had[87] taken just Revenge upon *Tristan de Melo,* who was carrying[88] by two blacks to the Archbishops, had not a Judge stopp'd them to gain Time for *Tristan* to Escape, cry'd out to them, In the King's Name to Stand. This hapned, because the Admiral's ill Tongue, as was said, had gain'd him many Enemies.[89] However, the Judge was Imprison'd some time after. *Machado* was generally lamented, and Particularly by Me, who having Travell'd with him, in 1689, from *Madrid* to *Genoa,* and receiv'd many Civilities from him, expected still greater in *India.* He was the Terror of the *Moors* and *Arabs,* and kept in Awe several Thousands of Vagabond Soldiers, who having Rebell'd in the *Mogul's Dominions,* threatned to Plunder the *Portuguese* Dominions. He gain'd many Victories over the Fleet of the *Arabs* of *Mascate,* and the most considerable of them was in the Bay of *Suratte,* in *April* 1694, when with only three Ships he Fought fourteen *Arabs* a whole Day ; and not so satisfy'd cast Anchor at Night, to renew the Battle the next Day ; but found the *Arabs* had stole away, with the Loss of some Hundreds of Men, and several of their Ships disabled. Several Boats full of *French, English* and *Dutch,* went out to Sea to see this Fight, because it hapned opposite to *Damam.*

Thursday 17th, we went with *F. Francis,* to Divert us out of Town ;[90] and on *Friday* 18th, I saw a good Procession in *Bazaim,* and heard a Sermon in our Church.

CHAPTER V

THE AUTHOR'S VOYAGE TO GOA.

Saturday 19th, the Convoy being ready to Sail, I caus'd my Baggage to be put Aboard a Vessel of War they there call a *Manchuca,*[1] Aboard which, *Nuno d' Acuna,* the Captain of it very Civilly gave me my Passage. *Sunday* 20th, I heard Mass, and a Sermon in the *Jesuits* Church, and then went with the Procession of the Holy Cross that was going[2] to the Church of St. *Augustin,* whence it set out the Day before. *Monday* 21st, the Fleet Sail'd an Hour before Day. It consisted of thirty six *Parangas,*[3] two Galiots which were Admiral and Vice-Admiral, and four *Manchucas* of War. These *Manchucas* had such a Main Sail as the *Leutis* of *Trapani,*[4] in the Kingdom of *Sicily,*[5] 12 Oars, and four small Guns, with fifteen *Portuguese* Soldiers, the aforesaid Captain *Nuno*'s Company being distributed Aboard them. The North, or Northwest Wind prevails almost all the Year in those Seas, so that it being seldom Fair for *Goa,* we made but little way. After eighteen Miles Sailing, we pass'd by the Island and Fort of *Bombaim,* seated on the Point of the Island of *Salzete,* being about nine Miles in length, and little less in breadth. Nine Miles further, I saw another small Island, or Rock as big as *Nisida,* at *Naples ;* and on it a Fort, with some Dwellings of *Savagis,* who being at War with the Great *Mogul,* are continually in Action against the *Sydi,*[5] and Garrison of the Fort on the Continent. This *Sydi* is a Black Subject to the Great *Mogul,* who, has given him the Government of the Country between *Bombaim* and *Chaul,* to defend it against the Invasions of *Savagi,* for which purpose he maintains 2000 Horse and Foot at his own Cost. These two Forts in the Island, and on the Continent are call'd *Undrin,*[6] and *Canderin,*[7]

Tuesday 22nd, after Sailing nine Miles further, we Anchor'd opposite to the City and Fortress of *Chaul.* It is seated on a Plain, six Miles from the Sea, on the Bank of a River,[8] which at Flood will carry any Ships up to the City. It is enclos'd with good Walls, and other Works, and furnish'd with excellent Cannon. A Fort call'd *El Morro,*[9] secures the Entrance of the Harbour, being Built by the *Portuguese,* in the Year 1520, on the Hill by their General *Sequeira,*[10] with leave of the Tyrant *Nizzamaluc ;*[11] who granted it upon Condition they should bring him over three hundred Horses at reasonable Rates out of *Persia,* or *Arabia,* because of the Scarcity of them there was in *India,* to Serve him in his Wars against *Hidalcan.*[12] *Jassi,*[13] Governour of *Diu,* hearing what the *Portuguese* were doing, sent fifty Sail to Obstruct the Building of the Fort, which *Sequeira* by his Industry had already made Tenable. The Fleets had several

Chaul City.

Mall. desc. de l'Unis. t. 2. p. 55.

Maff. Hist. Ind. lib. 8. pag. 184. lit. D.

Engagements, but always with Loss to the *Turks,* so that at last they went back Disabled. Afterwards the *Portuguese* made themselves Masters of the City with Ease. Its Territory does not Extend above six Miles in length ; on the South it borders on *Savagi,* and on the North with another Fort belonging to the *Sydi.*

Wednesday 23rd, it was late before we Sail'd, waiting for some Vessels of *Chaul ;* and the Wind failing, made but little way. The Calm continu'd *Thursday* 24th, and we were oblig'd to lie close by the Coast of *Savagi,* who is a mortal Enemy[14] to the *Portuguese.* This *Savagi,* whom his Subjects call *Raja,* which signifies petty King, is so Powerful, that he maintains War at one and the same time with the Great *Mogul,* and the *Portugueses.* He brings into the Field 50000 Horse, and as many, or more Foot, much better Soldiers than the *Moguls ;* for they Live a Day upon a piece of dry Bread, and the *Mogul's* will March at their Ease, carrying their Women, abundance of Provisions, and Tents, so that their Army looks like a moving City. The *Raja,* as to his Religion is an Idolater, as are most of his Subjects. All the Coast from *Chaul* to *Goa,* for the space of 250 Miles belongs to him, and from thence to *Visapor,*[15] he has several Forts, most of them among inaccessible Mountains, besides Cities and Towns,[16] defended both by Art and Nature.

Savagi, or Ragia.

This Prince's Dominion is but of a late Date, for it began in *Savagi's* Father,[17] to whom succeeded *Sambagi,*[18] his Eldest Son, who was afterwards kill'd in Battle by the Great *Mogul's* General, and so *Ramrao*[19] now Reigning, ascended the Throne. *Savagi* first rais'd his Fortune by Serving under the King of *Golconda ;*[20] then having gather'd vast Wealth, and scouring the Country with a great Number of Men like an Out-Law, he seiz'd some Places belonging to the King of *Visapor,* and fortifying themselves in them among the Mountains, at length gather'd a mighty Army, then making War on the *Mogul,* the *Portugueses,* and other Princes his Neighbours, he usurp'd all he now stands Possess'd of. They say he was Born in *Tana,*[21] a Subject of the King of *Portugal,* and kept Shop there. But *Ramrao* pretends he is Descended from *Rajapours,*[22] and endeavours daily to enlarge his Dominions, along the Coast of *Undrin,* and *Candrin,* as far as the Bay of *Galas,*[23] besides what he has up the Land. His Subjects are Robbers both by Sea and Land, that being the Pay he allows them, and make it dangerous Sailing along that Coast, so that it is not to be done without a good Convoy ; for being[24] to pass by their Forts, they run out in small Boats well Man'd, and Rob Friends and Foes, because, as has been said, their King gives them leave. Nor is the Voyage safe on Account of the *Malabars.*[25]

These are Pyrates of several Nations, as *Moors, Gentils, Jews,* and Christians, and fall upon all they meet with a great number of Boats full of Men. Their large Country reaches from Mount *Delhi,*[26] (bordering on the Kingdom of *Canara,* ever govern'd by a Queen, and never by a Man) to *Madrastapatan,*[27] a considerable City and Fort. They Live under several Monarchs, among which the most Powerful is the Emperor *Zamori,*[28] and the King's of *Tanor,*[29] *Porca,*[30] and others. These People take poor Passengers, and lest they should have swallow'd their Gold, tho' they have no need of it,[31] give them a Potion, which makes them Digest all they have in their Bodies, which done, they search the stinking Excrements to find the precious Metal. I was very much afraid of the *Malabar* Receipt,[32] having never taken any Purge, and therefore thought best to expect[33] the Convoy. *Malabars.*

About Sun-set, the North-west Wind freshned, and brought us in sight of *Dabul.*[34] This City is seated six Miles from the Sea, after the same manner as *Chaul,* and eight Miles from it; both in the Kingdom of *Decan.* The *Portugueses* took it under their General *Almeida,*[35] from *Hidalcan,* who Reign'd at *Goa,* in the Year 1508, burning the City, and putting the *Turkish*[36] Garrison to the Sword. Now it is Subject to *Savagi.* *Dabul* City. *Maillet. desc. de l'Univers. Tom.* 2, p. 55. *Maff. Hist. Ind. l.* 4. p. 9. *lit. A.*

Friday 25th, the same Wind continuing, we came in sight of the Fort of *Visapor,* in which River[37] the Viceroy Burnt the three *Arab* Vessels before-mention'd. Then we pass'd by *Lambuna,*[38] and the Fort of *Maliandi,*[39] belonging to *Savagi,* and after Mid-night the *Ysleos-quernados,*[40] which are three Rocks, 36 Miles from *Goa.*

The Wind freshning all Night, on *Saturday* 26th, at break of Day, we came to an Anchor in our Port, having Sail'd 280 Miles from *Chaul.* Having put my Baggage into a Boat call'd a *Ballon,*[41] to carry it up the Channel to *Goa,* I met two *Ballons* of the Custom-House coming to visit that I was in; but having been fore-warn'd to write a Superscription[42] upon one of my Parcels for *F. Salvador Galli,*[43] a *Milanese Theatin,*[44] and Superior of the Monastery of *Goa,* they went away. Being come to the City, I caus'd my Eqipage to be carry'd to the Monastery, where I was Courteously receiv'd by the said Father.

CHAPTER VI

THE DESCRIPTION OF THE CITY GOA, *AND ITS DELIGHTFUL CHANNEL.*

Goa City.

Thevenot voyage des Indes. c. 3.

Goa is seated in the Latitude of fifteen Degrees, and twenty Minutes, and 104 of Longitude,[1] in an Island nine Leagues about in the River *Mandova,*[2] which six Miles below it falls into the Sea. It stretches two Miles in length along the Channel upon uneven Ground; being but half a Mile broad. It is under the Torrid Zone, which the Antients thought Inhabitable,[3] by reason of the excessive Heat of the Sun; but Providence, which has dispos'd all Things in the best manner, has qualify'd it with continual Rains, which fall so plentifully from *June,* till *September,* or *October,* that the great Floods dam up the Harbour, and obstruct Navigation; besides the Skies being darkned whole Weeks with the thick Clouds. When the Rains cease at Sun-rising, the Heat is intollerable; and therefore it is most violent in *April,* and *May,* when the Sun is in the Zenith, and the Rains are not yet begun.

Alfonso de Albuquerque,[4] took *Goa* from *Hidalcan,* without Blood-shed, in the Year 1508,[4a] a *Dominican* Father setting up the Standard of our Holy Faith. *Hidalcan* afterwards Retook the City, but in 1510, *Albuquerque* recover'd it again, with the Slaughter of 7000 Barbarians, and Built a Fort there, as he did at *Malaca,* which was lost in 1641.[5] Then considering the goodness of the Country, and commodious Situation of the Place, he constituted it the Metropolis of the *Portuguese* Empire in *India.* To Establish his Master King *Emanuel*[6] in the Possession, by gaining the Love of the Subjects, he moderated the Tribute they paid to *Hidalcan;* and to Breed up Soldiers for the Wars, he contriv'd that the *Indian* Maids should be Baptiz'd, and Marry'd to the *Portugueses;* that the *Indians* might be united to his Nation by Affinity, and there might be no need of bringing fresh Supplies[7] still out of *Portugal,* to the Depopulating the Kingdom. *Goa,* the Center of all the *Portuguese* Conquests, grew in Wealth and Renown, being become the Key of all the Trade of the East, and the chief Mart of *India.* This plainly appears by the compass of its Walls, which Extend full four Leagues, with good Bastions, and Redoubts; which from the Church of the *Madre de Deos,*[8] or the Mother of God, run along for twelve Miles to the Powder-House,[9] passing by the Castles of St. *Blase,* and St. *James;*[10] a Work of a vast Expence; as are the others next the Channel, which divides the Dominion of the *Mogul,* from that of *Portugal,* beginning at Fort St. *Thomas,* and ending three Miles off, at that of St. *Christopher.* It may be objected that these last Fortifications, were rais'd to defend the Borders, as is true, but the first Walls were made to no other purpose but to defend, and inclose the City, as the Marquiss *de Villa Verde,* the Viceroy inform'd me, when I enquir'd into it, thinking that City did not stand in need of such large Walls. But it is certain the City is not now what it was formerly; for the great Losses the *Portugueses* sustain'd, whilst their Forces were employ'd in War at home, made their Trade decline, and impair'd the Wealth and Grandeur of the City to such a degree, that it was reduc'd to a miserable Condition.

Inhabitants of *Goa.*

The Houses are the best in India,[10a] but at present it does not contain above 20000 Inhabitants of several Nations, Habits, and Religious. There are fewest of the *Portugueses,* who go over with Employments, and then Marry and settle there: because the *Indian* Women, by reason of the ill Qualities of those Born in *India,* chuse rather to Marry a poor *Portuguese* Soldier, than a rich Country Man of their own, tho' Born of *Portuguese* Parents. The *Mestizos* are more numerous; and those are so call'd that are Born of *Portuguese* Men, and *Brachman* Women, whom they marry'd after reducing *Goa;* and tho' the *Canarine* Women were Black, yet marrying Whites, their Race by degrees became lighter Colour'd. About the fourth Part of the People are *Mulattas,* that is, Born of Whites and Blacks.

Canarines.

The *Canarines*[11] are[12] as black as *Ethiopians,* but have long Hair, and good Faces. Many of them, both in *Goa,* and the Islands are Priests, Lawyers, Attorneys, Scriveners, and Sollicitors, and very Diligent in the Service of their Masters. They are Descended from several Generations[13] of Gentils, and according to their Nobility, or Meanness,[14] they continue their Customs. Most of them are the Off-spring of *Brachmans, Banienes,* and *Charados,*[15] and these have good clear Understandings, being apt to Learn all Sciences, Sharp-witted, Ingenious, and Ready, and therefore every Body endeavours to have some of them for their Servants. On the contrary, those that are of low Extraction, as the *Langottis,* are the very Reverse of the Others. All *Asia* does not afford greater Thieves and Ruffians, or more faithless ill[16] Christians than they are. They go Naked, covering only their Privities with a Clout, which they call *Langoti,*[17] and passing betwixt their Thighs, is ty'd behind with a Cord hanging down from the Waste. These Till the Land, Fish, Row, carry *Andoras,* and follow such mean Employments; but, as was said, they are so addicted to Thieving, and do it so Dexterously, that it is almost impossible to Escape them. Were it for the Love of God they led so miserable a Life, they would be accounted living Saints. They Sleep naked Day and Night on the bare Ground; they Feed on a little Rice swimming in the Dish; never tasting Bread as long as they Live, unless they be extreamly Sick. All this proceeds from their Laziness, for no sooner have they got as much Rice as will keep them a Week, but they give over Work, living Idly as long as that lasts.

The *Portugueses* tell us, That these *Canarines,* when they were first discover'd, went to Advise with their Idols, that is, the Devil, to know what they were to do with the new People that had subd'd them, and receiv'd for an Answer, that they were not able to deal with them by open Force, and therefore pretending not to understand the impertinent *Portuguese,* they should give them Water when they ask'd for Bread, and Rice when they demanded Wine. Experience soon shew'd how frivolous the Advice was; for the *Portugueses* readily found the way to cure them of their Stupidity, taking a *Bamboo,* which is a very hard Cane in *India,* and beating them so severely, that afterwards they flew at every beck. And whilst I was at *Goa,* I perceiv'd the aforesaid Cane perform'd Wonders; for being beaten, they understood a Man's thoughts and serv'd readily, but to give them fair Words was time lost. Beating is so agreeable to these Wretches, that it makes up a part of their amorous Delight; for when they Marry, the Couple lies down upon their hard Bed, and the Kindred and Friends come and thrash them,[18] shewing them so much of this brutal Kindness, that they are unfit for any business for some time.

Most of the Citizens and Merchants of *Goa,* are *Idolaters* and *Mahometans,* who live in a quarter of the Town apart, and without any publick use of their Religion. We shall speak of them both at large hereafter. There are also abundance of

Blacks. *Cafres* and Blacks; for there are *Portugueses* that keep thirty, or forty, and the least six or twelve; to carry their Umbrella, and *Andora,* and other mean Employments; nor are they at any other charge to keep them, but a Dish of Rice at Noon,[19] and another at Night; for they have no other Garments but what they brought out of their Mothers Wombs. These Slaves are carry'd to sell at *Goa,* and all along the *Portuguese* Towns,[20] by the Company's Ships belonging to *Lisborn* and *India,* who buy them at *Monbaza, Mozambique, Zofala,*[21] and other Parts along the Coast of *Africk;* for those Nations being at War among themselves, take Slaves on both sides, whom they afterwards sell to the *Portuguese.* There are others whom their Parents out of meer want sell, for only a *Zecchine;* and others who in despair, Barbarously sell themselves. There would be abundance of this last sort, did not they foolishly conceit,[22] that at *Goa* they make Powder of them. They being very cheap, that is, fifteen or twenty Crowns of *Naples* a Head, it is no wonder there should be such numbers of them, and that the very Vintners keep them to sell their Wine; besides the *Canarines* they have for other uses. As to their Religion they are Idolaters, but are easily induc'd to embrace the Catholick Faith, there being no need of many persuasions, for they presently yield, and readily consent to be Baptiz'd. On the contrary, those of the Coast of *Africk* opposite to *Spain* are perverse. There are some of them who besides eating one another, when it Thunders, shoot Arrows towards Heaven, brutishly challenging God to fight with them.

But those Blacks we speak of, tho' of an ill aspect, have some of them[23] such a noble and genteel Disposition, that it were a Blessing that every *European* Gentleman were like them. D. *Francisco de Taverno,* Earl of *Alvor,*[24] who was afterwards Vice-Roy of *India,* being Governor of *Angola,*[25] the Son of a Neighbouring King, came once to visit him, and understanding that the *Portugueses* were precise in matter of Compliments, and that he should be receiv'd standing, as was accordingly done, he took along with him two Slaves well instructed what they were to do. Being come into the Governor's Room, and seeing no Chair brought him, he caus'd his two Slaves to squat down and sate upon them. The *Portuguese* admir'd the *Cafres* Ingenuity, and presently order'd Chairs to be brought. After the visit the two Slaves stay'd in the Count's House ; and their Master being told of it by the Count's Servants, that he might call them away, he answer'd, he did not use[26] to carry away the Chairs he sate on. A genteel Action of a Black.

In the same Kingdom of *Angola,* two Brothers of the King *de las Pedras* being made Prisoners by the *Portugueses,* were sent to *Lisbon,* where in a visit they made to the Marquis of *Marialva* seeing no Chairs were brought them ; they drew them themselves and sate down, telling the Marquis, that he was a Marquis, and they Princes. Another.

As their Princes and Gentry are endued with Generous and noble Thoughts, so the Commonalty are Couragious, and Cunning,[27] for they with poor Weapons overcome Elephants,[28] and the fiercest Lions. To kill the first of these they make a narrow Path, along which they by means of several contrivances drive the Beast, and then dexterosly wound it with a Javelin from off a Tree. When it has blead to Death and falls, all the Inhabitants of the neighbouring Village, resort to the place, and live there in Tents till they have eaten all the Flesh. Others finding the Elephant lying on the Ground, get upon him, and Stab him with a long Dagger, holding fast upon him till he is dead, which cannot be done without much Courage. They kill the Lions for sport ; for when they see one astray in the Woods, one of them advances with two small Cudgels in his Hand, and clapping one of them into the Lions Paw, plays with the other: In the mean while the next Black to him very dextrously takes the Beast by the Testicles, and then they beat him to death. So when they would have a Lion quit a Killing of Elephants and Lions.

Cow he has seiz'd, they draw near, and saluting him after the same manner as is us'd in *Africk,* to Persons of the greatest Note; that is, lying down on their side, holding up one Foot, and at the same time making a Noise with Hands and Mouth. This was generally told me by the *Portugueses;* the Reader may believe what he pleases; for I do not assert those things for Truths, which I have not seen. Since we are speaking of these Blacks, it is to be observ'd that in *Africk* there are some call'd *Nudoy, Macua,*[29] who are so fierce and inhuman, that they eat the Flesh of the Enemies they take, or kill in Battle. They go quite naked, except their Privities; and curl their thick Hair, winding it about small sticks, which makes them look like Devils. They lye in the open Fields[30] on Trees, being us'd to this dangerous Bed, for fear of the Wild Beasts that Country is full of. No[31] part of the World is richer in Gold; for in some Kingdoms it is found upon the surface of the Earth, so that there is no need of digging for it, and therefore instead of Iron they[32] use Golden Nails.

Inhuman Blacks.

The Port of *Goa.*

To return, after so long a digression, to *Goa,* its Port is compar'd by *Tavernier,*[33] to the best in our Continent, such as *Constantinople,* and *Toulon.* And to say the Truth, besides what Nature made it, the *Portuguese* have taken much Pains to Compleat, and Fortify it by means of many Castles and Towers furnish'd with good Cannon; for at the Entrance on the left upon the point of the Island of *Bardes,*[34] is a good Fort call'd *Aguada,*[35] with strong Works, and Guns levell'd with the Water; on the top of the Hill, near the Channel, is a long Wall, all planted with Cannon; and opposite to it the Castle call'd *Nossa Sinhora do Cabo,*[36] or our Lady of the Cope, built in the Island of *Goa.* Two Miles within the Channel, above the Island of *Bardes,* is another Castle call'd *dos Reys,*[37] or of the Kings, well Fortify'd and with Cannon level with the Water. Here the new Viceroys take Possession at their first Arrival. Near this Fort is a Monastery of *Franciscans.*[38] Opposite to it, and within common[38a] Shot, is the Fort of *Gaspar Dias;*[39] but two Miles distant from that of the King's. Beyond these Castles the Channel grows narrower, sometimes to one, sometimes to two Miles, and its Banks set out with the best Fruit and Trees *India* affords, yield the finest Prospect imaginable. Besides, there are delicate[40] Country Houses call'd *Quintas,*[41] and abundance of dwellings of the Country People. The delightful Scene holds for Eight Miles up to *Goa.*

Half way up on the right side is a Palace call'd *Passo de Daugi,*[42] where formerly the Vice-Roys resided; at present it serves to quarter the Garrison Souldiers. There begins a thick Wall two Miles in length, for[43] a Foot-Path when the Country is overflow'd; and there a great deal of Salt is gather'd: Opposite to this Wall, or Dike, is a Hill, on which the *Jesuits* have their Noviceship.[44] The Vice-Roy has his Palace call'd *la Palvereira,*[45] on the same Channel, and so has the Arch-bishop. Here begins the City, and so far Ships can come up after lightning some part of their Load.

This Channel that makes so noble[46] a Port, runs many Miles up the Country, dividing it into several Fruitful Islands and Peninsulas, which do not only plentifully supply the City[47] with necessaries,[48] but delight the Pallate with rich Fruit,[49] afford a curious[50] Prospect, and yield much profit to the Gentry, to whom for the most part they belong. In short, this Channel for Pleasure is no way inferiour to our *Posilipo,* as well on account of those advantages here mention'd, as for the many Boats there are on it to take the Air.

Adjoyning to this Port is that of *Murmugon*[51] form'd by the other Channel that runs between the Island of *Goa* and Peninsula's of *Salzete ;* to give a safe retreat to the Ships that come from *Portugal* and other Parts, when they are shut out of the Port, by the Sands the River *Mandua* brings down, when swollen by the first Rains of *June,* the Passage not being open till *October.*[52] This Port of *Murmugon* is defended by the Castle of the same Name, seated in the Island of *Salzete,* with a good Garrison and Cannon.

These two Channels which meet at St. *Laurence*[53] make the length from East to West of the Island of *Goa,* which is twenty seven Miles in compass and contains thirty Villages. Entring the Port on the right Hand is the Peninsula of *Salzete,* which is sixty Miles about, and twenty in length, containing 50000 Souls in fifty Villages, where the *Jesuits* administer the Sacraments.[54] On the left is the other Peninsula of *Bardes,* in which are the Forts of *Aguada,* and *Reyes.* It is fifteen Miles long, and about forty five in compass with 28 Villages, Govern'd in Spirituals[55] by the Clergy.

Saturday 26th, going to the Custom-house to find the Commander of the *Manchuca,* and tell him that his Men had stolen a Coat, and a Silver Case[56] for the Table out of my Portmantue ; I saw *F. Francis*'s Man carry'd away Prisoner, for having spoke saucily to the Officer of the Customs on account of his Masters Goods. He was discharg'd upon my request ; and the Customer very civilly told me, that if I had any Baggage I might take it away without searching ; a piece of Courtesy not used towards Strangers in our Custom-houses.

After Dinner, I went to see the Cathedral.[57] It is very large, Arch'd, divided into three Isles[58] by twelve Columns, and all curiously adorn'd with Figures, as are the Chappels. The Arch-bishop's Seat is in the Choir, but[59] rais'd a great height above the Ground. The Palace is Magnificent and Spacious, with curious Galleries and noble Apartments, for **Cathedral.**

what *India* affords; but the Archbishop, for the conveniency of the cool Air, lives in that we said was upon the Channel, near the Powder House. A few paces from the Cathedral is the little Church of the *Misericordia.*[60]

Recolets.

Sunday 27th, I went two Miles from the City to see the Monastery of the *Recolets,* call'd *A Madre de Deos,*[61] or the Mother of God. The Dormitories are large and sightly, and their Gardens furnish'd with several sorts of *European,* and *Indian* Fruit. The Church tho' small is Beautiful, with 3 handsom[62] Altars; one in the middle rail'd in, and two on the sides. In the Garden where S. *Jerome*'s Hermitage stands, there is a Fish-pond well stor'd.

The Great Wall.

Near this Monastery, at the place call'd *Daugi,*[63] begins the Wall built by the *Portuguese* when the City[64] was in it. Flourishing condition along the Channel, to secure it from being invaded by Enemies. It is about four Miles along, reaching to S. *Blase,* S. *James*'s Fort, and S. *Laurence,* with Towers at convenient distances furnish'd with Cannon.

Dominicans.

Returning home I went into the Church and Monastery of S. *Dominick.*[65] The first has three Isles,[66] made by six Columns on a side. The Arches are gilt, especially that of the Choir, where Gold glitters in every part. The high Altar and Chappel are well adorn'd. The Convent is Magnificent, for the long Arches of the Dormitories, Cloister and other Spacious places, necessary for a great number of Fathers. The Gardens are also pleasant and curious.[67]

Augustinians.

After Dinner I saw the Monastery of S. *Augustin,*[68] seated on a high Ground, that commands the City. A large ascent of steps leads up to the front of the Church, where there are two high Towers with great Bells. The Church has but one Isle[69] set off with good Images. As well the Altars of eight side-Chappels, as the high Altars, and only[70] on each Hand of it, are all richly gilt. The stately Choir is above, over the great Gate. The Monastery has a good Cloister with vast great Dormitories, and an infinite number of Cells. Add to all this the Beauty of the Gardens, always green, and beautify'd with the best Trees *India* produces. Near this Monastery is the College for Novices with a decent Church and dwellings.

Theatins.

The little Church of the *Theatins*[71] is built after the Model of S. *Andrew della Velle* in *Rome,*[72] Four Columns support the *Cupola,* which is adorn'd with Images, as are the Arches. Both the high Altar and beautiful Chapples on the sides are gilt, The Choir is over the three Doors coming in. The Monastery also small, and has a Garden.

Sagu root.

Monday 28th, F. *Salvador* gave me a taste of the Root *Sagu,*[73] boil'd with Coco-nut, Milk and Sugar. Tho' when dress'd it looks like Glew,[74] yet it is very Nourishing and well-tasted. It comes from *Malaca* and the Island of *Borneo* bruis'd small like Millet, and white.

Barefoot *Franciscans.*

Tuesday the 1st of *March,* the Vice-Roy return'd from visiting the Northern Coast. Two Vessels arriv'd from *China,* having spent a long time in their Voyage, for fear of the *Arabs.* I went to the Barefoot *Franciscans,* which is one of the best Churches in *Goa:*[75] For tho' small it looks like one entire Mass of Gold, there is so much of this Metal about the high Altar, and Sepulcher for *Maundy Thursday,* and in the eight Chappels on the side. The Roof is curiously adorn'd with Fretwork.

Jesuits College.

The *Jesuits* College, call'd S. *Rock,* has a small Church[76] with six little Chapples; but the House is large and capable of[77] seventy Fathers, who live in it, there being but twenty five at the profess'd House.

Augustinian Nuns.

S. *Monica*[78] of the *Augustinian* Nuns, is an arch'd Church, with three gilt Altars. Here is a miraculous Crucifix. Sister *Mary of Jesus*[79] dy'd in this Monastery with the reputation of Sanctity: She having the signs of our Saviour's Wounds found upon her, and on her Head, as it were the goreing of Thorns; whereof the Archibishop took authentick Information.

S. *Paul Jesuits.*

After Dinner I went to St. *Paul,*[79a] the first Church founded by the *Jesuits* in *India,* whence they took the Name of *Paulistas.* Afterward they left it on account of the ill Air, and because it was out of the City, so that only two Fathers reside there at present; Having formerly been a College, the Dormitories still standing are magnificent. In the Garden there are 2 *Jaqua,*[80] and some *Mango* Trees caused to be planted by *S. Francis Xaverius.* There is also a Chappel[81] built in Memory of the Extasy or Rapture the Saint had in that place. In this Church, tho' formerly Magnificent, there is at present only the high Altar, with two small ones on the sides. Here the Catechumens are instructed; for whose sustenance the King allows four hundred Pieces of Eight a Year.

In *India* all Christians wear their Beads about their Necks, like Religious Men. The *Jesuits* instead of a Priest's Cap, wear a long round one, broad at the top.

Miraculous Cross.

The Miraculous Cross,[82] is a Church built on the Hill, on the place where a wooden Cross being formerly fix'd on a Stone foot; it is reported that seventy four Years since the Crucifix was found with its back Miraculously turn'd towards Goa, which City from that time has very much declin'd.

St. *Thomas Dominicans.*

Wednesday 2d *March,* I went to the Church of S. *Thomas* of the *Dominicans,*[83] a good Fabrick on the Bank of the Channel. It has seven Altars; the Monastery is large, and Beautiful, inhabited by 25 Fathers.

S. Bonaventure Franciscans.

S. *Bonaventure*[84] of the *Observants* of S. *Francis,* is a small distance from it, has a little Church, and indifferent Dormitories. It was the first built at *Goa* in Honour of S. *Francis* by *Edward de Merses.*[85]

The Hospital of *Goa*[86] is small, and ill Govern'd,[87] tho' the King allows it four hundred pieces of Eight a Year. For this reason, and through the Pestilential Air of the Country there dye Thousands of sick Persons in it, and particularly of wretched *Portuguese* Souldiers.

Thursday 3d, I went in an *Andora,* to Our Lady of the Pillar,[88] seated on a Hill six Miles from the City. This is the School of the *Recolets.* The Church though small is Beautiful, and has three gilt Altars. Returning home one of the *Bues* or Porters that carry'd me in the *Andora* being got drunk, I was forc'd to make the Peasants, I met by the way carry me ; they obeying readily upon sight of a Cudgel.

It is to be observ'd that all the Monasteries in *Goa* and throughout all the *Portuguese* Dominions in *India,* have some allowance[89] from the King, more or less, according to the number of the Religious.

CHAPTER VII

OF THE ANTIENT AND MODERN DOMINION OF THE PORTUGUESE *IN* INDIA.

Discovery of *India Portuguese Asia.*

Vasco de Gama a *Portuguese* Gentleman, whose Statue is over one of the Gates of *Goa,*[1] was the first that perform'd this tedious Voyage ;[2] and King *Emanuel* of *Portugal* had the good Fortune to see that accomplish'd which his Predecessors had in Vain attempted for seventy five Years before. *Gama* had the Title of General, or Admiral of four Ships,[3] three whereof were well fitted for War,[4] and the fourth loaded with Provisions ; and being furnish'd with all necessaries for so long a Voyage he sail'd from *Lisbon* on the 9th of *July* 1947 ;[5] a Season, as afterwards was found by experience, most improper to go to *India ;* for want of those general Winds that forward Ships on their way thither. After some dangerous Storms he touch'd at the Island of St. *James,*[6] the biggest of the ten of *Cabo Verde,* where having taken what he wanted, he continu'd his Voyage to the *Cape of Good Hope,* which he found very stormy, as *Bartholomew Dias*[7] had call'd it, as well by reason of its being in thirty four Degrees and a half of South Latitude,[8] as because the two Oceans here break one upon another. Nevertheless King *John,*[9] under whom *Diaz* discover'd it, would not

Vita Alberque.

have it call'd the Stormy Cape for fear of discouraging Sailers for the time to come ;[10] but on the contrary gave it the Name of the *Cape of Good Hope.* There a worse Storm than that of the Sea, was rais'd aboard the Ship by the Sailers against *Gama,* for they daunted with the present Danger, and fearing greater, if they went further, conspir'd together to throw him over Board and return home. *Gama* having Intelligence of it, clapt the chief of the Conspirators in Irons, and sitting down himself at the Helm, play'd both the parts of the Captain and Pilot, till he had weather'd the *Cape,* and brought them all out of that Danger. Then steering North East, still Coasting along *Africk,* this Eastern *Columbus* came at last to the Island of *Mozambique,* and then boldly crossing a Gulph of 2500 Miles[11] on the 18th of *May* 1498, came to an Anchor in a Port thirty Miles from *Calicut*[12] a City in the Kingdom of *Malabar,* after ten Months Sail from *Lisbon.* The *Portuguese* continu'd this same way to *India* for several Years after, still going on to the discovery of more remote Countries, as far as *China*[13] and *Japan;* and to the Southward opened a way to the Infinite Number of Islands in that great Archipelago. Their Discoveries were follow'd by Conquests, with an incredible increase as well of Souls brought to the Faith, as of Glory and Dominions added to the Crown of *Portugal.* Having by repeated Voyages settled the means of getting the necessary supplies out of *Europe,* the *Portugueses* began to subdue the Kingdoms of *Decan, Cambaya,* and *Guzaratte,*[14] taking the Forts of *Diu, Cambaya, Suratte, Damam, Trapor, Maim, Bazaim, Tana, Chaul, Dabul,* and other places[15] for Two hundred Miles along the Coast ; as also the Islands of *Goa, Salzete, Bardes, Andegiva,*[16] and others ; the small City of S. *Thomas,* the Kingdoms of *Cochin* and *Calicut,* and the Island of *Ceylon.* *Portuguese* Conquests.

Further on towards *China,* they made themselves Masters of the important place of *Malaco,*[17] of the *Molucco*[18] Islands, and the Islands of *Timor,*[19] and *Solor,*[20] building the Colony of *Macao*[21] with the consent of the Emperor of *China.* The Dominion also extended on the Coast of *Africk* over *Angola* and *Mozambique.* This last is an Island three Miles in compass, and a Mile in length,[22] where only the *Jesuits* have a Garden of Palm-Trees. The Fort is seated on the Mouth of the Channel,[23] which runs between the said little Island, and the Continent. The Castle has four good Bastions, with seventy four choice pieces of Cannon. The Governor is honour'd with the Title of General of the River of *Senna,*[24] where he has his Lieutenant, which employment is worth to him several hundred thousand Crowns ; there are but a few Houses about the Fort,[25] the Inhabitants keeping their effects on the Neighbouring Continent. But notwithstanding the narrowness of the place there are Monasteries of *Jesuits, Dominicans,* of S. *John* *Mozambique de Dios*, besides the chief Church and that of the *Misericordia*. The Merchandize brought to this Port by the Ships of the Company,[26] are bought at a set Price by the Royal Factory; which afterwards sends them to *Chilimani*, the Mouth of the River of *Senna*, running three hundred Miles along the Coast in Galiots and small Vessels, because of the Flats. From *Chilimani*,[27] the Goods are sent up the River against the Stream in *Almandies*[28] or little Boats, which are ten Days going up, and but five coming down. It is very difficult going up for those that are not well acquainted with the Shallows, and Windings of the River. *Cafres*, or Blacks resort to this Port from Provinces and Kingdoms three or four Months Journey distant to buy or take up Goods upon Trust for so much Gold; which they never fail to bring punctually the next Year, unless Death prevent them. This Trade yields above *cent. per. cent.* so that the *Portugueses* may be said to have another *India* in *Africk*.

Senna[29] is a little Town on the right Hand of the River, inhabited by fifty *Portuguese* Families, who make it Populous enough by the great Number of Blacks they keep. These till the Ground, and dig in the Mines, and by that means maintain their Masters instead of being kept by them. The *Dominicans* and other Missioners, when they return from this place carry away Gold, in Ingots and Plates, so great is the Plenty of it, especially a Months Journey up the Country, where they say the Beasts Shooes are set on with Gold Nails, as was said elsewhere.

Zofala. On the same Coast, fifteen Days journey from *Mozambique*, the *Portugueses* have the Fort of *Zofala*,[30] the first Place they discover in this part of *Africk*, as also the small Island and Fort of *Mombaza*.

Mascate. In *Arabia Fœlix* the *Portugueses* once had the important Place of *Mascate*,[31] and its Dependances; the Kingdom of *Ormuz*,[32] the Islands of *Recca, Kescimi*,[33] and others in the *Persian* Gulph; where they made the Island of *Baharem*[34]
Bassora. Tributary, as also the considerable City of *Bassora*,[35] which still pays five Thousand five Hundred Crowns and a Horse yearly Tribute to the King of *Portugal*; besides two *Zecchines* a Day for the subsistence of the *Portuguese*'s Factor; but whensoever their Fleet, does not appear powerful in the Gulph the *Mahometans* refuse to pay.

They also made themselves Masters in the Kingdom of *Canara* of the Forts of *Onor*,[36] *Brazalor*,[37] and *Cambolin*;[38] in the Country of the *Naires* of the Castles of *Cananor*,[39] *Caranpanor*,[40] *Palepor*,[41] and *Coilon*;[42] and of the Fort of *Manar* on the Island of that Name.[43]

In the Island of *Ceylon,* of seven Provinces (or *Carolas,*[44] as the *Indians* call them) three were brought under the *Portugueses* Dominion; with the rich Country of the Cinnamon, and the Forts of *Calaturre,*[45] *Columbo,*[46] *Cilau,*[47] *Jafanapatan,*[48] *Trichil,*[49] *Mall,*[50] and *Batticall;*[51] and this by the last Will of the King of *Acota,*[52] who was Sovereign thereof. The *Dutch* with the assistance of the neighbouring Kings afterwards made themselves Masters, if not of all, at least of a considerable Part of the said three Provinces. *Ceylon.*

The *Portugueses* further subdu'd the City and Fort of *Negapatan*[53] in the Kingdom of *Madure; Tambulin*[54] in the Kingdom of *Bengala,* and *Macassar*[55] in the Kingdom of that Name. So that being become formidable to all the Princes of *Asia,* they had made all the Country about *Tributary;* and being Sovereigns of that vast Ocean by means of their mighty Fleets, no Ship of any Nation whatsoever could sail those Seas without their Leave and Pass; seizing the Ships and Goods, and Imprisoning the Men for presuming to Sail without their Protection.[56] This Authority the *Portugueses,* tho weak, still exercise over all Ships of *Moors* and *Gentils;* for the *Europeans* are got above it. These Conquests gain'd at the Expence of many Lives, and with the effusion of much Blood scarce lasted an Age and a half; for the *Dutch* falling into the *India* Trade,[57] instead of extending their Conquests among so many Islands and Kingdoms of *Mahometans* and *Pagans,* they only Robb'd the *Portugueses* of what they had gain'd with so much Valour; making this ungrateful return to a Nation, which with so many Dangers and Sufferings, taught and secur'd to them that tedious Voyage. *Negapatan.*

Another cause of the decay of the *Portugueses* Power in *India* was their Conquest of *Brazil;*[58] for finding there more Profit, they slighted *India,* and neglected to send thither sufficient Supplies[59] to preserve what they had, much less to make new Conquests. This is so certain, that the King of *Portugal* was several times in the Mind absolutely to abandon it, which had certainly been done, had not the Missioners made him sensible[60] that if he did so all the Christians of those Countries would again fall into Idolatry and *Mahometanism.* *Brazil.*

If we look upon what remains to the *Portugueses* at present in *India,* it is very inconsiderable, and instead of being Profitable scarce pays its own charge. At *Goa* they have the small Island of that Name, with those of *Salzete, Bardes, Angediva,* and others.[61] On the Northern Coast the Fortresses of *Damam, Bazaim,* and *Chaul;* in the Kingdom of *Guzaratte* the City of *Diu.* Near *China* the Islands of *Timor* (abounding in *Sandal*)[62] and *Solor;* and the Colony of *Macao,* Subject to the Emperor of *China.* In *Africk, Angola, Sena, Sofala, Mozambique* and *Mombaza;* many in number, but of no great

Present Dominions of *Portugal* in *India.*

value. Those that envy the Honour of the *Portugueses* ascribe their losses to their want of Zeal for Religion, and their not persisting long in the propagation of it; for they say that the *Portugueses* entring *India* with the Crucifix in one Hand and the Sword in the other, finding much Gold, they laid aside the Crucifix to fill their Pockets; and not being able to hold them up with one Hand they were grown so heavy, they dropp'd their Sword too. Being found in this Posture by those that came after, they were easily overcome. This is an excellent contrivance of ill Tongues; but the chief cause of their Ruin was their having made so many Conquests so far divided from one another; and next the War at home, which obstructed the relieving of *India*.

Government. Viceroy. Courts or Councils.

All that remains under the *Portugueses* Dominion from the Cape of *Good Hope* in *Africk*, to the City of *Macao* in *China*, is Govern'd by a Vice-Roy, with the Title of Captain General,[63] who resides at *Goa* as the Metropolis of *India*. There are six, and sometimes eight *Desembargadores*,[64] or Judges that attend the Government, as a sovereign Court or Council, who wear a Gown down to their Heels over a Cassock of the same length, the Gown with wide Sleeves down half way their Arms.[65] They wear *Golillas*[66] and huge Periwigs after the *French* Fashion. The chief Court these Gown-Men sit in is call'd a *Relacaon*, which administers Justice in Civil and Criminal Cases; having Power over all Ministers, and tries all Appeals brought from any Parts of the Dominions. The Vice-Roy sits as Chief of this Court under a Canopy; the Gown-Men sit on Benches plac'd on the plain Floor. The Council *de Facenda*,[67] is like the Court of Exchequer, where one of the Gown-Men sits as the Vice-Roy's Deputy.

There is the *Matricula-General*,[68] the *Procurador-Mor-dos-Contos*,[69] and the Committee of the new Company of Traders. These have put in several Sums to carry on the Trade of *Mozambique*, *Mombaca*, *Macao*, and other Parts of the *Portugueses* Dominions; and have the Privilege that none should Trade but they, because they pay the Salaries of the Governours. The Viceroy and Archbishop put in many thousand *Pardaos*[70] into this Company, to encourage others to do the like; but it can scarce last long, because the Stock is but small. The profit is to be divided every three Years.

Inquisition.

The *Inquisition*[71] is much respected and dreaded by the Christians at *Goa*, and about it; as is the Archbishop, or Primate.

The Viceroy goes by Water in a *Ballon*, or Barge row'd by twenty two *Canarines*, with Trumpets before him, and sits on a Velvet Seat, with several of his Domesticks about him. When he lands he is carry'd in a Sedan by four Men. He has a

Guard of ten Horse, and several of the Gentry and Officers attend him in *Palanchines.*

Tho' the *Portuguese* Dominions be small ; yet the King appoints several Generals who have very little advantage besides the Honour. One of them is call'd of the Gulph of *Ormuz,* and commands four Ships ; another of the North, who is like a *General*[72] over all those Towns, and resides at *Bazaim ;* another of *Salzete,* who commands in that Island ; one of *China,* who commads only in the Town of *Macao ;* one in the Islands of *Timar* and *Solor ;* and lastly one of *Goa,* who has the care of the Channels, that no Person may come in or pass by from the *Mogul's* Country. And this because it is a difficult Matter to secure the Passage between so many small Islands ; for besides those of *Goa, Bardes* and *Salzete,* there are, that of *Charon,*[73] where are two Villages, the Noviciate of the *Jesuits,* and a Parish of Seculars ; *Divar,* or *Narva*[74] with three Villages, where the Seculars have the Cure of Souls ; *Capon,*[75] belonging to the Nuns of *S. Monica ; Combargiva,* and *Juvari*[76] belonging to the *Jesuits ; S. Stephen,*[77] where there is a Fort, Village and Parish of Seculars ; the small Island of *Emanuel Lobo de Silveira,*[78] with a few Houses on it ; that of *Emanuel Motto,*[79] which is the Stews of *Goa,* being inhabited by *Pagan* Dancing-Whores ; and lastly the small Island of *Dongarin*[80] belonging to the *Augustinians.* These for the most part abound in Palm or Coco-Trees, under which the *Canarines* and *Gentils* build Cottages to live in ; so that every Palm-Tree Grove looks like a little Village. They say the Breath of Man makes the Palm-Tree more Fruitful.

Not only the Viceroy but all the Officers Civil and Military, and Church-Men have sufficient Allowance from the King to maintain them handsomely. The Viceroy's Salary is 30000 *Pardaos,* which are the third part of a piece of Eight. The Archibishop 12000 ; the Officers of the Inquisition, Canons, Monasteries, and Parishes a Competency ; but all the Tithes belong to the King.

CHAPTER VIII

OF THE FRUIT AND FLOWERS OF INDOSTAN.

It must not be thought strange that, being to speak[1] of the Fruit and Flowers of so vast a Country as *Indostan,* I should bring it in immediately after *Goa ;* because all those sorts, which are found[2] in the several Parts of that Tract, being to be had about *Goa,* and even some that are not elsewhere ;[3] it is proper we should give an account of them before we leave that City. I will endeavour to explain their *Portuguese* Names the best I can,[4] and add the Cuts of them,[5] that they may appear the plainer to the Reader.

Coco-Tree. To begin then by the *Palmera de Cocos,*[6] or Coco-Tree, the first Place being due to that Plant which is most beneficial to Man: It is to be conceiv'd that this Tree fits out and loads a Ship for Sea, without borrowing any think[7] elsewhere. Of the Leaves, which some of the People on that Coast use instead of Paper,[8] they generally make Sails; of the Wood the Vessel: The Fruit, which is well known in *Europe,* yields Meat[9] and Drink, and a good Commodity;[10] besides its outward Case or Rind[11] steep'd in Water is Spun to make all necessary Cordage for a Vessel, tho' there are some sorts of it which they eat like other Fruit.[12] This first Rind, when Ripe is yellow; the Shell which is hard, makes Dishes[13] to drink Chocolate and for other Uses.[14] Within it is a white Pulp or Nut sticking round the Shell about half an Inch thick, which tasts like an Almond.[15] In the midst of it is a clear Water very good to drink. Of this same Fruit they make several sorts of Sweetmeats, and Oyl, both to Burn[16] and Eat for want of Olives. Cutting a Branch of it and putting the end into a Vessel,[17] the moisture that should feed the Nut runs into it and is call'd *Nira,* and *Sura.* The *Nira* is white and sweet just of the taste of the Liquor made of the Grapes, by putting Water to them after they have been press'd, and is taken before the Sun rises. The *Sura* is the same Liquor turn'd sower, and is taken after the Sun is up and has heated the Air. It must be put to the Fire before it is drank, or else its Coldness would give the Gripes. It is so nourishing that the *Indians* live upon it several Days without any other Sustenance.

This *Sura* Distill'd makes Wine, and when it decays Vinegar; but the Distilling being several times repeated it becomes a strong Water:[18] Boil'd it turns to Sugar,[19] and they use it as Leaven to their Bread. Pressing the Pith of the Tree they draw Milk out of it, as we do from Almonds, to Boil Rice, and for several other uses.[20] This Fruit keeps the Year about.[21] Thus the Coco-Trees yield the best Revenue in *India,* because the Country does not produce much Rice, Cotton, or Corn. They grow strait to sixty Spans in height, of an equal thickness from the Bottom to the Top. The *Indians* use them for Timber to build their Houses, and the Leaves to cover them,[22] or to burn.

Palm-Tree. The Palm, or Date Tree[23] in *India* bears no Fruit, but they draw *Nira,* or *Sura* from them. There are several other sorts of them that yield little Fruit. One they call *Palmeira de*

Transolin. *Transolin,*[24] whose Fruit is ripe in *May.* This is smaller than the Coco, the outside Rind to make Ropes black;[25] and full within of the same substance as the other Cocos. Every

Transolin bears three little Coco-Nuts in a Triangle ; the Pulp whereof press'd yields a cold white Water. This grows as high as the Coco-Tree, but is thicker of Leaves, which grow like a Broom, and produces Fruit but once a Year, whereas the other does four times. This Tree also affords *Nira* and *Sura,* both of them naturally excessive Cold.

The *Palma de Coco de Bugios,*[26] or the Monkey Coco-Tree, has Boughs like large Disciplines. Of the Fruit they make curious Beads, because the *Paters* have a natural Work on them, than which nothing more curious could be made by Art. There are other Palm-Trees in *India* that do not bear, and the *Indians* run up and down them by the help of a Rope ty'd about the Tree, and the Man so nimbly that none can believe that has not seen it. *Palma de Bugios.*

The *Arequeira,* or *Areca*[27]-Tree is like the Palm, but slenderer and not so high. It bears[28] a sort of Fruit necessary for chewing with the *Betle,* like a Nutmeg and enclos'd in a Case or Rind, like that of the Coco-Nut, and on a Bough as thick of them as that which produces Dates. This Fruit is gather'd four or five times a Year. *Areca* Tree.

The *Figueira,* or Fig-Tree[29] is a Plant as soft as a Bulrush, as thick as a Man's Thigh, and between fifteen and twenty Spans high, with Leaves above a quarter Broad.[30] It is generally believ'd there that *Adam* and *Eve* cover'd what should not be seen with them in Paradice,[31] they being not only big enough to cover what should be hid, but to make a small Cloak for their Nakedness. The *Indians* use them for Dishes,[32] and have new ones every Meal ; others for Paper to Write on.[33] It bears Fruit but once, for when it has produced sixty, seventy, and sometimes a hundred Figs on a Branch, they cut down the Plant and a young Sprout grows out again. But there are two sorts of them. Those that are a Span long, and about the thickness and shape of an Egg, are call'd *Figos de assar,*[34] or roasting Figs ; and these are as sweet as a wild Fig, and very nourishing, being eaten roasted with Cinnamon and Sugar. The Pulp or Flesh within is white and red, with some small tender black Seeds, which are also eaten. They are gather'd green, and ripen and turn yellow in the House, like Winter Melons. The other sort is call'd *Figos de Orta,*[35] or Garden Figs ; these are sweeter, better tasted, and eaten Raw, but not so large as the others, tho' they have the same Seeds. As for their Nature, these are Cold, and the others Hot ; both of them ripen at any time of the Year. Fig-Tree.

The *Manguera* or *Mango*-Tree[36] is as high as a good Pear-Tree, but has larger and softer Leaves. The *Mango* it bears is weighty and flat, and hangs downwards by a long Stalk. Without they are green, and the Pulp within the Shell is white *Mango*-Tree.

and yellow. There are several sorts of them and variously Tasted.

Some are call'd *Mangas Carreiras* and *Mallaias,* others of *Nicholas Alfonso,* others *Satias,*[37] and others by other Names, all of them exceeding any *European* Fruit in delicate Taste.[38] They are Ripe in *May, June* and *July,*[39] tho' there are some in *January* and *February.* They are of a very hot Nature, and are gather'd from the Tree like all other *Indian* Fruits, green,[40] coming afterwards to their Maturity and Perfection in three Days keeping in the House.

Carambola-Tree. The *Caramboleira,* or *Carambola*-Tree,[42] is as big as a Plum Tree, and bears such a Leaf. The Fruit call'd *Carambola,* when Ripe is white within and yellow without, shap'd exactly like a Lemmon, with four or five Kernels, and it has a sour Taste like a Lemmon. The *Portugueses* preserve them because they are Cooling. The Tree Blossoms and bears several times a Year.

Anona-Tree. The *Anoneira,* or *Anona*-Tree[43] is very large and produces the Fruit call'd *Anona* in *March* and *April.*[44] It is as big as a Pear, red and yellow without, whitish within, and full of a soft, sweet, and pleasant Substance, which is eaten with a Spoon ; but it has some hard black Kernels. I do not know how to describe it better ; because it is nothing like any sort of Fruit in *Europe.*

Ata-Tree. The *Ateira,* or *Ata*-Tree[45] is as big as an Apple-Tree, but with small Leaves. Its Fruit call'd *Ata* is like that of the Pine-Tree, green without, and within white and soft with black Seeds, so that it is eaten with a Spoon. It is sweeter than the *Anona,* smelling both of Ambar and Rose-water. It Ripens in *November* and *December.*

Cajus-Tree. The *Cajuyera,* or *Cajus*-Tree[46] is not very Tall, but thick of Boughs and Leaves. The Fruit is like an Apple red and yellow without. It is singular in this, that all other Fruit having the Stone within, this has it at the Top rais'd like a green Crest ; smelling to which a *Spanish* Preacher and Missioner told me did much help the Memory ; and that he by that means soon made himself Master of the longest Sermon. I never had experience of it, nor will I vouch for what he said. What I can safely attest is, that breaking the Stone, the Kernel within it roasted tastes like an Almond, and raw like a new Nut. This Fruit Ripens between *February* and *May.* Cutting it in quarters, steeping it in cold Water, and then chewing it, there comes from it a cool Juice, good for all Obstructions in the Breast.[47]

Jambolon-Tree. The *Jamboleira,* or *Jambolon*-Tree[48] grows wild and has the Leaves like a Lemmon-Tree ; but the Fruit is so delicious, that an *Indian* Woman coming to *Lisbon,* loath'd all the best Fruit in Europe, remembring her lov'd *Jambolon.* They hang on the Boughs like Cherries, or Olives, and have the red Colour of the one and the Shape and Stone like the other. The *Indians* eat it with Salt, but I tasting them in the Garden of the *Theatins* where I was entertain'd, did not think them so pleasant to the Pallate of *Europeans;* because they taste somewhat like a service Apple, and to eat many of them makes the Belly swell extreamly. Their Season is generally in *April* and *May.*

Jangoma- Tree.

The *Jangomeira,* or *Jangoma*[49] Tree is very large, all prickly, and with small Leaves. The *Jangomas* the *Portuguese* call *Adam's* Fruit, being of the shape of a Walnut, Purple without and Red within, and has two Stones. The tast of it is a mixture of sour, sweet, and bitterish like a Medlar. They are in Season *November, December,* and *January.*

The *Brindeiera,* or *Brindon*-Tree[50] is as tall as a Pear-Tree, but has smaller Leaves. The *Brindones* or Fruit it bears in *February, March* and *April,* are a sort of Fruit like our Golden Pippins; but their Rind his harder, tho' the Pulp or Flesh of it is Red, Viscous and Sharpish, which they chew and suck the Juice, and has three soft Kernels within it. The *Portuguese* make Sauce of the Rind.

Caranda- Tree.

The *Carandeira,* or *Caranda*-Tree[51] is Low and Thorny, with Leaves like an Orange-Tree. The Fruit of it call'd *Caranda* is no other than wild Grapes of *Indostan;* Reddish without and White within, with Seeds. It is Ripe in *April,* and *May.*

The *Jambos* of *Malaca*[52] are tall Trees with long slender Leaves. The Fruit of it call'd also *Jambos,* are as big as small Apples and of the same taste, but smell like Rose-water. The outward Rind is Yellowish, within of a Cinnamon Colour, and there are two Stones loose from the Pulp. They begin to Ripen in *January,* and hold to the end of *April.*

Papaya- Tree.

The *Papayera*[53] is a Plant that does not grow above twenty Spans high, and the Body of it is under a Span Diameter, but so soft that it is easily cut with a Knife. The Leaf is broad like that of a *Pompion.*[54] The *Papayas* it produces, hang like clusters of Grapes about the top of the Trunk, where they Ripen and grow bigger, one after another. In the *Portuguese* Dominions in *India* they call these the *Jesuits* Melons, because they taste like Melons, and those Fathers like them so well, that they have them every Day at Dinner.[55] They are shap'd like them a *Berengena*[56] (a Fruit well known in *Spain,* but not in *England*)[57] but twice, or three times as big. As to Colour they are Green and Yellow without, and Yellowish within, with little black Seeds or Stones in them, like Elder-Berries. This Fruit grows all the Year about.

Jaqua- Tree.

The *Jaquera* or *Jaqua*-Tree[58] is as big as a Laurel with Green and Yellow Leaves. The Fruit it produces is the biggest in the World, or at least[59] that ever I saw ; for no Man can carry above one of them ; and some of them are four Spans long, and a Span and a Half Diameter. It being impossible for the Boughs to bear such a weight, Nature has providently order'd it should grow out at the Foot of the Tree ; and in the Island of *Ceilon* and at *Malaca,* under Ground upon the Root ; and they know when it is Ripe by the Smell that comes from it. The Rind is Yellow and Green, but Prickly, and with some stiff Points like those about the Collars of Mastiffs.[60] Within it there are many yellow Separations like those in an Orange, with each of them a Kernel in it, like an Acorn ;[61] which roasted tasts like a Chestnut. This Fruit is gather'd from *May* till *September.*[62]

*Jambo-*Tree. The white *Jamboyera,* or *Jambo*-Tree[63] of *India* is as high as a Laurel. The Leaf is small, the Blossom like the Orange-flower, and the Fruit like a Pear, White and Red without, and White within (with a Stone) of the smell and taste of a Cherry. They are Ripe in *January, Ferbuary,* and *March ;* and two or three times from the same Plant.

Pear-Tree. The *Pereira* or *Pear*-Tree[64] is no large Tree, but thick and has small Leaves. The Fruit without is Green and Yellow, like a Pear ; within it is white and soft, with tender Seeds, and tasts like an over-ripe Pear. It makes excellent Conserve, or Preserve, and lasts all the Year.

*Cinnamon-*Tree. The *Cinnamon*-Tree,[65] tho' it bears no Fruit is precious for its Bark ; which being taken off grows on the Tree again, to yield the Owner more Profit. The best grows in the Island of *Ceylon ;* for that of *Manila* and other Places is Wild, and has not so fragrant a Smell.

*Toranja-*Tree. The *Toranja*[66] is a Tree brought from *Africk,* small and prickly. Its Fruit is like a large round Lemmon, with a thick yellowish Rind, and Red within, of the taste of an Orange. 'Tis in Season in *October* and *November.*

*Bilimbin-*Tree. The *Bilimbeira*[67] is as big as a Plumb-Tree, with thin Leaves, and bears *Bilimbiries* all the Year. The Colour of it is greenish ; its shape like a long Pompion ; the tast sharp, and good to make Sauce, or Preserve. They are all eaten, because they have no Stone.[68]

*Amcale-*Tree. The *Amcaleira* or *Amcale*-Tree[69] is as big as a Pear-Tree. The Fruit of it by the *Portugueses* call'd *Amcale,* grows out of the thick part of the Branches. Its shape is like a golden Pippin, with streaks like a Melon on the outside ; the Flesh within is white, and has a Stone. They make good Sweetmeats of it, the natural tast being a pleasant Tartness. They are Ripe in *February, March,* and *April.*

*Anana-*Plant. The *Ananamzeira*[70] is a Plant like our House-Leek,[71] producing *Ananas,* which the *Spaniards* call *Pinas,* one, two, three, or more according to the bigness of the Plant.[72] This

Fruit is round and prickly, a Span long, and above a Span Diameter,[73] rising like a very great Artichoak.[74] The pulp within which smells like Musk, is hard, yellow, and partly whitish. Its taste between sweet and sower, but very pleasant, especially if peel'd and put into Sugar and Water. Some gather it before it is Ripe, and make it very sweet with Sugar ; and from *India* they send great Quantities into *Spain*, where it is much valu'd. It is wholsom, but so hot, that if a Knife be left sticking in it a Day, it loses its Temper and is spoiled.[75] The Season of Ripening is from *April* till *July*.

The *Mogoreira*[76] is a Plant which from *February*, till the end of *May*, bears a most beautiful white Flower call'd *Mogorin*. Its Smell, tho' like it, is much more fragrant than that of the *Jasmin*[77]; besides this difference, that the *Jasmin* has but six Leaves, and the *Mogorin* above fifty. *F. Salvador Galli* told me that several Plants were sent to *Lisbon* in earthen Pots, for some *Portuguese* Lords ; and particularly for the Duke of *Tuscany*,[78] who had a great Mind to them ; but that it was not known whether they arriv'd there fresh, being to cut the equinoctial Line twice.[79] The Flower very well deserves to be[80] in any Royal Garden, and the more because it is found no where but in *Indostan*. *Mogorin-Plant.*

The *Asafreira*[81] is bigger than a Palm-Tree,[82] and in *India* produces *Safron*.[83] The Flower has a yellow Bottom and six white Leaves, and serves the *Portugueses* as ours does in *Europe* to season their Meat, but is not so good. There is this singular in this Tree, that the Flowers come out in the Night, and almost all the Year about. Safron-Tree.

The *Pimenteira*[84] is but a low Plant which grows against any Tree or Wall, and bears the Pepper in clusters like Grapes. When Ripe it is Red, but the *Indians* burn and make it Black, that it may not serve for Seed elsewhere.[85] It comes in *March*, *April* and *May*. Pepper-Plant.

The *Beteleira*[86] is a tender Plant like Ivy, which runs up a Stick. Its Leaf is the delight of the *Asiaticks ;* for Men and Women, from the Prince to the Peasant delight in nothing more than chewing it all Day in Company ; and no Visit begins or ends without this Herb. Before it they always chew the *Areca* above describ'd, that the coolness of this, as they say, may temper the heat of the other ; and they lay a little dissolv'd Lime on the *Betel*-leaf to colour, and soften its biting Taste. It spends not so well in any part of *Asia* as in the *Phillippine* Islands,[87] where the *Areca* is soft and easie to chew, and the *Betel* extraordinary good. The *Spaniards* make a Composition of both Herbs with Lime, which they call Buyo,[88] and carry it in curious little Boxes, to chew it every moment aboard and at home.[89] The *Betel* makes the Lips so Fine, Red, and *Betel-Plant.*

Beautiful, that if the *Italian* Ladies could they would purchase it for the weight in Gold.[90]

Puna-Tree. The Trees and Flowers hitherto describ'd are the best in *Indostan ;* but there are many more not to be despis'd. One of them they call *Puna,*[91] so tall and strait that it may serve for Masts for Ships. It produces a red Fruit, in which there are twelve or more Seeds, as big as Acorns, and of the taste of Pine-Apple-Kernels. But they eat them boil'd that they may not cause the Head-ach.

Indian-Apples. There are also *Indian* Apples[92] as big as a Walnut, with a Stone as a Plum, and ill tasted. The Tree is small and has very little Leaves.

Tamarinds. The *Tamarinds*[93] of *Indostan* are extraordinary good, and there is plenty of them about the Fields. The Tree is large and bears the Fruit with a Cod,[94] like our Beans.

Undi-Tree. The *Scararagam*[95] Tree bears Fruit of a greenish Colour, and as big as a Walnut. They are call'd *Undis,* and are of a pleasant tast.

Chiampim-Flowers. The *Chiampim*[96] of *China* is an odoriferous white Flower, which Preserv'd, contrary to the nature of other Flowers, grows hard, and is sweet and pleasant in the Mouth. This Tree is like a little Plan Tree. There is another sort of *Chiampims* with two Leaves strait, white, and long, and as many red winding about below, and this grows not on a Tree, but on a low Plant[97] on the Ground.

Omlam-Tree. The *Omlam*[98] Tree bears a sort of Fruit like a ruddy Almond, and a long Flower beautiful[99] and fragrant enough.

Quegadam cheroza *Quegadam cheroza*[100] is an odd sort of a great yellow Flower, with long green and prickly Leaves.

Majericam. The *Majericam*[101] is a Flower of small esteem, green and growing out of a little Herb.

Padolim. The *Padolim*[102] is a green Plant, producing a sightly[103] Flower, and a long Fruit, like an *European* Cucumber.[104]

Pachaa. The *Pachaa*[105] is also a green Flower, coming from a low Plant.

Tindolim. The *Tindolim,*[106] is a Plant bearing a red Flower, and a Fruit of the same Colour, of the shape of a small Lemmon.

Inhama Cona. The *Inhama Cona*[107] is a Fruit white within, growing under Ground like Potatas ; but much bigger and weighing many Pounds. Boil'd it is better[108] than Potataes.

There are many more sorts of Fruit, besides those here mention'd, as well of the Country, as brought from other Parts ; as the *Batatas,*[109] the *Inhame,* which boil'd or roasted taste like Chestnuts, Pomgranates, Lemmons, and some few Grapes ; and as for Garden-wear,[110] *Berengenas* (before mention'd) Pompions,[111] Beets, Raddishes, Coleworts,[112] Mellons of all sorts, Cucumers, and many more brought out of *Persia* and *Europe.*

A
VOYAGE
ROUND THE WORLD

By Dr. JOHN FRANCIS GEMELLI CARERI.

PART III

Containing the most Remarkable Things he saw in

INDOSTAN

BOOK II

CHAPTER I

THE AUTHOR'S JOURNEY TO GALGALA.

Having resolv'd with my self ever since my first setting out, to see the Court and Camp of the Great *Mogul,* who is one of the greatest Princes in *Asia,* without regarding Danger or Expence; tho' Friends several times endeavour'd to Disswade me, by representing the many Hazards and Hardships I must meet with in Travelling over rugged Mountains, and among *Pagan* and *Mahometan* Princes; yet I held my first Purpose, and resolv'd to venture upon it whatsoever hapned. In order to it, I hir'd a *Begarine,*[1] or *Canarine* of St. *Stephen,* a Village near *Goa,* to carry my Provision for some Days, and Utensils[2] for Dressing of Meat; being sure to find nothing by the way; and because he Spoke not the Language of the *Moguls,* I took a Boy of *Golconda;* who, besides his Mother Tongue, had learn'd *Portuguese,* to be my Interpreter there. This done, I committed my Baggage to *F. Hippolito Visconti,* a *Milanese,* and regular Clergy-Man of the *Theatins;* desiring him, during my Absence, to Change my Money into Pieces of Eight, to serve me, when I came back, in my Voyage to *China;* carrying along with me no more than was just necessary for my Journey, as I was advis'd by *F. Galli,* who told me it would be all taken from me on the Mountains by the Custom-House Officers; and that when his Mony was gone, they had taken from him the very *Andora.*

Friday 4th, the Porter and Interpreter coming to tell me all was ready, I set out, leaving my own Servant in the Monastery, that I might have the less to Care for. I found the Pass of *Daugi,*[3] where I was to take Boat for *Ponda,*[4] was stopp'd by Order of the Arch-bishop[5]; who Governing during the Viceroy's Absence, had directed that no Person should be suffer'd to Pass into the Infidel's Country, without his particular Leave. Therefore leaving the Porter and Interpreter to look to my Things, I went in a Boat to Speak to that Prelate at his little Country-House; where he presently gave me a Pass under his own Hand. Then taking another Boat about Noon, I coasted along the City Wall on the Channel, passing at the end of four Miles, by the Fort of St. *Blase,*[6] on which there are eight Pieces of Cannon; and two Miles further, by the Castle of St. *James,*[7] where there are twelve Guns. Here shewing the Governour my Pass, he gave me Leave to cross the Channel into the *Mogul*'s Country.

We stay'd a long while in a Cottage belonging to the Guards, there being neither Man nor Beast to be found, to carry the Baggage of an *Armenian,* and a *Moor* that had joyn'd me. At last, seeing Night drew on, we forced some Gentils of the Village of *Arcolna*[8] to carry them. There being nothing to be Bought in this Place, the *Armenian,* and the *Moor* made shift with a little Rice half Boil'd, and so little of it that the Grains swam on the Water, which afterwards serv'd them for Drink.[9] I pass'd the Night under some Coco-Trees without Sleep, because of the great Noise of Drums, and Cries of the Idolaters, who Celebrated the Feast of *Siminga,*[10] at the full Moon.

Saturday 5th, before we set out, the *Armenian* and *Moor* fill'd their Bellies with *Cachiari;*[11] which is a Composition of Rice, Kidney-Beans, and Lentils Pounded and Boil'd together, as was said, at the end of our second Part. For want of Beasts to carry my Luggage to *Ponda,* which was twelve Miles off, I took three Gentils; and was forc'd against my Will to make use of a Cudgel upon them, because they will never do good Service either for fair Words, or Mony, but run away as soon as they can; and on the other side, when Thrash'd, they will Load themselves like Asses.

The Sun was so hot, that at very short Distances we were oblig'd to Rest, and Refresh us with Melons, and Fruit of the Country. At *Mardol*[12] it took us up much Time to Eat a *Jacca,* which was so large, that a Man could scarce carry it. The Idolaters would Eat none of it, for they will not Taste any thing that is Cut by us, tho' Starving for Hunger; and I was told some of them had been so Obstinate, as to continue five Days without Eating on this Account.

A *Pagod.* In this Village of *Mardol,* there is a famous *Pagod.* The way into the Court is over a cover'd Bridge of three Arches, up to which there are two Stair-cases. On the right of this

Court is an octangular Structure, consisting of seven Rounds of small Columns, with handsome Capitols, and little Windows in the Intervals, one of which serves for a Door. They say this was Built to put Lights in on the Festivals of their Idols, as was the other Place, like it, on the left, not yet finish'd. About the Porch, and before the Arches of the aforesaid Bridge, there are several Shops ; but all is gone to Ruin since the *Mogul* has taken that Country from the King of *Visapor,* on account of the Wars with *Savagi.* The *Pagod* is at the further end of the Court. The first Room is like a little Hall, longer than it is broad, the Roof supported by six small wooden Columns on each side, curiously carv'd with Figures on them, about them there are low Branches[13] to sit down. Within it is another Room, like the first, but less ; and further on upon the right is a little Room curiously painted, with several Figures, which have on their Heads, some of them Pyramidal Caps, and others a Crown like that the Pope wears. There is also a Figure with four Hands, two whereof hold a Staff, one a Looking-Glass, and the other rests on its side ; by it stand Women with five Vessels on their Heads, one upon another. There are besides several Monsters, Beasts and Birds ; as flying Horses, Cocks, Peacocks, and others. The *Pagod* stands[14] opposite to the Door in a little dark round Room, at the Foot of a small Tower, where there is a carv'd Stone cover'd like a Tomb. There is a winding Way on the out-side up to the top of the Tower, and to the Chambers of the Idolatrous Priests. One side of the second Room I mention'd, before a little Door stood the Bier they use to carry their Idol in Procession. On the same side is another *Pagod* shut up, with a Cistern before it, cover'd with a *Cupula,* and has a small Room in the Middle. Behind the aforesaid *Pagod,* is one of those Trees[15] they call of the *Banians,* and under it the Bath, or Pool, with large Stone-steps[16] about it for the Gentils to go down, and wash them of their Uncleanness.

Setting forward again, after Travelling a long time over Mountains and Plains, I came late, and very weary to *Ponda.* There I found a small Camp of the *Mogul*'s Forces ; and among them *Francis de Miranda,* Born in the Island of *Salzete,* who receiv'd me very Civilly. He had serv'd there as a Soldier of Fortune sixteen Years, with the Pay of 75 *Roupies* of Silver a Month, which are worth 45 Crowns of *Naples.* Those Troops were come that same Day from *Bichiolin,*[17] with the *Divan,* or Receiver of the King's Revenue of *Ponda,* and above 700 Villages, who has 7000 *Roupies* a Month, and 1000 Horse under him, whose Pay is a *Roupie* a Day, he was to take Possession of the Government of the lower Fort of *Ponda,* and of the Office of *Suba,*[18] of that Territory, which among us is like a Major General ; and this because the true Governour had sent some of his Soldiers to *Bichiolin,* to commit Acts of Hostility against the *Divan,* so that there had been Men Kill'd and wounded on both sides. *Ech-lascanpani-Suba*[19] refusing to Obey, unless he were first Paid what was Due to his Soldiers, and the more, because the *Divan* had no Commission from the King, but only a Letter of Advice from his Solicitor, therefore the two Parties contended, and threatned one another. The *Divan* now said he would drive him out of his Fort with the Cannon from the upper; when on *Sunday* 6th, about Sun-setting there was heard a confused Noise of Drums and Trumpets, such that I taking it for a warlike Sound, laid hold of my Gun, but it was for the coming of a Messenger sent by the King, who brought the *Divan* a Vest, and Commission for both Employments.

The Ceremony of receiving a Commission and Vest from the *Mogul.*

Seven Hundred Horse and Foot stood at their Arms before the *Divan*'s Tent, and two Companies of sixteen Gentils each Danc'd confusely to the Sound of Drums, Fifes, and Trumpets.[20] It being then a sort of Carnaval those People observe every Year for five Days,[21] they went about like Mad-men, in red Vests, and little Turbants of the same Colour call'd *Chiras,*[22] throwing red Dust upon all they met to Die them; as we use among us to do with black Dust.

The *Divan,* who was a Grey Headed old Man about Sixty five Years of Age, mounted[23] a Horse-back, with a pair of Kettle-Drums a Horse-back, before him; and follow'd by a *Palankine,* another pair of Kettle-Drums on a Camel, and a medley of Horse and Foot naked, who went in a Disorderly manner, like so many Goats. They had several Colours,[24] some of Calico, with a Trident on them, and some of Silk, with *Persian* Characters and Flames in the middle, all carry'd by Foot Soldiers. The *Divan* being come to a Tent, erected for that purpose near a *Mosch,* two Musket-shot from his own, he alighted, and after passing[25] some Compliments with the King's Messenger, and Persons of Note that were with him, put on the *Chira* himself on his Head,[26] whilst the Messenger held the Sash[27] to him. Then the latter[28] took a vest, or[29] Garment of green Silk, with Gold Stripes, and put it on the *Divan,* and then two Sashes about his Neck, his Scimiter hanging by his Side. The *Divan* laid his Hand on the Ground five times, and as often on his Head, in Thanksgiving to the King who had Honour'd him with that Present. Then sitting down, his Friends and Retinue came to Congratulate with him, and some to Present him with *Roupies,* which he gave to the Messenger, but they were very few. They call this Present *Nazar,*[30] that is, a goodly Sight; and the Custom is deriv'd from the Coronation of Kings, when the Noble Men present a great deal of Gold Coin; and some Pieces weighing above three Hundred Ounces, to Rejoice the *Mogul* that Day, who sits on a Throne studded with Jewels of an excessive Value. When the Solemnity was over, the

Divan mounted a Horse-back ; and alighted again by the Pool near the *Mosch ;* where sitting on a Carpet with Pillows at his Back, he diverted himself with the Singing, and Musick of the Mask'd *Gentils.* I was told this Honour cost him 20000 *Roupies* (each of them worth six *Carlines*[31] of *Naples*) which he sent the Secretary, who had pass'd the Commission in the King's Name ; for he never writes to his Subjects. For all this the *Suba* would not deliver up his Post, but keeping Possession of the lower Fort, said it was all Counterfeit.

The City *Ponda* is made up of Cottages, and Mud Houses seated in the midst of many Mountains. The Fort, which is also of Earth, and govern'd by the *Suba,* has a Garrison of about 400 Horse and Foot, and seven small Pieces of Cannon. There was formerly another Fort on a higher Ground ; but *D. Francis de Tavora,*[32] Viceroy of *Goa,* Besieging it twelve Years before this time with a Body of 10000 Men,[33] in a short time made a large Breach in it. *Savagi,*[34] to whom it belong'd, coming to the Relief of it with 12000 Horse, oblig'd the Viceroy to raise his Siege, and draw off. Then he went over to the Island of *Salzete,* St. *Stephen,* and others near *Goa* and having Plunder'd and Burn'd several Places, carry'd many Hundreds of the Natives Captives into his own Country ; and making them carry the Stones of the Fort that had been Demolish'd to the top of a Hill two Miles from *Ponda* Southward, built the small Fort now standing, calling it *Mardongar,*[35] that is, the Fort of Valiant Men. This Castle is held for the King, by a Garrison of 300 Men, under a *Kilidar,*[36] or Castellan, who has 200 *Roupies* a Month Pay, assign'd him out of certain Villages. It being a Place held upon Oath, he may not upon any Account go out of the Gate.

Ponda City.

The upper Fort.

The lower Fort, and Country depending on it, taken from *Savagi* by the Great *Mogul,* is govern'd as was said by a *Suba,* or General of the Field, who receives the Revenue of above 700 Villages, being therefore oblig'd to Maintain a certain Number of Soldiers ; so that he Drains the poor Country People, making a few Cottages sometimes pay Thousands of *Roupies.*

Monday 7th,[37] I saw the dismal Spectacle of a wretched *Pagan* Woman, the Kindred[38] of her dead Husband had obtain'd at the Price of great Presents from the *Suba,* to be Burn'd with the dead Body, according to their wicked unmerciful Custom.[39] In the Afternoon[40] the Woman came out well Clad, and adorn'd with Jewels, as if she had gone[41] to be Marry'd, with Musick Playing, and Singing. She was attended by the Kindred of both Sexes, Friends, and *Brachman* Priests. Being come to the Place appointed, she went about undaunted, taking Leave of them all ; after which she was laid all along;[42]

An *Indian* Woman Burn'd with her Husband.

with her Head on a Block, in a Cottage twelve Spans square, made of small Wood wet with Oil,[43] but bound to a Stake, that she might not run away with the fright of the Fire. Lying in this Posture, chewing *Betelle,* she ask'd of the Standers by, whether they had any Business by her to the other World ; and having receiv'd several Gifts, and Letters from those Ignorant People, to carry to their dead Friends, she wrapp'd them up in a Cloth. This done, the *Brachman,* who had been Encouraging of her, came out of the Hut, and caus'd it to be Fir'd ; the Friends pouring Vessels of Oil on her, that she might be the sooner reduc'd to Ashes, and out of Pain. *Francis de Miranda* told me, That as soon, as the Fire was out, the *Brachmans* would go gather all the melted Gold, Silver, and Copper.[44] This Barbarous Action was perform'd a Mile from *Ponda.*

A pannick Fear.

When I return'd to my Tent, the[45] Camp had a false Alarm, on account of one *Moor*'s cutting of another's Nose. Some *Gentils* fled upon the Mountains, and so did *Miranda,* leaving all he had behind, and I endeavouring to perswade him to stay, he answer'd, he must do as the rest did. Taking my Gun, Powder and Ball, I stood under a Tree to defend my self. *Miranda's* Cook in the mean while Laugh'd at his Master's Cowardice, saying, *What a brave Soldier the* Mogul *has, to allow him two* Roupies *and a half a Day : If he flies now no Body pursues,*[46] *what will he do when he sees an Enemy?* Here I saw them drink the Juice of an Herb they call *Banghe,*[47] which, mix'd with Water, stupifies like *Opium.* To this purpose they keep it in Glass-Bottles of a violet Colour, made on[48] the Mountains of *Gates,*[49] in the *Mogul*'s Territories, and in *China.*

There being no other conveniency of Carriage all the way I was to go, but on[50] Oxen, I bought a Horse at *Ponda* for sixty *Roupies.* Having got a Pass from the *Bachei,*[51] that I might not be stopp'd by the Guards on the Frontiers ; and leaving my Gun to be sent to *Goa,* that I might not be made Prisoner by *Savagi's* Men, I set out on *Tuesday* 8th, and Travelling eight Miles came to *Chiampon,*[52] a Village of a few Mud Houses, with a Fort of the same sort.[53] Here I caus'd some Meat to be Dress'd,[54] but my Porter going about[55] to take a Fig-Leaf to make use of instead of a Dish, after the manner of *India,* the Heathen Woman to whom the Fig-Tree belong'd, and the rest of the People, who came to her assistance, made such a Noise, that we were forc'd to depart. We Travell'd through Woods, as we had done before, and at last getting out of them, cross'd over an Arm of the Sea[56] in a small Boat, and entred the Territory of a *Pagan* Prince call'd *Sonde-kirani-karaja,*[57] Lord of some Villages among the Mountains, but Tributary and subject to the Great *Mogul,* being oblig'd to Serve him in his Wars. At the end of two *Cosses*[58] (each *Cosse* is two *Italian* Miles) we lay at the Village of *Kakore,*[59] consisting of a few Cottages under the Arch of a *Pagod.* At the upper end of it, under a small *Cupula*, was a thing like a Chamber-Pot of Copper, on a Stone Pedestal, with a Uizor like a Man's Face of the same Metal nail'd to it. Perhaps it might be an Urn containing the Ashes of some Hero of theirs. In the midst of the little *Cupula* hung a small Bell and without many small Lights.

At Night, Troops of Monkeys came leaping from one Tree to another ; and some of them with their young Ones so close hugg'd under their Belly, that tho' we threw many Stones at them, we could not fetch down one ; nor did they fly any further than from one Tree to another. The Inhabitants of these Villages being for the most part *Gentils* (for in *India*[60] there is scarce a *Mahometan* among fifty Men, they feed them and take care they shall not be kill'd ;[61] so that being grown Tame they walk familiarly in the Villages and even in the Houses. There are such incredible Stories told of these Creatures, that it is no wonder some blind Philosophers should allow Beasts some sort of understanding. All the *Cafres* and Blacks along the Coast of *Mozambique* in *Africk* are of this Opinion, saying they do not speak, because they will not work.[63]

In the Kingdom of *Canara* a Baboon[64] taking a kindness to a Woman, did so infest her Father's House, breaking all he found in it ; that not knowing what to do,[65] they at last permitted him to have carnal Copulation with her, and ever after to have free access to her. A *Portuguese* hapned to pass by that way, and lie at Night in the *Pagan*'s House, where seeing a great Baboon come in, and make such a disturbance, he inquir'd into the meaning of it. The young Woman's Father answer'd with a sigh, This Creature has taken away my Daughter's honour, and makes all this noise when he does not find her at home. The *Portuguese* reply'd, Why do you not kill it? The Peasant said he was a *Gentil*, and that the Queen being of the same Religion would punish him severely should he do it. The *Portuguese* without making more Words of it, waited till the Beast came in, and shot it, and the Idolater being afraid to be punish'd, he carry'd it himself out of the Cottage and bury'd it.[66] The *Portuguese* was requited for this kindness with a great quantity of Rice, as he himself told me fifteen Years after it hapned. A Story of a Baboon.

F. Causin writes that a Ship being cast away on the Cape of *Good Hope*, soon after *India* was discover'd by the *Portugueses*, a woman holding fast by a Plank, was drove by the Sea upon an Island. There a Baboon had to do with her, and maintan'd her for a long time in a Cave with what he found abroad, so that after some Years he had two young Ones by her. A Ship afterwards hapning to touch there, the wretched Woman by signs call'd for help and was deliver'd ; but the Baboon returning and finding she was far from the Another.

Shore was so enrag'd, that it took the two young Monsters and kill'd them in her sight.

A third.

It is well known that a Woman in *Brazil* having had to do with a Baboon,[67] and conceiving, she was deliver'd in due season of a Child with all the Limbs of a Man, but hairy, and tho dumb it did all it was commanded. The *Dominicans* and *Jesuits* had hot disputes about this Creature whether it ought to be Baptiz'd or not, and at last they concluded in the Negative, because begot by an irrational Sire; and that had the Father been a Man, and the Dam a Baboon it might have been Baptiz'd.

A fourth.

D. Antony Machado de Brito, Admiral of the *Portuguese* Fleet in *India* told me, that one of these Creatures continually troubling him, and breakig all it found in the Kitchin, he once to be even with it, order'd a *Coco*-nut to be put upon the Fire, which sort of Fruit the Monkies are most greedy of, and hid himself to see how that Beast would take it without burning his Paws. The cunning Creature coming at the usual hour[68] and finding its beloved Food on the Fire, look'd about and seeing a Cat by the Chimney held her Head in his mouth, and made use of her Paws to take off the *Coco*-nut, and then cooling it in Water, Eat it; the *Portuguese* laughing to see the Cat mewing about all Day with the Pain it had been put to.

How they take Monkeys.

The Monkeys being so greedy of *Coco*-nuts has taught the *Indians* how to catch them. They make a hole in the Shell, into which the Monkey runs its Paw, and not being able to fetch it out full of the Nut, rather than quit the hold it suffers itself to be taken by those that lye in wait for them. Nor is that true which is reported, that if one of them be kill'd in the Field the rest will fall upon him that kill'd it; for when I made one fall, the rest fled.

Wednesday 9th, I set out through thick Woods, and travelling eight *Cosses* came to the foot of the Mountain of *Balagati* where I found the Guards and other Custom-House-Officers so fond of other Mens Goods, that they took twelve *Roupies* for two strings of Pearls. Having climb'd the Mountain for eight Miles among dreadful thick Woods, I came to the second Guard and Custom-House, where they took a *Roupie* without examining further. There being no dwelling to be found, I lay all Night in the thickest part of the Wood (wherein *India* differs from *Persia,* which is bare of Tree) after travelling twelve *Cosses,* that is twenty four *Indian*[69] Miles.

A Caravan of Oxen.

Thursday 10th, the *Bojata*[70] set out three Hours before Day, and I went along with it for the more safety. This *Bojata* was a *Caravan* of above three hundred Oxen loaded with Provisions for the Camp at *Galgala.* The Woods we pass'd through abounded in Fruit, quite different from any in *Europe.* There were some not unpleasant;[72] and among the rest one sort they call *Gulara,* which tasts like an *European* wild Fig, and Grows and Ripens without any Blossom at the Body of the Tree. That Day I saw some wild Hens,[73] which I had never seen before, with a Crest and Feathers that inclin'd to black. At first I thought they had been tame, but was afterwards undeceiv'd, there being never a House for many Miles about. Having travell'd fourteen *Cosses,* we came two Hours before Sun set to the Village of *Bombnali,*[74] belonging to the same Prince *Kirani ;* where tho' there was a Guard call'd *Chiaruci,*[75] they took nothing of me ; perhaps because the Chief of it was not so Barbarous as the rest. *Gulara-Fruit.*

The Road I travell'd on *Friday* 11th, was through more open Woods in which there were Iron Mines. Having gone eight *Cosses* we came to the Village of *Chiamkan,*[76] where there was a Market and Custom-House kept by the *Gentils,* who search'd my Luggage. I lay four *Cosses*[77] further at *Sambrani.*[78] In this place resides the aforemention'd Prince *Sonde-Kirani-karaja* in a Fort made of Earth, encompass'd with Walls seven Spans high. The Village is nothing better than the rest of that Territory, but it has a good Market or *Bazar.* The Prince makes three *Lecches* of *Roupies,* that is 180000 *Neapolitan* Crowns a Year of this only Village ; by which the Reader may judge how cruelly the Idolaters and *Mahometans* oppress the People with heavy Taxes.

Setting out[79] late on *Saturday* 12th, after four Miles travel we came into the *Mogul's* Territories. Having pass'd the Prince *Kiranis* last Guards on the Road, I rested till Noon near the Fort of the Town of *Alcal ;*[80] but being ready to set forwards was inform'd the Road I was to go was infested with Robbers, and therefore I resolv'd to stay[81] for the *Bojata.* At this place there was a *Pagod,* and in it an Idol with a human Body, but the Face of a Monkey,[82] and a vast long Tail winding about to the top of its Head, with a little Bell hanging at the end of it. One Hand was on its side, and the other lifted up as it were to strike. They call it the Animating[83] Monkey, because according to the fabulous Traditions of those People, he once fought with much Bravery. When I perceived no Body took notice of me, I us'd to break all the Idols that came in my way ; especially those the Peasants, that conducted the *Bojata,* carry'd hanging about their Necks, wrapp'd up in a Cloth, which were of Stone, ill shap'd, and weighing 2 Pounds.

Sunday 13th, I set out four Hours before Day with the *Caravan* of Oxen, and at the end of six *Cosses* came to *Kancre*[84] a Village consisting of a few Houses, where I Din'd. Then I went five long *Cosses* further and lay[85] at the Village of *Etchi*[86] which tho' made up of Cottages has excellent Land for Tillage and Sport ; the Stages and other Game feeding about[87] tamely.

Monday 14th, setting out early with another *Bojata,* at the end of five *Cosses* all the way a fertile Soil,[88] I stopp'd at *Tikli*[89] a small Town defended by a Fort of Earth, and after Dinner proceeded to the little Village of *Onor.*[90]

Tuesday 15th,[91] I travell'd five *Cosses* through a Country full of green and delightful Trees to *Mandapur,*[92] a City made up of Mud Houses and enclos'd with a low Wall; but has a good Fort of Lime and Stone on a Hill. After Dinner I went two *Cosses* further to *Betchè*[93] a Wall'd Town, where I lay.[94]

Bad travelling in *India.*

It is far different Travelling through the *Mogul*'s Country, than thro' *Persia* or *Turky,* for there are no Beasts for carriage to be found, nor *Caravanseras* at convenient distances, nor Provisions; and what is worse there is no safety from Thieves. He therefore that has not a Horse of his own must mount upon an Ox, and besides that inconveniency, must carry along with him his Provision and Utensils to dress it; Rice, Pulse and Meal being only to be found in great Towns inhabited by the *Mogulstans*:[95] At Night the clear Sky will be all a Mans covering, or else a Tree. Add to all this the great Danger of Life and Goods, by reason of the Excursions *Savagi's* Souldiers make quite as far as the Camp at *Galgalà.* Besides, the *Moguls* themselves are such crafty Thieves,[96] that they reckon a Traveller's Mony and Cloaths their own; and they will keep along with him many Days till his security[97] gives them an opportunity to Rob him at their ease. Sometimes one of them will pretend to be a Traveller that is going the same way, and bears a Stranger company, that he may Rob him with more safety; for when he lyes down to sleep the other artificially[98] lets down a noose from the top of a Tree, and drawing him up a little way slips down to dive into his Purse.[99] Had not very powerful Motives press'd me forwards to see the Court of so great a King, I should not easily have expos'd my self to so many Dangers and Hardships. 'Tis true that excepting only this of *Visapor,* which is continually harass'd with Wars, the other Kingdoms subject to the *Great Mogul* are not so inconvenient for Travelling; especially about *Suratte,* and *Amadabat,* where necessaries for Life are to be had.

Edoar-City.

Wednesday 16th, having travell'd three *Cosses* I pass'd through a Village[100] call'd *Kodelki,*[101] where at a dear rate I tasted ripe Grapes of *Europe;* and three *Cosses* further came to *Edoar,*[102] the biggest City I saw in that short Journey. Within the first enclosure it has a Stone Fort ill Built, and a *Bazar;* in the second a Fort with a Garrison and Houses about it made of Mud and Straw. All the Merchants that come from the southern Parts to sell their Goods use to stay here, and afterwards go over to the Camp at *Galgalà* like *Retailers.*[103] When I pass'd that way this City was actually infested with the Plague.

After Dinner I went five *Cosses* further to the Town of *Muddol,*[104] seated on the left hand of a River, a matter of great Consideration on a Road where I sometimes drank Water muddy'd by the Cattle. There is a Mud Fort, as are the Walls of the Town, nor do the Cottages of the Natives deserve better Fortifications. As I was getting off my Horse I fell so violently upon my side that I could not breath for a quarter of an hour, and was in some danger of Death ; I was ill of it many Days after, tho' I Blooded, and us'd other Remedies.

CHAPTER II

THE AUTHOR'S ARRIVAL AT GALGALA, *WHERE THE* GREAT MOGUL *WAS INCAMP'D.*

Thursday 17th, after Riding five *Cosses* I pass'd through a Wall'd Town call'd *Matur,*[1] and two *Cosses* further to the Village of *Galgala*[2] where the *Moguls* Camp was. Crossing the River *Kiscina*[3] I came into the Quarters of the *Mahometans* call'd *Lascaris,*[4] and some Christian Souldiers of *Agra* entertain'd me.

Friday 18th, I went to the Christian Gunner's Quarter to hear Mass, and found a convenient Chappel of Mud Walls, serv'd by two *Canarine* Priests, maintain'd by the Catholicks. After Mass *Francis Borgia*[5] by extraction a *Venetian* but born at *Dehli,* invited me to his House. He being Captain of the Christians, an hour after[6] caus'd two *Mahometans* that had made themselves Drunk to be cruelly beaten before me, bound to a Stake. When they were set loose, they return'd him thanks for chastizing them, laying their Hands on the Ground first, and then on their Heads, after the Country Fashion.

That same Day the King put the Question to the *Kasi,*[7] or Judge of the Law, whether it was more for Gods service to go fight his Enemies to spread the *Mahometan* Sect, or else to go over to *Visapor* to keep the *Ramazan,* or their Lent. The *Casi* requir'd time to answer, which pleas'd the *Mogul,* who was a great Dissembler and Hypocrite, and never did as he said.

Saturday 19th. I went to *Gulalbar*[8] (so they call King's Quarters) and found the King was then giving Audience, but there was such a Multitude and Confusion that I could not have a good sight of him. The King's and Princes Tents took up three Miles in Compass, and were defended every way[9] with Palisadoes, Ditches and five hundred Falconets. There were three Gates into them one for the *Aram*[10] or Women, and two for the King and his Court, The King's Quarters.

The *Moguls* Camp.

I was told the Forces in this Camp amounted to 60000 Horse, and 1000000[11] Foot, for whose Baggage there were 50000 Camels, and 3000 Elephants; but that the Sutlers, Merchants and Artificers were much more numerous, the whole Camp being a moving City containing 500000 Souls, and abounding not only in Provisions, but in all things that could be desir'd. There were 250 *Bazars* or Markets, every *Omrah*, or General having one to serve his Men. In short the whole Camp was thirty Miles about.[12]

Omrahs

These *Omrahs* are oblig'd to maintain a certain number of Horse and Foot at their own Expence; but the *Mogul* assigns them the Revenues of Countries[13] and Provinces, whilst they continue in that Post. Some of them make a Million and a half a Year of these *Giaghers,*[14] or Feofs; others less, according to the Number of Souldiers they are to maintain. But the Princes of the Blood have the best, some of which are worth a Million and a half of *Roupies* a Month. They are not only oblig'd to serve in War, but to attend the King at all times, tho' he only goes abroad to divert him. To this purpose they all keep Spies at Court, for upon every failure a *Gari*[15] is taken from them, which is 3900 *Roupies,* or less proportionably to every Man's Pay.

Tho' these Generals are in so fair a way to heap Wealth;[16] yet when they are found faulty, as keeping a smaller Number of Souldiers than is their *quota* they are Punished[17] by pecuniary Mulcts. And tho' they should combine with the Commissaries that Muster them, it would avail but little: Because when they dye the Exchequer is their Heir, and only a bare subsistance is allow'd the Wife,[18] and for the Children they say the King will bestow more Riches on them, than he did on their Father, whensoever their faithful Services shall deserve it.[19] These Generals command every one his own Troops, without being subordinate to another; only obeying a Lieutenant of the Kings, when he is not there in Person, call'd *Gium-Detol-Molk,*[20] who receives the King's Orders, to communicate them to the Generals. Hence it is that they being lazy and undisciplin'd, go upon service when they please, and there is no great Danger. Many *French* men belonging to the Army, told me[21] it was a Pleasure and Diversion to serve the *Mogul,* because they that will not Fight, or do not keep their Guards are Subject to no other Penalty, but losing that days Pay, that they are convicted of having Trangress'd; and that they themselves did not value Honour much in the Service of a Barbarous King, who has no Hospital for the wounded Men. On the other side there being no Prince in the World that pays his Souldiers better, a Stranger that goes into his Service soon grows Rich, especially an *European* or *Persian*; but once in, it is a very hard matter to get a discharge to go home to

The *Mogul's* good service.

enjoy what is got, any other way than making an escape. The Country not affording so many Horses as are requisite for so great an Army, they bring them out of *Persia,* and *Arabia,* some at 1000, or 2000 *Roupies* purchase, and the lowest at 400. And because no Barly grows in *Indostan*[22] they give them four Pounds of boil'd Lentils[23] a Day, and in Winter they add half a Pound of Butter, and as much Sugar, four ounces of Pepper, and some dry Straw. *With the Author's leave, he seems here to impose upon the Reader, or be himself impos'd upon worse than* Tavernier *was with the Crabs.*[23a] Horses.

It is also a vast expence to maintain so great a Number of Elephants; for every one of them Eats at least 140 Pounds of Corn every day, besides Leaves, Green Canes, Sugar and Pepper so that the King allows 7 *Roupies* a day for every one. He has 3000 throughout his Empire, and three General Elephants. Each of these has half a Million of *Roupies* allowance a Month which are spent in keeping 500 other Elephants that are under him, and 200 Men that look to them. At this time there were but 500 belonging to the King in the Field; besides those belonging to the Princes and Omrahs,[24] who keep some 400, some 200, and others more or less. Elephants.

Sunday 20th, going to the Tents of the King's Eldest Son, whose name was *Scialam.*[25] I found about 2000 Souldiers Horse and Food drawn up, expecting[26] the Prince, who came from his Fathers quarters. Waiting I saw his Son[27] come out and Mount a Horse-back to go meet his Father; as soon as he saw him he alighted[28] in token of respect. *Scialam* was 65 Years of Age, Tall, and full Body'd,[29] with a thick long Beard, which began to be Grey. Having such a Title to the Crown, many Thousands of the Souldiers are of his Faction; who being imprison'd, continu'd resolute, refusing to receive any other Pay, notwithstanding he reliev'd them but meanly. *Mogul's* Son.

Monday 21st, by the means of a Christian of *Agra,* and an Eunuch his Friend I had the Fortune to be admitted to a private Audience of the King. In the first Court of the King's Quarters, which had two Doors, in a large Tent I saw Kettle-Drums, Trumpets eight Spans long, and other Instruments,[30] which use to sound at certain Hours of the Day and Night, according as occasion requires; and that day made their noise before Noon.[31] There was also a Gold Ball[32] between two Gilt Hands,[33] hanging by a Chain; the King's Ensign, which is carry'd on the Elephants, when they March. I pass'd on into the second Court, and then into the Royal Tents, and King's Apartments, adorn'd with Silks and Cloth of Gold. Finding the King in one of these Rooms, sitting after the Country manner, on Rich Carpets, and Pillars Embroider'd with Gold, Having made my Obeisance after the *Mogul* Fashion, I drew near, the same Christian being my Interpreter. He ask'd me The King's Quarters.

of what Kingdom of *Europe* I was, how long I had been come thence, where I had been, and what[34] I came to his Camp for, whether I would serve him, and whither I design'd to go? I answered accordingly, that I was a *Neapolitan,* and came thence two Years before; during which time I had seen *Ægypt,* the Grand Signior's Dominions, and the *Persian* Monarchy, that I was now come into his Camp, only out of curiosity to see the greatest Monarch in *Asia,* as his Majesty was, and the Grandeur of his Court and Army; that I should have reckoned it a great Honour[35] to serve him, did not affairs of the greatest Importance call me home, after seeing the Empire of *China.* He then ask'd me concerning the War betwixt the *Turk* and *European* Princes in *Hungary,*[36] and having answer'd to the best of my Knowledge, he dismiss'd me, the time of the Publick Audience drawing near. I return'd into the second Court, enclos'd with painted Calicoes, ten Spans high all about. Here on the side next the King's apartment, the Tent to give Audience in, was supported by two great Poles, being cover'd on the outsides with ordinary red Stuff, and with finer within, and small Taffeta Curtins. Under this Tent was a square place, rais'd four Spans above the Ground, enclos'd with silver Banisters, two Spans high, and cover'd with fine Carpets. Six Spans further in the middle was another place rais'd a Span higher,[38] at the Angles whereof there were 4 Poles, cover'd with silver reaching to the top of the Tent. Here stood the Throne, which was also square, of gilt Wood, three Spans[39] above the rest; to get up to it there was a little silver Footstool. On it there were three Pillows of Brocade, two to serve on the sides, and one at the back. Soon after the King came leaning on a Staff forked at the top, several *Omrahs* and abundance of Courtiers going before him. He had on a white Vest ty'd under the right Arm, according to the fashion of the *Mahometans,* to distinguish them from the Gentils, who tye it under the left. The *Cira* or Turbant of the same white stuff, was ty'd with a Gold Web,[40] on which an Emeraud of a vast bigness, appear'd[41] amidst four little ones. He had a Silk Sash, which cover'd the *Catari*[42] or *Indian* Dagger hanging on the left. His Shooes were after the *Moorish* Fashion, and his Legs naked without Hose. Two Servants put away the Flyes, with long, white Horse-tails; another at the same time keeping off the Sun, with a green Umbrello. He was of a low Stature, with a large Nose, Slender, and stooping with Age.[43] The whiteness of his round Bear'd, was more visible[44] on his Olive colour'd Skin. When he was seated they gave him his Scimiter, and Buckler, which he lay'd down on his left side within the Throne. Then he made a sign with his Hand for those that had business to draw near; who being come up, two Secretaries standing, took their Petitions, which

The *Mogul* gives Audience.

they deliver'd to the King,[45] telling him the Contents. I admir'd to see him[46] Indorse them with his own Hand, without Spectacles, and by his chearful smiling Countenance seem to be pleas'd with the employment.

Review of the Elephants.

In the mean while the Elephants were review'd, that the King might see what condition they were in, and whether the *Omrahs,* they were committed to, manage them well. When the *Cornaccia*[47] (that is he who rides them) had uncover'd the Elephants Crupper, for the King to view it, he made him turn his Head towards the Throne, and striking him on it three times, made him do his Submission as often, by lifting up and lowering down his Trunk. Then came *Scialam*'s Son and Grandson,[48] who having twice made their Obeisance to the King, each time putting their Hand to the Ground, on their Head, and on their Breast, sate down on the first floor of the Throne on the left. Then *Azam-Scia*[49] the King's Son coming in, and making the same submissions,[50] he sate down on the second Step, which we said was rais'd above the other.[51] These Princes wore silk Vests with Flowers of several Colours, *Ciras* adorn'd with precious Stones, Gold Collars, Jewells, rich Sashes, Scimiters, and Bucklers hanging by their sides. Those that were not of the Blood Royal, made[52] three Obeisances.

On the right Hand without the Tent, stood 100 *Musketiers* and more Mace-bearers, who had Clubs on their Shoulders with silver Globes at the Ends. These were clad in Cloth of several colours. There were also several Porters with Staves in their Hands, that no Person might go in without being introduc'd.

On the left of the Tent were the Royal Ensigns held up on Spears by nine Persons, clad in Vests of crimson Velvet, all adorn'd with Gold, and with wide Sleeves, and sharp Collars hanging down behind. He that stood in the middle held a Sun ; the two on his sides two gilt Hands ; next them stood two others, each holding two Horses Tails dy'd Red.[53] The other four had the Spears cover'd, so that there was no seeing what they held. Without the enclosure of the Royal Tents, several Companies and Troops of Horse and Foot stood at their Arms ; and Elephants with vast Standards, and Kettle-Drums on them, which were beaten all the time. When the Audience was over, the King with-drew in the same Order he came out ; so did the Princes ; some getting into *Palankines,* and others mounting stately Horses, cover'd with Gold and precious Stones. The *Omrahs,* who had stood all the while, return'd also to their Tents, follow'd by many Elephants, some with Seats on them and some with Colours flying, and attended by two Troops of Horse, and two Companies of Foot. The *Cattual,*[54] who is like a Provost-Marshal against Thieves, rode with a great Trumpet of green Copper, eight Spans long, carry'd before him by a *Moor* a-foot. That foolish Trumpet made me Laugh ; because it made a Noise much like that our Swineheards make, to call together their Swine at Night.

CHAPTER III

THE ARTIFICES, AND CRUEL PRACTICES OF THE MOGUL *NOW REIGNING, TO POSSESS HIMSELF OF THE EMPIRE.*

Experience has long since made it Notorious enough, that the Succession of this great Monarchy rather depends on Force than Right ; and that, (if it so happen, that the Sons expect their Father's Death[1]) they at last Determin the Title of Birth-right by the Event of a Battle ; but this *Mogul* we have spoken of, added Fraud to Force, by which he destroy'd not only his Brothers, but his Father.

Scia-gehan, Father to *Aurenge Zeb.*

When *Scia-gehan*[2] had Reign'd forty Years, more like a Father than a King,[3] being at the Age of seventy Years,[4] fitter for any thing than Love ; he became desperately Amorous[5] of a *Moorish* young Woman.[6] His unruly Passion prevailing, he gave himself up so entirely to her, beyond what became his Age, that being reduc'd to extream Weakness, and despairing of his Recovery, he shut himself up for three Months in the *Aram,* without shewing himself to the People, according to Custom.[7] He had six Children ; four of them Sons call'd,[8] *Dara,* or *Darius ;* the second *Sugiah,*[9] that is, valiant Prince ; the third *Aurenge Zeb,* that is, Ornament of the Throne, and the last *Morad Baksce.* The two Daughters were[10] *Begum Saheb,*[11] that is, supream Princess ; and[12] *Rausenora Begum,*[13] that is, lightsom Princess, or Light of Princesses. They take these Names, because there being no Titles of Earldoms, Dukedoms, or the like, as is us'd in *Europe ;* they cannot like our Princes take the Name of those Lands, for they all belong to the King, who gives all those that Serve him Assignments at Pleasure, or Pay in ready Mony. For the same Reason the *Omrahs* Names are[14] such as these, those that follow, Thunderer, breaker of Troops, faithful Lord, the Wise, the Perfect,[15] and the like.

He devides his Sons.

Bernier. Revolution des estats du G. Mogul. Tom. 1. *p.* 20.

Scia-gehan seeing his Sons Marry'd, grown Powerful, aspiring to the Crown, and consequently Enemies to one another, and in such a Condition that it was impossible to shut them up in the inaccessible Fortress of *Govallor,*[16] according to the antient Custom, after much thinking, for fear they should kill one another before his Face, he resolv'd to remove them from Court. He sent *Sultan Sugiah* into the Kingdom of *Bengala; Aurenge Zeb* into that of *Decan; Morad Baksce* into *Guzaratte,* and to *Dara* he gave *Cabul* and *Multan.* The three first went away well pleas'd, and acted like Sovereigns in their Governments; keeping to themselves all the Revenues, and maintaining Armies under Colour[17] of awing the Subjects, and bordering Princes. *Dara,* being the Eldest, and design'd for[18] Empire remain'd at Court, where the Father feeding him with hopes of the Crown, permitted all Orders to pass through his Hands, and allow'd him a Throne below his own among the *Omrahs;* for having offer'd to resign up the Government to him, *Dara* refus'd it out of Respect.

They Arm against him.

The Report being spread abroad upon *Sciah-gehan*'s shutting himself up, that he was Dead, his Sons immediately arm'd to contend for their Father's Kingdom. The cunning Fox *Aurenge Zeb,* whilst Things were in this Confusion, that he might the better surprize his Brother, gave out, that he had no pretensions to the Crown, but had chosen to become a *Fachir,* or Poor, to serve God in Peace. At the same time he writ to his Brother *Morad Baksce* acquainting him that he had always been his real Friend, and had no Pretensions to the Crown himself, being a profess'd *Fachir;* but that *Dara* being unfit to Reign, and a *Kafar*[19] or Idolater; and *Sultan Sujah* a *Refesis*[20] or Heretick, and Enemy of his Fore-fathers[21] Religion, and unworthy of the Crown, he thought none but *Morad* deserv'd it, to whom all the *Omrahs* being acquainted with his Valour would willingly submit. As for himself, provided he would give him his Word, that when he came to the Throne, he would leave him in Peace to pray to God in some corner of the Kingdom[22] the rest of his Days, he would not only endeavour to assist him with his Advice, but would joyn his Forces with him to Destroy his Brother;[23] in Token whereof he sent him 100000 *Roupies;* advising him to come with all Expedition to make himself Master of the Fort of *Suratte,* where the Treasure was. *Morad Baksce,* who was neither Powerful nor[24] Rich, freely accepted his Offer and Mony, and began immediately to Act like a King, promising great Rewards to those that would side with him; so that he rais'd a powerful Army in a short time. Then giving the Command of 3000 Men to *Scia-Abas,*[25] a valiant Eunuch, he sent him to Besiege the Castle of *Suratte.*

Aurenge Zeb his Artifices.

Dara would have Reliev'd it, but forebore it to attend his Father in his Sickness, and curb *Sultan Sugah,* who after subduing the Kingdom of *Bengala,* where he was Governour, was advanc'd with a powerful Army into the Kingdom of *Lahor.*[26] He sent his Eldest Son *Soliman Scecur*[27] against him with considerable Forces; who routed his Uncle, and drave him back into *Bengala,* and leaving good Garrisons on the Frontiers, he went back to his Father *Dara.*

On the other side, *Aurenge Zeb* sent his Son *Sultan Mahmud,*[28] Son-in-Law to the King of *Golconda,* to *Emir Gemla,*[29] who[30] lay by Order of *Sciah-gehan,* at the Siege of *Kaliana,*[31] to desire[32] him to meet him at *Daulet-Abad,*[33] where he would communicate a Matter of great Moment to him. The *Emir,* who was well acquainted with *Aurenge Zeb*'s Artifices, excus'd himself,[34] saying, his[35] Father was not yet Dead ; and that all his Family was left at *Agra,* in the Hands of *Dara,* as Hostages for his Fidelity ; for which Reason he could not Assist him without the Ruin of what he held most dear. Having receiv'd this Answer, *Aurenge Zeb* was no way discourag'd, but sent *Sultan Mazum,*[36] his second Son to the Emir ; who manag'd Things so well, that he perswaded him to go with him to *Dolet Abad,* with the Flower of his Army, he having[37] made himself Master of *Kaliana. Aurenge Zeb* receiv'd him with extraordinary Demonstrations of Affection and Honour ; calling him *Baba,* and *Babagi,* that is, Father, and Lord and Father ; and after giving him an hundred Embraces, taking him aside he told him, It was not reasonable that his Family being in *Dara*'s Hands, he should venture to do any thing for him Publickly ; but that on the other Hand there was no Difficulty but might be overcome. I will therefore propose a method to you, said he, which will not appear strange to you, when you think on the Safety of your Wife and Children ; which is, that you permit me to Imprison you,[38] which all the World will think is in Earnest, believing you are no Man that will take it in Jest,[39] and in the mean while I will make use of part of your Troops, of your Cannon, and some of your Mony, which you have so often offer'd me, and will try my Fortune. The *Emir,* either because he was a sworn Friend to *Aurenge Zeb,* or on account of the great Promises he had made him at other times ; or else by reason he saw *Sultan Mazum* well arm'd standing by him, and *Sultan Mahmud* looking upon him with a stern Countenance ; submitted to all his Will, suffering himself to be confin'd to[40] a Room. The News being spread abroad, his Men ran to Arms to Rescue him, and being very numerous would have done it had not *Aurenge Zeb* appeas'd them with fair Words, Promises, and Gifts ; so that not only the *Emir*'s Troops, but most of *Sciah Gehan*'s seeing Things in Confusion, sided with him. Having therefore Possess'd himself of the *Emir*'s Tents, Camels, and Baggage, he march'd to take *Suratte ;* but hearing within a few Days that the Governour had already surrendred it to *Morad Baksce,* he sent to Congratulate with him, and tell him what had hapned with[41] *Emir Jemla ;* what Forces and Mony he had ; and what secret Intelligence at Court ; desiring him, that since he was to go from *Brampur*[42] to *Agra,* he should[43] endeavour to meet, and Confer with him by the way,

This fell out to his Mind,[44] the two Armies joyning with much Satisfaction. *Aurenge Zeb* made *Morad Bakscé* fresh Promises, protesting over again that he did not Aspire to the Crown ; but only come to help raise him to the Throne, in Opposition to *Dara,* their common Enemy. They both mov'd towards *Brampur,* where coming to a Battle with the Army of *Sciah-gehan,* and *Dara,* which came to hinder them passing the River *Ogene ;*[45] the Generals, *Kasem* and *Cham,*[46] and *Gesson-senghe*[47] were overthrown by the Valour of *Morad,* with the Slaughter of 8000 *Ragipu*'s.[48]

Dara's Forces defeated.

Morad Baksce flush'd with the Success of the Battle, coveted nothing but Fighting ; using all possible means to overtake the Enemy ; whilst *Aurenge Zeb* grown vain, encourag'd his Soldiers, giving out he had 30000 *Moguls* of his Party among *Dara*'s Forces. Having taken some Rest, they Fought the second Battle at *Samongher,*[49] where *Morad Baksce,* tho wounded by the General *Ram senghe-rutle,*[50] fighting Couragiously kill'd him.[51] Whilst the Event[52] of the Battle was still Dubious, the Traitor *Calil-ullah-kan,*[53] who Commanded 30000 *Moguls,* with whom he might have routed the Enemy, did not only go over to *Aurenge Zeb,* but falsly[54] perswaded *Dara* to come down from his Elephant, and get a Horse-back, and this to the end that the Soldiers not seeing him, might suppose he was kill'd, and so dismay 'em.[55] It fell out as he design'd, for being all seiz'd with Fear,[56] they fled to escape *Aurenge Zeb.* Thus *Dara* on a sudden lost the Victory he had almost gain'd, and was overthrown ; and seeing himself forsaken, was forc'd to fly to save his Life. So that it may be said, that *Aurenge Zeb* by continuing stedfast on his Elephant, secur'd to himself the Crown of *Indostan ;* and *Dara* was thrown out of the Throne by coming down from his.[57] A Diversion Fortune often takes, to make the greatest Victories[58] depend on the most contemptible Accidents. The unhappy *Dara* returning to *Agra* in Despair, durst not appear before his Father, who, when he took his Leave, had said to him, *Be sure* Dara *never to come into my Sight unless Victorious.* Nevertheless the good old Man did not omit to send to Comfort[59] him, and assure him of his Affection.

Himself routed.

Four Days after, *Aurenge Zeb,* and *Morad Baksce* came to a Garden[60] a small League from the Fort of *Agra ;* and thence sent an ingenious and trusty Eunuch to pay their Respects to *Sciah-gehan ;* and to tell him they were very much troubled at all that had hapned, being compell'd to it by *Dara*'s Ambition ; but[61] were most ready to Obey his Commands. *Sciah-gehan,* tho' he well knew how eager his Son was to Reign, and that there was no trusting to his fair Words ; yet shew'd a good Countenance to the Eunuch, designing to intrap *Aurenge Zeb,* without coming to open Force, as was then proper to have

Aurenge Zeb comes to *Agra.*

done. But he, who was thorough skill'd in all Frauds, took his Father in the same Snare; for putting off the Visit from Day to Day, which had been agreed upon between them by the Eunuch, spent the mean time in gaining the Affections of the *Omrahs* underhand. When he thought Things were Ripe, he sent his Eldest Son *Sultan Mahmud* to the Fort, on Pretence to speak to *Sciah-gehan* from him.[62] This bold young Prince coming to the Gate, fell with his Men that lay in readiness upon the Guards, and putting them to Flight, went resolutely in, and made himself Master of the Walls. *Sciah-gehan* perceiving he was fallen into the Snare he had laid for his Son, try'd to Bribe *Sultan Mahmud* with the offer of the Crown, but he, without being mov'd, carry'd the Keys of the Fort to his Father, who made the same Governour[63] *Ekbar-kan*,[64] Governour of it. He presently shut up the old King with his Daughter *Begum Saheb*, and all the Women; so that he could neither Speak nor Write to any Body, much less go out of his Apartment.[65] As soon as this was done, all the *Omrahs* were oblig'd to make their Court to *Aurenge Zeb*, and *Morad Buksce*, and to declare for the first of them. He being now well Establish'd, took what he thought fit out of the King's Treasure; and leaving his Uncle *Scia-hest-kan*[66] Governour of the City, went away with *Morad Baksce* in Pursuit of *Dara*.

Imprisons his Father.

The Day they were to set out of *Agra*, *Morad Baksce*'s Friends, and particularly his Eunuch *Scia-Abas*, told him, That since he was King, and *Aurenge Zeb* himself gave him the Title of Majesty; he should send him against *Dara*, and stay himself with his Troops about Agra and Dehli.[67] But he had so much Confidence in his Brother's Promises, and in the mutual Oath of Fidelity they had taken to one another upon the *Al-coran*; that despising all good Counsel, he set out towards *Dehli*, with *Aurenge Zeb*. At *Maturas*,[68] four Days March from *Agra*, his Friends again endeavour'd to Convince him, that his Brother had ill Designs[69] in his Head; and advis'd him to forbear Visiting him, tho' it were but that Day[70] upon pretence of Indisposition; but he continuing Incredulous, and in a manner infatuated with his sweet Words,[71] did not only go, but staid to Sup with him. The false Wretch shew'd him all manner of Kindness, even to the wiping off his Sweat with his Handkerchief, always talking to him as King, and giving him the Title of Majesty; but as soon as he saw him overcome by the Fumes of *Sciras*,[72] and *Cabul* Wine, he arose from Table, and encouraging his Brother to carry on the Debauch with *Mircan*,[73] and other Officers there present, went away, as if he had gone to take his Rest. *Morad Baksce*, who lov'd Drinking, making himself Drunker than he was, at length fell asleep; which was what *Aurenge Zeb* expected,[74] in order to take away his *scimiter*, and *Gemder*,[75] or Dagger. Then returning into the Room, he

Seises *Morad Baksce*.

began to upbraid him in these Words, *What a Shame, what a Disgrace is this! for a King as you are to be so Debauch'd, as to make himself thus Drunk? What will the World say of you, and of me? Let this base Man, this Drunkard be bound Hands, and Feet, and shut up to Digest his Wine.* This was immediately Executed, and *Morad Baksce*'s Commanders being offended at his Imprisonment, *Aurenge Zeb* pacify'd[76] them with Gifts and Promises, and took them all into his Pay. His unfortunate Brother was shut up in an *Ambri*,[77] which is a little wooden House they set on an Elephant to carry Women, and so convey'd to *Dehli*, to the little Fort of *Salemgher*,[78] seated in the middle of the River.

Having secur'd *Morad Baksce*, he pursu'd *Dara*; leaving *Sultan Mahmud*, and *Emir Gemla* to Destroy *Sultan Sujah*. But *Mahmud* aspiring to those Things he ought not yet to have aim'd at, and being naturally Proud, fell at Variance[79] with *Emir Gemla*, about commanding in Chief, which he pretended to belong to him alone; and now and then let slip some Words of Contempt and Threatning against him, and such as did not become a dutiful Son. Then fearing that his Father on account of his ill Behaviour had given Orders to the *Emir* to secure him; he with-drew with a few Followers to *Sultan Sujah*,[80] making him great Promises, and swearing to be Faithful; but he fearing some Contrivance of *Aurenge Zeb*, and the *Emir*, caus'd all his Actions to be observ'd;[81] so that *Mahmud* in a few Months return'd to the *Emir*'s Camp. Others say it was a Project of *Aurenge Zeb*'s, to send him to his Uncle, to Ruin them both, or at least a specious Pretence to make sure of him; because afterwards, besides the threatning Letters he writ to recal him to *Dehli*, he caus'd him to be Arrested upon the River *Ganges*, and sent close shut up in an *Ambri*, to *Gavaleor*.

Imprisons his Eldest Son.

Aurenge Zeb having perform'd this Work, sent to warn his other Son *Sultan Mazum* to continue in his Duty, unless he would be serv'd[82] in the same manner; because it was a nice Point to Reign, and Kings ought to be jealous[83] of their own Shadows. Then going to *Dehli*, he began to Act as King; and whilst the *Emir* press'd *Sugiah*, who made a brave Opposition, securing the Passage of the River *Ganges*, he contriv'd to get *Dara* into his Power by Fraud, forcing him to quit *Guzaratte*. He made the *Raja Gessen Sanghe* write a Letter to tell him, he would speak with him about a Matter of great Moment on the way to *Agra*. *Dara*, who had gather'd an indifferent Army, unadvisedly came out of *Amed-Abad*, and hasted to *Asmire*,[84] eight Days Journey from *Agra*. Here too late discovering *Gessen Senghes Treachery*,[85] and seeing no Possibility of returning so soon to *Amed Abad*, which was thirty four Days[86] Journey distant, in Summer, with scarcity of Water, and through the Hands[87] of several *Raja*'s Friends to *Jessem*; he at last

Dara defeated again.

resolv'd, tho' he knew himself to be inferior in Forces to Fight him.[88] In this Battle Dara was betray'd, not only by *Scia-Navazekan,*[89] but by all his Officers, who fir'd his Cannon without Ball,[90] so that he was forced to fly to save his Life, and to cross all the Countries of *Raja*'s there are from *Asmire* to *Amed Abad;* without Tents, or Baggage, in the hottest Season, and with only 2000 Soldiers, who were most of them stripp'd by the *Kullys,*[91] Peasants of the Country, who are the greatest Thieves in *India.* Being come with so much Difficulty within a Day's Journey of *Amed Abad,* the Governour, who was corrupted by *Aurenge Zeb,* sent him Word to come no nearer, for he would find the Gates shut. *Dara* much concern'd at this News, and not knowing what to Resolve on, he bethought him of a Powerful *Patan,* call'd *Gion-Kan,*[92] whose Life he had twice sav'd, when *Scia-gehan* had commanded him to be cast to the Elephants for Rebellion. Him he purpos'd to repair to, notwithstanding his Son *Sapesce-Kuh,*[93] and his Wife's Disswasions. Coming thither he was at first Courteously receiv'd; but the next Morning the false and ungrateful *Patan* fell upon him with many arm'd Men, and killing some Soldiers that came to his Assistance, Bound him, his Wife and Son, seizing all their Jewels, and Mony. Then setting him on an Elephant, with an Executioner behind, who was to Kill him if he attempted to Escape, he conducted him to the Camp at *Tatabakar,*[94] where he deliver'd him up to the General *Mirbaba,*[95] who caus'd him to be carry'd in the same manner to *Agra,* and thence to *Dehli.* When he was come to the Gate of that City, *Aurenge Zeb,* and his Council differ'd in Opinions, whether they should carry him through the City, or not, in order to send him to *Govaleor,* and at last it was resolv'd to set him scurvily Clad, with his Wife and Son, on a pitiful Elephant, and so carry him through the City, with the infamous *Patan* by him. In the mean while *Aurenge Zeb* was inform'd, that all the City was Incens'd against him, on account of his many Cruelties; and mis-doubting the first,[96] he summon'd his Council, to Determine whether it was better to send him to Prison, or put him to Death. Many were of the first Opinion; but *Dara*'s old Enemies, especially *Nakim Daud,*[97] a Physitian, flattering the Tyrant's Inclination, cry'd out aloud, it was convenient for the safety of the Kingdom, that he should Die, and the more because he was no *Musulman,* but a *Kafer,* or Idolater.[98] *Aurenge Zeb* readily comply'd, immediately ordering that *Sapesce-Kuh* should be carry'd Prisoner to *Govaleor,* and *Dara* put to Death by the Hands of a Slave, call'd *Nazar.*[99] He going in to Execute the barbarous Command, *Dara,* who was himself dressing some Lentils for fear of Poison, foreseeing what was coming upon him, cry'd out to his Son, see he comes to Kill me.[100] Then taking a Kitchin Knife, he would have defended himself; but the

Betray'd.

Executioner fell on, and throwing him down, cut off his Head,[101] which was carry'd to the Fort to *Aurenge Zeb,* and he ordering it to be put into a Dish, wash'd[102] it with his own Hands, to be sure it was his Brother's, and when he found it was, began to Lament, saying, *Oh unhappy Man; take it out of my Sight, and let it be Bury'd in the Tomb of Humagon.*[103] At Night he caus'd his[104] Daughters to be put into the *Seraglio,* and afterwards sent her to *Scia-gehan,* and *Begum Saheb,* who desir'd it; and *Sapesce-Kuh* was carry'd to *Govaleor. Gion-Kan* was rewarded for his Treachery;[105] but was kill'd in a Wood as he return'd home, to prove that Men love the Treason, but hate the Traitor. His Sons secur'd.

There was none left of *Dara*'s Family, but *Soliman Scekuh,* who was not easily to be drawn from *Serenagher,*[106] had the *Raja* kept his Word; but the underhand Practices of the *Raja Gessen Senghe,*[106a] the Promises and Threats of *Aurenge Zeb,* the Death of *Dara,* and the neighbouring *Raja*'s made him break his Faith. *Soliman* understanding he was betray'd, fled over desert Mountains, towards the Great *Tibet,* but the *Raja's* Son[107] overtook, and stopp'd him, wounding him with a Stone; after which he was convey'd to *Dehli,* where he was shut up in *Salengher,* with *Morad Baksce,* not without Tears of all the *Omrahs.*

Aurenge Zeb perceiving there were Poems handed about in Commendation of *Morad Baksce*'s Valour, it rais'd such a Jealousy in him, that he presently contriv'd his Death. *Morad,* at the beginning of the War had kill'd one *Sajed,*[108] a very wealthy Man at *Amed Abad,* only to Sieze upon what he had.[109] The Tyrant made his Sons appear in a full Assembly, and demand that Prince's Head, in Revenge for their Father's Death. Not one of the *Omrahs* oppos'd it, as well because *Sajed* was of *Mahomet's* Family, as to comply with the will of *Aurenge Zeb,* whose invention[110] they knew that was. Accordingly they were permitted without any manner of Process to have *Morad*'s Head cut off; which was immediately perform'd at *Govaleor.* *Morad Baksce* kill'd.

There is now none left to oppose *Aurenge Zeb,* but only *Sultan Sujah,* who tho' he held out some time in *Bengala,* yet was at last forc'd to submit to his Brother's Power and good Fortune; for the *Emir Gemla* pursuing him with his Forces[111] into the Islands the *Ganges* makes near its Mouth, forc'd him to fly to *Dake*[112] the last City of *Bengala* on the Sea side. Here, having no Ships to commit himself to the Ocean, and not knowing which way to escape; he sent his eldest Son *Sultan Banche*[113] to the King of *Aracam* or *Mog,*[114] a heathen Prince, to pray him to give him Protection for the present in his Country, and in the proper Season a Vessel to carry him to *Moka,*[115] he having a mind to go to *Mecca.* The King of *Aracam* presently sent a number of Galeasses[116] or half Galleys with *Sultan Banche,* The end of *Sultan Sujah.*

and a civil Answer as to the rest. *Sujah* went aboard with his Women, and being brought to that King was well receiv'd; but when the Season came he perform'd not his Word[117] of furnishing him a Ship to go to *Mecca;* but appearing every Day more cold to him, began to complain that *Sujah* did not visit him, and tho' *Sultan Banche* often made his Court with great Presents, yet it avail'd nothing. Then asking one of *Sultan Sujah*'s Daughters in Marriage, and fiinding she was not immediately granted him, the Barbarian was so inrag'd, that he oblig'd the poor fugitive Prince to act a desperate Part. He thought with 300 Souldiers he brought from *Bengala,* and the assistance of the *Mahometans* of the Country whom he had corrupted to break into the Palace, kill all he found, and make himself King of *Arracam;* but the Day before he was to put this in Execution, the Design was discover'd, and he oblig'd to fly towards *Pegu* to save his Life, tho' it was impossible to come thither by reason of the vast Mountains and Forrests he was to pass through. That same Day he was overtaken by the King's Men, and tho' he defended himself with much Bravery, killing a great number, yet so many fell upon him, that at last he was forc'd to submit to his Fate. *Sultan Banche* who was not gone so far, made his defence too, but being hurt[118] with Stones, and encompass'd on all sides, was taken, with two little Brothers, a Sister and his Mother. As for *Sultan Sujah* himself there are different Accounts;[119] some say he was wounded on the Mountains, only four of his Men being left about him, and that an Eunuch having dress'd the Wound on his Head, he fled across the Woods; others will have it that he was found among the Dead, but not perfectly known;[120] others that he was afterwards seen at Maslipatan; others near *Suratte;* and others in fine that he was fled towards *Persia;*[121] so that by reason of these different Accounts, *Aurenge Zeb* one Day in jest said that *Sujah* was turn'd Pilgrim. The most receiv'd Opinion is that he dy'd in the Fray, if he was not kill'd by Robbers, or wild Beasts, of which those Forrests are full. After this Disaster all his Family was Imprison'd, and the King took his eldest Daughter to Wife; but another Conspiracy of *Sultan Banche*[122] being afterwards discover'd, he was so inrag'd that he caus'd them all to be put to Death, even to her that was his Wife and with Child. The Men were put to the Sword, and the Women starv'd to Death.

Exact Justice of a *Mahometan.*

The unnatural War being thus at an end after it had lasted through the ambition of Rule,[123] among the four Brothers from the Year 1655 till 1660.[124] *Aurenge Zeb* remain'd peaceable Possessor of that vast Empire; for after so much Blood shed and so many Enormities committed, it was easie to cause himself to be declar'd King with the consent of all the great Ones. The greatest Obstacle he found was the Grand *Cadi*[125] who was to put him in Possession, and pleaded that according to the Law of *Mahomet* and that of Nature, no Man could be declar'd King, whilst his Father was yet living ; much less *Aurenge Zeb,* who had put to death his elder Brother *Dara,* to whom the Crown belong'd after the Death of his Father *Scia-gehan.* To overcome this difficulty he assembled the Doctors of the Law, and told them, that as for his Father he was unfit to Rule by reason of his Age ; and for his Brother *Dara*'s Death he had caus'd him to be executed for contemning the Law, by drinking Wine, and favouring Infidels. Adding Threats to these Reasons he made the *Mahometan* Casuists agree, that he deserv'd the Crown and ought to be declar'd King. The *Cadi* still opposing him, he was depos'd[126] and another put in his Place, who for the kindness[127] receiv'd consented to all that was requir'd of him. *Aurenge Zeb* accordingly coming to the *Mosch* on the 20th of *October* 1660[128] seated himself on the richest Throne[129] that ever was seen in the World,[130] being the same that was begun by *Tamerlan* and finish'd by *Scia-gehan,* receiving there the Homage of all the great Men, as is the custom of the Country. Afterwards there was great rejoycing at *Jehanabat*[131] and throughout all the Kingdom.

Aurenge Zeb Enthron'd.

Aurenge-Zeb considering the heinousness of the Crimes he had committed for the compassing of his Ends ; voluntarily impos'd on himself a rigorous Abstinence, not to eat for the future any Wheaten-Bread, Fish, or Flesh ; and to live upon Barley-Bread, Rice, Herbs, Sweetmeats and such things ; nor to drink any sort of Liquor but Water.[132]

His Penance.

Ambassadors from the prime[133] Princes of *Asia* and *Africk* came to his Court to Congratulate his Accession to the Crown ;[134] but he was much offended at the Letter sent him by the King of *Persia,*[135] upbraiding him with the Murder of *Dara,* and Imprisonment of *Sciah-Gehan,* as being Actions unworthy a *Musulman,* and the Son and Brother of a *Musulman ;* and reflecting on[136] him for the Title he had assum'd of *Alem-Guire,*[137] that is, Lord of the World, concluded[138] challenging him in these Words, Since you are *Alem-Guire,* I send you a Sword and Horses that we may meet.

Is reprovd by the King of *Persia.*

Sciah-Gehan dy'd in the Fort of *Agra* about the end of the Year 1666.[139] and *Aurenge-Zeb,* who had long wish'd to be deliver'd from that continual Reproach of his Tyranny, went thither immediately to secure all his Father's Jewels. He receiv'd his Sister *Begum-Saheb* into favour, because she having an influence over her Father, being his[140] Wife and Daughter,[141] had preserv'd to him so many Jewels of incredible value, when *Sciah-Gehan* offended that he had sent for them whilst he was living, to adorn the Throne he had usurp'd, was about to reduce them to Powder in a Mortar. Besides she had given him much Gold, and set out[142] the *Mosch* he went into before his entring

Sciah Gehan dies *Tavern. l.* 2. p. 252.

the Fort, with rich Carpets. She was afterwards carry'd in honourable manner to *Jehanabat*, and there dy'd,[143] with suspition of being Poison'd.[144]

Divine Justice.

If we now look back into the Life of *Sciah-Gehan*,[145] we shall find that he was punish'd by the Hand of God as he had deserv'd, for the wrong he had done his Nephew *Bulaki*,[146] usurping the Crown from him.

Sciah Gehan an Usurper.

Gehanghir King of *India* Son of *Acbar*, and Grandson of *Humagion*, after having reign'd twenty three Years Peaceably was disturb'd by the Ambition of his Sons, who thought that Life lasted too long, which obstructed their getting into Power. The Eldest[147] rais'd a mighty Army about *Lahor* to possess his Father's Throne before it was his Due ; the King to punish his Presumption march'd against him with numerous Forces, and defeating his Troops, brought him away Prisoner with those great Men that had espous'd his Cause. But being of a merciful Disposition and unwilling to imbrue his Hands in the Blood of his Son, whom he could not but love, he was satisfy'd with holding a Red hot Iron to his Eyes, and keeping him in that Condition about him ; designing[148] to raise his[149] Son *Sultan Bulaki* to the Throne. But *Sultan Curom*,[150] who afterwards took the Name of *Sciah Gehan*, believing that he as second Son to *Gehan Ghir*, ought to be prefer'd in right before his Nephew ; resolv'd to leave no means unattempted to cast him down[151] and raise himself, without expecting[152] his Father's Death. He conceal'd his wicked Design under the Cloak of a counterfeit Obedience, till he gain'd his Father's good Will ; and when he thought himself well grounded in his Favour, desir'd he would give him leave to carry his blind Brother into the Kingdom of *Decan*, where he was Governour ; saying, he should by this means take out of his sight a displeasing Object, and his Brother would live[153] more Peaceably. The King not diving into *Curom*'s Design, consented to it ; but he having got the poor Prince into his Hands, contriv'd to make him away[154] in such manner, that no Man could imagine he had been so cruel as to Poison him.[155] This done he chang'd his Name into that of *Sciah-Gehan*, that is, King of the World, and raising a numerous Army, set forward to make War on his Father, who was justly provok'd, and the more for his Son's Death. *Jehanguir* went out in Person with a great Strength,[156] against the Wicked and Ambitious *Curom* ; but Age[157] and Grief to see himself so much wrong'd ended his Days by the way, and made it easie for the other to compass his Designs. However *Jehanguir* before his Death recommended his Grandson *Sultan Bulaki* to *Asuf-Kan*,[158] Generalissimo of his Army, and prime Minister of State, and to all the great Officers, commanding them when he was dead, to acknowledge none for their true and lawful Sovereign but *Bulaki* ; and[159] declaring

Sultan Curom a Rebel, and incapable of Succeeding in the Throne.[160] Besides he made them swear and particularly *Asuf-Kan,* that they would never consent that *Bulaki* should be put to Death ; which he afterwards faithfully perform'd, but not to settle him on the Throne,[161] having design'd that for *Scia Gehan* his Son in Law. The Death of *Jehan Guir*[162] being known all the great Men acknowledg'd the young *Sultan Bulaki* for their King. Two of his Cousins, soon perceiving the wicked design of *Asuf-Kan,* were the cause of their own Death, and his loosing the Crown, by discovering the Secret to him ; because he being unskill'd in the Mystery[163] of Reigning, ask'd the question of *Asuf-Kan* himself, who having swore he would ever be faithful to his King, privately contriv'd the Death of the two Princes. Then considering that the King having notice of the Conspiracy, it was dangerous to defer the Execution of it, and finding himself Powerful in the number of his Followers, he gave out that *Scia Gehan* was Dead,[164] and his Body would be carry'd to be Bury'd at *Agra,* with the Bones of *Jehan Guir,* as he had desir'd before his Death. He himself brought the News to *Bulaki,* persuading him when it was to be done to go[165] two Leagues out of *Agra* to meet the Body, that Honour being due to a Prince of the Blood tho' an Enemy. *Scia Gehan* came himself in disguise, and when he was in sight of the Army near *Agra* was lay'd on a Bier and carry'd as if he were Dead. All the principal Conspirators came with *Asuf* into the Tent, where he was lay'd, as[166] it were to do Honour to the dead Prince, and when they saw the young King was come out of *Agra,* uncovering the Bier, they made *Scia Gehan* stand up in the presence of all the Army, and declaring him King with a loud Voice, they and all the rest by their example swore Fealty to him. *Bulaki* receiving this dismal News by the way, being in a consternation had no hopes of safety but in flying ; which was easie to be done,[167] because his Enemies thought not proper to pursue him. He wandred about *India* a long time, becoming a *Fachir* ;[168] but at last tir'd with that painful Employment he retir'd into *Persia,*[169] where he was nobly receiv'd and entertain'd by *Scia Sofi.*[170] *Scia Gehan* being left without any Rival, yet fearing the Factions there might be for the lawful King, by degrees put to death all those that were well affected to his Nephew ; making the first Years of his Reign famous[171] for Cruelty. Thus his being in his Life time depriv'd of his Kingdom by his Son, is to be look'd upon as a just Judgment of God, which the longer it is defer'd the heavier it falls.

These are the Methods of securing the Throne of *Indostan,* not found out by any ill Custom of that People, but proceeding from the want of good Laws, concerning the Title of Birthright. Therefore every Prince of the Blood thinks he has a sufficient Claim to the Crown, and exposing himself to the cruel necessity of Overcoming to Reign,[172] sometimes involves an infinite number of Lives in his own Ruin, that another may be the more securely establish'd.

CHAPTER IV

THE GENEALOGY OF THE GREAT MOGULS, *AND OTHER THINGS THE AUTHOR OBSERV'D AT THAT COURT.*

The Empire of the *Mogul.*

The vast Empire of the *Mogul,* which in the *Indian* Language signifies white,[1] contains all the Country between the Rivers *Indus* and *Ganges.* It borders on the East with the Kingdoms of *Aracan, Tipa,* and *Assen ;*[2] on the West with *Persia,* and the *Usbeck Tartars ;* on the South of it is the great *Indian* Ocean, and some Countries[3] held by the *Portugueses* and other petty Kings ; and on the North it reaches to Mount *Caucasus,*[4] and the Country of *Zagotay ;*[5] on the North East of it is the Kingdom of *Butan,*[6] whence the Musk is brought. So that the Length of it from *Bengala* to *Candahor*[7] is no less than six Months Journey, and its Breadth from North to South at least four.

Tamerlan Founder of the Monarchy.

The first that lay'd[8] the Foundation of this mighty Monarchy was *Tamerlan,* otherwise call'd *Teymur ;* who by his wonderful[9] Conquests from *India* to *Poland,*[9a] far surpass'd the Renown of all former Commanders. He had one Leg shorter than the other, and was therefore call'd the Lame ; and here we may take notice of his sharp[10] Saying to this effect, to *Bajazeth*[11] Emperor of the *Turks,* whom he overthrew and took Prisoner. Causing him to be brought into his presence the same Day, and looking him steadily in the Face he fell a Laughing : Whereat *Bajazeth* offended said, *Do not Laugh at my ill Fortune* Tamerlan ; *know that it is God who bestows Kingdoms and Empires, and that all that has befallen me to Day may happen to you to Morrow. Tamerlan* without the least Concern answer'd, *I know very well* Bajazeth, *that it is God who bestows Kingdoms and Empires. I do not Laugh at your Misfortune, but because considering your Countenance, I perceived that these Kingdoms and Empires are very inconsiderable things with God ; since he bestows them on such ugly Fellows as we are, you a squinting Clown, and I a lame Wretch. Tamerlan* was not of mean Extraction, as some imagine, but of the Race of *Scia guis Cham,*[12] King of *Tartary.* He was born at *Samarcand* a Country of *Zagatay,* or of the *Usbeck-Tartars,* where he was afterwards Bury'd.

Bern. Revol. des estats du G. Mogul Tom. 2. p. 78. *Teixeira de Imp. Mogul. sive India vera* p. 162.

Tamarlan's Successors.

Mirumxa[13] his Son succeeded him in the Throne; his successor was his son *Mahomet*;[14] and *Mahomet*[15] *Mirza Sultan Absuid*[16] his Son, who was kill'd by the *Persians* in the Year 1469. *Mirza Sultan Hamet*[17] Son to him ascended the Throne next, and dy'd in 1495. The next[18] was *Hamet's* Son, call'd *Sultan Babir*,[19] which signifies brave Prince, who in 1500 was Dethron'd by *Kay-bek-Cham*[20] an *Usbeck*, but recover'd the Kingdom again after wandring a long time about *India*, and was the first *Mogul* that became so very Powerful. He dy'd in 1532.

Thevenot Voy. des. Indies. L. I. c. 3

His Son *Homagion*, that is, the Fortunate, succeeded him, who Conquer'd the best and wealthiest Kingdoms in *India*. *Kirkan*[21] his General Rebell'd and forc'd him to fly to the King of *Persia*; by whom being assisted with 12000 Men under the Command of *Beuran-Cham*,[22] he defeated the Rebel, and recover'd his Kingdom; then dy'd in 1552.[23]

After his Death his Son *Gelaladin*[24] commonly call'd *Akbar* ascended the Throne. He Reign'd 54 Years, and dy'd in 1605. since the Birth of Christ, and 1014, of the *Mahometan Epocha*, leaving the Kingdom to his Son *Sultan Selim*, call'd by another Name *Jehan-Guir-patsia*,[25] that is, Conquering Emperor of the World; at his Death he left four Sons, *Sultan Kosru*, *Sultan Kurom*, *Sultan Peruiz*, and *Scia Daniel*.[26]

Sultan Kurom succeeded his Father *Jehan Guir*, by means of the ill Practices above mention'd and was acknowledg'd for their Sovereign by the great Men of the Kingdom in the Fort of *Agra*, by the Name of *Sultan Sciabedin Muhammed*;[27] but he would be call'd *Scia-Gehan*. Next to him came *Aurenge-Zeb* ascending the Throne of *Indostan*, through such cruel Practices. He took the Name of *Aurenge-Zeb-Alem-Ghire*, That is, Lord of the World, believing he possess'd three parts of it. For this reason he carry'd as his peculiar Ensign a Golden-Globe, and had it in his Seal; and always tore off one corner of the Paper he wrote on, to express that the fourth part of the World was not his. He added to his Empire the Kingdoms of *Visapor*, and *Golconda*, the Kings whereof he kept Prisoners in my time, part of the Territory of *Savagi*, and of other petty Principalities in *Indostan*.

Aurenge Zeb's Conquests.

Aurenge Zeb labour'd to gain the Reputation of being a strict Observer of the *Mahometan* Law, and a lover of Justice. He had so distributed his time that he could scarce ever be said to be Idle.[28] Some Days in the Week he bath'd before break of Day; then having pray'd he eat something.[29] After that having spent two hours with his Secretaries, he gave publick Audience before Noon, and then pray'd again. This done he Din'd, and soon after gave Audience again, when follow'd the third and fourth time of praying. Next he was employ'd in the Affairs of his Family till two Hours after it was Dark.

His employments.

Then he Supp'd and slept only two Hours, after which he took the *Alcoran* and read till break of Day. This was told me by several Eunuchs belonging to the Court, who knowing their Prince was skill'd in Negromancy,[30] believ'd he was assisted by the Devil in that Painful Course of Life ; else he could not have gone through so much fatigue in his decrepit old Age. This might serve as an Example to some Princes of *Europe*, who are so reserv'd,[31] that they give Audience but twice a Week, and then will not stay a Moment to hear their Subject's Grievances ;[32] as if it were not their duty to listen to them with Patience. And it is certain the *Mogul* did not feed on such Dainties as they do, but on Herbs and Pulse ; fasting every Day at those Years, tho' made of Flesh and Blood like the *Europeans*.

His change of Life.

After Aurenge Zeb had prescrib'd himself this sort of Life, he ceas'd to be Bloody as before, and on the contrary became so mild, that the Governors and *Omrahs* did not pay him the Duty they ought ; knowing his Mercy would never suffer him to punish them. Thus the Poor were oppress'd by the great Ones without knowing who to have recourse to ; because the King when advis'd to be less merciful towards those that transgress'd his Commands, Answer'd, That he was no God, that his Ministers might not Contradict him,[33] and that if they misbehav'd themselves, Heaven would punish them. A Government far different from that of *Turky,* and *Persia,* where the stain of Disobedience is wash'd away with Blood. Those that saw but into[34] the outside, said, *Aurenge Zeb* was a great *Mahometan* Saint,[35] who after his Death must be put into the Martyrology of their false Sect. But I am of opinion he conniv'd at the failings of his Ministers, and Omrahs, that they might love the present Government, under which they were suffer'd to Act as they pleas'd, and consequently there might be no way for any of his Sons, to usurp the Throne.

His continency.

On the other side, to speak the Truth, he did not give himself up in his Youth to sensual Pleasures, as his Predecessors had done ; tho' according to their barbarous Custom, he kept several hundred Women[36] in the *Aram,* for ostentation. To this purpose they tell us,[37] that he having pitch'd upon[38] a Woman in the *Aram* to lye with him that Night, she dress'd her self the best she could to receive that Honour. The King coming at the appointed hour into her Chamber, instead of going to bed, fell a reading the *Alcoran* all Night. The Eunuch coming in the Morning to tell him the Bath was ready, as is us'd by[39] the *Mahometans* after they have had to do with Women ; the Woman who had been disappointed cry'd out, there was no need of a Bath, because the King had not broke Wind ; to signify, he had been at Prayers, which if interrupted by Wind, the *Mahometans* are to Bath.[40] The King hearing her went away asham'd, the Lady telling him that was no Room to pray in ; and he never after look'd her in the Face.[41] The Kings of *Indostan* are at a vast Charge in maintaining so many Women ; for they have many Thousands and thousands[42] of *Roupies* a Year out of the Treasury ; some of the best belov'd even to a Million and a half, which they spend in maintaining abundance of Elephants, Horses and Servants.

Besides *Aurenge Zeb*'s abstinence, after so many horrid crimes committed, his Table was not maintain'd out of the Revenue of the Crown ; he said that Food was not good,[43] which cost the sweat of the Subjects, but that every Man ought to work for his living. For this Reason he work'd Caps, and presented them to the Governors of his Kingdoms and Provinces ; who in return for the Honour done them, sent him a Present of several Thousands of *Roupies*. When I was there, his decrepit Age rendring him inable to work, he had reserv'd the Revenues of four Towns for his Table. His expence was but small, for a Vest of his did not cost above 8 *Roupies*, and the Sash and *Cira* or Cap, less. He work'd for his Bread.

The Great *Mogul*'s usual place of Residence is at *Agra*, and sometimes at *Dehli*, and *Lahor*, in which Cities the King is always guarded by an *Omrah*, with a Body of 20000 Horse, who incamp about those Cities, and this Guard is reliev'd every eight days. But when *Aurenge Zeb* who kept alwas in the Field, was to decamp from any place, where he lay with his Army, a Tent was carry'd before by a hundred and twenty Elephants, 1400 Camels, and 400 small Carts, to be set up where he was to go, and several thousands of Horse and Foot, went with 70 Elephants to secure the Ground to incamp on. Eight other Elephants carry'd eight Chairs, more like Biers, wrought with Gold and Silver, or Gilt Wood, and clos'd[44] with Cristal. There were three others[45] carry'd by 8 Men each, in one of which the King went, when he did not Mount an Elephant, especially if it rain'd, or the Way was dusty. All the great Men attended him afoot ; but when they went out of Town, and the Journey was long ; he us'd to command them to Mount a Horseback.

Aurenge Zeb got several Children. His eldest Son, (as we said elsewhere) was *Mahmud*, who following the Example of his Predecessors, in aiming at the Crown before his Fathers death, proceeded so openly, towards taking away his life, that he thought good to prevent him ; and accordingly caus'd him to be Poison'd one day,[46] when he went a Hunting ; and mistrusting he was not really dead,[47] when he was brought to the Palace, he cruelly caus'd a red hot Iron to be run in from the sole of his Foot to his Knee. His Children. 1st Son.

Scialam the 2d Son, by the death of *Mahmud*, had the right of Eldest, and with it entertain'd the same Thoughts, the The 2d.

other had done, of destroying his Father. To this purpose he once caus'd a great Trench to be dug near *Aurenge Zeb's* Tent, that he might fall into it, as he pass'd by; but he being told of it by an Eunuch, escap'd death; and put the wicked *Scialam* into a dark Prison,[48] where he continu'd six Years, tho' 60 Years of Age, till a few Days before I came into the Camp.

The 3d. *Azam-scia*[49] third Son to *Aurenge Zeb,* play'd his part in Plotting against his Father, with the King of *Visapor* his Kinsman, before he was taken, and[50] lost his Kingdom; so natural is it to this Race to hate their Father. He is now about 55 Years of Age.[51]

The 4th. The 4th Son is call'd *Akbar,*[52] now 45 Years of Age, more ambitious than all the rest; for being sent by his Father in the Year 1680, with an Army of 30000 Men to make War on the *Ragia Lisonte,*[53] who borders on the Kingdom of *Asmire,* belonging to the *Mogul;* instead of subduing him, he suffered himself to be persuaded by that Idolater, and by his own Ambition, to turn his Arms against his own Father. Having thus join'd his Forces with those of *Ragia* against *Aurenge Zeb,* who could never have believ'd it, and making a Body of 70000 Horse, and a competent number of Foot, most of them *Ragipurs,*[54] he came into *Asmire,* where his Father was. Here whilst he rested his Army much fatigu'd with the long March, the Crafty Old Man having no sufficient Force to oppose him, had recourse to Stratagem. He therefore sent a Confident of his into the Enemies Camp, with a Letter directed to his Son; in which he commended his extraordinary wise Conduct in drawing the Idolaters to that place, to be all cut off, as had been agreed; and that he would advance the next day, to put it in Execution. The Eunuch had orders to behave himself so that the Enemy growing jealous, might secure him, and intercepting the Letter rely no more on *Akbar.* It fell out accordingly; and tho' he swore upon the *Alcoran,* that it was an invention of his Fathers to distract them, the chiefs of the Gentils would never believe him. These jealousies kept them so long employ'd, that *Aurenge Zeb,* as he had expected,[55] gain'd time to call his 2d Son to his defence with a powerful Army, who being come up, he defeated the *Raja* and *Akbar.* He putting himself with 4000 Horse under the Protection of *Samba,*[56] a Pagan Roicolet.[57] *Aurenge Zeb* made War so furiously on the said *Samba,* that he at last took him Prisoner, and caus'd his Head to be cut off, for having utter'd some indecent expressions in his presence. This Man's ruin was caus'd by Drunkenness; for as he was drinking in his Tent with his Women-dancers, being told by the advanc'd Guards that the *Mogul's* Army was advancing, instead of going to Arms, he caus'd their Heads to be cut off; saying, they[58] would not dare to come where he was ; the same he did by a second Centinel. His Son,[59] whose Head was not so full of Wine, sav'd himself with a 1000 Horse, leaving his Father behind, who was carry'd away Prisoner, and not long after to his Grave.

Akbar escaping this Storm[60] went to *Goa,* where the *Portugueses* furnish'd him with Ships to go over to *Ormus.* There he was nobly receiv'd by the *Cham,* and afterwards by Order of *Scia-Selemon,*[61] then King of *Persia,* attended by many Troops of Souldiers to the Court of *Ispahan ;* where he was courteously entertain'd, and had an allowance to maintain him suitable to his Quality ; as I observ'd in the 2d Part.[62] The Old Man fearing this Son's Valour, us'd several Arts[63] to draw him out of *Persia,* but with small hopes of Success, because *Akbar* was not so weak as to be ensnar'd by his Father. Whilst I was at *Ispahan,* some Eunuchs told me, they were sent by a certain *Omrah,* who Govern'd on the Borders of *Candahor,* with a Present of several thousand *Roupies* to this Prince, which he would not accept, and therefore they were going back with the Mony. They offer'd to carry me into *India* by Land, but I refus'd their kindness. I was afterwards inform'd by others, that this was a contrivance[64] of *Aurenge Zeb,* who had order'd the *Omrah,* of whom *Akbar* had desir'd to borrow some thousand *Roupies,* to make him a Present of them, and to endeavour by fair means to draw him into *India :* which *Akbar* understanding by means of his Sister, he refus'd the Present. *Aurenge Zeb* took many Towns from *Savagi* for having assisted this Prince ; and continuing the War, had besieg'd him in his Court of *Gingi.*[65] The City is seated between 7 Mountains, each of which has a Fort on the top, and can be reliev'd by ways unknown to the *Moguls,* so that they lay before them to no purpose with 30000 Horse and as many Foot. I have not hear'd since I left the Country, what was the event of the Siege, which had then lasted seven Years.

Aurenge Zeb's youngest Son is *Sikandar*[66] now about 30 Years of Age, and infected like the rest, with the contagious Distemper of Ambition. Therefore the Old Man, tho' after subduing the Kings of *Visapor,* and *Golconda,* he had no Enemies left, but *Savagi,* who is inconsiderable in regard of him ; yet fearing with much reason the perverse Inclination of his Sons, he had continu'd in Arms in the Field for 15 Years ; and particularly four Years at *Galgala,* after defeating *Akbar.* He said his Father *Sciah-Gehan* had not so much discretion ; for he might have learnt by many years Experience, that the Kings of *Indostan* when they grow Old, must keep at the head of Powerful Armies, to defend themselves against their Sons. Yet I am of Opinion that notwithstanding all his precautions, he will come to no better end than his Predecessors. All I have hitherto said concerning the intestine Wars between the *Moguls* was told me and affirm'd by several Souldiers in the Camp, who had been Eye-witnesses, and some gather'd out of creditable Authors.

CHAPTER V

OF THE GOVERNMENT OF THE GREAT MOGUL.

4 Secretaries of State.

For the better management of Publick Affairs, and due Administration of Justice, the King keeps four Secretaries of State, who are to acquaint him with all that happens in the Empire, and to receive his Orders.[1] The first of them is call'd *Bagsci,*[2] and has the Charge of Warlike affairs, and looks that the Souldiers be pay'd, punish'd, and rewarded, as also that the *Omrahs* keep their full complement of Men. The 2d is call'd *Adelet,*[3] who takes care that Justice be administered, both in Civil and Criminal cases, giving the King an account what Ministers behave themselves well, and what ill.[4] The 3d they call *Divan,*[5] and to him it belongs to divide the *Jagors*[6] or Feofs among the *Omrahs, Subas,* and other Commanders; and to see they do not oppress the Inhabitants of the places committed to them with too heavy[7] Impositions. The 4th is known by the name of *Cansamon;*[8] who is a Treasurer General,[9] that causes all the Revenues of the Empire to be brought into the Treasury, and every Week, lays before the King what every Province is worth, and what it yields, and what Mony remains in the King's Coffers.

Distribution of business.

There are particular days appointed for these Secretaries to inform the King because a private Audience would not suffice for such multiplicity of business. *Monday,* therefore is lay'd aside for the Affairs of *Lahor, Dehli* and *Agra; Tuesday* for *Cabul; Wednesday* for the Kingdoms of *Bengala* and *Patna; Thursday* for that of *Guzaratte; Saturday* for that of *Brampour;* and *Sunday* for *Decan;* no business being done on *Friday,* because it is the *Mahometan* Festival.

Audiences.

Aurenge Zeb notwithstanding his continual application to these private Audiences with his Ministers, yet never fail'd of the Publick, except on *Fridays,* for the good of the Subjects; and this sometimes he did in three several places, one call'd *Divanxas,*[10] the other *Gosalxana,*[11] and the 3d *Adalet.*[12]

Absolute Power.

The Great *Mogul* is so absolute, that there being no written Laws, his Will in all things is a Law, and the last decision of all Causes, both Civil and Criminal. He makes a Tyrannical use of this absolute Power; for being Lord of all the Land, the Princes themselves have no certain place of aboad, the King altering it at Pleasure ; and the same with the poor Peasants who have sometimes the Land they have cultivated taken from them, and that which is untill'd given them in lieu of it ; besides that they are oblig'd every year to give the King three parts of the Crop.[13] He never admits any Body into his Presence, empty handed ; and sometimes refuses admittance to draw a greater Present. For this reason the *Omrahs* and *Nababs* appointed to govern the Provinces, oppress the People in the most miserable[14] manner imaginable.

CHAPTER VI

OF THE REVENUES AND WEALTH OF THE GREAT MOGUL.

An infinite quantity of *Roupies,* is continually flowing into the Great *Mogul*'s Exchequer ; for besides the usual Taxes and excessive Imposts, the Subjects must pay for their Land, which is all his. Besides when a General, or any other Person who has receiv'd the King's Pay dyes ; all his Goods fall to the King, without leaving the Children so much as a maintenance ; a Custom *Aurenge Zeb* condemn'd, when he spoke of his Father, and yet all employments both Civil and Military are sold. For this reason no Family can continue long great ; but sometimes the Son of an *Omrah* goes a begging. Add to all this, that tho' in so vast an Empire, there be some Barren Lands, yet there are some Kingdoms wonderful[1] Fruitful, as is that of *Bengala,*[1a] which exceeds *Egypt,* not only in Plenty of Rice, Corn, Sugar, and all other necessaries for the support of Humane Life ; but in the richest Commodities, as Silk, Cotton, Indigo and the like. Besides the Country is so Populous, that the Handicrafts,[2] tho' naturally given to sloath, are forc'd either by necessity or choice, to apply themselves to work on Carpets, Brocades, Embroidery, Cloth of Gold and Silver, and all sorts of Manufactures in Silk and Cotton, generally worn there ; besides those transported every Year, by an infinite number of Ships, not only into other Parts of *Asia,* but into *Africk* and *Europe.* *Mogul's great Revenue.*

That the Reader may form some Idea of the Wealth of this Empire, he is to observe that all the Gold and Silver, which circulates throughout the World, at last Centers[3] here. It is well known that as much of it as comes out of *America,* after running through several Kingdoms of *Europe,* goes partly into *Turky,* for several sorts of Commodities ; and part into *Persia,* by the way of *Smirna*[4] for Silk. Now the Turks not being able to abstain from Coffee, which comes from *Hyeman,*[5] and *Arabia* *Gold and Silver centers in this Empire.*

Fœlix ; nor Persia, *Arabia,* and the *Turks* themselves to go without the Commodities of *India,* send[6] vast quantities of Mony to *Moka*[7] on the Red Sea, near *Babel Mandel ;*[8] to *Bassora* at the bottom of the *Persian* Gulgh ; and to *Bander Abassi* and *Gomeron,* which is afterwards sent over in Ships to *Indostan.* Besides the *Indian, Dutch, English,* and *Portuguese* Ships, that every Year carry the Commodities of *Indostan,* to *Pegu, Tanasserri, Siam, Ceylon, Achem,*[9] *Macassar,* the *Maldive* Islands, *Mozambique* and other Places, must of necessity convey much Gold and Silver thither,[10] from those Countries. All that the *Dutch* fetch from the Mines in *Japan,* sooner or later, goes to *Indostan ;* and the goods carry'd hence into *Europe,* whether to *France, England,* or *Portugal,* are all purchas'd for ready Mony, which remains there.

I was told that the *Mogul* receives from only his Hereditary Countries, eighty *Carores*[11] of *Roupies*[12] a Year (every *Carore* is ten Millions) they could give me no certain account what the Conquer'd Kingdoms yield.

Thevenot. Voy. des. Ind. c. 3. p. 12. De. Imp. Mog. sive India vera. p. 142.

There is an Author,[13] not well acquainted with this Affair, who reduces this Monarch's Revenue to 330 Millions: Another[14] on the other side makes it infinite, and that alone which he says is in the Treasury, seems Fabulous. But they that will judge of it, by his expences must consider that the *Mogul* has dispers'd throughout his Empire 300000 Horse, and 400000 Foot, who have all great Pay.[15] At Court the daily expence is 50000 *Roupies,* to maintain the Elephants, Horses, Dogs, Hawks, Tigers, and Deer ; as also some hundreds of black and white Eunuchs to look to the Royal Palaces, Musitians, and Dancers. I am therefore of Opinion, that next to the Emperor of *China,* no Monarch in the World is equal to the Great *Mogul* in strength and Riches.

CHAPTER VII

OF THE WEAPONS, AND FORCES OF THE GREAT MOGUL.

Weapons us'd by the *Moguls.*

The Arms offensive of the Moguls are broad heavy Swords,[1] bow'd[2] like Scimitars ; and those made in the Country, being apt to break, the *English* furnish them with such as are made in *Europe,* ill shap'd Daggers, which they always wear hanging to their Girdle ; Bows and Arrows, Javelins, Pistols, Muskets ; and Pikes 12 Foot long, for the Foot ; but most of the Souldiers have Bows and Arrows. They have also Cannon in their Cities, and Armies.

Their Arms defensive,[3] are a round Buckler two foot Diameter, made of black Hides of wild Buffalos; with many Nails with large heads to ward off Arrows or Swords; Coats of Mail, Breast-Plates, Head-pieces,[4] and covering for their Arms down to their Wrists. Arms defensive.

As for the Souldiers pay, the *Mogul* manages it after a different manner than all other Princes in the World; for he pays them not himself, but gives the *Omrahs Jaghirs,* that is, Tenures of Lands[5] to maintain a certain number, as was said elsewhere, and this even to the Princes of the Blood. Souldiers how pay'd.

The *Omrahs* are divided into *Hazariis,*[6] *Cuhzariis, Panges, Hechets, Deh-Hazariis,* and *Duazdehazariis,*[7] of which last sort the King's Eldest Son was. Their pay is proportionable to the number of Horse they keep; besides which the King allows them a Pension for their own use. But they always cheat the Souldiers of part of their Pay, and by that means grow vastly rich; especially if they happen to have a good *Jaghir.* Some are oblig'd to keep 500 Horse, and have about 5000 *Neapolitan* Crowns Revenue a Month. 'Tis true they spend all they get in Presents they are forc'd to make the King every year, upon certain Festivals, every Man according to his condition; and in keeping so many Women, Servants, Camels, and Horses of great value. Degrees of *Omrahs.*

The Number of *Omrahs* throughout the Empire is not settled, but they are generally under 40. They are prefer'd to the greatest Governments, and chief Posts at Court, and in the Army; and therefore are, as they themselves say, the Pillars of the Empire. They appear abroad with noble Equipages; some on Elephants, others a Horseback, or on *Palankines,* attended by a considerable number of Horse, and by the Guards of their Palaces; as also by abundance of Servants, some of whom go before to clear the way, others drive away the Flies, or keep off the Dust with Peacocks tails, others carry Water to drink, and other things. All that reside at Court, are oblig'd to go twice a day to pay their respects to the King; that is, at ten in the Morning, and about Sun sent, in the place where he administers Justice; or else they lose part of their Pay. They are also to Mount the Guard once a Week for 24 Hours; and that day the King sends them their Meat, which they receive with much respect, doing the *Taslim*[8] three times, that is, an obeysance after their manner towards the Royal apartment, laying their right Hand on the Ground, and then on their Head. They are also oblig'd to attend the King at all times, as was said above. Their number and duty.

The *Mansebdars* are Gentlemen, or Horse,[9] who have very honourable Pay, and is call'd *Manseb,*[10] but less than the *Omrahs.* They are much respected in the Camp, because they *Mansebdars.*

may easily rise to the degree of *Omrahs*, and own no superiour but the King. They differ from the others in this particular that they are not oblig'd to maintain above 4, or 5 Horse. As for their Pay they have 150 *Roupies* a Month, and sometimes 700, but instead of having them in ready Mony, they are forc'd to take the old Furniture of the King's House, at excessive Rates. There is no fix'd number of them,[11] but they are more than the *Omrahs* ; there being 2, or 300 of them very often at Court, besides those in the Provinces, and Armies.

Rowzinders. The 3rd degree is of the *Rowzinders*,[12] who are also Horse,[13] but paid by the day, as their Name imports. Their Pay is not inferior to that of the *Mansebdars*, but the Post is not so honourable. The number of them is very great, and many of them are Clerks and under Clerks.

The light Horse are subject to the *Omrahs*, and those are counted the best, who have two Horses,[14] branded with their *Omrahs* mark on the Leg. Their pay is not fix'd, and depends on the generosity of the *Omrah*, but they stand[15] the *Mogul* in at least 25 *Roupies* a Month, considering the Revenues he assigns for their maintenance.

The Foot. The Foot and Musketiers are in a miserable condition, some of them having 20, some 15, and others ten *Roupies* a Month. They carry their Rest ty'd to[16] the Musket, which they make but ill use of, for fear of burning their great Beard. The

Cannon. Artillery is divided into two sorts, the heavy Cannon, and the light, as they call it. The heavy consists of between 60 and 70 Guns, without reckoning 300 Field-pieces, fix'd on Camels,[17] as Pedreroes are on our Backs.[18] The other, 50 or 60 small Brass[19] Guns, which are the 2d sort, are on Carriages, with little red Banners, each drawn by two Horses ; a third being led by,[20] to rest sometimes the one, and sometimes the other. Tho' the heavy Cannon cannot always follow the King, who sometimes goes out of the Road, to hunt, or take some other diversion, the light always does ;[21] and when he is near the place appointed to Incamp, it is fir'd, that the Army may know he is arriv'd. All this Artillery, especially the heavy, is under the direction of *Franks*, or Christian Gunners, who have extraordinary pay ; especially the *Portuguese, English, Dutch, Germans*, and *French*, who go from *Goa*, or run away from aboard Ships. Some of them formerly had 200 *Roupies* a Month ; but now the *Moguls* have learnt somewhat of the Art they have less.[22] There is a General of the Artillery whose Pay is a Million a year, out of which he is to keep 200 Men.

Rajapurs. Besides the *Mogul* Souldiers, there are the Strangers, hir'd of the *Rajas*, who serve the *Mogul* for very great Pay, bringing with them a certain number of *Rajapurs*, and doing the same Duty as the *Omrahs* do ; but with this difference, that they will not keep Guard in Forts, but in their own Tents, that they may not be shut up 24 hours. The *Mogul* keeps them in his pay, as also the *Patens,* because they are Men of Courage; and there are *Rajas* that can raise 20000 Horse[23] upon occasion; as also to sow Discord and Jealousies among them, by favouring one more than another, and by that means be the safer from their contrivances,[24] and from the others who are not in his Pay.

The Souldiers of the Country differ neither in Offices nor Discipline from that already mention'd, but that they never follow the King; but every Kingdom keeps its own to secure the Frontiers against Strangers, as the *Persians, Oganis,*[25] *Baluccis* and others. Country Troops.

All Souldiers whatsoever[26] receive their Pay duly every 2 Months from the King's Treasurer, except those that are pay'd by the *Omrahs,* as was said before. Nor is there any Danger their Pay should be kept from them; for all People here living either by their Industry, or by serving the King (for want of private Revenues)[27] if they were not well[28] paid, they must either starve, or Mutiny. And to say the Truth, the greatest wonder in that Country is to see so many thousands live on the King's Pay. It is not so in *Europe,* for sometimes Souldiers have something of their own; or when they want[29] Pay live upon others. Forces duly Paid.

The number of Troops they said the *Mogul* kept when I was there mounted to[30] 300000 Horse and 400000 Foot. Part of these were[31] in the Camp at Galgala; 60000 Horse and Foot at the Siege of *Gingi.* The third Camp was of[32] 7000 Horse and 10000 Foot; the 4th of[33] 12000 Horse, commanded at *Pernala*[34] by *Azam-Scia*'s Son the King's Grandson, and the rest were distributed about the Frontiers and in Garrisons.[35]

CHAPTER VIII

THE MANNERS, HABIT, MARRIAGES AND FUNERALS OF THE MOGULS.

There are two Principal Festivals kept in the Court of the Great *Mogul,* the one call'd *Barsgant,*[1] the other *Tol.*[2] The first is on the King's Birth day, or those of the Princes of the Blood, because *Bars* in the Country Language signifies Year, and *Gant* a Knot, and those People every Year make a knot in a Cord, they[3] either wear about them or keep at home, to know their Age. This Solemnity is kept with great Pomp, all the great Ones coming to wish the King many Happy years with Presents of Mony and Jewels. *Sciah Gehan* was mightily pleas'd they should present him with Gold Vessels set with The *Mogul's* Birth day.

Jewels, to hold sweet Waters,[4] which he plac'd in the Chamber that serv'd for his leud Practices. It was set out with Looking Glasses[5] adorn'd with precious Stones, and all the Roof sparkling with Diamonds. That Day the *Mogul* sits on the famous Throne begun by *Tamerlan* and finish'd by *Sciah Gehan.* It is all over set with Diamonds, Emerauds, Rubies, Pearls and Saphires ; especially the Pearls on the twelve little Pillars, which close the three sides, are beyond all that can be imagin'd.[6] Then the Roof of it and all other Parts is so orderly[7] enrich'd with jewels of inestimable Value, all found within the Empire, that some make the Value of it to rise to fifty Millions, but in reality it is not to be Valu'd.[8]

Taver. Voy. des Indes l. 2. c. 8.

The Festival call'd *Tol.*

The second Festival is that of *Tol,* which in that Language signifies Weight. Some suppose it to be so call'd because the King weighs himself in a pair of Scales, to see whether he is grown Fatter, but having ask'd the question in the Camp of several credible Persons, and particularly of Christians born at *Agra* and *Dehli,* who had serv'd there many Years, they told me it was a meer Romance ;[9] for not only *Aurenge Zeb,* but none of his Predecessors ever weigh'd themselves.[10] 'Tis true this Festival is kept in the King's House ; but they weigh Mony, Jewels, and other Things of value presented by the great Men and Favourites, which are afterwards distributed among the Poor with great Solemnity. It is done some Days after the *Barsgant,* either sooner, or later, as the King thinks fit.

Description of the *Indians.*

The *Indians* are well shap'd, it being rare to find any of them crooked,[11] and for Stature like the *Europeans.* They have black Hair, but not Curl'd, and their Skin is of an Olive Colour ; and they do not love White, saying it is the Colour of Leprousie. They wash often, anointing themselves after it with rich Oyls and Oyntments. They live in low Houses, with Trees about them, so that their Cities at a distance look like Woods.[12] There are no Inns for Travellers among them as was said at first ;[13] but in the Cities and great Towns they have some Places call'd *Sarays,* where Strangers may have Houseroom. They use Carts to travel in (which are shut when there are Women in them,) drawn by Oxen, and Asses when the Journey is short. The great Men and those that are well to pass[14] are carry'd upon Elephants, or in *Palankines.* There is none of them but endeavours the best he can to go to *Mecca,* to become a *Hagi*[15] or Saint. They delight very much in Hunting, and make[16] use of Dogs and tame Leopards. They take Water Foul[17] after this manner. They go into the Water up to the Chin, covering their Faces with Birds of the same sort they would take, artificially made ; Then the Bird coming near his likeness they draw him down by the Legs and stifle him. The *Chineses* and *Mexicans* do the same, as shall be said in its Place. Being excellent Archers they shoot Birds flying, with Arrows.

The *Mahometans* of *Indostan*, tho' barbarous in other Respects, are not so Deceitful, so Proud, or such Enemies to Christians, as the *Turks*; and a Christian may therefore keep them company with safety. The *Pagans* are still more just to Travellers. As for Courage neither *Mahometans* nor *Gentils* have much of it. The best of them are the *Baluccis* Borderers on *Persia*, the *Patans* of the Kingdom of *Bengala*, and the *Rasbootis*[18] very great Thieves. Their Disposition.

The Languages spoken at Court are the *Arabian* and the *Persian*. As for Sciences they can make no progress in them for want of Books; for they have none but some small manuscript Works of *Aristotle* and *Avicenne*[19] in *Arabick*. They hold Astrology in great account, in so much that the King undertakes nothing without the advice of his Astrologers. In Physick they have but small skill, and cure several Diseases by Fasting. They also delight in Musick, for which they have[20] several sorts of Instruments. Language and Learning.

They spend all they have in Luxury keeping a vast number of Servants, but above all of Concubines. These being many every one of them strives to be belov'd above the rest, using all manner of Allurements,[21] Perfumes and sweet Oyntments. Sometimes to heighten their Masters Lusts they give him Compositions of Pearl, Gold, Opium and Amber; or else much Wine that he may require Company in Bed. Then some drive away the Flies, others rub his Hands and Feet, others Dance, others play on Musick, and others do other things; and hence it is that for the most part they take the lawful Wifes place; who sitting near her Husband modestly winks at this Affront, till she has an opportunity to revenge herself. These Women are committed to the custody of Eunuchs, but it is delivering up the Sheep to the Wolves; so lascivious are the Women. And yet they are excusable, because the Husbands, tho' they be Peasants, lye apart from their Wives, and only call them when they have occasion.

The great Men have noble Structures, with several Courts, and the Tops of the Houses flat to take the Air, and Fountains with Carpets about them to sit and receive Visits from their Friends. Inferiors salute laying their Hand on their Head, but Equals only bow their Body. In their Discourse they are modest and civil; not using so many actions with their Hands, nor talking so loud as some *Europeans* do. The Table is spread on the Ground without Napkins or Table-Cloth; nor do they Drink till they have done Eating. Their greatest delight is to chew *Betlè* all Day.

The Vests both of Men and Women are narrow towards the Waste, and hang down half way the Leg; under them they wear long Breeches down to their Ankles, so that they serve for Stockins. The Foot remains bare, with a sort of flat Shooes, Habit.

like our Slippers; which are easily slipt off when they go into Rooms, to keep them clean, they being cover'd with Carpets. They wrap a very fine piece of Muslin or Calico about their Head, and never uncover it to do Reverence to Superiors, but bow their Body, putting their right Hand on the Ground and then on the Head, as if they said they submitted themselves to be trampled on by them. They generally wear the Vest and Turbant of Cotton, but the Sash is of Silk and Gold.

Women. The *Mahometan* Women do not appear in publick, except only the vulgar Sort, and the leud Ones. They cover their Heads, but the Hair hangs down behind in several Tresses. Many of them bore their Noses to wear a Gold Ring set with Stones.

Marriages. The *Mahometan Indians* Marry very Young, but the Idolaters at all Ages. These last may not have several Wives at once like the *Mahometans;* but when the first is Dead may take another, provided she be a Maid, and of the same Race, or Tribe. The Ceremony is thus, If they be Persons of Quality they make the Cavalcade at Night with Lights, abundance of People go before making a displeasing Concert with several Instruments, as Pipes, Kettle-Drums as long as a Barrel, and Copper-Plates, which they beat.[22] Then follow abundance of Children a Horseback, next to whom comes the Bridegroom, well Clad and Mounted, with several *Banians* about him, with their Vests and *Civas*[23] dy'd in *Zafran,*[24] and other Persons carrying Umbrellos, and Banners; and having taken a round about the City goes to the Brides-House. Here a *Brachman* having said some Prayers over them both, puts a Cloth between the Husband and Wife, and orders the Husband with his bare Foot to touch the Wifes,[25] and then the Wife the Husbands, which done the Marriage is concluded. When the Woman is carry'd home, the Goods go before, being for the most part Stuffs of several Colours, and a Cradle for the Child that is to be got;[26] all this with the noise of several Instruments. Rich People make a Hut before their Houses, cover'd both inside and outside with Stuffs and Carpets, to entertain their Guests under Shelter. Sometimes they treat them for eight Days together.

Women Fruitful. All the Women are Fruitful, which is caus'd by the Air and Provisions,[27] and are so easily deliver'd, that some of them go wash[28] in the River the same Day. They bring up their Children naked till seven Years of Age, nor do they take much care to teach them to go,[29] but let them tumble about the Ground as much as they will, as soon[30] as they are Born.

Barbarous Liberty. In *Malabar* the Women (even those that are of Quality and Kings Sisters) have the liberty to choose a Man to lye with them. When a *Naire*[31] or *Gentil* is in a Ladies Chamber, he leaves his Staff or his Sword at the Door, that others who would go in may see the Place is taken up; and no Man has the boldness to disturb him. Thus there being no possibility of knowing who is the Father of the Child that is born into the World, the Succession is order'd after another manner ; that is, when one dies his Sisters Children Inherit, because there can be no doubt made of the Kindred. *Thev. Voy. des. Ind.* l. 2. p. 258.

When a Man or Woman has committed such a Crime as to be expell'd their Tribe ; as if a Woman had lain with a *Mahometan,* she must live for a certain time only upon Corn found in the Cows Dung, if she will[32] be receiv'd again. Punishment.

As to the manner of Burying, the most usual is to wash the Body first in a River, or Pool ; then burn it in a neighbouring *Pagod,* and throw the Ashes into the same Water. In some Places they leave them by the River side. The manner of carrying them is also different, according to the Fashions of each Country. In some the Body well Clad, and sitting is carry'd with Drums beating, and a long Train of Kindred and Friends ;[33] and after being wash'd is encompass'd with Wood. The Wife who has been that while[34] near the Body singing, and expressing a desire to Die, is afterwards bound by a *Brachman* near the dead Body and burnt with it ; the Friends pouring Oyl[35] on them that they might consume the faster. Burials.

In other Places the Bodies are carry'd cover'd on a Bier to the River side ; and after they have been wash'd they are put into a Hut full of sweet Wood, if the dead Person has left Mony to defray the charge ; then the Woman that is to be burnt, takes leave of her Kindred and Friends, showing a contempt of Death, and sits down in the Hut, bearing up her Husband on her Knees. Then recommending herself to the Prayers of the *Brachmans,* desires them to set Fire speedily. A Barbarous Inhumanity ! And yet they make a scruple of killing Flies and Pismires.

In other Places they fill wide deep Trenches with combustible Matter, where laying the Husbands Body the *Brachmans* cast in the Woman, after they have Sung and Danc'd. Sometimes there are maiden Slaves, that throw themselves in after their Master to show the love they bear him, then the Ashes are cast into the River.

There are other Places where they Bury the Husband's Bodies with the Legs across ; they put the Woman into the same Grave, and when they have cover'd them up to the Neck[36] the *Brachmans* come and strangle her. Those wretched Women that refuse to be Burnt, are[37] to shave their Heads, and remain Widows all their Lives ; are despis'd by their Family and Tribe, because they have fear'd Death, and can never recover their Reputation, whatsoever good Actions they do, unless some young Woman of singular Beauty should happen to get a second Husband. Yet there are some that transgress the Laws of

Widowhood ; and because their Kindred expell them,[38] they have recourse to the *Mahometans* or Christians, forsaking their own Religion. In short the Gentils make the Widows Honour consist in being Burnt wth the Bodies of their Husbands, and if they be ask'd the Reason they can alledge none but antient Custom.

Since the *Mahometans* are become Sovereigns of *India* they do not easily consent to this Inhumanity,[39] which the *Brachmans* would have held up for their own Interest ; for as was said above, they who alone may touch the Ashes, carry off all the Gold and Silver the wretched Woman had about her. The great *Mogul*[40] and other Princes have commanded the Governours of their Towns to hinder[41] the Practice of this Abuse, but they do not so strictly observe it,[42] provided they have considerable Presents made them, and thus the difficulty they find in getting the leave saves many Women the Dishonour.

Mourning. The Mourning us'd[43] by the *Gentils* is Shaving their Beard and Head, when any Kindred within the third degree Dye. The Women break their Glass and Ivory Bracelets they wear on their Arms, as they also do at their King's Death. Having before spoke of[44] the *Mahometan* Ceremonies it is needless to repeat it in this Place.

CHAPTER IX

OF THE CLIMATE, FRUIT, FLOWERS, MINERALS, BEASTS AND COIN, OF INDOSTAN.

Heats and Seasons. Generally throughout all *Indostan* the Heat is Excessive, except near the Mountains. We *Europeans* fare ill there because of the Seasons differing from ours ; because their Winter begins in *June* and ends in *September ;* tho' there falls less Rain than at *Goa*. Before and after Winter there are dreadful Storms and Hurricans, three Months from the North and three from the South,[1] so that there is no Sailing[2] about *India* but[3] six months in the Year.

Clear Air. Between *Suratte* and *Agra* the Metropolis of the *Mogul*'s Dominions, it only Rains at one certain time of the Year, that is, during those three Months the Sun is about the Tropick of *Cancer ;* the other nine Months the Sky is so clear, that there is scarce a Cloud[4] to be seen above the *Horizon*.

Product. Having spoke of the Fruit when I was at *Goa*, there is no need of adding any more. *Indostan*[5] abounds in Rice, excellent Wheat, and all sorts of Grain,[6] vast Flocks and Herds of Cattle, Butter and Cheese. There being no Grapes, the Wine is brought out of *Arabia* and *Persia ;* or is made in the Country of *Raisins,* which being also brought from abroad, they steep[7] and boil in Water. The common Drink of the Country is distill'd *Sura,* but not very wholesome.

Flowers and Herbs.

The Flowers are very fragrant, and much better Colour'd than any in *Europe.* There are many Simples,[8] which they carry into *Europe* for Physical Uses, which I do not describe, because I will not Treat of what others have given an Account of.

Metals.

As for Metals the *Mogul's* Country affords none but Copper, Iron, and Lead, but the want of others is abundantly made amends for by the rich Mines of Diamonds and other precious Stones. The best is that in the Kingdom of *Golconda,* seven Days Journey East of *Agra,* which the Natives call *Gani,* and the *Persians Cular.*[9] It is in a Plain five Miles in Compass, between a Village and some Mountains, which produce nothing at all. They say it was discover'd 140 Years since after this manner. A Peasant sowing in that Plain, found such a rich Diamond, that tho' he did not understand those things, yet he would carry it to a Merchant of *Golconda* who delighted in them. The News was immediately spread about the City, and every one that had Mony digging in that Place, there were Stones found from 12 to 40 Carats ; and particularly that great Diamond of some hundred Carats, which *Emir Gamla,* the King of *Golconda's* General gave *Aurenge Zeb* when he came into his Service.[10] Afterwards the King took the Mine to himself, and now the Merchants buy it of him by Spans.

Diamond Mines.

How the Diamonds are found.

The Manner of Digging[11] the Stones is this. First they enclose a spot of Ground much bigger than that they Buy to Dig, with a little Wall two Spans high ; then they dig the Ground mark'd out by the King's Officers 12 or 14 Spans down to the Water, below which there is no hopes of any Diamonds, and carry the Earth into the aforesaid Enclosure in great Baskets. When it is all together they fill the Place full of Water, and leave it so till it is all Mud. Then they add more Water, and opening the Holes which are at every Step in the Wall, the Mud runs out, and the Cravel remains ; which is again cover'd with Water, if it be not clean. When dry they put it into Baskets for the Sand to drop through, and then putting it into the same Place they beat it with long Staves. Then they take it up again and sifting it,[12] they spread it and pick out the Diamonds in the presence of the Buyer, and of the Officers, who take those that are above a certain weight for the King.[13]

Diamonds in *Borneo.*

There are Diamond Mines at a Place call'd *Raolconda,*[14] in the Province of *Carnasica,* in the Kingdom of *Visapour,* but they do not work at them. The King of *Succadan* in the Island of *Borneo*[15] has some better, but there are few of them, and they are found in the Sand of the River *Succadan.*

Gazellers.

Besides the Birds and Beasts *Europe* affords, *India* has others peculiar to it; as for instance the *Gazellers,* of which we have spoke in the two precedent Volumns; they have Horns a Span and a half long, and twisted or spiral. To take them they make use of the tame Leopard,[16] or of the Male *Gazelle* thus. They tye him with a Rope wound about under his Belly; and when they see a Flock of *Gazelles* let him go among them. The Male that is in the Flock, being jealous comes out to attack him, and his Horns being spiral or winding does so intangle himself,[17] that not being able to retire when he would, the Hunters have time to take him.

Other Beasts.

There are also wild Cows and other wild Beasts we spoke of when we gave an account of the Game at *Damam,* Camels, Dromedaries, Rhinocerots,[18] as tall as a large Ox, and Elephants. There are several ways of taking these;[19] sometimes they dig Trenches and cover them, into which when they fall they cannot get out. In other Places they carry a Female[20] into the Woods just at the time when she is in her Lust;[21] at her Cries the wild Male comes, and couples with her contrary to[22] other Beasts, Belly to Belly,[23] in the narrow Place where she was left. When the Male would be gone, he finds the way stopp'd up, and the Hunters at a distance, throw over him great and small Ropes;[24] so that his Trunk and Legs being secur'd they can come near without Danger. However they lead him away between two tame Elephants,[25] and beat him if he makes a noise. Afterwards he grows tame among the rest of his kind; and then he that has them in charge, teaches him to Salute Friends with his Trunk, to Threaten, or Strike whom he pleases, and to kill a Man Condemn'd to that sort of Death, with an Iron fix'd at the end of a Pole, and then the Manager[26] sits upon his Neck. It is of it self a very tractable Creature, when it is not Enrag'd or in Lust; for then he that Rules it[27] is in Danger. They quiet him with Artificial Fire-works, or directing him into a River, where, tho' so large, he swims extraordinary well. The She Elephants carry their young 12 Months;[28] they live 100 years;[28a] and carry about 3200 Pounds weight *Spanish.*[29] Those of *Ceylon* tho' smaller are the most valu'd of any in India,[30] because they have more Courage, and as the *Indians* imagine are respected by the others. But those of *Golconda, Cochinchina, Siam,* and the Island *Sumatra* are stronger, and more surefooted on the Mountains. It is dear keeping of them;[31] for besides the Flesh they eat,[31a] Paste made of Meal with Sugar Canes,[32] and other things, they give them *Aqua-vitae* to drink.

Elephants.

There are also Stags, Lions, Tigers, and Leopards, which they hunt with good Dogs, and several[33] Creatures not to be found in *Europe,* of which mention was made among the Game of *Daman.*

I must not omit here to give an account of the Musk Wild Goat[34] found in the Country of *Azmer*. Its Snout is like a Goat, the Hair like a Stag, and its Teeth like a Dog. Under the Belly it has a little Bladder, as big as an Egg, full of a thick congeal'd Blood, which being cut off is ty'd up in a Skin, that the scent may not evaporate. After which the Beast lives but a short time. They are also taken on the cold Mountains of the Kingdom of *Butan,* in the Latitude of 56 and 60 Degrees, but the greatest quantity and the best comes out of the Country of the *Tartars* bordering on *China,* where they make a great Trade of it. The Sent is so strong that having bought a little at *Peking,* it was smelt at a great distance, as if my Portumantue had been full of it, which caus'd some dispute with the Customers. They so adulterate it,[35] mixing it with other Blood, that when it comes into *Europe* it is not a quarter Musk. Musk-Goat.

As for Foul, there are all[36] in *India* that *Europe* affords, and many peculiar to the Country. In the Woods there are abundance of Peacocks, several sorts of Parrots and green Pigeons. There are most Beautiful Birds, to be kept in Cages, both sightly for their Feathers, and Pleasant for singing sweetly. I saw some half as big as Wheat-ears, all spotted like a Tiger.[37] Besides the Wild Hens, there is a sort of tame ones whose Skin and Bones are very black, but they are well tasted.[38] Foul.

The Mony Coin'd in *Indostan* is, *Roupies,* half *Roupies,* and quarter *Roupies* of Silver ; as also *Roupies* of Gold, worth 13 Silver *Roupies* and a quarter, or six pieces of Eight *Spanish* Mony, half *Roupies,* and quarters. On, both sorts there are *Persian* Characters[39] with the Name of the City, where it is Coin'd, and the King's name on the Reverse. There are also Copper Pieces, call'd *Pesies,*[40] 54 whereof make a *Roupie* of silver. The *Rajas,* or Pagan Petty Kings, in their Dominions Coin Gold pieces call'd *Pagods,*[41] because they have a little *Pagod* stamp'd on them, and these are worth a *Zecchine* of *Venice.* Both the Gold and Silver, are much finer than the Gold of the *Spanish* Pistoles,[42] and Silver of their Pieces of Eight. Foreign Coin is also current in the *Mogul's* Country ; as *Zecchines,* by which there is much got,[43] Pieces of Eight, *Abassis*[44] of *Persia,* and other sorts ; but more particularly in the Ports, and places of Trade. Coin.

They reckon by *Leckes,* each worth 100000 *Roupies ; Crous* or *Crorores,* which are 100 *Leckes ;* and *Arebs,*[45] that are ten *Crous.* The *Batman,* and *Man,*[46] are Weights of 55 Pounds. Another smaller Weight is call'd *Goer* or *Keer,*[47] but they sometimes change according to the Princes will.[48]

A VOYAGE ROUND THE WORLD

BY DR. JOHN FRANCIS GEMELLI CARERI.

PART III

Containing the most Remarkable Things he saw in

INDOSTAN

BOOK III

CHAPTER I

OF THE SEVERAL RELIGIONS IN INDOSTAN.

This vast Empire, besides the Natives, is inhabited by *Persians, Tartars, Abissinians, Armenians, Jews, Christians, Mahometans,* and others[1] ; but the most universal Religions are the *Mahometan,* and the *Pagan ;* for the first is profess'd by the *Mogul,* and the other by the antient Lords and People of the Country. Having discours'd fully of the *Mahometan* in the first Volumn, and these Emperors being of the *Turkish* Sect,[2] it only Remains to give a short Account in this Chapter of the

Transmigration of Souls.

Pagan. All the *Gentils* in *India* hold the Transmigration of Souls, like the *Pythagoreans,*[3] by which means, in their Opinion, the Souls after Death receive the reward or punishment of their good or evil Actions, being put into good or bad Creatures. And therefore they pay singular Honour to the Cow, by the Advice of *Ramak*[4] their Legislator, as being Creatures that, besides the good they do to Men, shall receive the Souls of good Men. By reason of this same opinion, they take special Care of all other Creatures ; not only forbearing to Eat them, but using all means to prevent others Killing them ; and as was said before, in some Cities they have Hospitals, where they are at a vast Expence in looking after sick Creatures.[5]

84 Tribes.

Tho' they all Profess one Religion, yet they are divided into 84 Sects,[6] or Tribes ;[7] each of which has its particular Rites and Ceremonies ; and some peculiar Profession or Trade, which their Children never leave, without[8] they would be for ever reputed Infamous ; as I was told by a *Brachman,* I sent for on purpose to be inform'd in what relates to them.

Brachmans the first Tribe, 10 Sects of them.

The first and principal Tribe is that of the *Brachmans,* who are Professors of Learning, and Priests of their Religion, which is divided into ten several Sects. The first five feed on Herbs, and Grain,[9] without ever Eating any Thing that has Life ; and are call'd, the first *Maratas,*[10] the second *Telanga,*[11] the third *Canara,*[12] the fourth *Drovaras,*[13] and the fifth *Guzaratti ;*[14] the four first Eat in one anothers Houses, but not in those of the *Guzarattes.* The other five Sects Eat of all living Creatures, except Fish ; and are call'd *Gauri,*[15] *Canogia,*[16] *Triatori,*[17] which are the *Brachmans* of *Goa; Gagavali,*[18] and *Ponzaput,*[19] none of which Eat in the House of another.

Whom they may Marry, and whom not.

In these 10 Sects, or Orders of *Brachmans,* no Man may Marry out of his own Tribe. In the cross Line, in which only they may take Wives, the Prohibition reaches to the seventh Degree[20] of Consanguinity, or Affinity ; but the Daughter of a Brother may Marry the Son of a Sister, that is, her Cousin ;[21] yet not the contrary that is the Son of the Brother with the Daughter of the Sister, that the same Blood may not come into the Family. The *Guzarattis* are not Subject to this law.

All these 10 Tribes of *Brachmans* Converse with one another; but if one comes that is not wash'd, he may not touch any Body, lest he Defile them ; it being a Precept among them to wash their Body Morning, Noon and Night. Their Widows do not Marry again, and if they will Burn themselves with their Husbands Body, they gain much Reputation ;[22] such as will not are look'd upon as Cowardly, and Infamous.

Rajapours the second Tribe.

The second Tribe is that of the *Rajapours,* or Princes descended from warlike Men. These only Eat in the Houses of their own Tribe, or in those of the *Brachmans,* in which all the others may Eat, each according to its Quality. The Wives of *Rajapours* cannot avoid being Burn'd with their Husbands, if they have no Male Issue ; and if they refuse, are carry'd by Force. Tho' other Tribes are allow'd but one Wife ;[23] the *Rajapours,* as being free Princes may have as many as they please. Some of these *Rajapours* Border on the Lands of *Goa ;* for besides *Savagi,* there is *Chiotia,*[24] near *Daman ;* and *Grasia,*[25] not far from *Suratte,* both Robbers, living among Mountains, like Beasts. The King of *Portugal* allows *Chiotia* 30000 *Mamudis,*[26] which make 5500 Ducats of *Naples,* and the *Mogul* gives the other a like Sum out of the Neighbourhood of *Suratte,* that they may not Rob, but defend Travellers against Thieves. The King *Penti,*[27] near *Bazaim,* might more properly be call'd King of the Woods, he Living in them, like an Out-law. There is some difference of Sects among the *Rajapours ;* but they all agree in eating Fish, except Beef, and tame Swine.

Banians the third Tribe. The third Tribe of Banians is divided into twenty Sects, none of which Marries into the other. They Eat nothing that has Life, but only Herbs and Pulse. Almost all these are Merchants; and being bred up to it from their Infancy, they are much greater Cheats than the *Armenians* and *Jews.*

Paravous 2 Tribes. There are two Tribes of *Paravous,*[28] the one call'd *Patara,* the other———— (*Here the Author wants the Name of the Second*). These Eat all sorts of Flesh, but Beef;[29] one of them[30] neither Eats with, nor Marries into the other; and their Wives when the Husband Dies may Marry again.

Sutar 2 Tribes. There are also two Tribes of *Sutars,*[31] or Timber-Men; the one call'd *Concanas,* the other *Guzaratti,* The first Eat all sorts of Flesh, except Beef; the others only Fish. They do not Marry out of their own Tribe, nor do they Eat with one another, and the Widows Marry.

Cansars 2 Tribes. The *Cansars,*[32] or Brasiers, are also divided into *Concanas,* and *Guzarattis,* differing even in their Trade in some measure, and Eat all Flesh,[33] except Beef. But they do not intermix in Marriages, or Eat together, and the Widows Marry again.

Gaulis. The *Gaulis,*[34] who sell Milk, and are Herdsmen, are another Tribe, that Eats every Thing but Beef, and tame Swines Flesh. Their Widows Marry again.

Malis. The *Malis,*[35] or Sellers of Flowers, are another Tribe, that Eat all Things with the same Exception as the last, and their Widows Marry again without any Dishonour.

Sonars. The *Sonars,*[35a] or Goldsmiths, are divided into *Concanas,* and *Guzarattis,* and observe the same as the *Braziers.*

Valuoris. There is another Tribe of *Valuoris,*[36] or Gardiners, who Eat all Flesh, but Beef and Pork. They neither Eat with, nor Marry into another Tribe; their Widows Marry again.

Columbines. The *Columbines,*[37] or Peasants make up another Tribe. They Eat Flesh with the same Exception, and are divided into *Chodris, Matares, Pateis, Routas, Naichis, Morias, Gorels,*[37a] who go a Horseback[37b] when they are to be Marry'd, and *Doblas*[38] great Wizards, inhabiting the Woods, where they Eat Rats,[39] Lizards, Snakes,[40] Moles, and all sorts of Vermin, tho' never so Stinking. Their Women go Naked, only covering their Privities with a Leaf. These, and other Tribes of labouring People do not intermix in Marriages, but may Eat together, and the Women[41] Marry again.

Batala's. The *Batala*'s[42] are also Country People who wear a Line like the *Brachmans,* being one[43] made up of three, which seems to signify the Unity of God in three Persons. They Eat nothing that has Life, but Herbs; nor do they Marry into other Tribes. The Widows do not Marry again.

Bandarines. The *Bandarines,*[44] who Prune[45] the Palm, or Coco-Trees, and draw the *Sura* from it, are divided into *Rautis, Chodris, Shiadas,*

Kitas, Charadas, and other sorts which do not Marry into one another ; but Eat together, and of all sorts of Flesh, except Beef, and tame Swine. The Widows Marry again.

The *Doblis,*[46] or Washers of Linnen, are divided into *Concana's*, and *Guzarattis*. They Eat together, but Marry each in their own Tribe, and Eat any Flesh but Beef and Pork. The Widows Marry again. *Doblis.*

The Fisher-men[47] are divided into many Races, or Tribes, call'd *Coles, Mavis, Purubias, Vaitis,* and *Birmassis*. They Eat in one anothers Houses, of all Flesh with the usual Exception, and the Widows Marry again. Fishers.

The *Sotrias*[48] make two distinct Tribes ; the one call'd *Salunkis,* the other *Coles*. They neither Eat nor Marry together. They Eat Flesh like the rest, and their Widows Marry again. When the Elder Brother Dies, the Younger takes his Wife ; but if the Younger Dies, the Elder does not so. *Sotrias.*

Those that carry Salt are call'd *Charanas,*[49] and make several Tribes. They take Wives out of any of them, Eat Flesh as above, and their Widows have the Liberty to Marry again. *Charanas.*

The *Bangasalis,*[50] or Salt Merchants Eat all living Creatures except Beef, tame Swines Flesh, Crabs, Lobsters, Crevisses,[51] and all Shell Fish. They do not Marry out of their Tribes, but the Widows may have second Husbands. *Bangasalis.*

The Tribe of *Gantias,*[52] who are all Traders, Eat nothing but Fish. Neither Marry into, nor Eat with another Tribe ; so that for want of another, a poor Man sometimes gets a Wife with 50000 Crowns. *Gantias.*

In *Suratte* there are *Babrias,*[53] *Catis,*[54] and *Rajapours,* who Eat only Fish, and wild Flesh. They Eat together, but do not Marry out of their Tribes. Their Wives do not Marry again, but Burn themselves, if they will.[55] *Babrias.*

The *Farasis,*[56] make Sandals like those of the *Recolets*. Eat any sort of Flesh, tho' Rotten, Eat together, and inter-mix in Marriages, without any Prohibition ; but their Tribe being reputed very Vile, they are not allow'd to enter the Houses of other Gentils, or touch them ; and must keep at a great distance. *Farasis.*

In the Country of the *Naines*[57] of Cape *Comori,*[58] they are call'd *Polias,*[59] and as they go along the Streets, if they will not venture to be Beaten,[60] must cry *Po, Po,*[61] that the other Gentils may take care their very Shadow does not touch them, which would Defile them, and they would be forc'd[62] to Wash.

This Custom makes the *Jesuits* that are Missioners there lead a very uneasy Life ; for being oblig'd to imitate the ways of that Tribe, the better to ingratiate themselves with those Barbarians,[63] they are forc'd to Wash themselves as many times a Day as the others do ; to feed upon raw Herbs ; and when two Fathers meet in the Street, one acting the *Naires,* and the other the *Polias,* they keep at a distance from one another, that they may not be suspected. There is no doubt they Convert very many ; but abundance[64] of them not being us'd to that Hardship, fall into dangerous Distempers.

Of all the Tribes here mention'd, only the *Brachmans* and *Banians* are so Precise[65] about killing of all Creatures ;[66] that even those that are Venemous may Bite them without receiving any Harm from them ; but the others[67] in this Case kill them.

Jogis.

The *Jogis* are People of all Tribes, who have impos'd on themselves a most painful sort of penitent Life. Besides, being continually Naked, some of them hold up their Arms in the Air, without ever letting them down ; others hold them behind, till in time they cannot move them. Some hang themselves up with Ropes ; others close their Mouths with Padlocks, so that they must be fed[68] with Liquids ; others run an Iron-Ring through their Prepuce, and hang a little Bell to it ; which, when the silly barren Women hear, they run to see, and touch him, hoping by that means to become Fruitful.

The Gentils pay so great a Respect to these Penitents, that they think themselves happy, who can Prostitute Daughters, Sisters, or Kins-women to their Leudness, which they believe lawful in them ;[69] and for this Reason there are so many Thousands of Vagabond *Fakirs* throughout *India.* When the *Fakirs* meet with *Baraghis*[70] (which is another sort of Penitents, differently habited, with their Hair and Beard shav'd) they Fight desperately. They never Marry, and Eat in the Houses of all Sects, except the *Polias.* They go into the Kitchin, and take what they will, tho' the Master be not at Home. They come together like Swine by beat of a Tabor, or at the blowing of a Horn, and march in Companies with Banners, Lances, and other Weapons, which, when they rest, they lay down by their Master. They Boast they are Descended from *Revanche-Ram,*[71] who wandred about the World Poor and Naked ; and these Vagabonds for imitating him, are look'd upon as Saints, and Live a loose Life, with the Priviledge of committing any Crime their Brutality suggests.

Now considering so great a Number of Sects, and such variety of Manners, which makes it Impracticable for them to be unanimous in Government, it is not to be thought strange that so small a Number of *Mahometans* should subdue such a Multitude of Gentils ; since Divisions and Discord have ever been the most efficient Causes in the World to overthrow the greatest Monarchies.[72]

CHAPTER II

OF THE OPINIONS AND SUPERSTITIONS OF THE IDOLATERS.

These Gentils are so blinded with profound Superstition, that they do not think it inconsistent to make their Gods be Born of Men, and Assign them Women; believing they love the same Things Men delight in. They Esteem *Ram* a mighty Deity, on account of the Wonders he wrought whilst Living, by means of a Monkey,[1] which crossing the Sea at one Leap, Burnt *Rhevan*'s[2] Palace, and Leap'd back again, to which purpose[3] they tell a long and tedious Fable. Among the Goddesses they count *Malachiche*,[4] who they say never refus'd any Body that ask'd it, the use of her Body; as if[4a] she had perform'd some extraordinary Penance; and so[5] a Man call'd *Cunsunu*,[6] because whilst he Liv'd he enjoy'd 16000 Women.

Ram, a Deity.

Malachiche Goddess.

Cunsunu.

Some of them believe there are *Elisian* Fields, and that in order to come thither, a River[7] is to be pass'd like the *Styx*[8] of the Antients, where they are to receive new Bodies. Others are of Opinion the World will end very soon, after which they shall Live again, and go into a new Country. They all believe there is but one God, who has 1000 Arms, 1000 Eyes, and as many Feet;[9] not knowing any better way how to Explain the Thoughts of his Omnipotency. They say they have four Books[10] sent them by God, above 6000 Years since, through the Hands of their Prophet *Ram*; two of which Books are shut, and two open; but that they can only be Read by those of their Religion. Besides,[11] that there are seven Heavens,[12] in the highest of which God sits; and that he does not take Notice of the particular Actions of Men, because they are not worthy to be the Object of his Divine Thoughts. They also say there is a Place where he may be seen, as it were through a far distant Cloud. As for Evil Spirits they believe they are so chain'd up, that they can do them no Harm.

Opinions concerning one God.

They Talk of a Man call'd *Adam*,[13] who was the first and common Father, and they say that his Wife, having yielded to the Temptation of Eating of the forbidden Fruit, made her Husband Eat too; but that as the Mouthful he took was going down, the Hand of God stopp'd its passing further, and thence comes the Knot Men have in their Throat, which they therefore call *Adam*'s Apple.[14]

Adam.

The Priesthood among them is Hereditary, as it was formerly among the *Jews*; for, as was said before, when a *Brachman* Marries, he must take the Daughter of another *Brachman*. They are distinguishable from all other Gentils, by a String or Rope made of three Threads of new Cotton,[15] which they wear hanging about their Neck, and wound about[16] the

Priesthood.

left Arm. It is put upon Boys of Nine, or Ten Years of Age with great Solemnity, but never upon Girls. This String or Line is to signify the Unity of God in three Persons, which they call *Brama, Vistu,* and *Mayessu.*[17] They will never Eat a Bit without they have it on ;[18] and some of them have been known to Fast several Days,[19] because their Rope broke before they could get another of[20] the Priests.

Brachmans how expell'd.

When any one is to be Expell'd the Tribe of the *Brachmans, Banians,* or *Bangasclines,* for some heinous Crime, they take away his Line thus. All that are of the Tribe in that Place meet before the *Boto,*[21] or Priest, and accuse the Criminal of such a Crime. He replies, and if his Defence be not good, the *Boto* takes away his Line, wipes off the *Tilla,*[22] or Colour on his Forehead. Then all the Company falls to chewing of *Betelle,* eating of *Coco*-Nuts, and smoaking Tabacco, without giving the Criminal any ; only out of Pity they throw him down on the Ground a Leaf of Tabacco.

How receiv'd again.

If he desires to be again admitted into the Tribe, he must go from House to House, begging Pardon and Absolution of those that Voted, making them sensible of his Resignation, and soothing the *Boto* with the Present of a Cow. This done, he gives all the Tribe a Treat, who receive him again,[23] and the Priest gives him the Line and *Tilla.*

Gentils will not Eat with others.

All the Sects of *Gentils* on this side *Ganges,* are very scrupulous as to Eating with Christians, and *Mahometans,* or making use of the same Utensils. But those beyond *Malaca* make no Difficulty[24] of it.

A foolish Opinion of theirs.

They are so Silly, or Ignorant as to conceit[25] a Woman may Conceive by strength of Imagination ; and that tho' they are many thousand Miles distant, and that for several Years, yet their Wives imagining they Lie with them, may become with Child, and therefore when they hear of their being brought to Bed, they make great Rejoycing.

A pleasant Passage.

To this purpose, *F. Galli,* Prefect of the *Theatins* of *Goa,* told me a pleasant Story. *D. Francis de Tavora,* Earl of *Alvor,* arriving from *Portugal,* to be Vice-Roy of *India ;* News was brought that his Wife, whom he left big with Child, was deliver'd of a Son. Among the rest a *Pagan* Merchant went to Congratule him, and thinking to make the Vice-Roy a great Complement said, *I wish your Excellency Joy, and hope you will have News every Year of the Birth of a Son.* This would have put him in a Passion, had not some told him that the Idolaters held that preposterous Opinion. The Women are Happy, that can take their Liberty, and make their silly Husbands believe they Conceiv'd by thinking on them.

Dying Men.

When an Idolater is Dying, his Kindred place a Cow near the Bed, and shake her Tail till she Pisses ; if it reaches the Dying Man's Face, it is look'd upon as a good Token of his future State ; otherwise, but particularly if the Beast does not Piss, the Obsequies are perform'd in a very Melancholy manner. Besides, they put the Cow's Tail into the Dying Man's Hand,[26] thinking his Soul may go into her Body. In short, they believe every Man may be sav'd in his Religion, and his Sect, so he exactly observe God's Commandments, and the Light of Reason ; which Judgment, tho' False, some Divines would follow, were it not condemn'd by the Church.

Trial of Theft.

The Trial upon suspicion of Theft among them, is by making the Party swim over a River that is full of Crocodils, and if he gets over safe, he is reputed not Guilty. The *Naires* call this the Passage of Crocodils.[27]

Naires Sorcerers.

These *Naires* are great Wizards, nor do they ever Expose themselves to any Feats of Arms, without first consulting the Devil. To this purpose they let their Hair fly, and draw some Blood out of their Forehead with a Knife ; then Dancing to the Musick of a Drum, they call him aloud, and he comes to Advise them whether they had best engage their Enemy. But when the Enemy repents he gave the Challenge, and makes a Sign to beg Peace, they easily grant it.

Women in Common.

Their Women are in Common. When any of them is with her, he leaves his Sword and Buckler at the Door, that every Body may know the Place is taken up ;[27a] and therefore there being no certainty whose the Children are, they alter the manner of Inheritance, as was said before. But if the Women are found to have to do with Men of another Sect, they become Slaves to their Queen of *Canara.* When a Brother Marries, his Wife is Common to the rest.[28]

Security for Travellers.

By a Priviledge granted them by their Queen, they accompany Travellers through those Parts that are infested with Robbers, and if they happen to presume to Rob any Man, they all Meet, and Pursue the Felons till they utterly Extirpate them. Thus one Boy with a Rod in his Hand makes it safe Travelling throughout all *Canara,* tho' it be through Woods, and over Mountains ; and a Traveller for a small Matter may have one from one Village to another.

Barbarity to Infants.

The Superstition of all the *Gentils* in *India,* makes them Murderers of their own Children ;[29] for it is their Custom when the Infant will not Suck, to carry it into the Field ; and there they leave it from Morning till Night, in a Cloth ty'd up on high by the four Corners, that the Crows may peck its Eyes out, and this is the Reason why there are so many Blind in Bengala. Where there are Monkeys, the Danger is not so great, because they being Enemies to the Crows throw all their Eggs down from the Trees, and hinder their Multiplying. At Night the Infant is carry'd Home, and if he will not Suck is expos'd a second, and third time in the Field, and at last hated as if it were some Snake, or Adder, and cast into the River.

CHAPTER III

OF SEVERAL PAGODS *OF THE* GENTILS.

Variety of Idols.

In all the Temples or *Pagods* of these Idolaters, which for the most part are Round, there are Figures of Devils, Serpents, Monkeys, and several[1] Monsters hideous to behold. In the Villages, where there are not Carvers to cut them, they take a Stone shap'd like a Cilinder, or small Pillar, colour'd Black, and placing it on a Column, adore it instead of an Idol, offering to it Sacrifice of *Betle, Arecca,* and other Things ; as I observ'd in Travelling over dismal Mountains,[2] where the Country People had made Choice, some of a Stone,[3] others of a Tree,[4] and some of an Herb[5] for their Idol.

First great Place of Pilgrimage.

The chief *Pagods,* to which they go in Pilgrimage are four ; *Giagrane,*[6] *Benarus, Matura* and *Tripeti.*[7] That of *Giagrane,* is upon one of the Mouths of the River *Ganges,* where the Great *Brachman,* or High Priest resides. There they adore the great Idol *Kesora,*[8] adorn'd with many Jewels. Its Revenues maintain all that vast Multitude of Pilgrims that Resort thither, on account of the Conveniency of the River *Ganges,* washing in whose Water they think cleanses them from Sin more than any other.[9]

Second Pilgrimage.

The *Pagod* of *Benarus* is Built on the Bank of *Ganges,* in the City of the same Name, and there is a Stair-case from the Door of it down to that River, to wash or Drink. The Vagabond *Fakirs* carry on their Backs Vessels full of this Water, stopp'd and seal'd by the Great *Brachman,* to prevent all Frauds, for several hundreds of Miles, to be well Paid for it by rich People and Merchants they Present it to. At Weddings they spend the Value of 500 Crowns of it, or more, it being the Custom to give a Glass or two of it about after Dinner ; which they drink with as great a Gust, as we should do some rich Muskadine, or Hippocrass. The Idol is call'd *Bainmadu,*[10] held in such Honour by the *Gentils,* that as soon as the *Pagod* is open'd, the *Brachmans* fall flat on their Faces ; and some with vast great Fans go to drive the Flies from about the Idol. A *Brachman* Marks the Forehead of all the Pilgrims with a yellow Liquor. No Women may go into it, but only those of one certain Tribe. There is another *Pagod* near it call'd *Riscurdas,*[11] from the name of the Idol adorn'd there.

Third Pilgrimage.

The *Pagod* of *Matura* is 35 Miles from *Agra,* on the Road to Dehli. Within it is a Place hemm'd in with Marble Bannisters,[12] with the Idol *Ram*[13] in the middle, and two others by him ; and both within and without abundance of Monsters, some with four Arms, and some with four Legs ; and others with a Man's Head, and a long Tail.[14] They carry this Idol upon solemn Festivals on a Bier, to visit the other Gods, or the River.

The fourth *Pagod,* is that of *Tripeti,*[15] in the Province of *Carnatica,* on the Coast of *Cormandel,* and Cape *Comori* ; it is remarkable for the many Buildings and Pools about it. Fourth Pilgrimage.

In the Kingdom of *Bisnaga,*[16] there is a *Pagod* with 300 Marble Pillars in it.[17] A *Portuguese* Gentleman, who had liv'd forty Years in *India,* and was an Eye Witness to it, told me, they formerly laid out 10000 *Roupies* there every Year, in making a Cart with eigheen Wheels, on which, when the Festival of the Idol was kept, the *Brachmans* mounted with 200 impudent Women Dancers, skipping in Honour of the Idol.[18] The Cart was drawn by 500 Men, and some Idolaters, believing that Death the direct Road to Heaven, threw themselves under the Wheels, and were crush'd to Pieces. Besides, that when the King of *Golconda* Possess'd himself of that Country, under the Conduct of the General *Emir Gemla,* he found in that Temple an infinite Number of Gold Vessels, and three Diamonds of an inestimable Value ; one of which the said *Emir Gemla*[19] presented to the Great *Mogul* ;[20] and that this General advancing into the Country of the *Naiche* of *Tanjaur,*[21] a *Gentil,* and taking the City of that Name, Thousands of Women threw themselves into Wells on account of Religion. *Bisnaga Pagod.*

He told me further, That near the Island of *Ceylon,* there is another small Island call'd *Ramanacor,*[22] with a *Pagod* of the same Name ; at the Entrance whereof is a Trough of black Stone, and in it a Statue of Metal, with the Eyes made of Rubies ; and that the *Gentils* break over it *Coco*-Nuts full of Water ; and lay Figs there, to Eat them afterwards, as if they were Sanctify'd, and Drink that Water, as Holy. Within the further part of this *Pagod,* is another which they open once a Year ; and there they adore a Brazen Idol call'd *Lingon,*[23] which is a very lewd Figure, the Parts of Man and Woman appearing join'd together. Some *Gentils* wear it hanging about their Necks, out of Devotion, as the God of Nature. *Ramanacor Pagod.*

All the *Gentils* are oblig'd to go once in their Life, at least, in Pilgrimage, to one of the four Principal *Pagods* ; but the rich go several times, carry the Idols of their Places of Aboad in Procession, attended by Hundreds of People, and *Brachmans;* who, with long Fans made of Peacock's Feathers, drive away the Flies from the Idol lying on the Bier. Manner of going in Pilgrimage.

Three Days before an Eclipse[24] happens, the *Brachmans* having Notice of it, break all the Earthen Vessels,[25] to use new Ones afterwards ; and run all of them to the River to boil Rice, and other Things, and throw it in for the Fishes, and Crocodils, when they find the fortunate Hour is come, by their Magical Books,[26] and several Figures they make on the Ground with the Noise of Drums, and Latten[27] Plates they beat. They cast themselves into the River to Wash whilst the Eclipse lasts ; the *Brachmans*[28] attend the richest Persons with clean Cloths Superstitions at the Eclipse.

to dry them, and then make them sit down on a piece of Structure six Spans square, daub'd all about with liquid Cows Dung, that the Pismires may not run upon it in danger of being Burnt, whilst they Dress the Rice, and other Pulse. They cover several Figures made with Powder'd Lime, on that Square with the same Dung, and then lay on two or three small Sticks of Wood to burn several Blades of Grain, with a great deal of Butter ; and from the Manner of the Flame to judge what plenty of Rice, and other Corn[29] that Year will afford.

Divalis, or Festivals.

The chief *Divalis*, or Festivals are two,[30] when the Moon decreases in *October*, and when she increases in *March*. All those Heathen Sorcerers work Wonders by the help of the Devil, but particularly their Juglers and Tumblers, who, without all doubt, deceive the Eye. They plant the Stone of any[31] Fruit, and within two Hours the Tree grows up, Blossoms, and bears ripe Fruit.[32] Others lay the Eggs under the Hen, and Hatch them at the same time ; which can be nothing but meer illusion. But I never saw it.

Sorcerers.

Pagan Kings.

The Princes of *Asia* that are Idolaters, are the Kings of *Cochinchina, Tunkin, Arachan, Pegu, Siam, China*, and several *Chams* in great *Tartary ;* in the Islands the King of *Japan*, and *Ceylon*, and some Roytelets[33] of the *Molucco* Islands ; as also all the *Rajas* in the *Mogul*'s Empire, but of several Sects, some less Superstitious than Others.

CHAPTER IV

THE AUTHOR CONTINUES THE ACCOUNT OF WHAT HE SAW IN THE CAMP OF GALGALA.

Having desir'd a Christian Captain of *Agra*, to let me know when an Opportunity[1] offer'd of seeing the King of *Visapor*, he sent on *Tuesday* the 22d of *March*, to appoint me to be at his Tent in the Morning,[2] that we might go together to the King's Quarters to satisfy my Curiosity. I went accordingly,[3] and he being ready, we both set out. Being come to the King's Tents, we waited for him to Pass by, to go pay his Respects to the *Great Mogul*. In short, within an Hour[4] I saw the unhappy King, whose Name was *Sikander*,[5] come with a handsome Retinue. He was a sprightly Youth 29 Years of Age,[6] of a good Stature, and Olive colour'd Complexion. *Aurenge Zeb* depriv'd him of his Liberty and Kingdom, as he did him of *Golconda*, in the Year 1685,[7] upon Pretence that he had given *Savagi* Passage through his Country, which he could not have hindred, if he would. The true Original of the King of *Visapor*'s Misfortunes was, That the Queen being left a Widow, and without Children,

Original of the King of *Visapor*'s Misfortunes.

Savagi, who was offended at the King Deceas'd, for having caus'd his Father *Nair Savagi,*[8] then Captain of the Guards to Die in a Goal, took the Field with a small Army of Scoundrels ; and soon made himself Master of the Fortresses of *Rajapor, Rasigar, Crapaten, Dabul,*[9] and part of *Malabar.* Some think that raising[10] the Fortifications of *Rasigar,* he there found a great Treasure,[11] which enabled him to continue the War. The Queen finding her self in that Condition, thought it convenient during the Minority of *Sikandar,* whom she had adopted for her Son,[12] and bred up in the Doctrin of *Hali,* before the King's Death, to make a Peace, tho' Dishonourable, leaving to *Savagi,* the Country he had Conquer'd yet to hold of her,[13] and to pay half the Revenue as Tribute.

At the same time *Pamniach,*[14] who was Tributary to the same Crown, took up Arms to shake off that Yoke ; relying on the natural Strength of his Country, lying between 27 in accessible Mountains, call'd *Settais-pale,*[15] among which there are Villages, and Lands Till'd by *Gentils* of the vile Tribe of *Faras.*[16] *Aurenge-Zeb* seeing the Forces of the Kingdom, amounting to 30000 Horse, and as many Foot, employ'd against these Rebels, he laid hold of the Opportunity, and Besieg'd the City and Castle of *Visapor ;* which he took after a vigorous Defence of three Years, made by *Sidi Mansutu,* a Black, who govern'd during the King's Minority, and carry'd away *Sikandar* Prisoner, to whom he afterwards allow'd a Million of *Roupies* a Year, to maintain him Decently.

Of the King of *Golconda.*

Tanascia,[18] King of *Golconda,* who, in my Time was sixty Years of Age, had the same Misfortune. His General *Emir Gemla* being Disgusted,[19] invited *Aurenge Zeb* to invade the Kingdom through his means. The Ambitious *Mogul* hasted thither, but notwithstanding his Intelligence with the Traitor, could not compass his Design ; and was forc'd to return to his Country[20] with Dishonour. He afterwards again attempted the Fortress of *Golconda,* but the Besieg'd making a resolute Defence, and an Army of 70000 Horse, and as many Foot keeping *Aurenge-Zeb*'s Army in the Field within Bounds ; both Sides thought fit to conclude a Peace on this Condition, that *Mahmud,*[21] Son to *Aurenge-Zeb,* should take the King of *Golconda*'s Daughter to Wife, and receive the Kingdom as a Portion,[22] after the Father's Death.

When the War with *Akbar*[23] was concluded, *Scialam* was sent[24] with a powerful Army, to Attack *Golconda* a-new ; but he either thinking the Conquest difficult, or overcome by *Tanascia*'s Promises, to give him his Daughter in Marriage, and Assist him to secure his Father's Throne ; so manag'd Affairs, that he obtain'd his Father's Consent to settle Peace, and tho' afterwards he receiv'd never so many repeated Commands, could never be prevail'd on to return to the Siege, but casting his Scimiter at his Feet, told him, He was a *Musulman,* and could not break the Peace he had Promis'd to keep.[25]

Scialam thus refusing, *Aurenge-Zeb* march'd in Person, after he had Conquer'd the Kingdom of *Visapor,* with a mighty Army to Besiege *Golconda.*[26] At his first coming, he secur'd the Pass on the River, and *Bagnagor,*[27] where the Palace was, and then without staying to Fortify it, by the Advice of the *Franks* he had in his Service, who gave me this Relation, he went on to Besiege the Fortress, whither the King was retir'd This being Built with vast great Stones,[28] and encompass'd with a deep Ditch, held out a Siege of nine Months,[29] tho' Batter'd by many Pieces of Cannon, and particularly by three Pieces of such a prodigious Bigness, that each of them was drawn by 500 Elephants, and 200 Oxen, if we may believe what the Soldiers told me ; for they could make but a small Breach in a Fort that was not enclos'd with Walls, but with a Rock. At length, want of Provisions, and Distempers that rag'd in the Place, besides the Presents and Promises *Aurenge-Zeb* made, did not only prevail with the Defendants to Desert to him by degrees, letting themselves down from the Wall with Ropes in the Night, but corrupted the Governour, who surrendred the Fortress against the King's Will ; he offering to pay a Tribute of three Millions, and 700000 *Roupies,* which *Aurenge-Zeb* refus'd, entring the Place Victorious in the Year 1686. *Azamscia* carry'd away the King Prisoner, who having a Collar of inestimable Value on, presented it to him ; but his Father *Aurenge-Zeb* perceiving he carry'd him on an Elephant, cry'd out to him, because he had not Bound his Hands behind him. The Son answer'd, that he[30] was a King, and he ought to be satisfy'd with depriving him of his Kingdom and Liberty.[31] Having shut him up in the Fort of *Dolet-Abad,* the *Mogul* allow'd him a wretched maintenance of 20 *Roupies* a day ; but a Son being Born to him in Prison, which he never had whilst on his Throne, in pitty to the Infant Born at such an unfortunate time, he rais'd his allowance to 500 *Roupies* a day.

Pannaich,[32] who had with considerable Forces assisted the *Mogul* in Conquering the Kingdom,[33] was rewarded with death, upon very slight jealousies ; which enraging his Son, he refus'd to pay the Tribute, and retir'd among inaccessible Mountains ; but a few years after, the greater Power prevailing, he submitted to Pay Tribute, and receive a Governour appointed by the *Mogul* into his Dominions.

Wednesday 23d, I din'd with the Captain of *Agra,* who treated me very handsomly, after the Country manner. *Thursday* 24th, I was conducted to a Neighbouring *Pagod,* to see a Penitent, who held up his Arms, the Joints being hardned, or knit together so that he had no use of them. *Friday* 25th, I look'd out for some Company to go back with me to *Goa,* because the *Begarian* of St. *Stephen* and my Interpreter were both fled ; but could find none. I spent my time[34] in vain on *Saturday*, also seeking for Company.

CHAPTER V

THE AUTHOR'S RETURN TO GOA, *THE SAME WAY HE CAME.*

The Season was now so far advanc'd that to spend any more time at *Galgala* would have made me Slip the opportunity of going over to *China;* therefore bearing patiently with my Indian's running away, I made the best of it, and resolv'd to venture all alone thro' a Country invested with Robbers and Enemies of Christianity. Having heard Mass on *Sunday* 27th, I mounted but very Melancholy ; and believing when I came at Night to *Edoar,*[2] I should find the *Caravan* of Oxen for *Bardes,* or some Christian of *Goa,* was disappointed of both. Setting out hence on *Monday* 28th, I came before Noon to the Village to *Rodelki ;*[3] where desiring a *Gentil* by signs to make me a Cake of Bread, the Knave instead of Wheaten Flower made it of *Machini,*[4] which is a black Seed, that makes a Man giddy, and so ill tasted, that a Dog would not eat it. Whilst it was hot necessity[5] made me eat that Bread of Sorrow ; but could not swallow it cold, tho' I had none[6] for three days, At Night I lay near the *Pagod* of *Mandapour.*[7]

Tuesday 29th, meeting the Caravan of Oxen beyond *Onor,* I travel'd with it till Sun-set ; but being necessitated[8] to alight, and the *Caravan* going on, I lost sight of it, the Night growing dark. Then being left alone in the open Field, without anything to eat, or place to take shelter, and in much dread of Robbers, I lay'd me down[9] among the Bushes.

Wednesday 30th, when day appear'd, I went on alone without any knowledge of the Road, but what the track of the Oxen show'd, and come betimes to *Beligon.*[10] This City tho' made up of Mud Houses thatch'd, is[11] very Populous, because of its Trade. It has a large *Bazar* and a good Fort, considering it belongs to *Moors,* all built of Stone, and encompass'd with a deep ditch full of Water ; but it has little Canon in proportion to its bigness, and Garrison. Here I expected to have found the *Caravan* of Oxen belonging to S. *Stephen,* or at least to hear some News of it ; but no Body understanding me, I was disappointed. *Thursday* the last of the Month, a *Moor* conceiving[12] what I could not express, conducted me to *Sciapour,*[13] a Mile thence, where I found the *Caravan,* ready to set out for *Bardes*: The *Canarines* belonging to it, who were subjects to

Beligon City.

Portugal show'd me a great deal of kindness ; and finding I was spent with three days want,[14] plentifully provided me with Foul and Rice ; but could get no Bread, because the Natives do not eat any. The worst of it was, I must set out with them immediately, and tho' a *Canarin* help'd to hold me a Horseback, because of my Weakness, yet it went very hard with me. That Night we lay in a Wood near the Village of *Jambot,*[15] belonging to a *Say*[16] or Prince of the same name ; the *Mogul* permitting some Lords to Possess these Barren Countries for a yearly Tribute.

Friday the first of *April,* after a few hours riding we pass'd by some Cottages, where were the Officers of the Custom-house and Guards of the Roads, who are worse than Thieves. That Night we lay on the Mountain, near some little Huts of the Country People ; of whom I could not buy a Chicken, or any thing else to support me.

Saturday 2d, we went down the steep and tedious Mountain of *Balagati,* and travell'd all day through *Savagi*'s Country. The Guards, who like *Banditti* lay skulking about the Woods, stopp'd me, and by signs ask'd whether I could Shoot out of a Musket, or understood the Art of Gunnery ; and answering by signs that I did not, they at last let me go, fearing the *Portuguese* should[17] stop their People at *Goa,* because I pass'd for a *Portuguese.* Having travel'd a few Miles further, we lay in the Field, and had an ill Night of it, near a Lake.

Sunday 3d, being *Easter*-day, after several hours Travelling, we pass'd by the *Mogul*'s Guards and Custom-house. There I was again detain'd ; not because they had any need of Gunners or Souldiers, but to make me pay Toll like a Beast ; at length some Idolaters telling them, the *Portuguese,* who were but a Musket shot from thence would do the same,[18] they let me go.

I went away to *Tivi,*[19] and thence to Fort S. *Michael,*[20] where the Castellan and his Wife perceiving I was sick, would not suffer me to go any further ; but by all means would have me be their Guest ; sending away immediately to *Pumberpa,*[21] a Farm of the *Theatins* for a *Ballon,* or *Andora* to carry me to *Goa.*

As the *Ballon* or Boat was coming,[22] an unmannerly *Portuguese* Souldier carry'd it away by force, and there being no *Andora* to be had, returning thanks to the Captain and his Wife, for the favour they had shew'd me, I desir'd them to order a Souldier to bear me Company to the aforesaid Farm. They were much displeas'd at the *Portuguese* rudeness,[23] and caus'd his Captain to punish him, and perceiving I would stay no longer with them, sent a Souldier of the Castle to convoy me ;[24] who brought me to *Pumburpa* on *Monday* the 4th at

Sun-setting. Here I was very lovingly receiv'd by the Factor, who gave me a good Supper, and after it an easy[25] Bed to rest me.

Tuesday 5th, I cross'd the Canal[26] in a *Ballon* or Boat, and return'd to *Goa* to the aforemention'd Monastery of Fathers in a very ill condition. The Father *Prefect* seeing me so sick, told me that had happned[27] because I would not take his advice; I answer'd *Heu Patior telis vulnera facta meis.*[28] Both he and *F. Hippolitus* endeavour'd to recover me with good Fouls, to which the best Sauce was their kindness; and thus I recover'd my flitting[29] Spirits. Weakness oblig'd me on *Wednesday* 6th to hire four *Boes,* or Porters to carry me in an *Andora,* to see what remain'd worth observing in *Goa.* They were all four satisfy'd with 15 *Pardaos,* which are worth six Crowns of *Naples* a Month.

S. *Francis Xaverius's* Body.

Thursday 7th, I went to visit the Body of S. *Francis Xaverius,* at the Church of *Bon-Jesu,* or Good Jesus,[30] being the profess'd House of the *Jesuits.* The Church is indifferent[31] large and Arch'd, but has nothing of good Architecture,[32] being more like a great Hall than a Church. It has an high Altar, with two on the sides all well Gilt; and on the left a Chappel where the precious Body of S. *Francis* lies. It was in a Crystal Coffin, within another of Silver, on a Pedestal of Stone; but they expected a noble Tomb of Porphiry Stone, from *Florence,* order'd to be made by the Great Duke. Since, with the Pope's leave, the Saints Arm was cut off, the rest of the Body has decay'd, as if he had resented it; and therefore the *Jesuits* for nine Years[33] past, do not shew it to any but the Vice-roy, and some other Persons of Quality. Being told as much at my first coming to *Goa,* I so far prevail'd, as to have the Vice-roy use his Power with the Provincial; and he not knowing how to refuse him, would at least defer the favour till that Morning; shewing me the Holy Body, with the Church shut, cloath'd in its Habit, which is chang'd every Year.

Friday 8th, I went to see the Church of the *Italian Carmelites,*[34] on a pleasant Hill. Tho' small, it is very Bautiful, and Arch'd as are all the Churches in *India,* with 6 Chappels, and an high Altar, well Gilt. The Monastery is handsome and well contriv'd,[35] with excellent Cloisters and Cells, and a delicious Garden, in which there are *Chinese* Palm-trees which yield a pleasing shade, with their low and thick Leaves. There are also two Cinnamon Trees, like that of *Ceylon.* At present it is decay'd from what it was, before the *Italian* Fathers were confin'd by the King's Order, because only one *Portuguese* Father cannot take so much Pains. The first[36] had been again receiv'd into Favour, but four of them Dy'd at Sea, coming from *Portugal.*

Saturday 9th, there being some Apprehension of the coming of *Arabian* Ships, all the Religious Men and Priests went down arm'd by Order of the Archbishop to the Fort of *Aguada*, to make good that Pass among the Soldiers.[37]

Sunday 10th, I went to pay my Respects to the Vice-Roy, who receiv'd me very Courteously, and Discours'd with me in *French* about two Hours, about News from *Europe* and *Asia*, and when I took my Leave made me very civil Offers.[38]

Monday 11th, the Commadore, a small Vessel, and a Fireship Sail'd out of the Harbour for the Gulph of *Persia*, to assist the King of *Persia* against the *Iman*[39] of *Mascate*; who, with five Ships had Burnt the *Portuguese* Factory,[40] and several Houses; robb'd the Custom-House, and carry'd away four Pieces of Cannon there were in the Fort, with the Arms of *Spain* on them, brought thither from *Ormus*. The King of *Persia* had then 90000 Men ready to send into *Arabia Foelix*, against the *Iman*.

Vice-Roys Palaces.

There are three Palaces at *Goa*, for the use of the Vice-Roy. The chief of them, call'd the Fort,[41] near the Church of the *Theatins*, and *Vasco de Gama*'s Gate, has the Prospect of the Channel, and consists of excellent Apartments, and a Royal Chappel. In the Hall of it are the Pictures[42] of all the Vice-Roys, and Governours of *India*, and in another all the Ships and Vessels[43] that ever came out of *Portugal*, since the first Discovery of those Countries. In the same are kept the Courts of Judicature, or[44] Exchequer, and others, and they Coin Mony,[45] such as *Pardaos* of Silver, and St. *Thomases*,[46] and *Pardaos* of Gold. The small Mony is made of a Metal brought from *China*, which is neither Copper, nor Latten,[47] nor Lead, nor Pewter;[48] but a Substance differing from them all, not known in *Europe*, and call'd *Tutunaga*,[49] which they say has some mixture of Silver. The *Chineses* use it to make great Guns, mixing it with Brass.[50] Of this, as was said, they make a very low sort of Coin at *Goa*, call'd *Bazaruccos*,[51] 375 whereof make a *Pardao*, whose Value is four *Carlines* of *Naples*; and yet any small Matter,[52] or Fruit may be Bought for one of these.

Coins.

The Vice-Roys do not Live in the aforesaid Palace, because of the ill Air, but in that call'd *Polvereira*, or the Powder-House, two Miles from it, at the Entrance of the City, as was said elsewhere.[53] Being at first design'd to make Powder in, it was not then fit to entertain a Vice-Roy; but has been enlarg'd by degrees. The third is the Fort of Pangi, near the Fort of *Gaspar Diaz*. The Vice-Roys have not Liv'd in it for many Years past, and at present the Garrison Soldiers are Quarter'd in it.

Tuesday 12th, News was brought of the loss of a Ship of the *Portuguese* Fleet,[54] which had run upon some Rocks in the Port of *Varsava*. My *Armenian* Servant being Indispos'd,

I Purg'd him with the excellent *Rhubarb* I Bought in *Persia*, where the best in the World grows, and he was soon well.

Wednesday 13th, I went with the Fathers to Divert me at[55] the Farm of *Pumburpa,* and *Thursday* 14th, enjoy'd the good Company of some Friends that came thither from *Goa. Friday* 15th, we went a walking in the Noviciate of the Fathers of the Society, opposite to the said Country House. Walking there on *Saturday* 16th, I pitty'd so many poor Christians and Idolaters, who Live in wretched Cottages under the Coco-Trees, to make them Fruitful, Man's Breath helping them to bear ; without hopes of ever removing with their Family from the Place where they are Born, because if they go to another place, their Masters bring them back by force, worse than if they were Slaves. *Sunday* 17th, after Dinner, we went to see a Farm of the *Augustinians* close by, where an ingenious Father[56] had Built a good House, and Furnish'd it handsomly.

Monday 18th, we went a Fishing on the Channel, which does not only abound in all other sorts,[57] but several kinds of Shell Fish, and particularly Oisters,[58] so large that the very Fish of some of them weighs half a Pound ; but they are not so well tasted as ours. The *Portuguese* use the Shells in their Windows instead of Glass, making them thin, and Transparent.[59] *Tuesday* 19th, after Dinner, we return'd to *Goa.*

Wednesday 20th, two Vessels from *Macao,* Loaded with *Chinese* Commodities arriv'd in the Port ; and *Thursday* 21st, I went Aboard one of them, call'd the *Pumburpa,* to see several Rarities[60] it brought. *Friday* 22d, I went in an *Andora,* to Visit our *Lady del Cabo,* or of the Cape, standing on the point of the Island of *Goa,* where the *Franciscans* have a good Church and Monastery. Here Night overtaking me, I was forc'd to lie in the Monastery, and return'd to *Goa,* on *Saturday* 23d.

Our Lady of the Cape.

Sunday 24th, I heard Mass at the *Augustinians,* to visit my Friend and Fellow-Traveller for several Months *F. Francis of St. Joseph. Monday* 25th, I went over to Divert my self[61] to a little Country House, seated on the Island of *Bardes,* where on *Tuesday* 26th, I saw the Convoy of several Vessels return from *Canara,* with a good Stock of Rice, because the Islands of *Goa* do not produce enough. *Wednesday* 27th, I took the Air in a Boat upon the Channel.

Thursday 28th, was the Procession of *Corpus Christi,* which is made here with much Solemnity in *April,* because of the Storms, and great Rains in *June.*[62] Before it went a Soldier a Horse-back in bright Armour. Then follow'd an Image of St. *George* in Wood, about which some Persons in Masks Danc'd and after them six Canons, with six Silver Maces, and lastly, six Gentlemen carry'd the Canopy.

Friday 29th, I went to see a Lion brought the Vice-Roy[63] from *Mozumbique,* who was about to send it as a Present to the

Emperor of *China.* And still continuing to Divert my self after my late Sufferings, on *Saturday,* the last of the Month I saw the Powder-House, where they were then actually making Powder.

Sunday the first of *May,* I went to the Cathedral to hear some indifferent Musick, on account of the Festival of St. *Philip* and *Jacob ;* and *Monday* 2d, Din'd with *F. Francis,*[64] being invited by him, because the time of my Departure drew near. On *Tuesday* 3d, *F. Hippolitus Visconte* took care to Change what Mony I had into Pieces of Eight, because there is a great deal lost by carrying Gold into *China ;* and a *Portuguese* Merchant well skill'd in that Trade, made a small Purchase of Diamonds for me, they being cheap at *Goa. Wednesday* 4th, I went with *F. Salvador Galli, F. Visconti,* and the General of *Salzette,* to speak to *Jerom Vasconcellos,* Captain of the Vessel call'd *The Holy Rosary,* bound for *China.* For their Sakes he undertook to carry me ; but refusing to find me Provisions for my Mony, I was forc'd on *Thursday* 5th,[65] to lay in a Stock for so long a Voyage. *Friday* 6th, I went to the Church of the Miraculous Cross,[66] to beg of God a good Voyage, and *Saturday,* 7th diverted my self on the Channel. *Sunday* 8th, some Friends din'd with me, and *Monday* 9th, I din'd with *F. Francis,* and after drinking to my good Voyage, we took leave of one another with much Concern.[67] *Tuesday* 10th, I went to the Powder-House to pay my Respects to the Vice-Roy, and desire him to give me a Letter of Recommendation to the General of *China.* He granted it very Civilly, offering to do me any other Kindness.[68]

My *Armenian* Servant refusing to go to *China,* on *Wednesday* 11th, I Bought a Cafre, or Black Slave for eighteen Pieces of Eight, and there being a Necessity to get a License to Ship him off, because we were to touch at *Malaca,* where the *Dutch* Hereticks Command,[69] I went on *Thursday* 12th, to the Inquisitors to have it Pass'd. They made a great Difficulty of granting it, and dispensing with the Prohibition they themselves had been Authors of ; alledging that some *Cafes,* who had been Shipp'd at other times, being taken, had turn'd *Mahometans. Friday* 13th, I took Leave of my Friends, the Vessel being already fallen down to the Mouth of the Channel,[70] in order to Sail very speedily ; and *Saturday* 14th,[71] having return'd Thanks, and bid Adieu to the Fathers *Theatins,* I went Aboard with my Goods. There speaking to the Captain, to order my Equipage and Provisions to be taken Aboard, he order'd it to be deliver'd to the Master's Mate, for him to dispose of it as the Pilot should direct, he having undertaken to keep me by the way, I putting my Provision to his. This done, I return'd to the Farm of *Pumburpa,* to have the Satisfaction of lying Ashore one Night longer.

Sunday 15th, I went over to the Island *Charon,*[72] where the Novitiate of the *Jesuits* is, to hear Mass. Meeting there with some *Italian* Fathers, who were Bound for *China,* Aboard the same Vessel, they very Civilly shew'd me all the House. The Church is small, and has three Altars well Gilt ; but the Sacristy has curious Chests of Drawers about[73] it made of *Indian* Wood, varnish'd, with the Apostles[74] painted on it. The House is small, and the Cells for thirty Novices very little. I din'd in the Farm of the *Augustinians,*[75] and lay that Night in that of the *Theatins.*

CHAPTER VI

THE AUTHOR'S VOYAGE TO MALACA.

Munday 16th, the Vessel being under Sail I went Aboard. Towards Evening came Aboard *F. Emanuel Ferreira,* a *Portuguese,* Missioner to *Tunchin,*[1] who wore a Reverend long Beard ; *F. Joseph Condoni,* a *Sicilian,* going to his Mission of *Cochinchina,* which Fathers had been Summon'd to *Rome,* by his Holiness Pope *Innocent* the 11th,[2] because they had refus'd to Obey the *French* Bishops and Vicars Apostolick in those Kingdoms, to the great Scandal of the Christians, who saw the Church-Men Excommunicate one another, and eight other *Jesuits* of several Nations, who were[3] going to *China ;* besides ten others who went in the Vessel of the Merchants of *Goa,* call'd *Pumburpa,* which carry'd the Lion above-mention'd.

The Fathers of the Society[4] are in such Esteem and Reputation in *India,* that at Night the Vice-Roy came to Visit those that were Aboard the two Ships, and stay'd still Midnight in these two Visits. Laying hold of this opportunity, he himself recommended me to the Captain, telling him, I was a curious Gentleman, that Travell'd only to see the World, and therefore he should use me well. His Recommendation had but little Effect, because the Captain, who was Bred in *China,* had quite forgot the *Portuguese* Civility, which in all places I found they Practis'd more towards me, than towards their own Country-Men ; nor did he value another Man's Merit, or Qualifications. As soon as the Vice-Roy was gone they weigh'd Anchor, and the Vessels were tow'd by several *Paraos,*[5] which are long Boats with sixty Oars, and *Ballons,* which are smaller ; the City Pilots being aboard, to carry the Vessels beyond the Flat, which is before the Fort of *Gaspar Diaz,* near which we lay all *Tuesday,* because the Wind blew hard.

Wednesday 18th, the same Wind continuing, and the City Pilots having no hopes it would fall, weigh'd Anchor two Hours before Day, and began to have the Ships tow'd again by the *Ballons* and *Paraos*. But the Wind rising, to avoid the Rock, they both run[6] upon the Sand.[7] There being danger that the Ship might split at the Flood, it being then Ebb, every one endeavour'd to carry off his Goods, especially Mony, and to get it Ashore ; and it would go hard with the City Pilots, if once the Vessels were stranded, and they did not fly. I[8] put my Baggage Aboard a Coaster, and leaving my Slave with my Provisions, went to *Goa* for a new License from the Inquisition, to put the Black Aboard the Coaster, in case the Ships that were stranded should be rendred unfit to perform their Voyage ; which I got with some[9] Difficulty for the Reasons above alledg'd.

Whilst I was still at *Goa,* the Vice-Roy gathering abundance of *Paraos* and *Ballons,* went in Person to get off the Vessels with the Flood ; which being done, they came up again to take in as much Water as they had thrown over Board to lighten themselves. The honest Pilot, and Master's Mate of our Ship had also thrown over the Passengers Provision and Fruit ; but not their own, which afterwards they did Eat till they were ready to Crack.[10] Taking leave again of the Fathers *Galli* and *Visconti,* I return'd Aboard with my Baggage, but was not told they had thrown over Board three great Baskets of Wine[11] full of *Mangos,* for had I known it, I would have provided other Fruit.

We got not out on *Thursday* 19th, through the Fault[12] of the City Pilots ; but about break of Day, on *Friday* 20th, the Wind blowing fair at N.W. our Vessel call'd the *Rosary,* the *Pumburpa,* and four Coasters put out to Sea. The *Jesuits,* as they were the first that went off, so would they be the last to return Aboard. The same fair Wind continu'd *Saturday* 21st, and *Sunday* 22d.

Monday 23d, the Pilots by Observation found we were in the Latitude of *Cochin.* We had great Rains, and stormy Winds every Day and Night, but they did not last above an Hour. They call these Tempests *Sumatras,*[13] from the Island of that Name. Holding on our Course South on *Tuesday* 24th, the Pilots judg'd we were in the Latitude of Cape *Comori ;* which is like that of *Good Hope.* It is to be observ'd that in this Place they find a most unaccountable work of Nature ;[14] which is, that at the same time it is winter at *Goa,* and all along that Coast, it is Summer upon all the opposite Coast, as far as the Kingdom of *Golconda,* and thus in a few Hours they go from Winter to Summer ; which is experimentally known to be true every Day, by the Natives of *Madure, Tiar, Tanjaur, Ginge, Madrastapatan,*[15] the People of the *Naiches,* and other *Pagan* Princes.

Wednesday 25th, making an observation we found our selves in the Latitude of Cape *Galli*[16] in the Island of *Ceilon,* which was joyful News to all abroad, as being then sure they should continue their Voyage ; for had the South Wind started up before we reach'd that Place, we could have gone no further, but must have run away to Northward, as happen'd to two Ships of *China,* which set out in the Year 1693, and put in to refit after the Storm, the one at *Damam,* and the other at *Bombaim.* On the contrary being once in the Latitude of Cape *Galli,* no Wind could put us by our Voyage.[17] We were here according to the Pilots Computation 600 Miles from *Goa.*

The Island of *Ceilon* besides its rich Cinnamon, which is carry'd all the World over, has the best Elephants, as was said above, and a Mountain that produces Rock Crystal,[18] of which at *Goa* they make Buttons, Beads, and other Things. *Ceilon* Island.

Thursday 26th, we found our selves in the Latitude of 6 Degrees opposite to the Bay of *Bengala ;* and all the Mouths of the River *Ganges*[19] running into it, whilst at the same time the natural Current of the Water is from South to North, that Sea is very rough. This made the Ship often lye athwart the Waves, and kept us all continually watching for fear. This Kingdom of *Bengala* is accounted the most Fruitful the *Mogul* has, by reason of its Rivers. It has a great Trade for Silk, Calico, and other Stuffs. Finding our selves in this Latitude we stood to the Eastward, and[20] on *Friday* 27th, were off the *Maldive* Islands.[21] *Saturday* 28th, the same fair Wind continu'd, but with the same Rowling.[22] *Sunday* 29th, the Wind held on, and a Sailer dying was thrown over Board. *Monday* 30th, we were Becalm'd, but *Tuesday* the last of the Month the Wind came up again, blew harder on *Wednesday* the first of *June,* and held fair on *Thursday* 2d. *Bengala* Kingdom.

Friday 3d, we were in sight of the Island of *Nicobar,*[23] the Wind blowing fresher. This Island pays a Tribute of a certain number of human Bodies to the Island of *Andemaon,*[24] to be eaten by the Natives of it. These Brutes rather than Men, use[25] when they have wounded an Enemy, to run greedily to suck the Blood that runs. The *Dutch* are[26] Witnesses of this Cruelty of theirs ; For they going with 5 ships to subdue them and landing 800 Men, tho' they were well Intrench'd to defend themselves against those wild People ; yet they were most of them kill'd, very few having the good Fortune to fly to their Ships. *Nicobar* Island and *Andemaon.*

Sieur Francis Coutinho General of *Salzete* told me that the chief Motive the *Dutch* had to attempt the Conquest of that Island, was a Report spread abroad, that there was a Well[27] in that Island, whose Water Converted Iron into Gold, and was the true Philosophers Stone. The ground of this Rumour was, an *English* Ship putting into that Island after a dreadful Storm, where they[28] observ'd that a little Water[29] which an

Islander carry'd being split upon an Anchor, that part of it which was wet with it, turn'd into Gold; and asking him where he had that Water, he told them out of a Well in the Island, after which they kill'd him. I can neither affirm nor deny that there is such a Well;[31] but only declare this Story[32] was told me by *F. Emanuel Ferreira,* and by *Coutinho* a Knight of the Order of Christ, before *F. Galli* at *Goa,* who had also heard of it before. No Man in *Europe* or *Asia* can give any more certain Account of it, because those People have no Commerce with any Nation in the World.

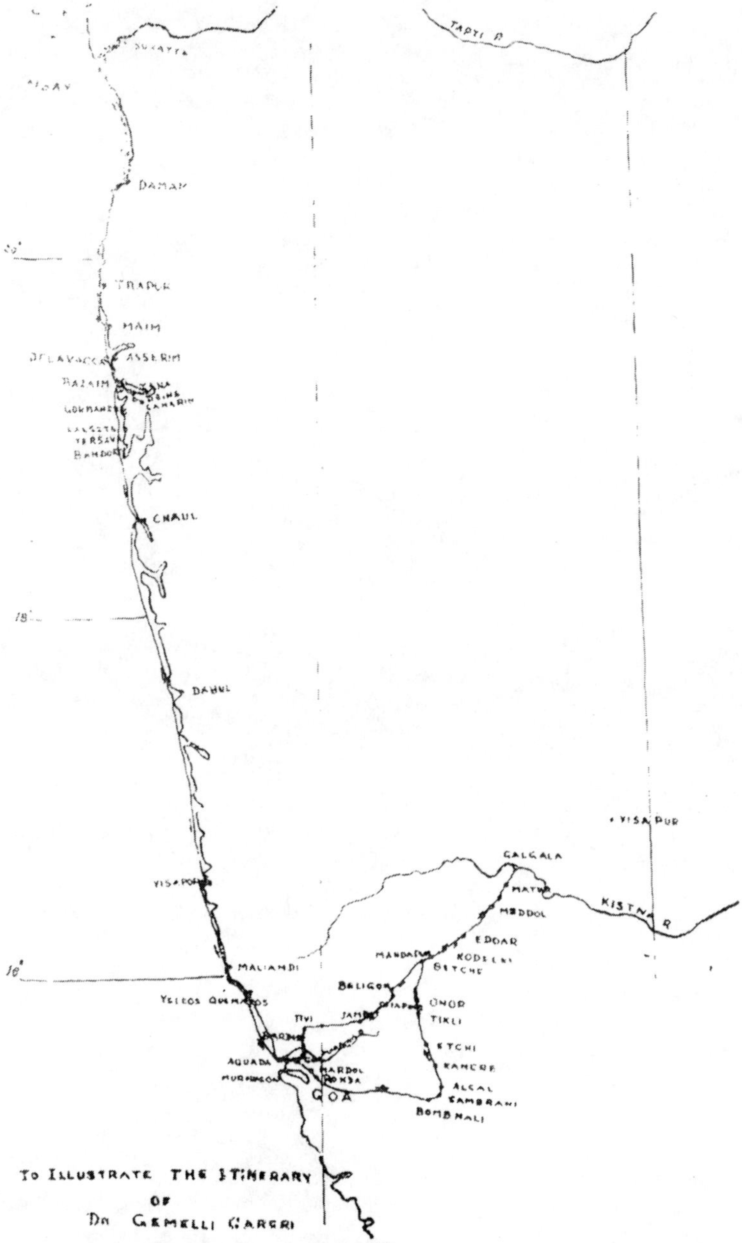

Map illustrating the itinerary of Dr Gemelli Careri

NOTES

INDIAN TRAVELS OF THEVENOT

BOOK I

CHAPTER I

1. The well-known port of Basra on the Persian Gulf. c.f. Balbi (quoted in *Hobson-Jobson*, "Balsara otherwise called Bassora"). Linschotén uses both the old and new forms, Balsora and Bassora (Vol. I, p. 45). Also see Tavernier, Vol. I, p. 5.
2. Opfel in the French text.
3. Wrongly translated. Six days *after* and not *before* the beginning of the monsoon.
4. Monsoon from Arabic *mausim*, season. "The name given to the periodical winds of the Indian seas, and of the seasons which they affect and characterise" (*Hobson-Jobson*). For the proper season for sailing from Persia to Surat, see Tavernier, Vol. I, p. 4.
5. See Chap. XV; also Ovington, pp. 100-101 and Forbes, *Oriental Memoirs*, Vol. I, p. 146.
6. At half past ten in the morning.
7. Waist deep.
8. First.
9. Examined.
10. Sir Thomas Roe refers to the "custome of the Kings officers to search everie thing that came ashoare, even to the pocketts of mens cloathes on their backs, for custome" (Foster, *Embassy*, pp. 28-29). Tavernier observes, "The officers are very strict and search persons with great care." (Vol. I, p. 7). Also see Pietro Della Valle, Vol. I, pp. 23-24.
11. First.
12. A guard.
13. Guard.
14. *Abbasi*, a Persian coin worth about 1s. 6d., named after Shah Abbas II. Fryer calls it 'a Sixteen penny piece of Silver' (Vol. I, p. 143). According to Dalgado, an *abbasi* was equivalent to three hundred Portuguese *reis*.
15. Immediately.
16. However it is open only from ten in the morning till noon.
17. Only one.
18. She.
19. Quay.
20. Kiosk, "from the Turki and Persian *kushk*, a pavilion, a villa." *Hobson-Jobson*, p. 485.
21. Peons (mod. sp.), from the Portuguese *peao* and Spanish *peon*, 'a footman'. *Hobson-Jobson*, p. 696.
22. Staffiere, Italian word for a footman or groom.
23. A French livre was equivalent to 1s. 6d. of English money at the time Thevenot wrote. See Tavernier, Vol. I, p. 327.
24. Much earlier.
25. They do not wait.
26. A couch with cushions.
27. First.
28. Tavernier says, "Gold and silver are charged 2 per cent." (Vol. I, p. 7) as does Mandelslo. (p. 18). Ovington indirectly corroborates Thevenot when

he says, "All strange Coyn, whether Imported or Exported, pays to the Mogul's Officers Two and an half *per Cent.*" (p. 132).

29. First.
30. Compare Tavernier who points out that "Private individuals pay as much as 4 and 5 per cent duty on all their goods; but as for the English and Dutch Companies, they pay less." (Vol. I, p. 7). According to Mandelslo the import and export duty on merchandise at Surat was 3½% (p. 18).

CHAPTER II

1. Mekran, which forms now a part of Southern Baluchistan (*Imp. Gaz.,* Vol. I, pp. 6 ff.).
2. Sind (mod. sp.).
3. Kabul and Kandahar are outside India now.
4. A misprint for 'on'.
5. It is to be noted that in early Portuguese writings the coast of Malabar was called India, and the rest of the country was designated Asia.
6. Cf. Baldaeus: "*India* was anciently divided into two parts by the river *Ganges;* thence the more eastern part was called *India* beyond the Ganges, and the western part India on this side of the *Ganges,* now known by the name of *Indostan.*"
7. Much useful information on the source of the river Indus has been supplied by recent explorations in Tibet. The Indus rises from "*Singi-kabab*" or 'the Lion's mouth' according to Sven Hedin (*Trans-Himalaya,* Vol. II, p. 210). Swami Pranavananda, in a recent book '*Exploration in Tibet*', however, argues that its real source is *Topchhen la.* The source of the Ganges in the Central Himalayas is known as the *Gomukhi* or the Cow's mouth. Here the river is locally known as the Bhagirathi.
8. Chagtai Khan, son of Chingiz Khan, governed Transoxiana, Balkh, Badakshan, and Kashgar, and the mountain ranges in these areas are collectively referred to as the Chagtai mountains.
9. Cape Comorin.

CHAPTER III

1. Mughal (mod. sp.). Bernier's remarks in this connection are interesting. "To be considered a *Mogol,* it is enough if a foreigner have a white face and profess Mahometanism." The Timurid rulers of India were not strictly speaking Moguls or Mughals. Timur himself was a Turk and Babar did not think highly of the Mughals though his mother was a Mughal princess.
2. Timur the lame.
3. The modern Khorasan (i.e. "land of the sun") in Persia. Originally it meant the eastern of the four quarters of the Sassanian monarchy but the expression is now limited to the north-eastern portion of Persia.
4. Chingiz Khan.
5. More than two centuries.
6. The modern Ghazni or Ghazna in Afghanistan, south west of Kabul. The statement however is hardly accurate. Sultan Mahmud of Ghazni annexed a part of the modern province of the Punjab. After the fall of the Ghaznavide kings Sultan Shahabuddin Muhammad Ghori extended his sway over N. India, but after his death an independent sultanate was founded at Delhi. Babar conquered N. India from Kabul, but after his death Kamran held Kabul independently of Delhi. Only in Akbar's time Kabul and Ghazni definitely became dependencies of the Delhi empire.

7. The grandson of Timur, through his eldest son Ghiyasuddin Jahangir. During the lifetime of Timur, he was in charge of the province of Balkh. (Ref. the genealogical chart on p. 268 of *"The Mohammadan Dynasties"* by S. Lane-Poole).
8. Ghiyasuddin, eldest son of Timur, others being Omar Sheikh, Jalaluddin Miran Shah and Shah Rukh.
9. Babar, as the author correctly points out, was descended directly from Jalaluddin Miran Shah, third son of Timur.
10. Mā-warā-l-nahr according to Lane-Poole or more correctly 'Māwarā-un-nahr', which means 'beyond the river', and is equivalent of Transoxiana.
11. Where.
12. *Lubbu-t-Tawarikh* written by Yahya Bin 'Abdul Latif in 1541 (Elliot and Dowson, Vol. IV, pp. 293-297).
13. Shah Alam. Sher Shah, who had assumed that title either after the battle of Chausa or after his accession to the throne of Delhi, is meant.
14. 'Decan' in the French original. This is a mistake, for Sher Shah did not rule over the Deccan.
15. Shah Tahmasp I (1524-1576), son of Shah Ismail, the founder of the great Safavi dynasty of Persia. Humayun did not marry the Shah's sister.
16. Delhi.
17. Akbar.
18. Akbar died in October 1605 and not in 1604.
19. Jahangir (1605-27) died in the twentysecond year of his reign. The date however is correctly stated.
20. Bulāqī (Dāwar Bakhsh), son of Khusrau, eldest son of Jahangir. Immediately after Jahangir's death he was raised to the throne by Asaf Khan to enable his son-in-law Prince Khurram to return from the Deccan and to foil the plans of Nur Jahan in favour of Shahriyar her son-in-law and the youngest son of Jahangir. He was 'a mere sacrificial lamb' and was put to death at the instance of Shah Jahan on 21 January 1628 (Saxena, *History of Shah Jahan*, p. 62). A pretender resided at the Persian Court and Mandelslo (p. 42) among others claims to have met this Polagi or Bulaqi in Persia.
21. Khurram ('Joyous'), the third son of Jahangir unsuccessfully rebelled against his father in 1622 and continued in arms till the death of the emperor. For details see Saxena, *op. cit.*, p. 40 ff.
22. Shah Jahan.
23. The reference here is obviously to the 'war of succession' among the four sons of Shah Jahan in Sept. 1657.
24. Aurangzeb.
25. Murad.
26. According to Abdul Hamid Lahori the total revenue of Shah Jahan's empire amounted to 200 millions of rupees, each rupee being computed by Moreland as equivalent to 2s. 3d at the date. Also see Bernier pp. 445-458; Manucci, Vol. II, pp. 413-415 and Mandelslo, p. 38. Roe contents himself with a statement that the Mughal is richer than the rulers of Persia and Turkey.
27. Obviously an incorrect rendering of the Persian *qanun-nama*. Elaborate "descriptive rolls" of the army were prepared since the days of Akbar, and the author is perhaps referring to one of these registers on the basis of which he estimates the number of forces of the Mughals.
28. It is not possible, in the present state of our knowledge of the sources, to arrive at any satisfactory, much less an accurate, estimate of the strength of the Mughal army or its component parts. Thevenot records the opinion of other travellers that the Mughal could send to the field a force of 300,000 horse. Careri was told that Aurangzeb's camp in the south had 60,000 horse. Bernier speaks of 100,000 horse in the camp during Aurangzeb's journey to Kashmir (p. 380). Manucci refrains from giving any figures and crisply describes the camp thus: "It looks like a great city travelling from place to place." He also adds that "the numbers of an army do not consist solely in cavalry and infantry soldiers. . . . . When you talk of a division

of 8,000 cavalry, the reader may assume that there are always 30,000 persons" (Vol. II, p. 75 and *n.*). The available figures are therefore to be scrutinized with great circumspection.

The Indian sources also do not help us much. The *Ain.* gives the details of the army but not the requisite figure. In Qazvini's *Padshahnama* (1666) we find that the cavalry maintained directly out of Imperial treasury consisted of 200,000 men. Sarkar holds that in 1648 the Imperial army comprised 200,000 cavalry besides 185,000 cavalry maintained by the princes and the nobles (*Studies in Mughal India*, p. 20).

29. According to Lahori's *Padshahnama* the Mughal empire was divided into 22 subahs or provinces out of which in the latter part of the reign of Shah Jahan, Qandahar was recovered by the Persians, and Balkh and Badakshan remained with the Mughals only for a short time. Thus in 1666, the empire could not have contained more than twenty provinces.

CHAPTER IV

1. Gujarat.
2. Correctly, 1572-73.
3. Itimad Khan, Abdul Karim, who invited Akbar in 1572 to occupy Gujarat.
4. Sultan Mahmud Shah III called 'the Martyr' (1538-1554).
5. The reference is to Changez Khan and his supporters.
6. Muzaffar Shah III (1561-1573).
7. The Sultan was about 23 years old at the time of Akbar's invasion.
8. This statement seems to be of doubtful accuracy and appears to have been borrowed from Mandelslo (p. 48).
9. Muzaffar effected his escape in 1578 and organised a formidable resistance to the Mughal government in Gujarat (1583) which was completely suppressed. A fugitive for ten years, hotly pursued from place to place, he committed suicide in 1593 (Smith, *Akbar the Great Mogul*, p. 208; *Cambridge History of India*, Vol. IV, p. 133; Commissariat, *A History of Gujarat*, pp. 527-28).
10. The Narbada and Tapti.
11. Cambay, more correctly Khambayat, capital of the state of the same name, 52 miles south of Ahmedabad. Tavernier writes that the port is famous for agates and indigo (Vol. I, p. 56).
12. North gate of Surat leading to Broach.
13. 'Variao' called 'Periaw' by De Laet, a small village, where travellers cross the Tapti, in Broach District, Bombay.
14. A river with a course seventy miles in length which falls into the Gulf of Cambay ten miles south of the estuary of the Narbada.
15. Oklesar, the modern Ankleshwar, a town about six miles south of Broach.
16. From Sanskrit *krosa*, 'a call'. A unit of distance which varies in different localities but is commonly considered to be equivalent to two miles. The author says it was only half a league, but Tavernier makes it equal to about one league. The Akbari 'kos' was equivalent to 5000 *gaz* or yards (*Hobson-Jobson*, pp. 261-262).
17. Broach (Sanskrit *Bhrigukachha*). More correctly Lat. 21° 42′.
18. Slope.
19. Bazaars.
20. Derived from the Persian *bafta* meaning 'woven' and is specially applied to a kind of calico manufactured in Broach. Besides Broach, Charpata and Noakhali in the Chittagong division of Bengal were famous for their cotton 'baftas'.
21. According to traditional accounts, the fortifications of the town are ascribed to Siddharaj Jai Singh of Anhilwara (1094-1143) but these were rebuilt and strengthened by Bahadur Shah (1526-1537). In 1660, a few years before Thevenot arrived in India, parts of the wall were dismantled under the

orders of Aurangzeb, but in 1685, he was forced to rebuild them in order to save the town from the ravages of the Marathas (*Surat and Broach Dist. Gazetteer*, p. 551).

22. Pagodas; this word is differently used for (1) a temple; (2) an idol; and (3) a coin formerly current in S. India. Here it is used in the first sense (*Hobson-Jobson*, pp. 652-657).
23. Compare Tavernier's account of Broach, its fort, the *bafta* manufactured there, the peculiar property of the river water, etc. (Vol. I, p. 54).
24. The Dutch Factory was established at Broach in 1617.
25. Two per cent according to Baldaeus.
26. Sarbhon, four miles east of Amod in the Amod sub-division of Broach district. Forbes (*Oriental Memoirs*, Vol. I, p. 390) describes it as "one of the best villages in the Baroche Purgunna".
27. River Dhadhar which rises in the Vindhya range and falls into the Gulf of Cambay.
28. Dabka is a village eighteen miles distant from Baroda on the left bank of the river Mahi (*Bombay Gazetteer*, Vol. VII, Baroda, pp. 542-544).
29. Persian *murdakhor*, literally eater of the dead or *maradkhor*, eater of man. Among Europeans, Herodotus was the first to suggest that there were cannibals in India. James Forbes (*Oriental Memoirs*, Vol. I, p. 390), however doubts the accuracy of Thevenot. The French traveller was in all probability imposed upon. We cannot trace any evidence of cannibalism in Gujarat. The lawless habits of tribes like Grassias, Bhils, Kolis etc. who infested this wild area may have given them a bad repute among their neighbours (James Douglas, *Bombay and Western India*, Vol. II, pp. 354-57).
30. Petlad town in Baroda State.
31. Mahi (the Mophis of Ptolemy), which rises in the Gwalior state and falls into the Gulf of Cambay.
32. Road.
33. *Tanki* (Gujarati), a reservoir of water, an artificial pond, commonly known to Europeans in India as a tank.
34. Reservoirs.
35. Sojitra, town in Petlad taluka, Baroda state. Mandelslo calls it Sejuntra (p. 22).
36. Matar, head-quarters of Matar taluk in Kaira district (*Bombay Presidency Gazetteer*, Vol. I, p. 280).
37. François de la Boullaye le Gouz. When he first came to India is not precisely known but he was at Goa in 1648 according to Tavernier (Vol. I, p. 164). His *Les Voyages et Observations* was published in 1653 and apparently secured him some reputation. As a person conversant with Indian affairs he was appointed one of the envoys to the court of Agra where he arrived in 1666. Towards the close of that year he was assassinated near Dacca on his way to China. Tavernier's story of his death (Vol. I, p. 169) is inaccurate (Manucci, Vol. II, pp. 150 ff and note; Tavernier, Vol. I, pp. 164-180).
38. Banyan tree (*Ficus bengalensis*). Is it the Kabir-Vad situated on an island in the Narbada river near Broach which James Forbes describes in *Oriental Memoirs*, Vol. I, pp. 16-18? Mr. J. Copland wrote of the same tree in 1814. Vide article entitled 'Account of the Cornelian Mines in the neighbourhood of Broach' printed in *Transactions of the Literary Society of Bombay*, Vol. I, 1819, pp. 313-14, cited at pp. 489-91 by Commissariat.
39. Jitbagh, 'garden of victory' to the south of the lake at Sarkhej, laid out in 1584 by Abdur Rahim Khan-i-Khanan in commemoration of his victory over Sultan Muzaffar III (*Ahmadabad Dist. Gazetteer*, p. 292). For a description of the garden, see Mandelslo (p. 34).
40. A primitive tribe with many sub-sections with different professions. The Kolis of Gujarat were turbulent people inhabiting hills and committing robbery. Traders were therefore compelled to buy their protection. (Forbes, *Oriental Memoirs*, Vol. II, pp. 162-163).

CHAPTER V

1. Arrian (Flavius Arrianus), famous Greek historian (c. 96 to c. 180 A.D.). His best known work is *Anabasis of Alexander* though his *Indica* is of more direct interest to students of Indian history. Thevenot's identification of Ahmadabad with '*Amadavistis*' of Arrian is however wrong.
2. Sultan Ahmad Shah (1411-1442) of Gujarat, the founder of Ahmadabad. It is said that the city occupies the site of an older one named Ashaval which is popularly attributed to Solanki Raja Karan of Anhilwada.
2a. See Tieffenthaler, *Description de l'Inde*, p. 373. "*Guzarat*, called *Ahmadabad* in Persian, after its founder *Ahmad*, is counted among the largest cities of India."
3. From *gard*, 'dust'. The author ascribes the nick-name to Shah Jahan, and his statement is repeated by Forbes (*Oriental Memoirs*, Vol. II, p. 119). His father was no less disgusted with its dirt and climate. Jahangir called it a "dustbin", "the place of the simoom", "abode of sickness", "the thorn bed" and "the house of Hell" (*Memoirs of Jahangir*, Vol. II, p. 13).
4. Governed the province for 6 years (1662-1668) (Sarkar, *History of Aurangzib*, Vol. V, p. 429).
5. Ahmadabad is situated in 23° 2′ North Latitude.
6. The river Sabarmati, on the left bank of which Ahmadabad stands.
7. Before entering the town I found myself in a pleasant avenue planted with trees, ending in a mosque.
8. The reference here is obviously to the Hauz-i-Qutb or Kankariya tank at Ahmadabad, which perpetuates the memory of Sultan Qutbuddin of Gujarat. It is said to have been completed in 1451, and is one of the largest of its kind in India, each of its 34 sides, according to Sir T. C. Hope, measuring 190 feet. There is an island in the centre of it, which formerly had a small garden called Nagina—"the jewel". Mandelslo visited it in 1638. (Burgess, *The Muhammadan Architecture of Ahmedabad*, Pt. I, pp. 52-53).
9. The more important tombs at Ahmadabad are those of (i) Ahmad Shah I; (ii) Ahmad Shah's queen; (iii) Darya Khan; (iv) Azam Khan; (v) Mir Abu; and (vi) Shah Waziruddin. See *Bombay Presidency Gaz.*, Vol. I, p. 257.
10. According to De Laet, Badur (Bhadwar) is 10 kos from Dayta (Dhaita) and eight kos from Nandurbar. In Akbar's time it formed a part of the territories of Pratap Shah (*The Empire of the Great Mogol*, pp. 28-29).
11. Khandesh.
12. *Caravanserai*, from Persian *karwansarai*, a serai for reception of caravans.
13. Does he mean the richly carved marble tomb of Mughali Bibi, queen of Muhammad Shah II, in the Rani ka Hazira or the queens' cemetery?
14. Maidan Shah or the King's square, which formed the outer courtyard of the palace. It originally covered an area 620 yards × 330 yards and was surrounded in 1638 by two rows of trees. Its main approach is through the Tin Darwaza or the Triple Gateway (Burgess, *op. cit.*, Pt. I, p. 25).
15. Obviously the Tin Darwaza.
16. Cotwal or kotwal, a police-magistrate. Thevenot writes of this official in greater detail in Chapter X. The duties of the kotwal, as given in the *Ain* (Vol. II, pp. 41-43) represent, according to Sarkar, 'the ideal'. Also see Manucci, Vol. II, pp. 420-21.
17. Are paltry.
18. Octagonal.
19. The Jami Masjid or the cathedral mosque, constructed by Ahmad Shah I (1411-1442), founder of the city, in close neighbourhood of the Tin Darwaza. It forms one of the best examples of the adaptation of the local Jain architectural style for purposes of Muslim worship. Previous to the great earthquake of 1918 it had four 'shaking minars'. See Burgess, *op. cit.*, Pt. I, pp. 30-36, Commissariat, pp. 107-110.
20. This is a common mistake. Jumah is Friday but Jami, that which collects or assembles.

21. Arabic *'mu'adhdhin'*, criers who call the faithful to the congregational prayer at specified hours.
22. From Arabic *imam*, 'an exemplar' or 'leader'; hence originally the first four Khalifas who were leaders *par excellence* of the faithful and subsequently a divine whose function is to lead the daily prayer of the congregation (*Hobson-Jobson*, p. 432).
23. Muluk Khana, or the Royal Gallery, which is "shut off from the mosque by a perforated screen." (Commissariat, p. 110; Burgess, *op. cit.*, Pt. I, p. 34).
24. Fakirs, from Arabic *fakir*, 'poor'. The term is usually applied to a Muslim religious mendicant but sometimes indiscriminately used by western writers for all Indian ascetics irrespective of their faith (*Hobson-Jobson*, p. 347).
25. Temple of Chintaman built by Shantidas, a Jain merchant, about 1638, at a cost of 9 lakhs of rupees. In 1644-46, Aurangzeb, then Viceroy of Gujarat converted it into a mosque, after effectively defiling and desecrating it. The temple was however subsequently restored to the Jains under the orders of Emperor Shah Jahan. Shantidas had succeeded in saving the principal image and he built another temple for it in the city, (*Ahmadabad Dist. Gazetteer*, p. 285). For a contemporary account see Mandelslo, p. 23.
26. Broken.
27. Thevenot refers to Shah Alam's mausoleum at Rasulabad, a mile and a quarter from the city, built by Taj Khan Narpali in 1531-32. Shah Alam (1415-1475) was the leader of the Bukhari Saiyads in Gujarat. His vast wealth, reputation for piety and family alliances secured for him unprecedented political power. Muslims claim that the conversion of a Hindu chieftain was due to the spiritual power of the saint (Commissariat, pp. 168, 208-9. *Ahmadabad Dist. Gazetteer*, p. 286).
28. Ostrich eggs are still used for similar purposes in Muslim tombs.
29. About sixty yards from Shah Alam's is another mausoleum, where his descendants lie buried. It is built on the same plan and scale as the saint's. (Commissariat, p. 209; Burgess, *op. cit.*, Pt. II, p. 20).
30. The Masjid at 'Shah Alam' described in Commissariat, p. 211.
31. The Shahi Bagh, a garden palace constructed by Shah Jahan while Viceroy of Gujarat. Mandelslo (1638) found the garden "very large, shut in by a great wall with ditches full of water, with a beautiful house having very rich rooms." For a more detailed description see Forbes, *Oriental Memoirs*, Vol. II, pp. 205-208 and Burgess, *op. cit.*, Pt. II, pp. 57-60.
32. A large pavilion.
33. Tank.
34. Though the king is not mentioned by name, the reference is obviously to the tomb of Ahmad Shah I.
35. Sarkhej, about six miles from Ahmadabad. The village came to fame as the residence of the celebrated saint Shaikh Ahmad Khattu Ganj Bakhsh. (Burgess, *op. cit.*, Pt. I, p. 46).
36. The ancient capital of Gujarat was Anhilvada (Patan).
37. There is a large number of tombs at Sarkhej including those of Shaikh Ahmad Khattu, Sultan Mahmud Begada, Muzaffar II and Mahmud III. For the Sarkhej group of buildings, see Burgess, *op. cit.*, Pt. I, pp. 46-51.
38. Shaikh Ahmad Khattu. The construction of the tomb and the mosque was commenced by Muhammad Shah in 1446 and completed by his son five years later.
39. And as many doors.
40. The mosque at Sarkhej has been described as "the perfection of elegant simplicity". "Except the Moti Masjid at Agra, there is probably no mosque in India that surpasses this in simple elegance." It "may fairly be considered an improvement on the plan of the Jami Masjid". (Burgess, *op. cit.*, Pt. I, p. 49).
41. It is flanked by.

41a. The great tank at Sarkhej measuring 700′ × 830′ feet was constructed by Mahmud Begada.

42. In fine, only tombs are to be seen in that place.
43. Designed.
44. Mandelslo also writes: "The best *Indico* in the world comes from about *Amadabath,* from a Village call'd *Chirchees* (Sarkhej)".
45. The reference here is to Dada Harir's or Bai Harir's well (Burgess, *op. cit.,* Pt. II, pp. 4-6; *Ahmadabad Dist Gazetteer,* p. 282).
46. Stages.
47. Square.
48. Winding.
49. The lady was the chief superintendent of the sultan's harem and the cost, according to a Sanskrit inscription, amounted to 329000 of an unspecified coin.
50. Almost all the foreign travellers of the period refer to the animal hospital of Ahmadabad.
51. More accurately, cheeta.
52. Chintz or printed cloth. Portuguese, *chita;* Marathi, *chit,* and Hindi, *chint.* Derived from Sanskrit *chitra* 'variegated, speckled' (*Hobson-Jobson,* 201 f).
53. Masulipatam in the Kistna district, Madras, once famous for its manufactures, specially chintzes.
54. Mylapore, a suburb of the Madras city. Linschoten says "The aforesaid place called S. Thomas was in time past a towne of great traffique, (and as then) called (by the name of) Meliapor" (Vol. I, p. 82). Conti calls it Malepur (*India in the Fifteenth century*).

CHAPTER VI

1. Bareja in the Daskroi sub-division of Ahmadabad district.
2. I took the Cambay road on the right hand.
3. Nagra, a village north of Cambay.
4. Baldaeus emphatically though wrongly asserts that "*Cambaja* is a different province from Gusuratte" (*Description of the Coasts, etc.,* p. 505).

4a. In 1638 Mandelslo found it "much greater than *Surat*" (p. 31).

5. And all have gates at the two ends. See Tavernier (Vol. I, p. 56) who also says, "at two hours after dark every street was closed by two gates." Also see Mandelslo, p. 31.
6. Limodra commonly called Nimodra now in the Rajpipla state. The celebrated cornelian and agate mines are three miles east of the village, and lie about five miles south-west of Ratanpur (Commissariat, pp. 262 and 268 *n.*). Barbosa visited "Limadura" and wrote of the cornelian rock (Vol. I, p. 143). Tavernier refers to the agates of Cambay (Vol. I, p. 56).
7. Banias and Rajputs.
8. The tomb of 'Umar bin Ahmad al Kazaruni, who bore the title of Zaur-al Malik. From an inscription on the tomb it appears that he died on 21 October 1333. (Burgess, *The Muhammadan Architecture of Bharoch, Cambay, Dholka etc.,* pp. 27-28).
9. Manucci also refers to the "hospital for sick birds" at Cambay (Vol. I, p. 156).
10. This is confirmed by Tavernier (Vol. I, p. 56): "Indigo of the same kind as that of Sarkhej is made, also, in the vicinity of the town (Cambay), and it was celebrated for its traffic when the Portuguese flourished in India."
11. Tavernier also assigns the decay of Cambay to the same cause. (Vol. I, p. 57).
12. Thevenot obviously refers to the 'bore' or rushing tide. See *Imp. Gaz.,* Vol. IX, p. 297.
13. The Dutch come there only at the end of September.

14. Faces.
15. The reference is to the south-west monsoon winds which blow from June to October, during which rains fall. These are accompanied by heavy storms in the month of September.
16. Wrecked.
17. Sought advice as to.
18. Almadia, from Arabic *al-madiya*, 'a raft'. In India, it is generally used for a canoe (*Hobson-Jobson*, p. 15).
19. Normally only at night time.
20. The pirates of Malabar were notorious for their ravages. They were particularly cruel to the Christians, as many of them were fanatical Moplah Mussalmans (Fryer, Vol. I, p. 164 and *n*; Biddulph, *The Pirates of Malabar*; Tavernier Vol. I, pp. 143-144).
21. Sand banks.
22. *Charans* who are found all over Gujarat. They acted as guards to travellers and goods. Their persons were held sacred and it was believed that a Charan's blood brought ruin on him who caused to it be split (R. E. Enthoven, *The Tribes and Castes of Bombay*, Vol. I, pp. 271 ff. Also see Heber, *Narrative of a Journey through the Upper Provinces of India*, Vol. II, pp. 40-41).
23. Outcaste.
24. Detour.
25. Obviously Petlad.
25a. Bilpad, south of Borsad, about 2 miles from the river Mahi.
26. 'Grasias' or 'Garasias', an epithet said to be derived from the term *grasa* (lit. a mouthful), which was used throughout Gujarat and Kathiawar to indicate lands and villages given to junior members of the Rajput ruling families for their maintenance. The term came to acquire a bad odour in the 17th and 18th centuries when it was applied to armed bands of robbers who exacted contribution, analogous to Marathi *chauth* and *rakhi* of the Sikhs, from villages as the price of their protection and forbearance.
27. Sili, a village in the Anand taluk of Kaira district near the Mahi river.
28. A very ill-clad fellow.
29. Paisa, a small copper coin current in India. It is now equivalent to 1/64 of a rupee. Thevenot elsewhere mentions that a rupee was worth 32½-33½ paisa only. According to Tavernier the value of a rupee varied from 46 to 56 paisas (Vol. I, pp. 22-23). At Surat "the Company's Accounts are kept in Book-rate *Price, viz.* 32 to the *Mam.* and 80 *pice* to the *Rupee*" (Fryer, Vol. II, p. 126).
30. Normally.
31. Immediately.
32. Toll.
33. "Ragout" in the original, stewed meat or fish, or stews in general.

CHAPTER VII

1. The correct latitude is 21° 12" N.
2. Shivaji. (For details see Chap. XVI).
3. The construction of the outer wall began in 1664 and was completed about 1675. (*Surat and Broach Dist. Gazetter*, p. 89).
4. Claim large compensation.
5. Moderate size.
6. The estimated population of Surat was about 2 lakhs in the later half of the 17th century (Ibid, p. 90).
7. November, December, January and February, etc.

8. Comfortable lodgings.
9. Used comprehensively for Europeans in general.
10. Muslims.
11. Though literally the term is applied to a person who is neither a Christian nor a Jew nor a Muslim here it refers to Hindus only.
12. Shias.
13. See Part II, Book II, Chap. XIII of *The Travels of Monsieur de Thevenot,* where he points out that the Sunnis acknowledge the first four Caliphs as the lawful successors of the Prophet while the Shias believe that Ali, the first of their twelve *Imams,* was his rightful successor.
14. From Persian *gabr,* 'infidel', a term of opprobrium generally applied to the Zoroastrians. See Dalgado, Vol. I, pp. 446-447. For Thevenot's account of *Gabrs* still resident in Persia, see Part II, Book II, Chap. XIV of the English translation.
15. *Atash-parast,* 'fire-worshipper'. The Parsis however deny that they worship fire as such.
16. The Parsis migrated to India in 716 A.D., and settled later at Navsari (Murzban, *The Parsis in India,* pp. 43 ff).
17. The second Caliph who was at the head of the Muslim state from 634 to 644 A.D. Persia came under his rule in 641 A.D. after the battle of Nehawand.
18. Virji Vora, the richest merchant and banker of his time. The English had dealings with him as early as 1617, and he was the Company's largest creditor in Surat. He had agents at Agra, Ahmadabad and other places. In 1643, the Court of Committees sent an 'iron chest from Nuremburg' as a present to Virji (Pant, *The Commercial Policy of the Moguls,* p. 137). He died probably in 1677, and is frequently mentioned in the letters of the time (Foster, *The English Factories in India*). Thevenot's statement that Virji was a "Banian" leaves no doubt about his religion.
19. The first English factory at Surat was founded in 1612. The Dutch established theirs four years later. For a sketch of the English factory, see Ovington, p. 226.
20. In the 17th century, there were two important officers in Surat. The officer in charge of the castle commanded the soldiers of the garrison only and possessed no authority in the city. The city had a separate governor who received the customs duties and other Imperial revenues on behalf of the Mughal emperor. Ovington (p. 136) says that the governor of the castle "is always confin'd a Prisoner within its Walls". See also Tavernier, Vol. I, p. 6.
21. The author's description of the houses in Surat is confirmed by Ovington (p. 130) and other European travellers.
22. Are expensive.
23. Portuguese settlement and town in Gujarat about 100 miles north of Bombay. It possesses stately forests about two-thirds of which consist of teak.
24. Obtained from.
25. Bambous split into two.
26. Rainy season.
27. Solidifies.
28. Cloths, "des toiles" in the French text. See p. 48, Part III of *Les Voyages de Mr de Thevenot,* Paris, 1689.
29. Game.
30. The common thistle of India cultivated all over the country for its oil producing black seeds (Watt, Vol. II, p. 378). Wild saffron does not bear oilseeds.
31. *Sesamum indicum.* Hindi, *til, tel* etc. Its small flattish seeds yield an oil and are used as food. See Watt, Vol. VI. Part II, pp. 502 ff.
32. Bitter.
33. Navapur-petha in Nandurbar taluk in Khandesh district, Bombay. It was renowned for its grapes and melons in the 17th century.
34. Brandy.

35. Jaggery, "coarse brown (or almost black) sugar made from the sap of various plants", such as *khajur*, the palmyra, the coco-palm etc. (*Hobson-Jobson*, p. 446).
36. *Babul* or *kikar*, the *Acacia arabica*.
37. 'Tari' or 'toddy', the fermented sap of the *tar* or palmyra, and also of other palms, such as the date, the coco-palm (*Hobson-Jobson*, p. 927).

CHAPTER VIII

1. *Khajur* (*Phoenix sylvestris*) which yields toddy, and is grown freely in several parts of Surat district.
2. More accurately cocoa-nut tree.
3. Take.
4. Bitter.
5. If he wishes to occupy.
6. There are sold etc.
7. Omit "to be sold there also".
7a. Myrrh—"A gum-resin highly esteemed by the ancients as an unguent and perfume, used for incense in temples and also in embalming." "True myrrh is the product of *Balsamodendron Myrrha*, a small tree of the natural order Amyridaceae that grows in eastern Africa and Arabia" (*Encyclopaedia Britannica*, Vol. 19, pp. 114-115).
8. A sweet exudation obtained from certain trees. The European *manna* is now obtained mainly from Sicily. The article referred to here seems to be of Persian or Arabic origin. Persian and Arabic *manna* "is the produce of *Alhagi maurorum*, a small, spiny, leguminous plant growing in Arabia, Asia Minor, Persia, Afghanistan, Baluchistan and northern India." (*Encyclopaedia Britannica*, Vol. 17, pp. 587-588).
9. Ammonium chloride or Sal ammoniac, said to have been prepared from camels' dung near the temple of Jupiter Ammon in Africa.
10. Mandelslo also mentions "*Roenas*, which is a root that dies red" (p. 19). 'Rohina', 'rohna', 'rohan' etc. are all vernacular names of *Soymida febrifuga*, the 'Indian red-wood tree'. The bark and *not the root* is responsible for the dye. See Watt, Vol. VI, Part III, pp. 318-319.
11. Are retailed.

CHAPTER IX

1. *Khandi*. This weight is common in southern India, and is equivalent to about 500 lbs (*Hobson-Jobson*, p. 155).
2. Maund (Eng.), *man* (Hind.). According to Tavernier the Surat maund varied between 40 and 42 seers (Vol. I, p. 334).
3. There is no standard seer in India; it varies from province to province. According to Mandelslo a Gujarat seer was equivalent to "about 12 ounces" in 1638 (p. 67). Tavernier says that the Surat seer was equal to ¾ livre or 13 French ounces (Vol. I, p. 334). Fryer (Vol. II, p. 126) makes it slightly less than a pound (40 seers=37 pounds).
4. Tola from Sanskrit *tula*, a balance. It is equivalent to 96 *rattis*, a ratti, according to E. Thomas, being equal to 1·75 grains. 80 tolas now equal 1 seer in India (*Hobson-Jobson*, p. 928).
5. Mangelin, seed of *Adenanthera pavonina*. According to Yule (*Hobson-Jobson*, p. 553) a seed of mangelin was equal to about 4·13 grains in weight. For its varying weights at Goa, Bijapur and Golkonda, see Tavernier, Vol. I, p. 333. See also Watt, *Dictionary of Economic Products*, Vol. I, pp. 107-108.

6. From Arabic *kirrat*, a bean of the carob tree, that formerly served as a unit of weight equivalent to 1/24 of an ounce. It is now used to indicate the proportionate quality of gold. A diamond carat is however 3⅙ grains nearly (*Hobson-Jobson*, pp. 160-161).
7. A val is equivalent to 3 *rattis* or about 5·733 grs. troy in weight (Tavernier, Vol. I, p. 333).
8. *Ghungchi*, Sanskrit *gunja*, the seed of *Abrus precatorius*. Its weight varies between 1·91 and 1·94 grs. troy, according to Ball. See Watt, Vol. I, pp. 10-14.
9. Rupee (mod. sp.). In Thevenot's time it was equivalent to 2*s*. 3*d*. The weight is still a tola.
10. Lakh (Sanskrit *laksha*), one hundred thousand.
11. Crores, 10 millions or one hundred lakhs.
12. *Padam* (Sanskrit *padman*).
13. Gold mohur, which equalled 14-14½ silver rupees in value. Tavernier also gives the same exchange value of a gold mohur as Thevenot.
14. 20 sols=1 livre, equivalent to 1*s*. 6*d*. See Ball, Vol.I, p. 327.
15. Hardly.
16. Tavernier mentions that 49 to 50, and sometimes 46 *paisas* went to the rupee. On an average, a *paisa* was equal to 1/50th of the rupee. The value of a *paisa* at Agra was about 1/55th or 1/56th of a rupee (Tavernier, Vol. I, pp. 22-23).
17. *Mahmudi*, equivalent to about 20 paisas or two-fifths of a rupee. Fryer says it was "somewhat less than an English shilling." (Vol. II, pp. 125-126). Its exchange value constantly fluctuated. Mahmudi was originally a Persian coin but it was later minted by the Gujarat kings. It was not a Mughal coin properly speaking.
18. One twelfth of a sol or 3/40*d*.
19. *Badam*, 'bitter almonds'. Tavernier disagrees with Thevenot. According to him, "Sometimes 35, sometimes 40, of them are given for the Paisa", (Vol. I, p. 23).
20. A Spanish coin of the same value as the French *ecu* and therefore equal to 4½*s* (Tavernier, Vol. I, p. 328).

CHAPTER X

1. Arabic *mufti*, "The officer who expounds the law. He assists the qazi, or judge, and supplies him with *fatwas*, or decisions. He must be learned in the Quaran and Hadis, and in the Muslim works of law" (Hughes, *A Dictionary of Islam*, p. 367). Prof. P. Saran is of opinion that the mufti in India was "a sort of unofficial legal referee recognised by public opinion" and he was not a regular official in the judicial department. (*The Provincial Government of the Mughals*, pp. 344-347; Sarkar, *Mughal Administration*, pp. 26-28 and 114).
2. Supervision.
3. The qazi was the chief judge in criminal suits and tried them according to Islamic laws. All cases between Muslims as well as all suits between Muslims and non-Muslims came before him. For qualifications and functions of a qazi, see P. Saran, pp. 339 ff; Sarkar, *op. cit.*, pp. 26-27.
4. Dispute.
5. Maintains.
6. Derived from Latin *intendere* meaning 'to watch over'. The intendents controlled practically the entire civil administration, including the judicial, and revenue machinery, of the province.
7. *Waqai-Navis* (sometimes written as *waqai-nigar* also) was one of the agencies through which the central government kept itself informed of the day-to-day happenings in the provinces. The *waqai-navis* was stationed at the provincial

headquarters and reported to the emperor every occurrence of note. Sarkar says that his reports were first "communicated to the subahdar or, in the case of a field-army, to the general in command, before being despatched to the Emperor." (Sarkar, *op. cit.*, pp. 71-75).

8. *Nawab*, (English 'Nabob'), as the provincial governors were officially styled during the Mughal period.
9. The Quran or Qoran.
10. On arrival one lays before him.
11. *Sir Bashi*, an ancient military title in Turkey. The officer exercised police control over the inhabitants of the district under his charge.
12. Formerly the supervisor of a department was styled *darogha* but now the designation is limited mainly to the lower ranks in the British Indian police service.
13. Shields.
14. This is fully confirmed by Ovington (p. 138) and *Mirat-i-Ahmadi* quoted in Saran, *op. cit.*, p. 388.
15. Part II, Book II, Chapter IV, p. 79.
16. *Khabar-dar.*
17. A similar.
17a. See also Ovington, p. 137.
18. Manucci also bears testimony to the kotwal's responsibility for thefts and robberies, and describes how the kotwal utilised sweepers who went to clean every house twice daily as his spies (Vol. II, p. 421).
19. Means.
20. 'Sequin', a coin of Venice worth about 9*s.* 3*d.* in English money. (See Tavernier, Vol. I, p. 328).
21. Khojah Minaz.
22. Every possible enquiry.
23. Had taken refuge with.
24. *Faujdar*, police magistrate in charge of a sarkar. His functions are briefly described in the *Ain*, Vol. II, pp. 40-41. See Manucci, Vol. II, pp. 450-451; Ovington, p. 139.
25. Who is responsible for the security of the country about.
26. *Dohai* or *Duhai-Padshah*, an exclamation or expression used in prohibiting in the name of the Padshah (*Hobson-Jobson*, p. 321), somewhat similar to the Portuguese invocation 'Aqui el Rei'.
27. Court.
28. Few penalties.

CHAPTER XI

1. Addressed.
2. The French Company.
3. Manucci (Vol. I, p. 62) calls him "Brother Ambrozio", and Irvine identifies him with "Father Ambroise of Preuilly". During the sack of Surat (1664) Shivaji did not plunder his house saying "The *Frankish* Padrys are good men, and shall not be molested" (Bernier, p. 188). Dr. Dellon also knew Father Ambrose and got from him a letter of introduction to Juan de Fonseca, Rector of the Jesuit College at Daman (*Relation d'un Voyage fait aux Indes Orientales*, p. 233).
4. Capuchins, a section of the great Franciscan order.
5. The reference is to the formation of the famous Compagnie des Indes at the instance of Colbert and Louis XIV in 1664 with the object of trading with India and the east.
6. Hubert Hugo, a Dutch pirate. Originally in the employment of the Dutch Company at Ahmadabad he returned home in 1654 and sailed from Amsterdam for the east (1661) in the *Black Eagle*. On his way he called at Havre where

he enlisted a number of Frenchmen who had brought a commission from the French Admiral, the Duc de Vendôme. The *Black Eagle* was driven by adverse winds to the Red Sea (April, 1662) where Hugo and his crew captured a number of merchantmen. It was probably on this occasion that the dowager queen of Bijapur was robbed (*The English Factories in India*, 1661-1664, pp. 189-190 and *n*. *Court Minutes of the East India Company*, 1664-1667, p. 7).

7. On board his ship.
8. Mocha or Mokha, a port in Arabia on the Red Sea.
9. Caesar, Duke of Vendôme (1594-1665), Admiral of France.
10. Badi Sahiba, widow of Muhammad Adil Shah and regent during the minority of Ali Adil Shah II. She went on pilgrimage to Mecca four times, according to Manucci (Vol. II, p. 300). The incident mentioned here probably relates to her journey commenced in February 1661. See *The English Factories in India* 1661-1664, p. 88 *n*.
11. Socotra or Sokotra, an island in the Indian Ocean belonging to Great Britain. It is situated in 12·30′ N (not 11° 40′ as Thevenot puts it) and is on the direct route to India via the Suez Canal.
12. Mecca.
13. The *Bantam*.
14. He did not despair.
15. Awaited.
16. Carried.
17. To the Grand Sheikh. The reference is to the dynasty founded at Mecca in the 11th century by Ibn Qitada who claimed descent from Hashim, the Prophet's great grandfather. This house continued to rule there until 1925 when King Hussain abdicated. The Hashimite family still rules in Iraq and Transjordan. (Gerald de Gaury, *Arabia Phoenix*, p. 24).
18. Others.
19. Spoke strongly about.
20. And said.
21. Aden, fortified town on the south coast of the province of Yemen, Arabia, situated in 12° 47′ N. Lat. It was acquired by the British in 1839 (*Imp. Gaz.*, Vol. V, pp. 9 ff.).
22. Charles de La Porte (1602-1664), first Duke of Meilleraye and Marshal of France. Thomas Reynardson wrote from Mokha on 20 July 1656 that "The last yeare a French Pyratt was forced by foule weather and want of provisions into Aden, where they were all put in prison and afterwards sent up to the Great Emaun, where they were all circumsized." Sir William Foster suggests that the vessel referred to above probably formed "part of the squadron sent out by the Duc de la Meilleraye for the Red Sea" (*The English Factories in India*, 1655-1660, pp. 58-59). The letter also mentions another ship of 26 guns from which the boat in question was separated by stress of weather. This almost confirms Thevenot's statement.
23. For la Boullaye, see *supra* Note, 37, Chapter IV. Boullaye was the king's envoy while Beber was the nominee of the new French East India Company. They arrived at Surat on 1 April, 1666 and left for Agra about a fortnight later, to secure a *farman* from the Mughal emperor in favour of the French Company. According to a contemporary English account, the envoys were not treated well; "They have had neither respect nor countenance shewed them, but tossed from post to pillar." From Agra, Boullaye proceeded to Bengal and was murdered near Decca.

    Beber left for Surat and was robbed of all his belongings while a day's journey out of Agra. The emperor then recalled him and granted him the *farman* he wanted. After a brief residence at Surat Beber went to Goa where he died. (Manucci, Vol. II, pp. 151-152; *The English Factories in India*, 1665-1667).
24. Sir George Oxenden. For details regarding his administration, see *The English Factories in India*, 1665-1667.

CHAPTER XII

1. Probably Muhammad Beg Khan who held this office in 1666.
2. Umara or Omrah (plural of *Amir*). The term was applied to the higher officials and nobility at Muhammadan Courts, specially those of the Mughals. In the accounts of European travellers, it is used for a lord or noble of the Imperial Court (*Hobson-Jobson*, p. 637). The premier noble was ordinarily styled as *Amir-ul-Umara* (*Ain-i-Akbari*, Vol. I, p. 240).
3. Obviously a misprint for cymbals in the original French which has been repeated in the translation.
4. Fifteen days.
5. And which.
6. Decorated.
7. The same as Barbosa's Reynel and Peter Mundy's Raneile. Rander, situated on the right bank of the Tapti, 2 miles above Surat city, and an important trading centre before Surat rose to prominence (*Bombay Presidency Gazetteer*, Vol. I, pp. 344-345).
8. Fountains.
9. Blue.
10. Shot up.
11. Arabic *maula*, Hindi *mulla*, 'a Muslim doctor of law'.
12. Ovington was more favourably impressed with the performances of the *kanchanis* or dancing girls of Surat (see p. 153).
13. Nimbler ones.
14. Punishment.

CHAPTER XIII

1. Like to adorn.
2. Large sums were spent by the English and the Dutch on tombs. The instance mentioned by Thevenot was a comparatively insignificant one. An idea of their expenditure can be had from the fact that a bill of Rs. 6,000/- was charged to the Dutch Company for merely repairing the tomb of Baron Van Reede, one of their early chiefs.
3. Read "a certain drinker" instead of "a great drinker." Ovington also refers to this tomb (p. 236) but Mr. Rawlinson suggests that he derived his information from Thevenot. An anonymous writer (*Calcutta Review*, Vol. IX, 1848, p. 125) says that the tomb was built over the grave of a "notorious tippler" who, according to one account, was a ship's butler, while others believed him to have been a person of distinction. The tomb has not survived to our times; whether it ever existed is a moot point.
4. *"Vrati"*, literally a person who has taken some vow, but used in a general sense for all 'sanyasis' and mendicants.
5. With the intention.
6. The name 'Tapti' is derived from *tap*, 'to heat'. According to mythology, it is said to have been created by the sun to protect himself from his own warmth. The river has a reputation for sanctity, and the chief places of pilgrimage are Changdeo, and Bodhan (*Bombay Presidency Gazetteer*, Vol. I, pp. 174-175).
7. Sanskrit *yogin*, and Hindi *yogi*, 'a Hindu ascetic, (*Hobson-Jobson*, p. 461).
8. From Persian *darvesh*, 'a Muslim mendicant'.
9. Mahadeva or Siva, the third deity of the Hindu trinity.

CHAPTER XIV

1. A Banian had it made.
2. It is mentioned by most of the 17th century travellers. Mandelslo (p. 18)

and Roe (p. 90) refer to it briefly. But Pietro Della Valle devotes one entire section (VII) to this famous reservoir (Vol. I, pp. 32-35), and Peter Mundy also gives a fairly detailed description of the tank and its environs (Vol. II, pp. 31-32). Fryer says that "were it filled, the best Ship that swims in the Sea might ride in it" (Vol. I, p. 261). The tank is now dry and has been converted into a garden. Strangely, however, Ovington is silent both about the tank and the famous banyan tree near it. See also *Surat and Broach Dist. Gazetteer*, p. 312.

2a. "Seze" (Sixteen) in the French original, was the correct number of sides.
3. Three fathoms in height, length and breadth.
4. On the southern bank of the reservoir, there are Muslim monuments of which the most famous is the mosque of Nav Syed Pir. Pietro Della Valle also refers to some Muslim tombs near the tank (Vol. I, p. 33).
5. Pietro Della Valle rightly identifies Gopi, whose name the tank bears, with Malik Gopi of the Portuguese chroniclers. Longworth Dames similarly identifies him with Barbosa's "Milocoxim" who governed Surat (Barbosa, Vol. I, p. 149 f.n. 2). He was, according to the local traditions, an Anavla Brahman and not a Bania as Thevenot suggests. Malik Gopi served under Mahmud Begada, and his successor Muzaffar by whom he was put to death. Though Gopi's tank is now dry a suburb of the city of Surat still commemorates his name.
6. The tank was in a fairly good condition when Mandelslo visited it in 1638 (p. 18) but it seems to have steadily deteriorated for lack of repairs and by the beginning of the next century it was completely in ruins. *Surat and Broach Dist. Gazetteer*, p. 312.
7. The reference perhaps is to one of the gardens owned by Jahanara Begam, the sister of Aurangzeb, who was assigned the revenues of the port of Surat for her betel expenses. (Manucci, Vol. I, p. 216).
8. Portuguese *mangueiras*, 'mango trees'.
9. Portuguese *palmeira*, 'the palm-tree'.
10. The dried unripe fruit of *Terminalia chebula.*
11. Probably maça or ber.
12. *Calotropis gigantea,* Vern. *ak, akond* etc. The plant is described in Part II, Book II, Chapter XVI. A woodcut of the flowering twig will be found opposite p. 116 of the English edition. "Querzehre" is obviously a corruption of the Persian *Khar zahrah.*
13. Brilliance.
14. Our.
15. *Vat tree,* the Indian fig (*Ficus indica*), which is particularly sacred to the Hindus. This particular tree has been noticed by Mandelslo (p. 18), Pietro Della Valle (Vol. I, p. 35), Peter Mundy (Vol. II, p. 34), Dellon (Supplement, p. 27), Tavernier (Vol. II, pp. 155-156) and Fryer (Vol. I, p. 265). Sir Richard Temple, Grey and Crooke wrongly identify it with the *Kabir Barh* which was near Broach.
16. Space.
17. Or more than.
18. Thevenot's *Mameva* and Tavernier's *Mamaniva* are probably bad corruptions of Mahamaya. Dellon calls the goddess the "Mother of Mankind" and Pietro Della Valle states that the Hindus called her "Parvete, whom they hold to be the wife of Mahadeu" (Vol. I, p. 35). There cannot therefore be any doubt about the identity of the goddess who is variously known Bhavani, Durga, Kali etc.
19. Coloured red all over.
20. French *goujon,* 'a small fresh water fish generally used as a bait'.
21. There.
22. Skins.
23. The rainy season.
24. Is it *Gahara Kunda,* deep tank? "The Tapti is believed to rise in the sacred tank of Multai (*Mul-tapi,* the source of the Tapti) on the Satpura

plateau, but its real source is two miles distant." A description of the tank is to be found in *Betul District Gazetteer*, p. 255.

25. Burhanpur.
26. But at high tide.

CHAPTER XV

1. Right up.
2. Suvali, the "Swally" of the old records, the sea-port of Surat, about 12 miles from the city.
3. According to Ball, a French livre was equivalent to 1s. 6d. when Tavernier visited India (1631-1662) and a rupee was worth 2s. 3d. Thevenot's calculation is therefore obviously wrong, for the exchange value of the rupee could not possibly fall to such an extent during the four years between Tavernier's sixth voyage in 1662 and Thevenot's visit to India in 1666.
4. Guards.

CHAPTER XVI

1. Predicament.
2. Shivaji's father began his career in Ahmadnagar and later entered the service of Bijapur.
3. Shivaji was born at Shivner near Junnar. Cosme da Guarda, a Portuguese writer, asserts that the Maratha prince was born at Virar (now on B. B. & C. I. Ry.) near Bassein. Thevenot's error may be due to the same source (Sen, *Foreign Biographies of Shivaji*, p. 1 and *n*.).
4. He resisted successfully in the mountains of Visiapour those that came to attack him.
5. Was acting in collusion.
6. The cause of Shahaji's arrest is a subject of controversy. It is also alleged that he was himself guilty of insubordination while participating in the seige of Jinji.
7. This is incorrect. Shahaji was released and died many years later from injuries caused by a fall from his horse while hunting.
8. Powerful.
9. Badi Sahiba. It was at her instance that Afzal Khan led his disastrous expedition against Shivaji.
10. Shaista Khan, appointed viceroy of the Deccan in 1659. He was the son of Asaf Khan, brother of the celebrated Nur Jahan and father-in-law of Shah Jahan and was thus maternal uncle of Aurangzeb.
11. 5 April, 1663.
12. Contemporary authorities differ on this point. While some chroniclers assert that Shaista Khan slept in a tent that fateful night, others are of opinion that he used to reside in a small building.
13. Abul Fath was killed while he rushed to his father's rescue.
14. The story is inaccurate but gained wide currency in the European settlements. L'Escaliot heard it and a letter from Surat to Madras dated 25 May 1663 (*English Factories in India*, 1661-1664, p. 238) also reports that Shivaji "killed 50 great persons, wounded Shasta Ckaun, killed 12 of his weomen and wounded 6, 'killed his eldest sonn and sonn in law, wounded 2 more,

carried away his daughter and a great treasure of jewells and money." The European travellers obviously relied on bazar rumours which greatly exaggerated Shivaji's achievement and the discomfiture of the Mughals.

15. Was hatching.
16. If he did not withdraw.
17. Shaista Khan was, in fact, transferred to Bengal, an unhealthy province, the climate of which did not suit the Mughal grandees.
18. Bassein (from *vasai*, 'settlement') in Thana district, Bombay. Bahadur Shah ceded the city and its neighbourhood to the Portuguese in 1534. Under them Bassein became famous for its wealth and magnificence. The ancient buildings in the city have been described in detail by Da Cunha (*History and Antiquities of Chaul and Bassein*).
19. Chaul (*Cheul*) in Kolaba district, about 30 miles south of Bombay. The Portuguese appeared for the first time at Chaul in 1505 and it was the scene of a naval fight between the Portuguese and the Muslim three years later in which the former were defeated.
20. Fakir, Arabic *fakir* (poor), a mendicant.
21. To distract.
22. Contemporary English and Dutch accounts of the first sack of Surat are available in print. (Letter of L'Escaliot in *Indian Antiquary*, Vol. L; *English Factories in India*, 1661-1664, pp. 298-316; Forrest, *Selections from the Bombay Records, Home Series*, Vol. I; Sen, *Foreign Biographies of Shivaji*).
23. Decided to march off.
24. He had amassed.

24a. Bernier (p. 188) gives no definite estimate of the value of the booty but says that it amounted to several millions. The English President and Henry Gary estimated it at a crore of rupees. (*The English Factories in India*, 1661-64, pp. 303-307).

25. According to an anonymous French writer who visited Surat six years later, Shivaji relieved one merchant of forty pounds of fine pearls (Sen, *Foreign Biographies of Shivaji, p.* 179 *f.n.* 2). L'Escaliot in a way confirms Thevenot, for Thevenot's pounds and seers are equivalent.
26. Might.
27. If one did not know that.
28. Thevenot forgets that the Marathas were also Indians.
29. Inayat Khan, the governor, made no effort to defend the town but deserted his post at the earliest opportunity.
30. Stood firm at.
31. Bernier (p. 188) corroborates Thevenot on this point. Carré says that the Capuchin Fathers were not molested on account of the general esteem in which they were held. He does not, however, mention Father Ambrose in this connection (*Foreign Biographies of Shivaji*, p. 199).
32. Allowing.
33. Pretended that.
34. Throwing.
35. Shivaji had been defeated by Jai Singh who induced him to visit the imperial court.
36. Coolness.
37. But while waiting for them to do so.
38. For the correct story, see Sen, *Siva Chhatrapati*, pp. 217-20.
39. Because most of them came to court only upon the King's word.

39a. Command.

40. Orme follows Thevenot (*Historical Fragments of the Mogul Empire*, p. 14). There is good reason to believe that Shivaji had offered to recover Kandahar for the emperor.
41. Baskets.
42. Ferry-man.
43. Rode.
44. According to Sabhasad, Shambaji was left with trusted friends at Muttra.

(See Sen, *Siva Chhatrapati*, p. 71). Shivaji had himself caused a rumour to this effect to be spread to ensure his son's safe return.

CHAPTER XVII

1. Father Ambrose is mentioned also by Bernier, Carré, Manucci and François Martin.
2. Resolves.
3. Shab-i-Barat, "The Persian title for the fifteenth day of the month Sha'ban." "On this night, Muhammad said, God registers annually all the actions of mankind which they are to perform during the year; and that all the children of men, who are to be born and to die in the year, are recorded." The night is to be spent in prayer and the next day is to be one of fasting. But actually it has become the Muslim "Guy Fawkes Day" in India (Hughes, *A Dictionary of Islam*, p. 570).
4. Alms-giving.

CHAPTER XVIII

1. Baroda. Barodora of John Jourdain (Pt. I, 174), Brodra of Mandelslo (p. 21), also called 'Brodera' by some English travellers (Forbes, *op. cit.*, Vol. II, Chap. X). Tavernier (Vol. I, p. 58) who calls the town Broudra says it was noted for 'a considerable trade in calicoes.' Jourdain refers to its indigo trade.
2. Rajapur. The modern town of Baroda was built at a short distance from the old town. Mandelslo calls the old town 'Radiapora' (p. 21). De Laet has "Radiapore or rather Brodera" (p. 25).
3. Plenty.
4. Lac, Hindi *lakh*, "the resinous incrustation produced on certain trees (such as *dhak*, *peepul* and *kusum* or *kusumb*) by the puncture of the lac insect." It contains "10 per cent of dark red colouring matter from which is manufactured *lac-dye*." (*Hobson-Jobson*, pp. 499-500; Watt, Vol. IV, 570-577).
5. Sindkheda in Baroda State. Mandelslo (p. 21) says it is 'eight Leagues from the City' (Baroda).
6. A port on the Gulf of Cambay in Ahmadabad district, once an important commercial centre, now superseded by the rival port of Bhavnagar (*Imp. Gaz.*, Vol. XII, pp. 301-302).
7. Headquarters of the taluk of the same name, Baroda state. Famous for the manufacture of *patolas* (variegated saris), embroidery and pottery.
8. A town at the east end of the island of the same name.
9. The correct latitude is 20° 43′ No.
10. It was Nuno da Cunha and not Albuquerque who built a fort at Diu in 1535-36. The date also is therefore wrong.

10a. Affonso d'Albuquerque, Governor of Portuguese India, 1509-1515.

11. Kansuh-al-Ghori, who ruled Egypt from 1501-1516, sent a naval expedition under Mir Hashim against the Portuguese in 1507. Hashim was joined by Malik Ayaz, Governor of Diu. The joint Egyptian and Gujarati armada encountered a Portuguese squadron commanded by Dom Lourenço d'Almeida, son of the viceroy, near Chaul in 1508. In the battle that followed the Portuguese were defeated and Dom Lourenço was killed. Next year the viceroy avenged his son's defeat and death by routing the allied fleet at Diu (Whiteway, *The Rise of Portuguese Power in India*, pp. 115-125).
12. Turkish and Circassian slaves trained in arms by Sultan Malik as-Salih. They later captured the government of Egypt in 1254 and ruled the country till 1517 A.D., when it was conquered by Salim I, emperor of the Turks (Hughes, *A Dictionary of Islam*, p. 312).

13. Incited.
14. Sultan Sulaiman I, surnamed 'the Magnificent', emperor of the Turks from 1520 to 1566 A.D.
15. The Portuguese occupied Diu in 1537 after Sultan Bahadur's death. It was besieged by a joint Turkish and Gujarati force by land and sea late in September 1538. The stubborn resistance of the defenders and the news of the arrival of reinforcement led to the Turkish withdrawal early in November. (Whiteway, *op. cit.*, pp. 254-265).
16. Bahadur Shah, Sultan of Gujarat, from 1526 to 1537.
17. From Turkish *'Yeni Cheri'*, new troops, 'an organised military force constituting until 1826 the standing army of the Ottoman Empire.' The fleet had a force of 7,000 Janissaries.
18. Now called 'pasha', Turkish officer of high rank.
19. Sulaiman Pasha al-Khadim participated in the Egyptian campaign of the Ottoman Sultan Salim I (1516-17) and was appointed governor of Egypt in 1525. He was 82 years of age when he was appointed to command the naval expedition to Diu. *J. R. A. S.*, 1921, pp. 17-18. See also *J. R. A. S.*, 1922, pp. 12-17.
20. Amir ibn Daud, lord of Aden was invited to Sulaiman Pasha's flagship and there treacherously put to death. While the Amir was held prisoner by Sulaiman Pasha, one of his officers captured Aden. See *J. R. A. S.* (1922), pp. 15-16.
21. One hundred and fifty pieces of Cannon.
22. Antonio da Silveira, brother-in-law of Nuno da Cunha.
23. Flags.
24. Several Portuguese and French writers refer to the snake stone and the popular belief that it is found in the head of a snake (Dalgado, *Glossario Luso-Asiatico*, Vol. II, pp. 201-202). Ovington, however, corroborates Thevenot about the artificial origin of the stone. He says, "The Composition of it is Ashes of burnt Roots, mixt with a kind of Earth, which is found at Diu" (p. 155). The stone is supposed to remove the venom by absorption when applied against the wound. Also see Fryer, Vol. I, pp. 138-139.
25. Nadiad, in Kaira District, 29 miles south-east of Ahmadabad. In the 17th century, it was a large town with cotton and indigo manufactures (*Imp. Gaz.*, Vol. XVIII, pp. 282-283).
26. Mahmadabad or Mahmudabad, in Kaira District, 17 miles south of Ahmadabad.

CHAPTER XIX

1. One of the twelve provinces into which Akbar's empire was divided; its area was 176 *kos* by 100 *kos*.
2. The correct latitude is 27° 10′ N.
3. The Jumna.
4. Allahabad.
5. To make Agra famous by an ancient name.
6. Akbarabad or Agra. No definite information is available regarding the foundation of the city. Tradition ascribes the building of the old fortress named Badalgarh to Badal Singh (1475) on or near the site of which the present fort was built by Akbar in 1566. (*Agra Dist. Gaz.*, p. 137).
7. Claimed.
8. Twenty-five.
9. Square.
10. Rooms.
11. Sports.
12. Which contribute much to the length of the town.
13. Akbar's tomb at Sikandra. It was commenced during the lifetime of the

emperor and completed by his son and successor Jahangir (E. W. Smith, *Akbar's Tomb, Sikandarah*).
14. Arjumand Banu Begam, better known as Mumtaz Mahal.
15. François Bernier, physician and traveller (1620-1688). After travelling widely in Europe, Palestine and Egypt he came to Surat, circa 1658. He was in India till 1667. His *Travels* published in 1670 received wide popularity and went through ten editions in different languages before his death. See Bernier (Ed. V. A. Smith), pp. xix-xlii.
16. The Taj garden has been described by Sleeman, *Rambles* (pp. 317 ff). For gardens in medieval India, see Stuart, *The Gardens of the Great Mughals*, 1913.
17. This is a mistake. Begun early in 1632, the Taj was completed in January 1643 (Sarkar, *Studies in Mughal India*, p. 30).
18. As many men as necessary for so great a work.
19. Jahangir was buried at Shahdara, near Lahore. Tavernier (Vol. I,* p. 91) commits the same error when he writes, "When you reach Agra from the Delhi side you meet a large bazaar, close to which there is a garden where the King Jahangir, father of Shahjahan, is interred. Over the gate of this garden you see a painting which represents his tomb covered by a great black pall with many torches of white wax, and two Jesuit Fathers at the ends." The building to which the French travellers refer cannot, however, be identified.
20. Unpleasant.
21. However great the aversion he had to it.
22. Shah Jahan passed the last seven and a half years of his life as a prisoner in Agra Fort where he breathed his last.
23. That misfortune befell him through Aurangzeb, his third son.
24. Introduced.
25. Formed.
26. This is slightly incorrect, as Shah Jahan died on 22 January, 1666.
27. The peacock-throne is probably meant.
28. Jahanara Begam, the favourite daughter of Shah Jahan, and a partisan of Dara, died in 1681. Bernier (p. 199) says she presented Aurangzeb "with a large golden basin, full of precious stones." The story of her death by poison is unfounded, though Tavernier mentions it (Vol. I, pp. 275-276).
29. Finally.
30. This is incorrect. Shah Jahan was buried by the side of his wife in the Taj at Agra, and the two tombs were enclosed with a marble screen by Aurangzeb. It is, however, popularly believed that Shah Jahan intended to build another mausoleum in black marble on the opposite bank of the river and connect it with the Taj by a marble bridge. Dara was buried in an unidentified vault in Humayun's tomb.
31. This need surprise no one.
32. Mansabdars from Persian *mansab*, office. The mansabdari system was introduced by Akbar. (*Ain-i-Akbari*, Vol. I, pp. 236-249; Irvine, *Army of the Indian Moghuls*, Chap. I).
32a. Bernier speaks only of twenty-five or thirty Christian families settled at Agra (p. 286).
33. In comparison with.
34. These latter.
35. For the Dutch factory, see Bernier, pp. 292-293.
36. We have seen.

CHAPTER XX

1. As those of the Persians are.
2. *Cabaya*, from Arabic *kaba*, 'a vesture'. The word is not used in India now. (*Hobson-Jobson*, p. 137).

3. Convenient.
4. Turkish *arqaliq*, 'a coat with sleeves' (Tavernier, Vol. I, p. 132 and *n* 3; Irvine, *op. cit.*, p. 29).
5. Chhit.
6. 'Jupe' in the French text means 'skirt'.
7. Spreading.
8. For a description of *Cadeby*, see Thevenot, *Travels into the Levant*, Part II, Chap. IX, p. 92.
9. Shawl, Persian and Hindi *shal*.
10. Thin cloth.
11. Kashmir.
12. An obsolete measure of length. English ell=45 inches, the old French ell was about 47 inches.
13. Very thin.
14. The colour of fallen leaves.
15. Read "great" for "the".
16. Sometimes will not weigh.
17. Thevenot devotes Chapter VII of Part II, Book II, of his *Travels* to "Moneys weights and measures" of Persia. "The *Toman*", he says there, "is worth fifteen *Piastres*, or fifty *Abassis*" (p. 89). Tavernier supports Thevenot (Vol. I, p. 20) and adds, "If you take 6¼ tomans to India you receive for each toman 29¼ rupees." Also see Fryer Vol. II, p. 139.
18. In front.
19. Whose head-gear closely resembled that kind of turban.
20. Unlike.
21. Persian *pa-posh*, 'foot-garment', slippers. Thevenot (Pt. I, p. 30) writes that Turkish shoes are "made almost like Slippers, the heel is equal to the rest of the sole, only it is shod with a piece of Iron made purposely half round, and these Shoes they called *Paboutches*."
22. Wish to.
23. Difficult enough.
24. Red velvet.
25. Decoration.
26. Chains, necklaces.
27. Set in the bezel.
28. Quite naked. The reference is to the Malabar regions.

CHAPTER XXI

1. Afford.
2. A great deal.
3. The majority.
4. With raising.
5. The common black buck (Sanskrit *krishnasara*) is meant.
6. From Hindi *sant*, a holy man.
7. Two-ended staff.
8. When they do not wish to use.
9. Involved.
10. Difficult.
11. There are several species of green pigeons in India. See Stuart Baker, *Fauna of British India, Birds*, Vol. V, pp. 180-211. The species meant here is most probably Indian green imperial pigeon, *Muscadivora ænea sylvatica* (pp. 208-209).
12. Hunting and fishing.
12a. A similar method of catching waterfowls is described by Terry (Foster,

Early Travels, p. 312), and Ovington (p. 162). It is also described in the *Ain*, Vol. I, p. 295.

13. Wait.
14. Narwar. The mountain is 'a steep scrap of the Vindhyas' near the town of the same name in Gwalior State, Central India.
15. Meru is the Marathi name of Sambar (*Rusa aristotelis*). Dalgado derives it from Sanskrit *mriga* and further opines that this name was invariably given to the Sambar by the Portuguese on account of its large size.
16. Profit from them.
17. Pietro Aretino (1492-1556), an Italian author who wrote a set of obscene sonnets to accompany an equally immoral series of drawings by Romano.
18. Materials.
19. Skilfully.
20. Solid.
21. Wish to surround.
22. Telugu *Ghurie-ghenza*, ghungchi. See *supra*, Chap. IX, N. 8.

22a. Fatehpur Sikri, 23 miles west of Agra. The word 'Fatehpur' does not mean 'the enjoyment of what one desires', but 'City of Victory' (*Imp. Gaz.*, Vol. XII, pp. 84-86; E. W. Smith, *The Mughal Architecture of Fatehpur Sikri*).

23. Jahangir was born at Fatehpur Sikri. Akbar was at Agra at the time.

23a. Sikandar Lodi had made Agra his residence. So it was not an insignificant village, as Thevenot suggests, before Akbar's time.

24. The Buland Darwaza is probably meant though it is a city gate rather than an "entry of Akbar's palace." All the state buildings of the deserted city are still intact.
25. The cathedral mosque at Fatehpur Sikri (Jama Masjid) has been described by Ferguson as "the glory of Fatehpur Sikri." For details see E. W. Smith, *The Mughal Architecture of Fatehpur Sikri*, Pts. III and IV.
26. An order of Muslim wandering monks.
27. Shaikh Salim Chisti known as *Shaikh-ul-Islam* was greatly revered by Akbar and his courtiers. He was an apostolic descendant of Shaikh Farid Shakarganj. The mosque at Sikri was built at his instance by Akbar. He died a few years after its completion and lies buried in the courtyard.
28. The huge lake formed by constructing a dam across the valley of the Khari Nadi. It supplied water to the city and fed many irrigation canals. The dam however burst while Akbar was still alive. For details see Keene, *Handbook to Delhi, Agra etc.*, pp. 222-223.
29. Firozabad, in Agra District, United Provinces, so named after Malik Firoz, an officer of Akbar (*Agra Dist. Gaz.*, p. 274). Previously known as Chandwar, it was under the Sarkar of Agra in the Mughal days, *Description Historique et Géographique de l'Inde* by Tieffenthaler, pp. 166, 198.
30. Sidhpur (?) in Baroda state, famous for the manufacture of Chintzes or coloured cottons.
31. It is difficult to identify the place. Ball says (Vol. I, p. 31) that this is probably Baglana but this cannot be reconciled with the distance (15 kos) given by Tavernier (Vol. I, p. 71) between Bargant and Bimal (Bhinmal in Marwar state). It is probably Barmer, an historic fortress in Marwar state and capital of an independent tribe during the Mughal period.
32. Jalor, a town in Jodhpur state in Rajputana.
33. Bharatpur, capital of the state of the same name in Rajputana. Tavernier (Vol. I, p. 72) describes it as "a very old town where they make woollen carpets," and places it at 12 coss from Agra.
34. Merta, town in Jodhpur state, Rajputana (Erskine, *Rajputana Gazetteer*, Vol. III A, pp. 203-204).
35. Ludana, on the Bandi river in Jaipur.
36. Hindaun, in Jaipur state, Rajputana (*Imp. Gaz.*, Vol. XIII, p. 135).
37. Kanwa, near Bayana, where the Rajput confederacy led by Rana Sanga was decisively defeated by Babar in 1527.

38. Bayana, ancient town in Bharatpur state (*Imp. Gaz.*, Vol. VII, p. 137).
39. Sikandra, a village five miles from Agra on the road to Muttra. It derives its name from Sultan Sikandar Lodi. The place is famous on account of Akbar's tomb (*Agra Dist. Gaz.*, pp. 325-331).
40. Obviously Sultan Sikandar Lodi, but Sikandarabad was not his capital city.
41. This is an obvious mistake, for Sultan Salim Shah Sur (1545-1554), better known as Islam Shah, never fought against Akbar. The prince who held Agra when it was captured by Akbar was Adil Shah Sur.
42. Hamida Bano Begam, commonly known as Haji Begam.
43. Sironj, a town in the Tonk State of Rajputana. Situated on the Agra-Deccan road. It was an important place in the Mughal days. Its trade and industry have since completely disappeared.
44. Is it Banganga, commonly called Ganga?
45. Chambal-nadi—river Chambal, which rises on the northern slopes of the Vindhyas near Mhow. It joins the Jumna as a tributary in Etawah District.
46. Obviously Tavernier's Iagou-nadi. Ball and Crooke identify Iagou with Jajau between Agra and Dholpur. The river that passes by this place is the Utangan otherwise known as the Banganga.
47. Sengar river, which rises near Ratauli, and leaves Agra district near Kotla. (*Agra Dist. Gaz.*, p. 9).

CHAPTER XXII

1. Shahjahanabad, so named after Shah Jahan who built the present city of Delhi.
2. Highway.
3. Shaikh or Shah-ki-Sarai, a travellers' resting place at Mathura. (Growse, *Mathura*, p. 118). Thevenot does not mention the city of Mathura though he refers to the temple. He obviously relies on Tavernier (Vol. I, p. 85), who confuses the city with the Sarai and applies the name only to the temple. The earlier traveller also mentions the "asylum for apes."
4. This information is also borrowed from Tavernier who says, "The Jumna then flowed at the foot of the Pagoda. . . . But for some years back the river has taken a northerly course and flows at a good coss distance from the Pagoda." Growse, however, is not inclined to give this statement much credence (*Mathura*, p. 120).
5. Receded.
6. Obviously the Thugs. They are known to have been operating in the Delhi province as early as the days of Jalal-ud-din Khilji.
7. Skill.
8. Heaving sighs.
9. The number is incorrect. Several capital cities have been built and later abandoned round about Delhi. Thevenot obviously attributed one city to the Hindus, a second to the so-called Pathans and the third to Shah Jahan.
10. One after another.
11. The site is certainly very old and is traditionally identified with Indraprastha, the capital of the Pandavas, but King Porus who fought Alexander near the Jhelum had nothing to do with it.
12. Humayun's tomb is one of the most famous extant monuments of Delhi. It probably marks one limit of the town of his time though Thevenot is wrong in calling it the second city.
13. The reference is obviously to the pyramidal structure on which Firuz Tughluq placed the inscribed monolith pillar of Asoka which he removed from Tobra. De Laet refers to the popular belief that the inscription was in Greek character and that the pillar had been built by Alexander. Tom Coryat gave currency to this error with less justification. The language of the inscription

is Prakrit and the script Brahmi. The pyramid is situated almost midway between Humayun's tomb and Shah Jahân's Red Fort.

14. The Delhi Fort, known also as Lal Qila or Qila Shahjahanabad. For a contemporary account of the fort, see Bernier, pp. 256-258.
15. Insignia.
16. Unlike.
17. Bernier also refers to "two large elephants of stone, placed at either side of one of the principal gates." The two warriors riding the elephants were Jaimal and Patta who defended Chitor with conspicuous valour (Bernier, pp. 256-257). The stone elephants and the two effigies are no longer in the fort. Manucci says that one of the elephants was broken by an infuriated elephant during Aurangzeb's reign (Vol. II, pp. 10-11).
18. The Diwan-i-Am or the Hall of Public Audience with its pillars is built of red sandstone while the Diwan-i-Khas or the Hall of Private Audience is in white marble. Thevenot borrows this ambiguous name from Bernier (p. 259) who should have known better. Manucci (Vol. II, p. 461) also uses this word to signify the Hall of Public Audience. The Hall of Public Audience has, however, no marble pillars as Thevenot says. For the buildings in the Red Fort see Carr Stephen, *Archaeology of Delhi.*
19. Hands crossed in front of them.
20. Diwan-i-Khas or Private Hall is obviously meant. Fergusson describes it as "if not the most beautiful, certainly the most highly ornamented of all Shah Jehan's Buildings."
21. It is doubtful whether the local people could make so absurd a statement. The person responsible for it is Tavernier (Vol. I, p. 305) who, however, does not mention the source of his information. For his account of the Peacock throne, see Vol. I, pp. 303-305.
22. Tavernier's estimate is 160,500,000 livres of French money, while Bernier says that "the throne is estimated at forty million *roupies,* worth sixty millions of pounds (livres) or thereabouts" (P. 269).
23. Convenient.
24. The Jami Masjid of Delhi. See Carr Stephen, *op. cit.*, pp. 250 ff, and Bernier, pp. 278-280.
25. Bernier has not failed to describe Jahanara Begam's serai (pp. 280-281). It was demolished soon after the Mutiny.
26. Tavernier also mentions (Vol. I, p. 79) the two principal streets (Chandni Chowk and Faiz Bazar).
27. Amongst its beautiful sights.
28. Inconvenient.
29. Like.

CHAPTER XXIII

1. Rounded iron.
2. Spherical.
3. It is a dagger commonly known as *katar*. For illustration see Egerton, *A Description of Indian and Oriental Armour,* plate X.
4. Fail to have.
5. Smaller.
6. This name does not occur in Irvine's list (pp. 81-85). Is it by any chance *sang* (a kind of spear)? Or is it *zaghnol,* a battle-axe with a pointed and two-edged head? (Irvine, *The Army of the Indian Moghuls,* p. 80).
7. This reference to 'pistol' by Thevenot is interesting as the prevailing belief is that it was unknown in India earlier than the 18th century. See Irvine, *op. cit.,* pp. 111-112.
8. See Irvine, *op. cit.,* Chap. X, p. 114 where an account is given of the founding of a cannon by Ustad Quli Khan.
9. Contrivance.

CHAPTER XXIV

1. Birds of prey.
2. Properly speaking *elks* do not belong to India. The sambar deer is meant.
3. Courageous.
4. Uzbegs.

4a. Daylight.

5. Light.
6. Hindi 'dana' literally 'grain'. The *Ain* (Vol. I, pp. 134-35) gives details of a horse's fodder. "In winter, they give boiled peas or vetch ; in summer, grain. The daily allowance includes two sers of flour, and one and a half sers of sugar. In winter, before the horse gets fresh grass, they give it half a ser of *ghi.* Two *dams* are daily allowed for hay; but hay is not given, when fresh grass is available."
7. Trappings.
8. Obviously yak tails or *qutas* (*Ain,* Vol. I, p. 128).
9. Bows of the saddle.
10. Give the finest effect in the world.
11. Other travellers also state that Ceylon elephants were held in greater esteem. See Bernier, p. 277 and Tavernier, Vol. I, p. 221.
12. Rogue elephants are notoriously dangerous animals but I do not know of any instance of their eating their victim's flesh.
13. A false step.
14. Expensive.
15. Pistole, from French *pistolet* foreign gold coin, specially Spanish. Sir Isaac Newton valued it at 16*s.* 9*d*. (Tavernier, Vol. I, p. 328).
16. Possess.
17. Meghdambar. Bernier describes it as 'a small house, or square wooden tower, gilt and painted' (p. 370). The *Ain* (Vol. I, p. 129) defines it as "an awning, to shade the elephant driver, an invention by His Majesty."
18. The keeper will.
19. Various.
20. When they have once been well-entangled.
21. Moves back and forth.
22. For an interesting account of capturing wild elephants in a *kheda* see Sanderson, *Thirteen years among the Wild Beasts of India.*

CHAPTER XXV

1. More respectable.
2. Well enough.
3. The personages have suitable attitudes.
4. Thevenot here repeats Bernier's criticism who says, "The *Indian* painters are chiefly deficient in just proportions, and in the expression of the face" (p. 255). The Mughal portraits were, but for rare exceptions, always drawn in profile.
5. Quite well.
6. Well paid.
7. Compare Bernier (p. 255) who writes, "These unhappy men are contemned, treated with harshness, and inadequately remunerated for their labour."
8. Add to.
9. "The Chinese have a peculiar alloy of copper consisting of copper 40·4, zinc 25·4, nickel 21·6, iron 2·6, and occasionally some silver and arsenic. It seems white or silver-like in the finish and is hence called *pai-t'un* (white copper). In Anglo-Indian it is *tootnague,* Tamil *tutunagam,* Portuguese *tutanaga*" (Berthold Laufer, *Sino-Iranica,* p. 555, quoted by Dalgado, Vol. II). This alloy was used both by the Portuguese of Goa and the English of Bombay for their coins.

10. Because.
11. Citrouille in French means a pumpkin, *Cucurbita pepo* or is it *Citrullus vulgaris?*
12. A kind of comb having rows of metallic teeth or serrated ridges, used in currying a horse.
13. Cited.
14. May be seen walking.

CHAPTER XXVI

1. In Part II, Book I, p. 35, Thevenot says that the word literally means 'ornament'. If so, the correct spelling should be *Zinat*. The festival at Aleppo lasted for seven days.
2. A Hindu practice which was adopted by Akbar. See Roe, pp. 378-379; Terry, p. 376; Tavernier, Vol. I, pp. 301-302; Bernier, p. 270; Ovington, pp. 109-110.
3. Precious stones.
4. Afterwards.
5. Festivals.
6. Scarcely lessens.
7. Far more frugal.
8. A dancing girl, from Portuguese *Balladeira* (*Hobson-Jobson*, p. 75).
9. Benares.
10. Shalamar Garden near village Haidarpur. Bernier describes it as "the King's country-house, a handsome and noble building, but not to be compared to *Fontainebleau, Saint Germain, or Versailles.*"

CHAPTER XXVII

1. This is a mistake, for Ajmer lies to the south-west of Delhi.
2. The subah of Lahore. Manucci says that the province was called the "Punjab" (Vol. II, p. 424).
3. Bundi state in the south-east of Rajputana. It was a part of the subah of Ajmer under Akbar (*Ain*, Vol. II, p. 268 and note 1).
4. Jaisalmer state in western Rajputana. It was a part of Ajmer subah. (*Ain*, Vol. II, p. 271).
5. 'Soret' of the European travellers may be identified with Sorath in Kathiawar. But it was not under the subah of Ajmer. Abu-l-Fazl mentions a place named Sojhat in the subah of Ajmer (*Ain*. Vol. II, p. 281).
6. Ajmer, an important city in Rajputana and the administrative head-quarters of the British province of Ajmer-Merwara.
7. The stages are :—Agra to Fatehpur-Sikri, Barambad (a village in Bayana tahsil, Bharatpur state), Hindaun 75 miles south-east of Jaipur (*Imp. Gaz.*, Vol. XIII, p. 135), Mughal Sarai ('Mogulserai' of Rennell's map, 1788 reproduced in Phillimore, *Historical Records of the Survey of India*, Vol. I, Plate 6), Lalsot (town in Jaipur state, *Imp. Gaz.*, Vol. XVI, p. 134), Chatsu or Chaksu (*Imp. Gaz.*, Vol. X, p. 182), Piplo in Tonk state, Mozabad (Jaipur state), Bandar-Sindri in Kishangarh state, Manderi and Ajmer.
8. Ajmer lies in 26° 27″ N. Latitude.
9. Taragarh hill, the highest point of the Aravalli range in Ajmer-Merwara district, 2,855 feet above sea-level (See *Rajputana Gazetteer*, p. 448).
10. Taragarh believed to be built by Raja Aja, who is probably to be identified with Ajayadeva, son of Prithviraja I.
11. Ajmer, one of the earliest acquisitions of Akbar, was probably occupied by the Mughals in 1557-58. For the controversy regarding the date of its capture, see Harbilas Sarda, *Ajmer : Historical and Descriptive*, pp. 153-54,

12. Haji Khan, a slave of Sultan Salim Shah Sur, held Ajmer before its annexation by Akbar.
13. Khwaja Muinuddin Hasan Chisti (1142-1236).
14. The tomb of Khwaja Muinuddin Chisti is popularly known as the *Dargah Khwaja Sahib*. The shrine contains a mosque by Akbar and another by Shah Jahan built of marble. For an account of the annual *Urs*, see *Rajputana Gazetteer*, pp. 488-489.
15. Employed.
16. In fulfilment of his vow Akbar walked to the tomb of the Chisti saint at Ajmer in 1570. (*Akbar Nama*, Vol. II, pp. 510-11; Elliot & Dowson, Vol. V, p. 334; Briggs, Vol. II, p. 233; Beni Prasad, *Jahangir*, p. 8).
17. Impulsive.
18. Slowly.
19. Salim, Murad and Daniyal were all born at Sikri.
20. Nauroz, the Persian New Year's day. The festivities lasted for nineteen and not nine days as some European travellers have suggested.
21. Jahangir spent three years at Ajmer from November, 1613 to November, 1616 and all the festivals were as usual celebrated during the emperor's stay there.

CHAPTER XXVIII

1. Allowed.
2. Bernier also refers to this fair (p. 272). For a description of the fair in Akbar's time, see *Ain*, i, pp. 276-277. Similar fairs (*meena bazar*) used to be held at Lucknow as late as the 19th century.
3. Many had an opportunity while selling.
4. Bargain for.
5. The remark within the bracket is the translator's.
6. Kanchani from *kanchan*, 'a dancing-girl'. According to Bernier (p. 273) the word signifies 'the gilded, the blooming'. See Crooke, *Tribes and Castes of N. W. P. and Oudh*, Vol. IV, p. 364, for the *Kanchan* caste.
7. Held.
8. An opportunity.
9. Trifles.
10. However good a humour they put him in, he received presents from them as from the others.
11. Magnificently.

CHAPTER XXIX

1. The Musk deer is an animal of the upper Himalayan ranges and is not to be found below 8,000 feet level. The animal referred to is very probably the *mashk billi* or civet cat. Dellon refers to the trade in civet perfume (*op. cit.*, p. 112) and Linschoten says "civet is much found in India" (Vol. II, pp. 95-96). Sir Thomas Roe mentions both civet and civet cats as articles of trade and he says that plenty of civet was available at Agra (pp. 23, 116 and 320).
2. The animal does not live long.
3. The black-boned poultry has naturally attracted notice of more than one western traveller and forms a subject of comment among modern annotators. It occurs in different parts of India and is mentioned in at least three Tamil works on medicine. Linschoten and François Pyrard found it at Mozambique in Africa. It is not certain whether Thevenot and Careri saw the fowl they

describe. Thevenot may have derived his information from Bernier who says that the skin of the bird is quite black, but is silent about the colour of the bone (p. 251). Thevenot and Careri, however, observe that the bone as well as the skin is black. Careri says nothing about the colour of the flesh, which, according to Thevenot, is "very white". Fryer, who first saw the bird at Tanore in Malabar, corroborates Thevenot. "The outward skin", he says "was a perfect *Negro,* the Bones also being as black as Jet; under the Skin nothing could be whiter than the Flesh, more tender, or more grateful" (Vol. I, p. 140). James Forbes found this fowl abounding in Calicut and hints that the flesh was white in contrast to the black skin and bone of the bird (*Oriental Memoirs,* Vol. I, p. 205). Linschoten and Pyrard, on the other hand, are definite that the flesh also is black. Linschoten says, "There are certain Hennes that are so blacke both of feathers, flesh, and bones, that being sodden they seeme as black as inke" (Vol. I, pp. 25-26). Pyrard observes, "There is also good store of fowls, very good and delicate, but all of black plumage; and the flesh is the same, whether cooked or raw. This is strange to those who have not been used to see and eat it; it seems as if the flesh had been cooked with some black dye, and the soup is the same" (Vol. II, Pt. I, p. 231). The late Dr Burnell, annotating Linschoten, roundly contradicted both the Dutch and the French travellers. He notes, "This is incorrect; the flesh is white, like that of other fowls" (Vol. I, p. 25), and again, referring to Pyrard, "but this is incorrect; the black plumage is an accident, and the flesh is white; the bones are black" (Vol. I, p. 26). William Crooke supports Burnell and notes, "Fryer does not fall into the error of Linschoten and Pyrard de Laval who say that the flesh is black" (Fryer, Vol. I, p. 140, *n.* 1). Vincent Smith also seems to be of the same view (Bernier, p. 251, *n.* I). It might be suggested that the flesh of the African "nigger fowls" (Bernier calls it 'Ethiopian') was black while that of the Indian variety was white, but Linschoten says that the same bird was to be found in India also.

I referred the question to Mr. A. J. Macdonald, Officer-in-charge, poultry Research Section, Indian Veterinary Research Institute, Izatnagar, and he writes: "I came across birds with black feathers and dark flesh in Madras and the North West Frontier Province. It is not quite correct to say that the flesh is black but the skin and flesh are pigmented to give a purplish black colouration. It would probably be best to say that the flesh and skin are pigmented purplish black. The bones are also much darker than normal. There is also a common belief that the flesh of these birds has a special medicinal value." Obviously the comments of Burnell, Crooke and Smith were based on insufficient information. Answering to further enquiries from me Mr. Macdonald wrote: "The pigmentation mentioned in the previous correspondence has no connection with feeding. It would be hardly correct to state that the birds with dark flesh belong to any one breed, for one characteristic does not make a breed." I may here quote also from a letter I received from Dr. B. N. Chopra of the Zoological Survey of India, "In *Ibis* Ser. 7, Vol. VI, p. 360 (1900) an entirely black specimen of the common Jungle Red Fowl has been described from Negros in the Philiphines, but there is no mention about the colour of its bones . . . . . . Several years ago I also remember having come across a fowl of this kind in Kashmir. Its skin was entirely black and the bones were of a smoky colour. I cannot, however, be quite sure after such a long lapse of time." I think that the discrepancy between Thevenot, Careri and Fryer on the one side and Linschoten and Pyrard on the other may be explained by the difference in pigmentation referred to by Mr. Macdonald. Not being a scientist I cannot say whether the term melanism may be appropriately used here. As the birds with black skin, bone, flesh and feather do not belong to any particular breed and as the degree of darkness apparently differs in different individuals it is quite possible that in some specimens the pigmentation occurred in skin and bone only while in others it affected the flesh as well.

About the medicinal properties of its flesh I received the following communication from Dewan Bahadur C. S. Srinivasachariar: Re. the pullet whose feathers, flesh and bones are all black, "It is called 'Kannikkozhi or Vidaikkozhi'. I have been able to get at Bhoga Muni's *Vaittiyam-700* (Ezhunuru) in which stanzas 388 to 392 inclusive are devoted to the preparation of the *churana* or *churna* known as *kukkuta-churna*, which should be taken for a period of six weeks or 45 days. The pullet which should be mature in growth should be brought, its legs, hair and head should be removed and it should be opened on the back and intestines and liver removed and mixed with substances like rocksalt, *kayam* (either asafoetida or pepper), garlic, black cumin, ammonia etc., and boiled with a number of other substances and reduced to *churana* and a little powder taken morning and evening. It is said to cure gastritis of the stomach, anaemia, jaundice, cough, dropsy, diseases of the lungs and rheumatism, colic, etc."

4. Where the majority have sexual relations.
5. Almost all the foreign travellers bear testimony to child-marriages in India.
5a. Many of the roads.
6. Cast them down.
7. A frame.
8. Hindi *khichri*, "a mess of rice, cooked with butter and *dal* and flavoured with a little space, shred onion, and the like" (*Hobson-Jobson*, p. 476). The word is not derived from the name of any grain used in preparing the dish.
9. Moreover.
9a. This is borrowed from Mandelslo who writes :—"Most of the *Saltpeter* which is sold in *Guzuratta* comes from *Asmer*, sixty Leagues from *Agra*, and they get it out of Land that hath lain long fallow. The blackest and fattest ground yields most of it. . . . ." (p. 66).
10. According to Manucci the province paid an annual revenue of 17 lakhs of Rupees (Vol. II, p. 425).

CHAPTER XXX

1. The modern Tatta in Sind, a taluk in the Karachi district. Throughout the 17th century it was a busy entrepôt but decayed during the later half of the 18th century. In Akbar's reign Tatta was a sarkar of the subah of Multan. (*Ain*, Vol. II, p. 336 ff.).
2. The Arabian Sea.
3. Seistan or Sistan, the ancient *Sacastane*. Part of it is Persian territory and part belongs to Afghanistan.
4. Jalaluddin Mangbarni, Shah of Khwarizm (Khiva), 1220-31. In his flight from his own territories he had come as far as the Indus and was defeated on the banks of that river (1221 A.D.) by Chingiz Khan.
5. The ruling house of Khwarizm or Khiva founded by Qutbuddin Muhammad in 1097.
6. Debal or Debal Sindhi. The position of this famous port, "the emporium of the Indus during the middle ages", is a matter of dispute. Abul-Fazl identifies it with Tattah. "Sir H. Elliot places Debal at Karachi" (*Ain*, Vol. II, p. 337 and *n.* 1). Foster (*The Embassy of Sir Thomas Roe to India*, p. 75, *n.*) writes, "Diul-Sind was the name given by the Portuguese to Lahribandar, the port of Tatta in the Indus delta." De Laet (p. 3) mentions that it was about 15 miles from the sea. It appears that "Debal occupied a site between Karachi and Thatha" (Crow cited in Cunningham, *Ancient Geography of India*, ed. Majumdar, p. 341).
7. Trade.
8. Pleasant.
9. Lahari-Bandar or Lari-Bandar, ancient port of Sind near Debal, which is now in ruins. "The present port of the western half of the (Indus) Delta

is Dharaja, which is only a few miles to the east of Lari Bandar" (Cunningham, p. 346). Ibn Battuta in 1333 describes it as "a fine town on the coast where the river of Sind discharges itself into the ocean. It possesses a large harbour, visited by men from Yemen, Fars, and elsewhere" (Ibn Battuta, trans. Gibb, p. 187).

10. *Palki* in Hindi from Sanskrit *paryanka* (Portuguese *palanchino*). For a description, see Chapter XXXI; also Ovington, p. 152 and Tavernier, Vol. I, pp. 37-38.
11. Conveyance.
12. If it come to lean in some bad place.

CHAPTER XXXI

1. Conveyance.
2. Bamboo.
3. Surrounded.
4. Compensate.

CHAPTER XXXII

1. Bukkur (Bakhar), fortified island in the river Indus, in Sukkur district, Sind. During the middle ages, owing to its insular position, it was a stronghold of some importance and "frequently a bone of contention between different States" (See *Imp. Gaz.*, Vol. IX, pp. 46-47).
2. The Indus and its tributaries, Jhelum, Chenab, Ravi and Sutlej.
3. Head-quarters of the Multan district in the Punjab. It was the capital of a province of the same name in the Mughal days.
4. Trade.
5. The reference is to the galls of *Tamarix articulata* (known variously as *faras*, *farash*, etc. in the Punjab) from which a dye is obtained and which are collected and sold in the bazars. See *Gazetteer of the Multan District* (1884), p. 10; Watt, Vol. VI, Part III, pp. 409-410.
6. More correctly, 30° 12′ North.
7. Kahror, also spelt Khardar, south-east of Multan, reputed to be the site of the battle between Vikramaditya and the Sakas in 79 A.D. (Cunningham, *op. cit.*, p. 277). Abu-l Fazl (*Ain.* Vol. II, p. 329) mentions this town under the sarkar of Multan.
8. Khanewal (?) in the Kabirwala tahsil of Multan district.
9. Probably Sitpur now in the Alipur tahsil of Muzaffargarh district. It was once famous for paper manufacture. "A certain amount of *Kamangari* work —painting over varnished wood or paper is applied to bows, saddles, paper, shields and toys." (*Punjab Provincial Gazetteer*, Vol. II, p. 256).
10. Compare Tavernier who, writing about Multan, says, "Numerous Baladins and Baladines, who hail from this town, spread themselves in divers parts of Persia" (Vol. I, p. 74).
11. Making profit.
12. Khatri caste of northern India claims Kshatriya descent, but is a mercantile caste (See Rose, *A Glossary of the Tribes and Castes of the Punjab and N. W. F. P.*, Vol. II, p. 501 ff.). This caste had its origin in the Punjab as the author correctly points out, but is found in large numbers in other parts of India also (Crooke, *The Tribes and Castes of the N. W. P. and Oudh*, Vol. III, pp. 264 ff; *Hobson-Jobson*, p. 482).
13. The reference is to the famous temple of the sun which was one of the earliest buildings in the Multan fort but of which no trace now remains. It was intact when the famous Chinese traveller Hiuen Tsang passed through the city and Alberuni says that the idol "was of wood and covered

with red Cordova leather." According to the *Chach-nama,* Muhammad bin Kasim in 712 A.D. found "an idol made of Gold, and its two eyes were bright red rubies" (Elliot and Dowson, Vol. I, p. 206). The temple was probably destroyed sometime in the 11th century but was restored later. In Thevenot's time (1666) it was still standing, but shortly afterwards it was pulled down by Aurangzeb who built a Jami Masjid on its site. The Sikhs in their turn converted it into a powder magazine which was blown up by the British in 1848. (Maclagan, *Gazetteer of the Multan District,* p. 336 ff.).

14. Is of very considerable importance.

CHAPTER XXXIII

1. The Timurid rulers of India long contended with Safavid princes of Persia for its possession on account of its strategic and commercial importance derived from its geographical situation. Kandahar commands the main road from India to Kabul and Herat.
2. Abbas II recaptured Kandahar in 1649, and all attempts to regain it on the part of Shah Jahan proved futile.
3. We get a different account of the death of the lady in a letter from John Lewis and Thomas Best at Gombroon to the President and Council at Surat dated October 19, 1648. (*The English Factories in India,* 1646-1650, p. 218). "The 11th instant wee had news in this place that the King, beinge weary of his grandmothers accustomed presumption over him, not consideringe that hee was now growne to more maturity, to be freed therof commands that she, together with the ould Sheckles loving mother, should bee poysoned; which was accordingly put in execution."
4. Balkh, now called Wazirabad.
5. The correct position is 31° 27′N.
6. Lacks.
7. Claim.
8. Of the neighbourhood.
9. Trade.
10. Part II, Book II, Chapter XIV, pp. 110-111.
11. Part II, Book II, Chapter XI, pp. 102-103.
12. Light.
13. Mr. Kohzad, Director of Archaeology, Kabul Museum informs me that Peria is likely to be Parian in the Upper Panjshir river valley, while Col. A. S. Lancaster is of opinion that Peria is in the Ghor district, north-east of present day Farah.
14. Not traceable on modern maps.
15. Not traceable.

CHAPTER XXXIV

1. Hindukush, also known as the Indian Caucasus.
2. From Zabul, which according to Abul-Fazl (*Ain,* Vol. II, p. 408) was another name of Ghazni. Jarrett in a footnote (*Ain,* II, p. 115) mentions that this appellation includes "Kabul and the adjacent territory as far as Ghazna and even beyond."
3. Add "It was formerly under the rule of the Persians."
4. Rivers Kabul and Kurram, the former of which joins the Indus near Attock (See Thornton, Vol. I, pp. 316-318 and 420; *Imp. Gaz.,* Vol. XIV, pp. 246 ff; XVI, p. 48).
5. Kabul was for some time Babar's capital. Humayun made it his headquarters prior to his return to India. His three immediate successors had resorted there from time to time.

6. Holi, the Hindu carnival which is celebrated for two (sometimes more) days before the full moon of *Phalguna* (corresponding with February-March).
7. The reference is to Kansa's dread of Krishna and the evil emissaries he sent to encompass the death of the divine child.
8. Trace.

CHAPTER XXXV

1. Kashmir was conquered by Akbar in 1586 from Yakub Khan the last of the Chak rulers.
2. It has received the waters discharged from a Lake.
3. Obviously the Jhelum (and not the Chenab), on the banks of which the capital city Srinagar stands, is meant. The river passes through the Wular lake and after traversing the level plain runs for many miles through a deep gorge between the mountains of the Kazinag and Pir Panjal ranges. It does not however go as far west as Attock but joins the Chenab at Trimmu. The Sindh which falls into the Jhelum at Shadipur is probably confused with the Indus or Sindhu. The joint river joins the Ravi and the Sutlej near Sidhu and at Madwala respectively and then falls into the Indus at Mithankot.
4. Kabul river.
5. Again wrong. The Jhelum was known to the Muslim writers variously as the Bihat, Wihat or Bihatah, undoubtedly mispronunciation of its old Sanskrit form *Vitasta*. Its modern Kashmiri the name is Veth (*Punjab Provincial Gazetteer*, Vol. I, p. 193).
6. Srinagar. The city is situated in 34° 5′ N. Latitude and 74° 50′ E. Longitude. (*Imp. Gaz.*, Vol. XXIII, pp. 99-105).
7. Compare Bernier (p. 398) who says "the houses, although for the most part of wood, are well-built and consist of two or three stories" and refers to the gardens as well as a "canal communicating with the lake."
8. Omit "lovely".
9. Very likely the Shalimar which is specifically mentioned by Bernier (pp. 399-400).
10. For "that" read "because".
11. Yusuf Khan, son of Ali Khan Chak, lost his throne to a rival, Sayyid Mubarak, and took asylum with Akbar. A counter-revolution restored him to power for a short while but he had ultimately to yield to an invading army from Delhi. He later entered the Mughal army and served under Man Singh in Orissa and Bengal. (*Ain*, Vol. I, pp. 478-480).
12. Yakub Khan son of Yusuf Khan became king for a brief period after his father's submission to the Mughals. *Ain*, Vol. I, p. 480.
13. Defiles.
14. Passes.
15. Guidance.
16. Bhimbar pass in the Pir Panjal range. Abul-Fazl writes "Twenty-six different roads lead into Hindustan but those by *Bhimbar* and *Pakli* are the best and are generally practicable on horseback." (*Ain*, Vol. II, p. 347).
17. To amuse that of prince Jacob.

CHAPTER XXXVI

1. A good hundred leagues.
2. The correct latitude is 31° 35′ North.
3. The Ravi river, the *Hydraotes* of Arrian, the *Parushni* of the Vedas, and the *Iravati* of classical Sanskrit authors. (*Punjab Provincial Gazetteer*, Vol. I, pp. 190-191).
4. Ptolemy in the French text and not Pliny.

5. Acesines, Vedic *Asikni* is the Chenab river; Cophis or the *Kubha* is the Kabul river, Hydraphes is the *Vitasta* or Jhelum; Zaradras is the *Satadru*, modern Sutlej; and Hispalis is the *Vipasa* or Beas.
6. The Behat is the Muslim name for Jhelum, Canab is probably a corruption of Chenab, Sind is the Indus and Van may be the Beas.
7. This evidently refers to the change in the course of the river Ravi. Thevenot's statement is based on that of Bernier (pp. 383-384).
8. Both Akbar and Jehangir held their court at Lahore but it can hardly be asserted that they preferred it to Delhi and Agra. Bernier says: "Unlike the buildings of *Delhi* and *Agra,* the houses here are very lofty, but the court having resided during the last twenty years or more in one of those two cities most of the houses in *Lahor* are in a ruinous state." (P. 384). Thomas Coryat found Agra, though "a verie great citie; in everie respect much inferior to Lahore" (Foster, *Early Travels,* p. 244).
9. The reference is obviously to the fort built by Akbar about 1568.
10. According to Manucci also the city of Lahore had twelve gates which he mentions by name (Vol. II, pp. 185-186). William Finch corroborates this. (Foster, *Early Travels,* p. 161). Dr Vogel suggests that Thevenot might have copied Herbert, for all the twelve gates were of the fortified city. See *Tile-Mosaics of the Lahore Fort,* p. 17.
11. See Bernier, p. 384.
11a. The paintings do not exist to-day. They were first noticed by William Finch in 1611. (Foster, *Early Travels,* pp. 162-64). De Laet and Herbert (pp. 69-70) in their turn copied Finch's account of Lahore and Thevenot's statement is obviously based on that of Herbert. Thevenot is unfair to Jahangir. Jesus is one of the Prophets highly revered by the Muslims and *Hazrat Maryam* (Mary) also shares their respect. See Vogel, *op. cit.,* pp. 63-64 and Payne, *Jahangir and the Jesuits,* Pt. I, Chapter VIII.
12. The castle was built by Akbar and not by Humayun as Thevenot asserts.
13. See Manucci, Vol. II, p. 424.
14. Bernier estimates the revenue of Lahore at 2,46,95,000 (p. 456) and Manucci at 2,24,53,302 Rupees (Vol. II, p. 416) per year.
15. Sign.
16. Ash tree (*Flaxinus excelsior*).
17. Thanesar or Thaneshwar in Karnal district of the Punjab about 100 miles from Delhi.
18. Bernier (p. 316) also refers to these vows of 'chastity, poverty, and submission'. The word Vartia is probably a corruption of Sanskrit *vratin.* Contemporary travellers' accounts leave little doubt that the reference is to the Jains.
19. They refuse it.
20. Take nothing but what is cooked.

CHAPTER XXXVII

1. Oudh. The boundaries of this province (*subah*) as given in the *Ain* (Vol. II, pp. 170 ff.) are as follows: "To the east is *Behar,* to the north, the mountains, to the south, *Manikpur,* and to the west, *Kanauj.*" The province was named after its chief town "*Avadh*", modern Ajodhya or Sanskrit *Ayodhya.*
2. Berar. The identification however is doubtful. Berar is not watered by the tributaries of the Ganges and it is not unlikely that the contiguous province of Bihar, Bernier's "Beara", is meant as Thevenot mentions Berar in Chapter XLII.
3. Probably he means the Gakkar country which was outside the limits of the Mughal province of Oudh. Kakori in Sarkar Lucknow is mentioned by Abu-l-Fazl (*Ain,* Vol. II, p. 93), but it is doubtful whether Thevenot knew the place.

4. May be identified with Bangash in N.W. Kohat. The Bangash Afghans settled in the area round modern Farrukhabad much later.
5. Nagarkot or Kangra.
6. De Laet (p. 12) describes it as a province, whose capital is "Hardwair" (Hardwar) lying to the south of Nagarkot. Siba is now in Kangra, Punjab. In Baffin's map of Indostan Siba is placed between Banchish and Pitan.
7. In Baffin's map Gor is placed at the north-eastern limit of India. De Laet's Gor may safely be identified with Gaur, the capital of the province of the same name. But if Varad is identified with Berar, Gor may be Garah near modern Jubbulpore which is much nearer Berar than Gaur.
8. In Baffin's map Pitan is located due north of Patna and may therefore be identified with Pattan in Nepal, but Baffin's map is full of inaccuracies and should not be treated as a reliable guide. Pitan may be the Patna State in Chhattishgarh district, if Varad is identified with Berar.
9. Gondwana, tract in Central Province and Central India. Baffin places it north of Bengal but the capital is correctly named Karahkatank or Garahkatanga.
10. The temple of Devi (Mahamaya) in the lower suburb (called Bhawan) of Nagarkot (Kangra) "ranks among the oldest and most wealthy shrines in India." Both Nagarkot and Jwalamukhi are outside the territorial limits of Oudh. The temple of Nagarkot dates back to very old times and was pillaged by Sultan Mahmud. Abu-l-Fazl refers to the sacrifice of tongues made by pilgrims here and their miraculous regrowth (*Ain*, Vol. II, pp. 312-313). De Laet (p. 12) and Terry (in Foster, *Early Travels*, p. 294) also mention this practice. Also see William Finch (in Foster, *op. cit.*, pp. 179-180) who calls the goddess "Je or Durga".
11. Jwalamukhi, in Kangra district, Punjab. De Laet also calls it Callamaka "which is also a celebrated place of pilgrimage", he says "for every day flames are seen to break forth from amongst some high rocks where there is a spring of cold water" (p. 12). Also see Terry (in Foster, *op. cit.*, p. 294).
12. *Mata*, 'the mother'. This is the name mentioned by De Laet and Terry. Abu-l Fazl says that the goddess was known as Mahamaya.
13. Bara Bangahal. Balaghat literally means upper passes. The Jwalamukhi temple is situated in the Bara Bangahal ridge.

CHAPTER XXXVIII

1. The identification of this province is fraught with no little difficulty. Sir William Foster (*Early Travels*, p. 294) whose opinion is not to be lightly treated has identified it with the modern state of Bikaner in Rajputana. De Laet (pp. 11-12), Terry (Foster, *op. cit.*, p. 294), Roe (p. 493) and Thevenot all agreed that the chief city was Bikaner. According to the first three writers the city is to the west of the Ganges. But Thevenot asserts that it lies not only to the east of Delhi but also includes Udese. Baffin locates Udessa with its capital *Jekqnat* on the eastern frontier of Indostan. He makes a separate province of Orixa. I wonder whether Udese has anything to do with Sanskrit *Udichi?* But Thevenot mentions among its principal towns Sambal, which according to De Laet, Roe and Terry formed a separate province and is in the modern Moradabad district, United Provinces and Rageapoor, capital of Roe's Jesual, which Sir William Foster identifies with Jaswan in Hoshiarpur district. Baffin who has contributed substantially to later geographical confusion places Jeswall and Raiapore, north of Bengal between Sambal and Mevat! Where to locate Becar, the last province on the eastern limit of the empire, which has for its capital Bikaner (on the western banks of the Ganges!) and has for its principal towns Sambal in the Moradabad district of U. P. and Rajapur, which Sir William Foster places in the Punjab and Blochmann locates in C. P.? Obviously such a province did not exist in reality. Baffin's Bakar and Thevenot's Becar cannot be identical,

2. Doab. As Becar is placed east of Delhi probably the Ganges-Jumna doab is meant.
3. It is also spelt as Jesual. De Laet says "It lies to the east of Patna and marches with Bengal on the south-east" (p. 14). Foster (p. 295, *n*. 4) identifies the place with Jaswan in Hoshiarpur District. Van den Broucke (cited in De Laet, p. 14, *n*. 23) puts Jesual east of Morang in the Himalayan tract.
4. Probably Orissa, as the capital is Jekanat i.e. Jagannath.
5. De Laet, Roe and Terry wrongly make a province of it. It was only a sarkar in Akbar's time, now in the Moradabad district of U. P.
6. May be Mainpuri in the district of the same name in Agra division, U. P. Finch mentions "Menepore 20 kosses from Allahabad alongst the river Ganges" (Foster, p. 178) which Foster identifies with Manihpur. Moll (*India*, p. 251) writes "the chief town of Sambal is Minapour, in the latitude of 27 degrees."
7. Rajpur, capital of Jesual. For its identification see *n*. 1, *supra*.
8. Probably a corruption of Jagannath the chief city of Udesse.
9. Bikaner, the capital of the state of the same name.
10. These are included.
11. A confusion probably with the common Hindu belief in *chaturasiti yoni* or 84 forms of life through which the soul has to pass before it attains salvation. In Bengal the castes in common parlance are estimated at 36. Hutton says (*Caste in India*, p. 128) "2378 (castes) were actually counted at the Indian Census of 1901 some numbering millions, others only a very few individuals. To say that there are some 3000 different castes in India is probably to run little risk of exaggeration."
12. Kshatriya or Rajput.
13. The reference here is to the Khatri caste of northern India.
14. Sanskrit Sudra—the fourth caste of the Hindus.
15. Probably Kahars (?) or more likely Kolis who used to carry palanquins who still carry on the old vocation.
16. Banjaras (Vanjaras), a tribe, mainly nomadic, of grain and salt dealers and carriers. They used to move in large hordes with their cattle from one part of the country to another and to supply provision to the armies on march. The Banjaras were very much in evidence during the eighteenth and the first half of the nineteenth centuries when the fighting forces depended mostly on them for regular supply of food grains. Wilson derives the word from Sanskrit *vanij* "trade" and *kara*, doer. There are various Anglo-Indian corrupt forms e.g., Brinjarry, Binjaree, Bunjaree, etc. (*Hobson-Jobson*, p. 114).
17. Artisans.
18. Pariah, Paraiyan. A low caste of Hindus in southern India. Some scholars derive the word from Tamil *parai*, "a drum", but this has been questioned (E. Thurston, *Castes and Tribes of Southern India*, vi, 77 *et seq*). The Pariah was condemned to a very low status in the Hindu caste system on account of his filthy habits (e.g. eating carrion etc.) but he is not, as was commonly believed, an outcaste and his was by no means the lowest caste either (*Hobson-Jobson*, pp. 678-680; Risley, *op. cit.*, p. 139).
19. Dher or Dhed are the scavengers and their position is one of the lowest in the Hindu society. "If he looks at a water jar he pollutes its contents; if you touch him by accident, you must bathe" (Risley, pp. 138-139).
20. Halalkhor, sweepers. They are so termed because they consider every food lawful (*halal*) (*Hobson-Jobson*, p. 409; Tavernier, Vol. II, pp. 145-146). Abu-l Fazl (*Ain*, Vol. I, p. 139) writes: "Sweepers are called in Hindustan *Halalkhur;* His Majesty brought this name *en vogue*."
21. Dirtiness.
22. Leather-workers.
23. Scavengers.
24. "Of Office" is the translator's addition,
25. Explanation.
26. Dirty.

27. Bairagi from Sanskrit *vairagin*, 'one devoid of passion'. A Hindu religious mendicant, of Vaishnava persuasion, but the term is applied indiscriminately to Hindu recluses of all sects and orders (Thurston, Vol. I, pp. 130-133; Russell, Vol. II, pp. 93 ff.).
28. Dislike.
29. Kurmis or Kunbis. A caste of cultivators claiming Kshatriya origin. The name is said to be derived from the Sanskrit *krishi*, cultivation, or from *kurma*, the tortoise incarnation of Vishnu (Russell, Vol. IV, p. 55 ff.).
30. A Greek neo-platonist of the third century A.D.
31. The four Vedas, *viz.*, the Rigveda, the Samaveda, the Yajurveda and the Atharvaveda.
32. They believe only in one.
33. The Hindus have a story of the deluge and they also believe in the descent from a common ancestor, Manu.
34. The doctrine of transmigration of soul was known in one form or other in many parts of the world. In India it is not limited to Hinduism only but it forms an important part of the Buddhist and the Jaina creeds as well.
35. A famous Greek philosopher who lived and taught in the 6th century B.C. There is no reason to believe that India borrowed the doctrine of metempsychosis from Pythagoras or his disciples.
36. Dasaratha.
37. Kausalya.
38. Sita, the ideal Hindu wife.
39. The Church of Nossa Senhora dos Remedios is situated midway between Bassein and Agasi and many miracles are attributed to the Lady after whom it is named. Da Cunha (pp. 162-4) says that it is the largest parish church in the Thana District and it was rebuilt in almost the same style as the original one burnt by Kakaji about 1690. Careri visited this church after it was rebuilt (Book I, Chap. III).

CHAPTER XXXIX

1. A corruption of *Illahabas* or *Ilahabad*, the modern Allahabad. The boundaries of the province in Mughal times have been described in the *Ain*, Vol. II, p. 157.
2. A corruption of Sanskrit *purva*, 'east'.
3. Narwar, historic town and fort, now in Gwalior state (see *Imp. Gaz.*, Vol. XVIII, p. 396). Abu-l Fazl mentions that it formed a sarkar under the subah of Agra (*Ain*, Vol. II, pp. 189-190).
4. The country of the Meos, divided in Akbar's time between the sarkars of Alwar and Tijara in the subah of Agra. It now comprises the greater part of Alwar and a small slice of the Bharatpur state besides parts of the British Indian districts of Muttra and Gurgaon.
5. Chrysobara. Pliny calls the river Jumna as "Jomanes and states that it flows into the Ganges through the Palibothri, between the towns of Methora, and Chrysobara (Krishnapura?)". See *Ancient India as Described by Ptolemy*, p. 98.
6. The construction of the fort was commenced in November 1583 and was completed shortly afterwards (Smith, *Akbar*, p. 224).
7. The reference is to the Asoka pillar which bears not only the inscriptions of that king but also those of Samudra Gupta and Jahangir. The texts of the Asokan and Gupta inscriptions have both been deciphered.
8. The king's palace is also well built.
9. Hindu pilgrims still visit the Patalpuri temple, 'the temple of the nether world' and the Akshaya Vat, 'the imperishable Banyan tree' in the fort. See also Finch (Foster, *Early Travels*, p. 178).

10. The same statement has been made by other European travellers, see De Laet, p. 63; William Finch (Foster, *Early Travels*, p. 177).
11. Shave.
12. Either Narwar or Narwal in the modern Cawnpore district of U. P. The other town is Gohad in Gwalior state.
13. Haughtily.
14. For a similar statement see Tavernier, Vol. II, p. 152 and Ovington, p. 210, Ravana, the demon-king of Lanka went to Rama's cottage in the guise of an ascetic and abducted Sita. It is probably on that account that he is credited as the originator of some ascetic orders. For the Ravanvanshi Gosains, see Russell, *Tribes and Castes of C. P.*, Vol. III, pp. 155-156. According to the Ramayana story, Ravana did not survive his defeat but was killed by Rama.
15. Hanuman, the monkey-god.
16. The reference is to the "Magh-Mela", which is held when the sun enters the sign of Capricorn ('Makar') and attracts thousands of pilgrims who bathe at the holy *sangama* or confluence of the Ganges and the Jumna at Allahabad.
17. One leg.
18. The reference is obviously to the monks of the Naga sect who go about naked and armed.

CHAPTER XL

1. Sarkar Jalesar in Orissa. According to Abu-l Fazl Orissa was divided into five sarkars by Akbar and incorporated in the province of Bengal (*Ain*, Vol. II, p. 126).
2. The famous temple of Jagannath (Sanskrit 'Lord of the Universe') at Puri in Orissa. The present temple was built about 1100 A.D. by Ananta Chodaganga (1076-1147). For contemporary accounts of the temple, see, Tavernier, Vol. II, pp. 175-178; Bernier, pp. 304-306.
3. Omit "pilfering and".
4. Omit "and debauch".
5. Because they are mostly handsome and well-dressed.
6. The Pathans were also Muslims.
7. Dacca in E. Bengal on the banks of the Buriganga river. For contemporary accounts, see Bowrey, *A Geographical Account*, pp. 149-150, 230 and Tavernier, Vol. I, pp. 105 and 107.
8. Tavernier (Vol. I, p. 105) writes :—'the church of the Rev. Augustin Fathers is all of brick, and the workmanship of it rather beautiful.'
9. Is it Pipli near Balasore in Orissa?
10. Satgaon, in Hooghly District, Bengal, 'Porto Pequeno' of the Portuguese, formerly an important commercial centre now fallen to ruins.
11. Patna, chief city of Bihar on the right bank of the Ganges.
12. Kashimbazar or Cossimbazar a town in the Murshidabad District, Bengal, was of great commercial importance before the foundation of Calcutta.
13. Chittagong, 'Porto Grando' of the Portuguese.
14. The bird Thevenot describes is the Indian Grackle or *Paharia Maina* (*Eulabes Javana intermedia*). The bird he saw on his way from Masulipatam to Hyderabad was the Southern Grackle (*Eulabes religiosa*) which occurs throughout the forested hills of south India as far north as Goomsur and the Northern Circars on the east and as far as North Kanara on the west (Stuart Baker, *Fauna of British India, Birds*, Vol. III, pp. 17-20).
15. And it has a similar tone and voice.
16. Bhagnagar (Hyderabad), the 'Fortunate city' called after Bhagmati, the favourite mistress of Qutb Shah Muhammad Quli. See Briggs, *History of the Rise of the Mahomedan Power*, trans., Vol. III, pp. 451-452.

17. Thevenot repeats the error of Tavernier (Vol. II, p. 175) who writes "Jagannath is the name of one of the mouths of the Ganges." Bernier, however, was better informed; he mentions that it was "situated on the Gulf of Bengale" (p. 304).
18. The reference here is to the celebrated shrine dedicated to Siva known as Visvesvara, which was destroyed by orders of Aurangzeb in 1669. (Sarkar, *History of Aurangzib,* Vol. III, p. 266). For a contemporary description of the temple, see the account of Tavernier (Vol. II, p. 180 ff.).
19. Hundreds of thousands.
20. Bernier, describing the camp of the Great Mughal, refers to 'the Ganges water' and 'the saltpetre with which it is cooled' among other things, which formed the equipment of the camp household (p. 364). Also see Terry (Foster, *Early Travels,* p. 299).
21. According to Bernier, *"Jagannat* in which is included *Bengale"* yields 72,70,000 Rupees (p. 457).
22. In Aurangzeb's time Bengal was regarded as a penal province where officers were transferred as a mark of imperial disfavour. William Finch mentions three prison fortresses one of which 'Rotas' was in Bengal (Foster, *Early Travels,* p. 145).

CHAPTER XLI

1. Malwa. Properly speaking the plateau "lying between 23° 30′ and 24° 30′ N. and 74° 30′ and 78° 10′ E." In Muslim times the province also included parts of Rajputana and the modern Central Provinces. Its boundaries nowhere touched those of Bengal though Baffin makes the same error.
2. Gwalior, capital of Gwalior state. At the time of Thevenot's visit Gwalior fort was a state prison.
3. Chitor, former capital of Mewar.
4. Mandu or Mandogarh, in the Dhar state, Central India, formerly the seat of a Muslim sultan. Under Akbar it became the head-quarters of a sarkar in the subah of Malwa (*Ain,* Vol. II, p. 112). But it was in partial ruins during the next reign when Sir Thomas Roe's quarters used to be infested by a lion and a wolf (p. 365).
5. Thevenot's statement is not quite accurate. Mandu first came under Muslim occupation in 1305 and Humayun conquered Malwa in 1535 after an interval of two centuries and three decades.
6. Humayun's adversary in Malwa was Bahadur Shah of Gujarat and not Salim Shah son of Sher Shah. When Akbar conquered the province Baz Bahadur was the ruler. Thevenot may have copied here William Finch who commits the same error (Foster, *Early Travels,* pp. 141-142).
7. Humayun never recovered the province, its reconquest for the Mughals was achieved by his son Akbar.
8. The reference is obviously to the splendid cathedral mosque built by Hoshang Shah which is still extant.
9. The mausoleum of Mahmud Khilji in the close neighbourhood of Hoshang Shah's mosque where the father and two successors of Mahmud Shah were also interred.
10. Sultan Mahmud Khilji's tower of victory of which only the base now remains.
11. William Finch found the city "ruined all save only tombes and meskites" (Foster, *Early Travels,* pp. 140-141). Roe took his residence at Mandu in one of the deserted *"mosquites"* (p. 354 f.n. 1).
12. The French original has temples only and not two temples. The remains of one near the Lahori Darwaza still survive. "Two piers marking the site of a doorway are still intact; they are elaborately carved, bearing figures of acrobats, animals, birds, and fabulous beings" (Yazdani, *Mandu, the City of Joy,* p. 122).

13. Mandu can still boast of many big tanks.
14. May be identified with Rantipore of De Laet and Baffin and Finch's Rantimore or Ranthambhor in Jaipur state though it was not the provincial capital. For the practice of giving the condemned prisoner a drink of milk before he was hurled down see De Laet (p. 36) and Finch (Foster, *Early Travels*, p. 145).
15. The ruling family of Mewar claims descent from the hero of the Ramayana and not from Porus.
16. I took pleasure in examining it in the house of a person who kept one out of curiosity.
17. In front.
18. The bat described here is the flying fox (*Pteropus medius*) seen all over India. According to Blanford, "The head is generally reddish brown, the hind neck and shoulder paler, generally pale brownish yellow to straw colour: Head and body about nine inches. The expanse of the wings is about 4 feet. Ears naked and acutely pointed." He adds: "The flesh is eaten by many classes of natives of India, and is said by some Europeans, who have tried it, to be well flavoured and delicate" (Blanford, *Mammalia*, Fauna of British India, Pt. II, pp. 257-259).

CHAPTER XLII

1. Khandesh. For an account of the subah under Akbar, see *Ain*, Vol. II, pp. 222 ff. It was also known as Dandes after prince Danyal.
2. Orissa. Baffin wrongly makes Orissa contiguous to Berar and Khandesh and Thevenot follows suit.
3. Memorandum.
4. Burhanpur in Nimar District, Central Provinces, famous for silk embroidery and the seat of the Mughal viceroy of the Deccan till 1635 (see, *Imp. Gaz.*, Vol. IX, pp. 104-106; Bernier, p. 31; Tavernier, Vol. I, pp. 42-44). The correct latitude is 21° 18′ North.
5. The distance between Surat and Burhanpur varies with different travellers. Tavernier (Vol. I, p. 43) gives 132 kos; Mundy makes it 170 kos (Vol. II, p. 50 f.n. 1); De Laet (p. 30) 233 miles and Sir Thomas Roe 223 miles (*Embassy of Sir Thomas Roe*, p. 68). Sir William Foster says that the actual distance as measured by General Goddard's surveyors is 237¾ miles. (*Ibid*, p. 68, f.n. 5).
6. The fort, commonly known as the Badshahi Qila, stands on the right bank of the Tapti. See Mundy, Vol. II, p. 50; Finch (Foster, *Early Travels*, p. 138) and De Laet (p. 30).
7. To enjoy the lovely view. Compare Peter Mundy, Vol. II, p. 50. He says that the king used to watch from here fighting elephants, buffaloes, antelopes and horse and hare racing.
8. De Laet (p. 30), Peter Mundy (Vol. II, p. 51) and Finch (Foster, *Early Travels*, p. 138) also describe this stone figure.
9. The water was delivered into a large square reservoir, known as *Jali Karanj*, "and from here was distributed to the town by earthen tile pipes surrounded with masonry." The Mughal waterworks were constructed between 1618 and 1650 and "form perhaps the most important monument of the past glory of Burhanpur" (See, *Nimar Dist. Gazetteer*, pp. 219-220).
10. See Manucci who says, "In this province they make much very fine white and coloured cloth, also printed cloth, which are exported in quantities by Persian and Armenian merchants to Persia, Arabia and Turkey. The soil is productive in grain" (Vol. II, p. 429).

CHAPTER XLIII

1. Balaghat is evidently the subah of Aurangabad.
2. Aurangabad in Hyderabad state. Founded by Malik Ambar in 1610 Fateh-

nagar was renamed Aurangabad by Aurangzeb when he transferred his headquarters there as viceroy of the Deccan. (See *Imp. Gaz.*, Vol. VI, pp. 148 ff.).

3. Baglan, a hilly tract comprising the present Baglan and Kalyan taluks of Nasik district, Bombay (*Imp. Gaz.*, Vol. VI, p. 192; also Foster, *Early Travels*, pp. 78-79, *n.* 2 and 136).
4. Telingana. Its capital was Warangal.
5. To rest.
6. The identity is not clear. We find mention of one Signor David Bazeu or Bazu, a Dutch man who followed Tavernier to India (see, Tavernier, Vol. I, p. xlix; Vol. II, p. 99; *The English Factories in India*, 1665-1667, p. 16 and *n.*).
7. Mahua (*bassia latifolia*) indigenous to many parts of India and yields valuable timber. Its flowers are eaten and yield a strong and cheap drink, (*mahua arrack*), Watt, Vol. I, pp. 406-415.
8. Cashew-nut; *Anacardium occidentale*, Hindi *kaju*. The tree was introduced into India by the Portuguese. (Watt, Vol. I, pp. 232-233).
9. Hindi *babul, babur, kikar*, the wild *Acacia arabica*. (Watt, Vol. I, pp. 18-27).
9a. See *supra* Chapter XXI, Note 15.
10. Navapur in the Pimpalner sub-division of Khandesh dist., Bombay. Tavernier writes that Navapur is the place where 'the best musk-scented rice in the world grows'. (Vol. I, p. 116).
11. The places on the route are :—Surat, Bardoli, Valod, Vyara, Sarkna, Navapur, Khanapur, Pimpalner, Taharabad (on the Mosam river), Satana, Umbrane, Ankai, Tankai, Devthan, Lasur, and Aurangabad.
12. *Chaukis*=guards.
13. Ox is the vehicle of Siva and not of Rama.
14. May be either a viragal or a sati stone.
15. Filth.
16. Satana, the head-quarters of the Baglan sub-division in Nasik district, Bombay about 30 miles west of Malegaon. (*Nasik Dist. Gazetteer*, Part II, pp. 646-647).
17. François Pallu, Bishop of Heliopolis passed through India in 1663 on his way to Siam where he went to supervise the mission work. He returned home in 1666 via Surat and Aleppo. (See, *The English Factories in India*, 1661-1664, p. 270; 1665-67, pp. 127 and 219). For details of M. Pallu's career, reference may be made to Hutchinson, *Adventurers in Siam in the Seventeenth Century* (London, 1940).
18. M. Lambert, Bishop of Beyrout in Syria who, according to Tavernier (ii, p. 232), was in Siam in 1665. For his career in Siam, see Hutchinson, *op. cit.*, Chapter III.
19. Aurangzeb's first viceroyalty of the Deccan with head-quarters at Burhanpur lasted from 1636 to 1644. His second viceroyalty of the Deccan, with the seat of Government at Aurangabad, lasted for a shorter term from 1653 to 1658. See, Sarkar, *History of Aurangzib*, Vol. I, pp. 54 and 170-171.
20. Dilras Banu Begam, Aurangzib's first wife, "died at Aurangabad on 8th October, 1657 from illness following child birth" (Sarkar, *op. cit.*, Vol. I, p. 61). Tavernier (Vol. I, pp. 118-9) also describes the tomb. According to the *Cambridge History of India* (Vol. IV, p. 567), the tomb was built in 1679. This is wrong. An inscription on the gateway of the mausoleum says that it was built in 1071 A.H. (1660 A.D.) by Ataullah (Cousens, *Archaeological Survey of India*, New Series, Vol. XXXI, p. 3).
21. Of the mosques at Aurangabad, the most famous is the Jama Masjid built by Malik Ambar.
22. Bains in the French text. Baths.
23. If the animal came from Ceylon it was either a Ceylon Sloth (*Loris tardigradus tardigradus*) or an allied species; two are found in South India also. See Pocock, *Mammalia, Fauna of British India*, Vol. I, pp. 181-182.

CHAPTER XLIV

1. Ellora (Verul), village in the district of Aurangabad, Hyderabad state about 15 miles north-west of Aurangabad famous for its rock temples and caves, which are among the finest in India. See Burgess, *Archaeological Survey Reports of Western India,* Vol. V (Elura Cave Temples).
2. Slowly.
3. Daulatabad in Hyderabad state 28 miles northwest of Hyderabad city, also known as Deogir or Deogarh. See, Bilgrami and Wilmott, *op. cit.*, Vol. II, pp. 397 ff.
4. Thevenot evidently refers to the tombs at Khuldabad or Rauza near Ellora. The original name of the place was Rauza, "which was changed to Khuldabad in consequence of the title of *Khuld Makan* conferred on Aurangzeb after his death." The most notable of the tombs in Thevenot's time were those of Malik Ambar, and Saiyed Hazrat Burhanuddin. Later, Aurangzeb and his son of Azam Shah were buried at Khuldabad (*Hyderabad State Gazetteer,* p. 213).
5. Tank near the Pangra gate of the city-walls, Rauza. (Bilgrami and Willmott, ii, p. 715).
6. The reference is apparently to the two gigantic *Dwarapalas* (door-keepers) on the north side of the court of the Kailash temple. These *Dwarapalas* are shown "with several arms, and wearing high *mukutas* or tiaras". See Burgess, *Archaeological Survey of Western India,* Vol. V (Elura Cave Temples), p. 34.
7. The well-known court of the Kailash temple. For a description see, Burgess, *Archaeological Survey of Western India,* Vol. V, pp. 28 ff.
8. On either side of the detached porch in the Kailas temple, "there are two pillars or dhvajastambhas (literally banner staves)" and "two elephants about the size of life" (Fergusson, *History of Indian and Eastern Architecture,* Vol. I, p. 343).
9. I could make nothing connected of it.
10. The Kailash temple which has been described as "by far the most extensive and elaborate rock-cut temple in India." The temple was built by Krishna I, the Rashtrakuta king of Malkhed (757-783). For a detailed description of the temple, see, Burgess, *Archaeological Survey of Western India,* Vol. V, pp. 26 ff.; Fergusson, *op. cit.*, pp. 342-349.
11. Ordinary size.
12. The reference here is to the 'Tin Thal' or three-storeyed cave-temple, the last of the twelve Buddhist caves at Ellora. It was "adapted for worship rather than as a monastery". Mr. Burgess writes "In no other series do we find a three-storeyed *vihara* carried out with the same consistency of design and the like magnificence as in this example." (*Archaeological Survey of Western India,* V, p. 16).

12a. Yogis.

13. At the time of Thevenot's visit, it was not certain when the caves at Ellora were excavated, but due to modern researches, we may safely say that the Buddhist cave-temples (the earliest chronologically) were excavated between A.D. 450 to 650 or 700. (See Burgess, *op. cit.*, p. 4). The Hindu caves were constructed during 650-800 A.D. and the Jain caves between 850-1100 A.D.
14. Modern Khuldabad (?) formerly known as Rauza.
15. Not traceable on modern maps.
16. Houses whereof are built of a blackish freestone with which its streets are also paved. At some distance from there I encountered the difficult descent, which I have mentioned.

CHAPTER XLV

1. Moderately large.
2. For a description of the fort, see Bilgrami and Wilmott, Vol. II, p. 422 ff.

3. Seventy and not three score leagues and more.
4. Kalvaral (18° 27′ N. and 78° 16′ E.). Orme has marked this place on his map as 'Calvar'. (*Historical Fragments of the Mogul Empire*).
5. The stages on the route are Ambad (34 miles south-east of Aurangabad), Ashti, Lasina (Nander Dist.), Nander (on the north bank of the Godavari), Lisa, Dentapur, Indur (now known as Nizamabad), Kondalwadi (Nizamabad Dist.) and Indalwai. Out of these places, Lisa and Dentapur are not traceable on modern maps, but they are marked in Orme's map. Thevenot's route from Aurangabad upto Nander is the same as that of Tavernier (Vol. I, p. 119). Earlier, he mentions only eight towns, but actually he refers to nine between Patoda and Indur.
6. Three hundred and thirty.
7. Are usually there.
8. Thevenot here refers to the invasion of Bijapur by the Mughals under Raja Jai Singh. On 7 Jan. 1666, the Mughals forced their way to within 12 miles of Bijapur, but a few months after Jai Singh had to return baffled. (*Cambridge History of India*, Vol. IV, pp. 254-255).
9. Patoda south-east of Nander. Tavernier calls it "Patonta", 9 kos from Nander. (Vol. I, p. 119).
10. Perilous feats.
11. For tricks of jugglers, see Jafar Sharif, *Islam in India*. Most of the European travellers have described with admiration the performances of the Indian jugglers.
12. Roll.
13. Took a whim to remove the basin.
14. Indur now known as Nizamabad situated in 18° 40′ N. and 78° 6′ E. (*Hyderabad State Gazetteer*, p. 132).
15. Because when he wishes he is maintained by the King of Golkonda.
16. Not traceable on modern maps.

CHAPTER XLVI

1. Sitanagar, city of Sita, cannot be located in a modern map. Moll, (*India*, p. 239) mentions the town of 'Chitinagar' which 'stands about 63 leagues to the southward of Aurengabad, and is remarkable only for a fine pagoda. . . . . .' Cousens mentions only one temple dedicated to Rama, Lakshmana and Sita situated to the south-west of Indur. This may be the temple that Thevenot visited (Cousens, *List of Antiquarian Remains in His Highness the Nizam's Territories*, p. 63).
2. Loaded.
3. Decorations.
4. It hath a nave, a choir.
5. Style.
6. Chikalthan, Rohilagadh, Ambad, Dhasalkher, Ashti, Manwat, Parbhani, Purna river (a tributary of the Godavari), Lasina, Nander, the Godavari river. (In the Deccan the Godavari is sometimes called Godaganga), Patoda, Kondalwadi (north-east of Biloli), Manjra river, Lisa, Dentapur, Indur or Nizamabad, Phulang river, Indalwai, Kalvaral.
7. Hyderabad iron became famous for its quality in very early times, as it formed the raw material for the Damascus blades. According to the *Ain* (Vol. II, p. 230) Nirmal and Indore (Indalwai) possessed mines of iron and other metals. The best steel, according to Bilgrami and Willmott (Vol. I,

p. 399) is produced at Kunasamudram near Nirmal in the Nander District. Also see Ball's note, Tavernier, Vol. I, p. 127 and *Relations of Golconda*, p. 34.

8. Kalaghat.
9. This is probably a mistake. Shivaji had a brother, Sambhaji and a step brother, Ekoji (Vyankoji), both of whom were in the Bijapur service. Shambhaji was not alive at the time. Probably one of the principal officers of Shivaji or a natural son of Shahaji, of whom there was more than one, is meant.
10. Nuts or a pullet's eggs.
11. The Balaghat (*bala* 'above', *ghat* 'a mountain pass'). It has been used to denote various parts of India. In Berar, the name is given to the upland country above the Ajanta Hills, and this is the northernmost portion of 'the tableland of the Deccan'. The Muslims of Bijapur applied this term to territories conquered by them from the Hindu kingdom of Vijayanagar in the 17th century. This 'comprised the north-east part of Mysore and the Bellary, Anantapur, Kurnool, and Cuddapah Districts of Madras.' It is also applied, as mentioned before, to the range of hills, in the western half of Hyderabad in which sense it is used here. (*Imp. Gaz.*, Vol. VI, p. 222).

CHAPTER XLVII

1. Telingana (*Telinga*, Sanskrit *Trilinga*). The Muslims vaguely applied it to the country of the Telegus, in the north-eastern part of the Madras Presidency. (*Imp. Gaz.*, Vol. XXIII, pp. 275-276; *Hobson-Jobson*, pp. 912-913). Sarkar (*Aurangzeb*, Vol. I, p. 43), describes Telingana as one of the four provinces of Mughal Deccan at the time of Aurangzeb's first viceroyalty of the Deccan.
2. Seat of the Portuguese government in India.
3. Bidar, head-quarters of the district of the same name in Hyderabad state, formerly capital of the Bahmani kingdom.
4. Kalyani, the ancient Chalukyan city now in Hyderabad state. It was captured by Aurangzeb in 1656.
5. Vijayanagar.
6. "When Aurangzeb invested the place, Bidar was described as 4,500 yards in circumference, having three deep ditches 25 yards wide and 15 yards deep, cut in the stone." (Bilgrami and Willmott, Vol. II, p. 380).
7. The castle was built by Ahmad Shah Wali. Its building commenced in 1428, and was completed in 1432. (Burgess, *Archaeological Survey Reports of Western India*, Vol. III, p. 42; Yazdani, *The Antiquities of Bidar*, p. 4).

7a. Thevenot probably refers to Shaista Khan who was Shah Jahan's brother-in-law. Shaista Khan was recalled from the Deccan in January 1664 before Thevenot's visit to Bidar, but it is hardly accurate to describe him as governor of that place. Mr. Ghulam Yazdani informs me that the first governor of Bidar on the part of the Mughal emperor was Iftikhar Khan who held his office for a little over two years. The next governor, Khan Zaman Mir Khalil-ullah left Bidar in 1660 to assume the governorship of Malwa. He was succeeded by Shams-ud-Din Mukhtar Khan who held his charge from 1660 to 1672. Thevenot could not possibly have met his successor in 1666. Nor was Shaista Khan succeeded by an old Persian in the viceroyalty of the Deccan, Prince Muazzam being his successor.

8. Sandalwood.
9. I do not know on what evidence Thevenot's statement is based. I have not been able to trace this custom nor could I find any reference anywhere to the practice of eating a cow made of paste and honey.

9a. Enjoins.

10. Fasting among both savage and higher races is a recognized practice. For the origin of fasting and its prevalence among the various races of the world, an excellent summary is contained in the article by A. J. Maclean entitled "*Fasting*" in the *Encyclopaedia of Religion and Ethics*, Vol. V, pp. 759-771. Among the Hindus, fasts are frequently observed. The days of the new and full moon (*amavasya* and *purnima*) are fast-days and so also the eleventh day of each lunar month, which is called the *ekadasi* day. (See Dubois, *Hindu manners*, pp. 271 ff.).
11. Five, six or seven days.
12. *Chirata swertia, charayatah, chireta.* It is commonly found in temperate regions of the Himalayas from Kashmir to Bhutan, and in Khasia mountains. The basis of Thevenot's statement that it grows towards Cambay is unknown. (Watt, Vol. VI, Part III, pp. 390-392).

CHAPTER XLVIII

1. The province lay between Khandesh and the Surat coast. Sarkar (*Aurangzeb*, Vol. I, pp. 50-51) describes it as "a small tract, stretching north and south for about 160 miles from the Tapti river to the Ghatmata hills of the Nasik district, and 100 miles east and west across the Ghats." Its Rathor Rajas styled themselves *Shah* and used the title of *Baharji.* They became vassals of the Mughals in 1638. (Sarkar, *Aurangzeb*, Vol. I, pp. 52-3). For a description of Baglana, see, *Ain*, Vol. II, p. 251.
2. Mulher on the Mosam river.
3. Portuguese settlement and town in Gujarat at the entrance of the Gulf of Cambay. (*Imp. Goz.*, Vol. XI, pp. 128-131).
4. Moderately large.
5. Slavery was not abolished in Portuguese India till 25 February, 1869. (Danvers, *The Portuguese in India*, ii, pp. 467-468).
6. Bombay was acquired by the Portuguese in 1534 from Bahadur Shah.
7. The fortified hill of Korle called by the Portuguese "*Morro de Chaul*" (Da Cunha, *Chaul and Bassein*, pp. 85-87).
8. Dabhol in Ratnagiri District, Bombay situated in 17° 35′ North Lat.
9. Shivaji took Dabhol in 1660.
10. Rajapur (Ratnagiri Dist. Bombay) was sacked by Shivaji in 1660. (Grant Duff, *History of Marathas*, I, p. 139). Vengurla, famous for spices, had a Dutch factory for many years. Ball's identification of Rasigarh with Rakshasgudda is obviously wrong.
11. Cloth.
12. The reference here is to *Coconut day* (*Nariali Purnima*) celebrated in coastal areas on the full moon day of *Shravan.* The idea underlying it is to keep the sea calm and smooth, and traders think that by offering coco-nuts, flowers, betel-nuts, etc., they please the sea-goddess or god. (See, Manohar Lall, *Among the Hindus*, pp. 149-151; Mrs. Stevenson, *The Rites of the Twice-born*, pp. 309 ff.).
13. And some of them have been known to have children at that age.
14. Otherwise.

14a. There is no legal bar to a Hindu having a plurality of wives.

15. For marriage preliminaries, procession, feast, rites etc., see, Mrs. Stevenson, Chapters III-V.
16. That appear.
17. Walk.

CHAPTER XLIX

1. The custom of shaving a widow's head differs in various parts of India. In Gujarat, the hair of a widow are cut off on the tenth day. In certain castes, the head is shaved on the day of the husband's death. (Mrs. Stevenson, *op. cit.*, p. 204).
2. The reference is to the *sati* rite abolished by Lord William Bentinck.
3. Ball (Tavernier, Vol. II, p. 168, *n.* 2) suggests that the custom referred to by Thevenot here probably gave rise to the story of Sindbad's burial with his dead wife.
4. On Mughal efforts to suppress *sati,* see, Bernier, pp. 306-307; Tavernier, Vol. II, pp. 163-164; Peter Mundy, II, pp. 179-180; Manucci, II, p. 97; Ovington, p. 201. Akbar prohibited the burning of a widow against her inclination, and so did his son Jahangir (Hawkins in Foster, *Early Travels,* p. 119).

BOOK II

CHAPTER I

1. The Deccan. This name is "a corruption of the Sanskrit *dakshina*" (southern), and "includes, in its widest sense, the whole of India south of the Narbada river" (See, *Imp. Gaz.*, Vol. XI, pp. 205-208). Thevenot obviously refers to Bahmani kingdom here.
2. These principalities owed their allegiance to the Hindu rulers of Vijayanagar and not to the Bahmani kings.
3. Calicut in the Malabar District, Madras. Vasco da Gama landed here in 1498 (*Imp. Gaz.*, Vol. IX, pp. 289-291).
4. Cochin situated in 9° 58′ N. and 76° 14′ E. The original town was swept away in 1341 by violent floods. It played an important part in the history of Portuguese and Dutch expansion in India. The Portuguese appeared at Cochin in 1500. In 1663, the town was captured by the Dutch. It is now the chief port of Malabar. (*Imp. Gaz.*, Vol. X, pp. 353-355).
5. Cannanore in Chirakkal taluk of Malabar district, Madras, once 'the capital of the Zamorin's principal rival the Kolattiri Raja and one of the earliest Portuguese settlements on the coast'. (*Imp. Gaz.*, Vol. IX, pp. 298-299).
6. Quilon (Kollam) An important port now in Travancore state, which once formed the capital of an independent principality.
7. The first two syllables are the ordinary Dravidian word, *mala* (hill, mountain), and *bar* is the Persian for country. The native name is *Malayalam* (hill-country).
8. The kingdom of Vijayanagar was so called by the Portuguese after Narsingha Saluva, the founder of the second ruling dynasty. Here the name of the kingdom has been applied to the capital, the ruins of which are still to be seen about the village of Hampi near Hospet in the Bellary district. (See, Longhurst, *Hamp. Ruins;* Barbosa, Vol. I, p. 128).
9. The reference is again to the Bahamani King.
10. Vasco da Gama (1469-1524), famous Portuguese navigator and discoverer of of the sea-route to India. For his voyage to India and dealings with the Malabar princes see Danvers, *The Portuguese in India,* Whiteway, *The Rise of the Portuguese Power in India* and Prestage, *Vasco da Gama.*
11. Zamorin, the title of the Hindu raja of Calicut, from Malayal, *Samutiri* abbreviated to Samuri, which again is derived from *Samudrin.* 'The Sea-Lord'. (See, *Hobson-Jobson,* p. 977). Ball suggests that "it is more likely to be a transliteration of the Malayalam *Samutiri,* itself a corruption of Swami-Sri, Lord-Master" (Tavernier, Vol. I, p. 89 *n.* 2).

12. This is approximately correct, the actual latitude being 11° 15′ N.
13. Are detached.
14. Anxious to supplant his rival the Zamorin from the predominant position in Malabar the raja of Cochin readily allied himself with the Portuguese. In 1503 the Portuguese built a fort at Cochin and soon afterwards the raja acknowledged the suzerainty of the king of Portugal. Amity between the two powers long remained unbroken until the advent of the Dutch in Malabar upset the existing political balance. See, Panikkar, *Malabar and the Portuguese,* Chap. IV and Logan, *Malabar,* Vol. I, pp. 304 ff.
15. In 1663.
16. The Cochin River. This is hardly a river. The *Malabar and Anjengo Gaz.* (Vol. I, p. 6) says it is the only outlet of the great system of lagoons and backwaters which extends along this part of the Coast.
17. From early times, pepper, particularly *piper nigrum* (black pepper) formed the chief article of export from Malabar. (Watt, Vol. VI, Pt. I, pp. 260 ff.). Duarte Barbosa (Vol. II, p. 92) writes that in the kingdom of Cochin, "there is much pepper which grow throughout the land on trees like unto ivy." Hamilton (*A new Account of the East Indies,* Vol. I, p. 183) found the state "producing great Quantities of Pepper" in the next century.
18. This is obviously a reference to the disease known as elephantiasis or 'Cochin-leg'. Ralph Fitch (1583-91) writes "This bad water causeth many of the people to be like lepers, and many of them have their legs swollen as bigge as a man in the waste, and many of them are scant able to go." (Foster, *Early Travels,* p. 44). Hamilton, (Vol. I, p. 181) also refers to this disease.
19. Nayars. Probably derived from the Sanskrit *Nayaka,* a leader. The Nayars were originally a martial caste well known for their warlike spirit. Burke compared them to the Mamelukes of Egypt. For details see Barbosa, Vol. II, pp. 38157; *Malabar Anjengo Gas., Vol.* I, pp. 114-123; Thurston, *Castes and Tribes of Southern India,* Vol. V, pp. 283 ff; Logan, Vol. I, pp. 131 ff.
20. Almost every European traveller who visited the Malabar coast refers to this custom. See Nicolo de Conti (*India in the fifteenth century,* Conti's narrative, p. 20); Linschoten, Vol. I, p. 280, Barbosa, Vol. II, p. 47; Pyrard, Vol. I, p. 384; Ceasar Frederick in Purchas, Vol. X, p. 104; Hamilton, Vol. I, p. 173 and Grose, Vol. I, p. 243. Logan (Vol. I, p. 136) says that "the custom was adopted to prevent alienation of property."
21. The reference is to Goda Varma the last of the four princes adopted by the Rani in 1658. The last king to be crowned in the Portuguese cathedral was Rama Varma. (*Cochin State Manual,* pp. 88 ff.).
22. General Hustaart installed Vira Kerala as king of Cochin on behalf of the Dutch, and entered into a treaty with him on 22 March 1663 (*Cochin State Manual,* p. 95). For the terms of the treaty see Panikkar, *Malabar and the Dutch,* pp. 17-18.
23. Tanur or Vettat in Ponnai taluk, Malabar Dist.
24. The origin of the Nayars is a disputed point. The generally accepted idea is that "they are the same as the Sudras of the east coast and that the term Nayar is etymologically identical with Naick or Naidu." (*Cochin State Manual,* p. 31). As they are analogous to the Kshatriyas or fighting castes of north India probably they claim like their confreres in the north descent from heroes of the solar race.
25. The dress of the Nayars is scanty. 'By custom the Nayar women go uncovered from the waist; upper garments indicate lower caste'. (Logan, Vol. I, p. 134; Thurston, Vol. V, pp. 365-366).
26. The Pulayan from Mal. *pula,* pollution, also known as Cheruman, forms one of the polluting castes in Malabar. The word Cheruman means a slave and perhaps indicates still their social and economic status. (Thurston, Vol. II, p. 45 ff; *Malabar and Anjengo Dist. Gaz.,* Vol. I, pp. 133-134).
27. "They pollute the high castes at a distance of 64 feet" (*Malabar and Anjengo Gazetteer,* Vol. I, p. 134).

28. Go, go, see Mandelslo, p. 88.
29. Mr. Poduval, Director of Archaeology, Travancore state informs me that "Coucouya" is the same as *hoi hoi* which a man of high caste shouts as he walks about the road to avoid pollution by a low caste man.
30. Literally the big river, the reference is obviously to the Periyar (the great river) of Cochin which is about 142 miles in length (*Cochin State Manual,* pp. 5-6).
31. Trial by ordeal was common in civil and criminal cases in Cochin as in other parts of India. The most common form was the ordeal by fire, but there were several forms of ordeal by water. Achyuta Menon says that "the accused had to swim across the ferry at Uzahavam in Cranganur, or that at Pillipuram in Vaipin island which used to swarm with crocodiles, and if he escaped unhurt by these creatures he was declared innocent." (*Cochin State Manual,* pp. 339-340, 377). Thevenot's account however is fanciful. The "Alligator pagoda" known as the temple of Trikkatakkapilli was on the Cranganor river to the south of Paliport (Pallipuram). See, K. P. Padmanabha Menon, *History of Kerala,* Vol. II, pp. 258-261. Col. H. Temple Drury writes on the ordeal as follows : "a small pagoda, or heathen temple stands on the bank of the river, in which two alligators were specially supported, their daily food having been thrown into the water in order to keep them there. To undergo their ordeal the accused was compelled to swim across this river and back, which if he refused to do, he was dragged through, holding on with his hands to a boat. If the alligator pulled him under the water, it was considered a sign of guilt, if otherwise he was released as innocent." (*Life and Sport in Southern India,* p. 70). Dellon refers to a similar ordeal prevailing among the inhabitants of Madagascar "If there be any Contest betwixt two parties, they appear on the Shoar of a Lake or River; he that is to confirm the Truth of his Affirmation by Oath, plunges himself into the River, Conjures and Prays the *Jacaret,* (Crocodile) to be Arbitrators betwixt him and his Enemy, and to decide their Quarrel; to let him Live if he speaks Truth, and to devour him instantly if he affirms anything contrary to it. And this they make use of for a Tryal of the Guilt or Innocency of him who thus commits himself to the decision of the Crocodile in the Water." *A Voyage to the East Indies* (English edition 1698), p. 27. *Nouvelle Relation d'un Voyage fait aux Indes Orientales, Amsterdam,* 1699, p. 35.
32. The Christians of the Syrian and Romo Syrian sects are sometimes called the Christians of St. Thomas in the belief that their ancestors were converted by the apostle himself.
33. Headquarters of the district of the same name in Madras. (*Imp. Gaz.,* Vol. XVI, pp. 404-7).
34. Kayangulam or Kayankulam in Travancore State. It was formerly the capital of an independent principality known as Onad, which had the same status as Travancore. (*Imp. Gaz.,* Vol. XV, pp. 195-196).
35. The ruler of Cannanore bore the title of Kollattiri. He was the chief rival of the Zamorin.
36. Badagora or Vadakara (north bank) north of Kotta river in Kurumbranad taluk of Malabar district. (*Malabar and Anjengo Dist. Gazetteer,* Vol. I, pp. 432-433).
37. Kottakkal, three miles south of Badagra. It was once "the stronghold of the Kotakkal Kunhali Marakkars, famous pirates whose deeds are the theme of many ballads." (*Ibid,* pp. 433-434).
38. Muttungal north of Vadakara on the sea coast.
39. *Areca catechu,* Vern. *supari,* Tamil, *adaikay* from *adai* 'close-clustering' and '*kay*', 'nut'. (*Hobson-Jobson,* p. 35; Watt, Col. I, pp. 291 ff.).
40. The Palmyra palm; brab tree, *Borassus flabelliformis* Vern. *tel, tala, tar, tari,* commonly cultivated in South India and Ceylon. The leaf gives a material which is a substitute for paper. (Watt, Vol. I, pp. 495-504; *Hobson-Jobson,* p. 664). Palm leaves or cadjans are still used for keeping state records.

41. During the Onam festival, "the men, particularly those who are young, form themselves into parties, and shoot at each other with arrows. These arrows are blunted, but exceedingly strong, and are discharged with such force, that a considerable number are generally wounded on both sides." (Thurston, V, p. 373).
42. Banghel (Bangar) near Mangalore. The Bangar family ruled over Mangalore and were under Vijayanagar. Subsequently, they allied themselves with the Portuguese. For a description of the place see Pietro Della Valle, p. 302. (See also *Manual of South Canara District*, Vol. I, pp. 71-73).
43. Ullal situated on the Netravati river, now a village in the Mangalore taluk of South Kanara district, Madras. It was the seat of a Jain family of some local importance and was ruled by a queen when Pietro Della Valle, the Italian traveller visited the place (pp. 303-304). (See also *Madras Provincial Gazetteer*, Vol. II, p. 399).
44. Mangalore, South Kanara district, Madras. The Portuguese captured the town in 1596 and maintained a footing there for the next two centuries. The correct latitude of the city is 12° 52′ North. (*Madras Provincial Gazetteer*, Vol. II, pp. 396-397).
45. Basrur (the Barcelore or Barkalur of early geographers), now a village in South Kanara district, Madras. Formerly it was an important trade centre. It was sacked by Shivaji in 1665.
46. Honavar or Onore, in North Kanara district, Bombay situated in 14° 17′ N. The place was visited thrice by Ibn Batuta and is mentioned by Duarte Barbosa (Vol. I, pp. 185-187). Pietro Della Valle (pp. 202-203) describes the town.
47. Kanara or Canara from Kannada literally "the black country" so named on account of its black soil and probably also for its long association with Kanarese princes. The part of the western sea-board to which the name is popularly applied is now divided into two districts (1) North Kanara in Bombay and (2) South Kanara in Madras.
48. Worthless.

CHAPTER II

1. Sher Khan better known as Sher Shah. He defeated Humayun at Chausa (1539) and subsequently assumed the title of Shah Alam. His power however never extended beyond the Vindhyas and it is wrong to call him "King of Deccan".
2. Another inaccurate statement. Mahmud Shah was not put to death by Sher Shah.
3. Humayun was the second Mughal emperor of India.
4. Thevenot is again wrong. Sikandar and not Selim Shah lost Delhi to Humayun.
5. Neither Humayun nor Sher Shah ever conquered any part of the Carnatic.
6. Purely a fiction.
7. Sher Shah died in 1545 A.D. Humayun returned to India in 1555 during the troublesome period that followed Selim Shah's death in 1554.
8. Malik Ahmad or Ahmad Nizam Shah became independent ruler of Ahmadnagar in 1490.
9. Quli Qutb Shah founded the ruling dynasty of Golkonda either in 1512 or 1518.
10. Yusuf Adil Shah, the first king of Bijapur declared his independence in 1489-90. Thevenot's information about the ruling houses of the Deccan was hopelessly confused. He found two independent Muslim principalities Bijapur and Golkonda in the Deccan and must have heard of another—Ahmadnagar which had already been annexed by the Mughals. All these

principalities were founded long before Babar's invasion of India. Sher Shah and his successors had nothing to do with them. Vijaynagar was conquered by the allied Muslim princes in 1565.

11. The reference is obviously to Fathullah Imad Shah of Berar and Qasim Barid of Bidar.
12. The reference is probably to the victory gained by Malik Ambar, in alliance with the Deccani powers, over the Mughals in 1620 when he drove them back to Burhanpur (Sarkar, *Aurangzib*, Vol. I, p. 34).
13. Balaghat and Telingana must have been conquered during the Mughal campaign of 1631-1632. Telingana formed one of the four Deccan provinces of the Mughal Empire in 1636, and the whole of it, according to Sarkar (Vol. I, p. 43) was upland (*Balaghat*). Baglana was annexed in 1638.
14. For Aurangzeb's conquests in Bijapur during his second viceroyalty of the Deccan, see, Sarkar, Vol. I, Chapter XI.
15. Name applied to the east coast of Madras, although its boundaries were not clearly mentioned. The derivation of the word has been in dispute, but it is now regarded as a corruption of *Cholamandalam*, 'the country of the Cholas'. (See *Imp. Gaz.*, Vol XI, pp. 51-52).
16. Famous sea-port, now in Tanjore district, Madras.
17. Again a mistake. Adil Shah and Qutb Shah conquered the remnants of the Vijayanagar kingdom in the Karnatak.
18. Vellore, taluk and town, now in North Arcot district, Madras, Bijapur and Golkonda were captured by Aurangzeb in 1686 and 1687 respectively. At the time of Thevenot's visit Adil Shah could not be a fugitive at Vellore which formed the fief of one of his nobles. The fort fell to Shivaji's troops in 1678. Vellore was for several years the headquarters of Shri Ranga III of Vijayanagar and he is probably confused with Adil Shah. (Sarkar, *Aurangzib*, Vol. IV, pp. 217-218; Vriddhagirisan, *Nayaks of Tanjore*, pp. 132-3).
19. Gingee (Gingi), a famous rock-fortress in South Arcot district, Madras. Originally a stronghold of Vijayanagar it was later annexed by Bijapur. Shivaji secured the place from Nasir Muhammad Khan a Bijapuri noble in 1677.
20. Riza Quli, surnamed Neknam Khan was a 'trusty eunuch' of the sultan of Golconda and not an officer of Bijapur. He was appointed governor of Karnatak in 1661. See Irvine's note, Manucci, Vol. IV, p. 451.
21. The reference is to the joint invasion by Bijapur and Golkonda of Shri Ranga Rayal's territories.
22. The principality of Madura was originally a part of the Vijayanagar kingdom. Viswanath the founder of the ruling dynasty rose to prominence after the decline of Vijayanagar. After the death of the famous Tirumala Nayak in 1659 the rulers of Madura lost their former power and importance.
23. Tanjore, headquarters of Tanjore district in Madras, was like Madura once a dependency of Vijayanagar. A Nayak dynasty was founded early in the 17th century. It was later supplanted by Ekoji or Vyankoji, step-brother of Shivaji. See Vriddhagirishan, *Nayaks of Tanjore*.
24. Tranquebar, Vernacular *Tarangampadi*, in Tanjore District, Madras, 18 miles north of Negapatam. It became a Danish settlement in 1620.
25. *Pattamar, partimar*, 'a foot-runner, a courier.' (*Hobson-Jobson*, p. 687).
26. Tirupati town in the Chandragiri taluk of North Arcot district, Madras. The town contains several temples, the chief of which are those of Govindrajaswami and Ramaswamy. (*Manual of North Arcot Dist*, Vol. II, pp. 326-328). Tirupati is not, strictly speaking, near Cape Comorin.
27. Kareputtun in the Devagad sub-division, Ratnagiri District, Bombay. It has lost its former importance now.
28. Crocodiles were often kept in the deep moats of forts in India as a defensive measure. According to Sabhasad there were numerous crocodiles in the ditch of the Vellore fort. See Sen, *Siva Chhatrapati*, p. 127.
29. Ali Adil Shah II of Bijapur. On the question of his parentage, see, Sarkar, Vol. I, pp. 285-286; Bernier, p. 197; Tavernier, Vol. I, p. 148.

CHAPTER III

1. Tissuari a corruption of *Tisvadi* or a district comprising thirty village communities (Fonseca, *An Historical and Archaeological Sketch of Goa,* p. 111).
2. There is a slight error. The correct latitude is 15° 30′ North.
3. The Mandavi or the river of the toll post rises at the Parvar *ghat* in the district of Satari, and falls into the Bay of Aguada. (*Bombay Presidency Gazetteer,* Vol. II, p. 563).
4. Goa was, as a matter of fact, conquered by the Portuguese from the Bijapuris. Zabaim, Sabaio or Savai, as the name is variously written, is no other than Yusuf Adil Shah the first king of Bijapur. (Fonseca, *op. cit.,* pp. 130-131 and note, Danvers, *The Portuguese in India,* Vol. I, pp. 186-187).
5. Duarte Barbosa's account of Goa confirms that of Thevenot. "The city is very great, with good houses, well girt about with strong-walls, with towers and bastions. Around it are many vegetable and fruit gardens, with fine trees and tanks of sweet water, with mosques and heathen temples." (Vol. I, p. 175). One of the best accounts of Goa is that of the Frenchman Dellon (*Relation de l'Inquisition de Goa,* 1698). François Pyrard (Vol. II, pt. I, Chapter I-VII) describes the city in great details.
6. Xavier, Francisco de (1506-1552), the famous Jesuit missionary and Saint, died at Sancian, off China, in 1552. His body was first buried at Molucca whence it was transferred to Goa Velha two years later where it still remains. The body is supposed to be incorruptible and is still periodically exposed for the benefit of pilgrims.
7. Tavernier also says almost in identical language "Many of these idolaters worship monkeys". "As I have elsewhere said pagodas have been built . . ." etc. The reference in both cases is to the worship of the monkey god Hanuman or Mahavir. Hon. Emily Eden mentions a case of some villagers in northern India insisting on worshipping a tame langur monkey belonging to a military officer (*Up the Country,* Vol. I, p. 107).
8. See Thevenot's account of Muttra. Pt. III, Book I, Chapter XXII.
9. This is still a well-known custom in orthodox Brahman families. Nobody who has not taken his bath is allowed to enter the *chauka.* If somebody touches the circle, the cooked food is defiled and no orthodox Brahman would partake of it.
10. Shares.

CHAPTER IV

1. Biknur town, north-east of Medak in Hyderabad state.
2. Nawab. 'Nabad' in the French text is obviously a printer's error.
3. Medchal, in Hyderabad state in the north-east of Atraf-i-balda district. (*Hyderabad State Gazetteer,* p. 112).
4. The places on the route are :—Chinna Mallareddi, Biknur, Melur and Jidpalli (Meliver and Jalpeli of Orme's map), Medchal (Orme's Mersel), Bhagnagar or Hyderabad.
5. Hyderabad (Haiderabad). The city was founded in 1589 by Muhammad Quli, the fifth Qutb Shahi king.
6. This is approximately correct, the exact latitude being 17° 22′ N.
7. Waited.
8. Probably Huq-Nazar.
9. This cannot be the Purana Pul over Musi of which 23 arches still exist. Of old bridges with three arches there are several in the neighbourhood.
10. Thevenot again mentions the river in Chap. X and places it between Danec and Tchelcour. It must be a very small stream and is not shown in modern maps. Both Danec and Tchelcour are shown in Orme's map but not the

river. Mr. Ghulam Yazdani tells me that there are several nullahs near Hyderabad which fall into the Musi but none of them bear a name that may approximate to Nerva.

11. This serai must have been in the Karwan suburb which contains ruins of many buildings.
12. The Char Minar. The most striking monument of the Qutb Shahs, occupies a central position with four roads radiating from its base. These four minarets rise to a height of about 180 feet, and were erected in 1591 A.D. by Muhammad Quli Qutb Shah. For a detailed account, see, Bilgrami and Willmott, *Historical and Descriptive Sketch of the Nizam's Dominions*, Vol. II, pp. 560-562; *Archaeological Report* (Hyderabad), 1918-1919, pp. 3-4.
13. The majority.
14. Mud.
15. Fountains.
16. Gul-i-Daudi. This word is used by Indians for both *Chrysanthemum coronarium* and *c. indicum* (Watt, Vol. II, pp. 272-273).
17. Thick.
18. Include.

CHAPTER V

1. Settled.
2. We get stray references to Englishmen at Golkonda in the factory records. Mr. Nathaniel Chumley or Cholmley was engaged in the diamond trade for several years and Mr. Andrews was sent to Golkonda from Surat (*The English Factories in India*, 1661-64, pp. 274 n and 391).
3. Manucci refers to the Dutch factory at Golkonda, (Vol. III, pp. 132-133), Bernier to their power and influence (pp. 195-196).
4. Kettle-drums.
5. Tavernier estimated their number at more than 20,000. (Vol. I, pp. 127-128).
6. See Sen, *Administrative System of the Marathas*, pp. 393-396, 556-558, and 651-653.
7. Fryer (Vol. II, p. 132) puts its value at 8*s.* in the last quarter of the 17th century. According to Tavernier, the value of a pagoda varied from 6 to 9½ francs (Vol. I, p. 130 and p. 329).
8. Regarding the location of Golkonda diamond mines, see Ball's note (Tavernier, Vol. II, pp. 352 ff.).
9. In Golkonda, according to Ball, it weighed 5½ grains, which is slightly less than Thevenot's estimate.
10. The French text is wrong here. (*sept mangelins sont sept carats*) for seven mangelin could not be equal to seven carats. The translator has made the necessary correction.
11. The French text has 'ecus' for 'crowns'.
12. Fifty five.
13. Nine.
14. Dutch *gulden*. According to Ball, its value was about 1*s.* 9*d.* to 1*s.* 9½*d.* (Tavernier, Vol. I, p. 328).

CHAPTER VI

1. The old fortress is about 5 miles west of Hyderabad city. Originally constructed by a raja of Warangal the fort was ceded to Muhammad Shah Bahmani in 1364. It later passed to the Qutb Shahi Sultans early in the sixteenth century and was captured by Aurangzeb in 1687. (Bilgrami and Willmott, *op. cit.*, Vol. II, pp. 469 ff; *Hyderabad State Gazetteer*, pp. 113-114).

2. Sultan Quli Qutb Shah (1512-43). See, Briggs, *op. cit.*, Vol. III, pp. 339-378; Bilgrami and Willmott, Vol. II, pp. 470 ff.
3. The name 'Golkonda' is a compound of Telegu 'golla', (a shepherd) and 'konda', (a hill). It thus means 'shepherd's hill' (*Relations of Golconda*, Introduction, pp. xv-xvi).
4. The fort of Golkonda is surrounded by a stone wall about three miles in circumference, 'having high bastions eighty-seven in number at the angles'. There were originally eight gates, out of which only four are in use (Bilgrami and Willmott, Vol. II, pp. 510 ff.).

   Bowrey confirms Thevenot "The fort of this Metropolitan is an admirable One, noe lesse then 5 English miles in Circuit, the walls of Vast height and Substance proportionable thereunto, gunned all round. . . ." (*A Geographical Account*, p. 110).
5. This large tank near the Banjara gate is said to have been built by Ibrahim Qutb Shah. (Bilgrami and Willmott, Vol. II, p. 511).
6. The Banjara gate, 'a massive structure of granite' about 50 ft. high, with platforms and chambers on either side for the guards.
7. The King's Palace, now in ruins, was built on the summit of the hill. (Bilgrami and Willmott, Vol. II, p. 514).
8. Probably Pitre de Lan, a young Dutch Surgeon, with whom Tavernier, (Vol. I, pp. 240-243) stayed for a few days at Golkonda.
9. Are busy with.
10. Emery stone. "This the industrial form of the mineral, is a granular alumina, with which a small amount of magnetic iron is associated. It is very freely distributed among the crystalline rocks of Southern India. . . . . A large quantity is employed by the cutters and polishers of stones, both precious and ornamental" (Watt, Vol. II, pp. 572-73).
11. Yule derives the word from Persian *padzahr or pazahr* (*Hobson-Jobson*, p. 90). It may also be *bezahr,* without poison or anti poison. The name is applied "to certain hard concretions found in the bodies of animals, to which antidotal virtues were ascribed, and specially to one obtained from the stomach of a wild goat in the Persian province of Lar." Thevenot's account of Golkonda *bezoars* reads like a summary of Tavernier's more detailed narrative which mentions the porcupine besides, goat, cow and monkey as a *bezoar* producing animal (Vol. II, pp. 115-120). Fryer also was told (in Persia) that the stone found in the stomachs of wild goats was "occasioned by some Plant they delight to feed on." He says "The Persians there call this Stone *Pazahar,* being a Compound of *Pa* and *Zahar,* the first of which is *against,* the other is *Poyson*" (Vol. II, pp. 193-195). Manucci however asserts that the stone was named after the place of its origin. "In Gulkundah . . . . . is a district call Bezoar, near the country of Chanda. In that part goats are very numerous, and in them grow *bezoar* stones. It is from this place that the stones take their name" (Vol. II, p. 431). Manucci claims to have "strengthened" a patient with "Chicken broth and *bezoar* stone" (Vol. II, p. 178). Garcia da Orta also used it as a stimulant (Vol. I, p. 266). For his discourse on *bezoars* see Vol. II, pp. 231-235. It does not appear that Orta knew of Golkonda *bezoars*. See also *Relations of Golconda,* pp. 34-35.
12. Thevenot could have seen the Mausolea of five kings only as the sixth ruler of the Qutb Shahi dynasty was alive when he visited Golkonda. The tombs stand on a plain about half a mile from the fort and they have suffered badly from the ravages of time and man alike.
13. Porcelain.
14. Muhammad Quli Qutb Shah who died in 1625. For description of his tomb see Bilgrami & Willmott, Vol. II, p. 520.
15. *Ghati* or *Ghari.* The day and night are divided into 60 and not 64 *gharis* as Thevenot asserts. The gong or bell that announces the time is also called *ghari.* See Terry (Foster, *Early Travels,* p. 317).

CHAPTER VII

1. Shia.
2. Abdullah Qutb Shah (1626-1672) was the sixth and not the seventh ruler of the Qutb Shahi line. Bernier gives us an account of the king's character. (pp. 18-19). He writes "The King has lost all mental energy, and has ceased to hold the reins of government" (p. 194). Tavernier, (Vol. I, pp. 128 ff) also refers to the sultan. For a modern estimate of his character; see, Sarkar, *History of Aurangzib*, Vol. IV, pp. 330 ff.
3. This is wrong. See N. 1, Chapter II.
4. Hayat Baksh Begam, Abdullah's mother was a daughter of Ibrahim Quli the fourth king of the Qutb Shahi dynasty and not a Brahman lady as Thevenot imagined.
5. Thirteen, according to Sir Richard Burn (*Cambridge History of India*, Vol. IV, p. 261) and twelve according to Sir Jadunath Sarkar (*History of Aurangzib*, Vol. IV, p. 330).
6. This is a mistatement. Abdullah was the eldest son of his father. There is no reference to a palace intrigue engineered by Hayat Bakhsh Begam as Thevenot writes. There was, however, some disorder and disturbance caused by 'the people of the *bazar* and the vagabonds' which was quickly put down.

6a. Aurangzeb began his campaign against Golkonda in January 1656, and not in 1658. For details of the campaign, see, Sarkar, *op. cit.*, Vol. I, Chap. X.

7. An obvious exaggeration.
8. By the treaty of 1636 the king of Golkonda undertook to pay the emperor of Delhi an annual tribute of two lakhs of pagodas.
9. Prince Muhammad Sultan, entered Hyderabad unopposed on the 24th January 1656. Abdullah Qutb Shah had fled to the fort of Golkonda two days previously and the Mughal army reached the environs of the city on the 23rd. The king of Golkonda therefore, had a very narrow escape (Sarkar, *op. cit.*, Vol. I, pp. 230-231; also Tavernier, Vol. I, p. 135).
10. Prince Muhammad Sultan was married to the second daughter of Abdullah Qutb Shah in 1656.
11. Syed Muzaffar was one of the leading generals of Golkonda. He was mainly instrumental in raising Abul Hasan to the throne and the grateful sultan made him his prime minister. (See Sarkar, *op. cit.*, IV, p. 333).
12. The reference is to Mirza Raja Jai Singh's invasion of Bijapur (1665-1666).
13. Bernier, who was at Golkonda in 1667 refers to an unknown English ship, the seizure of which by the Dutch was prevented by the governor of Masulipatam by arming the whole population (pp. 195-196).
14. Abul-Hasan, popularly known as Tana Shah, married the youngest daughter of Abdullah Qutb Shah and succeeded him on the throne of Golkonda in 1672. (Tavernier, Vol. I, p. 138; Sarkar, *op. cit.*, Vol. IV, pp. 331 ff.).
15. The reference is probably to Shah Raju Saheb who had prophesied Abul Hasan's marriage and helped him in securing the throne. The accuracy of the rest of the story is more than doubtful. (See Bilgrami & Willmott, Vol. II, pp. 571-572).
16. Omit "prostrating themselves".
17. Gain.
18. Ma Sahib, the eldest daughter of Sultan Abdullah Qutb Shah, was married to Sayyid Ahmad. Tavernier calls him 'one of the relatives of the Grand Shaikh of Mecca' and gives an interesting account of the events preceding the marriage (Vol. I, pp. 131-132). On Abdullah's death, he was one of the candidates to the throne, but was defeated and thrown into prison.
19. Bernier wrongly says that the prince married the eldest daughter of the king of Golkonda (p. 21).
20. Tavernier calls him Mirza Abdul Cosing and says that he had two sons by the princess (Vol. I, p. 138).

21. Thevenot is wrong. There was no fourth daughter.
22. Madras.
23. Tavernier (Vol. II, p. 46) writes "Two per cent. on all purchases is paid to the King, who receives also a royalty from the merchants for permission to mine." The merchants paid a duty of 2 pagodas (16s.) per day for fifty men, and 4 pagodas when they employed a hundred men to work in "an area of about 200 paces in circumference." Thomas Bowrey, a contemporary of Tavernier, says that the land in the diamond mine fetches a much higher price, ". . . any Merchant adventurer may purchas a piece of land of halfe an Aker, a whole Aker or more, but at deare rates, as it Sometimes fall out. The Merchant giveing 8,10,20 thousand Pagodes for a Small Spot of land, hath the liberty to digge soe deep as he pleaseth, and wash out the Earth Searchinge for what hidden treasure he may happilie find, but severely inspected by the King's Officers, soe that if he meet with a rough Diamond that weyeth about 70 or 72 Conderines, the Exact weight of one Royal of 8, it must be for the King's owne Use. . . . ." (p. 112).
24. Tavernier gives a detailed account of the diamond mines. The most famous of the mines in the Carnatic was at Vajra-Karur in the Guti taluk of the Bellary district. The mine was privately worked by the sultan, and "the stones produced from it were large and wellspread." For other mines in the Carnatic, see, Tavernier, Vol. II, pp. 352-354.

CHAPTER VIII

1. Concluded.
2. Places himself in.
3. Omit "by him".
4. Betel, "the leaf of the *Piper betel* chewed with the dried areca-nut." (*Hobson-Jobson*, pp. 89-90).
5. Means.
6. Nevertheless.
7. Mir Muhammad Said, better known as Mir Jumla, first came into prominence as a diamond merchant. He later rose to be Abdullah Qutb Shah's prime-minister, and earned a high reputation as a military leader in the Carnatic campaign. The plunder of the Carnatic made him "the richest private man in the South", and he then turned a traitor and entered the Mughal service (1656). In the war of succession he espoused the cause of Aurangzeb, though he did not forget to safeguard his own interests. Aurangzeb appointed him governor of Bengal whence he led an expedition into Assam. He died on 31 March 1663. For a detailed account, see, Tavernier, Vol. I, pp. 133 ff; Bernier, pp. 16-19; Sarkar, *Aurangzib*, Vol. I, pp. 216 ff.
8. Muhammad Amin.
9. Gandikota, ancient fortress in the Cuddapah district, Madras. For a description of the fort see Tavernier, Vol. I, pp. 227-228. Tavernier visited the place shortly after its reduction by Mir Jumla and he does not refer to the story told by Thevenot here. Tavernier ascribes Mir Jumla's success to the skill of European gunners in his service, and the weakness of the defenders in artillery as they had only two iron guns.

   It is not correct to say that Mir Jumla's conquests stopped at Gandikota. He later took Sidhout, east of Cuddapah, "and his troops advanced as far as Chandragiri and Tirupati in the North Arcot District" (See, Sarkar, *Aurangzib*, Vol. I, pp. 217-218).
10. Almost.
11. The Musi river.

CHAPTER IX

1. This place is not shown in modern maps. Is it Ambarpet Kalan near Hayatnagar, about 14 miles from Hyderabad?
2. Tavernier (Vol. I, p. 139) writes that this place is "called in Persian Coulour and Gani in the Indian language." The site is now known by the name of Kollur; it is situated on the Kistna river in lat. 16° 42′, long. 80° 5′. According to Ball although "very wild suggestions" have been made about the Kollur diamond-mines, "its position is correctly indicated on several maps of the beginning of the eighteenth and end of the seventeenth centuries" (*Ibid*, f.n. 4).
3. This place is also mentioned by Tavernier (Vol. I, pp. 139-40) and its buildings are described by him, but it is not traceable on modern maps. Mr. Ghulam Yazdani (cited by Crooke in Tavernier, Vol. I, pp. 139-40 f.n.) identifies it with Sarurnagar or Sururnagar which is about 10 miles from Golkonda. Several old Qutb Shahi buildings and gardens still exist there.
4. Pangal, about 4 miles N.E. of Nalgonda town. (Dodwell, cited by Crooke in Tavernier, Vol. I, pp. 140-41 f.n.).
5. Not traceable on modern maps.
6. Penuganchyprolu on the Muneru river.
7. The Kistna river.
8. The Musi river.
9. *Cassia fistula* (Hind. *amaltas*) is well known for its lovely yellow flower. Its long pods when ripe yield a valuable laxative. (Watt, Vol. II, pp. 217-219). It is one of the common flowering trees of India.
10. Masulipatam (Hind. *Machhlipatan*='Fishtown'). The correct latitude is 16° 11′ North. For a contemporary account, see, Tavernier, Vol. I, pp. 141-142. Masulipatam was once well known for its printed cloth but it has lost its former importance. (*Imp. Gaz.*, Vol. XVII, pp. 215-217).
11. The main route is clear, although it is difficult to identify some of the towns or villages:—Ambarpet Kalan (?); Chalkapalli; Pangal; Amangal; Surchel-Quipentche (not traceable); Musi river; Gurglur; Anantagiri; Penuganchiprolu; Pendyala; Madduru; the Kistna river; Vuyyuru; Nidumolu, 10 miles north-west of Masulipatam; Guduru and Masulipatam.
12. Masulipatam, according to Tavernier had the best anchorage in the Bay of Bengal. (Vol. I, p. 141).
13. Cape Palmyras or Palmyras Point in the Kendrapara sub-division of Cuttack district which constitutes "a landmark for vessels making for the Hooghly from the south." *Imp. Gaz.*, Vol. XIX, pp. 370-371.
14. This is a mistake; the correct latitude is 10° 46′ North.
15. Is it mumps?
16. Pulicat in Chingleput district, Madras. The Dutch settled here in 1610. For a contemporary account see Tavernier, Vol. I, p. 214.
17. The Dutch fort, Geldria was built in 1613-15 and was named after the native place of the builder (Manucci, Vol. IV, p. 458). According to Tavernier (Vol. I, p. 214, and f.n. 1) the Governor of the fort in 1655 was Sieur Pite, a German of the town of Bremen. Ball, in a footnote suggests that he must have been Laurens Pit (the elder) who was Councillor Ordinary from 1660-1678. For a note on Laurens Pit the younger see f.n. 1 in Manucci, Vol. II, p. 296.
18. Fanam, a small coin used in South India, "Malayal and Tamil *fanam* meaning 'money'." Its value differed, "but according to old Madras monetary system prevailing till 1818; 42 *fanams* went to one star pagoda." (*Hobson-Jobson*, pp. 348-349). Tavernier, Vol. I, p. 329) makes it equivalent to 4½*d.*, but some were worth double i.e., 9d.
19. It is not clear what copper coin is meant. The word is probably a corruption of 'cash' "a name applied by Europeans to sundry coins of low value" current in South India. (80 cash=1 fanam). See, *Hobson-Jobson*, pp. 167-168.

20. Palakollu in Kistna district, Madras 6 miles from Narsapur. The Dutch had a factory here in the middle of the seventeenth century. (*Madras Provincial Gazetteer*, Vol. I, p. 327).
21. Probably Draksharamam (?) in Godavari district, Madras. There are two Dutch tombs in the village. (*Godavari Dist. Gazetteer*, Vol. I, pp. 250-252).
22. Bimlipatam in Vizagapatam district, Madras. The Dutch established a factory here in the 17th century. For its imports and exports, see *Madras Provincial Gazetteer*, Vol. I, pp. 261-262.
23. Chicacole (*Srikakulam*) in Ganjam district, Madras. "Its muslins were at one time as famous as those of Dacca or Arni", but the industry has now declined (*Madras Provincial Gazetteer*, Vol. I, pp. 222-223).
24. See Tavernier, Vol. II, pp. 120-121.
25. Imam Husain, the second son of Ali, and grandson of the Prophet of Islam; the anniversary of his martyrdom is observed by the Shias in the month of Muharram. Bilgrami and Willmott suggest that Thevenot alludes here to the langur procession which takes place on the fifth of Muharram. (Vol. II, pp. 575-578). The first ten days of the Muharram are considered sacred, and the 10th of Muharram is specially consecrated by the death of Husain.
26. Yezid I, the son of Muawia, the founder of the Ummayad dynasty of Caliphs.

CHAPTER X

1. An old town north of Hyderabad. It is not traceable on modern maps, but is marked in Orme's map.
2. Momanpet and Panchnigal. Under their old names. they are shown on Orme's map.
3. Kohir (24 miles south east of Bidar), and Sajjapur (Senjavurd of Orme's map).
4. The stages on the route are :—Hyderabad; Danec; Nerva (?) river; Chilkur; Penu(?) river; Shekerdeh and Yakut-kepensh (both traceable in Orme's map); Eniktala; Momanpet; Panchnigal; Kohir, Sajjapur; Mamadgi; Bidar. The two rivers are not traceable in any map.
5. Etour (Hatnur); Manjra river; Morg (Marrag); Oudeguir (Udgir); Helly (Hali); Rajoura (Rajura now known as Ahmadpur); Sourgong (Sawargaon); Careck (the Galati river); Ganga (the Godavari); Caly (Khalli on the Godavari); Raampouri (Rampuri Buzurg, 'Rampoor' of Orme's map); Patry (Pathri Parbhani District).
6. All the places on the route are marked in Orme's map, and are also available in large-scale modern maps. They are :—Pathri; Gohegaon; Dudna river; Putah; Ner; Seouny (Shivni); Chendeque (Sindkhed); Ourna river (Amna river); Jafarabad; Piply (Pimpalgaon); Deoulgan (Devalghat); Rouquera (Rohankhed); Malkapur; Nervar River (Nalganga river); Pourna river (Purna river); Papour (Dapora); Tapti river and Burhanpur.
7. Pathri, in Parbhani district, situated in 19° 15′ N. and 76° 27′ E. (*Hyderabad State Gazetteer*, p. 223).
8. Manjra, the largest tributary of the Godavari; the Galati and the Godavari.
9. Udgir in Bidar District. The fort formerly held by Bijapur kings was captured by the Mughals in 1635. (*Hyderabad State Gazetteer*, p. 292).
10. Rajura now known as Ahmadpur.
11. Dudna, which joins the Purna; Nerver (the Nalganga); the Purna, and the Tapti.
12. Cholera, from Konkani and Marathi *Modyachi*. For details see, *Hobson-Jobson*, pp. 586-589; Pyrard, Vol. II, Part I, pp. 13-14. Garcia da Orta also recommended cauterization of the patient's feet (Vol. I pp. 264-265). Dr. Fryer confirms the account of Thevenot when he says—"They apply cauteries most unmercifully in a *Mordisheen*" (Vol. I, p. 286). Linschoten mentions the disease (Vol. I, pp. 235-236) and Dellon refers to the common treatment.

13. *Rheum emodi,* Vern. *Hindi-revand chini* used as a purgative. (Watt, Vol. VI, part I, pp. 485-486).
14. *Cuminum cyminum; zira, jiraka*: The plant is cultivated throughout India 'except perhaps Bengal and Assam'. The seeds are useful in dyspepsia and diarrhoea. (Watt, Vol. II, pp. 642-645).
15. Linschoten also found this distemper quite common at Goa (Vol. I, p. 236).

INDIAN TRAVELS OF CARERI

BOOK I

CHAPTER I

1. Literally "roof".
2. Also known as Black Friars. The fourth mendicant order so-called because they lived according to the rule of St. Augustine. They were governed by a general elected by chapter, and provincials looked after the order in different countries. Originally their manner of life was comparatively mild but later reforms imposed great austerity and some of the congregations used to go bare-footed. Martin Luther was originally an Augustinian and friars of this order did considerable missionary work in India under the aegis of the Portuguese.
3. Daman.
4. 'Martedi' in the Italian original means Tuesday and not Monday.
5. Congo-Bunder, Kongun on the Persian Gulf, 100 miles west of Gombroon. It is mentioned as a port for Lar in the *Persian Travels*, pp. 232-4 (cited in Ball's Tavernier, Vol. II, p. 85 *n* 6). See also Curzon, *Persia*, Vol. II, p. 408; *Hobson-Jobson*, p. 246.
6. This appears to be an exaggeration. The customs duties never exceeded 5 per cent. Tavernier writes: "Private individuals pay as much as 4 and 5 per cent duty on all their goods; but as for the English and Dutch Companies, they pay less" (Vol. I, p. 7).
7. This word is a corruption of the Portuguese *gentio*, 'a gentile' or heathen which they applied to the Hindus (*Hobson-Jobson*. pp. 367-369).

7a. Father Francis of St. Joseph and Father Constantine of the Holy Ghost were both Portuguese Augustinians. They were with Careri at Ispahan and sailed for Surat in November 1694. (Careri, *A Voyage Round the World*, pp. 167 and 187).

8. The Damanganga.
9. Detached.
10. 'e tutta la costa' (and the whole coast) has been omitted in the translation.
11. Old writers constantly applied the term 'winter' to the rainy season, a usage which has now become obsolete.
12. Daman has two forts originally erected for the defence of the two banks of the river Damanganga. Careri refers to the old fort, inside which the governor's palace and important churches and hospitals were situated.
13. The governor of Daman is still the civil and military head of the administration subject to the authority of the governor-general of Goa.
14. A half-caste or Eurasian now called misturados at Goa. Dalgado explains the term as offspring of parents of different races. In India, he adds, the term applies to those who have for their ancestors, near or remote, a European man and an Indian woman or vice versa (Vol. II, p. 51). Careri himself explains this term in Chapter VI.
15. Recollects. Tavernier (Vol. I, p. 183) describes the Capuchins as a kind of Recollects. They are members of an Observantine branch of the Franciscan Order, which originated in Spain towards the close of the 15th century and were so-named because of their detachment from creatures and recollection in God which the founders aimed at. (T. Arnold and W. E. Addis, *A Catholic Dictionary*, p. 774).
16. Ostend, "the second port of Belgium" situated on the North Sea. It was strongly fortified in the middle ages and underwent a famous siege during 1601-1604.

17. 'In Picardy' is not to be found in the Italian text which has 'Cales, ed altri di quell Oceano'—Calais and other ports of that ocean.
18. Wrongly translated—more correctly 'unless there is a strong favourable wind' (purche non vi sia un gran vento favorevole).
19. No mention of the "Spring Tide" in the text. The more accurate rendering ought to be—"because of the greater change in the sea at that time and the increase of waters."
20. Bislunga in the text means oblong. More accurately it is of the shape of an oblong.
21. Martim Affonso de Sousa came to India in 1534 with a fleet of five vessels and had a commission as admiral of the Indian Sea. The same year he was sent against Daman at the head of a large fleet and reduced the fort without much difficulty. Next he was invited by Bahadur Shah of Gujarat to fortify Diu. (Danvers, Vol. I, pp. 405-406). Subsequently he was appointed governor of the Portuguese territories in India (1542-45). For details, see R. S. Whiteway, *The Rise of the Portuguese Power in India*, pp. 279-290.
22. Dom Constantino de Braganza. Danvers (Vol. I, p. 511) mentions that he was the brother of Theodosius, Duke of Braganza. He was appointed governor in 1558 and sailed from Lisbon on 7 April with four ships and 2000 men, and arrived in India early in September. The city and the fortress of Daman were occupied on 2 February, 1559 by the Portuguese (*Bombay Presy. Gaz.*, Vol. II, p. 582, Danvers, Vol. I, pp. 511-12).
23. Sayful-Muluk Miftah, an Abyssinian noble (called Cide Bofata by Portuguese historians). Francisco Barreto had obtained a grant of the territory of Bassein, and Daman from the king of Gujarat for the Portuguese, but Sayful-Muluk refused to surrender Daman even when ordered by Imad-ul-Mulk Arslan (Commissariat, pp. 4623). No sooner had the Portuguese landed than the enemy fled abandoning the city as well as the fortress, which the governor immediately occupied (1559) see Danvers, Vol. I, pp. 511-12.
24. The earliest attempts to conquer Daman were made by the Mughals under Akbar soon after the conquest of Gujarat. Akbar in 1572 threatened an attack, but this was soon followed by a treaty. (Danvers, Vol. II, pp. 3-4). Eleven years later (1583) on his final conquest of Gujarat, Akbar again attempted to acquire Daman and Bassein. But the Portuguese forced the Mughals to retire. (Faria in Kerr, Vol. VI, p. 442 cited in *Thana District Gazetteer*, Part II, Thana, p. 453). Under Jahangir in 1613, in consequence of an injury done to their fleet at Surat, the Mughals besieged Daman and other Portuguese ports, desolated the country and had to be bought off. (Danvers, Vol. II, p. 162; *Thana Dist. Gaz.*, Vol. II, p. 453).
25. 'Fiftyfive' and not 'fifty', 'cinquanta cinque anni' in the text.
26. The reference is to the siege of Daman in 1638 by the Mughals during Aurangzeb's first viceroyalty of the Deccan (1636-1644). The siege lasted for four or five months without any success, and the Portuguese had the better of the Mughals in many sallies. In spite of this, the Portuguese were obliged to pay "the same rent they were accustomed to give the Raja of that Country viz. 60,000 Mahmudis." Peace was made through the intervention of President Fremlin, the chief of the English Factory at Surat. (Foster, *The English Factories in India, 1637-1641*, p. 214; Saxena, *Shah Jahan*, p. 302).
27. 'Seis mesi' (six months) in the text.
28. 'Archibusi e moschetti' (Arquebuses and Muskets) in the text.
29. Not 'cockle-shells' but 'young pigs', 'porcelletti' or small pieces of pork.
30. Spanish 'pedrero', an engine for flinging stones, later a piece of ordnance for discharging pieces of broken iron etc., and for firing salutes. Fryer, Vol. I, p. 271 *n* 3).
31. 'Con molta splendidezza'—with much splendour.
32. Kafris, ('cafri' in Italian original) a common appellation for Negroes from Arabic *kafir*, an infidel.
33. They lie full length.
34. Bamboa—Bamboo ('bambu' in original Italian).

35. Portuguese 'Andor', 'a litter', used for palanquin by old Portuguese writers. It may have been derived from Sanskrit *hindola*, 'a swing or cradle'. (*Hobson-Jobson*, pp. 29-30).
36. From Italian 'cosa-llino', a thing of trifling value. Apparently this appears to have been the smallest coin of Naples, but I have not been able to evaluate it.
37. More correctly 'cloth' or 'canvas'.
38. 'Solamente' (alone, only) after 'pane' (bread) has been omitted in the translation.
39. Sanskrit *sura*, an alcoholic drink described by Careri in detail in Chap. VIII.
40. Between 'Coco-nuts' and 'Mansanas' add 'mangoes, figs, papayas, carambolas'. For a description of these fruits see Chap. VIII.
41. Casava. It is known as the sweet cassava. (See Watt, *Dict. of Economic Products*, Vol. V, p. 157). Hawkins has described a meal of cassava and the root (*Purchas His Pilgrimes*, Vol. XVII, pp. 99 and 523).
42. Instead of 'creatures of' read 'animals like'.
43. From Gujarati *bekri* or Marathi *bhenkre*, barking deer, *Cervulus muntjac* of Lydekker.
44. The sambar deer, *Cervus unicolor* (see Lydekker, *The Game Animals of India, Burma, Malaya and Tibet*, pp. 223 ff).
45. An animal of the genus antelope. The species mentioned here is most likely the *chinkara* or Bennett's gazelle (Lydekker, *op. cit.*, p. 201).
46. Careri's "dive" should be identified with Dr. Dellon's "adive", the South Indian jackal, *Canis aureus naria*. Dellon says that "adive is as big as a medium-sized dog, hides under earth during the day-time and comes out in search of food at night. It has a plaintive cry and dogs are at perpetual feud with it and keep it off the houses. He also refers to its supposed co-operation with the tiger. (*Nouvelle Relation d'un Voyage fait aux Indes Orientales*, pp. 109-110). Also see Pocock, *Mammalia*, Vol. II (Fauna of British India), pp. 100-109.
47. Meru is the Marathi name of sambar. (See *supra*, Thevenot, Part III, Book I, Chap. XXI, n. 15). Rose is the name of *nilgai* and not the female Sambar as Careri seems to think. He refers probably to the tuft of hair that hangs from the animal's breast as the rose.
48. Does he mean Caracal whose tufted ear may look like hairy horns? The animal however does not occur near Daman, but is to be found in Sind and Central India.
49. Probably flying squirrels. *Kal Manjar* or black tree-cat is without wing-like appendages.
50. From Marathi *bibia* and Konkani *Bibyo*, the Panther, *Panthera pardus fusca*, see Pocock, *Mammalia*, Vol. I (Fauna of British India), pp. 226 ff.
51. *Chita*, or a hunting leopard, *Acinonyx jubatus venaticus*. (Pocock, *op. cit.*, pp. 325 ff).
52. Obviously the Royal Tiger, *Panthera tigris* of Pocock (*op. cit.*, p. 197). It cannot be the Indian lion as Careri describes it as one of "the three sorts of Tigers each differing from the other in bigness of Body, and variety of Spots."
53. Slowly.
54. Add "which the terrain and the height of the trees allow": che lo permette il terreno, e l'altezza degli alberi.
55. Dalgado says that in Portuguese Asia, this name came to be associated with the common Myna. The city bird must be the common Myna, *Acridotheres tristis* with black head and neck and a broad white patch on the wings. The country species is probably the grey-headed Myna, *Sturnia malabarica*.
56. Lit. he who does business in India.
57. Add 'only' after 'fashion'.
58. Mort de Chien (Cholera) see Thevenot, Book II, Chap. X, n. 12.
59. It is not clear to what disease Careri refers here. Thevenot mentions four different types of colic (Part III, Bk. II, Chap. V) and it is not unlikely that

Bombaraki and Naricut are some forms of the same disease. Garcia da Orta has nothing to say about either of them.

60. Add here "and of their children".
61. From Portuguese 'candala', sort of covering for the legs. (Michaelis, *Portuguese-English Dictionary*, Pt. I, p. 131).
62. Correctly "cloth".
63. Portuguese *'cabaya'* or *'caba'* from Arabic *kaba*, vesture, a long coat or tunic of muslin. See Thevenot, Pt. III, Bk. I, Ch. XX.
64. Cotton or woollen cloth.
65. Brass.
66. Paid the expenses and gave a splendid dinner.
67. Derived from Portuguese *'galeota'*. In India it took the form of gallivat. For a description, see Sen, *Military System of the Marathas*, pp. 179 ff.

CHAPTER II

1. Ports.
2. Frigate.
3. About 9 P.M.
4. Suwali, a roadstead near the mouth of the Tapti, about 12 miles from Surat.
5. Sequin of Venice (See Thevenot, Pt. III, Bk. I, Ch. IX, Note 20).
6. Pilavoine was Director of the French Factory at the time. The home authorities decided in January 1695 to replace him by Jean Baptiste Martin (Paul Kaeppelin, *La Compagnie des Indes Orientales et Francois Martin*, p. 236), but Pilavoine could not leave till July 1696 (p. 341).

6a. Kept me in his house—'ritenne in sua casa'.

7. This is a mistake. Surat is situated in 21° 12′ N. Lat. and 72° 50′ E. Long.
8. Shivaji sacked Surat in 1664, and again in 1670. The wall was built after the first sack of Surat in 1664. Cf., Fryer's description, Vol. I, pp. 229 ff.; Thevenot, III, Chap. VII and *note;* Ovington, pp. 129 ff. Shivaji and Kakaji were two different persons. The latter was the ruler of the petty state of Jawhar in the Thana District.
9. Surat in the 17th century had two governors, one in charge of the castle, and another of the city. Cf., Ovington, p. 136. Thevenot also mentions these two officers.
10. Ahmadabad.
11. Seen in Europe.
12. The Portuguese were never masters of Cambay, Broach and Surat as the author suggests.
13. Not 'retired to the sea', the correct version is—'and the sea receded'.
14. 'Trade' and not 'splendour' in the original.
15. Broach, about 37 and not 10 miles from Surat. It was well-known for its cotton manufactures and the English and the Dutch had their factories there in the 17th century.
16. Inaccurate translation. It should be 'there is better sale for its commodities than at Surat'.
17. The Narbada.
18. For the French Capuchins at Surat, see Thevenot, Chapter X and *note*.
19. Banyan-tree. The Indian fig tree (*Ficus Indica* or *Ficus bengalensis*). According to Yule, the name was first bestowed upon a famous tree of this species growing near Gombroon in Persia under which the baniyas or Hindu traders had built a little pagoda (*Hobson-Jobson*, p. 65).
20. Called 'Mameva' by Thevenot. (Chap. XIV). Probably a corruption of 'Mahamaya'. Pietro Della Valle correctly calls her 'Parvete (Parvati) whom they hold to be the wife of Mahadeu'. (Vol. I, p. 35).
21. Rio Ram is obviously a misprint for Dio Ram—the god Rama—in the original.
22. Instead of 'quite naked' read 'everywhere naked'.

23. Tavernier, (Vol. I, pp. 63-4) mentions a few such hospitals at Ahmadabad. Fryer (Vol. I, p. 138), Linchoten (Vol. I, p. 253) and Ovington (p. 177) all refer to animal hospitals.
24. At 10 P.M.

CHAPTER III

1. "Martedi"—Tuesday and not Thursday.
2. Boys; palanquin-bearers, from Marathi caste name Bhoi (*Hobson-Jobson*, p. 110).
3. Add "by boat" after "thence".
3a. Portuguese 'religioso', a member of a religious order, a monk.
4. Add "for its defence" after "having".
5. Add "at ten o'clock" before "when".
6. Bassein (*Vasai*, from *Vasati*—'The Settlement') in Thana District, Bombay. (See Thevenot, Pt. III, Bk. I, Ch. XVI, Note 18).
7. Tarapur, a port in the Mahim sub-division of Thana District, about 15 miles north of Mahim.
8. Read "fort" after "this".
9. The great hill fort of Asheri about 8 miles from Manor on the Vaitarna. It was captured by the Portuguese in 1556. The fort was the head-quarters of one of the seven parganas under Bassein. It was captured by the Marathas in February 1739 (Danvers, Vol. II, p. 409).
10. Mahim or Kelve in Thana District, 56 miles north of Bombay town.
11. *Ilha de vaccas* of the Portuguese, otherwise known as "Arnalla". Hamilton mentions that it was 'of small Account in the Table of Trade'. (*A New Account of the East Indies*, Vol. I, p. 104). It commands the southern and main entrance into the Vaitarna river (Da Cunha, *Antiquities of Chaul and Bassein*, p. 159).
12. For 'and' read 'or'.
13. "Parangue", a small cargo boat common on the western coast of India. (Michaelis, *op. cit.*, p. 536).
14. For "the small island and the continent" read "the island of Salsette and the main land".
15. Add "finally on" before "Thursday".
16. More correctly 19° 20′ N. and 72° 49′ E.
17. Nuno da Cunha, Portuguese Viceroy in India (1529-38). He first opened up direct and regular trade with Bengal, and obtained possession of the island of Diu in 1535 from Bahadur Shah of Gujarat. (See Whiteway, *op. cit.*, Chap. XI).
18. John III (1502-1557), King of Portugal, ascended the throne in December, 1521. His reign was marked by the ascendancy of the clerical party and decline of trade and commerce.
19. Bahadur Shah of Gujarat. (See Thevenot, Pt. III, Bk. I, Ch. XVIII).
20. According to Fernandes (*A Guide to the Ruins of Bassein*, p. 4) the fortifications were completed towards the close of the 16th century, and had ten bastions.
21. Philip IV (1605-1665), King of Spain. It was during his reign that Portugal separated from the Spanish Empire (1640).
22. The reference is probably to the plague of 1689 (Elliot and Dowson, Vol. VII, p. 337). Between 1686 and 1696, there was a severe outbreak of plague in Western India which wrought great havoc in Bassein, Thana and Chaul (*Gazetteer of Bombay City and Island*, Vol. II, pp. 71-72).
23. The civil and military government was vested in the captain. The post of the general of the north was established about the year 1690. (Fernandes, *op. cit.*, p. 4, *n* 1).
24. For "or Governor" read "who is governor in charge of arms."
25. Portuguese 'ovidore', 'ouvidor' *i.e.*, supervisor. (*Hobson-Jobson*, p. 649).

26. A chief judge.
27. Add "of the same monastery" after "Fathers".
28. Read "the prodigy of" instead of "I did on".
29. More correctly "or".
30. "Wide" and not "long".
31. This is very common even now, "the stick" used is usually of *neem* and *babul* or *kikar.*
32. Read "coverlets" for "Blankets".
33. And "wood and" before "cords".
34. Lar in Persia about 40 miles from Teheran.
35. After "Martyrs" add "Visitor of the Augustinians".
36. Bhadrapur of the Marathas.
37. For "activity" read "dexterity" and omit "Tumblers and" before "rope dancers".
38. Read "after dinner" after "Wednesday 2nd".
39. Casabe from 'Kasaba' meaning a small town inhabited by decent people or families of rank (Da Cunha, p. 157). Casabe de Bacaim had according to Da Cunha eight *hortas* or orchards and sixteen *pacarias* or suburbs (p. 158). It was therefore a fairly big town.
40. Da Cunha says that this is "not to be found in the lexicons of the Italian language, the symptoms undoubtedly point to the plague" (p. 142 *n*).
41. Thana, chief town of the district of the same name on G. I. P. Railway, 21 miles north-east of Bombay city. It was a place of great commercial importance in the Muslim days. (Da Cunha, pp. 165 ff).
42. See Thevenot, Book I, Chap. XXXVIII, Note 39.
43. Kakaji. He ravaged several villages in 1690 and came close to Bassein. (*Thana Dist. Gaz.*, Part II, p. 481).
44. The Church of *Nossa Serhora das Merces* built by Dom Fr. Aleixo de Menezes, the archbishop, who fought 'the interesting sect' of the Syro-Chaldeans of Southern India (*Chronista de Tissuary*, Vol. I, p. 63 cited by Da Cunha, p. 161 n). Da Cunha says that this church was in charge of the Franciscans.
45. It has been described as 'the most handsome piece of architecture in Bassein'. The foundation was laid in 1549 and the present edifice was built in 1560 replacing the original one with thatched roof. (Fernandes, pp. 24 ff).
46. Paulist. The first and the principal Jesuit College at Goa was named after St. Paul. Many of their churches were also dedicated to the same saint and hence they were commonly known as Paulists. (P. Della Valle, Vol. I, p. 142; *Bombay Gaz.*, Vol. XI, Kalaba and Janjira, p. 294 *n*).
47. More accurately—'afterwards I went to see the Dormitory and the Cloister which are the best in the City.'
48. The church with the convent was built in 1588. The monastery is a massive pile, built in the form of a square. "It has a large and beautiful cloistered arcade enclosing a spacious courtyard completely shut in from the sight of the outer world." (Fernandes, pp. 22-23). Careri is wrong in stating that the church had three altars. Actually it has seven altars.

48a. "Next to those of the General of the North's palace, and separated from them by a large oblong area which was the garden of the palace are the ruins of the "Misericordia" and of the Hospital attached to it." The church was a handsome building. The hospital enjoyed a munificent grant from the treasury. It was very near the Church of Nossa Senhora da Vida where Careri heard Mass two days later (Da Cunha, pp. 225-226).

49. Now in ruins, the church and the monastery were to the right of the Augustinian church. The original monastery and a small church were built by Frei Antonio do Porto as early as 1536. St. Francis Xavier resided here on three occasions for a short while (Fernandes, pp. 30-31).
50. The parish church of Nossa Senhora da Vida was under the charge of the Augustinians. Also known as Nossa Senhora da Saude (Da Cunha, p. 161). According to Fernandes, "The church of Nossa Senhora da Vida came to

be known as the church of the *Misericordia* from the hospital of the same name in its vicinity." (*A Guide to the Ruins of Bassein,* p. 17). Careri however, mentions the churches of la vida and Misericordia separately. He heard mass at Misericordia on Sunday the 6th and at la Vida on the 8th. Fernandes's remark therefore refers to a later period.

51. The hospital of Mercy or of the Misericordia conducted by the Hospitallers or Brothers of St. John of God. Fernandes identifies it with a large building in front of the church of Nossa Senhora da Vida (p. 18). Da Cunha has, however, placed this hospital in the Dominican convent (p. 225). The date of the building is not known.
52. "Wednesday" and not "Monday". 'Mercordi' in the text.
53. Read "Took an andora and went" after 'I'.
54. The 'Matriz' or Cathedral of St. Joseph. This cathedral was built in or about the year 1546 during the governorship of Dom Joao de Castro. For description of the church see Da Cunha, pp. 214-216.
55. A piece of eight or a dollar.

CHAPTER IV

1. Salsette, a large island north of Bombay in Thana District having an area of 246 square miles. It was seized by the Portuguese early in the sixteenth century. Its name is derived from Sanskrit *Shashti* by which name it is still known among the Marathas as it was alleged to contain that number of villages. See Da Cunha, p. 188; *Hobson-Jobson,* pp. 786-788; *Imp. Gaz.,* Vol. XXI, pp. 411-12.
2. Kanheri caves in Thana District, Bombay, about 7 miles from Borivli on the B. B. & C. I. Railway. The name Kanheri is derived from Prakrit *Kanhagiri* and Sanskrit *Krishnagiri,* but the caves, more than one hundred in number, are of Buddhist origin. According to Cunningham some of them date back to the first century B.C. while several inscriptions refer to the Satavahana kings. For a full description of the caves, see *Bombay Gaz.,* Vol. XIV (Thana, Places of Interest), pp. 121-190; Fergusson, *History of Indian And Eastern Architecture,* Vol. I, pp. 162 ff.
3. This is purely imaginary. Garcia da Orta in his *Colloquios* (Vol. II, pp. 341, 346) says that the caves were attributed by some people to the Chinese who often visited this coast. Fryer (Vol. I, pp. 187-8) refers to the Alexander tradition but does not treat it seriously.
4. Careri was by no means the first European traveller to visit Kanheri. Garcia da Orta refers to the cave temples of Kanheri, Mandapeshwar and Elephanta in his *Colloquios* (Vol. II, pp. 340-342) first published at Goa in 1563. The Dutchman, John Huyghen van Linschoten, who spent five years in India, from September 1583 to January, 1589, gives a short account of the caves of Kanheri and Elephanta. His description substantially agrees with that of Garcia da Orta and may have been borrowed from him (Vol. I, pp. 289-291). Diogo de Couto, the famous Portuguese chronicler describes the caves in greater details. He however greatly exaggerated both the size of the place and the number of cells. Among later travellers who wrote about Kanheri, Fryer, Hamilton, Du Perron, Lord Valentia and Bishop Heber may be mentioned. Cunningham was of opinion that the celebrated Chinese traveller Yuan Chwang also visited the caves of Kanheri.
5. Pietro Della Valle (1586-1652) travelled widely over the near and the middle east. He spent nearly ten years in Turkey, Asia Minor, Egypt and Persia but his sojourn in India was comparatively brief (February 1623 to November 1624) and his travels in this country were limited to the west coast only. He visited Cambay, Ahmadabad, Chaul, Goa, Ikkeri, Barcelore, Mangalore and Calicut. The Indian part of his travels has been published by the Hakluyt Society.
6. Careri describes the ruins of Darius's palace in Chap. IX, Book II, of his

Voyage to Persia, pp. 170-172. He also copied some cuneiform inscriptions and sketched the ruins and some of the sculptures he saw. Pietro Della Valle did visit the ruins of Persepolis.

7. Chehil Minar or the Hall of Xerxes at Persepolis described by Fergusson as "the pride and glory of Persepolis and of Persian architecture". The hall contains forty columns. (*The Palaces of Nineveh and Persepolis*, pp. 138 ff). See also Thevenot, *Travels into the Levant*, Part II, Book III, Chap. VII.
8. Add "I can say truly that" before "tho' a poor man".
9. Jean Baptiste Tavernier, the famous French traveller (1605-1689). His first publication appeared under the title *Nouvelle Relation du Serrail du Grand Signior* in 1675, and a year later appeared his *'magnum opus'* the *Six Voyages*. For details of his life, see Ball's Introduction to Tavernier, *Travels in India;* Oaten, *op. cit.*, pp. 184-192.
10. Not traceable on modern maps. According to Careri's account, it was a mile (probably to the north) from Mandapeshwar and six miles from Bassein. There is a place called Dahisar about six miles to the south of Bassein and a mile to the north of Borivli. It is not unlikely that Dahisar is Careri's Deins.
11. Ghodbandar, a small village and port in Salsette, 10 miles north-west of Thana. The local church was named after St. John. (See *Bombay Gazetteer*, Vol. XIV, Thana, Places of Interest, pp. 99-100).
12. Thirsty. The sentence should begin as follows: "I having arrived hot and thirsty".
13. Mandapeshwar in Salsette, called Montpezier or Monpacer by the Portuguese, in the neighbourhood of Borivli. The cave-temple mentioned both by Garcia da Orta and Diogo do Couto was originally dedicated to Shiva. The sculptured figures were either defaced or plastered over by the Portuguese, but in a small room behind the main hall where an image of the Virgin has been installed a bas-relief of Nataraja attended by other gods can now be seen.
14. Lord Valentia (1804) has also given a description of it. "Under the church a small pagoda has been formed out of the rock; it is square and flat-roofed, with a few deities, and other figures, in basso-relievo." (*Voyages and Travels to India, Ceylon, etc.*, Vol. II, p. 182).
15. The college founded by the great Franciscan missionary, P. Antonio de Porto. Lord Valentia wrongly attributes it to the Jesuits. The monastery and college were abandoned when Anquetil du Perron visited the place in 1760, but the humanitarian work has now been resumed and the church restored.
16. Read "abominable" after "their".
17. Elsewhere Dr. Careri writes: "A *Murais* (Mura) is twenty five *paras*, and the *para* twenty four pounds Spanish". The actual measurement varied from place to place but ordinarily a *mura* was equivalent to half a *khandi* or ten maunds. According to Antonio Nunez, quoted by Dalgado, a *mura* of rice measured three *khandis* (Vol. II, p. 81).
18. Brothers—"Frati" in the original text.
19. Cashi, two miles south of Ghodbandar. The village has a church dedicated to St. Jerome (*Bombay Gaz.*, Vol. XIV, Thana, Places of Interest, p. 51).
20. "House" is obviously a misprint for "horse". ("Cavallo" in the original text). A more accurate rendering would be—I was forced to content myself with a wretched horse.
21. "Cibo"—food or nourishment and not "meat".
22. More correctly—as the gentile was not very experienced.
23. Read "who put us back into the lost road."
24. "erta" in the text means steep, not bare.
25. Translator's error, should be "west" and not "east". ("Occidentale" in the text).
26. The two pillars which support the front screen in Cave No. 1 at Kanheri *Bombay Dist. Gaz.*, Vol. XIV, p. 165.

27. Obviously a printing error. "20" in figures in the text.
28. Another printing error, should be "forty".
29. Grottos.
30. Add here—"entered by three doors".
31. Cannot be clearly discerned.
32. Cave No. 2A. See plate LVI of Fergusson and Burgess, *Cave Temples of India*. In the centre, Buddha is seated on the lotus, with his hands in the *vyakhyana mudra*. On one side is a *chauri* holder, on the other is Padmapani with a chauri. Over Buddha's head are two *Gandharva* figures with garlands while the stem of the lotus seat is upheld by two *nagas*.
32a. Cave No. 2 C. This description applies to three figures only.
32b. *Padmapani*. The lotus bud on a lengthy stem is wrongly described as a fruit and a tree.
32c. All Buddhas in *Vykhyanamudra*.
32d. Cave No. 2 D. Buddha and *Padmapani*.
33. The Great Chaitya Cave (Cave No. 3). (*Bombay Gaz.*, Vol. XIV, pp. 121 ff., Burgess, *op. cit.*, pp. 60-70, Fergusson and Burgess, *Cave Temples of India*, pp. 350-353).
34. Wide.
35. The capital of the northern column at the entrance to cave No. 3, supports three fat figures holding behind them something like a great bowl, and on the capital of the southern column are four seated lions. These two columns are known as *Sinha Stambhas* or 'Lion-Pillars'. The shield is now missing; probably it was a wheel—the *Dharma chakra*.
36. In circumference.
36a. Probably inscription No. 10 of Plate LI in Burgess, *Elura Cave Temples* which records that "it is the Stupa of the Thera, the venerable Dharmapala" dedicated by a goldsmith's wife.
37. Read "you pass through" instead of "there are".
38. Level.
38a. No. 4 of Plate II in Burgess: *Elura Cave Temples*. The work was executed during the reign of Gautamiputra Sri Satakarni by some merchants.
39. Two standing Buddhas about 23 feet high. They have long pendant ears but wear no pendents.
39a. No. 9 of Plate LI. The language is of the Gupta period.
40. Read "aisles" for "isles".
41. Read "by their diligence" after "never".
42. Cave No. 67. There are numerous figures sculptured all over the walls; their number is easily above 300.
43. More correctly "whose length is that of the pagoda and width eight spans."
44. "Fifty" in figures in the original text, not "five".
45. "Upon" and not "under".
46. This is still commonly done in India.
47. Read "my raging hunger" after "satisfy".
48. Read "About two hours and half of night".
49. Read "Had talked together".
50. Read "At this news, I began to have hope of restoring myself with something good".
51. Read "I was twice on the point of stretching my hand and changing plates with him".
52. Turnsole. Vern. *Shadevi, Sonballi, Subali* Hind; *Kukronda* Pb. etc. (See Watt, Vol. II, pp. 621 ff).
53. *Ghia-Kakri*, genus *Cucurbita* (Watt, Vol. II, pp. 638-64).
54. *Ananas sativa*, the pine-apple. See Book I, Chap. VIII.
55. Papaya. *Carica papaya* (*Hobson-Jobson*, pp. 670-71).
56. Add "if" between slaves and they and delete "and".
57. Rice *bhat, Oryza Sativa*.
58. Covado, a cubit or ell, a lineal measure which varies in different places. The Surat cubit, according to Ovington, was of 27 inches.

59. Read "for cloth" instead "for long measure".
60. The translation here is not quite accurate. It should be "But those who hold in fee pay an imposition according to the rents, *Los Foros* (Taxes) (which is equivalent to the Adoa in the Kingdom of Naples)."
61. Bombay. In Humphrey Cooke's report "it's some eight miles in length and five miles and a half broad." (*English Factories in India,* 1665-67, p. 46). Sir William Foster points out that the mile at that time had not its present definite length, and three to four miles, therefore, would be a correct estimate of Bombay's breadth. The actual width is about 3 miles.
62. By the recent construction of causeways and breakwaters, Bombay is now connected on the north end with Salsette. (*Bombay Presidency Gazetteer,* Vol. I, p. 210).
63. See Thevenot, Pt. III, Bk. I, Ch. XLVIII.
64. Bandra (*Bandora, Vandra*), nine miles to the north of Bombay city. For a contemporary account, see Fryer, Vol. I, p. 183.
65. Versova, a small village and port on the west coast of Salsette, 12 miles north of Bombay. (*Bombay Gaz.,* Vol. XIV, Thana, Places of Interest, p. 379).
66. *Tanushi,* a kind of striped cotton cloth, which is still known as Thana cloth.
67. Should be—"also for table linen".
68. Not to be found in modern maps.
68a. Fryer also refers to this tradition (Vol. I, p. 191).
69. The reference is obviously to the cave temple of Elephanta.
70. After "and" add "on arrival at the monastery".
71. Goa (not India) in the original text. Dom Pedro Antonio de Noronha, Conde de Villa Verde, Viceroy of India from 1693-98, fought several actions with the Arabs on the sea. (Danvers, Vol. II, pp. 371 ff., Fonseca, p. 93).
72. The city replied with another royal salvo.
73. Muscat, capital of Oman on the sea-coast situated in 23° 40′ N., 58° 25′ E. For a contemporary account see Ovington, *Voyage to Suratt,* pp. 245-251.
74. Sangameshwar in Ratnagiri District, Bombay. It was a port of some commercial importance and the headquarters of a Maratha fleet in the old days.
75. Manucci also refers to the murder of Antonio Machado de Britto but his chronology and facts are both inaccurate. The official letter communicating the news of the murder to Lisbon is dated 8th December, 1695 (*Livro das Monçoes do Reino,* No. 59 fol. 223, 1694-1699). Manucci's date (1696) is therefore obviously wrong. Nor was Antonio Machado in a room (Manucci, Vol. III, p. 170) when he was shot. Careri's account and date are corroborated by the official letter but he gives more details.
76. Melos were troublesome people. Two of them were in exile for murder about 1665.
77. This was erected about the year 1542 or 1543 at the expense of the public treasury. The church has nothing remarkable about it. (Fonseca, *op. cit.,* pp. 323-324).
78. "Or rather Admiral" does not occur in the original. It is the translator's improvement.
79. The first shot was fired from the window of the house of Padre Joseph da Silva Maciel who was also in the conspiracy. See *Livro das Monçoes do Reino,* No. 59, fol. 223 (1694-1699).
80. Literally "tobacco".
81. Born of white father and black mother.
82. Firing two more shots with a blunderbuss.
83. As usual, "general" in the original Italian text.
84. Add—"a weapon of the coast of Mozambique".
85. This is corroborated by the official account quoted in No. 79 but it does not mention the name of the Dominican.
86. Add—"ready to leave the following day" after "Aboard".
87. Would have.
88. Being carried.
89. Manucci writes: "The reason for killing Antonio Machado Supico was his

unbridled tongue, which spared neither priests, householders, nor widow women. He abused everybody in disgraceful language, and for this he was done to death by treachery." (Vol. III, p. 170).

90. More accurately—"on a pleasant trip into the country".

CHAPTER V

1. Manehua, a large cargo-boat with a square sail and single mast commonly used on the west coast of India, especially Malabar. It is the Portuguese from the original Malayan *Manji* (Skt. *Mancha*), so called apparently from its raised platform for cargo (*Hobson-Jobson*, pp. 549-50).
2. Returning.
3. Pangara, from Portuguese *Parangue*,—Tamil, *Padagu*, according to Dalgado; a small boat, commonly used on the west coast of India for carrying provision.
4. Trapani, capital of the Province of the same name in Sicily.
5. *Sidi*, Arab *Saiyid* "a Lord", a title of the Habshi or Abyssinian rulers of the island of Janjira, often described in Marathi records as "Shamal" or dark from their complexion. The struggle between the Marathas and the Sidi began in 1648, but neither Shivaji nor his successors ever accomplished the conquest of Janjira although they occupied the mainland (Sen, *Military System of the Marathas*, p. 186). The Sidis originally held Janjira from the Sultan of Bijapur but transferred their allegiance to the Emperor of Delhi in 1670.
6. Underi, commonly known as Henery, a small island near the entrance of Bombay harbour. Fryer mentions it in 1674. The island was fortified by Sidi Kasim in 1680 and remained in his hands till the close of the seventeenth century.
7. Khanderi (Kenery) island, eleven miles south of Bombay, and only 1½ miles from the sister island of Underi. The island is described by Dom Joao de Castro (1538) and Fryer (1674). It was captured by Shivaji's fleet in 1679 and held against the Sidis and the English of Bombay. Both of them are island fortresses. See, Sen, *op. cit.*, pp. 189-190.
8. The Kundalika.
9. The 'Morro de Chaul' or the fortified hill of Korle. For an illustration, see Da Cunha, p. 45. Careri's chronology is faulty here. Diogo Lopes de Sequeira was busy elsewhere in 1520 and did not arrive at Chaul until next year (1521) when he started fortifications with the permission of Burhan Nizam Shah.
10. Diogo Lopes de Sequeira, Portuguese governor of India (1518-1521). See Danvers, Vol. I, pp. 342 ff.
11. Nizam-ul-Mulk. Obviously Burhan Nizam Shah (1508-1553). For a detailed account of his career, see Briggs, Vol. III, pp. 210-236.
12. Adil Khan or Adil Shah, the title of the rulers of Bijapur who were often at war with the rulers of Ahmadnagar and Golkonda.
13. Malik Ayaz Sultani. Originally a slave, he rose very high in the service of the sultan of Gujarat by his uncommon ability. He won several victories over the Portuguese at sea, but his attempts to prevent the fortification of Chaul proved unsuccessful.
14. Shivaji was not always unfriendly to the Portuguese. The reference is obviously to Sambhaji who led his troops almost to the walls of Goa in 1683.
15. Bijapur.
16. More accurately—"districts".
17. The author refers to the reigning Maratha king Rajaram as Shivaji, and is correct in saying that his father viz., Shivaji was the founder of the kingdom.
18. Shambhaji (1680-89) was not killed in battle. He was captured and put to death.
19. More correctly "Rajaram".

20. This is wrong. Shivaji was originally a Bijapur subject.
21. Shivaji was born at Shivner. There was a rumour that he was born a Portuguese subject to which Cosme da Guarda gave currency. See Sen, *Foreign Biographies of Shivaji*, p. 1.
22. The Bhonslas claimed, on rather insufficient evidence, descent from a branch of the ruling dynasty of Mewar.
23. Not traceable on modern maps.
24. Read "it being necessary to pass" etc.
25. The Malaber pirates. See Thevenot (Part III, Book II, Chapter I).
26. Mount Delly, headland on the coast of the Chirakkal *taluk* of Malabar district, a few miles north of Cannanore.
27. Former name of Madras.
28. Zamorin. See Thevenot, Part III, Book II, Chap. I.
29. Tanur or Vettat in Ponnai Taluk, Malabar District, Madras. See Thevenot, *loc. cit.*
30. Porakad (*Porca*), town in Travancore State situated in 9° 22′ N. and 76° 22′ E. It was once the capital of the Chempakasseri Rajas, and passed to Travancore in 1748. The Portuguese and the Dutch had their settlements here. (*Imp. Gaz.*, Vol. XX, p. 188).
31. Though they have no sign of illness.
32. Recipe.
33. Wait for.
34. Dabhol, in Ratnagiri District, Bombay, fell to Shivaji in 1662. The distance between Chaul and Dabhol is nearly 70 and not 8 miles.
35. Dom Francisco de Almeida, the first Portuguese viceroy of India (1505-9). He burnt the city in 1508. The Portuguese sacked the place many times subsequently but it was never permanently occupied by them.
36. Loosely used for Muslims here.
37. The river seems to be the Shastri or Sangameshwar where the viceroy according to Careri (see Chap. IV) burnt the Arab ships.
38. Is not found on modern maps; the place should be somewhere between Vijayagad on the Shastri river and Maliandi or Malwan. It is therefore unlikely to be Vengurla. The place mentioned here is likely to be Vijayagad (Visiapur in the Italian text) on the Shastri or Sangameshwar river opposite Jayagad.
39. Malvan, a port in Ratnagiri District where Shivaji built his famous naval stronghold and arsenal of Sindhudurg.
40. Ilheos Queimados or Burnt Islands, a group of rocky islets nine miles off Vengurla. There are three large rocks and many small.
41. Baloon, Balloon etc. Probably derived from Gujarati *Baliyan* or Konkani *Baliyam*, a small light boat or canoe formerly used in different parts of India. Fryer mentions a baloon of two oars.
42. Read "To write the name upon one of my parcels of Father Salvador Galli".
43. Salvador Gallo, a native of Milan, appointed Prefect in 1672. He left Europe with four other Theatins in August 1673, and has been described as "the soul of the Theatine Mission in India." (Manucci, Vol. III, p. 127 *n.* 1).
44. The congregation of regular clerks, whose name is derived from Theati or Chieti of which one of their founders, John Peter Caraffa was Bishop. The order was founded in 1524 (Arnold and Addis, *A Catholic Dict.*, pp. 876 ff). The Mission at Goa was established in 1640 (Fonseca, p. 68).

CHAPTER VI

1. The situation of Goa as mentioned by the author is wrong. The correct position is 15° 30′ N. and 73° 57′ E.
2. The Mandavi river, literally the river of the custom-house, near the mouth of which stands Goa.
3 "Which the ancient philosophers considered uninhabitable." "Inabitabile" in the Italian text means uninhabitable.

4. Governor of Portuguese India (1509-1515). For a brief but brilliant review of his Indian career see Prof. Edgar Prestage's *Albuquerque*.
4a. This is wrong. In 1508 Almeida was the head of the Portuguese government in India. Goa was first captured by Alfonso de Albuquerque on 17 February, 1510, but Ismail Adil Shah recovered the place soon afterwards. The final conquest and annexation of Goa was effected by Albuquerque during the same year on November 25, St. Catherine's day.
5. Malacca on the west coast of the Malaya Peninsula. The city was conquered by the Portuguese under Albuquerque on 4 August 1511. It remained a Portuguese possession for 130 years, and was an important centre of their trade and commercial exploration in south-eastern Asia. It fell to a joint attack of the Dutch and the Achinese in 1641.
6. Emanuel I (Port. Manoel) king of Portugal (1469-1521), surnamed the Happy. His reign is marked by a number of notable achievements of Portuguese navigators, particularly Vasco da Gama's discovery of an all-sea route to India and Cabral's landing in Brazil.
7. Reinforcements.
8. "After the viceroy's (palace) comes that of *Madre de Dẹos*, i.e., Mother of God, otherwise called *Dạugin*", says François Pyrard (Vol. II, Part I, p. 33). It was a league and a half from St. Iago, he adds. It is not shown in Pietro Della Valle's chart. According to Fonseca "the convent of *Mae de Deus* in the suburb of Daugim" was built by Dom Gaspar de Leão Pereira, the first Archbishop of Goa (*Historical and Archaeological Sketch of Goa*, p. 207).
9. The *Casa de Polvora* or gunpowder factory. It is still in existence and stands near the archiepiscopal palace close to the river. Constructed by Francisco da Gama (viceroy, 1597-1600). See Fonseca, p. 326.
10. All the four forts mentioned in this para have been long abandoned. For the defensive fortification of Goa in the middle of the eighteenth century see Marquis De Alorna's *Instructions* (Sen, *Studies in Indian History*, pp. 240-243).
10a. Compare Fryer who writes "it (Goa) is modelled but rudely, many Houses disgracing it with their ruins" (Vol. II, p. 10). "The buildings of the city are good, large and convenient" (Pietro Della Valle, Vol. I, p. 155). Also see François Pyrard, Vol. II, Part I, p. 63.
11. People of Kanara district. But the Portuguese applied the name indiscriminately to the Konkanis inhabiting Goa. The term has now an offensive significance and is applied exclusively to native Christians (Pyrard, Vol. II, p. 35 *n.*, *Hobson-Jobson*, p. 154). For a contemporary description of the country and its people, see Fryer, Vol. II.
12. Add "Christians and" after "are".
13. Breeds.
14. Lowly birth.
15. Charados or Chardis roughly correspond to Sanskrit *sudra*.
16. Worse.
17. A small piece of cloth just sufficient to avoid nudity. Hence poorer castes who went about clad in langotis alone.
18. Prof. Pissurlencar writes that the custom of thrashing no longer exists at Goa. On the day following the wedding, the friends and relatives do sometimes make fun of the groom by throwing banana skins at him but this practice also is fast disappearing even among the poorer classes.
19. In the morning.
20. Empire.
21. Mombasa, the principal seaport of British East Africa; Mozambique a town of Portuguese East Africa under the administration of Goa, and Sofala in the east coast of Africa. The Italian original has "Senna".
22. Imagine.
23. Sometimes.
24. Francisco de Tavora, Count of Alvor, Portuguese viceroy from 1681 to 1686. In the Italian text, the name and the title are correctly given.

25. The general name of the Portuguese possessions on the west coast of Africa south of the equator. The word "Angola" is a Portuguese corruption of the Bantu *Nojola*. The Portuguese came there towards the close of the 15th century.
26. He was not accustomed to.
27. Add here "unlike the blacks of the opposite coast".
28. For a slightly different method of hunting elephants, see, *Purchas His Pilgrimes* (Extra Series), Vol. VI, p. 325.
29. The Nandi (?) and the Makua. The Makuas belong to the group of Wanyassa who live in the vicinity of Lake Nyassa and the watershed of the Zambesi. They are described as a well disposed people with an active sense of the family, and a strong feeling for the honour of their wives and daughters. I am indebted to Dr. B. S. Guha of the Anthropological Survey for this information.
30. Open country.
31. Before "No" read "on the other hand".
32. Between "they" and "use" read "sometimes".
33. Tavernier writes, "The port of Goa, that of Constantinopole, and that of Toulon, are the three finest ports in both the continents" (i.e. Europe and Asia), Vol. I, p. 150.
34. One of the three islands that formed the *Velhas Conquistas* or old conquests. Bounded on the north and east by Pernem and Sanquelim—two districts of the *Novas Conquistas* or new conquests and on the west by the sea, it is separated from the island of Goa by the Mandavi river. Bardez was annexed by the Portuguese in 1543. The coast line is defended by the forts of Chapora at the northern and Agoada and Reis Magos at the southern extremities.
35. In the province of Bardez opposite Pangim on the Bay of Agoada. It was built in 1612. As the name indicates it was a watering place for Portuguese vessels. See Pyrard, Vol. II, Part I, p. 30.
36. Literally the Cape—not far off from Pangim. The fort commanded the Bay of Marmagao on one side and Agoada Bay on the other and thus occupied a very important strategic point. It has long been abandoned and is now in complete ruins. (Fonseca, pp. 43-44 and Pyrard, Vol. II, Part I, pp. 30-31).
37. The fortress of Reis Magos constructed in 1551 in the province of Bardez. It is on the right bank of the Mandavi opposite Gaspar Dias. (Fonseca, pp. 44-45).
38. The church of the Franciscans built in 1550 still exists, but their college is not in good preservation. (*Ibid*, pp. 45 and 66).
38a. Cannon.
39. Constructed in 1598 by the viceroy, Dom Francisco da Gama, on a site owned by Gaspar Dias, about a mile from Pangim or New Goa. The fort has been entirely demolished.
40. Read "most beautiful" instead of "delicate".
41. Quintas are country houses with orchards around.
42. The fortress palace of Daugi continued to be the Viceregal residence till it was abandoned by Conde de Villa Verde in 1695 for Pangim. Fryer has described some of the painting that he saw there (Vol. II, p. 15). See Fonseca, pp. 194 ff; Manucci, Vol. III, pp. 168 ff; Pyrard, Vol. II, Part I, pp. 47-48.
43. To serve as.
44. The reference is to the novitiate attached to the college of St. Paul founded for the training of native converts. The college gained considerable eminence when the great St. Francis Xavier was placed at its head.
45. A small palace of recreation near the Casa de Polvora. See Fonseca, pp. 326-327.
46. Famous.
47. Citizens.
48. Add here "from the evergreen fields".
49. Add here "from a large variety of trees".

50. Pleasant.
51. Marmagao, peninsula, village and port in Salsette district, Goa, Portuguese India. The peninsula is situated on the southern side of the harbour of Goa on the left bank of the Zuari river. The fortress has been converted into a hotel. Marmagao is the terminus of the railway connecting British India with the Portuguese districts and is about an hour's journey from Pangim by sea. It has a very fine natural harbour.
52. This is about the same even now. See Fonseca, p. 4.
53. Sao Laurenco, the offshoots of the Mandavi and Zeari or Zuari rivers meet between Marcaim and Sao Laurenco.
54. The Jesuits made Salsette their main centre of activities as the Franciscans turned their attention mainly to Bardez. See Fonseca, p. 65.
55. Spiritual matters.
56. The silver cover.
57. Originally built in the days of Albuquerque and dedicated to St. Catherine, it became the archiepiscopal metropolitan church in 1557. In 1562 the viceroy Dom Francisco Coutinho started to rebuild it on a magnificent scale but it was still unfinished when Pyrard saw it (Vol. II, Part I, p. 53). Fryer says that "the Cathedral is not often excelled by ours at home for bigness of the Pile" (Vol. II, p. 10). Pietro Della Valle observes, "The see of Goa at the time of my being there was not finish'd, but scarce above half built and thence seem'd to me small and less stately ; but having since seen the intire design of the structure, I conceive that when 'tis finsh'd 'twill be a goodly church" (Vol. I, p. 156). Finished in 1631, the Cathedral is still in use (Fonseca, pp. 198 ff.).
58. Aisles.
59. Read "not" for "but".
60. *Santa Casa de Misericordia* (Sacred House of Mercy). Pietro Della Valle saw a solemn procession issue out of it in 1624. Pyrard mistook it for the church of Nossa Senhora de Serra (Vol. II, p. 51). Fryer mentions it (Vol. II, p. 16). Hamilton's (*New Account*, Vol. I, p. 140) "beautiful church, called Miserecordia" was probably a later building on the old site. See Fonseca, pp. 244 ff.
61. See Nō. 8.
62. Read "gilded" after "handsom".
63. See note No. 42.
64. In the 16th century.
65. The Dominicans arrived in Goa in 1548 and built their convent and church (1550-1564). Pyrard describes the church as "exceedingly well built and decorated" (Vol. II, Part I, p. 49). According to Fryer—"the church surpassed the cathedral" (Vol. II, p. 11). See also Fonseca, pp. 253-255. The Dominicans used to conduct the inquisition. They were expelled from Goa in 1841.
66. Aisles.
67. Beautiful.
68. The convent and church of St. Augustine, and its novitiate are in the neighbourhood of St. Roch and St. John of God. Mandelslo and Cottineau testify to their beauty. First built in 1572, they were abandoned in 1835, and are now a heap of ruins. (Fonseca, pp. 311 ff; Fryer, Vol. II, p. 13; Pyrard, Vol. II, p. 57). The Novitiate of the Augustinians was situated to the south of the convent. Among other travellers of recent times, Buchanan, Dr. Claudius, Capt. Franklin, and Dr. Wilson, have written about this group of buildings. The Augustinians came to Goa in 1572 and were suppressed in 1835 (Fonseca, p. 68).
69. Vaulted nave.
70. One.
71. The church and convent of St. Cajetan are situated very near the old viceregal palace. For a detailed description see Fonseca, pp. 248-250.
72. Other writers suggest that it was built after the style of the Basilica of St. Peter in Rome (Fonseca, p. 249).

73. Sago from Malay *Sagu*. Hind. *Sagu-dana*. It is prepared not from the root, as Careri was told, but from the pith of several genera of palm trees indigenous to the islands of the Indian Archipelago. See Watt, *Dict. of Economic Products*, Vol. VI, Part II, pp. 383 ff.; *Hobson-Jobson*, pp. 780-81).
74. Glue.
75. The Church of St. Francis of Assisi is situated to the west of the Cathedral near the ruins of the Palace of the Inquisition, and was built in 1521. Demolished in 1661, it was reconstructed a few years later. Fryer says the monks go about with cords instead of girdles and in sandals instead of shoes. The gold referred to by Careri is probably "the rich gilding of the altar-pieces", because its decorations were all of silver. See Fonseca, pp. 223 ff.
76. The reference is to the new College of St. Paul generally known as Convent of St. Roch. Pyrard writes: "The third house and church is founded in honour of St. Roch and is called the Novitiate where are the Portuguese novices who aspire to be Jesuits, to prove themselves whether they can persist in the observance of the rules" (Vol. II, pt. I, p. 61). The novitiate attached to the old College of St. Paul over which the great St. Francis Xavier once presided had been abandoned at the time of Careri's visit. Also see Fonseca, pp. 315-320.
77. Accommodating.
78. The convent of St. Monica was founded by Archbishop Alexio de Menezes in 1606 and completed in 1627. It was midway between St. Roch and St. John of God. It is barely mentioned by Francois Pyrard and Pietro Della Valle. For an account of the church, see Fonseca, pp. 310-311.
79. Sister Mary of Jesus, a German lady married to a Portuguese nobleman Dom Manoel de Souza; became a nun after her husband's death and died in the convent of St. Monica on 2 January 1683 at the age of seventy-eight. It was discovered that her corpse bore five marks of wounds on her hands, feet and breast resembling those of Christ. A subsequent examination by the chief physician at the instance of the governor confirmed the supernatural nature of the wounds (Fonseca, pp. 307-309).
79a. The reference is to the old College and Church of St. Paul.
80. It was commonly believed that a jack-tree at the foot of the Chapel was planted by St. Francis Xavier and miraculous healing power was attributed to it. (Fonseca, p. 267).
81. "Within the enclosure of the above college stood, on a small eminence, the celebrated chapel of St. Francis Xavier. It is related that on one occasion the saint, whilst at prayer, was so much overpowered by devotional fervour that he felt himself almost suffocated, and then, opening his soutane near the chest, burst into an exclamation *"Domine sat est* (Lord, it is enough)". The author of the *Oriente Conquistado* states that, according to a tradition, this chapel was erected to commemorate the above incident, on the very spot where it occurred, and that every year on a Friday in Lent high mass was celebrated, attended by the gentry of the city, but that, on the other hand, some writers, especially Father Manoel Xavier, affirm that the saint himself caused this chapel to be built, and was in the habit of saying mass there" (Fonseca, p. 266).
82. For the miracles associated with this cross see Fonseca, pp. 274-277.
83. Named after St. Thomas the Apostle of India. The reputed relics of the saint were transferred from Mylapore and enshrined here. As Careri points out it is near the college church of St. Bonaventura (Fonseca, pp. 270-272).
84. According to Pietro Della Valle's chart the college and church of St. Bonaventura stood on the Mandavi river next to the arsenal. It was built in 1602. For details see Fonseca, pp. 242-43.
85. Merses is obviously a printing mistake. The Italian text has "Eduardo Manesio" (Archbishop of Goa from 1595 to 1610). The Archbishop only directed it to be built with funds subscribed by the matrons of Bassein for founding a monastery for the nuns of St. Clare.

86. The well-known Royal Hospital begun by Albuquerque. Pyrard de Laval who was treated there has left a graphic account of it (Vol. II, Part I, p. 317). He says, "The hospital is, I believe, the finest in the world, whether for the beauty of the building . . . . or for the perfect order, regulation and cleanliness observed, the great care taken of the sick and supply of all comforts that can be wished for" (p. 5). Also see Fonseca, pp. 228-236.
87. Badly administered.
88. The Holy Pillar attached to the church of *Nossa Senhora de Cabo.* Fryer thus describes it "on an hanging Hill is a Sumptuous Structure of the Capuchins called *Sancto Pillar,* the Ascent to it is by a winding Staircase cut out of the Rock, and Railed with stone Banisters" (Vol. II, p. 22).
89. Add "called Quartelles" after "allowance".

CHAPTER VII

1. According to Danvers (Vol. II, p. 121), the marble statue of Gama was broken into pieces by the people of Goa in 1600 as a token of their disrespect for his grandson, the retiring viceroy. It was replaced by another statue soon afterwards which Manucci (Vol. III, p. 161) and Careri saw. Professor Pissurlencar tells me that this statue of Gama is still to be found in one of the niches of the Arco dos Vicereis at Velha Goa which was constructed under the order of Dom Francisco da Gama in 1599.
2. Add "and dangerous exploration" after "voyage".
3. The Italian text mentions only the title of "General". The correct designation according to the *Roteira* was "Captain Major", (Portuguese *Capitão Mor*) which approximates to English commodore.
4. Sao Gabriel, Sao Rafael, and Berrio. These were the three ships "fitted for war" (Danvers, Vol. I, pp. 42-43).
5. Careri seems to rely on Osorio. According to the *Roteiro,* the most authentic account of Vasco da Gama's first voyage, so far available, the journey began on Saturday, July 8, 1497. The unknown author of this incomplete journal served on board the *Sao Raphael* and his evidence may be accepted as fairly reliable. (See *Vasco da Gama's First Voyage,* p. 1 and the introduction). Barros gives the correct date (8th July). Osorio puts it one day later (9th July). Gaspar Correa antedates it by more than three months (25th March). Danvers accepted "the earliest date as the correct one", without assigning any reason for his conclusion. (Danvers, Vol. I, p. 44, Whiteway, p. 78).
6. The island of St. Iago (or English St. Jago) of the Cape Verde group is meant.
7. Diaz was the first Portuguese navigator to circum-navigate the cape which he named Cabo tormentoso or the Stormy Cape on account of the heavy gale he encountered there but the King renamed it Cabo da boa esperenza or Cape of Good Hope, as the voyage offered the Portuguese navigators a reasonable hope for finding an all-sea-route to India.
8. Instead of "a half of South Latitude" read "two thirds towards the Antarctic".
9. John II (1455-1498), *"the perfect",* ascended the throne in August, 1481.
10. Instead of "for the time to come" read "from coming".
11. The Arabian Sea.
12. Both the date of arrival and the distance of the port from Calicut seem to be inaccurate. According to the *Roteiro* (*First Voyage,* pp. 47-48) lofty mountains were sighted on the 18th May and on the 20th the ships anchored at a place called Capua two leagues from Calicut (identified by Whiteway with "Kappat a small village 8 miles north of Calicut", p. 78). Whiteway says that the fleet reached Kappat on the 17th May.

13. Before "China" read "the great empires of".
14. The Kingdom of Gujarat was known as the Kingdom of Cambay to the European travellers of the sixteenth and seventeenth centuries.
15. The Portuguese never became masters of Cambay, Surat and Dabhol like the other places mentioned here.
16. Anjidiva island, 5 miles S.W. of Karwar. Vasco da Gama visited the island in 1498 and in 1505 Almeida built a fortress here which was later on abandoned. It still forms a part of their possessions in western India (*Imperial Gaz.*, Vol. V, pp. 384-385. Danvers, Vol. I, pp. 117 ff.; Whiteway, p. 105).
17. Malacca, once a flourishing centre of commerce on the west coast of the Malaya Peninsula. It was captured by Albuquerque in 1511 and remained a Portuguese possession for the next 130 years, when it was lost to the Dutch. It finally passed into British hands in 1824.
18. Moluccas or Spice Islands. An exploratory expedition was sent by Albuquerque to the spice island immediately after the conquest of Malacca and trading posts were established in many islands of this group, with headquarters in Ternate. The native king formally ceded the Moluccas with all its dependencies to the Portuguese crown in 1564. By the beginning of the 17th century Dutch ascendancy was definitely established in the Moluccas.
19. An island of the Malay Archipelago, in the Lesser Sunda group. The island is partly Portuguese and partly Dutch. It is not certain when the Portuguese occupied the island but they came long before the Dutch.
20. An island, west of Timor.
21. It lies to the west of the mouth of the Canton River in China. Although the Portuguese were permitted to build factories at Macao as early as 1557, they did not assert their full sovereignty till 1849 until which date China used to receive an annual rent and also claimed judicial jurisdiction over the place. It was at Macao that Camoens wrote his immortal work.
22. After "length" add "and a stone-shot wide".
23. Mossoril Bay.
24. The Zambezi river in Africa (*Rio de Sena*).
25. The reference here is to St. Sebastian, at the northern extremity of the island built in 1510.
26. For "the ships of the Company" read "the trading ships".
27. Kilimane, or São Martinho de Quilimane, a Portuguese trading town in East Africa on the river of the same name. Vasco da Gama entered the river in 1498, and found a flourishing Arab settlement there. The Portuguese city founded in the sixteenth century became a big slave mart in the eighteenth. In 1861 David Livingstone began from Kilimane his journey up the Zambezi to Lake Nayasa.
28. *Almadia* from Arab. *Al-Madiya*, a ferry-boat. Tavernier describes it as "a kind of row-boat" (Vol. I, p. 142). See also Barbosa, Vol. I, p. 14.
29. Sena, an inland port in Portuguese East Africa on the Zambezi river.
30. Sofala is situated in 20° 12′ S. on the east coast of Africa at the mouth of the river of the same name. The coast of Sofala was visited by Cabral on the 16th July 1500. (Danvers, Vol. I, p. 68). Vasco da Gama did not touch at Sofala in 1498 but Covilhan had reached the port eleven years earlier from the Gulf of Ormuz down the east coast of Africa (Prestage, *Portuguese Pioneers*, p. 219). The fort was built in 1507.
31. Muscat or Muskat in Arabia, capital of the province of Oman, and a naval base of great importance commanding the entrance to the Persian Gulf. The Portuguese occupied it in 1508.
32. Ormuz—island in the Persian Gulf. On its importance and occupation by the Portuguese see Sir P. Sykes, *History of Persia*, 2nd ed., Vol. II, pp. 185 ff.
33. Larak (?) and Kishm islands in the Persian Gulf. The rest are Hormuz, Hengam, Furur, Kish, Hindrabi, Shaikh Shuaib, Jebrui, Kharak and Kharaku (Khorgu).
34. Bahrein Islands, a group of islands about 20 miles east of the coast of El Hasa in the Persian Gulf. The largest of the group is called Bahrein,

The Portuguese occupied the islands in 1507, but were dispossessed by Shah Abbas in 1622. (Encyc. Britt., Vol. II, p. 212).

35. Basra. See Thevenot, Pt. III, Bk. I, Chap. I, Note 1.

36. Onore or Honavar, town in North Kanara, Bombay, 50 miles south-east of Karwar fortified by the Portuguese in 1505. Pietro Della Valle says "Onor is a small place by the Sea-side, but a good Port of indifferent capacity." (Vol. II, p. 202). It later passed into the hands of the chiefs of Bednur from whom Haidar Ali acquired it.

37. Barcelore or Basrur—a village in the Coondapur taluk of South Kanara District, Madras. The Portuguese Viceroy Dom Luiz de Athaide built a fortress here in 1569.

38. Combolin which was lost by the Portuguese in 1652 (Danvers, Vol. II, p. 303).

39. Cannanore, town and port in Malabar Dist. Madras. The Portuguese built a fort here in 1505 during the viceroyalty of Almeida. By the middle of the 17th century the Dutch captured the place which they sold to Ali Raja in 1771.

40. Cranganor in Cochin State, the Muziris of Pliny. "Cranganor was already in decay when the Portuguese arrived. They eventually established themselves with a strong fort (1523) which the Dutch took from them in 1662." (*Hobson-Jobson*, p. 272). See also *Cochin State Manual.*

41. Pallipuram in Vaipin island; had a fortress in medieval times. *Cochin State Manual*, pp. 89, 90, 93 and 377.

42. Quilon now the second city in the Travancore state. It was formerly ruled by a queen. The Portuguese established their trade relations with Quilon and built a fort in 1505 soon after their arrival in India. They were ousted by the Dutch in 1662.

43. Island of Manar or Manaar off the north-west coast of Ceylon almost opposite Dhanuskodi on the Indian main-land. The Portuguese built a fort there in 1560.

44. The island was not divided into seven kingdoms when the Portuguese arrived. Mr. S. Paranavitane, Archaeological Commissioner, Ceylon, informs me that "the larger territorial units into which the kingdom of Kotte was divided for administrative purposes were mostly called Korales. The number of Korales was, however, more than seven and there were some territorial units to which the term 'Korale' did not apply. One of these units was, and is still, known as the Sat Korale i.e., the Seven Korales, for it comprised a group of seven territorial divisions. Another was similarly called, as it still is, the Satara Korale i.e., the four Korales. The Korales still retain, more or less, the boundaries which they had in fifteenth century and form units for administrative purposes."

45. Kalutara—south of Colombo on the west coast of Ceylon, nineteen miles from Mount Lavinia. It has a small Dutch fort.

46. Capital and chief port of Ceylon on the west coast of the island. The Portuguese first visited Ceylon in 1505 and built a fort at Colombo in 1517 with the permission of the king of Kotta. In 1656 the fort was captured by the Dutch.

47. Chilaw—about 30 miles to the north of Negombo on the west coast of Ceylon.

48. Jaffna at the northern extremity of the island. The town was first captured by the Portuguese in 1560. The Dutch expelled the Portuguese from Jaffna in 1658 and improved the fort which still exists.

49. "Trichil" and "Mall" should be read together—Trichilmalle appears to represent the Sinhalese name Tirikunamale i.e. Trincomalee.

50. See the preceding note, should not be confused with Galle.

51. Batticaloa, 60 miles S. S. E. from Trincomalee on the east coast of Ceylon. Constantino de Sae Noronha built a fort here in 1629. In 1638 the Portuguese commander capitulated to a joint force of the Dutch and the king of Kandi.

52. Kotta near Colombo, the capital of Ceylon during the 16th century.

53. Negapatam, seaport in Tanjore district, Madras, (See Thevenot, Pt. III, Bk. II, Ch. IX).

54. Tamluk, ancient Tamralipti, in Midnapore district, Bengal, situated on the southern bank of the Rupnarayan. In 1635 the Portuguese built a church there. Tamluk had a good slave market where the Arakan and Portuguese pirates brought their captives for sale. (Campos *Portuguese in Bengal*, pp. 96-97).
55. Macassar (Makassar, Mangkasar), the capital of the district of the same name in the island of Celebes.
56. For this practice see Sen, *Studies in Indian History*, pp. 15 ff and 184 and Sen, *Military System of the Marathas*, Chap. XIII.
57. Read "for the powerful Northern Dutch Company entering into the Eastern Trade".
58. It is not known who first discovered Brazil and when. That Cabral the Portuguese navigator reached the Brazilian coast in 1500 either by accident or by design is beyond dispute. It is also a fact that Brazil ultimately became a Portuguese colony and remained so until it asserted its independence in the 19th century. Prof. Edgar Prestage writes: "Though the first part of his (Cabral's) instructions are missing there is good reason to believe that he was charged to touch at the Brazilian coast, which thenceforth entered into the route of vessels proceeding to India, and officially discover it. We do not know when Brazil was first found and by whom, but Robert Thorne dates its discovery before 1494, which would explain the insistence of John II on having the dividing line moved farther to the west; and in 1498 King Manoel secretly despatched Duarte Pachero in the same direction. Owing to Spanish rivals it would have been imprudent to take formal possession of Brazil until India, a far more important 'conquest' had been reached, and the last step in the route to the east could not have been safely made previous to the settlement effected by the treaty of Tordesillas." For a brief but learned discussion of the subject see Edgar Prestage, *The Portuguese Pioneers*, pp. 277-291.
59. More accurately "forces".
60. Conscious.
61. The Novas Conquistas were acquired later.
62. Timor is famous for producing excellent sandalwood which, along with a noted breed of hardy ponies, form the chief articles of export. Barbosa refers to the white sandal of Timor and according to Garcia da Orta the major part of imported sandal comes from the island where it grew wild.
63. The head of the government was either a viceroy or a governor but there were interregnums when the administration was vested in a commission. At the time of Careri's visit to Goa there was a viceroy.
64. The *Relação das Indias* or the High Court with jurisdiction over all the Portuguese possessions in the east was established at Goa in 1544. The presiding judge was the chancellor but the number of ordinary judges or Desembargadores varied from time to time. There were ten of them in 1587, five in 1628 and only six in 1748. (Fonseca, p. 75).
65. "Down to the elbow" for "half way their Arms".
66. Golilla, a kind of collar forming part of the dress of the magistrates of some superior courts of justice in Spain. Read after Golillas "(inseparable from the nation)."
67. *Junta da Fazenda Publica* or council of public revenue.
68. From *Matricula*, a register, roll or statistical table. The officer was in charge of the registry office. Read "Matricula General like our Accounts office."
69. Director or chief of the Finance Department. This officer was later replaced by Vedor Geral de Fazenda.
70. A gold coin formerly current in Western India, variously known as Pardâo, Varaha and Pagoda. Pardao is probably a Portuguese corruption of Sanskrit Pratapa and the coin bore the figures of Varaha—the boar incarnation of Vishnu. Later the Portuguese minted a silver coin of the same name. According to Dalgado gold varaha was equal to 360 reis and silver, 300 reis. See *Hobson-Jobson*, pp. 673-678.

71. The Dominicans established the Inquisition in India in 1560 and its head-quarters were in the *Casa da Santa Inquisitione* or Palace of the Inquisition near the Cathedral. The inquisition was abolished in 1774. For an excellent modern account, see Fonseca, pp. 210 ff.
72. Governor of arms.
73. Chorao, island in Goa settlement between Goa and Bardez Islands. See map of Goa in Fonseca.
74. Divar, or Narva island about 2¼ miles N. E. of Goa city. Fryer (Vol. II, p. 19) mentions that it was "famous for Curtisans".
75. De Capan or Vanxim mentioned among the Goa islands by Fonseca. (p. 4).
76. Cumbarjua (Fonseca, p. 4) and Juarim (vide Fonseca's map).
77. Santo Estevâo—an island near Goa which was captured by Sambhaji in 1683.
78. Fryer (Vol. II, p. 21) also mentions this islet but Fonseca does not mention it among the islands of Goa.
79. A ilha de Manuel de Mota, locally known as Akaddo now.
80. Dongarim.

CHAPTER VIII

1. Treating in this chapter.
2. Grow.
3. Not found elsewhere.
4. Describe with the Portuguese and Italian names all their trees.
5. All the "cuts" in the Italian edition were not reproduced in the English version published by the Churchills. They are not however faithful representations of the original plants.
6. Palmera de cocos—or cocoanut palms, have been described in full by almost all the travellers of this period. Linschoten devotes one whole chapter to this tree, Vol. II, Chap. 56.
7. *Sic.* Anything. After "elsewhere" add "as it provides all that is necessary itself".
8. Palmyra leaves are commonly used for writing purposes and Linschoten also testifies to the same use of tender white coconut leaves. "This the Indians use for paper, and bookes, which continueth in the same foldes, whereon they write when it is greene" (Linschoten, Vol. II, p. 50).
9 Food.
10. Trading commodity.
11. The reference is to the coir fibre. The fibre is exceptionally good for making light, elastic, strong and durable ropes that will stand continuous exposure to moisture and rain. Also see Linschoten, Vol. II, p. 46. "This Huske being drie and pulled off, is haire like hempe, whereof all the cordes and cables that are used throughout al India are made, as well upon the land as in the ships, ..."
12. Pears.
13. Commonly called chiechere. See Linschoten, Vol. II, p. 45.
14. Among the food products obtained from the palm are (*i*) cocoa-nut cabbage, (*ii*) young cocoa-nut (vern. *dab*), (*iii*) mature cocoa-nut (vern. *jhuna narkel*), (*iv*) juice and (*v*) the root. (Watt, Vol. II, p. 448). Also see Linschoten, Vol. II, pp. 46-47.
15. Almost like Artichokes, according to Linschoten, Vol. II, p. 46.
16. Burn in lamps.
17. For a better account of the process see Linschoten, Vol. II, p. 48.
18. Brandy.
19. When boiled black sugar is extracted from it.
20. To make sauces and many kinds of stew.
21. Keeps fresh a whole year.

22. The roofs.
23. The wild date or date-sugar palm, *Phoenix Sylvestris,* Vern. *khajur* indigenous to many parts of India.
24. The fruit of this palm has ordinarily three stones which in their tender stage consist of a shell of soft pulp with a small quantity of liquid inside. Both the pulp and the liquid are highly relished during the hot months of the summer.
25. And with the rind black outside they make ropes.
26. Cocoa-nut, *cocos nucifera.* It is called the monkey-coco by some writers (Barros, Linschoten, Garcia da Orta etc.) with reference to the appearance of the base of the shell with its three holes. (*Hobson-Jobson,* p. 228).
27. *Areca Catechu* or betel-nut palm, Vern. *supari, supyari,* cultivated throughout India. (Watt, Vol. I, pp. 291 ff).
28. It bears the areca.
29. The "figos da India" of the Portuguese are not figs at all but bananas. Discoursing on "figos" Garcia da Orta says that in Konkani, Deccani, Gujrati and Bengali languages they are called "quelli" (*keli*), in Malabar tongue "palam" and in Guinea "bananas". He also adds that the 'figos" of Martaban and Pegu are very good and they are known in Bengal as *Figos martabanis* (*martamān kalā*) (Orta—Vol. I, pp. 329-331). Linschoten probably quotes Garcia da Orta when he says (Vol. II, p. 40), "The Gusurates, Decanijns, Canarijns and Bengalers call them Quelli, the Malabares, Palan." We are also told by Pietro Della Valle that the "tree which the *Arabians* and *Persians* call *Mouz* (*Musa*) the *Portugals* in *India Fichi d' India, Indian Fig trees.*" (Vol. II, p. 327).
30. More than four spans broad.
31. "Adam and Eve covered with these leaves what should not be seen in the earthly Paradise." Garcia da Orta refers to a story which he heard from a Franciscan monk (Vol. I, p. 331) that Adam ate this fruit when he first sinned. Linschoten repeats "And they do believe that this is the same fruits, which Adam did eate when hee sinned first." (Vol. II, p. 40). He prefers to identify it with the grapes from the land of promise mentioned in the Book of Moses. (Ibid).
32. It is still a common practice in Southern India to use the broad banana leaves instead of metal plates for serving the meals. Pietro Della Valle refers to this custom (Vol. II, p. 327). "Upon the said Leaf they had lay'd a good quantity of Rice, boyl'd, after their manner."
33. In Bengal small children used to be given big pieces of banana leaves to write on in the *pathshalas* before they were permitted the use of paper.
34. The cooking bananas. This was the variety known as figs of Cananore. See Linschoten, Vol. II, p. 39.
35. Linschoten also describes these figs which are "somewhat thicke". (Vol. II, p. 39).
36. *Mangifera Indica,* Vern. *ām, amba.* The name is derived from Tamil *man-kay* or *man-gay, i.e.,* man fruit. The Portuguese form is *manga* from which we have *mango.* (Watt, Vol. V, pp. 146 ff).
37. Manucci says—"The best mangoes grow in the island of Goa. They have special names which are as follows: mangoes of *Niculao Affonso, Malaiasses, Carreira branca, Carreira vermelha,* of *Conde,* of *Joani Pereira, Babia* (large and round) of *Araup,* of *Porta,* of *Secreta,* of *Mainato,* of *Our Lady,* of *Agua de Lupe* (Vol. III, p. 180). Of the four varieties mentioned by Careri only one the *Satias* does not occur in Manucci's list, unless it is to be identified with *Secreta. Niculao Affonso* otherwise known as *Afuz* or *Hafuz* still retains its popularity and fetches a very high price.
38. Flavour.
39. In April, May and June.
40. Unripe and green.
41. Read 'at' for 'to'.

42. *Averrhoa Carambola,* Bengali *kamranga.* Linschoten thus writes about it, "There is another fruit called Carambolas, which hath 8 corners, as big as a small apple, sower in eating, like unripe plums, and most used to make conserves." (Vol. II, p. 33).
43. *Anona Reticulata,* Bengali *nona,* English "Bullock's heart."
44. In February, March and April.
45. *Anona squamosa,* custard apple of Europeans in India. Vern. *sharifah* or *sitaphal,* Beng. *ata, luna.* See Watt, Vol. I, pp. 259 ff.
46. *Anacardium occidentale,* cashew or *kaju nuts,* indigenous to Brazil, was introduced by the Portuguese in India. It is fairly common in the west Malabar and Coromandel coasts and grows well in Hijli littoral and Chittagong forests of Bengal where the Portuguese once had some settlements. For another account see Linschoten, Vol. II, Chap. 52. See also Forbes—*Oriental Memoirs* Vol. I, pp. 232 & 238.
47. Chest diseases.
48. *Eugenia Jambolana,* "The fruit, which is sometimes as large as a pigeon's egg and of a purple colour, is eaten by all classes of people : it is sub-acid and rather astringent and is improved in taste by being pricked and rubbed with a little salt and allowed to stand an hour." (Watt, Vol. III, pp. 285-286).
49. *Flacourtia Cataphracta.* Vern. *jan-gama, paniamalak, paniaonvola, taliasptri, paniamalak.* Taylor writes, "The fruit of this tree, which is of a purple colour, and of the size and appearance of a plum, is sold in the city during the rains". (*Topography of Dacca* cited in Watt, Vol. III, p. 398). See also Linschoten, Vol. II, p. 32.
50. *Garcinia indica,* "A slender tree with drooping branches, found on the Ghats of the Konkan and Kanara, most commonly in Southern Konkan, and considerably cultivated in gardens of that district. It bears a conspicuous spherical purple fruit, the size of a small orange, which ripens about April." "The juice of the fruit has long been employed as a mordant by dyers in South-Western India." "A valuable oil, 'Kokam butter' is obtained from the seeds of the fruit to the extent of about 30 per cent." (Watt, Vol. III, p. 467).
51. *Carissa Carandas,* Vern. *karaunda, karamcha,* etc. See Watt, Vol. II, pp. 165-66.
52. The rose-apple. Lat. *Eugenia,* Sansk. *Jambos, jambu;* Beng. *golap jam.* Garcia da Orta (II, pp. 25, 27) mentions it under the name *jambos,* and says (1563) that it had been recently introduced into Goa from Malacca. See Watt, Vol. III, p. 287.
53. The Papaya tree, *Carica Papaya,* Vern. *Pappaiya, pepiya.* Atkinson (cited in Watt, Vol. II, p. 159) regards it as introduced into India by the Portuguese. Watt says, "The non-Asiatic origin of the Papaw is conclusively proved by its not having been known before the discovery of America; by its having no Sanskrit name, and by the modern Indian names being evidently derived from the American word *papaya,* itself a corruption of the *Carib ababai.*"
54. Gourd.
55. Omit "at dinner".
56. *Bergamot. Citrus aurantium,* "only rarely met with in India". (Watt, Vol. II, p. 347).
57. The bracketed comment is that of the translator, and does not occur in the original.
58. The jack-fruit tree. *Artocarpus integrifolia.* Vern. *kathal, kanthal, panas* etc. Manucci gives an interesting account of the tree and its fruit (Vol. III, pp. 182-183).
59. Omit "at least".
60. Rings for playing ball.
61. There are many yellow partitions, very sweet, and each of them with a kernel in it, hard as an acorn.
62. From March till September.
63. *Jambo*—Konkani *jambol,* Bengali, *jamrul, Inga xilocarpa* (?)

64. Not "Pear" but "guava tree". Bengali *peyara,* Hindi *amrud. Psidium Guyava,* indigenous to South America was introduced into India by the Portuguese. It now grows all over the country. (Watt, Vol. VI, Part I, pp. 351-353).
65. *Cinnamomum zeylanicum,* Vern. *dalchini.*
66. *Citrus decumana,* English 'pumelo', Bengali *batapi nebu.* Careri is wrong in suggesting that the tree was brought from Africa. "A native of the islands of the Malay Archipelago, more particularly abundant in the Friendly Isles and Fiji. Introduced into India from Java and into the West Indies by Captain Shaddock; hence the name *Shaddock.* . . The vernacular name *batavi nebu* suggests its having been originally brought from Batavia." (Watt, Vol. II, pp. 348-349).
67. Bilimbi tree, *Averrhoa Bilimbi*—Vern. *bilimbi, belambu.* See Watt, Vol. I, p. 359.
68. The whole fruit is eaten, because it has no stone.
69. Vern. *amlaki, anuli, aonla,* etc., *Phyllanthus Emblica,* the Emblic Myrobalan. (Watt, Vol. VI, Part I, pp. 217-221). 'Amsaleira' and 'Amsale' in the Italian text.
70. *Ananas sativa,* Pineapple. A native of Brazil, it was introduced into Bengal by the Portuguese in 1594. (Watt, Vol. I, pp. 236-239).
71. Like the everlasting flower (not "our House-leek").
72. Careri is obviously wrong. Each plant bears only one fruit; a big bush consisting of several plants may bear two or more. Manucci correctly states —"each plant yielding no more than one fruit." (Vol. III, p. 183).
73. and above half a span in diameter.
74. "Green", not "great" Artichoke.
75. This is obviously borrowed from Linschoten who says, "It is very hotte of nature, for if you let a knife sticke in it but halfe an hour long when you draw it forth again, it will be halfe eaten up." (Vol. II, pp. 19-20).
76. *Jasiminum Sambac,* the Arabian Jasmine. Vern. *Mogra, Motia.* It is not confined to India but is found in Burma and Ceylon also. (Watt, Vol. IV, pp. 544-545).
77. Besides this difference, that the jasmine has but six leaves.
78. Cosimo III, Grand Duke of Tuscany from 1670 to 1723.
79. Having had to cross the Equator twice.
80. To be planted or placed.
81. *Sephalika* (Sans.) *Nyclanthes arbor tristis.* Linschoten says of the tree called *Arbore Triste*—"the tree is as great as a Plum Tree. . . . . . The flower being white, and in the bottome (somewhat) yellow and reddish which in India they use for Saffron, therewith to dresse their meats, and to die with all as (wee doe) with (our) Saffron, but it is neyther so good nor of so pleasant to taste, yet it serveth there, for want of the other." (Vol. II, pp. 59-60). Linschoten doubtless derived his information from Garcia da Orta (Vol. I, pp. 69-72). Many travellers refer to this tree. For an account of the tree and its products, see Watt, Vol. V, pp. 434-435.
82. Plum tree.
83. Although the flower is used for dyeing it does not produce saffron.
84. *Piper nigrum, gulmirch, kalimirch.* For an account of the plant and its cultivation see Watt, Vol. VI, Part I, pp. 260-267. Linschoten as usual devotes a chapter to various kinds of pepper, Vol. II, Chapter 62.
85. For what purpose it is used is well known in Europe and it comes in March, April and May.

    Careri is wrong. The berries are not burnt to take off their seed value. "The fruit is gathered as soon as the berries at the base of the spike begin to change colour from green to red, since if allowed to ripen fully it becomes less pungent and easily falls off. . . . . They are then dried by exposure to the sun or more frequently by the heat of a gentle fire." (Watt, Vol. VI, Part I, p. 261).

86. Betel, Hind. *pan*, the leaf of the *Piper betel* chewed with the dried areca-nut by the Indians and the Indo-Chinese. Almost every traveller has referred to the Indian and Luso-Indian habit of chewing betel. Linschoten's Chapter 60 deals with betel and areca. See Watt, Vol. VI, Part I, pp. 247-256.
87. In no part of Asia is it consumed better than in the Philippine islands.
88. A compound of bonga-fruit, betel leaves and lime for chewing.
89. To chew it at every moment like oxen, abroad and at home.
90. If the Italian ladies could obtain it they would pay for it its weight in gold.
91. *Calophyllum inophyllum* popularly known as *puna* in Goa (Dalgado, Vol. II, p. 229) "used for masts, spars etc" (Watt, Vol. II, p. 31).
92. *Mele Indiane*—in the Italian text is a literal rendering of *Maça da India* which however is not a real maça or apple. Conde de Ficalho identifies it with *jatiphal* or nutmeg. Garcia da Orta (Vol. II, pp. 81-89) calls it *jaiphal*, the fruit of which was called apple according to Linschoten (Vol. II, p. 84). Mace may conceivably be therefore a corruption of Port. 'Maca'. Careri's apple is not nutmeg which does not grow in India but a common country fruit. Dalgado says that *ber* is vulgarly called *Maça* or apple in Goa (Vol. I, p. 496). He quotes Bernardo da Costa who says, "In India the Jajuba tree is called *Maceira* (apple tree) in Portuguese and *bori* in Concani." The Indian apple is therefore *Zizyphus Jujuba* of the Botanists (Watt, Vol. VI, Part IV, pp. 367-370). Peter Mundy also mentions this fruit (Vol. V, p. 58, also footnote) which according to him the Portuguese called Mansana.
93. The pod of the Tamarind tree, *Tamarindus indica*, Vern. *Amli, Imli*. (Watt, Vol. VI, Part III, pp. 404-9).
94. A misprint for pod; the Italian text is "L'albero è grande, e porta le frutta dentro una scorza, o guaina come i legumi." The tree is big and bears the fruit in a shell or pod like the bean.
95. Is *scararagam* a corruption of Deccani *Surpanka*? *Undi* is another name of *Puna*. Careri obviously did not see either the tree or its fruit.
96. *Michelia Champaca*. Vern. *Champa, Champaka*, etc. See Watt, Vol. V, pp. 241-43.
97. Grows not as a tree but as a low plant.
98. *Mimusops Elengi* Vern. *mulsari, maulser* etc. Known as *ovalli, wowli* etc. in Bombay and *bakula* in Bengal. In the summer months, the tree produces small fragrant flowers. (Watt, Vol. V, pp. 249-51). I am indebted to Prof. Pissurlencar for helping me in identiyfing this.
99. Strange.
100. *Quegada cheirosa* or sweet-scented quegada. *Pandanus Odoratissimus*, Bengali *keora, ketaki*. Konkani *kagad, kegdi*. "A common much branched shrub, frequently planted on account of the powerful fragrance of its flowers but wild on the coasts of South India, Burma and the Andamans. It is found abundantly in Bengal, Madras, the Straits Settlements and the South Sea Islands." (Watt, Vol. VI, Part I, pp. 5-6); see also Dalgado, Vol. II, p. 233.
101. *Origanum Marjorana*, the sweet marjoram, Beng. *ban tulsi*. Vern. *murru*. (Watt, Vol. V, pp. 493-94).
102. *Padolim* may be a corruption of Konkani *Panri* or *Pandhri* by which name two different plants are known. *Bauhinia alba* gives a showy flower like all *Bauhinias* but its fruit can by no stretch of imagination be likened to a water melon or cucumber. The fruit is somewhat like a broad bean. The other is *Strychnos Colubrina*, the 'snake wood' of Linschoten (Vol. II, pp. 104-5) and 'Pau de Cobra' of Garcia da Orta (Vol. II, pp. 181 ff), and is still less likely to be Careri's *padolim*.
103. Showy.
104. Water melon.
105. Green flowers are admittedly rare. Two occur in Bengal. Of the two only one can be described as "coming from a low plant" and is a garden flower as well. Careri's *Pachaa* may therefore be identified with the flower known as *kantali champa* (*Artabotrys Odoratissimus*) in Bengal. It is indigenous to southern parts of Western India but is cultivated throughout the country.

106. Marathi *tenduli* or *tendli,* Bengali *telakucha, Cephalandra indica* (Watt, Vol. II, p. 252; Dalgado, Vol. II, p. 366). Careri is wrong about the flower which is pure white and not red. The fruit when ripe is scarlet.
107. *Inhame do Cao.* English *yam* or sweet potato. It is a tuberous root and not a fruit. Dalgado suggests that it is probably *Dioscorea alata* (Vol. I, p. 469). See Watt, Vol. III, pp. 126-27; also *Hobson-Jobson,* p. 977. Linschoten also speaks of Iniamos and Batutas as fruits (Vol. II, p. 42).
108. Better flavoured.
109. Potato, *Solanum tuberosum,* Vern. *alu.* Bomb. *batata.* See Watt, Vol. VI, Part III, pp. 265 ff.) Linschoten's *batatas* were probably some kind of yams. "The Batatas are somewhat red of colour, and of fashion almost like the Iniamos, but sweeter, of taste like an earth Nut." (Vol. II, p. 42).
110. Herbs.
111. Pumpkins.
112. Cabbages.

BOOK II

CHAPTER I

1. Hind. *begari* from Pers. *begar,* 'forced labour' (*be*—without, *gar*—*kar,* 'one who works'); a person pressed to carry a load or do other work really or professedly for public service" (*Hobson-Jobson,* pp. 80-81).
2. Cooking utensils. Omit "for dressing of meat."
3. Pass of Daugim which lies about a mile east of Goa town on the Mandavi river and is shown on the map of Goa settlement inserted in Danvers, Vol. II. Passo is not really a mountain pass but a crossing place as Linschoten explains. There were five of these, (1) Passo de Saint Iago (2) Tebe de Passo (3) Passo de Daugijn (4) Passo de Norwa and (5) Passo de Paugijn (Linschoten, Vol. I, pp. 180-181). Careri took his boat at Daugim, went down the river and crossed to the main land at St. Iago.
4. A fortified town in the district of the same name about nine miles from Goa town (*Bombay Presidency Gazetteer,* Vol. II, p. 562; Manucci, Vol. II, p. 263 & *n* 3).
5. Dom Fr. Agostinho de Annunciaçao was the contemporary archbishop. He was also a member of the commission in charge of the administration prior to Conde de Vilaverde's arrival.
6. Sao Braz near Daugim.
7. St. Iago further south-east. For both these places see Danvers' map.
8. Cannot be found in a modern map. Is it Hurcun?
9. Probably Congee (the water in which rice has been boiled). See *Hobson-Jobson,* p. 245.
10. Mar. *Shimga,* the Holi festival.
11. Hind. *khichari.* See Thevenot, Part III, Book I, Chap. XXIX, Note 8.
12. Mardol in Ponda District, north of the town of Ponda.
13. Obviously a misprint for Benches; the Italian text has "all 'intorno sono bassi scanni per sedere."
14. Ends.
15. One of those great trees.
16. With a staircase of large stone steps.
17. Bicholim to the north of Goa. The Portuguese recaptured the fort from the Sardesais of Kudal in 1746 (Danvers, Vol. II, pp. 417, 429).
18. Subahdar. The head of the province under Akbar was officially styled the *sipah-salar.* He was popularly called subahdar and later only *subah.*
19. Ikhlas Khan Pani (?)
20. Drums, fifes, trumpets and other military instruments.

21. The reference is to the Holi festival. For a detailed account see Thevenot, Pt. III, Bk. II, Ch. XL.
22. Hind. *chira*, a turban made of parti-coloured cloth. See Platts, *Dict. of Urdu, Classical Hindi and English*, p. 470.
23. Then mounted.
24. Various flags.
25. Exchanging.
26. Put the *chira* with his own hands on his head.
27. Sash of gold brocade.
28. Envoy.
29. Omit "vest or".
30. Nazr, nazar, najar. "A present, an offering, especially one from an inferior to a superior, to a holy man, or to a prince" (Wilson's *Glossary*, pp. 595-96).
31. Carlina, Carlin (Fr.), Carlino (It.). A silver coin first struck by Charles (Carlo) of Anjou, King of Naples and Sicily, originally equivalent to about four pence.
32. Count of Alvor and Viceroy of Goa. For his attack on and discomfiture at Ponda see Manucci, Vol. II, pp. 262-263, also Sarkar, *History of Aurangzib*, Vol. IV, pp. 273-276; Danvers, Vol. II, p. 369.
33. "Eight hundred white soldiers and eight thousand Canarese", says Manucci. According to Danvers 1200 of the troops were Europeans but Manucci was better informed as he was at Goa at the time.
34. Shambhaji, not Shivaji. It should be noticed that Careri treats the personal name of the first Maratha king as a common title for his successors.
35. Shambhaji razed the fort to the ground and built another nearby. Careri obviously confuses Persian *mardan*, men, with Sanskrit *mardana*, crushing, destruction. The fort was probably so named because the Portuguese army was crushed here. *Mardan* does not necessarily mean valiant men.
36. Kiladar from Arabic *qala* "a fort" which is pronounced 'kila' in India. The commandant of a fort, castle or garrison.
37. Monday, March 7th.
38. Woman whom the kindred etc.
39. Free performance of "sati" was prohibited in the Mughal empire and the permission of the local governor had to be obtained before a widow could burn herself with the dead husband. The case witnessed by Careri appears to be an instance of voluntary self-immolation though his suspicions about "the price of great presents" may be fully justified. Also see Roe, pp. 105-271, Peter Mundy, Vol. II, pp. 24-36, 179-180, Pyrard, Vol. I, pp. 378, 394, Mandelslo, pp. 55-56, Manucci, Vol. III, pp. 60, 65-66, Tavernier, Vol. II, pp. 162-168, Bernier, pp. 306-314, Dellon, Ch. XVII.
40. About 9 o'clock in the evening, literally "about 21 hours".
41. Come.
42. Stretched out.
43. Small pieces of wood greased with oil.
44. Francois Pyrard however says, "The Gentile women, who burn themselves after the death of their husbands, first take off all their trinkets, and give them to whom they will" (Vol. I, p. 378).
45. Our little camp.
46. When nobody pursues.
47. *Bhang* from H. *bhang*, Skt. *bhanga*, the dried leaves and small stalks of hemp (*Cannabis indica*). For an account of the drug and its numerous preparations, see Watt, Vol. II, pp. 103 ff. For a 17th century account of the plant, its use and misuse, see Linschoten, Vol. II, pp. 116-117. Aurangzeb forbade its use, see Manucci, Vol. II, p. 7.
48. In.
49. Ghats.
50. By.
51. Bakhshi or paymaster of the forces. The officer at the imperial headquarters

was styled mir bakhshi. For the origin of the term and the functions of the bakhshi, see Ibn Hasan, pp. 213 ff.

52. Cianpon in the Italian text, not to be found in modern maps.
53. Material.
54. Food to be prepared.
55. Wishing.
56. Probably the Rachol river.
57. Ruler of Sonda. The contemporary chief was Sadashive Naik the ablest of his dynasty, who assumed the title of Raja.
58. At the end of nine cosses, (each cosse is two Italian miles) we spent the night at the village of Kakore.
59. Cacora in Chandrovaddi district, south-east of Ponda? (see Fonseca's map).
60. Like the Portuguese, Careri means by India the Malabar coast alone and not the entire country.
61. They feed the monkeys with particular care and arrange that they shall not be killed.
62. Or.
63. Do not wish to work.
64. Baboons or dog-headed monkeys are now to be found in Arabia and Africa. It had become extinct in India long before Careri visited this country. European travellers generally used the words baboon and ape indiscriminately for all monkeys. Of the apes or tail-less monkeys only the gibbon occurs in India. Gibbons however are not to be found in Malabar.

    The stories are in all probability apocryphal. Though it is not physically impossible for man-like apes to have such relations with human females authentic records of such cases are naturally lacking. There is however a widespread belief in its prevalence. The Tibetans think that they are descended from an ape. A story of another such union is to be found in the *Arabian Nights* (ed. Burton, Vol. IV, pp. 297-299). Burton refers to a case mentioned in the *Ajaib-al-Hind* of man having children by a she-ape. But *Ajaib-al-Hind* admittedly deals more with fiction than with facts and Burton heard of an incident which is more to the point. An Abyssinian baboon, he says, once "attempted to rape a girl in the public street and was prevented by a sentinel's bayonet". A mandrill, another African baboon, in the Calcutta Zoo invariably became obscene in its behaviour whenever a woman came in view. Briffault writes on the authority of de Garcia that Igorot girls of the Phillipines were believed to go into the woods and have connexion with monkeys (Elwin, *The Maria and their Ghotul*, p. 278).
65. Not being able to resist any longer.
66. The idolater being afraid that he would be punished, the Portuguese removed it himself out of the cottage and buried it.
67. Baboons are not to be found in Brazil, some other monkey is meant.
68. From the roof to the kitchen.
69. Read "Italian miles".
70. Bojata seems to be a corruption of Portuguese *boyada*, a train of transport bullocks. In Chapter V, Book II, Careri uses the words *bojata* and *caravana* as synonymous. In the English translation (p. 232) it is rendered as caravan of oxen, but bullocks seem more likely to have been used for this purpose.
71. Loaded like horses.
72. In flavour.
73. Careri might have seen a grey jungle fowl *Gallus Sonneratii* which occurs widely in South India.
74. Bomanhalli village in Supa sub-division of North Kanara dist., Bombay (*Kanara Dist. Gaz.*, Part I, p. 33).
75. Hind. *chauki*, a customs or toll station. Also a police station. (*Hobson-Jobson*, pp. 205-206).
76. Not shown in modern maps.
77. I stayed overnight four cosses further at Sambrani.

78. A large village about five miles south of Haliyal in North Kanara dist., Bombay. "Colonel Wellesley in 1799 described it as a large and well stocked village" (*Kanara Dist. Gaz.*, Part II, p. 340).
79. Setting out from Sambrani.
80. Fort of the territory of Alcal. Probably Haliyal, to the north of Sambrani, the headquarters of the Supa sub-division in North Kanara dist., Bombay (*Kanara Dist. Gaz.*, Part II, p. 304).
81. Wait.
82. Hanuman, the monkey-god, worshipped by Hindus throughout India.
83. "Animante" in the Italian text is obviously Careri's rendering of *Hanumanta* and is not to be taken in the literal sense as has been done by the translator.
84. Kakeri, a small village about twenty-eight miles south-east of Belgaum. (*Belgaum Dist. Gaz.*, p. 377).
85. Stayed overnight.
86. Itgi, twelve miles north of Kakeri (*Belgaum Dist. Gaz.*, p. 377).
87. Grazing.
88. Through fertile country.
89. Tigdi (*Belgaum Dist. Gaz.*, p. 378).
90. Vanur (Ibid, p. 378).
91. The Italian text has "Mercordi 15" which must be a mistake if Monday was the 14th. The translator's emendation is therefore quite justified.
92. Mamdapur, ten miles south-east of Gokak, in Belgaum district, Bombay. (*Belgaum District Gaz.*, p. 378).
93. Betgeri.
94. Stayed overnight.
95. Great Mughal towns.
96. Crafty and experienced thieves.
97. Negligence.
98. Dexterously.
99. Careri here obviously writes of the Thugs. It is interesting to note that in the closing years of the seventeenth century the operations of these gangs had spread so far south. Fryer mentions a gang of fifteen apprehended and hanged near Surat (Vol. I, pp. 244-245). A much bigger party, about 100 strong, was captured at Bangalore in 1799 (Mackenzie, quoted in *Hobson-Jobson*, p. 916). Their headquarters were mostly in Central and Northern India when they were finally suppressed by Sleeman.
100. Through a large village.
101. Kalligudi situated in 75° 6′ E. and 16° 9′ N.
102. Yadvad, twenty-five miles east of Gokak. (*Belgaum Dist. Gaz.*, p. 278).
103. The goods afterwards are transported to the camp at Galgala by retailers.
104. Mudhol, capital of a small state of the same name, on the left bank of the Ghatprabha river, now under the jurisdiction of Kolhapur. (See *Bombay Presidency Gaz.*, Vol. II, pp. 537-38).

CHAPTER II

1. Mantur (6° 23′ N. and 75° 22′ E.) midway between Mudhol and Galgali.
2. Galgali, a large village on the Kistna, 32 miles south-west of Bijapur in the Bijapur district, Bombay. After Shambhaji's execution in 1689, Aurangzeb moved with his grand army from Brahmapuri in Sholapur to Galgali hoping to draw the Marathas southward. See *Bijapur Dist. Gaz.*, pp. 648-649.
3. The Kistna or Krishna river.
4. Lascar. Pers. *Lashkar,* 'an army'· 'a camp'. Laskari is a corrupt form of the word prevalent among the Portuguese and other Europeans. It is vulgarly used for a sailor but here it means a military camp, see *Hobson-Jobson*, pp. 507-509.
5. Manucci mentions one Francisco Borges who was at San Thome in 1704 (Vol. VI, p. 67).

6. From then until 1 o'clock.
7. Qazi or Kazi, see Thevenot, Pt. III, Bk. I, Ch. X, Note 3.
8. Literally the red barrier by which name the red painted bamboo network screen put up around the imperial tents was known. The Imperial quarters as such were not called the gulalbar. See Irvine, *Army of the Indian Moghuls*, p. 199.
9. Defended on every side.
10. Harem. Ar. *harem, harim* commonly applied to the ladies' apartment and also to ladies (*Hobson-Jobson*, p. 411).
11. A misprint for 100,000. The Italian text has 10 m.
12. In circumference. For the strength of Mughal cavalry, see Thevenot, Book I, Chap. II, Note 28.
13. Many lands.
14. Jagirs. Assignments of land made to the officials of the State by way of payment of their remuneration. Moreland, *The Agrarian System of Moslem India*, pp. 92 ff.
15. Ghari (?) the subdivision of a village as in Delhi district. (Wilson's *Glossary*, p. 271).
16. Though these generals have so great rents to accumulate vast wealth.
17. Only by.
18. Widow.
19. The king of Persia follows a similar practice.
20. *Wakil-i-mutlaq* or *Divan-i-mutlaq*, vicegerent (Irvine, *The Army of the Indian Moghuls*, p. 37).
21. Told me in this connection that.
22. This is a mistake. Barley (Hind. *jau*, Lat. *Hordeum Vulgare*) grows in many parts of India.
23. Probably *chana* is meant. For horses' fodder allowed in the imperial stables. See *Ain*, Vol. I, pp. 134-135.
23a. The portion in italics is not in Italian original but inserted by the translator.
24. The system of making over elephants to the nobles was introduced by Akbar. "He (Akbar) therefore put several *halqahs* (groups of baggage elephants) in charge of every grandee, and required him to look after them." (*Ain*, Vol. I, p. 126). Elephants were classified into seven grades, and their food varied with the class. For instance, large *mast* elephants got as much as 2 maunds 24 seers, and *mokals* got 8-26 seers for food (*Ain*, Vol. I, p. 124).
25. Shah Alam, Muhammad Muazzam, the second son of Aurangzeb, who was born on the 30th Rajab, 1053 H. (October 14, 1643). He succeeded his father as Bahadur Shah I (1707) and died in 1712 (Sarkar, *Aurangzib*, Vol. I, pp. 71-72; Irvine, *The Later Mughals*, Vol. I, p. 135). At the time of Careri's visit (1695), he was the eldest surviving son, Muhammad Sultan, the first-born, having died in prison in 1676. He was 52 at the time and not 65.
26. Awaiting.
27. While I was waiting I saw the son.
28. Dismounted.
29. Stout.
30. *Naubat* and *Naubat khana*. "A free space, as extensive as may be convenient or practicable, is always kept in front of the royal entrance, and at its extremity there is a large tent called *Nagar Kane* (*Naqqar khana*= *Naubat khana*) because it contains the trumpets and cymbals" (Bernier, p. 363). The music was played eight times in twenty four hours, but sometimes to announce good news an extra blare was made (Irvine, *The Army of the Indian Moghuls*, pp. 207-209).
31. Made their noisy concert about 3 P.M. by Italian time.
32. This is the *Kaukabah* mentioned in the *Ain* (Vol. I, p. 50). Steingass describes it as "a polished steel ball suspended from a long pole and carried as an ensign before the king" (Irvine, *The Army of the Indian Moghuls*, p. 32).
33. *Panjah*. See Irvine, *The Army of the Indian Moghuls*, pp. 31-32.

34. For what purpose.
35. And fortune.
36. Emperor Leopold formed an alliance with John Sobieski, King of Poland, against the Turks in 1683, and soon after on March 5, 1684 a Holy League was formed with the addition of Venice, Russia and the Papacy. The war, which began with the famous siege of Vienna (July 14—Sept. 12, 1683), lasted for sixteen years and put an end to Turkish domination in Hungary.
37. I returned therefore at 4 P.M.
38. Forming a sort of dais.
39. Raised three spans above the rest.
40. Gold veil.
41. Shone.
42. *Katari, katar, katarah.* A dagger. For full description see Irvine, *The Army of the Indian Moghuls*, pp. 85-86.
43. Being eighty years old.
44. Conspicuous.
45. The officer in charge of petitions was the *mir arz.* There are very few references to this office in the *Akbarnama.* In the twentieth year of Akbar's reign, the officer was for the first time appointed. "An accomplished courtier was made Mir 'Arzi' so that he might during the time of his watch represent the petitions and requests of mankind without reference to his own ease, and also the public be freed from the pain of waiting and from various troubles." (*Akbarnama*, Vol. III, p. 208; Ibn Hasan, *Central Structure of the Mughal Empire*, p. 220, *n.* 1).
46. At so advanced an age.
47. Cornac. Elephant driver or mahout. See *Hobson-Jobson*, p. 256.
48. Shah Alam had five sons—Muizz-ud-din, Azz-ud-din, Muhammad Azim surnamed 'Azim-ush-shan', Rafi-ul-qadr, and Khujista-Akhtar Jahan Shah. With the exception of Azz-ud-din all the sons had children. (See genealogical table on p. 143 of Irvine, *The Later Mughals*, Vol. I).
49. Muhammad Azam Shah born in 1653, died at Jajau, in the war of succession following Aurangzeb's death (June 1707).
50. Obeisances.
51. One span above the other.
52. Had to make.
53. The ensigns at the entrance to the Emperor's camp, which the author describes, were collectively called the *qur.* The *aftab* or sun was adopted as a standard by Timur when the fire-worshippers were conquered. The gilt hand is the *panjah.* It represents the hand of Ali. The horse's tail is obviously the *chatrtoq* or the *tumantoq* mentioned in the *Ain* (Vol. I, p. 50). It is a small standard adorned with the tails of Tibetan yaks. See Irvine, *The Army of the Indian Moghuls*, pp. 31-35.
54. Kotwal.

CHAPTER III

1. If indeed the sons await their father's death.
2. Shah Jahan.
3. Compare Tavernier who writes "This great monarch reigned more than forty years, less as an Emperor over his subjects than as father of a family over his house and children." (Vol. I, p. 260). Shah Jahan ascended the throne in 1627 and had reigned only for thirty years when the war of succession began.
4. The actual age was 65 years and 8 months.
5. More fitted for other things than love, he became desperately enamoured of a young Muslim woman.

6. This is one of the fantastic stories to which the foreign travellers often gave currency. For similar or more baseless scandals see Manucci, Vol. I, pp. 194-196; Bernier, pp. 273-274; Manrique, Vol. II, pp. 141-44; Peter Mundy, Vol. II, p. 203; Tavernier, Vol. I, p. 260.
7. The Mughal emperors appeared at a balcony every day. The practice was discontinued by Aurangzeb.
8. The first.
9. Shuja.
10. Called—the first, Begum Saheb.
11. Jahanara Begam, surnamed the Begum Sahib. See Thevenot, Pt. III, Bk. I, Ch. XVIII, Note 28.
12. The second.
13. Raushanara Begam, literally "adornment of light", here of "serene mind."
14. Accustomed to be.
15. Barqandaz Khan, Sardar Khan, Itibar Khan, Danishmand Khan and Kamal Khan.
16. Gwalior. Princes of the imperial family, for political convenience of the reigning monarch, were usually lodged in the fort of Gwalior and there rendered imbecile by regular administration of drugs like "post". (Bernier, pp. 106 ff and note).
17. On the pretext of.
18. Succession to the empire.
19. From Ar. *kafir*, pl. *kofra*, 'an infidel, an unbeliever in Islam' (*Hobson-Jobson*, pp. 140-42).
20. Ar. *Rafzi*.
21. Country's (*della Patria*).
22. For the rest of his days.
23. Rival brothers.
24. Very rich.
25. Shahbaz (Manucci's Xaabas), an able officer of the rank of 5000. He reduced Surat on his master's behalf and warned him against the designs of Aurangzeb who had the faithful eunuch strangled. (Manucci, Vol. I, pp. 249, 252, 303).
26. This is a mistake. Shuja after taking Patna advanced towards Benares, but was defeated by Jai Singh and Sulaiman Shukoh near Bahadurpur five miles north-east of Benares, and fled towards Bengal.
27. Sulaiman Shukoh, son of Dara, was born in 1635. Jai Singh and Diler Khan deserted him after his father's defeat at Samugarh and he took refuge with the Raja of Srinagar, Prithvi Singh. Subsequently he was handed over to Aurangzeb who imprisoned him in the fort of Gwalior where he was poisoned.
28. Muhammad Sultan was the eldest son of Aurangzeb; born 1639, died 1676. As to his marriage with the daughter of Abdullah Qutb Shah, see Khafi Khan, Vol. I, pp. 746, 749. He was in charge of Aurangzeb's right-wing in the battle of Samugarh.
29. Mir Jumla, see Thevenot, Pt. III, Bk. II, Ch. VIII, Note 7.
30. Who was still occupied, by order of Shah Jahan, at the siege of Kaliana.
31. Kalyan, an important railway junction in Thana district, Bombay, about 30 miles from Bombay town.
32. Tell him.
33. Daulatabad. See Thevenot, Pt. III, Bk. I, Ch. XLV.
34. Ingenuously.
35. That the father.
36. Muhammad Muazzam surnamed Shah Alam, see *ante*.
37. Having already made.
38. Mir Jumla returned to Aurangabad about 1 January, 1658 and as soon as he entered the chamber of Aurangzeb, he was arrested by collusion on a false charge of 'treason' and all his artillery and property seized in the name of the state. For a discussion of the motives of Aurangzeb and the sham nature of the arrest, see Sarkar, *History of Aurangzib*, Vol. I, pp. 361-362.

39. That you are not the man to take it in jest.
40. In.
41. To.
42. Burhanpur.
43. Should make every endeavour.
44. As he wished.
45. The river at Ujjain, Sipra (*Imp. Gaz.*, XXIII, pp. 14-15). Thornton's *Gazetteer* (1854), Vol. IV, pp. 412-413, gives the position and character of the various crossings, and the width and depth of the stream. The reference is to the battle of Dharmat near Ujjain.
46. 'And' between Kasem and Cham is a printing mistake. The Italian text has Kasem Kan, Muhammad Qasim, surnamed Mutamad Khan in the first instance and then Qasim Khan (*Maasir-ul-Umara*, Vol. III, pp. 95-99).
47. Maharaja Jaswant Singh of Jodhpur, a staunch partisan of Dara who later submitted to Aurangzeb. He held a mansab of 7,000 and died at Jamrud near Peshawar in 1678.
48. Bernier estimates Rajput casualty at 7,400 (p. 39). Isardas's estimate is "24 eminent Rajput chiefs, 2,000 Rajputs of Marwar, and 6,000 troopers and officers of the Imperial service were slain." See Sarkar, *History of Aurangzib*, Vol. II, pp. 25-26 and *n*.
49. Samugarh, a village 8 miles due east of Agra Fort (*Indian Atlas*, Sheet 50 S.E. cited in Sarkar, *History of Aurangzib*, Vol. II, p. 31 *n*). According to the *Alamgirnamah*, (p. 94) cited in Manucci, Vol. I *n*., the battle was fought on the 7th Ramzan (June 8, 1658, N.S.; May 30, O.S.).
50. Ram Singh Rathor of Kishangarh, son of Karmsi, and nephew through his mother of Rana Jagat Singh of Udaipur. (*Maasir-ul-umara*, Vol. II, p. 266). Rutle or Rotella, according to Irvine (*Manucci*, Vol. I, p. 241 *n*), 'must be either a popular form of Rathor, or one of their subdivisions.' Khafi Khan has given a detailed account of the valour displayed by Ram Singh who was shot in the forehead with an arrow by Murad and killed. Also see Bernier, pp. 51-52.
51. With an arrow
52. Issue.
53. Khalilullah Khan, son of Mir Miran, Yazdi. Manucci, (Vol. I, pp. 280-82), and Bernier (pp. 53-54) also refer to his treachery at Samugarh. The contemporary Mughal authorities (cited in Sarkar, *History of Aurangzib*, Vol. II, p. 57 *n*) refute the story that Dara dismounted from his elephant at a time when he had completely defeated Aurangzeb, and maintain that Dara took to his horse when he had absolutely no chance of victory.
54. Treacherously.
55. Might lose heart.
56. Sudden fear.
57. Too quickly from his.
58. Great victories.
59. Send his consolation.
60. The garden of Nur-Manzil or Dhara, outside Agra city (Sarkar, *History of Aurangzib*, Vol. II, p. 70).
61. For the rest.
62. On the pretence of wishing to speak to Shah Jahan on his behalf.
63. His eunuch.
64. Not Akbar Khan, but I'tibar Khan (Manucci's Atbarcan) see Manucci, Vol. I, p. 296. Bernier says, "He immediately appointed his eunuch *Etbarkan* governor of the fortress" (p. 64). As Careri was familiar with Bernier's *Travels*, Ekbar in the Italian text is very likely a printing mistake for Etbar.
65. Without permission.
66. Shaista Khan.
67. This account is probably borrowed from Bernier (p. 66).
68. Mathura or Muttra on the right bank of the Jumna, about 30 miles from Agra.

69. Concealed evil designs.
70. At least for that day.
71. His (Aurangzeb's) honeyed words.
72. The Shiraz wine so called from the town in Persia.
73. Sayyid Mir entitled Amir Khan, brother of Shaikh Mir, and son of Mir Muhammad Khan Khwafi (*Maasir-ul-umara*, Vol. II, pp. 476, 668). Also see Bernier, p. 67.
74. Desired.
75. *Jamdhar* from Sans. *Yama*, 'death and *dhāra* 'a sharp edge'. It was a short, broad dagger. (*Ain-i-Akbari*, Vol. I, p. 110; Irvine, *The Army of the Indian Moguls*, p. 86). Egerton, *An Illustrated Handbook of Indian Arms* supplies useful information regarding eastern arms.
76. Succeeded in pacifying them.
77. 'Amari, 'a covered-in-howdah or litter'.
78. Salimgarh or Nurgarh fort, at the north end of the Delhi Fort (*Lal Qila*) built by Salim Shah in 1546. During Aurangzeb's reign it served the purpose of a state prison. (Carr Stephen, *Archaeology of Delhi*, pp. 195-6; *List of Muhammadan and Hindu Monuments in Delhi Province*, Vol. II, p. 300).
79. Came in conflict.
80. Prince Muhammad Sultan deserted to Shuja in June 1659. In February next year he left his uncle and returned to Mir Jumla's camp where he was put under arrest, and sent to Gwalior. Subsequently he was transferred to Salimgarh and poisoned (Sarkar, *History of Aurangzib*, Vol. II, p. 275; Bernier, pp. 82-83; Manucci, Vol. I, pp. 337-338, Vol. II, pp. 194-195).
81. Careri simply repeats Bernier's account here. The prince was warmly received by Shuja, married one of his daughters and became his chief commander. (Sarkar, *History of Aurangzib*, Vol. II, p. 261).
82. He wished to be treated.
83. Almost of.
84. Ajmer. The battle between Dara and Aurangzeb was fought at Dorai about 3 miles south of Ajmer (12th-14th March, 1659).
85. Jaswant Singh had not originally acted as an instrument of Aurangzeb as Careri suggests. He sincerely wanted to fight for Dara when he invited the prince in February 1659 to come to Ajmer but was later won over to Aurangzeb's side by Jai Singh. The result was the disastrous defeat of Dara in the battle of Dorai.
86. "35 days" in the Italian text.
87. 'Hand' is a misprint for 'land'. The Italian text is as follows: "fra le Terre dia molti Ragia, amici di Gessem."
88. Fight him anyhow. Dara fought Aurangzeb's army at Dorai pass and not Jaswant Singh who was at Jodhpur at the time.
89. Badi-uz-zaman, called Mirza Dakhini, governor of Ahmadabad. Careri following Bernier wrongly accuses Shah Nawaz Khan of treachery. It is said that Dara himself suspected Shah Nawaz's good faith probably because the old man was Aurangzeb's father-in-law and this suspicion was shared by some Indian chroniclers as well. But Shah Nawaz's death at Dorai in defence of a hopeless cause should set all such suspicions at rest. Manucci says that "he did, as a fact, lose his life for love of Dara" (Vol. I, p. 325) and was killed at Aurangzeb's orders (Vol. I, p. 344). Indeed he had willingly surrendered Ahmadabad to Dara when he could easily repulse the prince's insignificant force.
90. This statement is also based on Bernier, pp. 87-88.
91. Kolis, see Thevenot, Part III, Book I, Chap. IV. Bernier calls them "the greatest robbers, and altogether the most unprincipled people in the *Indies*" (pp. 88-89).
92. Malik Jiwan, son of Ayub, the chief of the Barozai Afghans. He was rewarded with the title of Bakhtyar Khan for his treachery. Manucci says, "Dara had three times rescued this man from death." (Vol. I, p. 347).
93. Sipihr Shukoh, son of Dara.

94. The island fortress of Bhakkar (now in Sukkur district) under the jurisdiction of Tatta in Sind.
95. Mirbaba or Bahadur Khan, the foster-brother of Aurangzeb.
96. Suspecting worse.
97. Hakim Daud, Taqarrub Khan, physician to Shah Jahan (*Maasir-ul-Umara*, Vol. I, p. 490). He came from Persia (Bernier, p. 100).
98. And without religion.
99. Nazar Beg Chelah. Manucci says that he was "one of King Shahjahan's slaves, brought up by him from childhood." Dara had once given him offence by rebuking him for his insolence (Vol. I, p. 358). Nazar Beg himself was later stabbed to death under Aurangzeb's instructions (Manucci, Vol. I, p. 383).
100. Us.
101. For the murder and burial of Dara, see Bernier, p. 102; Manucci, Vol. I, pp. 358-360; Tavernier, Vol. I, p. 283.
102. First washed it with his own hands.
103. Humagon—a misprint in the English translation for 'Humayon' (in the Italian text). Humayun's tomb has long served as a cemetery for the Imperial family. About 120 princes of the house of Timur including poor Dara were buried in its vaults but the exact place where Dara was interred cannot be located.
104. Daughters—a misprint for "daughter", the more accurate translation is—"That night the daughter of the unhappy man was made to enter the seraglio" (Italian text, p. 182).
105. See *ante*.
106. Srinagar in the Garhwal District of U. P. The ruler was Raja Prithvi Singh who treated Sulaiman Shukoh with all kindness and attention. For the intrigues of Aurangzeb and capture of Sulaiman, see Sarkar, *History of Aurangzib*, Vol. II, pp. 232-234.
106a. Confused with Jai Singh.
107. Medini Singh.
108. Saiyad (Bernier, p. 108). The person executed by Murad was Mir Ali Naqi, Diwan of Gujarat, (Manucci, Vol. I, p. 240 *n* and p. 382).
109. In order to seize his goods.
109a. Murad was executed after a mock trial on the complaint of Ali Naqi's second son.
110. Whose intention.
111. Everywhere, even into the islands.
112. Dacca, former capital of Bengal. See also Thevenot, Part III, Chapter XL, Note 7.
113. Sultan Bang, according to Manucci. Bernier calls him Sultan Banque (p. 109). Irvine suggests that he may be identified with Sultan Buland Akhtar, second son of Shuja whom the Dutch called Bon Sultan and the eldest son of his father. (Manucci, Vol. I, p. 369 *n*).
114. Arakan or Magh. Arakan is the country and the people inhabiting it are known as Maghs.
115. Mokha.
116. *Jalia*, a small trading or fighting craft commonly used by the Arakanese Portuguese in their expeditions to Bengal.
117. The King did not fulfil his promise.
118. Wounded.
119. For the different accounts regarding Sultan Shuja's death, see Bernier, pp. 112-114; Manucci, Vol. I, pp. 374-376, specially footnote 2, and Sarkar, *History of Aurangzib*, Vol. II, pp. 286-288.
120. Identified.
121. And others that he finally fled to Persia.
122. Bernier says that some of Sultan Banque's servants were responsible for this imprudence (p. 114).
123. Through the excessive ambition to rule.

124. The dates are wrong. The war began in 1657 and lasted till 1660. Careri as usual blindly follows Bernier.
125. The chief qazi, *Qazi-ul-quzzat*. The account of the resistance of the qazi is in line with Tavernier's account (Vol. I, p. 284), though not confirmed by other sources.
126. It was necessary to depose him.
127. Benefit.
128. Aurangzeb ascended the throne on 21 July, 1658 according to Sarkar but the coronation festival, *Jashan*, took place for the first time on 24 Ramazan, 1069 H. (15 June, 1659).
129. The celebrated Peacock-Throne of Shah Jahan. Careri wrongly attributes its construction to Tamerlane.
130. Seated himself on the richest and most superb throne that ever was seen in the world on account of the vast number of precious stones that adorned it.
131 Shahjahanabad or Delhi.
132. Tavernier also says, "From the moment that Aurangzeb took possession of the throne, he would eat neither wheaten bread, flesh, nor fish. He sustained himself with barley bread, vegetables, and sweetmeats, and would not drink any strong liquor" (Vol. I, p. 296). On the puritanical habits of Aurangzeb, see Sarkar, *History of Aurangzib*, Vol. III, pp. 84 ff; Manucci, Vol. II, p. 332.
133. Foremost.
134. Throne.
135. The Persian envoy Budaq Beg presented himself at the court on 2 June, 1661 (*Maasir-i-Alamgiri*, p. 35). Bernier gives the alleged purport of the letter, (p. 149) and Careri reproduces it here. Manucci also states that some people believed that the Persian monarch had reproved Aurangzeb for his misdeeds. (Vol. II, p. 52). See Manucci, Vol. II, pp. 47-54, Sarkar, *History of Aurangzib*, Vol. III, pp. 105 ff.
136. Laughing at him.
137. Alamgir. The Emperor's full title was—Abul Muzaffar Muhiuddin Muhammad Aurangzeb Bahadur Alamgir Padishah Ghazi. Alamgir literally means 'conqueror of the world'.
138. Concluded by challenging him.
139. Shah Jahan died, according to Sarkar, on 22 January, 1666 (*History of Aurangzib*, Vol. III, p. 140). Irvine in a footnote gives another date, February 1, 1666 (Manucci, Vol. II, p. 125 *note*). The discrepancy is accounted for by the difference between old and new calenders.
140. To him.
141. The originator of this scandal seems to have been the gossiping Bernier (p. 11) whom other travellers willingly copied. Manucci observes—"this has given occasion to Monsieur Bernier to write many things about the princess, founded entirely on the talk of low people" Vol. I, p. 217.
142. Adorned.
143. Where she died.
144. She died in 1681. The story of poison is baseless. The princess was buried in the *dargah* of Hazrat Nizamuddin near Humayun's tomb, Delhi.
145. If we now like to glance back at times past, and into the life of Shah Jahan.
146. Prince Dawar Baksh, son of Khusrau, surnamed 'Bulaqi' See Thevenot, Pt. III, Bk. I, Ch. III, Note 20.
147. Sultan Khusrau rebelled against his father five months after the latter's accession to the throne.
148. Designing one day.
149. Eldest son.
150. Prince Khurram, afterwards Emperor Shah Jahan. He was not the second but the third son of Jahangir, the second being Prince Parwiz, who died in 1626.
151. From the throne.
152. Awaiting.
153. Live the rest of his days.

154. Make away with him.
155 For details regarding Khusrau's death, see Beni Prasad, *History of Jahangir*, pp. 330-31 and note.
156. With a great number of soldiers.
157. Old age.
158. Asaf Khan, brother of Nur Jahan and father-in-law of Shah Jahan. Careri's account is very inaccurate here. Khurram was chased from province to province by his father's generals. Nur Jahan tried to secure the throne for the Emperor's youngest son and her son-in-law, the do-nothing Shahriyar and Asaf Khan proclaimed Bulaqi as emperor in furtherance of the interests of his own son-in-law Khurram then absent from Hindustan.
159. And on the contrary.
160. Crown.
161. But did not settle him (Bulaqi) on the throne.
162. The event occurred on 28 October 1627 (Beni Prasad, p. 423).
163. Art.
164. A fanciful story which Careri might have heard from some of his imaginative acquaintances. Jahangir was buried at Shahdara near Lahore. A very similar story of Shah Jahan's feigned death is told by Peter Mundy (Vol. II, p. 213).
165. At least two leagues.
166. As if.
167. Which was easy for him.
168. Leading the life of a fakir.
169. Bulaqi was put to death by Shah Jahan in January, 1628 and the person going by that name in Persia must have been an impostor. But more than one European traveller believed in the story of Bulaqi's escape to Persia. Mandelslo claims to have met Polagi (Bulaqi) at Qazvin (p. 256). Peter Mundy was more correctly informed but he shared the belief common among the travellers that Jahangir had nominated Bulaqi or Dawar Baksh his heir. (Vol. II, pp. 107, 206). Manucci also asserts that Bulaqi found his way to Persia and died there (Vol. I, p. 181). Tavernier (Vol. I, p. 272) says "I had an opportunity of conversing with him during my travels in Persia, and drank and ate with him." It is quite conceivable that the Shah entertained a pretender for political reasons.
170. Shah Safi or Safavi II (1629-42), ruler of Persia.
171. Notorious.
172. Conquering in order to reign.

CHAPTER IV

1. In no Indian language is the word used in this sense. The Marathas however referred to the Mughals as the *tambra* or red (fair) in contradistinction to the Abyssynians who were styled as the *Skamal*—black or dark.
2. Arakan, Tipperah and Assam.
3. Lands.
4. The Himalayas are probably meant.
5. Chughtai, so named after a son of Chingiz Khan.
6. Bhutan.
7. Kandahar.
8. To lay.
9. Great.
9a. The extent of Timur's empire is highly exaggerated. Though the Saiyad Kings pretended to rule on behalf of Timur, India never formed an integral part of his empire and he certainly did not carry his arms as far as Poland though he defeated the Ottoman ruler of Constantinople.
10. Clever.
11. Sultan Bayazid I, (1389-1403). His army was defeated by Timur near Angora, and he himself was taken prisoner (21 July, 1402). Lane-Poole, *Muhammadan Dynasties*, pp. 185, 266. Bernier also repeats the conversation (pp. 167-68).

12. Chingiz Khan, the great Khakan of the Mongols. Timur however did not belong to Chingiz's family. He was a Berlas Turk.
13. Miran Shah who survived Timur, his father, only three years.
14. Sultan Muhammad Mirza, son of Miran Shah. See Table in *Ain*, Vol. I.
15. Mahomet was succeeded by Mirza Sultan Absuid.
16. Sultan Abu Said Mirza, grandson of Miran Shah. He allied himself with the Uzbegs, seized Bokhara and entered Khorasan. He was eventually taken prisoner by Uzun Hasan and killed in 1469.
17. Sultan Omar Shaikh, father of Babar. Omar Shaikh held the small principality of Farghana. Timur's vast empire had already been divided among his numerous descendants.
18. The next ruler.
19. Babar, Zahiruddin Muhammad, who was defeated by Shaibani Khan in 1504. He died in 1530 and not in 1532 as wrongly stated by Careri. Babar in Turki means 'a lion' and not 'bold'. He did not succeed in recovering his ancestral territories as Careri suggests later.
20. Shaibani Khan, the Uzbeg leader.
21. Sher Khan or Sher Shah. He was not a general of Humayun although he had served for a while in Babar's army.
22. Bairam Khan, son of Saif Ali Beg. He was born at Badakshan and entered Humayun's army at the age of 16. The conquest of India may justly be ascribed to him. In 1556, he was appointed *ataliq* (guardian) of Akbar, and later received the title of *Khan Baba.* For details of his life, see *Ain*, Vol. I, pp. 315-317.
23. Humayun died in 1556, and not in 1552.
24. Jalal-ud-din Muhammad Akbar.
25. Jahangir Padishah.
26. The sons of Jahangir were Khusrau, Parwiz, Khurram and Shahriyar. Daniyal was a son of Akbar and brother of Jahangir. Khusrau and Parwiz had predeceased their father; only Khurram and Shahriyar were alive at the time of Jahangir's death.
27. Abul Muzaffar Shihabuddin Muhammad. He obtained the title "Shah Jahan" (King of the World) in 1617 during his father's lifetime.
28. For the daily life of the Mughal Emperors from Akbar onwards, see Ibn Hasan, *The Central Structure of the Mughal Empire*, pp. 65 ff. The *Ain* (Vol. I, passim) gives minute details of Akbar's daily life, and this served as a model for his successors. Details about the daily life of Shah Jahan and Aurangzeb are available in Sarkar, *Studies in Mughal India*, pp. 1-15 and 64-71.
29. He took some food.
30. Necromancy.
31. Aloof.
32. Needs.
33. To whom appeal could be made from the ministers.
34. Did not penetrate beyond the outside.
35. The emperor was venerated as *Zinda Pir* or living saint by his Muslim subjects.
36. Concubines.
37. In this connection it is reported.
38. Indicated.
39. Customary with.
40. Are expected to bathe.
41. A similar story is described by Moll (*India*, p. 214).
42. Omit "and thousands".
43. Salutary.
44. Bound with.
45. Three other chairs.
46. Poisoned by a eunuch one day.
47. And doubting whether he was really dead.

48. Shah Alam was imprisoned with his sons in 1687 after the alleged discovery of his correspondence with the King of Golkonda. He was formally released, according to Sarkar, *History of Aurangzib*, (Vol. III, p. 47) on 9 May, 1695. Careri arrived at Gagala on 17 March, 1695 and waited on the Emperor on Monday the 21st. The day previous he had seen Shah Alam returning from his father's quarters. His release therefore must be dated earlier than the third week of March.
49. The King of Bijapur was not a kinsman of Azam Shah. The mistake has probably arisen from the fact that Azam was proud of his descent from the royal blood of Persia through his mother, and the ruler of Bijapur was a Shia like the Persian Kings. No reference to Azam's being in league with Bijapur is traceable. He never rebelled against his father. According to Ishwardas (cited in Sarkar, *History of Aurangzib*, Vol. III, p. 51) "in 1683 he strongly resented a false suspicion of the Emperor that he was forming a disloyal intrigue with Dilir Khan, and the Emperor had to soothe his injured feelings."
50. Before the latter was taken prisoner and lost his Kingdom.
51. This is a mistake. Muhammad Azam was born in 1653. Azam was only 42 when Careri came to Galgala.
52. Sultan Akbar, the fourth son of Aurangzeb, was born in 1657. In March 1695, he was only 38 years old. He died an exile in Persia either in 1706 or in 1704. See Irvine, *The Later Mughals*, Vol. I, p. 1 and *n*.
53. The identification of this name is not clear. Is it Sonoegi of Manucci (Vol. II, p. 244) and Tod's 'Soning'? If so, he, along with Durga Das, was the leader of the Rajput forces. The name is spelt 'Sonig' in the *Maasir-ul-Umara* Vol. II, p. 873). Ojha (*History of Mewar*, Vol. II, pp. 556-57) identifies him with Soning, son of Vithaldas Champavata.
54. "Ragiaputi" in the original, Rajputs.
55. Planned.
56. Shambhaji, King of the Marathas. Akbar reached his court in 1681 but Careri makes an error when he says that he had 4,000 followers. The escort consisted of 500 Rathor horse. (Sarkar, *History of Aurangzib*, Vol. III, p. 367).
57. Kingling or chieftain. "Regolo" in the original means a ruler.
58. The enemy.
59. Shahu was not with his father Shambhaji when he was taken by surprise at Shangameshwar and he was too young at the time to participate in the war.
60. Violent storm.
61. Shah Sulaiman Safawi (1667-1694).
62. Part II, Book I, Ch. VII, p. 141.
63. Made several efforts.
64. Machination.
65. Gingee, the famous fortress in South Arcot District, Madras. Shivaji got possession of Gingee in 1677. The Mughal siege of this famous fortress lasted for eight years from 1690 to 1698 and was conducted by Zulfiqar Khan. Although the fort ultimately capitulated Zulfiqar Khan failed in his main objective—the capture of Chhatrapati Rajaram.
66. Kam Baksh, the fifth and youngest son of Aurangzeb, was born in 1667. He was slain in the war of succession near Hyderabad on 3 January, 1709. (Sarkar, *History of Aurangzib*, Vol. I, p. 72).

CHAPTER V

1. Requisite orders.
2. Bakhshi or pay-master. Manucci calls him "the commissary-general of the cavalry" (Vol. IV, p. 408). Towards the close of Aurangzeb's reign there were four bakshis, the chief of them being styled as mir bakhshi. A detailed account of their duties is available in Irvine, *The Army of the Indian Moghuls*, pp. 37 ff; Ibn Ḥasan, pp. 213 ff.

3. Mir'adl is meant. This office was peculiar to India and was not known in Turkey, Persia or Egypt. According to Abul Fazl, the actual appointment of that officer was conditional on the qazi being unable to carry on the whole work. It was not a regular appointment, and the only instance of a mir'adl has been mentioned by Badaoni. (Saran, *Prov. Govt. of the Moghuls*, p. 347).
4. An account of whether ministers behave themselves well or ill.
5. Diwan. For the functions of this officer see Ibn Hasan, pp. 147 ff.
6. A misprint for "Giaghir" in the Italian text.
7. Excessive.
8. *Khan-i-saman* or *Mir Saman*, high Steward. His duties are not mentioned nor his power defined in the *Ain*. Manucci writes, "He has charge of the whole expenditure of the royal household in reference to both great and small things" (Vol. II, p. 419). See Ibn Hasan, *op. cit.*, pp. 237 ff; Sarkar, *Mughal Administration*, pp. 48 ff.
9. He is a kind of Treasurer General.
10. Diwan-i-khas, Hall of Private Audience.
11. *Ghusal Khan*, 'Private Chamber'. "Between the Divan Khan and the female residences there was an apartment in which Akbar used to take his bath, after which a few trusted persons were admitted to see him. Later on, the divan and bakhshi were admitted for state business, and gradually certain nobles of the court were also allowed in. Thus state business came to be transacted there, and the chamber, by its proximity to the bathroom, came to be known as the *Ghusal Khana* (or bathroom)." Ibn Hasan, *op. cit.*, pp. 77 ff. Under Shah Jahan this was named *Daulat Khana-i-Khas*.
12. A court of justice from "adl', 'doing justice'.
13. This is highly exaggerated. The share of the State (land-revenue) was one-third.
14. The cruellest.

CHAPTER VI

1. Very fruitful.
1a. For a contemporary account of the province and its products see Bernier, pp. 437-46.
2. Craftsmen.
3. Remains.
4. Smyrna (Ismir), in Asia Minor.
5. Yemen. See Bernier, p. 202. "Turkey cannot dispense with the coffee, which she received from *Yemen*, or Arabia Felix."
6. They send.
7. Mocha or Mokha in Arabia.
8. Bab-el-Mandeb (Arab for "The Gate of Tears", the strait between Arabia and Africa which connects the Red Sea with the Indian Ocean. For the origin of the name, see *Encyc. Brit.*, Vol. III, p. 91.
9. Achin in the northern extremity of the island of Sumatra.
10. To India.
11. Eighty-two crores.
12. Various estimates have been given of the revenues of the Mughals towards the close of the 17th century. According to *Khulasat-ut-Tawarikh*, in 1695 the total revenue was a little over 20 crores. This is an underestimate as the revenues of only 17 subahs were taken into account. Manucci's estimate of about 38 Crores (1697) is probably nearer the true figure although he omitted the revenues of Bengal. See Sarkar, *India of Aurangzib*, p. xxxii.
13. Threvenot (See Part III, Book I, Chap. III).
14. De Laet. For the wealth of the Mughals, see pp. 107-12.
15. Pyrard heard that the Mughal could put into the field 30,000 elephants, 80,000 horse and 200,000 foot (Vol. II, Pt. I, p. 251). The foreign travellers

were prepared to accept any estimate of the Emperor's wealth and military strength.

CHAPTER VII

1. For the various kinds of swords and other offensive weapons used by the Mughals, see Irvine, *Army of the Indian Moghuls*, pp. 74 ff.
2. Curved.
3. See Irvine, *op. cit.*, pp. 62 ff.
4. Helmets.
5. With the obligation to maintain.
6. From *hazar*, 'one thousand'. It applied to a mansabdar of 1000 who was an officer of high rank. The word, according to Irvine (*op. cit.*), was also applied to "an officer of artillery, generally of garrison artillery" (p. 157).
7. Cuhzariis, probably a misprint for Du hazari (commander of two thousand); Panges, *Panj hazari* (commander of five thousand); Hechets, *hasht-hazari* (commander of eight thousand); Deh-Hazariis, *Dah-hazari* (commander of ten thousand); Duazdehazariis, *Dawazdah hazari* (commander of twelve thousand). In Akbar's time, Prince Salim was a mansabdar of 10,000, which was the highest mansab (*Ain*, Vol. I, p. 308).
8. "The salutation, called *taslim*, consists in placing the back of the right hand on the ground, and then raising it gently till the person stands erect, when he puts the palm of his hand upon the crown of his head, which pleasing manner of saluting signifies that he is ready to give himself as an offering." "Upon taking leave, or presentation, or upon receiving a *mansab*, a *jagir* or a dress of honour, or an elephant, or a horse, the rule is to make three *taslims*; but only one on all other occasions, when salaries are paid, or presents are made." (*Ain*, Vol. I, p. 158).
9. Horsemen.
10. Which is called *mansab*.
11. Careri has apparently no clear idea about the *mansabdari* system. He did not know that there were no less than sixty six different grades of mansabs in Akbar's time the lowest being that of 10 horses. Mânsabdars of superior grades were known as omrahs—the honorific plural of amir.
12. Bernier (p. 215) writes, "*Rouzindars* are also cavaliers, who receive their pay daily, as the word imports; but their pay is greater, in some instances, than that of many of the *mansebdars*."
13. Horsemen.
14. *Do-aspa* cavalry.
15. Cost.
16. Attached.
17. Shutarnal or camel swivel.
18. Like swivel-guns on our barques.
19. Bronze.
20. Led close by.
21. The light artillery always accompanies him.
22. Bernier says that their pay was limited to thirty-two rupees (p. 217).
23. The ruler of Chittor had a militia of 22,000 horse and 82,000 foot. (P. Saran, p. 266).
24. Machinations.
25. Doubtless Bernier's *Augans* or Afghans.
26. Of whatever kind.
27. Income.
28. Punctually.
29. Are short of pay.
30. More than 300,000 etc.
31. Were stationed.

32. Comprised.
33. Consisted of.
34. Panhala, historic hill-fort in Kolhapur State, Bombay (*Imp. Gaz.*, Vol. XIX, pp. 396-397). Bidar Bakht, the eldest son of Azam Shah, attacked the place in 1695. (Sarkar, *History of Aurangzib,* Vol. V, p. 37).
35. For Manucci's estimate of the strength of the army about the emperor's person see Vol. II, p. 422.

CHAPTER VIII

1. Sans. *varshagrantha*, the birth-day anniversary, from *varsha* 'year' and *grantha* 'knot'.
2. Hind. *Tol,* weight, 'custom of weighing'. See Thevenot, Pt. III, Bk. I, Chap. XXVI.
   Aurangzeb discontinued the custom of distributing his weight in money.
3. And those people are accustomed every year to make a knot in a cord which they etc.
4. Scented waters.
5. This room was quite filled with mirrors.
6. Beyond all belief.
7. Symmetrical and enriched etc.
8. For a description of the Peacock-throne see Tavernier, Vol. I, pp. 303-305.
9. Fable.
10. Aurangzeb as a puritan discouraged and discontinued practices of non-Islamic origin but it is not correct to say that none of his predecessors had ever weighed themselves. Both Roe and Hawkins refer to this custom. In fact Roe witnessed the ceremony. "September 1—was the kings birth-day and the solemnitie of his weighing to which I went" (p. 378). Terry was also with Roe and gives a description of the scene (cited in f.n. p. 378 of Roe's *Embassy,* ed. Foster). Also see Hawkins, p. 440. Careri wrongly describes the birth-day and weighing as two different festivals. The latter forms part of the former. The other festival was that of Nawroz or New year's day.
11. Hunchbacked.
12. More like woods.
13. This is the general complaint of contemporary European travellers who visited India.
14. Well-to-do.
15. *Haji,* a pilgrim to Mecca; from *hajj,* the pilgrimage, to Mecca made in the 12th month of the Muhammadan year. See Hughes, *A Dictionary of Islam,* pp. 155-159.
16. For which they make.
17. Waterfowl.
18. Rajputs.
19. Avicenna (Abu Ali al-Husain ibn Abdullah ibn Sina), Arabian philosopher and scientist (980 A.D.—1037 A.D.). His European reputation is based mainly on his *Canon of Medicine.*
20. Use.
21. Add "caresses" after "allurements".
22. Clash together. The instrument seems to be *karatals* or cymbals.
23. A misprint for *Cira* or turban.
24. Arab. Zafaran, saffron. The true saffron (*Crocus Sativus*) is cultivated in Kashmir only. *Haldi* or turmeric is known as country saffron.
25. The reference is to *saptapadi* or seven steps.
26. Born.
27. Food.

27a. Methwold also makes a similar statement: "They come into the world without much trouble to their mothers; for they are up againe about their business in three or foure days, some the same day." (*Relations of Golconda,* p. 26).

28. Go to wash.
29. Walk.
30. Almost as soon as they are born.
31. Nayar, see Thevenot, Part III, Book II, Chap. I.
32. If she wishes to be.
33. Is borne sitting, with drums beating, followed by a long train of kindred and friends.
34. Who has been meanwhile etc.
35. Scented oil.
36. With earth.
37. Have.
38. From their caste.
39. For Mughal efforts to suppress *sati,* see *ante,* p. 363, Note 39.
40. Read "Certainly" after 'Mogul'.
41. To their utmost power.
42. This Command.
43. Practised.
44. Noted.

CHAPTER IX

1. Hurricanes called typhoons, six (*sic.*) months from the South and as many from the North.
2. Moving.
3. Except for.
4. A tiny cloud.
5. Read "For the rest", before "Indostan".
6. And vegetables.
7. Press.
8. Simples=Medicinal herbs.
9. Kollur. See Thevenot, Part III, Book II, Chap. IX. Careri's account is obviously based on that of Tavernier.
10. See Tavernier, Vol. II, p. 58.
11. Discovering. Tavernier (Vol. II, pp. 59-61) gives the same method of digging. See also *Relations of Golconda,* pp. 30 ff.
12. Sifting it anew.
13. See Bowrey, *Countries Round the Bay of Bengal,* p. 112; Ovington, p. 121; and *Relations of Golconda,* p. 32.
14. Rammalakota, about 20 miles south of Karnul (Kurnool), the identification of which was a matter of dispute for many years. According to Ball, its "position is fairly indicated on the small map of India which accompanies the Revised French edition of Tavernier's Travels, published at Rouen in 1713." (Tavernier, Vol. II, p. 43 *n* 2).
15. Sukadana, a port of the island of Borneo. The principal port for export of diamonds is now Pontianak. Ovington (p. 121) says that Borneo diamonds were much superior to those of India.
16. More accurately cheetah, *Acinonyx Jubatus.*
17. With the rope.
18. Apparently Careri never saw the animal for even the largest ox cannot approach it in bulk and size. Finn writes of *Rhinoceros unicornis* "The largest of our rhinoceroses and the fourth largest land mammal, the other three being the African and Indian elephants and the African square-lipped or white Rhinoceros." (Finn, *Sterndale's Mammalia of India,* pp. 186-187). *Rhinoceros Sumatransis* which is confined only in a distant corner of the country is much smaller and is about 4 ft. 6 in. at the shoulder (Finn, p. 189). Terry also makes a similar statement (Terry in Foster, p. 304).

19. Sanderson mentions the following: Driving into *Kheddahs* or enclosures, hunting with trained females, pitfalls and noosing from trained elephants' backs (*Thirteen years among the Wild Beasts of India*, p. 70). Careri mentions only hunting with trained females and pitfalls.
20. A female animal, bound.
21. Sanderson definitely states that "the period of heat is not marked by any particular signs in the female. . . . . . In approaching a male elephant, a female desirous of his attentions utters certain sounds, and courts his society; but only those conversant with elephants would notice this." (Sanderson, *op. cit.*, p. 94).
22. The habit of.
23. Sanderson roundly contradicts this notion. He says—"I have myself, on four different occasions, witnessed the act—once by two animals belonging to a wild herd in the jungles; on the others, by animals which had just been caught, and which were at large within the Kheddah enclosures. On each, the female elephant stood to receive the male in the manner common to all quadrupeds" pp. 94-95.
24. According to Sanderson the operation needs a party of four or five steady females, ridden by their mahouts, and not one female elephant in lust, pp. 73-74.
25. To domesticate him.
26. Keeper.
27. Even its keeper.
28. The period of gestation is not definitely known. It varies according to Sanderson's information from 18 to 22 months according to the sex of the calf (p. 59). Abul Fazl says that the period of gestation is generally eighteen lunar months. In a recent case, well authenticated, the period was about 21½ months, the calf being female. "The period of gestation in this case is about 21 months and 18 days. In the case of a male calf reported by Corse (*Tr. Roy. Soc.* 1799) it was 20 months and 18 days." (A. Aiyappan, *Journal of the Bombay Natural History Society*, Vol. 46, No. I, April 1946, p. 182).

28a. "The general opinion of experienced natives is that it attains 120 years in exceptional cases, but more generally to about 80 years. . . . . . My own opinion is that the elephant attains at least to 150 years." Sanderson, p. 56.

29. Sanderson says, "Half a ton is a good load for an elephant for continuous marching", p. 87. He does not consider the elephant satisfactory "as a beast of burden".
30. Linschoten makes a similar statement. "In the Island of Seylon there are also great numbers, which are esteemed the best and sensiblest of all the worlde, for wheresoever they meet with any other Elephantes (the Indians report for a truth, that they have tryed it) those Elephants of other Countries do reverence and honour to the Elephants of Seylon" (Vol. II, p. 2).
31. Their maintenance is very expensive.

31a. Normally elephants are herbivorous. If the *Ain* is to be relied on, no meat was served to elephants in the imperial stables.

32. Butter, green sugarcane.
33. Very many.
34. Musk-deer, see also Thevenot, Pt. III, Bk. I, Chap. XXIX, Note 1. It is not found in Rajputana, nor does the beast survive the removal of the musk pod.
35. Afterwards.
36. Almost all.
37. Seems to be male Baya or weaver bird during the breeding season.
38. Of good flavour. Also see Thevenot for this black-boned chicken (Pt. III, Bk. I, Ch. XXIX, Note 3).
39. On one side.
40. *Paisas.* The value varied between 46 and 56 to a rupee during the 17th century. Thevenot, however, makes the rupee equivalent to 32½-33½ *paisas.* (Pt. III, Bk. I, Ch. IX, Note 16).

41. For the different meanings of the term see Thevenot, Pt. III, Bk. I, Ch. IV, Note 20. "The pagoda is an original Hindu coin, called *Varaha,* from the symbol on it of the varaha or boar, one of the incarnations of Vishnu, which formed the crest of the Chalukyas and of the Vijayanagar Kings." (Rice, *Mysore,* Vol. I, p. 801). Ball (Tavernier, Vol, I, p. 329) writes "Pagoda, new=3½ rupees; old=4½ rupees." In 1818 it was reckoned as equivalent to 3½ rupees. (*Hobson-Jobson,* p. 653). Manucci (Vol. IV, pp. 132-133) says that 150 pagodas was equal to 520 rupees, thus making a pagoda worth nearly 3½ rupees. Careri makes it worth a sequin which according to Sir Isaac Newton was worth 9s. 5·7d., and according to Yule, 9s. 3d. Since a rupee was equal to 2s. 3d., the pagoda of Careri would be equivalent to a little more than 4 rupees.
42. A Spanish coin worth 16s. 9d. according to Sir Isaac Newton.
43. Profit.
44. A Persian silver coin the exchange value of which fluctuated from 16 to 18 pence when Careri wrote. See Sen, *Administrative System of the Marathas,* pp. 125-126; Thevenot, Part III, Book I, Chap. I, Note 14.
45. Arab. This is equal to 100 crores, not ten.
46. Hind. *Man,* Maund. See Thevenot, Pt. III, Book I, Chap. IX.
47. Seers (*ibid*).
48. From time to time.

BOOK III

CHAPTER I

1. With free exercise of their religion.
2. The Mughals were Chagatai Turks. By Turkish sect Careri probably means *sunni* as opposed to the Persians who are mostly *shias.*
3. Most of the European travellers who wrote about India believed that the Hindu theory of transmigration of souls was borrowed from Pythogoras.
4. The identity is not clear. The most famous Hindu law-giver is Manu.
5. Animals.
6. Different sects.
7. Thevenot (Part III, Book I, Chap. XXXVIII) also mentions that the castes and tribes of the Indians "are reckoned in all to be fourscore and four in number."
8. Unless.
9. Vegetables.
10. The Maratha or Maharashtra Brahmans are meant. The three main subdivisions of the caste are, the Konkanastha, the Desastha and the Saraswata (*Census of India,* 1931, Vol. I, Part III Ethnographical, p. xxix). For a list of the Maratha Brahmans, see Wilson, *Indian Caste,* Vol. II, pp. 18-50.
11. Brahmans of Telingana or the districts inhabited by the Telegu-speaking people. They have eight main sub-divisions, among whom however neither inter-dining nor inter-marriage is permissible (Sherring, *Hindu Tribes and Castes,* Vol. I, pp. 91-92).
12. Kanarese Brahmans. (Sherring, Vol. I, pp. 95-97).
13. Dravida. Maharastra, Tailanga, Dravida, Karnata and Gurjara are grouped as pancha Dravida or the five branches of the Dravida Brahman caste. See Sherring, Vol. I, pp. 27 ff.
14. Gujaratis. The two main sections are the Audichya or the Northerners, and the Nagars. See *Census of India,* 1931, pp. xxvi-xxvii.
15. Gaud Brahmans who like the Dravidas have five main sections collectively known as Pancha Gaudas. (1) Kanyakubja or Kanaujiya, (2) Saraswata, (3) Gaud, (4) Maithila and (5) Utkala. (Sherring, Vol. I, pp. 19 ff.).

16. Kanaujiya or Kanyakubja Brahmans of the United Provinces. A well-known proverb *Tin Kanauji terah chulha* (Three Kanaujias require thirteen kitchens) refers to their exclusiveness. Risley, *The People of India,* p. 159.
17. Trihuti. See Brahmans of Goa who claim to be Gauda Saraswata, but are contemptuously called Shenwis on account of their fish-eating habit by other Brahmans of Maharashtra, believe that their ancestors migrated from Trihut or Mithila with the image of their patron deity Shanta Durga.
18. A misprint for *Gayavali* in the original, Gayali or Brahmans of Gaya.
19. Probably Gangaputra.
20. Hindus are not permitted to marry a *sapinda,* one entitled to pinda i.e. any person of seven generations in direct line of ascent or descent. Svagotra marriage or marriage within the same sept is also prohibited among the Brahmans and other high castes. See *Yājñavalkya Smṛiti,* Āchāra Adhyāya, *Sacred Books of the Hindus,* Vol. XXI, pp. 94 *et seq.*
21. Cousin marriage is common among the Saraswat Brahmans of Goa with which region Careri was particularly familiar. Other Brahmans hold such matrimony in abhorrence. The Deshasthas and the Konkanasthas—the Maharashtra Brahmans *par excellence,* would not even think of it.
22. Add 'for courage'.
23. Legally no Hindu is bound to observe the rules of monogamy. In practice however the poor people are monogamous for economic reasons.
24. Choutia. The Raja of Ramnagar was styled in the Portuguese records as the King Choutia since he used to receive Chauth. (Sen, *Administrative System of the Marathas,* 114 *n* and *Military System of the Marathas,* Chap. II).
25. Grassias.
26. Mahmudi—a silver coin of Persia. According to Mandelslo (p. 68) it was equivalent to a shilling. Fryer gives its exchange value at somewhat "less than an *English* Shilling." He further adds that "2¼ *Mamoodoes* is reckoned a *Rupee.* Yet to change *Mamoodoes* into *Rupees* there is sometimes given 3." (Vol. II, pp. 125-126). Ball suggests that its exchange value fluctuated from 8*d.* to 1*s.* (Tavernier, Vol. I, p. 330).
27. Formerly a small state ruled by a Rajput chief, now a *taluk* in the Nasik district, Bombay. Careri rightly describes it as full of woods. The town of Peint is about 73 miles from Surat. The state lapsed to the British Government in 1837. *Imp. Gaz.,* XX, pp. 100-101.
28. Prabhus or Chandraseniya Kayastha Prabhus as they prefer to style themselves. As early as Shivaji's time they claimed to be Kshatriyas. The Prabhus distinguished themselves both as men of arms and men of letters. Balaji Avji, Shivaji's Private Secretary, and Baji Prabhu the famous hero both belonged to this caste. In recent times also they have produced many distinguished men of whom Sir Mahadev Chaubal may be mentioned here. The Pathare Prabhus abound near Bassein and are essentially city people. In Maharashtra widows of all non-Brahman castes are entitled to remarry.
29. Meat except beef.
30. One of these tribes. The Pathare and the Chandraseniya Prabhu Kayasthas usually do not inter-marry. The latter are more numerous than the former who number only a few hundred.
31. Sutar or Barhai, carpenters. The two divisions mentioned by the author are Konkani and Gujarati. For proverbs regarding Sutars, see Risley, pp. 135, 316.
32. Kansars or coppersmiths, and workers in copper, brass and other metals.
33. All kinds of meat.
34. Gaulis or Gowalas, milkmen. (Enthoven, *Tribes and Castes of Bombay,* Vol. I, pp. 367 ff).
35. Gardeners who trade mainly in flowers and garlands.

35a. For the Sonars or goldsmiths and their subdivisions see Enthoven, Vol. III, pp. 338-344.

36. Should not be confused with the Vallalars of the Madras Presidency who try to observe the orthodox customs of the Brahmans. Careri probably refers

to the Valar, a section of the Mangs, among whom widow remarriage is common and who "eat all kinds of flesh except pork." See Enthoven, Vol. II, pp. 434-445.

37. Kunbi, Kalambi or Kurmi, the great agricultural caste of India known by various designations in different localities. (See Thevenot, Pt. III, Bk. I, Ch. XXXVIII, Note 29).

37a. Chaudhuris, Patels, Rauts, Naiks etc.

37b. The bridegrooms of some untouchable castes e.g., *mangs* were not permitted to ride a horse. They rode a bullock in their marriage procession. See Sen, *Administrative System of the Marathas*, p. 231.

38. Does Careri mean the *Vaidus* a nomadic tribe of professional medicine men divided into three main section—Jholiwalas (the sound approximates the Doblas), Dadichewalas and Chataiwalas? The Jholiwalas eat deer, jackals, rats and squirrels (Enthoven, Vol. III, pp. 406-410). The Dublas of Broach, Surat and Thana cannot be reasonably identified with the Doblas of Careri as they do not eat such vermin as rats and squirrels and refrain from beef and carrion. Moreover they are peasants and agricultural labourers and cannot be described as "Wizards inhabiting the woods."

39. A misprint for Bats.

40. Crocodiles?

41. Widows.

42. Bhathelas, a subdivision of the Brahman caste who are agriculturists by pursuit found mostly in Surat district and Baroda state. (Enthoven, Vol. I, pp. 225-228).

43. One thread.

44. Bhandaris, toddy-drawers and distillers. They are divided into eight endogamous sections of which the Kitte and Shinde correspond to Careri's *Kitas* and *Shiadas*. "They eat the flesh of Goats, sheep, fowls, hares, deer, wild boars and fish" and drink liquor. Enthoven, Vol. I, pp. 96-104.

45. Tend.

46. Dhobis, washermen.

47. The fishing tribes mentioned here are Kolis or Sonkalis, Gabits otherwise known as Kharuis, Vaitis, "a degraded section of the Sonkalis" inhabiting Thana District and Machhis.

48. Should not be confused with Sarothias of the Thana District. The reference to the two distinct tribes, the one called Salukis, the other Goles, indicate a fishing community. The Solankis and Koli form two of the ten endogamous divisions of the Machhis. Of these the Koli, Dhimar and Kharva inter-dine but "in the Panch Mahals Machhis are divided into two groups, Kharva and Solanki which do not generally intermarry." A *Machhi* widow "may marry a younger brother of her deceased husband" Enthoven, Vol. II, pp. 397-400.

49. A subdivision of the Lamanis or Vanjaris. (Enthoven, Vol. II, p. 341).

50. Bhansalis or Vegas, who are closely connected with the Lohanas and Lavanas. At present they are labourers and cultivaters rather than dealers in salt. Widow remarriage is permitted among them. but they are vegetarians as a rule (Enthoven, Vol. I, p. 113).

51. Crawfish and similar shell fish.

52. Obviously a misprint for Bhatias, an important trading community. Careri wrongly says that they eat nothing but fish. Except in some parts of the Punjab and Sind they are strict vegetarians. Wives still continue to be costly. "The supply of marriageable girls falls much short of the demand, consequently the bridegroom, besides presents to the girl in the shape of ornaments and clothes of the value of Rs. 4,000 to Rs. 5,000, has in some cases to pay the girl's father large sums in the shape of purchase money" (Enthoven, Vol. I, pp. 133-145).

53. A mixed tribe of the Kathis and Ahirs, found mostly in Bahiravad in Kathiawar. Careri wrongly asserts that their widows do not remarry. Widow remarriage is permitted and commonly practised among Babrias (Enthoven, Vol. I, pp. 44-48).

54. Kathis, a fighting tribe of professional marauders. Careri is again wrong about widow remarriage, which they permit and practice (Enthoven, Vol. II, pp. 165-70).
55. Only Rajput widows practise sati and are not permiited to remarry.
56. Not to be confused with Hindi *farash*—a menial. The translator has made an important omission here. The original Italian has in parenthesis *"Alparqueros detti da Portughesi"* or the sandal-makers of the Portuguese. The farashes are not sandal-makers. The caste or castes that go under the general name of Chambhar are probably meant but all these castes do not necessarily inter-dine or inter-marry though some of them may eat carrian. See Enthoven, Vol. I, pp. 260-271.
57. Nayars.
58. Cape Comorin from Sanskrit Kumari Devi, whose temple is situated there.
59. This is the Pulayan caste, also known as Cheruman, one of the lowest in social position in Malabar. Thurston, Vol. II, pp. 45 ff; *Malabar Gaz.*, p. 133. See also Thevenot, Part III, Book II, Chap. I).
60. If they do not wish to be beaten.
61. Compare Thevenot, Pt. III, Bk. II, Ch. I, Note 28. Also see Mandelslo, p. 88.
62. Forced immediately to wash.
63. Whom they are striving to convert.
64. Many.
65. Scrupulous.
66. Animals.
67. Other tribes.
68. By others.
69. Which the penitents are allowed to exercise everywhere.
70. Bairagi or Vairagi.
71. Ravana. Thevenot, Ovington, and Tavernier all support the legend that the fakirs traced their origin to him. (See Thevenot, Book I, Chap. XXXIX, Note 14).

    Careri may be referring here to Raghuvanshi Rama who did wander for many years in the forests as an ascetic; the sect in that case is the one known as Ramayet.
72. Republics or states.

CHAPTER II

1. Hanuman.
2. Ravana, king of Lanka (Ceylon). The story forms the theme of the great Indian Epic, the Ramayana.
3. On which theme.
4. Probably a corruption of Mahalakshmi. The character attributed to her is absurd.

4a. Exactly as if.

5. In the same way.
6. Krishna, one of the ten incarnations of Vishnu. The legend of his having 16,000 wives is to be found in *Bhagavata Purana*.
7. Vaitarani, the river of the Hindu nether world which corresponds to the Styx of Greek mythology, see *Sacred Books of the Hindus,* Vol. IX, Garuda Purana, pp. 11-12.
8. Or Acheron.
9. The reference is probably to Canto XI of the Gita where Srikrishna revealed himself to Arjuna as the supreme deity pervading the entire universe.
10. The four Vedas.
11. They believe.

12. To be more accurate there are seven regions including earth viz., *Bhu, Bhuva, Svar, Mahas, Jana, Tapas* and *Satva*.
13. Hindus believe in a common ancestor Manu from whose name the word *manava* or man is derived. But the story given here is fantastic in the extreme.
14. The Muslims believe in the story of Adam and Eve which they borrowed from the Christian scripture.
15. The sacred thread or Janeu. "The whole cord is tied together by knot called *Brahma-Granthi*, which has three parts, reperesenting Brahma, Vishnu and Siva" (Mrs. Stevenson, p. 32). Pyrard also speaks of "a cord of three strands of cotton which they (Brahmans) wear next the skin" (Vol. I, pp. 372-373). Pietro Della Valle also refers to "a fillet of three braids" but he knew that the distinction of wearing it was not confined to the Brahmans (Vol. I, pp. 88-89). The privilege of wearing the sacred thread is not the monopoly of the Brahmans but is shared by the first three castes.
16. Under.
17. Brahma, Vishnu and Mahesa, the Hindu trinity.
18. Eat any food unless they have it on.
19. Fast sometimes for several days.
20. From.
21. Sanskrit *Bhatta*, a learned Brahman.
22. Tilak.
23. He gives a feast to all the tribe who unitedly receive him again.
24. No great difficulty.
25. Believe that.
26. The Hindus believe that "it is only by holding on to the tail of a cow that the dying man hopes to cross the horrible river of blood and filth, called Vaitarani." "If the dying man has the physical strength, he should take the cow's tail in his hand and present it, together with a *tulasi* leaf, to a Brahman." (Mrs. Stevenson, p. 141).

26a. Provided that.

27. See Thevenot, Part III, Book II, Chap. I, f.n. 31.

27a. See François Pyrard (Vol. I, p. 384), "he leaves his arms or some other signal at the door, and the others will dare not enter until he be gone forth." Also Pietro Della Valle "The Gentile *Nairi* have no peculiar Wives; but all Women are common amongst them; and when any man repairs to visit one of them he leaves his weapon at the door, which sign sufficiently debars all others from entering to disturb him." Mandelslo also refers to this custom (p. 88).

28. Polyandry was once quite common among the Nayars. See Note 27a above. Pyrard observes, "The Nairs may have but one wife at the time; but it is not so with the women; for every woman may have as many as three husbands at once, if she likes" (Vol. I, p. 384).
29. Careri did not visit Bengal and his account of exposure of babies is based entirely on that of Tavernier (Vol. II, pp. 167-168), but whereas Tavernier says that the babies so left are liable to be tormented by the crows, Careri suggests that they are exposed with that very purpose. The large percentage of blindness in Bengal can however be otherwise explained. The practice is entirely unknown to-day and was by no means common all over the province even in the 17th century.

CHAPTER III

1. Various.
2. Very rough hills.
3. Round stone.
4. A fine tree.
5. Or other thing.

6. A misprint for "Giagranate" in the original text. English 'Juggur Naut'.
7. Jagannath at Puri, Benares on the Ganges, Mathura on the Jumna and Tirupati in the Madras Presidency. Careri commits the same error as Thevenot and Tavernier when he says that Jagannath is situated on one of the mouths of the river Ganges.
8. Kesava Raya, a name of Krishna. The most well known temple of Kesava Raya is at Brindavan.
9. Near there are other Pagodas and the tomb of their prophet Kabir.
10. Beni-madhava=Madhava or Krishna with braided locks (veni). Tavernier, (Vol. II, p. 181) thus describes the idol:—"Among the idols on the great altar one stands 5 or 6 feet in height; neither the arms, legs, nor trunk are seen, only the head and neck being visible; all the remainder of the body, down to the altar, is covered by a robe which increases its width below. Sometimes on its neck there is rich chain of gold, rubies, pearls or emeralds." The mosque built on the site of the old temple still bears the name of Beni-madhava. Benares, however, is specially sacred to Siva or Visvanath and not to Krishna.
11. Ranchordas. Careri's account of Benares temples is based on that of Tavernier who mentions two pagodas, those of Richourdas and Gopaldas. Ball and Crooke are obviously wrong (Tavernier, Vol. II, p. 185) in suggesting that the two idols were so named. Most likely the two idols were set up by two Vaishnavas Ranchordas and Gopaldas and the deities were named after them Ranchhor and Gopal—the god who ran away from battlefield and the god who looked after cattle—Krishna in his different manifestations.
12. Within it is a marble balustrade.
13. This is incorrect. The idol was that of Kesava or Krishna. Careri again repeats Tavernier's inaccurate statement.
14. Tavernier refers to "two courses of animals chiefly monkeys, carved in relief." (Vol. II, p. 187).
15. Tirupati, commonly called Tripetty. The principal temple is at Tirumala, 6 miles distant. Pilgrims flock from all parts of India there, bearing large offerings with them. (*Imp. Gaz.*, Vol. XXIII, p. 393 ff. It is not very near the coast and is certainly far from Cape Comorin.
16. Vijayanagar.
17. The reference seems to be to the Vitthala temple, "the most splendid building in the city", though the pillars are not of marble. Commenced by Krishna Deva Raya in 1513 the construction of the temple was probably not completed on account of the final disaster that befell the city about fifty years later i.e. in 1565 (Longhurst, *Hampi Ruins*, pp. 116 ff.).
18. The car festival was annually held at Vijayanagar (Sewell, *A Forgotten Empire*, 255, 262). Nicolo Conti, who visited Vijaynagar in 1420-21, writes:—"At a certain time of the year their idol is carried through the city, placed between two chariots, in which are young women richly adorned, who sing hymns to the god, and accompanied by a great concourse of people. Many, carried away by the fervour of their faith, cast themselves on the ground before the wheels, in order that they may be crushed to death—a mode of death which they say is very acceptable to their god."
19. Afterwards presented.
20. The great diamond which Mir Jumla presented to Shah Jahan was the celebrated Koh-i-Nur. (Tavernier, Vol. I, p. 315; Vol. II, App. I; Bernier, p. 22; Manucci, Vol. I, p. 237). It did not come from a Vijayanagar temple as Careri asserts but from the Kollur mine. Careri confuses it with one of the four large diamonds mentioned by Garcia da Orta which according to information received by him "had been seen at Bisnaguer" (See Dr. Ball's very learned examination of this subject in Appendix I, Vol. II of Tavernier).
21. Tanjore. It appears that the Nayak of Tanjore, Vijayaraghava became a vassal, by 1656 A.D., of Bijapur and not of Golkonda. Mir Jumla, therefore, could not have captured the place. Thevenot (Part III, pp. 91 and 105) writing in 1666 observes, "There are many Naiques to the South of St. Thomas who

are Sovereigns. The Naique of Madura is one. He of Tangiour (Tanjore) is at present a Vassal to the King of Vigianour." (Vriddhagirisan, *The Nayaks of Tanjore*, p. 140).

22. Rameswaram, in Madura District, Madras, on the island of Pamban. Tradition attributes the original shrine to Rama, the hero of the great Hindu epic. The present temple has been highly praised by Fergusson as a perfect example of Dravidian style of architecture.
23. *Lingam* from Linga. Siva is usually worshipped in the form of a phallus. The phallus is not infrequently represented to be standing on its female counterpart commonly called *Gauripatta.* The principal lingam is of stone while the one commonly attributed to Rama and his consort Sita is supposed to be of sand.
24. For the custom of cleaning metal pots after the eclipse is over and replacing old earthen jars by new ones, see Mrs. Stevenson, pp. 351 ff.
25. The Brahmans having given notice of it everybody breaks the earthen vessels.
26. Discovered by Brahmans from their magical books.
27. Brass.
28. Meanwhile attend.
29. Rice, grains and other produce.
30. The Divali and the Holi.
31. Some.
32. Careri is probably indebted to Bernier for this account of Mango trick (Bernier, pp. 153-154). Fryer (Vol. II, pp. 104-105) also mentions this trick of which a more detailed account is given by Tavernier (Vol. I, p. 55).
33. '"Reguli", petty princes.

CHAPTER IV

1. A favourable opportunity.
2. At 2 o'clock in the afternoon.
3. On horseback to the Captain's tent accordingly.
4. At 3 o'clock.
5. Sikander Adil Shah, son of Ali Adil Shah, the last Sultan of Bijapur was a minor when he succeeded his father in 1672. He was taken prisoner in 1686 when Bijapur capitulated and died in captivity about fourteen years later.
6. Obviously lunar years as the prince was born in 1668.
7. The date is wrong. Golkonda was annexed to the Mughal Empire on I October, 1687. (Manucci, Vol. II, p. 306 *n* 2).
8. Shahaji Bhonsle, Shivaji's father, did not die in prison, though he was once placed under arrest and put into prison. He died of an accident at a village in the Mysore state. See Sen, *Sivachhatrapati,* pp. 90-91.
9. Rajapur, Rajgad, Kharepatan and Dabhol.
10. Razing.
11. Probably an echo of a similar story about Shivaji's grandfather Maloji whose sudden and unexpected opulence was attributed to the discovery of buried treasure through divine grace.
12. An indirect hint about the popular suspicion about the young prince's legitimacy. See Sen, *Foreign Biographies of Shivaji,* pp. 4-5, f.n. 5.
13. In fief.
14. Pam Nayak, the Berad chieftain, inflicted a defeat on the Mughal general Dilir Khan in 1680. He loyally stood by his master the Sultan of Bijapur during his last war with the Mughals but had to submit to the latter in November 1687. He died in January 1688 (Sarkar, Vol. V, pp. 216-17). His nephew Pidia Nayak gave the emperor much trouble.
15. Twenty-seven villages. From "Sattais" (twenty-seven) and Sans. "palli" (Village). The headquarters were at Shorapur or Surapur now in Gulbarga District, Hyderabad State.

16. As in Book III, Chap. I Careri here uses the term indiscriminately for all low castes. The people meant here are obviously Berads. Fryer also groups *Coolies, Frasses* and *Hoiencores* together and calls them "the Dregs of the People". (Vol. II, p. 108. Also Iyer, *The Mysore Tribes and Castes,* Vol. II, 197 *et seq.*).
17. Sidi Masud, regent of Bijapur during the minority of Sultan Sikandar Adil Shah for five years. Careri is wrong when he says that Masud defended Bijapur against Aurangzeb, Sayyid Makhdum, surnamed Sharza Khan, was the general commanding the Bijapur troops. The siege lasted a little over seventeen months from 1 April, 1685 to 12 September, 1686. (Sarkar, *History of Aurangzib,* Vol. IV, Chap. XIV).
18. Abul Hasan (1672-1687) surnamed *"Tana-shah"*, "the dainty King." See Thevenot, Pt. III, Bk. II, Ch. VII, Note 14; Lane-Poole, *Muhammadan Dynasties,* p. 321.
19. Bitterly disgusted.
20. Own territory.
21. Muhammad Sultan, eldest son of Aurangzeb, who died in 1677-78. The reference is to the Mughal invasion of 1656. For his marriage with the daughter of the King of Golkonda, see Thevenot, Pt. III, Bk. II, Ch. VII, Note 10; according to Khafi Khan (Vol. I, pp. 746, 749) *sarkar* Ramgir on the borders of Berar and Bidar formed the dowry.
22. Dowry.
23. Prince Akbar sailed for Persia in February 1687. A written promise securing the succession to the throne of Golkonda for Muhammad Sultan was also obtained but kept secret all the time.
24. On the pretext of the passage given to *Savaji.*
25. Here Careri records nothing but bazar gossip.
26. The siege of Golkonda began on 7 February, 1687. (Sarkar, *History of Aurangzib,* Vol. IV, p. 362).
27. Bhaganagar or Hyderabad.
28. Cut stones.
29. The siege actually lasted seven months and a half. Golkonda was captured by bribery on 21 September, 1687. (Sarkar, *History of Aurangzib,* Vol. IV, p. 382).
30. The prisoner.
31. Manucci (Vol. II, pp. 306-308) also says that the Sultan was insulted and beaten at the instance of Aurangzeb. Ishwardas gives quite a different account. (See Sarkar, History of Aurangzib, Vol. IV, p. 385 *n*). Abul Hasan was sent to Daulatabad in February 1688 on a pension of Rs. 50,000 a year.
32. "Pannaich" a misprint for "Pamnaich".
33. Pam Nayak, on the contrary, loyally stood by Bijapur in 1686. See Sarkar, History of Aurangzib, Vol. V, p. 216.
34. Equally.

CHAPTER V

1. Lose.
2. See Book II, Ch. I.
3. See Book II, Ch. I.
4. Hind. *machin,* Marathi *nachni,* (*Lolium Temulentum*). The seeds are found mixed with those of wheat or other cereals. (See Watt, Vol. V, p. 90).
5. The hard law of necessity.
6. No food.
7. See Book II, Ch. I.
8. Compelled.
9. I concealed myself in great fear.
10. Belgaum, headquarters of the district of the same name in Bombay. It was not a very big place either under the Muslims or the Marathas. (*Belgaum Dist. Gaz.,* pp. 515 ff.).

11. Nevertheless.
12. Understanding.
13. Shahapur due south of Belgaum.
14. Fasting.
15. Jamboti, a small town eighteen miles south-west of Belgaum on the road leading by Kunkumbi and the Chorle pass into Portuguese territory (*Belgaum Dist. Gaz.*, pp. 572-573).
16. Desai, from Mar. *desai,* a hereditary officer with extensive powers in charge of a district, in western and southern India. (*Hobson-Jobson,* p. 306).
17. Likewise.
18. To them.
19. Tivi in Bardez district, Goa settlement.
20. S. Michael, one of the three forts of Tivi, mentioned in an official document of 1726 at Goa according to Cavaliero P. Pissurlencar.
21. Pumburpa, north of Goa. (See map attached to Fonseca's book).
22. From Pumburpa.
23. At the rudeness of the Portuguese soldier.
24. Escort.
25. A comfortable.
26. Channel.
27. This had happened.
28. Alas I am suffering from wounds inflicted by my own missiles.
29. Failing.
30. No. 13 of Pietro Della Valle's Chart, opposite St. John of God on the left side of the hill. Della Valle was at Goa when the news of canonisation of Francis Xavier arrived (Vol. I, pp. 170-171). A description of the reliquary containing the body is given by François Pyrard (Vol. II, Part I, p. 62). An illustration of the "Noble Tomb" ordered by the Grand Duke of Tuscany to which Careri refers, is given opposite p. 62 of Pyrard, Vol. II, Part I. Dr. Fryer also visited the shrine (Vol. II, p. 12) and Mandelslo refers to the miraculous preservation of the Saint's body (pp. 80-81). For a detailed account of the tomb and stories of the miracles, see Fonseca, pp. 286-301.
31. Fairly.
32. Of no architectural beauty.
33. Nearly nine years.
34. No. 35 of Pietro Della Valle's Chart. The Carmelites held a solemn mass in this church to celebrate the canonisation of St. Theresa when Pietro Della Valle was at Goa (Vol. I, pp. 172-174). They were expelled from Goa in 1707. The convent is now in ruins. See Fonseca, pp. 256-259.
35. Well designed.
36. The Italian fathers.
37. To defend that pass along with the soldiers.
38. Handsome gifts.
39. Imam.
40. The Captain's Galley, a small vessel and a fireship sailed out of the harbour for the Gulf of Persia, in aid of the King of Persia against the Imam of Muscat who with five ships had burnt the Portuguese factory at Congo.
41. Palace of the fortress or the Fortress of the viceroy (Fonseca, pp. 194-197).
42. As Fonseca observes, the pictures must have been very numerous for no less than 806 vessels had come to the east up to 1612 (Fonseca, p. 195).
43. And in another room paintings of all the ships and fleets.
44. Of the.
45. And there they coin money.
46. Portuguese gold and silver coin. "Garcia de Sa (1548-49) issued a gold coin called *Sao Thome* of the value of 1,000 reis (£1 2s. 4d.), followed by a silver piece bearing the same name." Subsequently a new gold coin, called *Sao Thome Novo* to distinguish it from the old coin was issued. "This was of three kinds, called double, single and half *Sao Thome* valued respectively at 8s. 4d., 4s. 2d. and 2s. 1d" (Fonseca, pp. 30-31). The coin was minted

for the last time in 1841. It derived its name from the figure of the apostle which it bore on one side (Dalgado, Vol. II, pp. 289-290).

47. Brass.
48. Tin.
49. See Thevenot, Part III, Chap. XXV, Note 9.
50. Bronze.
51. Port. *Bazarucco*. A small coin of diverse metals and fluctuating exchange value. About its etymology there is a difference of opinion. Some interpret it as *Bazar-rukka* or market money, others would derive it from Persian *buzurg* or big. The Bazarucco coined by Albuquerque in 1510 was worth two reis only. In 1554 it was worth 3 reis each but in 1712 five of this coin would bring only 4 reis. Fryer says 20 of these coins were equivalent to a fanam (Dalgado, Vol. I, p. 109; *Hobson-Jobson,* p. 121).
52. Article.
53. See Book I, Chap. VI.
54. Called the Fiscala.
55. On a pleasure excursion to.
56. A father of good taste.
57. Good fish.
58. But in several kinds of fruits; particularly large are the oysters.
59. Other contemporary travellers also testify to this practice.
60. Several very fine rarities.
61. I went on a pleasure trip.
62. Pyrard says—"They are obliged to have the fête-Dieu in February or March, because in the season we celebrate it there is too much rain" (Vol. II, Part I, p. 35).
63. Brought for the Viceroy.
64. Of St. Joseph's.
65. With the help of Father Visconti.
66. Situated on the hill of Boavista. For the miracles associated with the cross, see Fonseca, pp. 274-277.
67. Very cordially.
68. That I required.
69. Are in control.
70. The vessel having already descended to the Passo near the mouth of the channel.
71. After dinner.
72. Chorao island in the Goa settlement.
73. Around.
74. Holy Apostles.
75. On my return, going to take leave of Father Constantine, I lunched and dined in the Farm of the Augustinians.

CHAPTER VI

1. Tongking, French *Tonquin* or *Tonkin,* the northern division of the kingdom of Annam, which forms an integral part of French Indo-China.
2. Innocent XI, Pope from 1676-1689.
3. Likewise.
4. Society of Jesus, *i.e.,* the Jesuits.
5. *Parao, prow* etc. Yule gives it a double origin; the Malayal *paru* 'a boat', and the island word *prau or prahu* (*Hobson-Jobson,* p. 733).
6. Ram.
7. Confirming the saying "They struck Scylla in wishing to avoid Charybdis." (*Incidit in Scyllam cupiens vitare carybdim*).
8. I also put.
9. Great.

10. Burst.
11. A misprint for "mine".
12. Lack of.
13. "Sudden squalls accompanied by thunder and lightning, which are common in the narrow sea between the Malay Peninsula and the island of Sumatra." (*Hobson-Jobson*, p. 867).
14. The difference in the seasons is due to the south-eastern regions receiving the north-east monsoon winds instead of the south-west. Other travellers also noticed this contrast, *cf.* Mandelslo, p. 83, and Peter Mundy, Vol. V, p. 65.
15. Madura, Turaiyar, Tanjore, Gingee and Madras.
16. Point de Galle, Ceylon. A rocky cape, to the south of Colombo.
17. No wind could turn us from our course.
18. The island of Ceylon contains every variety of quartz, such as rock-crystal, amethyst, cat's eye etc., the first of which is abundant, of various colours and of good quality (Hamilton, *East-India Gazetteer*, Vol. I, p. 384).
19. And other rivers.
20. The same wind and rains continuing.
21. An archipelago of coral islets in the Indian Ocean, between 7° 6′ N., and 0° 42′ S. The hereditary Sultan of these islands is tributary to the British Government of Ceylon.
22. Called Bilanzo by the sailors.
23. Nicobar islands, a group of twelve inhabited and seven uninhabited islands in the Bay of Bengal between Sumatra and the Andaman islands. They have an area of 635 square miles.
24. Andaman islands, numbering 204, in the Bay of Bengal. "The traditional charge of cannibalism has been very persistent, but it is denied by the islanders themselves. It is however, undoubted that they massacred shipwrecked crews even in quite modern times".
25. Are accustomed.
26. Sufficient witnesses.
27. Nicolo Conti in the fifteenth century explains the name 'Andamans' to mean "Island of Gold", and speaks of a lake with peculiar virtues as existing in it (cited in *Encyclopaedia Britannica*, s.v. *Andaman Islands*).
28. The crew.
29. Being poured from a vase (carried by a native of the island) on to an anchor the part which was wet with it, turned into gold.
30. Out of gratitude.
31. And water.
32. Of the English.

ADDITIONAL NOTES

Page 16: *A rare Beast.* The rare beast described here is difficult to identify. Dr. Cockburn of the Zoological Society of London, thinks that "it is quite probably a Malabar Giant Squirrel". Dr. B. N. Chopra of the Zoological Survey of India writes: "Dr. M. L. Roonwal, our expert on birds and mammals, and I have carefully scrutinized the description of the animal mentioned by Thevenot, but its characters, as described, are so composite that it is extremely difficult to identify it. There is a superficial resemblance to *Hyrax* (order Hyracoidea) found in E. Africa and W. Asia (not India), but the teeth, tail etc. of Thevenot's animal are not like those of an *Hyrax*. The animal is more likely to be a rodent. The large size, as indicated by the tail-measurement, would appear to show that the animal might possibly be one of the giant squirrels of the *Rotufa* group, but these occur only in the Malaysian-Burma region. The presence of flat Primate-like soles is, however, a character not found in the rodents."

Page 177: *The Pagod is 100 Spans in length,* . . . . To be identified with Cave No. 10, the Great Darbar Hall. See plate No. LIV of Fergusson and Burgess.

Page 207: *F. Hippolito Visconti.* He is referred to as *Father Hippolitus, Father Hippolitus Visconte,* and *Father Visconti* in Book III, Chap. V (pp. 269 and 272 of the present reprint). Father Giuseppe Monticone of the Propaganda Fide Archives, Vatican tells me that Hippolito Visconti originally belonged to the Theatin Convent of Milan. In 1673 he joined the new expedition of Theatin fathers for India formed by the Sacred Congregation. Following Father Gallo's death he was appointed Vice-prefect in 1698 and subsequently Prefect of the Missions (1705) with his headquarters at Goa. Father Visconti incurred the displeasure of the Portuguese authorities at Goa for having dared to follow the decrees of the Papal Legate Tournon in respect of Chinese rites. He was thrown into prison and remained there till 1714 when he was set free on condition that he should recall his missionaries from San Thomé (Mylapore). In 1720 he was succeeded by Father John Cajetan Comini as Prefect.

Page 348, Note 43: *Salvador Gallo.* He is referred to by the author as *Father Salvador* in Book I, Chapter VI (p. 192 of the present reprint), as *Father Galli* in Book II, Chap. I (*Ibid,* p. 207), and simply as *Father Prefect* in Book III, Chap. V (*Ibid,* p. 269). Father Giuseppe Monticone, General Archivist of the Propaganda Fide, Vatican tells me that there are plenty of records relating to him in the Propaganda Fide Archives. It appears from these records that the expedition of Theatin fathers of which he was the leader was organised by the Sacred Congregation in 1673 and that Father Gallo continued to be the Director of the Theatin Missions till his death in 1697. The headquarters of the Missions were in the 'hospice' of Goa.

ITINERARY OF M. DE THEVENOT

November 6, 1665 ..	Embarks from Basra on board the Hopewell.
January 10, 1666 ..	Arrives at the bar of Surat.
January 12, 1666 ..	Lands at Surat.
February 1, 1666 ..	Leaves Surat for Ahmedabad, where he stays till February 16. Important towns en route Broach, Petlad etc. Visits Sarkhej, near Ahmedabad.
February 16, 1666 ..	Leaves Ahmedabad for Cambay by the land-route, and after losing his way, ultimately reaches Surat. (Exact date not mentioned). Speaks of the high-handedness of the Grassias.
February 25 (?), 1666 ..	Travels from Surat to Aurangabad in company with Monsieur Bazou via Navapur, Pimpalner, Satana, Deogaon and Suregaon. Meets Francis Fallu, Bishop of Heliopolis at Satana.
March 11, 1666 ..	Reaches Aurangabad performing the whole journey in a fortnight. The same day takes a night-journey to see the Ellora caves.
March 12, 1666 ..	Reaches Daulatabad at 2 A.M. where he stays till 5 A.M. Stays at Ellora for two hours and returns to Daulatabad the same day. Leaves Daulatabad and arrives at Aurangabad.
March 13, 1666 ..	Departs from Aurangabad to Calvar. Describes tank at Ambad. Sees feats of jugglers at Patoda. Reaches Indur after some days' stay at Bisetpuri.
March 25, 1666 ..	Reaches Indelvai.
March 26, 1666 ..	Arrives at Calvar. Leaves Calvar for Bhagnagar (Hyderabad). Writes of the exactions of the officers on the way. Journey takes six days.
April, 1666	Arrives at Hyderabad where he stays till October. Leaves Hyderabad for Masulipatam. The journey usually took a week during fair weather.
October 23-24 (?), 1666 ..	Returns from Masulipatam to Hyderabad and stays there for three weeks.
November 13, 1666 ..	Leaves Hyderabad.
November 20, 1666 ..	Arrives at Bidar and leaves for Pathri.
November 30, 1666 ..	Parts at Pathri from his fellow traveller Monsieur Bazou.

December 9, 1666	..	Arrives at Burhanpur and leaves for Surat. Suffers from Cholera during the journey. Comes across lions. The journey takes a fortnight.
December 23, 1666	..	Reaches Surat and rests for some time.
February, 1667	..	Embarks for Bandar-Abbas or Gombroon in the Persian Gulf. From Bandar-Abbas proceeds to Shiraz. Accidentally hit by a shot from his own pistol. Is treated at Shiraz without much relief whereupon leaves for Isfahan where his wound is cured.
February-October, 1667	.	Stays at Isfahan.
October 25, 1667	..	Leaves Isfahan for Sier (?). Suffers from fever and ague.
October 31, 1667	..	Leaves for Kashan and arrives there after four days.
November 8, 1667	..	Leaves Kum at 2 A.M.
November 16, 1667	..	Lodges at Farsank where he stops writing his memoirs.
November 28, 1667	..	Dies at Mianeh.

ITINERARY OF DR. GAMELLI CARERI

January 11, 1695	..	Arrives at Daman and stays in the monastery of the Augustinians.
January 12, 1695	..	Visits old Daman in company with F. Constantin.
January 15, 1695	..	Sails from Daman for Surat.
January 16, 1695	..	Anchors at Survali.
January 23, 1695	..	Returns to Daman after leaving Surat the previous day.
January 25, 1695	..	Leaves for Bassein.
January 26, 1695	..	Visits Tarapur. Passes through Mahim and the island of Vaccas or Arnalla.
January 27, 1695	..	Reaches Bassein.
February 13, 1695	..	Visits Ghodbandar in Salsette. Stops at Deins(?), six miles from Bassein. Describes the village of Mandapeshwar. Returns to Deins from Mandapeshwar.
February 14, 1695	..	Leaves Deins for Kanheri and returns the same evening.
February 15, 1695	..	Goes to Bassein again by way of Ghodbandar.
February 21, 1695	..	Departs from Bassein for Goa. Passes through Bombay.
February 22, 1695	..	Anchors at Chaul.
February 24, 1695	..	Reaches Dabhol.
February 25, 1695	..	Passes through Visapor, Lambuna(?) and Malvan.
February 26, 1695	..	Reaches Goa. Stays there till March 3.
March 4-5, 1695	..	Leaves Goa for Galgali; after passing through Mardol reaches Ponda.
March 8, 1695	..	Sets out for Chiampan (?).
March 11, 1695	..	Reaches Sambrani after passing through Bombuali and Chiamkan.
March 12, 1695	..	Arrives at Haliyal.
March 13-15, 1695	..	Passes through Kancre, Etchi, Tikli, Hunur and Mandapur.
March 16, 1695	..	Passes through Chikodi and Edur and arrives at Mudhol.
March 17, 1695	..	Arrives at Galgali.
March 19, 1695	..	Pays a visit to Aurangzeb's quarters.
March 20, 1695	..	Goes to see the tent of Shah Alam.

March 21, 1695	..	Is admitted to a private audience with Aurangzeb.
March 22, 1695	..	Has an opportunity to see Sikandar Adil Shah.
March 27, 1695	..	Leaves Galgali for Goa.
March 30, 1695	..	Reaches Belgaum after passing through Edur, Rodelki, Mandapur and Hunur.
April 3, 1695	..	Crosses the Mughal boundary into Portuguese territory.
April 5, 1695	..	Reaches Goa where he stays till May 15.
May 16, 1695	..	Sails from Goa for China.
May 23-24, 1695	..	The ship passes through Cochin and Cape Comorin latitudes.
June 4, 1695	..	Reaches Achin in Sumatra.
June 27, 1695	..	Arrives at Malacca.

BIBLIOGRAPHY

Abu-l Fazl: *Ain-i-Akbari,* tr. Blochman & Jarrett (Cal. 1873-94), 3 Vols.

———*Akbarnama,* tr. Beveridge in Bibliotheca Indica Series (Cal. 1904-39) 3 Vols.

Ain-i-Akbari: See under Abu-l Fazl.

Akbarnama: See under Abu-l Fazl.

Arnold, T. and Addis, W. E.: *A Catholic Dictionary.*

Baker, E. C. Stuart: *The Fauna of British India*: *Birds* (Lond. 1922-1930), 8 Vols.

Baldacus, Philip: *A Description of the East India Coasts of Malabar as also of the Isle of Ceylon.* (Amsterdam, 1672).

Barbosa, Duarte: *The Book of Duarte Barbosa,* ed. Dames (Hakluyt, 1918-21).

Beni Prasad: *History of Jahangir* (Lond. 1922).

Bernier, François: *Travels in the Mogul Empire,* ed. Constable & Smith (Oxford, 1934).

Biddulph, J.: *The Pirates of Malabar* (Lond. 1907).

Bilgrami, Syed Hussain and Willmott, C.: *Historical and Descriptive Sketch of His Highness the Nizam's Dominions* (Bombay, 1883), 2 Vols.

Blanford, W. T.: *The Fauna of British India*: *Mammalia* (Lond. 1888) 2 Vols.

Bombay Presidency Gazetteer, Imp. Gaz. of India: Prov. Series (Cal. 1909), 2 Vols.

Bowrey, Thomas: *A Geographical Account of Countries round the Bay of Bengal,* ed. Temple (Hakluyt, 1905).

Briggs, J.: *History of the Rise of the Mohamedan Power in India,* tr. from Firistha (Cal. 1908), 4 Vols.

Burgess, James: *The Muhammadan Architecture of Bharoch, Cambay Dholka, Champanir and Mahmudabad in Gujarat* (Lond. 1896).

———*The Muhammadan Architecture of Ahmedabad* (Lond. 1900-05), 2 Pts.

———*Archæological Survey of India Reports*: *Western India.* Vol. III (Lond. 1878).

———*Archaeological Survey of India Reports*: *Western India* Vol. V (Lond. 1883).

Burton, R.: *Book of the Thousand Nights and a Night* (1894).

Calcutta Review, The

Cambridge History of India, ed. Rapson, Haig & Dodwell (Cambridge, 1922-1932).

Campos, J. J. A.: *History of the Portuguese in Bengal* (Cal. 1919).

Carré Barthelemy: *The Travels of the Abbe Carre in India and the Near East,* tr. Lady Fawcett & ed. Fawcett & Burn. (Hakluyt, 1947), 3 Vols.

Census of India for 1931.

Cochin State Manual (Ernakulam, 1911).
Commissariat, M. S.: *A History of Gujarat* (London 1938).
Coryat, Thomas: *Coryat's Crudities* (Glasgow, 1905) 2 Vols.
Cousens: *List of Antiquarian Remains in His Highness the Nizam's Territories* in the New Imp. Series of Arch. Survey (Cal. 1900), Vol. XXXI.
Crooke, W.: *The Tribes and Castes of the North Western Provinces and Oudh* (Cal. 1896), 4 Vols.
Cunningham, Alexander: See under Majumdar, S.N.
Curzon, G. N.: *Persia* (Lond. 1892) 2 Vols.
Da Cunha, J. G.: *Notes on the History and Antiquities of Chaul and Bassein* (Bombay, 1876).
Dalgado, S. R.: *Glossario Luso-Asiatico* (Coimbra, 1919-21) 2 Vols.
Danvers, F. C.: *The Portuguese in India* (Lond. 1894), 2 Vols.
De Laet: *The Empire of the Great Mogol,* ed. Hoyland & Banerjee (Bombay, 1928).
Della Valle, Pietro: *The Travels of Pietro della Valle in India,* ed. Grey (Hakluyt, 1892) 2 Vols.
Dellon, Gabriel: *Nouvelle relation d'un voyage fait aux Indus Orientales contenant la description des Isles de Bourbon et de Madagascar, de Surate, de la côte de Malabar, de Calicut, de Tanor, de Goa &c.* (Amsterdam, 1699).
Drury, Heber: *Reminiscences of Life and Sport in South India* (London, 1890).
Douglas, James: *Bombay and Western India* (Lond. 1893) 2 Vols.
Dubois, J. A.: *Hindu Manners, Customs and Ceremonies,* tr. Beauchamp (Oxford, 1897) 2 Vols.
Eden, Emily: *Up the Country* (Lond. 1866) 2 Vols.
Egerton, W.: *An Illustrated Handbook of Indian Arms* (Lond. 1880).
———*A Description of Indian and Oriental Armour* (Lond. 1896).
Elliot, H. M. and Dowson, J.: *The History of India as told by its own Historians* (Lond. 1867-77) 8 Vols.
Elphinstone, *Kingdom of Cabul,* 2 Vols. (London, 1814, 1819).
Elwin, V.: *The Maria and their Ghotul* (Oxford, 1947).
Encyclopaedia Britannica (Eleventh Edition: Handy Volume Issue, New York, 1910).
Encyclopaedia of Religion and Ethics, ed. Hastings (Edinburgh & New York, 1908-18).
Enthoven, R. E.: *The Castes and Tribes of Bombay* (Bombay, 1920-22) 3 Vols.
Fergusson, J.: *The Palaces of Nineveh and Persepolis* (Lond. 1851).
———*History of Indian and Eastern Architecture,* ed. Burgess & Spiers (Lond. 1910) 2 Vols.
Fergusson, J. and Burgess, J: *The Cave Temples of India* (Lond. 1880).
Fernandes, Braz A.: *A Guide to the Ruins of Bassein* (Bombay, 1941).
Firistha, Md. Qasim: *Tarikh-i-Firistha,* tr. Briggs (Cal. 1908) 4 Vols.
Fonseca, J. N.: *An Historical and Archaeological Sketch of the City of Goa* (Bombay, 1878).

Forbes, J.: *Oriental Memoirs* (Lond. 1834) 2 Vols.

Forrest, George: *Selections from the Letters, Despatches and State papers preserved in the Bombay Secretariat: Home Series* (Bombay 1887).

Foster, William: *The English Factories in India* (1618-1669) (Oxford, 1906-27) 13 Vols.

———*Early Travels in India* (Oxford, 1921) See also under Roe, Thomas.

Fryer, John: *A New Account of East India and Persia,* ed. Crooke (Hakluyt, 1909-15) 3 Vols.

Gama, Vasco da: *A Journal of the First Voyage of Vasco da Gama,* tr. and ed. Revenstein (Hakluyt, 1898).

Gazetteers: *Imperial Gazetteer of India* Main Series (Oxford, 1908-9) Provincial Series (Calcutta, 1908-9).

———*District Gazetteers and Manuals* (Provinces and States).

Gerald de Gaury: *Arabia Phoenix* (Lond. 1946).

Gibb, H. A. R.: *Travels of Ibn Battuta* in Broadway Series (Lond. 1929).

Grant Duff, J. D.: *A History of the Mahrattas,* ed. S. M. Edwardes (Oxford, 1921) 2 Vols.

Grose: *A Voyage to the East Indies* (Lond. 1772) 2 Vols.

Growse, F. S.: *Mathura, a District Memoir* (Allahabad, 1880).

Hamilton, Alexander: *A New Account of the East Indies,* ed. Foster (Lond. 1930) 2 Vols.

Hamilton, Walter: *The East India Gazetteer* (Lond. 1828) 2 Vols.

Heber, Reginald: *Narrative of a Journey through the Upper Provinces of India* (Lond. 1828) 2 Vols.

Hedin, Sven: *Trans-Himalaya* (Lond. 1909-13) 3 Vols.

Herbert, Thomas: *Some Yeares Travels into Asia and Africa* (Lond. 1677).

Hobson-Jobson: See under Yule and Burnell.

Hughes, T. P.: *A Dictionary of Islam* (Lond. 1935).

Hutchinson, E. W.: *Adventurers in Siam in Seventeenth Century* (Lond. 1940).

Hutton, J. H.: *Caste in India* (Cambridge, 1946).

Hyderabad State Gazetteer, Imp. Gaz.: Prov. Series, (Cal. 1909).

Ibn Battuta: See under Gibb, H. A. R.

Ibn Hasan: *The Central Structure of the Mughal Empire* (Oxford, 1936).

Indian Antiquary, The

India in the Fifteenth Century, ed. Major (Hakluyt, 1888).

Irvine, William: *Army of the Indian Moghuls* (Lond. 1903).

———*The Later Mughals,* ed. Sarkar (Cal. 1922) 2 Vols.

Iyer, A. K.: *Tribes and Castes of Cochin,* 2 Vols.

Jafar Sharif: *Islam in India,* ed. Herklots & Crooke, (Oxford, 1921).

Jahangir: *Tuzuk-i-Jahangiri* (*Memoirs of Jahangir*), tr. Rogers & Beveridge (Lond. 1909-14) 2 Vols.

Journal of the Royal Asiatic Society of Great Britain, The

Jourdain: *The Journal of John Jourdain,* ed. Foster (Hakluyt, 1905).

Kaeppelin, Paul: *La Compagnie des Indes Orientales* (Paris, 1908).

Keene, H. G.: *Handbook to Delhi, Agra, etc.* (Calcutta, 1909).

Khafi Khan: *Muntakhab-ul-lubab* in Bibliotheca Indica Series (Cal. 1874) 2 Vols.

Lanepoole, S.: *The Mohammadan Dynasties* (Westminster, 1894).

Linschoten: *The Voyage of John Huyghen van Linschoten to the East Indies*, ed. Burnell & Tiele (Hakluyt, 1885) 2 Vols.

List of Muhammadan and Hindu Monuments in Delhi Province (Cal. 1916-22) 4 Vols.

Logan, William: *Malabar* (Madras, 1887) 2 Vols.

Longhurst, A. H.: *Hampi Ruins Described and Illustrated* (Cal. 1933).

Lyddekker: *The Game Animals of India, Burma, Malaya and Tibet* (Lond. 1907).

Maasir-i-Alamgiri: See under Muhammad Saqi Mustaidd Khan.

Maasir-ul-Umara: See under Shah Nawaz Khan.

Majumdar, S. N.: *Ancient India as described by Ptolemy* (Cal. 1927).

———*Cunningham's Ancient Geography of India* (Cal. 1924).

Mandelslo, John Albert de: *Voyages and Travels into the East Indies*, tr. Davies (Lond. 1669).

Manohar Lal: *Among the Hindus* (Cawnpore, 1933).

Manrique: *Travels of Fray Sebastien Manrique*, ed. Luard & Hosten (Hakluyt, 1927) 2 Vols.

Manucci, N.: *Storia do Mogor*, tr. & ed. Irvine in Indian Text Series (Lond. 1907-8) 4 Vols.

Menon, K. P. Padmanabha: *History of Kerala* (Ernakulam, 1924-37) 4 Vols.

Michaelis: *Portuguese-English Dictionary*.

Moll, Herman: *India*. See under Salmon.

Moreland, W. H.: *The Agrarian System of Moslem India* (Cam. 1929).

———*Relations of Golconda in the early Seventeenth Century* (Hakluyt, 1931).

Moreland & Geyl: *Jahangir's India* (Cam. 1925).

Muhammad Saqi Mustaidd Khan: *Maasir-i-Alamgiri* in Bibliotheca Indica Series (Cal. 1870-73); Eng. tr. Sir J. N. Sarkar (Cal. 1947).

Mundy, Peter: *The Travels of Peter Mundy in Europe and Asia*, ed. Temple and Anstey (Hakluyt, 1907-36) 5 Vols.

Muntakhab-ul-lubab: See under Khafi Khan.

Murzban, M. M.: *The Parsis in India* an English edition of Mlle. Delphine Menant's Le Parsis. (Bombay, 1917) 2 Vols.

Oaten, E. F.: *European Travellers in India* (Lond. 1909).

Ojha, G. H.: *Mewar-ka-Itihas* (Udaipur Rajya-ka-Itihasa) 2 Vols. Ajmer, 1931.

Orme, Robert: *Historical Fragments of the Moghul Empire* (Lond. 1805)

Garcia da Orta: *Coloquios dos Simples e Drogas da India* (Lisboa, 1891-92).

Ovington, J.: *A Voyage to Surat*, ed. Rawlinson (Oxford, 1929).

Panikkar, K. M.: *Malabar and the Portuguese* (Bombay, 1929).

———*Malabar and the Dutch* (Bombay, 1931).

Pant, D.: *The Commercial Policy of the Moghuls* (Bombay, 1930).

Payne, C. H.: *Jahangir and the Jesuits* in Broadway Series (Lond. 1930).
Phillimore, R. H.: *Historical Records of the Survey of India*, Vol. I (Dehra Dun, 1945).
Platts, J. T.: *A Dictionary of Urdu, Classical Hindi and English* (Lond. 1884).
Pocock, R. I.: *The Fauna of British India: Mammalia* (Lond. 1939-41) 2 Vols.
Pranabananda, Swami: *Exploration in Tibet* (Cal. 1939).
Prestage, E.: *The Portuguese Pioneers* (Lond. 1933).
Prestage: *Affonso de Albuquerque* (Watford, 1929).
——*Vasco da Gama.*
Ptolemy: See under Majumdar, S. N.
Punjab Gazetteer, Imp. Gaz. of India Prov. Series (Cal. 1908) 2 Vols.
Purchas, Samuel: *Hakluytus Posthumus or Purchas His Pilgrimes* (Glasgow, 1905-7) 20 Vols. Ext. Series.
Pyrard: *The Voyage of François Pyrard of Lavat*, tr. and ed. Gray (Hakluyt, 1887-90) 2 Vols.
Rajputana Gazetteer, Imp. Gaz. of India: Prov. Series (Cal. 1908).
Rawlinson, G.: *The History of Herodotus*, 4 Vols. (Lond. 1858-60).
Relations of Golconda in the Early Seventeenth Century, ed. Moreland (Hakluyt, 1931).
Rice, P. Lewis: *Mysore*, 2 Vols. (Westminster, 1897).
Risley, H.: *The People of India* (Lond. 1915).
Roe, Thomas: *The Embassy of Sir Thomas Roe to India*, ed. Foster (Oxford, 1926).
Rose, H. A.: *A Glossary of the Tribes and Castes of the Punjab and North-West Frontier Province* (Lahore, 1911-14) 3 Vols.
Roteiro: See under Vasco da Gama.
Russel, R. V. and Hira Lal: *Tribes and Castes of the Central Provinces of India* (Lond. 1916) 4 Vols.
Sacred Books of the Hindus, ed. Basu (Allahabad, 1911-19).
Salmon, Thomas: *Modern History; or the Present State of all Nations* 3rd edition, Vol. I, containing Moll's contribution (Lond. 1744).
Sanderson, G. P.: *Thirteen Years among the Wild Beasts of India*, 7th edition (Edinburgh, 1912).
Saran, P.: *The Provincial Government of the Moghuls* (Allahabad, 1941).
Sarda, H. B.: *Ajmer: Historical and Descriptive* (Ajmer, 1911).
Sarkar, Jadu Nath: *India of Aurangzib* (Cal. 1901).
——*History of Aurangzib* (Cal. 1912-25) 5 Vols.
——*Studies in Mughal India* (Cal. 1919).
——*Mughal Administration* (Cal. 1924).
Saxena, B. P.: *History of Shah Jahan of Delhi* (Allahabad, 1932).
Seely, John B.: *The Wonders of Elora* (Lond. 1824).
Sen, S. N.: *Siva Chhatrapati* (Cal. 1920).
——*Administrative System of the Marathas* (Cal. 1925).
——*Military System of the Marathas* (Cal. 1928).
——*Foreign Biographies of Shivaji* (Lond. 1927).
——*Studies in Indian History* (Cal. 1930).

Sewell, Robert: *A Forgotten Empire (Vijayanagar)* (Lond. 1900).

Shah Nawaz Khan: *Maasir-ul-Umara in Bibliotheca Indica Series* (Cal. 1888-91) 3 Vols. Eng. tr. H. Beveridge, completed and revised by Baini Prashad, Vol. I (Cal. 1911-41).

Sherring, H. A.: *Hindu Tribes and Castes* (Lond.-Calcutta, 1872-81) 3 Vols.

Sleeman, *Rambles and Recollections of an Indian Official,* ed. Smith (Oxford, 1915).

Smith, Edmund W.: *The Moghul Architecture of Fatehpur Sikri* (Allahabad, 1894-98) 4 Vols. No. XVIII in the New Imp. Series of Arch. Survey.

———*Akbar's Tomb, Sikandarah* (Allahabad, 1909) No. XXXV in the New Imp. Series of Arch. Survey.

Smith, Vincent A.: *Akbar the Great Moghul* (Oxford, 1917).

Stephen, Carr: *Archaeology and Monumental Remains of Delhi* (Simla, 1876).

Sterndale, R. A.: *Mammalia of India,* revised by F. Finn (Cal. 1929).

Stevenson, (Mrs.) Sinclair: *The Rites of the Twice-Born* (Lond. 1920).

Stuart, C. M. V.: *The Gardens of the Great Mughals* (Lond. 1913).

Sykes, P.: *History of Persia* (Lond. 1921) 2 Vols.

Tavernier, Jean-Baptiste: *Travels in India,* ed. Ball and Crooks (Oxford, 1925) 2 Vols.

Terry: *Voyage to East India* (Lond. 1655).

Thevenot: *Les Voyages de Mr. de Thevenot* (Paris, 1689).

———*The Travels of Monsieur de Thevenot into the Levant* (Lond. 1687).

Thornton, Edward: *Gazetteer of the Territories under the East India Company, etc.* (Lond. 1854) 4 Vols.

Thurston, E. and Rangachari, K.: *Castes and Tribes of Southern India* (Madras, 1909) 7 Vols.

Tieffenthaler, Joseph: *Description Historique et Geographique de l'Inde,* Vols. I-III (Berlin, 1786-88).

Valentia, George Viscount: *Voyages and Travels to India, Ceylon, the Red Sea, Abyssinia and Egypt* (Lond. 1811).

Vasco da Gama: See Gama, Vasco da.

Vogel, J. Ph.: *The Tile Mosaics of the Lahore Fort* (Cal. 1920).

Vriddhagirisan, V.: *The Nayaks of Tanjore* (Annamalai, 1942).

Watt, George: *Dictionary of Economic Products of India* (Cal. 1889-96) 6 Vols.

Whiteway, R. S.: *The Rise of the Portuguese Power in India* (Westminster, 1899).

Wilson, H. H.: *A Glossary of Revenue and Judicial Terms,* ed. Ganguli & Basu (Cal. 1940).

Wilson, John: *Indian Caste* (Edinburgh, 1877).

Yazdani, G.: *The Antiquities of Bidar* (Cal. 1917).

———*Mandu: the City of Joy* (Oxford, 1929).

Yule, Henry and Burnell, A. C.: *Hobson-Jobson,* ed. Crooke (Lond. 1903).

INDEX

INDEX

Abbas II, Shah of Persia, Kandahar captured by, 78-79, 310.
Abbasi (Abassi), Persian coin, xviii, xxii, 2, 26, 253, 279, 300, 381.
Abdul Karim, *Itimad Khan,* invites Akbar to occupy Gujarat, 8, 282.
Abdullah Qutb Shah (Abdulla Cotup Cha), King of Golkonda, 140, 332, 333.
—Mother of, *see* Hayat Baksh Begam.
Abu Said Mirza, *Sultan,* grandson of Miran Shah, 235, 374.
Abul Hassan, *surnamed* Tana Shah, King of Golkonda, account of, 141, 265, 332; Aurangzeb's war with, 265, 388.
Abyssinians, in India, 254.
Achin (Achem), in Sumatra, trade with India, 242, 349, 376.
Acuna, Capt. Nuno d', 183.
Adalat (Adalet), Court of Justice, 240, 376.
Aden, in Arabia, xliii, 30, 45, 292, 298.
Adil Khan, Adil Shah (Hidalcan), *see* Ismail Adil Shah.
Adil Shah Sur, descendant of Sher Shah, Akbar captures Agra from, 57, 302.
Afghans (Oganis), 245, 377.
Afuz, Hafuz, *see* Niculao Affonso.
Agates, trade at Broach, 8; from Cambay, 18, 164, 282, 286; mining near Limodra, 18, 286; sold at Surat, 25.
Agra, historic town in U. P., xxixn, xxxiii, xxxv, xlvii, lv, lvii, lix, lx, 68, 219, 224, 226, 298, 305, 306, 312, 315; practice of *Sati* at, xlix; situation, 46; fort and palace, 47, 299, 369; Jesuits at, 47; animal and elephant-fight at, 47, 53; baths, 48; Tajmahal, 48; royal tombs, 48-49; Caravanserai at, 49; climate, 49; population; houses; Dutch factory at, 49-50, 399; Christians and Parsis at, 50, 299; Beber robbed at, 50; dress and ornaments, 50-53; fauna, 53-55; hunting and fishing, 54-55; painting, 55; gold work at, 55-56; built by Akbar, 56, 301; captured by Akbar from Adil Shah Sur, 57, 302; revenue, 57; cotton textiles from, 103; capital of the Mughal kings, 236, 237.
Agriculture, at Surat, 36-37; at Bassein and Cassabo, 169; at Salsette, 179.
Aguada, fort in the province of Bardez, 190, 191, 350.
Ahmad, *Malik, see* Ahmad Nizam Shah.
Ahmad Khattu Ganj Baksh, *Shaikh,* venerated by Muslims and Hindus, 15; tomb at Sarkhej, 15, 285.
Ahmad Nizam Shah (Nizam-cha), *also known* as Malik Ahmad, liv, 127, 327.
Ahmad Shah (Ahmed, Amed), King of Gujarat, founds Ahmedabad, 11, 284, 285; tomb of, 11, 15, 284.
Ahmad Shah Wali, Bidar fort built by, 113, 322.
Ahmadabad (Amadabath, Amedabad, Amedabet), city in Bombay Presy., xix, xxxiii, xlvi, 8, 9, 10; English factory at, lviii, 13; textiles, 9, 13, 17, 164, 286, 340; tombs at; Jami Masjid at, 11, 13, 14, 15, 284; founded by Ahmad Shah, 11; situation and descriptive account, 11; Hauz-i-Qutb at, 11, 284; inroads by Raja of Bhadwar into, 12, 284; caravanserai at, 12; houses and temples, 12, 13-14, 164, 225, 340; Dutch at 12, 17; Maidan Shah at, 12; Tin Darwaza at, 12, 284; practice of archery at, 12; castle and king's palace at, 12, 13; fakirs at, 13; Shahi Bagh, 14, 15, 285; veterinary hospital, 16, 286; Dada Harir's well, 16, 286; hunting at, 16-17; fauna of, 16-17; trade and manufactures, 17, 286; city, 164, 340; Dara's flight to, 227-28.
—Governor of, see Badi-us-Zaman *Shah Nawaz Khan.*
Ahmadabad English Factory, lviii, 13.
Ahmadpur, *see* Rajura.
Ajmer (Adgemere, Azmer, Hasmer), xvii, xxxii, xxxiii, xxxv, xxxviii, xl, xli, lvii, 68-74, 305, 370; situation and history, 68-70, 305; pilgrimage of Akbar to, 69, 305; tomb of Khwaja Muinuddin Chisti at, 69, 306; fauna, 72, 73; saltpetre from, 73-74, 308; Dara defeated by Aurangzeb at 227-28.
Akbar (Ecbar, Schach Achbar), Mughal Emperor, liv, 68, 98, 281; legend re. necromancy, xxviii; imprisons Muzaffar Shah, liv; death, 6; occupies Gujarat, 8, 12, 282; tomb at Sikandra, 48, 56, 298, 299, 302; builds Agra, 56, 301; captures Agra from Adil Shah Sur, 57, 302; pilgrimage to Ajmer, 69; conquest of Kashmir, 83-84, 311; reign of, 235, 374.
—Mother of, *see* Hamida Bano Begam.
Akbar Sultan, fourth son of Aurangzeb, rebels against his father, 238-39, 265, 375, 388.
Akbarabad (Ecbarabad), *see* Agra.
Albuquerque (Albaquerque), Affonso de, Portuguese Viceroy of India, 45; buried in Goa, 129; takes Goa from Adil Shah, 186, 349; construction of Royal Hospital at Goa, 194, 353.
Alcal (? Haliyal), town in Kanara dist., fort and Hanuman temple at, 215, 365.
Alexander, *surnamed* the Great, Indian campaigns, xxiii, xxviii, 58; legends re. his excavation of Kanheri rock temples, xxiii, 171, 177; legends re. excavation

Alexander—*Contd.*
of passage by him through rocks at Bassein, 180.
Alfondica, custom house, xlii.
Ali Adil Shah, of Bijapur, reign of, 128, 328.
Ali Naqi, *Mir Saiyad* (Sajed), Diwan of Gujarat, 229, 371.
Allahabad (Halabas), xxxiii, xxxiv, lxi, 92-94; confluence of the Ganga and Jumna at, 46, 298; boundaries, 92; fort, 93; *Magh mela*, 93, 316; fakirs, 93-94; revenues, 94.
Allahabad fort, Asoka pillar in, xxiii, 92, 315; palaces, Patalpuri temple and Akshaya Vat at, 92, 315.
Almadia (Almadie, Almandies), a ferry boat used in Cambay coastal trade, 18-19, 196, 287, 354.
Almeida, Dom Francisco de, first Portuguese Viceroy of India (1508-10), takes Dabhol from Adil Shah, 185, 349.
Alvor, Don Francis de Tavora, Viceroy of Goa, attack on Ponda, 211, 363.
Amangal (Amanguel), near Hyderabad, 146, 334.
Amari (*Ambri*), a covered-in-howdah or litter, 227, 370.
Ambad, Ambar, town in Daulatabad, 108-09, 112, 321; tank at, 108; temple at, 109.
Ambar, *Malik*, Mughals defeated by, 127, 328.
Ambarpet Kalan (Elmas-Kepentch), in Hyderabad State, 146, 333.
Amber, sold at Surat, 25.
Ambrose (Ambroise, Ambrozio), Father, Superior of the Capuchins at Surat, 29, 30, 31, 41, 80, 291, 296, 299; service to Indians, 43-44; reputation and authority, 43, 297.
Amcaleira, Amcale (*Amlaki*) tree, 204, 360.
Ammonium Chloride, sold at Surat, 25, 289.
Amna (Ourna), river, 150,335.
Ananamzeira, ananas or pine apple, 161, 179, 204-05, 345, 360.
Anantagiri (Anendeguir), near Hyderabad, 147.
Andaman (Andemaon), island in Bay of Bengal, short account, 275, 276; cannibals in, 275, 391.
Andora, a kind of conveyance, 160, 168, 170, 172, 187, 188, 194, 207, 339.
Angola, on the west coast of Africa, 189, 195, 197, 350.
Anhilwara, in Gujarat, fortifications, 9, 282.
Animal husbandry, by the Mughals, 62-63.
Animante (Animating), *see* Hanuman.
Anjidiva (Andegiva), Island of, taken by the Portuguese, 195, 197, 354.
Ankai—Tankai (Enquitenqui), in Nasik dist., 102, 319.
Ankleshwar (Oclisser, Oklesar), in Broach Dist., Bombay, lx, 9, 21, 282.
Annunciacao, Dom Fr. Agostinho de, Archbishop of Goa, 208, 362.
Anoneira, anonas, 161, 202, 359.
Antelope (Antilope), at Agra, 54, 300; *see also* Meru.
Anthropo-phagi, *see* Cannibalism.
Apes (also mistaken for baboons), stories relating to, xiii, xxviii, 213-14, 364; hospital near Mathura for, 57, 302; at Aurangabad, 104.
Apples, Indian, 206.
Arabia, xliii, 62, 183, 196; trade with India, 241.
Arabian Sea (Indian Sea), xxii, 74, 308, 353.
Arabs, the, at Surat, 21, 38; defeated by the Portuguese, 180-82, 185.
Arakan (Aracam), in Burma, Shuja's flight to, 229, 230, 371.
Architecture, of Taj Mahal, 48, 299; of Delhi, 58-60; of Ellora, 104-07; of Sitanagar temple, 111-12; of Kanheri, 171-72.
Arco dos Vicereis, at Velha Goa, Vasco da Gama's statue at, constructed under Dom Francisco de Gama's orders, 194, 353.
Arcolna, village in the settlement of Goa, 208, 362.
Arequeira, Areca, betelnut-palm, 201, 205, 358.
Aretino, Pietro (Aretin), Italian author, 55, 301.
Arjumand Banu Begam, wife of Shah Jahan, *popularly* Mumtaz Mahal, tomb at Agra, 48, 299.
Armenians, the, at Surat, 21, in India, 254.
Arms and Ammunition, of the Mughals, 61-62, 242-43, 377; manufacture at Indalwai, 112-13; cannon at Bidar, 113.
Army, Mughal, 159, 182, 184; horses and elephants for, 219, 366; estimated strength, 242, 376; finances, 243.
Arnalla, near Bassein, 167, 341.
Arqaliq (*Arcaluk*), a coat with sleeves, 51, 300.
Arrian, *see* Flavius, Arrianus.
Asaf Khan (Asuf-Khan), father-in-law of Shah Jahan, proclaims Bulaqi as emperor, 232, 233, 281, 373; plans to help Shah Jahan to throne, 233, 373.
Asheri (Asserim), in Thana dist., Bombay, Portuguese castle at, 166-67, 341.
Ashti (Achty), town near Aurangabad, 108, 112, 321.
Asid Bosita Abyssino, *see* Miftah, *Sayf-ul-Mulk*.
Asoka pillar, at Allahabad fort, xxiii, 92, 315; at Delhi, 58, 302.
As-Salih, *Malik*, Sultan of Egypt, imparts training in arms to Mameluke slaves, 45, 297.
Atash-Parast (*Atech perest*), *see* Parsis, the.
Ateira, Ata tree, 202, 359.
Athaide, Dom Luiz de, fortress at Basrur built by, 196, 355.

Attock (Attack, Atek, Atoc), town in the Punjab, xxxii, xxixn, 82.
Augustinians, the, *also known as* Black Friars, monastery at Dacca, 95, monastery at Daman; mode of life, 157, 158, 337; at Bassein, 168, 342; monastery at Salsette, 179; at Dongorim, 199; at Goa, 273, 351.
Aurangabad (Aurangeabad, Aurengabad), capital of Balaghat, xix, xxxiii, 39, 101-02, 107, 151, 321, 368; revenues, 101; flora, 102; buildings, 103-04, 319; Dilras Banu Begam's tomb and Jami Masjid at, 103, 319; fauna, 104.
Aurangzeb (Aurengezeb), Mughal Emperor, xxxiii, liv, 57, 67, 99, 107, 281, 317, 320, 330, 333, 371, 375; at Galgala, xxiv, 220-22; Careri's interview with, xxiv, 220; religious intolerance 1; imprisons Shah Jahan, 6, 49, 226; treachery to Murad, 6, 223, 225-27, 229, 370; army of, 6-7; vandalism at Ahmadabad, 14; defeats and puts Dara to death, 9, 223, 225, 227, 228, 229, 370; expedition against Shivaji, 39; alleged present of treasure by Jahanara Begam to, 49, 231-32, 299; at Aurangabad, 103, 319; conquests in Bijapur and Golkonda, 127, 141, 142, 235, 265, 328, 332; besieges Daman, 159, 338; Deccan assigned to, 223, 322; deputes Muazzam to win over Mir Jumla, 224; appoints Shaista Khan as Governor of Agra, 226; imprisons Jahanara Begam, 226; sends Mir Jumla against Shujah, 227, 229; imprisons Muhammad Sultan, 228, 370; captures and imprisons Sulaiman Shikoh, 229; Dara's family captured by, 229; sends Dara's daughter to Jahanara Begam, 229; coronation, 231, 372; letter from King of Persia to, 231, 372; penance and piety, 231, 235-40, 372, 374; conquests and wars, 235, 238-39; sons of, 235-40; imprisons Shah Alam I, 237-38, 375; suspects Azam Shah's loyalty, 237-38, 375; wars with the Marathas, 238-39, 375; deposes Sikandar Adil Shah, 264-65; dismantles and rebuilds fortifications of Broach, 282-83.
Ayaz Sultani, *Malik* (Jassi), Governor of Diu, joins Egyptian expedition against the Portuguese in India, 45, 297; vain attempts to prevent Portuguese fortification of Chaul, 183-84.
Azam Shah (Azam-Scia), son of Aurangzeb, tomb at Ahmadabad, 11, 284, 320; alleged conspiracy against his father, 238.

Babar (Mirza Baber, Sultan Babir), Mughal Emperor, 58, 281, 301, 328; conquers Ghazni and N. India, 5, 280; succeeded by Humayun, 5; dethroned by Shaibani Khan, 235; early career of, 274.
Bab-el-Mandeb (Bab-el-Mandel), Strait between Arabia and Africa, 242, 376.
Babia, a variety of mangoes, 202, 358.
Baboons, *see* Apes.
Babrias, tribe in Kathiwar, 257, 383.
Babul (*Caboul, Baboul*), tree, 102, 319; bark used in preparing wine, 23, 289.
Baccareos, barking deer, at Daman, 161, 339.
Badagora (Bergare), village in Malabar, 125, 326.
Badam (*Baden*), bitter almonds, used as currency at Surat, 26, 290.
Badi Saheba, Dowager queen of Bijapur, robbed by Hubert Hugo on way to Mecca, 29, 30, 292; peace with Shivaji, 39, 295.
Badi-uz-Zaman, also called Mirza Dakhini, deserts Dara, 228, 370.
Bafta, a kind of calico, manufacture at Broach, 9, 282, 283.
Baglan (Baganala, Baglana, Benganala), hilly tract in Nasik dist., Bombay, xxxiii, 101, 113, 319, 328; revenues, 116, 323; situation, 116; marriages in, 117-18.
Bahadur Khan, *popularly known as* Mirbaba, foster brother of Aurangzeb, takes custody of Dara, 228, 371.
Bahadur Shah (Badar), King of Gujarat, surrenders Bassein etc. to the Portuguese, 167, 296.
Bahrein (Baharam), group of islands in Persian Gulf, Portuguese occupation of, 196, 354-55.
Bairagi (*Baraguy*), Hindu religious mendicant, 89, 258, 315, 384.
Bairam Khan (Beuran Cham), *Khan-i-Khanan*, Humayun's General, 235, 374.
Bakhshi (*Bachei, Bagsci*), Paymaster of the Mughal army, 212, 240, 363-64, 375.
Balaghat (Balagate, Balaquate), 23, 88, 101-04, 113, 322, 328; revenues, 101; fauna and flora, 102; missionaries, 103; *see also* Aurangabad.
Baloon, Balloon (*Ballon*), a kind of boat, 185, 198, 273, 274, 348.
Bandar Abbas (Bander Abbasi), Persian port, xviii, xix, 242.
Bandar-Sindri, in Kishangarh State, 68, 305.
Bandra (Bandora), village and fort near Bombay, 179.
Bangash (Bankich), Afghan tribe, settled in Farrukhabad, 87, 313.
Banghel (Banguel), near Mangalore, 125, 327.
Banias (Banians, Banienes, Baniyans, Bannyans, Benjans), Hindu traders, xli, xlii, xliii, xlv, xlvi, xlvii, lii; customs duty charged at Surat from 4; at Cambay, 18, 19; at Goa, 187; customs, 256.
Banjaras, Vanjaras (Bengiara, Binjaree, Brinjarry, Bunjaree), a nomadic tribe, 89, 314.
Bara Bangahal, ridge in Kangra, 88, 313.
Barambad, village in Bayana *tahsil*, Bharatpur State, 68, 305.

Barbosa, Duarte, xxxvi, 286, 293, 294, 325, 327, 329.
Bardez (Bardes), Island, 190, 191, 199; taken by the Portuguese, 195, 350-51.
Bardoli (Barnoly), town near Surat, 102, 319.
Bareja (Baredgia), in Daskroi subdivision of Ahmadabad dist., Bombay, 17, 286.
Barmer, historic fortress in Marwar State, Rajputana, 56, 301.
Baroda (Barodora, Brodera, Brodra, Broudra), Calico trade and indigo manufacture at, 44, 297.
Barqandaz Khan, one of the titles of the Mughal nobility, 222, 368.
Basra (Balsra, Balsora, Bassora), xviii, 1, 279, 355; tribute exacted by the king of Portugual, 196.
Basrur (Barcelore, Barkalar), in S. Kanara dist., Madras, sacked by Shivaji, 125, 327; taken by the Portuguese, 196, 355.
Bassein (Bassaim, Bazaim), in Thana dist., Bombay, former Portuguese settlement, xix, 38, 116, 171, 197, 199; Shivaji's camp near, 40; churches, 92, 169, 170, 315, 342, 343; captured by Nuno da Cunha, 167, 195, 296, 341; city and harbour, 166, 167; fortifications, 167, 341; government of, 167-68, 341; climate and dress of the people, 168; houses, 168; Dominicans at, 169; administration of justice, 170; channel of, 180; Portuguese ships at, 183.
—Archibishop of, *see* Menzes, Dom Fr. Aleixo de.
Bats, 98-99.
Batticaloa (Batticall), in Ceylon, bequeathed to the Portuguese by the King of Kotta, 197, 355.
Baya, weaver bird, 253, 380.
Bayana (Byana), ancient town in Bharatpur State, 56, 57, 301, 302.
Bayazid I (Bayazeth), Sultan, Emperor of the Turks, defeated by Timur, 234, 373.
Bazen (Bazon, Bazu), Signor David, 120, 150, 319.
Beas, river, 84, 312.
Beber, M. ——, of French E. I. Coy., granted farman by the Mughal Emperor, 31, 292; robbed at Agra, 50; at Burhanpur, 99, 100.
Becar (? Bihar), province of, 88, 313, 314; boundaries, 88; revenue, 88; castes and tribes, 88-92.
Begam Sahiba (Begam Saheb), *see* Jahanara Begam.
Begari (*Begarine*), labourer, 207, 362.
Behar, Behat, Bhat, *see* Jhelum.
Belgaum (Beligon), in Bombay Presy., town and fort, 267, 388.
Benares (Banarous, Benara, Benarous, Benarus), gambling at, 67, 305; temples of, 90, 262, 317, 386.
Bengal (Bengala), xxvii, xxixn, xxxiii, xl, 92, 94-97, 144, 148, 197; textiles from, 52, 96, 275; inhabitants, 94-95; trades and manufactures, 96; agricultural products, 96; flora and fauna, 96; rivers, 96, castles and temples, 96; revenues, 97; regarded as a penal province in Aurangzeb's time, 97, 317; assigned to Shuja, 223, 368.
Beni-Madhava (Bain-Madu), temple at Benares, 262, 386.
Berar (Varad, Varal), xxixn, xxxiii, xxxiv, 87, 99, 312, 313, 318, 322, 328; revenues of, 87; trade, 101.
Berengena, Bergamot tree, 203, 206, 359.
Bernier, François, physician and traveller, xxxii, xxxiii, xxxiv, xxxv, liv, lvii, 280, 281, 296, 297, 299, 305, 306, 316, 317, 318, 320, 324, 328, 330, 332, 333, 377.
Beteleira, betel plant, xliii-v, 144, 205, 333, 360.
Bets, see Vedas.
Bezat, *see* Jhelum.
Bezoar, an antipoison, 138, 331.
Bhadrapur (Madrapur), Muslim acrobats at, 168, 342.
Bhadwar (Badur), Raja of, inroads into Ahmadabad by, 12, 284.
Bhagirathi, *see* Ganges.
Bhagmati, mistress of Qutb Shah Muhammad Quli, Bhagnagar named after, 96, 148, 149, 316.
Bhagnagar (Begnagur), *see* Hyderabad.
Bhakkar (Tatabakar), fortress in Tatta, Sind, 228, 371.
Bhandaris (Bandarines), toddy-drawers and distillers, 256, 383.
Bhang (*Banghe*), hemp, used as intoxicant, xliii, 212, 363.
Bhansalis (Bangasalis), a caste in India, 257, 383.
Bhathelas (Batalas), a subdivision of the Brahman caste, 256, 383.
Bhatias (Gantias), a trading community, 257, 383.
Bhatta (*Boto*), a learned Brahman, 260, 385.
Bhimbar (Bambar), pass in Pir Panjal range, 83, 311.
Bhonslas, the, descent claimed from a branch of the rulers of Mewar, 184, 348.
Bhutan (Butan), musk from, 234.
Bibo, a kind of panther, 161, 339.
Bicholim (Bichiolin), town north of Goa, 209, 210, 362.
Bidar (Beder), in Hyderabad, 150, 328, 350; town, 113-14; fort built by Ahmad Shah Wali, 113, 114, 327.
—Governor of, *see* Shaista Khan.
Bidar Bakht, eldest son of Azam Shah, Panhala attacked by, 245, 378.
Bihat, Bihatah, *see* Jhelum river.
Bijapur (Visapor, Visiapour, Viziapour), 29, 38, 39, 109, 113, 116, 125, 126, 127, 151, 295; Aurangzeb's conquests in, 127, 328; Europeans in, 128; wealth, 128, 129, 130, 141, 145; short history, 128, 328;

Bijapur—*Contd.*
fort, 185; conquered by Aurangzeb, 235, 321, 322.
—King of, 184; alleged treacherous negotiations with Azam Shah, 238, 375; imprisons Shahji; Shivaji's wars with, 264-65; Pam Nayaka's rebellion against, 265; *see also* Yusuf Adil Shah.
—Queen of, peace with Shivaji, 265; *see also* Badi Saheba.
Bikaner (Becaner, Bikaneer, Bikanir), in Rajputana, xxxiv, 313, 314.
Biknur (Baquenour), in Hyderabad, 131, 329.
Bilimbeira, the Bilimbi tree, 204, 360.
Bilpad (Bilpar), village in Gujarat, Grasias of, 20, 287.
Bimlipatam, Dutch Factory at, 148, 335.
Birds, hospitals for, xlv-xlvi, 16, 286.
Biriguano, Prince of, *see* Sanseverino, Don Carlos.
Black Friars, *see* Augustinians, the.
Black Pepper, from Malabar, 122, 325.
Boars, at Daman, 161.
Bojata (? *Boyada*), caravan of oxen, 214-15, 364.
Bomanballi (Bombnali), village in N. Kanara Dist., Bombay, 215, 364.
Bombaraki, a disease at Daman, 162, 340.
Bombay (Bombaim, Bombayam), liii, 116, 125, 179, 180, 183, 275; short history, 179, 323; city and fort, 179, 346; fishing tribes, 257, 383.
Bon-Jesu, church of, St. Xavier's body at, 269, 389.
Borgia, Francis, invites Careri to Galgala, 217.
Borneo, island of, export of sago to Goa, 193; diamonds of, 251, 379.
Boullaye le Gouz, Francois de la, French envoy to India, 10, 31, 283, 292.
Boys (Boes), palanquin bearers, porters, 166, 194, 341.
Braganza, Dom Constantino de (Constantin), takes Daman from Sayf-ul-Mulk Miftah, 159, 338.
Brahmans (Brachman, Bramins), Hindu caste, xlvi, li, lii; females of, 186; at Goa, 187, 255, 382; subdivisions, 255, 381, 382; religious customs and beliefs, 258-60.
Brazil, in S. America, conquest by the Portuguese, 197, 349, 356; baboons in, 214, 364.
Brindeiera, the Brindon tree, 203, 359.
Britto, Antonio Machado de, murder of, 181-82; relates story re. apes, 214, 346.
Broach (Baroche, Barosce), city in Bombay Presy., liii, lx, 8, 21, 166; agate trade, 9; peacocks at, 9; situation, 9; customs duties, 9, 283; fortress, 9, 282-83; bazars, 9, 282, 283; Dutch factory at, 9, 283, 340; Calico manufacture, 9, 164, 282, 283, 340; trade, 164.
Brocade, trade at Surat, 164.
Brothers of St. John, *see* Hospitallers, the.
Bubo, a kind of disease, at Bassein, 169.
Bukhari Saiyads, in Gujarat, 14, 285.
—Leader of, *see* Shah Alam.
Bukkur, Bakhar (Bucor), fortified island in the Indus, Sukkur dist., Sind, 77, 309.
Buland Akhtar, Sultan (Sultan Banche), son of Shuja, 229, 230, 371.
Bulaqi (Boulloquoy, Polagi), *see* Dawar Baksh.
Bundi (Bando), town and state in Rajputana, 68, 305.
Burhan Nizam Shah, at war with Adil Shah, 183; permits Gen. Sequeira to build El Morro fort, 183, 347.
Burhanpur (Brampour), in C.P., xix, 37, 150-52, 295, 328, 335, 369; Beber and De La Boullaye at, 99, 318; buildings and roads, 100, 318; Aurangzeb at, 224; defeat of Dara's forces at, 225.
Burhanuddin, Saiyed, tomb at Khuldabad, 105, 320.
Buyo, a compound of bonga fruit, betel leaves and lime for chewing, 205, 361.

Cabaya (*Caba*), a kind of dress, 51, 162, 299, 340.
Cabo Verde, group of islands near Africa, 194.
Cacora (Kakore), village in Chandravaddi dist., 212, 213.
Cadeby, a kind of dress, 52, 300.
Caesar, Duke of Vendome, French Admiral, 29, 292.
Cajuyera, the *Caju* (Cashewnut) tree, 102, 202, 319, 359.
Calabria, *see* Radicena.
Calais (Calis), in France, 159, 338.
Calamac, *see* Jwalamukhi.
Calicoes, manufacture in Broach, 164, 282; trade in Bombay, 179-80; trade in Bengal, 275.
Calicut (Calecut), in Malabar Dist., Madras, Zamorin (Samorin) of, 121, 122, 324, 348; Vasco da Gama at, 195; conquered by the Portuguese, 195.
Calvar, in Golconda, 130.
Cambay (Cambaya), capital of the state of that name and former port in Bombay Presidency, xix, xxxi, xxxiii, xlvi, lx, 115, 121, 163, 166, 167, 286; gulf, xxxi, xxxii, 18, 116, 163; practice of *Sati* at, xlix; situation, 17; tombs, 18; veterinary hospital, 18; castle, 18; trade and manufactures, 18, 164, 282, 286, 340; ships and vessels, 18-19, 287; city and its inhabitants, 164, 340; loss of trade due to silting up of the harbour, 164; taken by the Portuguese, 195.
Cambolin, taken by the Portuguese, 196, 355.
Canara, Kingdom of, 185, 196.
Canarines, 166, 188, 198, 199.
Candales, a kind of dress, 162, 340.
Candavil (? Khanewal), in Multan Dist., Punjab, 77, 309.

Cannanore (Cananor), in Malabar dist., Madras, city, 121, 124, 125; harbour, 124, 326; taken by the Portuguese, 196, 324, 355.
Cannibalism, belief about, in Gujarat, 9, 283; in Andaman islands, 275, 391.
Cape of Good Hope, 194, 195, 198, 353.
Cape Palmyras (Palmyras Point), 147, 334.
Capes and headlands, Comorin, 4, 280; Cape Palmyras, 147, 334; Mount Delly, 185, 348; Cape of Good Hope, 194, 195, 198, 353.
Capital punishment, at Ranthambhor, 98.
Capuchins (Capucins), the, at Surat, 29, 41, 164, 166, 291, 296, 340; treated kindly by the Marathas during sack of Surat, 41, 296; at Daman, 158; at Salsette, 179; *see also* Recollects, the.
Caramboleira, Carambola tree, 202, 339, 359.
Carandeira, Caranda tree, 203, 359.
Carat, weight, 25, 290.
Caravanserai (Quervanseray), lvi, lvii, 284; at Ahmedabad, 12; at Agra, 49.
Carazzo, a kind of disease, *probably* plague, at Bassein, 169, 342.
Careck, *see* Galati river.
Careri, Giovanni Francesco Gemelli, life and works, xx-xxvii; estimate of his work, xxvii-xxviii; historical and topographical errors in his work, xxxi-xxxvi, liii-liv; errors in describing Indian fauna and flora, xxxvi-xl, 199-206, 250-53; on Indian people, their habits, food, dress, trades and professions, religious beliefs and tolerance, xl-xlvii, l-li, 245-50, 254-61; on early marriage in India, xlviii; on Indian women, xlviii-xlix, 247-49; on *Sati*, xlix-l; on caste system, li-lii, 254-58; on custom officers at Surat, lv-lvi; on Indian inns, lvi-lvii; on Indian transport, lvii-lix; on Indian roads, lix-lxiii; on Indian civility, lxiii; at Daman, 157-62; at Surat, 163-66; on Ahmadabad, Cambay and Broach, 163-64; visits Bassein, 166-70; visits Kanheri, 171-83; at Chaul, 183-84; on Shivaji, 184; on pirates in Arabian Sea, 185; at Dabhol, 185; at Goa, 186-94; on the history of the Portuguese in India, 194-97; on the government of Portuguese India, 198-99; journey to Galgala, 207-17; at Mughal camp at Galgala, 217-22, 264-67; on the history of Aurangzeb, 222-40; on Mughal geneology, 234-40; on Mughal government, 240-41; on Mughal revenues and wealth, 241-42; on Mughal arms and weapons, 242-45; on Mughal customs and manners, festivities, punishment, marriages, polyandry in Malabar, funeral rites, etc., 245-50; on Indian climate, mines and minerals and coins, 250-53; on Hindu superstitions, 250-61; on Hindu temples, 262-64; return to Goa, 267-73; voyage to Malacca, 273-76.
Carlina, Carlin, a silver coin of Naples, 211, 363.
Carmelites (Italian), church at Goa, 269.
Carnatic, the (Cornates), extent and government, 126, 127, 128.
Casabe (Cassabi), town near Bassein, Bombay, gardens and pleasure houses at, 168, 169, 342; Dominican church near, 169; sugar industry, 169.
Cashew-nuts (Quieson), of Balaghat, 102, 319.
Cashi (Cassi), near Ghodbandar, church of St. Jerome at, 172, 344.
Cassava (Cassaras), a kind of edible root, 161, 339.
Cassia, tree, 146, 334.
Castes and tribes, Hindu, xlii, li-lii, 88-92, 254-58, 314, 381; of Becar, 88-90; in Goa, 187, 188; of Multan, 77-78; in Telingana, 114-115.
Catechumen, at Goa, 193.
Cats, wild, at Daman, 161.
Causin, Father, story re. apes related by, 213.
Ceylon (Ceilon, Seylon), island of, 63, 204, 274, 275, 326; elephants of, 63, 252, 275, 380; conquered by the Portuguese, 195, 197; cinnamon of, 197, 275; trade with India, 242; rock-crystal from, 275, 391.
Chaalem, *see* Shah Alam.
Cha-Gehan, *see* Shahjahan.
Chaghtai (Zagatay), mountains, 4, 5, 234, 280.
Cha-Humayon, *see* Humayun.
Cham, *see* Muhammad Qasim, *Mutamad Khan.*
Chambal (Cham-Elnady), river, 57, 302.
Chambhars, caste in India, 257, 384.
Champson, Monsieur, 103.
Chandwar, *see* Firozabad.
Changez Khan, of Gujarat, 8, 282.
Char Minar, at Hyderabad, built by Muhammad Quli Qutb Shah, 131, 132, 133, 330.
Charados, Chardis, *see* Sudra.
Charanas (Tcherons), a caste in India, lx, 19, 257, 383; used as escorts by travellers, lx, 19, 287.
Chauki (*Chiaruci*), customs or toll station, 215, 364.
Chaul (Chaoul, Cheul), historic town in Kolaba dist., Bombay, 116, 184, 185, 197, 296-97, 323; port, 116, 323; Shivaji's camp at, 40; city and fortress, 183, 347; fortified by the Portuguese, 183-84, 347; taken by the Portuguese, 195.
Chawdis (Charados), low caste Hindus at Goa, 187.
Cheboular, in Afghanistan, 80, 310.
Chehil Minar (Celmenar), at Persepolis, 171, 344.
Chenab (Canab, Ychenas), river, xxii, 82, 84, 309, 311, 312.
Cheruman, *see* Pulayan.
Chiamkan, village on the way to Galgala, 215, 364.
Chiampin, *champa* tree, 206, 361.
Chiampon, village and fort on way to Galgala, 212, 364.

Chicacole (Cicacola), in Ganjam dist., Madras, 148, 335.
Chikalthan (Tchequelcane), near Hyderabad, 112, 321.
Chilan (Cilau), North Western Province of Ceylon, 197, 355.
Child-marriage, among Hindus, 72, 308.
Chilkur, near Hyderabad, 150, 335.
China, xxv, 4, 103, 193, 195, 197, 198, 199, 206, 207, 273, 275, 354; Careri's travels in, xxiv; Jesuits in, xxiv, 273; great wall, xxiv.
—Emperor of, Careri's interview with, xxlv; permits the Portuguese to colonise Macao, 195.
Chingiz Khan (Chingez Khan, Ginguis Can, Scinguis Khan), Mongol leader, 5, 234, 280, 373, 374; Jalaluddin Mangbarni defeated by, 74, 308.
Chintaman, temple of, built by Shantidas at Ahmadabad, 13, 285; desecrated by Aurangzeb and restored to the Jains by Shah Jahan, 13-14, 285.
Chintz (Schites), from Ahmadabad, 17, 286; trade at Masulipatam, 17, 146, 286, 334; at St. Thomas, 17, 286.
Chireta (*Criala*), a root, found in temperate regions of the Himalayas, 115, 323.
Chismer, *see* Kashmir.
Chita (*Cito*), leopard, 16, 161, 252, 286, 339, 379.
Chitor, former capital of Mewar, xxixn, xxxiii, 98, 317.
Chittagong (Chatigan), in E. Bengal, 96, 316.
Cholera, disease, 151, 335, 339.
Chorao (Charon), island in the Goa settlement, visited by Careri; Jesuits and Theatins at, 199, 273, 357, 390.
Choukis (*Tchogivis*), guards on the highways, 103, 319.
Choutia (Chiotia), *see* Ramnagar, Raja of.
Christians, the, at Surat, 21-22, 41, 287, 288; kindness of Jahangir to, 85, 312; at St. Thomas, 124, 326; in India, 254.
Chrysobara, Chrysobacra (? Krishnapura), 92, 315.
Cira (*Civa*), a turban made of particoloured cloth, 210, 248, 363, 378.
Cinnamon, 197, 204, 275, 360.
Citrouille (Citrul), a pumpkin, 66, 305.
Cochin, capital of Cochin State and chief port of Malabar, 122, 274, 324; elephants, 63; fort, 122; inhabitants, 122; law of succession in, 122; marriage customs, 122; pepper, 122; port, 122; trial by ordeal in, 124, 326; conquered by the Portuguese, 195, 325.
Cochin-China, French bishops and vicars apostolic in, 273; Jesuits in, 273.
Coconut, fruit and tree, 160, 161, 179, 339.
Coconut day, a Hindu Festival, 117, 323.
Cogea Mundy, *see* Muinuddin Hasan Chisti.
Coins and Currency, of India, 20, 253, 287, 290, 380; of Surat, 25; of the
Coins and Currency,—*Contd.*
Mughals, 26; of Golkonda, 136; of Southern India, 148, 334; of Goa, 270, 389-90.
Colewarts, Cabbages, 206, 362.
Colombo (Columbo), capital of Ceylon, xxxvn., 197, 355.
Comorin (Comori), headland in Madras, 4, 45, 257, 274, 280, 328, 384.
Compagnie des Indes, formation of, 29, 291.
Condoni, Father Joseph, a Sicilian missionary to Cochin-China, 273.
Congo-Bunder (Bander Congo), on the Persian Gulf, xxi-ii, 157, 158, 164, 168, 337.
Constantin, D., *see* Braganza, Dom Constantino de.
Constantin, Father, 162, 166, 337.
Constantinople, in European Turkey, xviii, xxi, 190, 349.
Conveyances and Transport, lvii-lix, 216; on way to Surat, 19-20; use of oxen, 73; use of chariots, 75; palanquins, 76-77, 309; coaches at Daman, 160, 341; of Goa, 188; in Balaghat, 214.
Cornac (Cornaccia), elephant driver, 221, 367.
Cornelians, sold at Surat, 25.
Corpus Christi, procession at Goa of, 271.
Coryat, Thomas, famous traveller, xvii, xxiii, xxxvii, xli, xlii, 302, 312; belief in Akbar's proficiency in necromancy, xxviii; attack on Islam and the prophet, 1; on Indian transport, lix; on robbers in European highways, lxi, lxii.
Cosimo III, Grand Duke of Tuscany, fondness for mogra tree, 205, 360.
Coslines, a coin of Naples, 160, 339.
Cosne, in Afghanistan, 80, 310.
Cossimbazar, Kasimbazar (Casambazar), in Bengal, 96, 316.
Costumes and dress, of the people at Agra, 50-53; used by Indian women, 53; of the inhabitants of Daman, 162; of the people of Bassein, 168; of the inhabitants of Salsette, 179; of Indians, 247-48.
Coulam, town in Malabar, 124.
Council de Facenda, *see* Junta da Fazenda Publica.
Coutinho, Gen. Sieur Francis, account of the Andaman islands by, 275, 276.
Covado (Covedo), a lineal measure, 179, 345.
Cow-worship, by the Hindus, 91.
Cranganur (Caranpanor), in Cochin, Madras, taken by the Portuguese, 196, 355.
Crore (*Crouls, courous*), Indian numeral, 25, 290.
Cumbarijiva (Cambargiva), island near Goa, Jesuits at, 199.
Curry Combes, a kind of comb used in currying a horse, 166, 305.

Custom houses, in Europe, lvi; at Suvali, 38; at Surat, 163.
Customs and beliefs, of the Indians, xl-liii, 245-50; of the inhabitants of Ponda, 211-15; of the Mughals, 245-50, 378.
—Muslim, relating to marriage, 31-33; relating to burial at Surat, 33-34.
—Parsi, funeral ceremony, lii.
—Hindu, *Sati*, xlii, xlix-l, 79-80, 119-20, 249, 324, 379, 384; transmigration of soul, xlii, 254, 381; relating to marriage, xlviii, 90, 255, 256-58, 382, 383; at Surat, 33-34; funeral rites, 33-34, 119-20; plant worship, 36; kindness to animals and insects, 36; child-marriage, 72, 117, 308; in Kandahar, 79-81, 311; idol-worship, 89, 90, 91; cow-worship, 91; animal sacrifices, 92; in Telingana, 114-15; at Bassein, 168; of Brahmans, 255; of Rajputs, 255, 384; of Banias, 256.
Customs duties, rates at Surat, lv, 3, 279, 280; discrimination between Hindus and Christians, 4; rates at Broach, 9, 283; from shipping at Suvali, 38; rates at Daman, 157, 337.
Cutch (Cache, Cachy, Caeche), island of, noted for its horses, xxxi.

Dabhol (Dabul), city in Ratnagiri dist., Bombay, 185, 354, 387; under Maratha occupation, 185; conquered by Gen. Almeida, 185, 195, 348, 354; conquered by Shivaji, 265.
Dacca (Dake), in East Bengal, Shuja at, 229.
Dah-hazari (*Deh Hazaris*), a rank of mansabdars, 243, 377.
Daman (Damam), Portuguese settlement in India, 197, 275; taken by Braganza from Sayf-ul-Mulk, 159; besieged by Aurangzeb, 159; taken by the Portuguese, 195.
Dancing Girls, at Emanuel Motto island, 199; in temples of India, 263.
Danishmand Khan, one of the titles of Mughal nobility, 222, 368.
Daniyal (Scia Daniel), son of Akbar, 235, 374.
Dara Shikoh, eldest son of Shah Jahan, 222, 368; Multan and Kabul assigned to, 223, 224; defeated by Murad in the battle of Dharmat, 225, 369; defeated by Aurangzeb at Burhanpur, 225; treachery of Khalilulla Khan towards, 225; defeated at Samugarh by Aurangzeb, 227-28, 368; flight to Ahmadabad, 227; betrayed by Jaswant Singh, 227-28, 370; deserted by Badi-uz-Zaman, 228, 370; defeated at Ajmer, 228; betrayed to Aurangzeb by Malik Jiwan, 228, 229, 370; sent to Agra by Bahadur Khan 228; assassinated by Aurangzeb and buried in Humayun's Tomb at Delhi, 229, 371.
Date, tree, 200, 358.
Daud Taqarrub Khan, *Hakim*, Shah Jahan's physician, persuades Aurangzeb to execute Dara, 228, 371.
Daugi, Passo de, former abode of the Portuguese viceroys of India near Goa, 190, 192, 208, 350, 362.
Daulat Khan-i-Khas, *see* Ghusal Khana.
Daulatabad (Dolet Abad), hill fort in Aurangabad Dist., Hyderabad State, Aurangzeb at, 244; King of Golkonda imprisoned in, 266.
Dawar Baksh, son of Khusrau, grandson of Jahangir, short account of, 6, 232-33, 281, 373.
Dawazdah-hazari (*Duaz-dehazaris*), a rank of mansabdars, 243, 377.
De Capan (Capon), island near Goa, 199, 357.
Deccan (Decan), the, kingdom of, subdued by the Portuguese, 195; assigned to Aurangzeb, 223.
Delhi, city, 58-59; Red fort, 59; Jami Masjid, 60; Chandni Chowk and Faiz Bazar, 60, 303; fauna, 62; elephants, 63-65; painters, 65; women of, 66, revenues, 68; Aurangzeb's coronation at, 231; Jahanara Begam at, 232.
Desai (*Say*), a hereditary district officer, of Jamboti, 268, 369.
Desembargadores, administrators of justice in Portuguese India, 198, 356.
Dharmat, battle of, 225, 369.
Dhobis (Doblis), washermen, 257, 383.
Diamonds, mines at Kollur, 146, 251, 334, 379; mines in India, 251; from Rammalakota, 251; of Borneo, 251, 379; trade at Goa, 272.
Diaz (Dias), Bartholomew, Portuguese Navigator, 194, 353.
Diu, Portuguese settlement in India, 195, 197.
Divar, *also named* Narva, island near Goa, 199, 357.
Diwali (*Divali*), Hindu festival, 264, 387.
Diwan (*Divan*), a Mughal official, at Ponda, 209; functions, 240, 376.
Diwan-i-Khas (*Divan Xas*), 'Hall of Private Audience', at Red Fort in Delhi, 240, 376.
Do-aspa, cavalry of the Mughals, 244, 377.
Dominicans, the, at Goa, 192, 193, 351, 356; monastery in Mozambique, 195; missionaries at Senna, 196.
Dongarim (Dongarin), island near Goa, 199, 357; St. Augustin Friars at, 199.
Dos Reys, *see* Reis Magos.
Du-hazari (*Cuhzaris*), a rank of mansabdars, 243, 377.
Dutch, the, coinage at Pulicat by, 148; in Malacca and Moluccas, 186, 195, 349, 354; capture Portuguese dominions in Ceylon, 197; trade with India, 242; encounter with cannibals of the Andamans, 275.

East India Company, xxix; efforts to suppress *Sati*, 1; factory at Surat, lviii, 22, 33-34, 38, 288, 293; factory at Ahmadabad, 13.
Echlas Canpani-Suba (? Ikhlas Khan Pani), 210, 362.
Eclipses, ceremonies and superstitions connected with, 263-64.
Edward, Father, Procurator to the nuns of St. Monica at Goa, 171, 172, 178, 180.
Egypt, xvii, xviii, xxi, 45, 297, 325.
—Governor of, *see* Sulaiman Pasha al-Khadim.
Ekoji, step brother of Shivaji, 112, 322.
El-Morro, 'Morro de Chaul' or the fortified hill of Korle, built by Gen. Sequeira, 183, 347.
Elabas, *see* Allahabad.
Elephanta (Elephant), cave temples, 180, 343, 346.
Elephant-fight, at Agra, 49; at Burhanpur, 100-01; at Hyderabad, 132.
Elephants, xxxvii; from India, Siam, Cochin, Sumatra and Golkonda, 63; from Ceylon, 63, 252, 275, 380; at Delhi, 63-65; capture of, 64, 65, 252, 304, 380; longevity, 65, 252, 304, 380; used in battles in Malabar, 124; hunting of 189-90, 350; for Mughal army, 219, 221, 366; courtship and gestation period, 252, 380; diet and maintenance, 252, 380.
Ellora (Elora), rock temples, xix, xxii, 104-07, 320.
Elmas-kepentch, *see* Ambarpet Kalan.
Emanuel I, King of Portugal (1469-1521), 186, 194, 349.
Emanuel Lobo de Silveira, island near Goa, 199, 357.
Emanuel Motto, island near Goa, 199, 357.
Emery stone (Emrod), of Golkonda, 138, 331.
England, xviii, xxi, 179, 203; trade with India, 242.
English, the, at war with the French, xxi; merchants, xlix, lv; shipping at Surat by, 38; at Dacca, 95; at Hyderabad, 135; at Golkonda, 136, 330; trade with India, 242; *see also* East India Company.
Eniktala, near Hyderabad, 150, 335.
Eunuchs, at Surat, 33.
Europe, xlv; customs houses in, lvi; village inns of, lvii; insecurity of roads in, lxi-lxii; grapes in, 216.
Europeans, the, travellers in India, xvii; at Surat, 21; at Hyderabad, 135-36.

Factories—
—Danish, at Tranquebar, 128, 328.
—Dutch, at Broach, 9, 283; at Ahmadabad, 12; at Surat, 22, 288; at Agra, 50, 299; at Patna, 96; at Vengurla, 128, 323; at Golkonda, 136, 330; at Pala-Kollu and Bimlipatam, 148, 335.
—English, at Ahmadabad, 13; at Surat, 27, 288.
Factories—
—French, at Surat, 163, 340.
—Portuguese, at Macao, 195, 354.
Fakirs (Faquirs, Faqirs), at Ahmadabad, 13, 285; at Allahabad and Puri, 93, 94; in Bengal, 94-95; in Telingana, 115; at Surat, 164-65; *see also Yogi*.
Fanam (*Fanon*), coin of Southern India, 148, 334.
Farasis, *see* Chambhars.
Fatehnagar, *see* Aurangabad.
Fatehpur (Fetipour), 56, 68, 69.
Fatehpur Sikri, in Agra dist., U.P., Buland Darwaza and Jami Masjid at, 56, 301, 305.
Fathers of the Society, *see* Jesuits.
Fathullah Imad Shah, of Berar, 127, 328.
Faujdar (*Foursdar*), Police magistrate in charge of a *sarkar*, at Surat, 28, 291.
Fauna, of Agra, 53, 54, 55; of Ajmer, 72-73; of Bengal, 96; of Daman, 161; of Delhi, 62-65; of Goa, 129; of Gujarat, 9, 23-24; of India, xx, xxxvi-xxxix, 252-53; of Kabul, 81; of Kanheri, 172, 177; of Malwa, 98-99.
Felicianus, Father, Prior of the Augustine Monastery at Bassein, 167, 170.
Ferreira, Father Emanuel, a Portuguese missionary to Tongking, 273, 276.
Festivals and fairs, Dewali, 264; Holi, 81, 208, 210, 264, 387; *Maghmela*, 93, 316; of Malabar, 125; of the Mughals, 66-68; *Muharram*, 148-49; *Nauroz*, 70-71, 306; *Ramzan*, 217; *Shab-i-barat*, 44, 297.
Figueira, banana tree, 201, 358.
Finch, William, xxiii, xxviii, xxxii, xxxvii, 313-18.
Firozabad (Beruzabad), in Agra Dist., U.P., 56, 301.
Flavius Arrianus, Greek historian, 11, 284
Flora, of Aurangabad, 102; of Bengal, 96; of Daman, 161; of Goa, 129, 199-206; of Golkonda, 130-31; of Hyderabad, 133-35; of India, xx, xxxvi-xl, 199-206, 251; of Lahore, 85; of Surat, 35-36.
Flux, a kind of disease, 151, 152, 336.
Footwears, used by the Indians, 52, 300; *see also Pa-posh*.
Fort St. Christopher, near Goa, 186.
Fort St. Thomas, near Goa, 186.
France, xxi, xxiv, 103; Indian trade with, 242.
Francis, Father, 157, 158, 162, 166, 182, 191, 337, 390.
Franciscans, the, church and monastery at Bassein, 169, 342; college and monastery at Mandapeshwar, 172, 344; monastery in Goa, 192, 193; order of the Observants, 194.
French, the, at war with the English, xxi; at Surat, 29-31; in Mughal army, 218.
French East India Coy, xxix, 163; factory at Surat, 29, 163, 291, 340; envoys to Mughal court, 50, 99-100.
Fruits, of Daman, 161; of Goa, 199-206; of India, 199-206.

Fryer, John, xxxvii, xliii, xliv, xlv, l, liii, 290, 330, 331, 335, 341, 343, 346, 348, 349.
Funeral rites, at Surat, 33-34; of the Hindus, 119-20, 249, 324.

Gabits, a tribe of fishermen, 257, 383.
Gabrs (Gaures), *see* Parsis.
Gahara Kunda (Geher Conde), supposed source of the Tapti river, 37, 294.
Gakkars (Caucares), 87, 312.
Galas, near Bombay, bay of, 184.
Galati, river near Hyderabad, 150, 335.
Galgala (Galgali), village on the Kistna in Bijapur dist., Bombay, Aurangzeb at, xxiv, 216, 217-22, 239; Careri's journey to, 207-17, 362-67, 375.
Galli, Father Salvador, a Milanese Theatin, 185, 192, 205, 207, 269, 272, 274, 276, 348, 392.
Gallivat (Galavetta, Galeota, Galiot, Gallavetta, Galliot), a kind of vessel, 162, 163, 166, 183, 196.
Gama, Dom Francisco da, Portuguese Viceroy of India (1597-1600), 190, 350, 353.
Gama, Vasco da, voyages of, 194; statue in Goa, 194, 353; discovery of a sea route to India, 194, 349, 353, 354; quells mutiny on board his ships, 195; at Calicut, 195, 324.
Gandikota (Guendicot), in Cuddapah Dist., Madras, fort at, 145, 146, 333.
Gangaputra (Pangaput), a low caste of India, 255, 382.
Ganges, the, river in India, xxx, xxxiv, li, 46, 87, 92-93, 96-97, 129, 229, 275, 313; source of, 4, 280; sacred character of 93, 315.
Gani, *see* Kollur.
Gardabad (Guerdabad), *see* Ahmadabad.
Gardens and Parks, at Jitbagh, 10, 283; at Ahmadabad, 11, 12, 14-15, 284-85; at Surat, 35-36; at Agra, 48, 290; at Delhi, 60; Shalimar Gardens, 68, 305; in Kashmir, 82-83, 311; at Lahore, 85; at Hyderabad, 132-35; at Bassein, 168-69, 342.
Garnets, kind of precious stone, in Delhi, 66.
Gaspar Dias, fort near Goa, 190, 273, 350.
Gaur (Gor), Province, xxxiii, xxxiv, 87, 313.
Gayali (Gagavali), Brahmans of Gaya, 255, 382.
Gazelles, a kind of animal, 161.
Gehanabad, *see* Delhi.
Geldria (Gueldria), Dutch fort at Pulicat, 148, 334.
Genoa, in Italy, xxiv, 182.
Gentis, the, *see* Hindus, the.
Ghari, Ghati (*Gary*), gong or bell, 139, 140, 331.
Ghazni, Ghazna, in Afghanistan, 80, 280, 310; ruled over by Pir Muhammad, 5; conquered by Babar, 5, 280.
Ghendas, *see* Rhinoceros.
Ghia Kakri (*Giacocharas*), a kind of fruit, 179, 345.
Ghiyasuddin Jahangir (Gayeteddin), son of Timur, 5, 281.
Ghodbander (Gormandel), village in Thana Dist., Bombay, 171, 180, 344.
Ghunghchi (*Gomtchi, Gongys, Gourghindel*), used as weight, 25, 290; used as soldering medium, 55, 301.
Ghusal Khana, private chamber of the Mughal Emperors near bathroom, *also known as Daulat Khana-i-Khas,* 240, 376.
Giagrane, *see* Puri.
Gingee (Gengi, Ginge), in S. Arcot dist., Madras, 127, 274, 328, 391; taken by Shivaji; Mughal siege of, 239, 375.
Ginger, exported from Ahmadabad, 17; trade at Surat, 164.
Goa, Portuguese settlement in India, xxiii, xxiv, xxxv, xxxvi, xl, 113, 116, 125, 166, 175, 185, 197, 273, 274, 275, 276, 332, 348; fauna and flora, xxxix, 129, 199-206, 358, 359; situation, 129; city, 129, 186, 274; fortifications, 129, 186, 349-50, 389; port, 129, 190, 191, 350; history, 129-30, 186, 195, 329, 349, 351; buildings, 129-30, 192, 270, 349, 389; inhabitants, 130, 158, 181, 187, 188, 255, 337; nuns of St. Monica at, 171; Portuguese ships at, 183; trade, 186; transport, 187, 194; castes and tribes, 187-88; merchants, 188; hunting at, 189-90; Cathedral of, 191-92, 351; church, college, convent and monasteries, 191-94, 269, 271, 272, 329, 350, 351, 352, 390; gates of, 194; Royal Hospital at, 194, 353; Inquisition at, 198, 356; government of 198, 356, 357; islands near, 199; coins of, 270, 389; diamonds at, 272; farm of the Augustinians, 273; pilots at, 273-74.
—Archbishop of, 192, 193, 198, 199; *see also* Annunciacao, Dom Fr. Agostinho.
—Viceroy of, 273, 274, 337; *see also* Alvor, Don Francis de Tavora.
Godaganga (Guenga, Ganga), *see* Godavari.
Godavari, river in S. India, 112, 150, 321, 335.
Goga, a port on the Gulf of Cambay, 45, 207.
Gohad (Gehud), town in Gwalior State, xxxiv, 93, 316.
Gohegaon (Gahelgaon), near Hyderabad, 150, 335.
Goldsmiths, workmanship at Agra, 55.
Golkonda (Golconda), Kingdom of, xix, 101, 108, 110, 113, 127, 147, 148, 207, 274; 328, 331; elephants, 63; situation, 130; extent, 130; collections of tolls at, 130; flora, 130-31, 145; currency, 136; Englishmen at, 136, 330; Dutch factory at, 136, 330; precious stones, 136-38, 330; diamond mines, 136, 137, 138, 142, 143, 330, 333; fort, 137-38, 330-32; manu-

Golkonda—*Contd.*
facture of 'bezoar' at; production of emery stone at, 138-39, 331; royal tombs, 139-40, 331; revenues, 142; Omrahs of, 143-44; climate, 145; inhabitants, 148; serpents at, 148; Muharram at, 148-49; conquered by Aurangzeb, 265-66, 332, 387, 388.
—King of, religion, 140; army, 140, 141-42; war with the Mughals, 141; served by Shivaji, 184; Shah Alam's alleged treacherous correspondence with, 237-38, 375; *see also* Abdullah Qutb Shah; Muhammad Quli Qutb Shah; Quli Qutb Shah.
Gondwana (Canduana), in Central India, 87, 313.
Gopi (Gopy), *Malik*, tank of, at Surat, 35, 294.
Goujon (Gudgeon), a small fresh water fish, used as manure for sugarcane cultivation at Surat, 36-37, 294.
Govindrajaswami temple, at Tirupati, 128, 328.
Gowalas (Gaulis), milkmen, 256, 382.
Grapes, of Surat, 23; of Europe, 216; of India, 296.
Grasias (Garasias, Gratiates), predatory inhabitants of Bilpad, 18, 20, 255, 283, 287, 382; dues exacted from travellers in lieu of protection, lxi; *ragout* served to travellers by, 21, 287.
—Raja of, lxii, 20.
Gujarat (Guzaratte, Guzerate), Kingdom of, *also known* as Kingdom of Cambay, xxixn, xlv, lii, lvi, lviii, 68, 163, 195, 197, 282, 286, 308, 324, 354; Mughal conquest of, liv, 8, 282; oxen from, lviii; roads, lxi, lxii; government, 8; ports, 8; towns, 8-10; buildings, 8-10; Cannibals of, 9, 283; inhabitants, 9-10; water works, 10, 35; rivers, 10-11; tombs, 12, 14-15, 45; revenues, 46; assigned to Murad, 223.
—King of, *see* Bahadur Shah; Mahmud Begada; Mahmud Shah III; Muzaffar Shah III.
Gulalbar, a red painted bamboo screen put up around the imperial camp, 217, 366.
Gul-i-Daudi (*Ghoul Daoudi*), a kind of flower, 134, 330.
Gwalior (Gualear), historic city and fort, xxixn, xxxiii, 97; Mughal state-prison in the fort, 97, 222, 317, 368; 370; Sipihr Shikoh imprisoned by Aurangzeb at, 228, 229; Murad put to death by Aurangzeb at, 229.

Haji (*Hagi*), a pilgrim to Mecca, 246, 378.
Haji Begam, *see* Hamida Bano Begam.
Haji Khan, a slave of Sultan Salim Shah Sur, 68, 308.
Hakim Daud (Nakim Daud), *see* Daud Taqarrub Khan, *Hakim*,
Halabas, *see* Allahabad.
Halalkhor (Halalkhur, Halalcour), sweeper caste in India, 89, 314.
Hali (Helly), village near Hyderabad, 150, 335.
Hamida Bano Begam, *commonly known as* Haji Begam, mother of Akbar, 57, 302.
Hanuman (Herman), the monkey god, 93, 130, 215, 259, 316, 329, 365, 384.
Haoud, *see* Oudh.
Harem (Aram), female apartments of the Mughals, 217, 366.
Hashim, Mir, expedition against the Portuguese in India, 45, 297.
Hasht-hazari (*Hechets*), Mughal *mansab*, 243, 377.
Hatnur (Etour), village on way to Burhanpur, 150, 335.
Hayat Baksh Begam, mother of Abdulla Qutb Shah, 140, 332.
Hazari, a rank of mansabdars, 243, 377.
Headgears, 52, 53, 210, 363.
Herbert, Sir Thomas, xxiin, xxiii, xxviii, xxix, xli, xlii, xlvi, xlviii, li, lii, liv, lix, 312.
Hermaphrodites, *see* Eunuchs.
Hindaun (Hindon), in Jaipur State, Rajputana, 56, 301, 315.
Hindukush, mountain range, 80, 310.
Hindus, the, xxxvi, 15, 16, 22, 165, 178, 179, 180, 199, 288; funerals, 33-34, 249, 260-61; women, 66, 165; castes and tribes, 88-92, 114-15; widows, 119-20; merchants, 165; peasants, 169, princes, 207; marriages, 248, 261, 382; *sati*, 249; religious beliefs and social customs, 254, 258-60, 263, 381; gods and goddesses, 259, 260; trial by ordeal, 261; infanticide, 261, 385; pilgrimage, 262, 263.
Holi, a Hindu festival, 81, 210, 264, 311, 363, 387.
Honavar, Onore (Onor), in North Kanara, 125, 327.
Honey, exported from Ahmadabad, 17.
Hopewell (ship), xviii, xix, 1, 279.
Horses, for Mughal army, 62-63, 219, 366.
Hoshang Shah, Jami Masjid at Mandu built by, 97, 317.
Hospitallers, the, at Bassein, 169, 343.
Hospitals, for birds and beasts, *see* Veterinary hospitals.
Hugo, Hubert, a Dutch pirate, 29, 30, 291, 292.
Humayun (Humagion), Mughal Emperor, 97, 232, 233, 281, 312; succeeds Babar, 5; tomb at Delhi, 58, 229, 299, 302, 317; wars with Sher Shah, 126, 235, 327; aided by Shah Tahmasp, 126; death, 235, 374.
Hunting, 16-17, 54-55, 161; of lions, 189-90; of waterfowls, 246, 378; of gazelles, elephants, etc., 252-53.
Huq-Nazar, (*Ak-nazar*), an official of the King of Golkonda, 131, 329.

Hurricane (Hurrican), 250, 379.
Hyderabad, capital of Golkonda, 96, 148, 149, 150, 316, 322, 329, 330, 335, 388; situation, 131; town and gardens, 132, 133, 134, 135; palaces, 132-33, 266; flora, 133-35; administration, 135; inhabitants, 135-36; trade and manufacture, 135, 136, 321; currency, 136; prostitutes, 136.
Hydraphes, *see* Jhelum.

Ibn Daud, *Amir*, Lord of Aden, death, 45, 298.
Idol worship, by the Hindus, 22, 89, 90, 91.
Ikhlas Khan Pani (Ech-las Can Pani), 210, 362.
Ilahabad, Illahabas, *see* Allahabad.
Ilha de Vaccas (De la Vaca), *see* Arnalla.
Ilheos Queimados (Ysleos Quernados), a group of rocky islets nine miles off Vengurla, 185, 348.
Imam, 13, 285, 288.
Inayat Khan, Governor of Surat, deserts his post, 41, 296.
Incense, sold at Surat, 25.
Indalwai (Indelvai), town near Hyderabad, 108, 321; iron mines at, 112.
India, xvii, 5, 6, 190, 213, 280; flora, xxxvi-xl, 199, 205, 206, 250, 251; fauna, xxxvi-xl, 252-53; social customs and religious practices, xl-liii, 245-50; caste system, xlii, li-lii; economic conditions in 17th Century, liv; roads and inns, lix, lx, lvi, lxiii, 216; inhabitants, lxiii, 245-50, 254-58, 381; boundaries and divisions, 4; trade, 242; languages, 247; women, 248; minerals and precious stones, 251; currency, 253.
Indian Caucasus (Caf-Dagai), *see* Hindukush.
Indigo, from Sarkhej, 16, 285; produced in Cambay, 18, 282, 286; trade at Surat, 25; from Khandesh, 101; trade at Baroda, 297.
Indur (Indour), *see* Nizamabad.
Indus river, xxx, xxxii, xxxiii, 3, 74-75, 84-85, 280, 309, 311, 312.
Infanticide, among the Hindus, 261.
Inhame do Cao (Inhama Cona), sweet potato, 206, 362.
Innocent XI, Pope, 273, 390.
Inquisition, the, at Goa, 198-99, 357.
Iran, 77, 78-79, 80, 102.
Iron, mine at Narwar, 54, 301; mines at Indalwai, 112.
Irrigation and Waterworks, tanks in Gujarat, 10, 283; at Ahmadabad, 11, 15, 16, 284, 285, 294; at Surat, 34-35, 294; at Lahore, 85; at Chitor, 98; at Sitanagar, 111; at Golkonda and Hyderabad, 134-35, 331; *see also* Tanks and Wells.
Islam Shah, *see* Salim Shah Sur.
Ismail Adil Shah, king of Bijapur, at war with Nizam-ul-Mulk, 183, 347; loses Dabhol to Gen. Almeida, 185, 348; conquest of Goa; surrenders Goa to Albuquerque, 186, 349.
Ispahan, in Persia, xvii, xviii, xxi, xxiv, xliii, 144, 158, 239, 337.
Italy, xviii, xxi, 168, 170.
Itgi (Etchi), village near Kakeri, 215, 365.
Itibar Khan, one of the titles of Mughal nobility, 222, 368.
Itimad Khan, *see* Abdul Karim.
Ivory, sold at Surat, 25; work at Cambay, 18, 286.

Jack fruit (Jaqua), 193, 350.
Jafarabad (*Zafravad*), village near Hyderabad, 150, 335.
Jaffna, Jaffnapatam (Jafanapatam), in Ceylon, 197, 355.
Jagannath (Jaganat, Jagannat, Jekanat), temple at Puri, Orissa, 94, 262, 313, 314, 316, 317, 386.
Jagir, 218, 240, 366.
Jahanara Begam, daughter of Shah Jahan, 49, 60, 222, 223, 226, 229, 231-32, 368, 372.
Jahangir (Gehanguir), Mughal Emperor, xxix, liv, lviii, lix, 6, 20, 312, 315, 327; tomb at Shahdara, 48, 299, 373; celebrates *Nauroz* in Ajmer, 70-71; kindness to the Christians and Portuguese, 85, 312; Khusrau and Shah Jahan's rebellion against, 232, 372.
—sons of, *see* Khurram; Khusrau; Parwez.
Jai Singh, Mughal General, defeats Shivaji, 42, 296; invades Bijapur, 141, 321, 332.
Jains, the, xlvi; in the Punjab, 86-87, 312; nuns, 87.
Jaisalmer (Jeselmeere), in Rajputana, xxixn, xxx, 68.
Jalaluddin Mangbarni (Gelaleddin), Shah of Khwarizm, defeated by Chingiz Khan, 74, 308.
Jalesar (Oulesser), in Orissa, inhabitants of, 94, 316.
Jamboleira, the Jambolon tree, 202-03, 359.
Jambos, Rose-apple tree, 203, 359.
Jamboti (Jambot), south-west of Belgaum, 268, 389.
Jamboyera, Jambo, the *Jamrul* tree, 204, 359.
Jamdhar (*Gemder*), a kind of dagger, 226, 370.
Jami Masjid, built by Ahmad Shah at Ahmadabad, 13, 284; at Delhi, 60, 303; built by Hoshang Shah at Mandu, 97, 317; built by Malik Ambar at Aurangabad, 103, 319.
Jangomeira, the Jangoma tree, 203, 359.
Janissaries (Janisaries), army of the Ottoman Empire, 45, 298.
Janjira, island, held by the Sidis, 183, 347.
Japan, 195, 242.
Jaquera, Jack-fruit tree, 203-04, 359.

Jasmine (Jasmin), *also known as* mogra flower, 205, 360.

Jassi, *see* Ayaz Sultani, *Malik*.

Jaswant Singh (Gessen Sanghe), Raja of Jodhpur, defeated by Dara, 225; betrays Dara, 227-29, 369-70.

Jehana, *probably* a corruption of Jagannath, xxxiv, 88, 314.

Jesual (Jesuat, Jesnoll), an unidentified province, xxixn, xxxiii, xxxiv, 88, 313, 314.

Jesuits (Paulistas), the, 129, 180, 193, 199, 274; church at Bassein, xxii, 169, 185, 342; in China and Cochin-China, xxiv, 273; monasteries at Daman, 158; at Goa, 190, 191, 192, 351; garden and monastery in Mozambique, 195; at Cumbarjiva and Juarim, 199; at Chorao, 273; novitiates, 273.

Jesus Christ, reverence of the Muslims for 85, 312.

Jewellery and Ornaments, at Cambay, 18; of the Mughal women, 53; workmanship at Agra, 55; at Delhi, 65-66; of women at Daman, 162, 340; of the Hindus of Bassein, 168.

Jews, the, at Surat, 22, 288; in India, 254.

Jhelum, tributary of the Indus, xxx, xxxii, 82, 84, 311, 312.

Jidpalli, village near Hyderabad, 131, 329.

Jitbagh (Gitbag), built near Sarkhej by Abdur Rahim Khan-i-Khanan, 10, 283.

Jiwan Khan *Malik* (Gion Kan), betrays Dara, 228, 229.

Jodhpur, Maharaja of, *see* Jaswant Singh.

John II, King of Portugal (1455-98), 194, 353.

John III, King of Portugal (1502-57), 167, 341.

Juarim (Juvari), island near Goa, 199, 357.

Jube (Muluk Khana), at Ahmadabad, 13, 285.

Jugglers and Acrobats, of India, li, 109-10, 165, 168, 264.

Jumna (Gemna, Geminy, Gomany), river, 46, 57, 92, 298, 315.

Junta da Fazenda Publica (Council de Facenda), Council of Public Revenue, at Goa, 198, 356.

Justice, administration of, at Surat, 27, 28, 29; at Bassein, 70, at Hyderabad, 135; in Portuguese India, 170, 198; of the Mughals, 240.

Jwalamukhi, in Kangra Valley, Punjab, a place of pilgrimage, xxxiv, 87, 313.

Kabul (Cabour, Caboulistan, Kaboul, Kabulistan), in Afghanistan, xxixn, xxx, xxxii, xxxiii, 4, 6, 280, 310; description, 80-81; short history, 80-81, 223, 280, 310.

Kabul, river, 80, 82, 84, 310, 311, 312.

Kafir (*Kafar*), unbeliever in Islam, 223, 368.

Kafris (Cafres), slaves, in Goa, 188-90; in Daman, 159, 338; in Mozambique, 196; at Sena, 196.

Kahars, caste in N. India, 88, 314.

Kahror, Khardar (Cordar, Cozdar), town near Multan, 77, 309.

Kailash Temple, at Ellora, 106, 320.

Kakaji, ruler of Jawhar State in Thana district, 169, 315, 342; sack of Surat by, 163, 340; plunders Surat, 163.

Kakeri (Kancre), village near Belgaum, 215, 365.

Kakore or Kakora, village in Chandrovaddi dist, southeast of Ponda, 212, 364.

Kakori (Cancares), in Lucknow Dist., U.P., 87, 312.

Kalambi, Kunbi, Kurmi (Columbines, Courmy), agricultural caste of India, 88, 89, 256, 315, 383.

Kaliana, in Thana dist. Bombay, besieged by Mir Jumla, 224, 368.

Kalligudi (Kodelki), village near Yadvad, 216, 365.

Kalutara (Calaturre), in Ceylon, 197, 355.

Kalvaral (Calvar), vilage near Daulatabad, 108, 112, 321.

Kalyani (Calion), in Hyderabad, ancient Chalukyan City, 113, 322.

Kam Baksh (Sikandar), fifth son of Aurangzeb, 239, 375.

Kamal Khan, one of the titles of Mughal nobility, 222, 368.

Kanara (Canara), districts in Bombay and Madras, 125, 261, 316, 327, 349.

Kanchani (*Quenchenies*), a dancing girl, 33, 71, 293, 306; *see also* Dancing Girls.

Kandahar (Candahar), xxixn, xxxiii, 4, 6, 7, 42, 77, 280, 296, 310; Mughal wars to capture it, 78-79, 282, 310; description, 78-80; revenues, 79.

Kanheri Caves, xxii, xxiii, xxvi, xxvin, xxvii, xxxviii, 171-82, 343, 344, 345.

Kansars (Cansar), Coppersmiths, 256, 382.

Kansuh-al-Ghori, ruler of Egypt, sends expedition under Mir Hashim against the Portuguese, 45, 297.

Kanwa (Canova), famous village near Bayana, 56, 301.

Karatals, Cymbals, 248, 378.

Kareputtnm (Carapatan), in Ratnagiri dist., Bombay, 128, 328.

Karwan, suburb of Hyderabad, 132, 330.

Kashmir (Cashmir, Chistmere, Kachemir, Kichmir), xxix; xxx, xxxii, xxxiii, 281, 307; shawls from 52, 300; physical aspects, 82-84; history, 83; Akbar's conquest, 83-84, 311; revenues, 84.

Katar, Katarah, Katari (*Cateri*), a dagger, 220, 303, 367.

Kathiawad, peninsula of, xxxi, 257, 383.

Kathis, a fighting tribe of professional marauders, 257, 383, 384.

Kaukabah, Mughal ensign, 219, 366.

Kayangulam, Kayankulam (Carghelan), in Travancore State, 124, 326.
Kelve, *see* Mahim.
Kesava Raya (Kesora), temple at Brindaban, 262, 386.
Khabardar (*Caberdar*), a cry of challenge, 27, 291.
Khajur (*Cadgiour*), date, used in preparation of Toddy, 23, 24, 289.
Khalilullah Khan (Calil-ullah-Kan), 225, 369.
Khalli (Caly), village on the Godavari river, 150, 335.
Khambayat, *see* Cambay.
Khanapur (Quanapour), village near Surat, 102, 319.
Khanderi (Canderin, Candrin, Kenery), island near Bombay, 183, 184, 347.
Khandesh, (Candeys, Candich, Candiche, Candisch, Dandes), xxxi, xxxiii, 12, 99-101, 151, 284, 318; revenues, 99; trade and manufacture, 99, 100, 101; cotton, 101; indigo, 101.
Khandi (*Candy*), a weight, 25, 289.
Khanewal (Candavil), town in Multan dist., Punjab, 77, 309.
Khan-i-Saman, Mir Saman, (*Cansamon*), High steward of the Mughals, duties of, 240, 376.
Kharak, Kharaku (Khorgu), island in the Persian Gulf, 133, 354.
Kharepatan (Crapaten), fortress in Bijapur, conquered by Shivaji, 265, 387.
Khatri (Catry), Hindu Caste, 78, 88, 309, 314.
Khichari (*Cachiari, Kichery, Kistery*), a kind of cooked food, xlv, 73, 208, 308, 362.
Khorasan (Corassan), in Persia, 5, 280.
Khuldabad, near Ellora, 105, 320.
Khurram (Schach Choram, Korom), *see* Shahjahan.
Khusrau, Prince, son of Jahangir, 235, 281, 374; rises against his father, 232, 372; death of, 232, 373.
Khwarizm (Carezmian), ruling house of, 74, 308.
Kikar, *see* Babul.
Kiladar (*Kilidar*), commandant of a fort, castle or garrison, 211, 363.
Kilimane (Chilimani), a Portuguese trading town in East Africa, 196, 354.
Kim, river, 9, 282.
Kiosk, Kushk (Kiochk), a pavilion, 2, 279.
Kishm (Kescimi), island in Persian Gulf, 196, 354.
Kistna (Kachkna, Kiscina), river, 146, 217, 334.
Kohir (Covir), near Bidar, 150, 335.
Kolis, the, a predatory tribe, lx, lxii, 88, 257, 283, 314, 370, 383.
Kollattiri Rajas (King of Cananor), rulers of Cannanore, 124, 326.
Kollur, on the Kistna river, diamond mines at, 146, 251, 334, 379.
Kondalwadi (Condelvai, Condelvaly), in Nizamabad dist., Hyderabad, 108, 112, 321.
Kongun, *see* Congo-Bunder.
Konkanies (Canarines), 187, 188.
Korales (Carolas), territorial units for administrative purposes in Ceylon, 191, 355.
Korle, (Moro di Ciaul), 116, 323.
Kotta (Acota), capital of Ceylon during the sixteenth century, Batticaloa bequeathed to the Portuguese by the king of, 197, 355.
Kottakhal, pirates of, 125, 326.
Kotwal (*Cattual, Catoual, Cotwal*), police magistrate, functions, 12, 27, 28, 29, 221, 284, 291, 367.
Krishna (Kansunu), one of the incarnations of Vishnu, 259, 384; belief of the inhabitants of Kabul in the legend of, 81, 311.
Krosa (*Coss, Cosse, Kos*), unit of distance, 9, 212, 215, 283.
Kshatriyas (Catry, Cuttery), Hindu Caste, lii, 88, 314.
Kurram, river, 80, 310.

La Boullaye (de la Boullaye), French envoy, at Surat, 10, 31, 283, 292.
La Palvereira, palace at Goa, 191, 350.
Lac, exported from Ahmadabad, 17; sold at Surat, 25; from Sindhukheda, 44, 297.
Lahari Bandar, Lari-Bandar (Loureebender), ancient port of Sind near Debal, 75, 308-09.
Lahore (Lahors), xxxii, xxxiii, xlvii, xlix, lix, 57, 223, 305, 312; textiles, 13; physical aspects, 84-85; city and fort, 84-85; Mughal paintings, 85; agriculture and manufactures, 85; flora, 85; revenue, 85.
Lakh (*Lak*), Indian numeral, 25, 290.
Lambert, Hugo, *see* Hugo, Hubert.
Lambert, M., Bishop of Beirut in Syria, travels of, 103, 319.
Lambuna, a place near Goa, 185.
Land Settlement, of Salsette, 179.
Langoti, lion cloth, 187, 349.
Langotis (Langottis), a poor caste of the Hindus, at Goa, 187, 349.
Lar, about 40 miles from Teheran, Persia, xxi, 168, 331, 342.
Lascar (*Lashkar*), a military camp, 217, 365.
Lasina (Lasana, Lazana), town in Nander dist., Hyderabad, 108, 112, 321.
Lasur (Sour), town near Hyderabad, 102, 319.
Law, Islamic, 26, 290; of Kandahar, 79; of succession in Malabar, 122, 324.
Leutis, a kind of vessel, 183.
Limodra (Limadur), in Rajpipla State, cornelian and agate mines near, 18, 286.

Linschoten, John Huyghen Van, xxii, xlvi, 279, 286, 306-07, 325, 335, 336, 341, 358; on fauna and flora of India, xxxvii, xxxix; on Kanheri and Elephanta, 343.
Lions, hunting method of the *kafirs*, 189-90.
Lisa (Lila), near Hyderabad, 108, 112, 321.
Lisbon (Lisborn), capital of Portugal, 188-89, 194-95, 202, 205.
Livourne (It. Livorno, Eng. Leghorn), xviii.
Livre, French coin, 3, 279, 289, 290, 295.
Louvre, town near Paris, 132.
Lovell, A., English translator of Thevenot's *Voyages*, xx.
Luigi, Don, Duke of Medina, Careri dedicates his book to, xxiv.

Ma Sahib, daughter of the King of Golkonda, 142, 332.
Macao, Portuguese Settlement on the coast of China, xxiv, 195, 197, 198, 199, 271, 354.
Macassar, in the island of Celebes, 197, 356; subdued by the Portuguese, 197; Indian trade with, 242.
Machini, machin seeds, 267, 388.
Madina (Medina), city in Arabia, 30.
Madras (Madrastapatan), 142, 185; climate, 274, 333, 391.
Madre de Deus (Madre de Deos), church at Goa, 186, 192, 349.
Madrid, capital of Spain, 182.
Madura (Madure), city and dist. in Madras, 124, 147, 197, 274, 326, 328, 391.
Magh-mela, at Allahabad, 93, 316.
Maghs (Mag), the, people of Arakan, 229, 230, 371.
Mahabat Khan (Muhabbat Khan), Governor of Ahmadabad, 11, 284.
Mahadeva (Madeo, Mahadev), Hindu deity, li, 34, 293; *see also* Shiva.
Mahalakshmi (Malachiche), Hindu goddess of wealth, 259, 384.
Mahamaya, Hindu deity, temple at Nagarkot, 87, 313.
Mahi (Mai), river in Western India, xxxii, 10, 20, 283.
Mahim (Maim), town in Thana dist., Bombay, 167, 341; fort, 195; taken by the Portuguese, 195.
Mahmud Begada, Sultan (Mahomed Begeran Sulthan), King of Gujarat, liv; constructs tanks at Sarkhej; tomb at Sarkhej, 14, 285.
Mahmud Khilji, tomb at Mandu, 97, 317.
Mahmud Shah, King of Bengal, 126, 327.
Mahmud Shah III (Sultan Mamcot), King of Gujarat, 8; tomb at Sarkhej, 14, 285.
Mahmudi (Mahmoudy), Indian coin, 26, 290, 382.
Mahua (*Mahova*), tree, at Balaghat, 102, 319.
Maidan Shah (Meidan-chah), the king's square at Ahmadabad, 12, 284.
Maina (*Meina*), a bird of grackle variety, 96, 316.
Mainpuri (*Menapur*), district in U. P., 88, 314.
Majericam, a kind of herb, *commonly known as* Ban Tulsi, 206, 361.
Makua (Macua), the, a cannibal race of Africa, 190, 350.
Malabar, 121-22, 195, 280, 324-25; pirates, 18-19, 125, 184-85, 287, 348; ports, 122; law of succession in, 122, 324; Dutch advent in, 122-23, 325; inhabitants, 122-25, 325; wealth, 124; festivals, 125.
Malabar Recipe (Malabar Receipt), administered to victims by the pirates, 185.
Malacca (Malaca), on the west coast of Malay Peninsula, 186, 203, 204, 273, 349, 354, 387, 390; export of sago to Goa, 193; conquered by the Portuguese, 195.
Maldive islands, an archipelago in the Indian Ocean, 275, 391; Indian trade with, 242.
Mali, gardener caste, 256, 382.
Malkapur (Melcapour), near Hyderabad, 150, 335.
Mall, *see* Trincomalee.
Mallaias, a species of mango, 202.
Malvan (Malinadi), fort in Ratnagiri dist., Bombay, 185, 348.
Malwa (Malva), province of, xxixn, xxxiii, 97-99; situation, towns, history, 97, 317; architectural remains, 98; revenues, 98; bats, 98.
Mamaniva, Mameva (? Mahamaya), Hindu goddess, temple at Surat, 36, 164, 294, 340.
Mamdapur ((Mandapour), a town in Bijapur dist., Bombay, 216, 267, 365.
Mamelukes (Mammelukes), Turkish and Circasian slaves of the ruler of Egypt, 45, 297, 325.
Man, maund, Indian weight, 25, 253, 289, 381.
Manar, island west of Ceylon, fort in, conquered by the Portuguese, 196, 355.
Mandapeshwar (Monoposser), in Bombay Presidency, cave temples at, xxii, 172, 344; road to Kanheri from, xxiii; underground church at, 172; college and monastery of the Fransiscans at, 172, 344.
Mandavi (Mendova, Mandua, Mandoua), river near Goa, 129, 186, 191, 329, 348.
Mandelslo, John Albert de, xvii, xviii, xxix, xxx, xxxi, xxxiii, xxxv, xxxvi, xxxvii, xlii, xliii, xliv, xlv, xlvi, li, lii, liii, liv, lv, lvi, lviii, lix, lx, lxi, lxii, 279-82, 283, 284-86, 289, 293-94, 297, 308, 325, 351; opinion on Hindu religious beliefs, xlvii; on marriage customs of the Hindus, xlviii; on *Sati*, xlix, l; on Indian highwaymen, lxi.

Mandu (Mando, Mandogarh), in Dhar State, C. I., xxxiii, lvii; history, 97, 317; Jami Masjid, 97, 317; tomb, 97, 317; town and fort, 97-98; ruins, 98; tanks at, 98, 318.
Manchua (*Manchuca*), cargo boat, 183, 191, 347.
Manesio, Eduardo, Archbishop of. Goa (1595-1610), 85, 352.
Mangalore (Mangalor), in South Kanara, 125, 327.
Mangas Carreiras, a specie of mango, 202.
Mangelin (Mangelis), seed of, used as a weight in various parts of India, 25, 289.
Mango tree, planted by St. Francis Xavier in St. Paul's church at Goa, 193.
Mangoes (Mangos), the well known fruit of India, 179, 274, 339, 358.
Manilla, in the Philippine Islands, xxiv, 204.
Manjra (Mandgera, Manjera), a tributary of the Godavari, 112, 150, 151, 321, 335.
Manna, sold at Surat, 25, 289.
Mansab (*Manseb*), rank in Mugal Army, 243, 377.
Mansabdari (*Mansebdari*), system under the Mughals, 49, 244, 299, 377.
Mansanas, a kind of fruit, 161.
Mantur (Matur), a town midway between Mudhol and Galgala, 217, 365.
Manucci, xxix, xlii, 1, 281, 283-84, 286, 291-92, 297, 303, 305, 308, 312, 318, 324, 330-31, 334, 346-47, 353, 358.
Manwat (Manod), near Hyderabad, 112, 321.
Marad Khor, Murda Khor (Merdi-Coura), a cannibal tribe in Gujarat, xxviii-ix, 9, 283.
Marathas, the, country of; struggle with the Mughals; menace in the Deccan, lxii; spare Capuchin monks from molestation during sack of Surat, 41, 296.
—King of, *see* Rajaram; Sambhaji; Shivaji.
Mardangarh (Mardongar), fort near Ponda, 211.
Mardol, in Ponda dist., Goa, description, 208, 362; temple at, 208-09.
Marialva, Marquis of, a Portuguese nobleman, 189.
Mariucca, Signora, travels with della Valle in India, lviii, lv.
Marmagao (Murmugon), peninsula, village, fort and port in Salsette dist., Goa, 191, 351.
Marrag (Morg), 150, 335.
Marriage Customs, among Muslims at Surat, 31-33; among the Hindus, 90; child marriage, 117; of Hindus and Muslims of Baglana, 117-18; of the Portuguese in India, 170; in Goa, 187, 349; among Indian Muslims and Hindus, 248, 378; of Brahmans, 255; among the untouchables, 256-58, 383.
Martinhos, a kind of bird, 161.
Mary, mother of Jesus, revered by the Muslims, 85, 312.
Mary of Jesus, Sister, appearance of sacred signs on her body at death, 193, 352.
Maryam, *Hazrat*, *see* Mary, mother of Jesus.
Masulipatam (Masulipatan), in Kistna Dist., Madras, xix, xxxii, 96, 113, 136, 142, 147, 148, 230, 316, 334; *sati* at, 1; textiles and chintz from, 17, 146, 286; situation, 146; diamond mines, 146; fauna, 146; people, 147; shipping at, 147; diseases, 147-48.
Mata, *see* Mahamaya.
Matar, town and taluka in Kaira dist., Bombay, 10, 283.
Matricula, General, Portuguese official at Goa, 198, 356.
Matriz, *see* St. Joseph, Cathedral of.
Maula, *Mulla* (*Moula*), a Muslim theologian, 33, 293.
Mawara-un-Nahr, Ma-wara-l-Nahr (Maurenahor), *see* Transoxania.
Mecca (Mecha), in Arabia, 29, 292; Shuja's intended pilgrimage to, 229-30.
Medchal (Marcel), in Hyderabad, 131, 329.
Medina, Duke of, *see* Luigi, Don.
Meghdambar (*Mickdember*), a kind of house, 64, 304.
Mehmadabad, Mahmudabad (Mamadebad), in Kaira dist., Bombay, cotton thread from, 46, 298.
Mekran (Macran), in Southern Baluchistan, 4, 7, 280.
Menzes, Dom Fr. Aleixo de, Archbishop of Goa, 194, 342, 352.
Meos, the, country of, in Alwar and Tijara, 92, 315.
Merta (Mirda), town in Jodhpur State, Rajputana, 56, 301.
Meru (*Merous*), wild deer, xxxix, 55, 161, 301, 339.
Mestizos, the, half caste, at Goa, 158, 187, 337.
Mewar, ruling family of, descent claimed from Rama, 98, 318.
Mewat (Menat, Mevat), the country of the Meos, xxixn, xxxiv, 92; *see also* Meos.
Miana, town in Persia, Thevenot's death near, xvii.
Miftah, *Sayf-ul-Mulk* (Asid Bosita Abyssino, Cide Bofata), surrenders Daman to the Portuguese, 159, 338.
Milan, in Italy, xxiv, 207.
Milocoxim, *see* Gopi, *Malik*.
Minaz, Khojah (Cogea Minas), an Armenian merchant, robbed at Surat, 28, 291.
Mines and Mining, in Borneo, of diamonds, 251, 379; in India, 251; of cornelian and agates near Limodra, 18, 286; of iron at Narwar, 54, 301; of iron at Indalwai, 112; of diamonds in Golkonda, 136, 137, 142, 143, 330, 333;

Mines and Mining—*contd.*
of diamonds in Kollur, 146, 251, 334; of precious stones, 251; in Mexico, at Pachuca, xxiv.

Mir Arz, Mughal officer in charge of petitions, 220-21, 367.

Mir Jumla (Emir Gemla), *see* Muhammad Said, Mir.

Miraculous Cross, church at Goa of, 193, 272, 352, 390.

Mir' adl (*Adelet*), an administrator of justice under the Mughals, 240, 376.

Miran Shah, son and successor of Timur, 235, 373-74.

Miranda, Francis de, in the Mughal camp at Ponda, 212.

Mirbaba, *see* Bahadur Khan.

Mirzababer, *see* Babar.

Misericordia, the, church of, at Bassein, 169, 342, 343; monastery in Mozambique, 196; *see also* Santa Casa de Misericordia.

Missionaries, in India, Jesuits, 257; in Cochin-China, 273; summoned by Pope Innocent XI to Rome, 273, 390.

Mocha, Mokha (Moca), port in Arabia, 29, 242, 292, 376.

Mogoreira, the *Mogra* tree, 205, 360, *see also* Jasmine.

Mohur, Indian coin, 25, 290.

Molucca (Molucco) islands, in Malay Archipelago, conquered by the Portuguese, 195, 329, 354.

Momanpet (Moumin), 150, 335.

Mombasa (Mombaca, Mombaza), seaport in Br. East Africa, 188, 196, 197, 198, 349.

Monasteries, at Daman, 157, 158; at Tarapur, 166; at Surat, 164; at Bassein, 168, 169; in Goa, 171, 192-93, 194; at Mandapeswar, 172; at Salsette, 179; in Mozambique, 195-96; at Sena, 196; at the islands near Goa, 199; allowance paid to, 199.

Monkeys, in Gujarat, 10; in Cambay, 18; worship at Goa, 130, 329; worship in India, 213, 364.

Monkey-catching, in Malabar, 214-15.

Monogamy, among Hindus, 256-57, 382.

Monsoon (Monson, Monseon, Mousim, Moussem), season, 1, 279, 287.

Mophis, *see* Mahi river.

Mort de Chien (Mordazin, Mordechin), cholera, 151, 162, 335, 339.

Moselle, river, *see* Kabul river.

Mount Delly (Mount *Delhi*), headland on the coast of Chirakkal *taluq* of Malabar dist., Madras, 185, 348.

Mozabad (Mosabad), in Jaipur State, 68, 305.

Mozambique, in Portuguese East Africa, 188, 195, 197, 198, 271, 306, 349; fort in 195; Jesuit garden in, 195; Portuguese Governor of, 195; houses in, 195; taken by the Portuguese, 195-96; monasteries in, 195-96; port, 196; description, 196; Kafris in, 196; Indian trade with, 242.

Muadhdhin (*Muezin*), criers who call the faithful to the congregational prayer at specified hours, xli, 13, 285.

Mudhol (Muddol), town in Kolhapur, 217, 365.

Mufti (Mufty), at Surat, 26, 290.

Mughal Serai (Mogulserai), 68, 305.

Mughali Bibi, queen of Muhammad Shah II, tomb in Rani Ka Hazira, 12, 284.

Mughals (Mogul), the, xxx, 4, 5, 61-62, 96-97, 280, 282, 321; extent and boundaries of the empire, xxix, xxx, xxxiv-v, 4, 5, 7, 130-31, 234, 373; efforts to suppress *Sati*, 1, 249, 379; officers, 210, 240, 280; conquest of Gujarat, liv, 8, 282; struggle with the Marathas, lxii, 183, 347; geneology, 5-6, 234-40; army, 6-7, 218, 242, 244-45, 281, 282; revenues and revenue administration, 6-7, 240, 241, 242, 376; provinces in the empire, 7; currency and coinage, 26; court at Delhi, 60; arms and weapons, 61-62, 242-43, 377; birds and beasts, 62-65; festivals of, 66-68; emperors, 120, 374; defeated by Malik Ambar, 127, 328; deserters from the army of, 182; princes, 207; French in the service of, 218; Omrahs and ranks of nobility, 218, 243-44, 377; standards and ensigns of, 221, 367; administration of justice, 240; government of 240-41; foreign trade, 240-42; trades and manufacturers, 241, 242; court expenses, 242; military finances, 243; religion, 254, 381; capture of Golkonda, 266, 388.

Muhammad Azam Shah (Azam-Scia), third son of Aurangzeb, 221, 367; suspected by Aurangzeb of disloyalty; alleged treacherous negotiations with the king of Bijapur, 238, 375.

Muhammad Beg Khan, Governor of Surat, marriage of his daughter, 31, 293.

Muhammad Mirza, Sultan (Mahomet), son of Miran Shah, 235, 374.

Muhammad Muazzam Shah Alam (Sultan Mazum Scialam), son of Aurangzeb, 219, 221, 322, 366; sons of, 221, 367; deputed by his father to win over Mir Jumla, 224, 227, 322; imprisoned by Aurangzeb, 237-38; 375; sent to attack Golkonda, 265-66.

Muhammad Qasim, *Mutamad Khan* (Kasim Cham), Mughal General, defeated by Murad, 225, 369.

Muhammad Quli Qutb Shah, King of Golkonda, Hyderabad city founded by, 329; Char Minar built by, 330, 331.

Muhammad Said, *Mir*, better *known as* Mir Jumla, career of, 144-45, 333, 370, 386; sides with Aurangzeb against Dara, 224; invited by Aurangzeb to Daulatabad, 224; Muazzam deputed by Aurangzeb to win him over, 224; siege of Kaliana by, 224, 368; sent by Aurangzeb against Shuja, 227, 229; Vijayanagar temple plundered by, 263.

Muhammad Sultan (Sultan Mahmud), eldest son of Aurangzeb, 141, 224, 226, 332, 368, 370, 388; deserts to Shuja, 227, 370; matrimonial alliance with Golkonda, 265; imprisoned and poisoned by Aurangzeb, 227, 370.
Muhammadans (Mahometans, Moors), the, at Surat, 21, 164, 288; wedding customs at Surat, 31-33; burial customs at Surat, 33-34; festivals of, 44; women at Delhi, 66; of Multan, 77; of Cambay, 164; of Bassein, 169; in Goa, 188; in India, 248, 254; marriage customs in India, 248.
Muinuddin Hasan Chisti, Khwaja (Cogea Mundy), Muslim saint, 69; tomb at Ajmer, 69, 306.
Mulattas, Mulattos, at Goa, 181, 187, 346.
Mulher (Mouler), town on the Mosam river, 116, 323.
Multai, Multapi, on the Satpura plateau, believed to be the source of Tapti river, 294; *see also* Gahara Kunda.
Multan (Moultan), town and district in Panjab, xxix, xxxii, xxxiii, 68; situation; satellite townships; inhabitants; trade and manufacture; dancers of, 77, 78, 309; Khatris at, 78, 309; sun-temple at, 78, 309, 310; revenues, 78; assigned to Dara, 223.
Muluk Khana (Jube), royal gallery, at Ahmadabad, 13, 285.
Mumtaz Mahal (Tadge Mahal), *see* Arjumand Banu Begam.
Mundy, Peter, xxix, xxxvi-ix, xl, xlvi, lvii, lviii, lx, lxi, 194, 293, 318.
Mura (*Murais*), a measure, 172, 179, 344.
Murad Baksh (Morad Baksca, Mourad), fourth son of Shah Jahan, imprisoned by Aurangzeb, 6, 226-27, 281, 370; Gujarat assigned to, 223; alliance with Aurangzeb, 223; Surat surrendered by its governor to, 224; defeats Muhammad Quasim Khan and Jaswant Singh at Burhanpur, 225; put to death by Aurangzeb at Gwalior, 229, 371.
Muscat (Mascate), capital of Oman Province in Arabia, 180, 196, 346, 354.
Muscat, Imam of, encounter with the Portuguese, 270, 354.
Musi (Mouci), river, near Hyderabad, 145, 146, 329, 330, 333, 334.
Musk, sold at Surat, 25; from Bhutan, 237; trade in India, 253.
Musk-deer, in India, xxxv, xl, 253, 380; of Ajmer, 72, 306.
Muslins, a kind of textile, 164, 168.
Muttra (Matura), famous city in U.P., Sambhaji left by Shivaji at, 43, 296; Murad captured by Aurangzeb at, 226-27; temple at, 262, 386.
Muzaffar Shah III (Mudafar), King of Gujarat (1561-73), taken prisoner by Akbar, liv, 8; effects his escape; commits suicide, 8, 282; tomb at Sarkhej, 15, 285.
Mylapore (Meliapore, Malepur), a suburb of Madras City, 17, 286, 352; chintz from, 17; *see also* St. Thomas.
Myrobalan (Mirabolan), export from Ahmadabad, 17.
Myrrh, sold at Surat, 25, 289.

Nadiad (Nariad), in Kaira Dist., Bombay, 46, 298.
Naga, sect of ascetics, at Allahabad, 94, 316.
Nagarkot (Nagracut), town in Kangra dist., Punjab, xxixn, xxxiii-iv; Mahamaya temple at, 87, 313.
Nagra (Canara), a village north of Cambay, 17, 286.
Naiks (Naiqs, Naique), of Madura and Tanjore, 128, 328.
Nalganga (Nervar), river, 150, 335.
Nander, town on the north bank of the Godavari, 108, 109, 112, 321, 322.
Naples, in Italy, xxi, xxiv, 160, 170, 175, 183, 188, 209, 339.
Narbada (Nardaba), river, xxxviii, 8, 9, 164, 282, 283, 340.
Nariali Purnima, *see* Coconut day.
Naricut, a kind of disease, at Daman, 162, 339-40.
Narva, *see* Divar.
Naubat Khana, music gallery, of the Mughals, 219, 366.
Nauroz (*Neurous*), Persian New Year's Day, 70-71, 306.
Nav Syed, *Pir*, mosque at Surat, 35, 294.
Narwar (Nerouer, Narva), historic town and fort in Gwalior State, xxix, xxx, xxxiv, 92, 93, 315-16; iron mine at, 54, 301; *merus* of, 55, 301.
Navapur (Naopura), town in Bombay, famous for rice, 102, 319.
Navapur-petha (Naapoura), in Khandesh Dist., Bombay, 23, 288.
Navy, of the Portuguese, 181-82; of the Arabs, 182; of the Sidis, 183.
Nawab (*Nabad*), 27, 291.
Nayars (Nairs), of Malabar, customs and manners, 122-24, 257, 325, 384; women, 248, 379; polyandry among, 261, 385.
Nazar Beg Chelah, a slave of Shah Jahan, 228, 371.
Nazr (*Nazar*), a present from an inferior to a superior, 210, 363.
Negapatam (Negapatan), sea-port in Tanjore dist., Madras, 127, 128, 147, 328, 355; taken by the Portuguese, 197.
Neknam Khan, *see* Riza Quli.
Ner, village near Burhanpur, 150, 335.
Nerva, river, 131, 150, 329, 330, 335.
Nicobar islands, in the Bay of Bengal, 275, 391.
Niculao Affonso (Nicholas Alfonso), a variety of mangoes, *also known as* Afuz or Hafuz, 202, 358.
Nilgau, a kind of Indian antelope, xxxix; *see also Meru*.

Nimet-ulla, a caravanserai, in the Karwan suburb of Hyderabad, 132, 330.
Nimodra, *see* Limodra.
Nira, preparation at Goa, 200.
Nisida, island near Italy, 183.
Nizamabad, town in Hyderabad State, 108, 112, 321.
Nizamshah (Nezam, Nizam-Cha), *see* Ahmad Nizam Shah.
Nizam-ul-Mulk (Nizzamaluc), *see* Burhan Nizam Shah.
Nossa Senhora da Vida (Our Lady de la Vida), church at Bassein, 170, 342-43.
Nossa Senhora das Merces (Our Lady da Merce), church at Bassein, 169, 342.
Nossa Senhora do Cabo (Lady del Cabo), fortress on the island of Goa, 190, 350, 353; church, 271.
Nossa Senhora dos Remedios (Our Lady of Remedies), church near Bassein; 92, 315.
Nudoy (? Nandi), a cannibal race of Africa, 190, 350.
Numerals, Indian, 25, 253, 290.
Nuns, of St. Monica and St. Augustin at Goa, 171, 193, 352.
Nurgarh, *see* Salimgarh.

Oath taking, in Cochin, 124, 326.
Observants, the, *see* Franciscans, the.
Omar (Calyfe Omar), second Caliph of Bagdad, conquers Persia, 22, 288.
Omar Shaikh (Mirza Sultan Hamet), father of Babar, 235, 374.
Omlam, *mulsari* (*bakula*) tree, xxxix, 206, 361.
Omrahs (Omras), Mughal nobles, 143-44, 218, 243, 377.
Onore, Honavar (Onor), in N. Kanara Dist., Bombay, 125, 327, 355; taken by the Portuguese, 196, 355.
Opfel, see Hopewell.
Opium, exported from Ahmadabad, 17.
Orissa (Orixa, Udese, Udessa), xxixn, xxxiii, 88, 99, 313, 314; women of, 95; trade, 101.
Ormuz (Ormus), island in Persian Gulf, 196, 199, 239, 354.
Ornaments, used by Indian women, 53; of the people of Delhi, 65; of women at Daman, 162, 340.
Ostend, in Belgium, 159, 337.
Ostrich eggs, use as embellishment of Muslim tombs, 14, 285.
Oudh (Ayoud, Ayoudh, Haoud), xxxiii-iv, 87-88; revenues, 87; boundaries, 87, 312.
Oulesser, *see* Orissa.
Our Lady da Merce, *see* Nossa Senhora das Merces.
Our Lady da Se, *see* St. Josheph, Cathedral of.
Our Lady de la Vida, *see* Nossa Senhora da Vida.
Our Lady De Los Remedios, *see* Nossa Senhora dos Remedios.
Our Lady of the Pillar, church and college of the Recollects, near Goa, 194, 353.
Ovidore (*Veedor*), an administrator of justice, 167, 341.

Pachaa, *Kantali champa* flower, 206, 361.
Padam (*Padans*), Indian numeral, 25, 290.
Padolim, *Panri* plant, 206, 361.
Pagoda, Indian coin, 253, 283, 381.
Paintings, Mughal, at Agra, 55, 65; at Delhi, 55, 65; at Lahore, 85.
Paisa (Peche, Pecha), Indian coin, 20, 26, 253, 287, 290, 380.
Palakollu (Palicole), in Kistna dist., Madras, Dutch factory at, 148, 335.
Palanquins (Palanchine, Palankeen, Palankines), lviii, 75, 76, 142, 144, 159, 160, 168, 181, 182, 199, 210, 221, 246, 309.
Pallipuram (Palepor), in Cochin, taken by the Portuguese, 196, 355.
Pallu, Francois, Bishop of Heliopolis, 103, 319.
Palmyra tree, leaves used as paper, 125, 326, 357, 358; different varieties of, 200, 201, 357, 358.
Pam Nayak (Pamnaich), a chieftain of Berad, 265, 266, 387, 388.
Pan, Pawn, see Beteleira.
Panchnigal (Pendigoul), 150, 335.
Pangal (Panguel), in Nalgonda dist., Hyderabad, 146, 334.
Pangara (*Paranco, Paranga*), a small boat, 167, 183, 341, 347.
Panhala (Pernala), historic hill-fort in Kolhapur State, 245, 378.
Panj-hazari (*Panges*), a rank of mansabdars, 243, 377.
Papagayo, a war-engine, 159, 338.
Papayera, Papaya tree, xxxix-xl, 179, 203, 339, 345, 359.
Pa-posh (*Paboutches, Pa-pouches*), slippers, 52, 300.
Parao, a kind of boat, 273, 274, 390.
Parbhani (Parboni), town and dist. in Hyderabad, 112, 321.
Pardao (Paradaos, Pardoes), a gold coin formerly current in western India, 198, 199, 270, 356.
Pariah, Paraiyan (Piriaves), a low caste of Hindus in S. India, 89, 314.
Parsis, the, lii, liii, 80, 288; trade and professions, liii; at Surat, 21, 22, 38, 288; at Agra, 50; in India, 254.
Parwez (Sultan Peruiz), son of Emperor Akbar, 235.
Patalpuri Temple, at Allahabad fort, 92, 315.
Patan, town in Baroda State, xxxiii, xxxiv, 45, 297.
Patel, caste in India, 256, 383.
Pathans (Patan), the, tombs, 58; Kings, 92; rule in Bengal, 95.
Pathri (Patry), town in Parbhani dist., Hyderabad, 150, 151, 335.

Patna (Patane, Pitan), in Bihar, xxixn, xxxiii, xxxiv, 87, 313, 314, 368; Dutch factory at, 96, 316.
Patoda (Patonta), near Nander, 109, 112, 321.
Paulists (Paulistas), the, at Bassein, 109, 342; at Goa, 193, 350; *see also*, Jesuits, the.
Peacock Throne, 59, 246, 289, 303, 378.
Peacocks, at Broach, 9; in Gujarat, 10.
Pearls, xxii, lvi, 25.
Pedras, de las, King of Angola, 189.
Pegu, in Burma, 230, 242.
Pendyala (Pentela), 147, 334.
Pengeah, *see* Punjab.
Penu, river, 150, 335.
Penuganchyprolu (Penguetchepoul), village on the Muneru river, 146, 334.
Pereira, the guava tree, 204, 360.
Peria, unidentified place in Afghanistan, 80, 310.
Periyar, river, 124, 326.
Persepolis, ancient capital of Persia, xxi, 171, 343-44.
Persia, xvii, xviii, xix, xxi, xxxi, xliii, 1, 5, 62, 77, 80, 102, 183, 206, 288, 300.
—King of, *see* Abbas II; Sulaiman Safavi I.
Peter, Father, 168.
Petlad (Petnad), town in Baroda state, 10, 20, 283, 287.
Phallic worship, by the Hindus, 263, 387.
Phat, *see* Jhelum.
Philip IV, King of Spain, 167, 341.
Philipatan (? Pipli), in Orissa, 96, 316.
Phillippine Islands, 205.
Philosopher's stone, in the Andamans, 275.
Phulang (Coulan), river, 112.
Picardy, in France, 159.
Pigeons, 54, 300.
Pilgrimage, by the Hindus, 262-63.
Pilots, the, at Goa, 273-74.
Pimenteira, black-pepper plant, 205, 360.
Pimpalgaon (Piply), 150, 335.
Pimpalner (Pipelnar), town in West Khandesh dist., Bombay, 102, 319.
Pipola, in Tonk State, 68, 305.
Pir Muhammad (Pir Muhemmed), grandson of Timur, rule over Ghazni, 5, 281.
Pirates, Arab, xviii; Baloche, xxii; in the Gulf of Cambay, 18-19, 185, 287; of Malabar, 18-19, 125, 287; Sanganian, xxii, xxxvi.
Pistoles, Spanish coin, 253, 381.
Pitan (Pattan), in Nepal, 87, 313.
Pliny, xxviii, xlviii, 84, 311.
Point de Galle (Cape Galli), in Ceylon, 274, 275, 391.
Polyandry, in Kanara, 261, 385.
Pompion, Gourd, 203, 204, 206, 359.
Ponda, town and dist. in Goa, 208, 209, 211, 363; inhabitants, 211-15.
Porakad (Porca), town in Travancore State, Portuguese and Dutch settlements at, 185, 348.
Portugal, xxi, 166, 186, 191, 195, 341; Indian trade with, 242.
Portugal, King of, 172, 180, 193, 194, 196, 197, 199; *see also* Emanuel I (1469-1521); John III (1502-1557).
Portuguese, the xxiv, xl, lv, 85, 116, 147, 161, 185, 189, 196, 286, 316, 323, 348, 356, 359, 389; at Daman, xxii, 116; decline of their power in India, xxiii, 197-98; trade, 18, 242; Egyptian expedition against, 45, 297; conquests in India, 45, 121, 129, 180, 186, 195-97, 298, 324, 327, 329; relations with the Mughals, 85, 312; relations with South Indian princes, 121-22, 125, 128; in Goa, 129; at Bhagnagar, 135; troops, 166, 183, 199; customs, 170; extent of dominions, 180, 186, 195-99, 350; ships, 183; at Chaul, 183-84, 296; in Moluccas, 195, 349, 354; at Macao, 195, 354; administration, 198-99; relations with the Imam of Muscat, 270; relations with Bahadur Shah of Gujarat, 296, 323; at Cochin, 325; in Ceylon, 355.
Porus, a king of ancient India, xxiii, 58, 98.
Posilipo, cape in Italy, 191.
Prabhus (Paravous), a caste of the Hindus in Bombay, 256, 382.
Precious stones, of Golkonda, 138; of Surat, 25; mines in India, 251; *see also* Agates; Cornelians; Diamonds; Garnets; Pearls; Rubies; Sapphires.
Primogeniture, Law of, absence among the Mughals, 232-34.
Prostitution, at Hyderabad, 136.
Pulayan (Poleas, Polias), a low caste in Malabar, 123, 124, 257, 325, 384.
Pulicat (Poliacate), saltpetre and gunpowder industry at; Dutch port at, 148, 334; trade, 148; coinage by the Dutch at, 148.
Pullets, black-boned poultry, 72, 253, 306-08, 380.
Pumburpa (Pumberpa), village north of Goa, 268, 271, 389.
Pumburpa, a kind of boat, 273, 274.
Puna, a kind of tree, 206, 361.
Punishment, of drunkards in Kandahar, 79; capital sentence at Ranthambhor 98, 318; for Hindu woman living with a Muslim, 119, 249; of Malabar robbers, 125.
Punjab (Penjab), the, xxixn, 68, 84, 280.
Purana Pul, over Musi, 132, 329.
Purdah System, among Indian Muslims, 248.
Puri, in Orissa, temple of Jagannath at, xxxv, 94, 262, 313, 314, 316.
Purna (Pourna, Pournanad), river, 112, 150, 321, 335.
Purva, (*Purop*), *see* Allahabad.
Putah (Patou), 150, 335.
Pyrard de Laval, Francois, xxiii, xl, 306, 307, 325, 329, 335, 349, 350, 351, 352, 353, 389.
Pythagoras, Greek philosopher, xlii, xlvi, xlvii, 91, 254, 315, 381.

Qanun-nama (*Canon Name*), descriptive rolls of the Mughal army, 6, 281.
Qasim Barid, of Bidar, 328.
Qazi (*Cady, Kasi*), a civil judge under Muhammadan government, 217, 366, 376; at Surat, 26, 290.
Qazi-ul-quzzat (Grand Cadi), chief civil judge under Muhammadan government, opposition to Aurangzeb, 230-31, 372.
Qila Shahjahanabad, *see* Delhi, fort.
Quay (Key), at Surat, 2, 279.
Quegada Cheirosa (Quegadam Cheroza), *ketaki* or *keora* flower, 206, 361.
Quick silver, sold at Surat, 25.
Quilon (Coilon, Kollain), in Travancore State, Madras, 121; taken by the Portuguese, 196, 324, 355.
Quintas, country houses, 190, 350.
Quli Qutb Shah (Cotb-Cha), Sultan of Golkonda, founder of the ruling dynasty of Golkonda, 127, 327, 331; conquered Vijayanagar Kingdom, 327, 328.

Radicena, in Italy, Careri's birth place, xx, xxi.
Ragia Lisonte (? Soning, Sonoegi), a leader of the Rajputs, war with Aurangzeb, 238, 375.
Ragout (*Ragoes*), stewed meat or fish, served to travellers by the Grasias, 21, 287.
Rajapur (Radiapora, Radiapore, Rageapour, Ragepur, Rajapar, Rajapour), town and fort in Ratnagiri dist., Bombay, xxxiv, 128, 387; artisans at, 44, 297; sacked by Shivaji, 116, 265, 323.
Rajaram (Ramrao, Savagi), Maratha ruler, 184, 185, 347.
Rajgad (Rasigar), fortress in Bijapur, conquered by Shivaji, 265, 387.
Rajputs (Ragiaputi, Rajapours, Rajpours, Rasbootis, Rasboutes), xlvi-vii, xlix, 88, 184, 238, 247, 314, 375, 378; predatory practices of, lx-lxii; at Cambay, 18; customs, 255, 384.
Raju Saheb, *Shah*, a Muslim saint at Hyderabad, 142, 332.
Rajura (Rajoura), 150, 151, 335.
Ram Singh Rathor (Ram Senghe-rutle), Mughal General, killed in the battle of Samugarh, 225, 369.
Rama Chandra, King of Ayodhya, worship of, 19; Ravana killed by, 93, 259, 316; descent claimed by Mewar ruling family from, 98, 318.
Ramak (?Manu), Hindu lawgiver, 254, 381.
Ramaswami Temple (Pagod of Trapety), at Tirupati, 128, 328.
Rameshwaram (Ramanacor), in Madras Presidency, temple of Rama at, 263, 387.
Rammalakota (Raolconda), near Kurnool, diamond mines at, 251, 379.
Ramnagar, Raja of, *also known as* King Choutia, 255, 382.
Rampuri Buzurg (Raampouri, Rampoor), a village near Pathri, 150, 335.
Ramzan, Muslim festival, 217.
Ranas, the, *see* Sanganian pirates.
Ranchordas (Risurdas), temple at Benares, 262, 386.
Rander (Renelle), town on the right bank of the Tapti, near Surat, Dutch magazine at, 32, 293.
Rani Ka Hazira, the queen's cemetery, tomb of Mughali Bibi at Ahmadabad, 12, 284.
Ranthambhor (Ratispor, Rantimore, Rantipore), in Jaipur State, Rajputana, trade; capital punishment at, 98, 318.
Rasigarh (Rasigar), captured by Shivaji, 116, 323.
Rasulabad, tomb of Shah Alam at, 14, 285.
Rauza, *see* Khuldabad.
Ravana (Ravan, Rhevan), demon king of Lanka, story of, 93; credited as originator of an ascetic order, 93, 259, 316, 384.
Ravanavanshi Gosains, 93, 316.
Ravi (Ravee), a tributary of the Indus, xxxii, 84-85, 309; change in the course of, 84-85, 311-12.
Recca (? Larak), island in Persian Gulf, 196, 354.
Recollects (Recolets), the, Observantine branch of the Franciscan order, monastery at Daman, 158, 337; school of Our Lady of the Pillar near Goa, 194, 353; *see also* Capuchins.
Red Wood, sold at Surat, 25, 289.
Refesis (*Rafzi*), a heretic, 223, 368.
Reguli (*Roytelets*), petty princes of Moluccas, 264, 387.
Reis Magos (dos Reys), a fortress in the province of Bardez, Goa, 190, 191, 350.
Relacao das Indias (Relacaon), Chief Court of Justice in Portuguese India, at Goa, 198, 356.
Reptiles, of Ajmer, 72; serpents at Golkonda, 148; *see also* Scorpions.
Revanche-Ram (? Raghuvanshi Ram), 258, 384.
Revand Chini, used as purgative, 152, 336.
Revenues, of the Mughals, 6-7, 240-42, 376; from Gujarat, 46; from Agra, 57; from Sind, 77; from Multan, 78; from Kabul, 81; of Kashmir, 84; of Lahore, 85; of Oudh and Berar, 87; from Allahabad, 94, of Bengal, 97; of Malwa, 98; of Khandesh, 99; of Subah of Aurangabad, 101; of Telengana, 114; of Baglana, 116; from diamond mines of Golkonda, 142; from Sambrani, 215.
Rhinoceros (Rhinocerots), in India, xxxvii, xxxviii, 252, 379.
Rhubarb, see Revand Chini.
Rice, used in preparation of wine at Surat, 23.
Rio Largo, *see* Periyar, river.
Rio Ram (? Raja Ram), Hindu deity, temple at Surat, 164, 340.
Riza Quli (Raja-Couli), *surnamed* Neknam Khan, 127, 128, 328.
Roads and Highways, of India, lix,

Robbers and Thugs, 9-10, 19-20, 28, 50, 58; *see also* Pirates.
Rock-Crystal, in Ceylon, 275.
Roe, Sir Thomas, xxx, xxxv, xxxvii, xli-ii, xliv, li, 279, 281, 294, 305, 313-14, 317-18; relates story of the 'Christian ape', xxvii-xxviii; on provinces of Mughal India, xxix; letter to Lord Carew re. errors in maps of India, xxxii; on Hindu belief in transmigration of soul, xlvii; on custom of *Sati*, xlix; on customs duties at Surat, lv-vi; at Mandu, lvii; on transport of India, lviii-ix; letter to Smythe re. Jahangir's tours, lix; story re. his cook, lxiii.
Roenas, *see* Red Wood.
Rohankhed (Rouquera), 150, 335.
Rohilagadh (Rovilag-herd), a town near Aurangabad, 112, 321.
Roicolet (*Regolo*), a ruler, 239, 375.
Rome, capaital of Italy, xviii, 96; church of St. Andrew della Velle in, 192; missionaries of Cochin-China summoned by Pope Innocent XI to, 273.
Rosary (ship), 274.
Rose, a kind of animal, at Daman, 161, 339.
Roshanara Begam (Rausenora Begum), daughter of Shah Jahan, 222, 368.
Rouzindars (*Rowzinders*), Mughal cavalry, 244, 377.
Royal Hospital, at Goa, 194, 353.
Rubies, sold at Surat, 25.
Rupee (Roupie), an Indian coin, 20, 26, 290, 295, 300.

Sabarmati (Sabremetty), river in Bombay Presidency, 11, 284.
Sacred Thread, worn by the Hindus, 259-60, 385.
Sadashiva Naik (Sonde-Kirani-Karaja), Chief of Sonda, 212, 215, 364.
Saffron, xl, 23, 288.
Sago (Sagu), imported into Goa from Malacca and Borneo, 192, 193, 352.
St. Andrew della Velle, church in Rome, 192.
St. Augustine, order of, garden at Daman, 162; monastery at Bassein, 167; church and image of Our Lady da Merce at Bassein, 169, 342; procession of the Holy cross at Bassein, 183; church and monastery at Goa, 192, 193, 351, 352; nuns at Ghodbandar, 171; nuns at Goa, 193, 352.
St. Blase, near Goa, castle of, 186, 192, 208, 349.
St. Bonaventura, college and church at Goa, 194, 352.
St. James (St. Jago), island near Goa, fort at, 192, 194, 208, 362.
St. Jerome, hermitage and church at Cashi, 172, 344; hermitage at Goa, 192.
St. John, church at Ghodbandar, 344.
St. John de Dios, monastery in Mozambique, 195-96.
St. Joseph (Our Lady da Se), Cathedral of, *also known as* the 'Matriz', at Bassein, 170, 343.
St. Michael, fort in Tivi, 268, 389.
St. Monica, convent and church of, at Goa and Ghodbandar, 171, 193, 199, 352.
St. Paul, church and college in Goa, 193, 352.
St. Roch (S. Rock), convent in Goa, 193, 352.
St. Sebastian, fort in Mozambique, 195, 354.
St. Stephen, island near Goa, 199, 207, 211.
St. Thomas, suburb of Madras city, 127, 128, 147, 195; chintz from, 17, 57, 286; *see also* Mylapore.
St. Thomas, church at Goa, 193, 352.
Sajjapur (Senjavourd), 150, 335.
Sal Ammoniac (Salarmanic), *see* Ammonium Chloride.
Salim (Selim), son of Emperor Akbar, *see* Jahangir.
Salim Chisti, *Shaikh*, popularly known as *Shaikh-ul-Islam*, tomb at Fatehpur Sikri, 27, 301.
Salim Shah Sur (Cha-Selim), son of Sher Shah Sur, 97, 302, 317, 370.
Salimgarh (Salemghar, Salengher), fort near Delhi, imprisonment of Murad at, 226-27; imprisonment and subsequent poisoning of Muhammad Sultan by Aurangzeb at, 227, 370; Sulaiman Shikoh imprisoned at, 229.
Salsette (Salzete), island near Bombay, 171, 179, 180, 183, 191, 197, 199, 209, 275, 341, 343, 346; centre of Jesuit activities, 191, 351; taken by the Portuguese, 195.
Saltpetre, export from Ahmadabad, 17; manufacture at Ajmer, 73, 74; industry at Pulicat, 148, 334; brought to Gujarat for sale from Ajmer, 74, 308.
Salvador, Father, *see* Galli.
Samarkand (Samarcand), famous city in Turkistan, 234.
Sambal (Sumbal), xxxiv, 88, 313, 314.
Sambhaji (Sambagi), son of Shivaji, 43, 184, 238, 296, 347, 357, 375; Ponda relieved by, 211, 365; Aurangzeb's war with, 238.
Sambhar (*Sambar*), a kind of Indian antelope, xxxix, 161, 339; *see also Meru*.
Sambrani, village in North Kanara dist., Bombay, revenues from, 215, 365.
Samugarh (Samongher), village near Agra, Dara defeated by Aurangzeb near 225, 369.
Sandalwood, from Timor, 197, 356.
Sandur (? Sitpur), in Punjab, 77, 309.
Sangameshwar (Zanghisara), river, 180, 185, 346, 348.
Sanganian pirates, *see* Pirates, Sanganian.

Sanseverino, Don Carlos, Prince of Biriguano and Duke of Sao Marco, Careri dedicates his works to, xxiv, xxv.
Santa Casa de Misericordia (Sacred House of Mercy), church at Goa, 192, 351.
Sao Laurenco (St. Laurence), 191, 192, 351.
Sao Thome (St. Thomas), coin of Goa, 270, 389-390.
Sapphires (Saphirs), of Golkonda, 138.
Sarbhon (Sourban), village in Broach Dist., 9, 283.
Sardar Khan, one of the titles of Mughal nobility, 222, 368.
Sarkhej (Serquech), village near Ahmadabad, 15, 16, 283, 285.
Sarkna (Charca), 102, 319.
Satana (Setana), in Nasik dist., Bombay, 102, 103, 104, 319.
Satgaon (Satigan), in Hooghly dist., Bengal, 96, 316.
Sati, custom of, practised by Hindu widows, xlii, xlix, 119-20, 211-12; practised at Agra, Cambay and Masulipatam, xlix, l; Mughal attempts at suppression of, l, 120, 249, 324, 379; prohibited in Kandahar, 79-80; at Ponda, 211-12, 363; practised among Rajput women, 255, 384.
Satias, specie of mangoes known as *safia*, 202, 358.
Satins, at Ahmadabad, 17.
Sattaispalli (Settais-pale), region in Hyderabad, 265, 387.
Sawargaon (Saudurgaon), 150, 335.
Sayyid Ahmad, son-in-law of Abdulla Qutb Shah, 142, 332.
Sayyid Muzaffar (Sidy Mezafer), a general of Golkonda, 150, 332.
Scaragam, a kind of tree, 206, 361.
Scorpions, of Ajmer, 72.
Seer (*Serres, Goer, Keer*), Indian weight, 25, 253, 289, 381.
Seine river, in France, 37, 132.
Seistan, Sistan (Segestan), ancient territory in Persia and Afghanistan, 74, 308.
Sena (Senna), river, *see* Zambezi.
Sena (Senna), port in East Africa on the Zambezi river, town, 196, 197, 354; Portuguese at, 196; Kafri slaves at, 196; gold at, 196; Dominican and other missionaries at, 196.
Sengar (Singour) river, near Agra, 57, 302.
Sequeira, Gen. Diogo Lopes de, Governor of Portuguese India (1518-21), El Morro Fort built by, 183, 347.
Sequin (Chequins), a coin of Venice, 28, 291, 340.
Sironj (Seronge), a town in Tonk State, Rajputana, 57, 302.
Shab-i-Barat (*Choubret*), Muslim festival, 44, 297.
Shah Alam (Chhalem), title adopted by Sher Shah, q.v.
Shah Alam (Chhalem), leader of the Bukhari Saiyads in Gujarat, mausoleum at Rasulabad, 14, 285.
Shah Alam (Scialam), *see* Muhammad Muzzam.
Shah Nawaz Khan (Scia Navaz-e-Kan), *see* Badi-uz-Zaman.
Shahapur (Sciapur), south of Belgaum, 267, 389.
Shahbaz (Scia-Abas), Murad's eunuch, 223, 226, 368.
Shahdara, near Lahore, tomb of Jahangir at, 48, 299.
Shahi Bagh, built by Shah Jahan at Ahmadabad, 14, 15, 285.
Shahjahan (Cha Gehan, Scia-Gehan, Sheich Choram), xlviii, liv, lxiii, 6, 11, 58, 78, 100, 281, 284, 306, 367, 369, 372; death, 6, 49, 231, 372, 373; Shahi Bagh at Ahmadabad built by, 14, 15, 285; imprisoned by Aurangzeb, 49, 226, 299; tomb, 49; Delhi built by, 57, 302; Kandahar wars, 78-79, 282, 310; sons and daughters, 222, 224, 225; war of succession among his sons, 223-31, 233, 281, 373; rebels against Jahangir, 232; succeeds Jahangir, 235, 374.
Shahjahanabad (Gehan-abad, Jehanabat), *see* Delhi.
Shahji (Nair Savagi), Shivaji's father, in Bijapur service, 38, 295, 322; imprisoned by King of Bijapur, 265, 387.
Shaibani Khan (Kay-bek-Cham), Uzbeg leader, Babar dethroned by, 235, 374.
Shaikh-ki-Sarai, Shah-ki-Sarai (Chekiserai), a traveller's resting place near Muttra, 57, 302.
Shaikh Shuaib, island in the Persian Gulf, 196, 354.
Shaikh-ul-Islam, *see* Salim Chisti, Shaikh.
Shaista Khan (Chasta Can, Scia-hesta Kan, Shasta Chan), Mughal Viceroy of the Deccan, 39, 40, 322, 369; unsuccessful expedition against Shivaji, 39, 40, 295, 296; appointed Governor of Agra by Aurangzeb, 226.
Shalamar (Chalimar), garden, near Delhi, 68, 305.
Shalimar Gardens, in Kashmir, 82, 83, 311.
Shantidas (Santidas), Jain merchant, Chintaman temple built at Ahmadabad by, 13-14, 285.
Shastri, river, Arab ships burnt by the Portuguese at, 348.
Shawls (Chal), from Kashmir, 52, 300.
Shekerdeh (Squequerdeh), village near Hyderabad, 150, 335.
Sher Khan (Tcher-Can), *see* Sher Shah.
Sher Shah, *Shah Alam* (Kirkam), 281, 374; wars with Humayun, 6, 14, 126, 235, 327.
Shia (Chiai), religious sect of the Muslims, 77, 140, 149, 288, 332, 338.
Shimga (Siminga), the Holi festival, 208, 362.
Ship building, at Daman, 162, 340.
Shipping, at Cambay, 18-19, 287; by the Dutch and the French, 29-30; at Surat, 37-38, 164, 166; by the English, 141, 332; at Masulipatam, 147; by the Portuguese, 270.

Shiraz, ancient city in Persia, ruins of, xviii, xxi.
Shiva, Hindu God, lix, 103, 317, 319.
Shivaji (Savagi, Sivagy), liv, 112, 116, 129, 180, 184, 209, 287, 296, 322, 323, 328, 346, 348; sack of Surat by, 21, 38-43, 163, 259, 291, 296, 340; wars with the Mughals, 39-43, 183, 239, 295, 296, 297, 375; physical appearance, 43; Basrur sacked by, 125, 327; wars with Bijapur, 265; born at Shivner, 295, 348; compassion for non-combatants, 41.
Shivni (Seouny), 150, 335.
Shuja (Sugiah), Sultan, son of Shah Jahan, Bengal assigned to, 222-23; defeated by Raja Jai Singh and Sulaiman Shikoh near Benares, 223, 368; Mir Jumla sent by Aurangzeb against, 227, 229; joined by Muhammad Sultan, 227, 370; flight to Arakan, 229-30; death, 230.
Shutarnal, camel swivel, 244, 377.
Siam, missionaries, 103; trade with India, 242.
Siba, in Kangra, xxxiii, 87, 313.
Sidi (Sydi), a title of the Habshi or Abyssinian rulers of the island of Janjira, 183, 184, 347.
Sidi Masud (Sidi Mansutu), regent of Bijapur during the minority of Sultan Sikandar Adil Shah, 265, 388.
Sikandar, *see* Kam Baksh.
Sikandar Adil Shah (Sikandar), King of Bijapur, deprived of his kingdom by Aurangzeb, 264-65, 387.
Sikandar Lodi, Sultan of Delhi, 56, 302, 327.
Sikandra (Scanderabad), town near Agra, 48, 56, 298, 299, 302.
Sili (Selly), village in Kaira dist., Bombay, 20, 287.
Silveira, Antonio da, brother-in-law of Nuno da Cunha, 45, 298.
Simples, medicinal herbs, export to Europe, 251, 379.
Sind (Sinde, Sindy), xxxii, xxxiii, xxxvi, 4, 7, 74-77; boundaries, 74; towns, 74-75, 308; trade, 74-75; arts and crafts, 75; transport, 75-76.
Sindkheda (Sindiguera), in Baroda State, lac from, 43, 44, 297.
Sindkhed (Chendeque), 150, 335.
Sipihr Shikoh (Sapesee-Kuh), son of Dara, imprisoned by Aurangzeb at Gwalior, 228, 229, 310.
Sipra (Ogene), river in Central India, 225, 369.
Sita (*Chita*), wife of Rama, 91, 92, 315, 316.
Sitanagar (Chitanagar), temple and palace, 111-12, 321.
Slaves, trade in Portuguese India, 116, 188, 323; in Daman, 159, 338; kafris and black slaves of Goa, 188-90; in Mozambique and Sena, 196; purchased by Careri at Goa, 272.
Smyrna (Smirna), in Asia Minor, xxi, 241, 376.
Snake-stone (Stone of Cobra), preparation and use, 46, 298.
Socotra, Sokotra, island in Indian Ocean, 29, 292.
Sofala (Zofala), on the East Coast of Africa, 188, 197, 349, 354; fort, 196.
Sojitra (Sousentra, Sonzentra), town in Baroda State, 10, 19, 283.
Sol, French coin, 26, 290.
Solor,, island in the Malaya, Archipelago, 197, 199, 354; conquered by the Portuguese, 195.
Sonda, ruler of *see* Sadashiva Naik.
Sonars, goldsmiths, 256, 382.
Sotrias, a fishing community, 257, 383.
Sousa, Martim Affonso de (Sousa, Martin Alfonso de), seizes Daman, 159, 167, 338.
Spain (Hispan), xvii, xxi, xxiv, 189, 203, 205.
—King of, *see* Philip IV (1605-65).
Spaniards, the, use of betel leaf by, 205.
Srinagar (Sirinakar, Srinakar, Syranakar), capital of Kashmir, xxx, xxxii, xxxiii, 82-83, 311.
Srinagar (Sereneghar), in Garhwal Dist., U.P., refuge taken by Sulaiman Shikoh at, 229.
Staffiere (Staffieri), footman, 2, 279.
Suba, Subahdar, governor of a province, 209, 362.
Sudra (Soudr), fourth caste of the Hindus, lii, 88, 314, 349.
Suez, port in the Red Sea, xviii, 45.
Sugar, exported from Ahmadabad, 17.
Sugarcane, cultivation at Surat, 36-37.
Sukadana (Succadan), port in Borneo, export of diamonds from, 251, 379.
Sulaiman I (Soliman), Sultan of Turkey, *surnamed* the Magnificent, 45, 297, 298.
Sulaiman Pasha al-Khadim, Governor of Egypt, commands naval expedition against Diu; treacherously kills Amir Ibn Daud; Aden captured by, 45, 298.
Sulaiman Safavi I (Scia Safi, Scia Selimon), Shah of Persia, Dawar Baksh entertained by, 233, 373; Prince Akbar's escape to, 239, 375.
Sulaiman Shikoh (Soliman Scecur, Soliman Scekah), son of Dara, Shuja defeated by, 223; takes refuge in Srinagar; captured by Aurangzeb; imprisoned in Salimgarh, 229, 371.
Sultan Bang, Sultan Banque, Sultan Bon, *see* Buland Akhtar, Sultan.
Sumatra, island in Indian Ocean, elephants of, 63.
Sumatras, 274, 391.
Sunnis, the, a sect of Muslims, at Surat, 22, 288; ill-treatment of the French at Aden by, 30; quarrel with Shias, 149, 335
Superstitions, of the Hindus, 259-61; during esclipse, 263-64.
Sura, wine, preparation at Daman, 161, 339, 357; preparation at Goa, 200; uses, 200, 357.

Surat (Suratte, Surrat, Soret), historic town in Bombay Presy., xxviii, xxix fn, xxxii, xxxiii, xliii, xliv, xlvi, l, lx, lxiii, 1, 8, 12, 17, 18, 19, 74, 77, 101, 102, 103, 104, 116, 125, 150, 163, 164, 169, 230, 317, 318, 319, 323, 354; Mandelslo's visit to, xvii; fare from Basra, xviii; *Hopewell* at, xix; customs duties at, xix, lv, 3, 279, 280; smuggling of pearls to, xxi, lvi; customs officers at, lv, lvi; custom house at, lv, lvi, 1-3, 163; English factory at, lvii, 22, 288, 310; bar of, 1-2, 37; situation, 21; fortifications, 21, 22, 163; Dutch factory at, 22, 288; inhabitants, 22; houses, 22-23, 163; streets and bazaars, 23; food and drink, 23-24; trade, 25, 163-64; currency, weights and measures, 25-26; officials, 26-29, 290-91; administration of justice, 27, 28, 29; French at, 29-31, 163, 340; marriage of governors' daughter, 31-33; Muslim wedding customs at, 31-33; eunuchs at, 33; dancing girls and Indian dancing at, 33; Broach gate at, 33; cemeteries and cremation grounds at, 33-35, 294; tanks and wells at, 34, 293, 294; irrigation and water works, 34-35, 37; Daman gate at 35; Pir Nav Syed at, 35, 294; tank of Malik Gopi at, 35, 294; buildings, 35; Jahanara Begam's garden, 35-36, 294; flora, 35-36; temple of Mahamaya at, 36; soil, 36-37; agriculture, 36-37; fauna, 36-37; Tapti river at, 37; shipping at 37, 164-66; port, 37-38, 163; revenues, 38; sacked by Shivaji, 38-43, 163, 291, 296, 340; Capuchins at, 41, 164, 296, 340; city, 163; plundered by Kakaji, 163, 340; European and Muslim merchants at, 163; government of, 163, 340; fakirs at, 164; veterinary hospital at, 164; jugglers at, 165; bay of, 182; taken by the Portuguese, 195; captured by Murad, 223, 224.
—Governor of, 22, 168; *see also* Gopi, *Malik;* Inayat Khan; Muhammad Beg Khan.
Sutar, carpenter caste, 256, 382.
Sutlej, tributary of the Indus, 84, 309, 311, 312.
Swally, Suvali (Suali), roadstead at the mouth of the Tapti, xliii, 37, 38, 163, 164, 295, 340; custom house at 38.

Taffeta, a kind of woven silk, at Ahmadabad, 17, 164.
Taharabad (Tarabat), village on the Mosam river, 102, 319.
Tahmasp Shah I (Tahmas), King of Persia, 6, 281.
Taj Mahal (Tadge Mehal), at Agra, liv; architecture, 48; Shah Jehan buried at, 48, 49, 299.
Tamarind, 179, 206, 361; exported from Ahmadabad, 17.
Tamerlane, *see* Timur.
Tamluk (Tambulin), in Midnapore dist., Bengal, conquered by the Portuguese, 197, 356.
Tana Shah (Tanscia), *see* Abul Hassan.
Tanjore (Tanjaur), city and dist. in Madras, lix, 274, 328, 387, 391.
Tanks and Wells, on way to Petlad, 10, 283; at Sarkhej, 15, 285; at Surat, 34-35, 293, 294.
Tanur (Tanor), town in Malabar dist., Madras, 123, 185, 307, 325, 348.
Tapestries, of Ahmadabad, 17.
Tapti (Tapty), river of Western India, 8, 9, 32, 37, 100-01, 150, 282, 293, 323, 335; supposed source at Multapi, 37, 294.
Taragarh, hill and fort in Ajmer, 68, 305.
Tarapur (Trapor), in Mahim dist., Bombay, 166, 195, 341.
Tari, see Toddy.
Taslim, salutation, 243, 377.
Tatabakar, *see* Bhakkar.
Tatta (Thatta), taluq in Karachi dist., Sind, xxix fn, xxxii, xxxiii, 74, 77, 308.
Tavernier, Jean Baptiste (1605-89), xxxii, xxxv, xxxix, xlii, xliii, xliv, xlvi, lvi, lvii, lviii, lix, lxi, 171, 190, 282, 287, 294-95, 297, 299, 300-01, 303-05, 309, 314, 316-19, 321, 324, 328-35, 337, 341, 344, 384, 385.
Tavora, Fransisco de, Count of Alvor (Taverno, Fransisco de, Earl of Alvor), Portuguese Viceroy of India (1681-86), 189, 349.
Tchenau, *see* Chenab.
Telingana (Talengand, Telenga), xxxiii, 101, 319, 328; boundaries; towns, 113, 322; revenues, 114; Hindu castes and tribes, customs and beliefs, 114-15.
Temples, at Benares, Muttra, Puri, Rameshwaram, Tirupati, Vijayanagar, 262, 263.
Tenasserim (Tansserri), trade with India, 242.
Terry, Edward, famous traveller, xxix, xxx, xxxi, xxxiii, xxxiv, xxxvii, xxxix, xli, xliii, xliv, xlviii, l, li, lvi, lx, lxiii, lxiv, 300, 305, 313, 314, 317, 331, 379.
Textiles, of Bengal, 96, 275; from Masulipatam, 146, 334; of Ahmadabad, 164.
—Cotton, manufactured by the Parsis, liii; *bafta* manufacture at Broach, 9, 282; trade at Ahmadabad, 13, 17; from Bengal, 52; trade at Firozabad and Sidhpur, 56, 301; of Khandesh, 99-101; from Agra, 103; trade at Surat, 163.
—Silk, manufactured by the Parsis, liii; trade at Ahmadabad, 17; trade at Surat, 163, of Bassein, 168.
—Woollens, from Kashmir, 52.
Thailand (Siam), elephants from, 63.
Thana (Tana), chief town of the dist. of the same name, Bombay, 169, 171, 180, 184, 342; fort, 179-80; taken by the Portuguese, 195.
Thanesar, Thaneswar (Tanassar), town in Punjab, 86, 312.

Theatins, the, 203, 207, 348; at Goa, 192, 354; at Chorao, 273.
Theban stone, *see* Garnets.
Thevenot, Jean de, life and travels, xvii-xix; influence of his uncle, xvii-xviii; works, xx; estimate of his work, xxvii-xxviii, lxiv; influence of his classical studies, xxviii-xxix; historical and topographical errors in his work, xxxi-xxxvi, liii-liv; errors in describing flora and fauna of India, xxxvi-xl; on Indian people, their habits, food, dress, trade and profession and religious beliefs and tolerance, xl-xlvi, l-li; on early marriage in India, xlviii; on Indian women, xlviii-xlix; on *Sati*, xlix-l, 119-20; on caste system, li-liii; on customs officers at Surat, lv-lvi; on Indian inns, lvi-lvii; on Indian transport, lvii-lix; on Indian roads, lix-lxiii; on Indian civility, lxiii; at Surat, 1-4, 152; on geography of India and history of the Mughals, 4-7; in Gujarat, 8-10; at Ahmadabad 11-17; departs from Cambay, 17-21; description of city, weights and money, officers, history, marriage ceremony, cremation and burial grounds, curiosities and port of Surat, 21-44; on the towns of Gujarat, 44-46; on province, town and inhabitants of Agra, 46-57; on province, city and inhabitants of Delhi, 57-66; on Mughal arms and weapons, 61-62; on Mughal festivities, 66-68, 70-71; on Ajmer province and city, 68-74; on Sind province, 74-75; on palanquins, 76-77; on Multan province, 77-78; on Kandahar province, 78-80; on Kabul province, 80-81; on Kashmir, 82-84; on Punjab, 84-87; on Oudh, Berar and Becar, 87-88; on Indian castes and tribes, 89-92; on Allahabad, 92-94; on Indian Fakirs, 93; on Orissa and Bengal, 94-97; on Malwa, 97-99; on Khandesh, 99-101; travels in Golkonda, Hyderabad and Balaghat, 101-04, 130-35; visits Ellora, 104-07; travels in the province of Daulatabad, 107-10; at Sitanagar, 111-13; on Telingana province, 113-15; on Baglana province, 116-18; on Hindu widows, 119; on the Deccan and Malabar provinces, 121-26; on the inhabitants and castes and tribes in the Deccan and Malabar, 123-24; on history of the Deccan, 126-29; visit to Goa, 129-30; on the inhabitants of Hyderabad, 135-37; on fortifications, mineral wealth and tombs of Golkonda; on history and nobility of Golkonda, 140-45; departs from Hyderabad for Masulipatam, 146-50; on Indian diseases, 150-52.
Thevenot, Melechisedech de, uncle of Jean de Thevenot, xvii-xviii.
Tigdi (Tikli), town and fort in Belgaum dist., Bombay, 216, 365.
Timor, island in the Malay Archipelago, 199, 354; conquered by the Portuguese, 195; sandalwood in, 197, 356.
Timur, the Lame, (Tamerlane, Teymur), 5, 289-81; succeeded by Miran Shah, 234; Sultan Bayazid I defeated and captured near Angora by; extent of his empire, 234, 373.
Tin Darwaza, the triple gateway at Ahmadabad, 12, 284.
Tindolim, tree and flower, xxxix, 206, 361.
Tirupati (Trapety, Tripti), in Madras, 128, 328, 333, 386; temples at, 128, 262-63.
Tissuari, Tisvadi (Tilsoar), a district comprising thirty village communities, a name of Goa, q.v.
Tithes and allowances, paid to the officers of Inquisition, to monasteries and clergy, 199.
Tivi, village and fort in Goa Settlement, 286, 390.
Toddy (Tari, Tadie, Terry), xliv, liii; used as liquor in India, 23, 24, 289.
Tol, Mughal custom of weighing the emperor on his birth day, 245, 378.
Tola (*Tole*), Indian weight, 25, 289, 290.
Tolls and transit duties, lxi, 20, 287.
Tombs, of Ahmad Shah I and his queen, Darya Khan, Azam Khan, Mir Abu, and Shah Waziruddin at Ahmadabad, 11, 284; of Shah Alam and his descendants at Rasulabad, 14, 285; at Sarkhej, 15, 285; at Surat, 33-35, 293-94; of Akbar at Sikandra, of Mumtaz Mahal at Agra, 48, 56, 298, 299, 302; of Jahangir at Shahdara, 48, 299; of Humayun at Delhi, 58, 299, 302; of Khwaja Muinuddin Chisti at Ajmer, 69, 306; of Mahmud Khilji at Mandu, 97, 317; of Dilras Banu Begam at Aurangabad, 103, 319; of Qutb Shahi Kings at Golkonda, 139, 331.
Tongking (Tunchin), in Fr. Indo-China, 273, 390.
Toranja, pumelo tree, 204, 360.
Toulon, port in France, 190, 350.
Town administration, of Surat, 26-29, 290-300; of Daman, 158, 337; of Bassein, 167-68, 341; of Goa, 198, 356-57.
Trade and Manufactures, of India, lii-liii; of Gujarat, liii; of Ahmadabad, 17, 164; of the Dutch at Cambay, 18, 286; of Surat, 25, 163-64; of Agra, 51-52, 55; of Ajmer, 73; of Sind; of Debal Sindhi, 74-75, 308; of Multan, 77-78; of Lahore, 85; in Bengal, 96, 275; of Ranthambhor, 98; of Khandesh, 99-101; of arms at Indalwai, 112-13; at Pulicat, 148, 334; of Cambay, 164; of Broach, 164; of Goa, 186; of Mozambique, 196; at Yadvad, 216, 365; of the Mughals, 241-42; of musk in Bhutan, 253; of diamonds at Goa, 272.
Tranquebar (Trangabar), town in Tanjore dist., Madras, 128, 147, 328.
Transmigration of soul, doctrine of, xlii, xlvi-xlvii, 91, 254, 315, 381.
Transoxiana (Mawara-un-Nahr), 5, 280, 281; hunting dogs from, 62.

Transport, in Seventeenth Century India, lvii-lix; of Bassein, 168; of Goa, 194.
Trapani, capital of the province of same name in Sicily, 183, 347.
Trial by ordeal, 124, 261, 326.
Trincomalee (Mall, Trichil), in Ceylon, 197, 355.
Turaiyar (Tiar), town in Trichinopoly dist., Madras, 274, 391.
Turkey, 281, 376; trade with the Mughals, 241.
—Sultan of, *see* Sulaiman I (1520-86).
Turks, the, at Surat, 21, 280.
Tutanaga (Tutunac), a kind of copper alloy, 65, 304.
Typhoon, *see* Hurricane.

Udesse, Udessa (? Orissa) province of, 88, 313.
Udgir (Oudeguir), in Bidar dist., 151, 335.
Ullal (Olala), in S. Kanara dist., Madras, 125, 327.
Umar bin Ahmad al Kazaruni, *Zaul-al-Malik*, tomb at Cambay, 18, 286.
Umbrane (Omrana), 102, 319.
Underi (Undrin), island near the entrance of Bombay harbour, 183, 184, 347.
Undi, a kind of tree, 161; 206; *see also* Puna.
Untouchables, the, marriage customs among, 256-58, 383.
Urs, annual fair at the tomb of Khawaja Muinuddin Chisti at Ajmer, 69, 306.
Ustad Quli Khan, founding of cannon by, 62, 303.
Uzbegs (Ulbecks), 62.

Vadakara, *see* Badagora.
Vaitarani, mythological river of Hindu nether world, 259, 384, 385.
Vaitis, a tribe of fishermen, 257, 383.
Val (*Vabs*), Indian weight, 25, 290.
Valars (Valuoris), a caste in India, 256, 382-83.
Valle, Pietro della (Peter de la Valle), xvii, xxii, xxiii, xxxii, xxxv, xxxvii, xxxix, xliv, xlvii, xlix, li, lv, lx, lxii, 171, 294, 327.
Valod (Balor), 102, 319.
Vanur (Onor), village in Belgaum dist., Bombay, 216, 365.
Varad, Varal, Varada, *see* Berar.
Variao (Beriao, Periaw), village in Broach dist., Bombay, 92, 282.
Varsha-grantha (*Borsgant*), birthday of the Mughal emperor, public observance of, 245, 378.
Vat tree (Wartree), at Surat, 36, 294.
Vedas (*Bets*), holy scriptures of the Hindus, 90, 315.
Vellore (Velour), 127, 328.
Velvet, of Surat and Ahmadabad, 17, 164.
Vendome (Vendosme) Duc de, see Caesar, Duke of Vendome.
Vengurla (Vingourla), port in Bijapur Kingdom, 116, 128, 323.
Venice, lv, lxi, 173, 291, 340.
Versova (Versava), port and village near Bombay, 179, 346.
Veterinary hospitals, xlv-xlvi, 254, 286; at Ahmadabad, 16, 341; at Cambay, 18; at Surat, 165; in Goa, 194; at Bassein, 343.
Vettar, *see* Tanur.
Vijayanagar (Bisnag), Kingdom of, xxxvi, 126-27, 145, 322, 324, 328; temple plundered by Mir Jumla at, 263, 386.
Vinegar, prepared at Surat, 23.
Virar, near Bassein, supposed birth-place of Shivaji, 38, 295.
Virji Vora (Varjivora), merchant and banker of Surat, 22, 288.
Visconti, Father Hippolito, 207, 269, 272, 274, 390, 392.
Vrati (Vartias), burial of, 34, 293; at Lahore, 86-87.
Vyara (Biaraa), 102, 319.

Wakil-i-mutlaq or Divan-i-mutlaq (*Gium-Detal-Malk*), Vicegerent of the Mughals, 218, 366.
Waqai-Navis, *Waqai-Nigar* (*Vaca-Nevis*), news writer, at Surat, 26, 290, 291.
Water-fowls, hunting of, 246, 378.
Weights and Measures, of Surat, 25; of India, 253.
Widows, Hindu, 119-20, 250, 256, 257.
Wine, distillation at Surat, 23.
Women, Methwold and Terry on, xlvii; dancing girls, 33, 71, 199, 293, 306; dress and ornaments, 53; used as decoy by robbers, 58; of Delhi, 66; of Bengal and Orissa, 95; Hindu, 119-20, 250, 256, 257; of Malabar, 122, 261, 325; of Golkonda and Hyderabad, 136; at Daman, 162; fecundity, 248; Rajput, 255, 284; polyandry among Nayars, 261; temple dancers, 263.

Xavier, St. Francis (Xaverius, S. Francis), buried at Goa Velha, 129, 329; tradition of planting Jack fruit and mango trees at St. Paul's church in Goa by, 193, 352; chapel at Goa, 352.

Yadvad (Edoar), in Belgaum dist., 216, 267, 365.
Yakub Khan (Jacob), Kashmir conquered by Akbar from, 83, 311.
Yakut-kepensh, 150, 335.
Yemen (Hyeman), in Arabia, xliii; export of coffee from, 241, 376.
Yezid I, Caliph, 150, 335.
Yogi, Yogin (*Jogis, Jogues*), Hindu ascetics, burial rites, 34, 293; sects and mode of life, 258.

Yusuf Adil Shah (Adil-Cha), King of Bijapur, conquers Bijapur, 127, 327-28; Goa conquered by the Portuguese from, 129, 329.
Yusuf Khan (Justaf-Can), King of Kashmir, 83, 311.

Zabaim, *see* Yusuf Adil Shah.
Zabulistan, 80, 310.
Zafran, Saffron, 248, 378.
Zagatay, *see* Chagtai.
Zagaye (Javelin), 61, 303.
Zakat, taxes, collected by rebel leaders from travellers in India, lxi.
Zambezi (Rio de Sena), river in Africa, 195, 196, 354.
Zamorin (Zamorri), ruler of Calicut, 122, 185, 324-26, 348.
Zoroastrians, *see* Parsis.

CORRIGENDA

Page	*Line*	*For*	*Read*
XX	32	CXCIII	LXCIII
XXXIII	2	.... Bember"	.... Bember"[37]
XL	35	.... Indies"[63]	.... Indies"[68]
XLIV	26	helps	helpe
,,	27	as	an
XLIX	36	Governours	Governeurs
1	8	Mousson	Meusson
8 margin	34	The ports Surrat	The ports of Surrat
20	16	he Coachman	the Coachman
25	12	also	also[7]
25	15	go off	go off[11]
26 margin	2	Insert 'Roupies of Silver'	
72	38	The ways	The ways[6a]
76	28	Pambou	*Pambou*
76	39	Livres	*Livres*
83	13	Justaf-can	*Justaf-can*
83 margin	20	Jacob	*Jacob*
88	12	Mogolistan	*Mogolistan*
90	8	*Rajpoutes*	*Raspoutes*
93 margin	14	*Faquir*	*Faquirs*
100	2	the	them
100 margin	16	House	Houses
103	19	*Caravanserai*	*Caravanseras*
107	32	mentioned	mentioned[16]
110	17	Boson	Bason
114	2	commanded	commanded in
123	43	Town	Towns
130	24	Golconda	Golconde
135 margin	17	Insert 'a hyphen' after 'Inhabi'	
135	36	taken up	taken up[1]
145	42	thay	they
148	6	Insert 'semicolon' after 'Factories'	
174	13	its side[32d]	its side
175	39	ancient	antient
178	36	Insert 'hope I should have something good to' after 'This word made me'	
181	29	Snuff	Snuff[80]
183	12	*Sicily*[5]	*Sicily*
185	37	Eqipage	Equipage
187	12	Religious	Religions
194	32	1947	1497
202	9	to	to[41]
205	47	aboard	abroad
213	17	and	and[62]
214	44	loaded	loaded[71]
220	15	return'd	return'd[37]
229	30	Death	Death[109a]
248	39	deliver'd	deliver'd[27a]
261	5	so he	so[26a] he
265	23	*Sidi Mansutu*	*Sidi Mansutu*[17]
267	8	Slip	Slip[1]
276	4	which	which[30]
292	52	Decca	Dacca
298	36	Mahmadabad	Mehmadabad
307	47	Philiphines	Philippines
308	44	Abul-Fazl	Abu-l Fazl
323	24	*Imp. Goz.*	*Imp. Gaz.*
323	34	*History of Marathas*	*History of the Mahrattas*

Line	*For*	*Read*
5	Satari	Satara
2	Linchoten	Linschoten
12	Chap. II	Chap. III
17	*Ghusal Khan*	*Ghusal Khana*
,,	Divan Khan	Divan Khana
26	Abul Fazl	Abu-l Fazl
2	Note 20	Note 22
32	f.n. 31	n. 31
41	255,262	pp. 255, 262
,,	Vijaynagar	Vijayanagar
58	pp, 91 & 105	BK. II Chaps. II & IX pp. 127-128, 147.
2	Vigianour	Viziapour
38, 42	History of Aurangzib	*History of Aurangzib*